# INTELLIGENT SYSTEMS

Edited by **Vladimir Mikhailovich Koleshko**

**Intelligent Systems**
Edited by Vladimir Mikhailovich Koleshko

**Published by InTech**
Janeza Trdine 9, 51000 Rijeka, Croatia



**Publishing Process Manager** Gorana Scerbe

**Technical Editor** Teodora Smiljanic

**Cover Designer** InTech Design Team

Additional hard copies can be obtained from orders@intechopen.com

Intelligent Systems, Edited by Vladimir Mikhailovich Koleshko
p. cm.
ISBN 978-953-51-0054-6

For EU product safety concerns:
IN TECH d.o.o., Prolaz Marije Krucifikse Kozulić 3, 51000 Rijeka, Croatia,
info@intechopen.com or visit our website at intechopen.com.

# Meet the editor

Professor Vladimir M. Koleshko is an esteemed scientist in the field of intelligent systems, solid state micro-nanoelectronics and integrated circuit technology. He made a fundamental scientific discovery in brain acoustoelectronic phenomena (USSR № 395, 18.02.1988), and his discovery on hyperconductivity of thin-film structures is protected by the patent "Thin-film structures of high-temperature superconductors" (T=82K) in the Russian Federation. Professor Koleshko is the author of 9 scientific-and-innovative monographs (1978-1988) and 5 electronic books "Cognitive technology of consciousness" with 3D films: "Brain nanoelectronics" (Vol.1), "Control of objects by power of thought" (Vol.2), "Intelligent systems in biometrics" (Vol.3), "Intelligent sensory micro-nanosystems and networks" (Vol.4), "Cell phones, smartphones and ageing of organism" (Vol.5), as well as 35 booklets and educational-methodological textbooks for students, Master's and PhD students, 550 scientific articles in reviewed journals and 620 innovative patents.

# Contents

# Preface

Human progress is characterized by passing through information innovation intelligent society at present. Machines (systems) produced by the genius of man in the near future will not only be smarter than a man, but will also exceed its intelligent mind. Intelligent machines will be of different sizes, shapes and functionality, equipped with an initial program (technogene), and their ability to learn and perform operations will not only depend on the technogene, but also on what the machines will be trained for. All of this is conditioned by the intellectualization of all systems and technological processes that humankind realizes, using the paradigm of developing by which everything must become sensory and motoric, with the ability to make decisions. Smart machines help people to not only make use of their own intellect, but to also grow smarter themselves. Intelligent systems are able to self-train, make their own decisions to support management activities in financial institutions, economics, energetics, logistics, industrial, commercial and social systems, remotely piloted satellite monitoring systems of the broad-spectrum application and communication systems with remote distribution of intelligence for improvement of reliability of an intelligent system in whole. In addition to that, they can also be used for governing a state, control of a holding company, a concern or a firm, as well as for early recognition and prediction of sustainability and prolongation of life, for achieving the maximum increase of functional creative and cognitive human life activity and supporting personal and social safety.

Intelligent systems can be used as authoritative advisers/consultants for all sorts of questions, but will also be able to solve a large number of incipient problems that are a result of human interference, can acquire new knowledge operating with semantic, pragmatic, heuristic and hyper-heuristic features of intelligent information in the process of generating and approximating to a functional model of natural intelligence. They can also produce adaptive, self-learning, self-organizing cognitive systems making it possible to disclose new secrets of nature and produce even more intelligent devices, machines, technologies and productions.

An intelligent system is an automatic or automated system with a possibility of internal and external sensing, based on using artificial intelligence, and includes the following features:

- Self-learning – being able to not only execute underlying and designed-in functions and programs, but also have the ability to adapt them according to the task assigned
- Self-organization – an ability to change its structure and architecture according to the task assigned, or for the purpose of improvement in the process of self-learning, self-diagnostics and self-preservation
- Capability of solving problems that standard methods and/or solution algorithms can not solve or are unknown

For the first time, the research presented in this book is that of scientists from many countries, like Argentina, Australia, Belarus, Brazil, Bulgaria, Czech Republic, Denmark, India, Iran, Italy, Japan, Greece, Mexico, Portugal, Russia, Slovakia, United Kingdom, USA and Vietnam. It will be useful to a wide range of readers, especially students, young scientists, engineers and businessmen/investors taking a great interest in innovations in the future.

**Prof. Vladimir Mikhailovich Koleshko**
Belarussian National Technical University, Mechanical Engineering Faculty,
Department of Intelligent Systems,
Minsk,
The Republic of Belarus

# 1

# Intelligent Systems in Technology of Precision Agriculture and Biosafety

Vladimir M. Koleshko, Anatolij V. Gulay, Elena V. Polynkova, Viacheslav A. Gulay and Yauhen A. Varabei
*Belarusian National Technical University / Dept. of Intelligent Systems*
*Minsk,*
*Belarus*

## 1. Introduction

The XXI century is based on developments of up-to-date intelligent systems and self-learning wireless distributed sensory networks for different purposes of the application to make the whole of space surrounding us sensory and motoric but also for the health and human life maintenance, the improvement of a production status, an output quality, and the product biosafety. A bedrock principle underlying precision agriculture is a wide application of intelligent systems for the control and the assistance of decision making in technological operations of an agricultural production [1, 2]. Precise positioning of agricultural machines using satellite systems gives an opportunity to produce an intelligent system of the agrarian production with dosed applying fertilizers but also chemical weed and pest killers depending on information patterns in a specific spot of the tillable field for the sensory control. Microsensory intelligent systems on a chip "electronic eye" (e-eye) with a LED technology of the data acquisition let form soil light-colour information patterns fast to get a maximal quantity of quality products, foods or biomatters (blood, saliva, sweat, urine, tears, etc.) for the ecological, personal and social biosafety as well as real-time monitoring the human health. The LED technology represents an optical microtomography of functional states of bioobjects on a chip of the type e-eye. The intelligent control in the agro-industrial production offers an opportunity to generate information electronic maps, e.g., the distribution of nutrients and organic fertilizers applied in soil, virtual maps of crop yield taking into account the technological preparation of land for growing crops and micronutrients carried-out from this one with early taken crops, electronic satellite maps of field, electronic maps of the quality, the information-microbial biosafety of foodstuffs, the human health, and ecological environmental conditions. The distributed wireless sensory systems and networks with a self-learning software make for the development of intelligent precision agriculture including the information pattern recognition of an agrotechnical technology, agricultural products and external ecological conditions in a space of multidimensional sensory data. The use of intelligent information CIMLS (Continuous Intelligent Management and Life Cycle Support) technology with developed intelligent systems of data superprotection maintains and controls the life cycle of all the agricultural production.

## 2. Intelligent sensory systems and networks of precision agriculture

### 2.1 LED technology in precision agriculture

The main principle of intelligent precision agriculture is the high-precision dosed fertilizer application in a specified small piece of the ground depending in a soil physical-chemical status (colour, structure, organics content, moisture, temperature) for an equal distribution of organic fertilizers and using controlled actuators, electronic, virtual and intellect-maps for the agro-industrial production, the foodstuff biosafety and the human life maintenance. The use of intelligent technologies in precision agriculture enables to achieve saving weed and pest killers, fertilizers, energy resources, ecological sustainability, raising the level of crop yield, the quality of fields, the biosafety of agricultural products, and the increased efficiency of the agricultural production. The most effective method for monitoring and the fast formation of soil information patterns consists in the estimation of its spectral reflectance as a set of optical parameters in the ultraviolet, visible and near infrared spectral ranges. The LED technology presented by us is intended for taking soil brightness coefficients in the broadband optical spectrum range ($10^{11}$–$10^{15}$ Hz) using a set of light-emitting and light-sensitive microelements for the illumination of a controlled small piece of soil and for recording the reflected optical signal. A wide application of intelligent sensory systems for precision agriculture and the fast control of soil information patterns in every spot of a cultivated agricultural field underlie the LED technology of precision agriculture with the differentiated fertilization [1, 3].

### 2.2 Mobile microsensory system for precision agriculture

A mobile microsensory system "ISSE" developed by us with the LED technology for the light-colour information pattern recognition can analyze a soil state from within and apply fertilizers on different spots of a field just that dosage which is required in a defined soil spot. The registration of soil optical characteristics is realized by means of light-emitting microdiodes with the emission wavelength 405 nm (violet), 460 nm (blue), 505 nm (green), 530 nm (green), 570 nm (yellow), 620 nm (orange), 660 nm (red) but also in spectral points of the sensory control of the infrared radiation (760-2400 nm) and white light (integrated index) [3, 4]. Light-emitting microdiodes irradiate the given electromagnetic waves in the broadband frequency range, but photosensitive microdiodes register a quantitative change of the reflected radiation. The optimal spectrum width corresponds to the wavelength range of 400-800 nm, so the oscillation spectrum effect of $H_2O$ molecules in soil begins to become apparent at the greater wavelength, and complementary errors are introduced in results of the diagnostics of a soil horizon. The multisensory system "ISSE" includes an electronic optical module for the formation and the registration of optical impulses consisting of the analog-digital transducer with a microcontroller and a pulse-shaping module (Fig. 1) but also for the comparison of obtained information sensory patterns with soil experimental characteristics on local field areas using a special self-learning software [3].

Light-emitting microdiodes are equispaced on a perimeter of circle in 20 mm over on the angle about 10° relative to the vertical line, so the placing height of these ones over a controlled surface is equal to 30 mm. Eight numbers in the binary-coded decimal notation in the range of 0...1000 corresponding to reflectivity factors of the radiation for each of eight spectrum lines are generated by the use of RS-232 or RS-485 interfaces. Then the value 1000

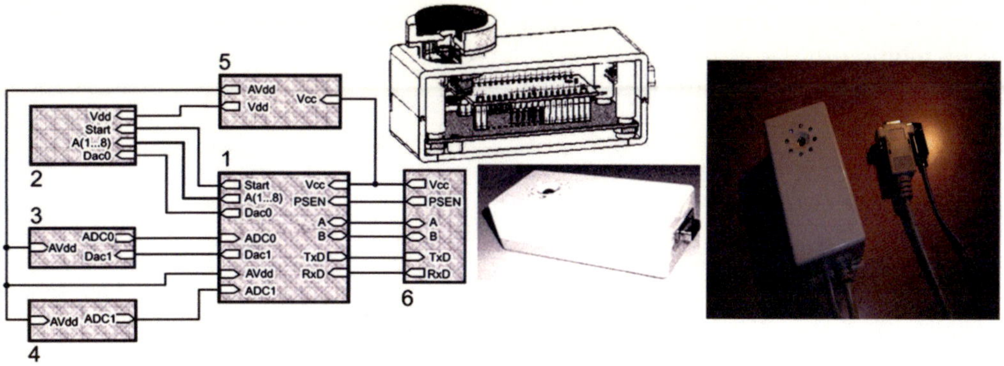


Fig. 1. Function circuit of the electron-optical module "ISSE" for a sensory system "CDOT": 1 - microcontroller for the control and information processing; 2 - light-emitting microdiodes control circuit; 3 - microphotodetector coupling; 4 – temperature monitoring circuit; 5 - secondary voltage source; 6 – COM-port connector

characterizes a reflection coefficient from a reference surface used for the calibration of the electronic optical module. The microprocessor-based device generating a soil sensory information pattern processes the output signal of the microphotodetector [4]. Using "ISSE" it is possible to analyze coefficients of absorption, refraction, light scattering, gradient change, and polarization but also coefficients of variation (intensity, amplitude, and phase) of the electromagnetic wave and a space-time field distribution. The obtained data of spectroscopic analysis enable to produce an information pattern of soil, agricultural products, foodstuff, and human biomatters. A gridded registrating unit periodic realizes the real-time satellite navigation and the control of soil parameters. The specifically developed software "ISSE" can be applied in an intelligent system "CDOT" (Control of Distribution of Organics and Temperature) on a chip "electronic eye" which is of interest in precision agriculture for the control of a soil humus-accumulative horizon at the depth of 20-30 to 180-200 mm. A small intelligent sensory "mole" ("CDOT") includes "ISSE" placed in the metal sheathing with the stone and sunlight protection. The optical beam output to a controlled soil surface is realized by the use of the sapphire transparent coating as the extra hard material, so "CDOT" can be attached, e.g., to a mini-tractor or any other agricultural units. "ISSE" explores the ground at the depth of 5-10 cm for the detection of organic substances, moisture, temperature, colour, granulometric composition and for the analysis of the fertile topsoil and using the GPS (Global Positioning System) navigation defines rapidly how much exactly fertilizers have to be applied with the micromechatronic system in the specific field place in process of optimal motion of the mini-tractor with an attached drawbar hitch (Fig. 2) [1, 3, 4].

The given depth of penetration of the multisensory system "CDOT" for topsoil copying is determined depending on structural features of the floor profile and on the location of the humus-accumulative horizon. The hydralift system of the mini-tractor is intended for the control of "CDOT" lifting and sinking actuators in soil. Positioning of the units is also based on data from ultrasonic, microwave, electrostatic sensory modules at the same time. The intelligent system "CDOT" fulfils data binding of a soil controlled information pattern to ground control points from a GPS receiver and stores obtained data in its memory for postprocessing and the sensory information pattern recognition. Principal parameters of the mobile multisensory system "CDOT" developed by us for the control of soil in precision agriculture are presented in the table 1 [4].

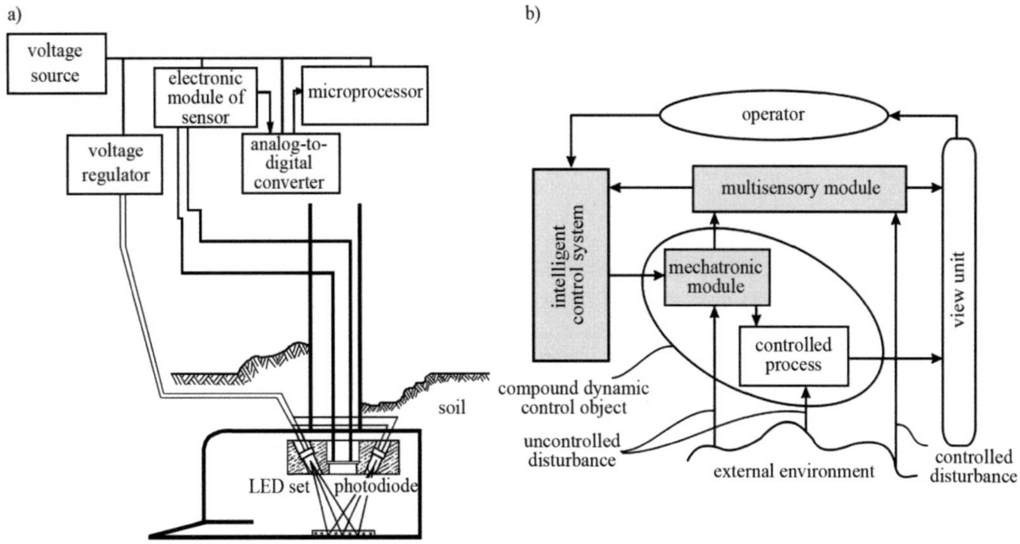


Fig. 2. Multisensory system "CDOT" for the light-colour soil control: (a) intelligent mechatronic system for precision agriculture; (b) block diagram of the intelligent sensory system

| Technical characteristics of "CDOT" | Data description |
|---|---|
| controlled spectrum width | 400-2400 nm |
| spatial resolution of agricultural unit location | 2-5 m |
| spatial resolution for the control of soil | 0,5 m |
| maximal output current of light-emitting microdiodes | 40 mA |
| duration of information pattern generating | 120 ms |
| space of time between impulses | 5 ms |
| depth of taken measurements | 8-15 cm |
| speed of the mini-tractor | 2,83 m/s |
| control of organic matter content in the soil humic-accumulative horizon | 0,1–6 % |
| control of soil moisture | 0-20 % |
| control of temperature | 3-50 $^0$C |

Table 1. Principal parameters of mobile multisensory system "CDOT"

Fundamental purposes of the developed intelligent multisensory system "CDOT" for precision agriculture is to ensure the processing quality optimization, in particular, for the control of the developed mechatronic mechanism of the agricultural unit and its positioning mechatronic system. The intelligent system analyses sensory processing information, carries out the computation of optimal motion and changes a control criteria preliminary programming a movement pattern and maintaining the power-saving engine behaviour. Solar energy converters can be used as an auxiliary supply source or the alternative energy one of the intelligent mobile system "ISSE" for the optical control of the soil quality. A soil light-colour information pattern is taken into account in the process of dosing introduced fertilizers and considered as a control parameter according to the model of the plants inorganic nutrition:

$$F_{IF}=F-F_{0}, \qquad (1)$$

where $F_{IF}$ - cumulative dose of introduced fertilizers, F - plants nutrition level, $F_0$ - initial fertility of soil.

Metering microdevices of the mechatronic module are intended for the fertilizer application in soil or for the power feed of weed and pest killers with annular ultrasonic microactuators, so that acoustic vibrations of ones put a diaphragm mechanism in motion for the control of the metering microdevice-delivered material flow (Fig. 3) [1, 5].

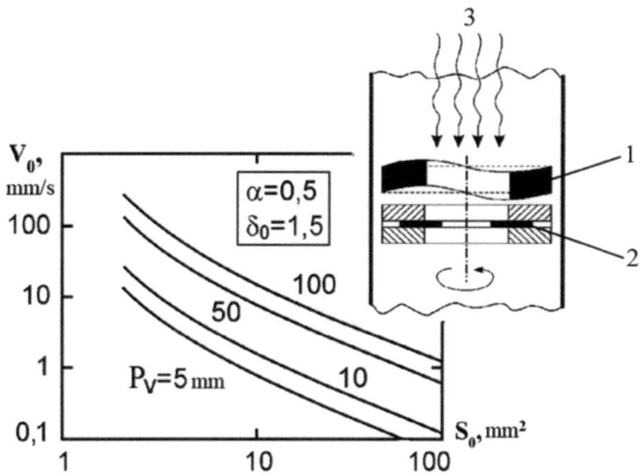


Fig. 3. Metering microdevice of the free-flowing material and the nomogram for its parameterization: 1 - electroacoustic element; 2 - diaphragm mechanism; 3 - flow of the dosed material

The intelligent system fulfils, e.g., dosing of introduced mineral fertilizers depending on the organics content in a field specified point by controlling impulse characteristics of a high-frequency generator which supplies the ultrasonic microactuator. The volumetric capacity $P_v$ of the metering device with the presented design is equal to:

$$P_v = (S_0 - P_1 \cdot \delta_0 / 2{,}3) \cdot V_0, \qquad (2)$$

where $S_0$, $\delta_0$, $V_0$ - flow area, diameter of granules, flow velocity of dosed materials; $P_1$ - part of the metering hole perimeter formed by fixed edges relative to the material flow. The form of a hole produced by blades of the dosing unit is presented as an approximate circle, so $P_1$ can be written in this form:

$$P_1=2 \cdot \alpha \cdot (\pi \cdot S_0)^{-0{,}5}, \qquad (3)$$

where $1 \geq \alpha \geq 0$ - coefficient characterizing the dosing performance degradation because of the reduction of the flow area. A value of the coefficient $P_1$ is taken into consideration on conditions that $P_1 > 0{,}025 \cdot S_0/\delta_0$ and for the considered dosing unit:

$$\alpha \geq 6 \cdot 10^{-3} \cdot \xi , \tag{4}$$

where $\xi = D_0/\delta_0$, $D_0$ - diameter of the metering hole.

Nomographic charts in the form of the $S_0$-$V_0$ relation for different values of granules sizes $\delta_0$ and the coefficient $\alpha$ were calculated for the metering device developed by us. The given dependences have a linear character for relatively low values $\alpha$ and $\delta_0$, but these ones take the nonlinear form for $\alpha > 0{,}5$ and $\delta_0 > 0{,}5$ mm especially in and around small values of the sectional area of the metering hole. The increase in $\alpha$ and $\delta_0$ requires rising in flow velocity of the dosed material to attain the same performance as for $\alpha=0$.

### 2.3 Recognition of soil light-colour information patterns

Every soil information pattern is characterized by inhomogeneous agrochemical and agrophysical values. We investigated soil multicomponent information patterns using soil reference patterns with contrast colour tones in accordance with a triangle of the soil coloration. This one is produced from the assumption that soil humus colours in grey and dark-grey tones, iron compounds - in brown, reddish, yellowish ones, but many soil components (silicon dioxide, quartz, carbonates, and calcium sulphates) have a white colour. Light-colour information patterns were obtained as a set of values of brightness coefficients in this form:

$$R = I / I_0, \tag{5}$$

where $I$, $I_0$ - light intensity reflected from a soil controlled sample and a standard white surface, respectively.

At the same time, a set of brightness coefficients in the soil humus-accumulative horizon defines its information light-colour pattern (Fig. 4). Histograms of a size distribution of soil particles and the soil microstructure registered by a method of scanning electron microscopy supplement a soil information pattern. We developed a special software for the data visualization of reflection indexes of the optical radiation, preprocessing, the data transmission [3, 5].

The following conclusions result from undertaken experimental studies of the developed intelligent multisensory system "CDOT" [1-5]:

- reflection coefficients increase in the examined broadband wavelength range if the irradiation intensity goes up especially fast when the wavelength rises, but soil is lighter;
- the more soil fine particles, the higher the reflection coefficient which exponentially increases when sizes of soil particles reduce from 2500 μm to 25 μm, so large particles reflect less energy of the optical radiation because of a long space between ones;
- there are significant changes of the organics content for the mixture with light soil, and there are especially more significant differences of information patterns in the range of 620-660 nm in contrast to the one of 460-505 nm;

- there are a quite strong correlation dependence between the organics content in soil and moisture of this one, so moisture is generally retained in organic components of soil, but soil mineral ones don't absorb water (Fig. 5a);
- water makes changes in the reflection, and there is especially significant increased light scattering by soil particles in the visible spectrum, so a brightness coefficient falls slowly, but soil becomes darker if the water content increases (Fig. 5b);

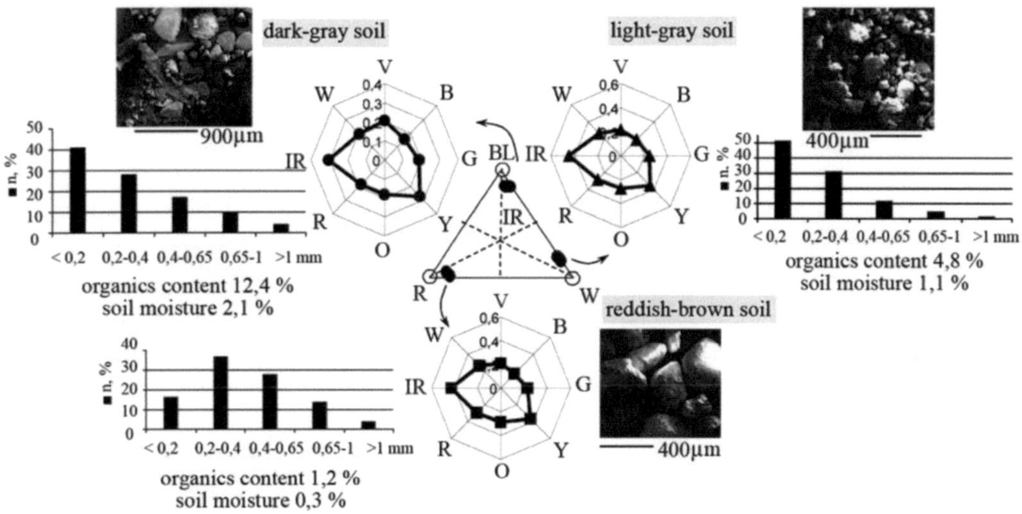


Fig. 4. Soil information patterns in the form of the triangle of the soil coloration: BL-black; W-white; R-red; reflected light: V-violet; B-blue; G-green; Y-yellow; O-orange; R-red; IR-infrared radiation

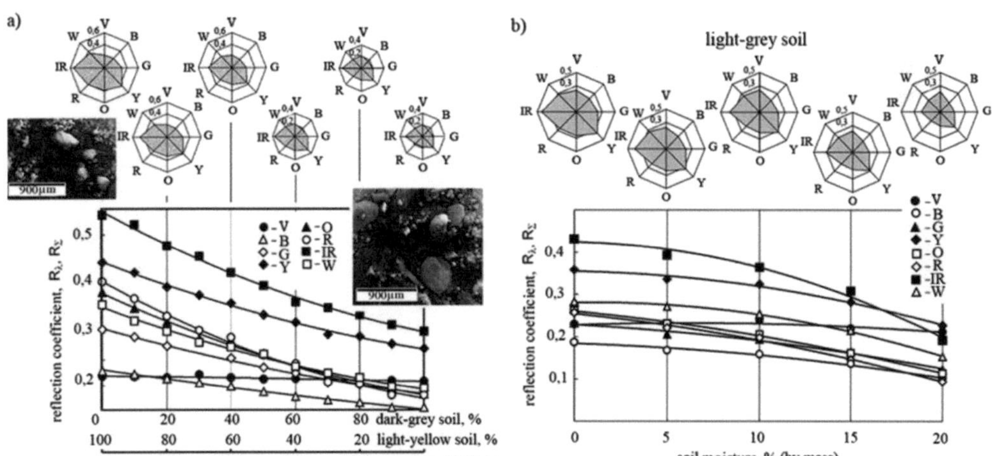


Fig. 5. Correlation of soil information patterns with the soil composition and moisture

- the ferric oxide content in soil considerably influences on reflection coefficients, so that there is the absorption with minimum energy in the range of 570-660 nm, but an absorption effect goes up if the organics content is more than 2 % (Fig. 6a,b);

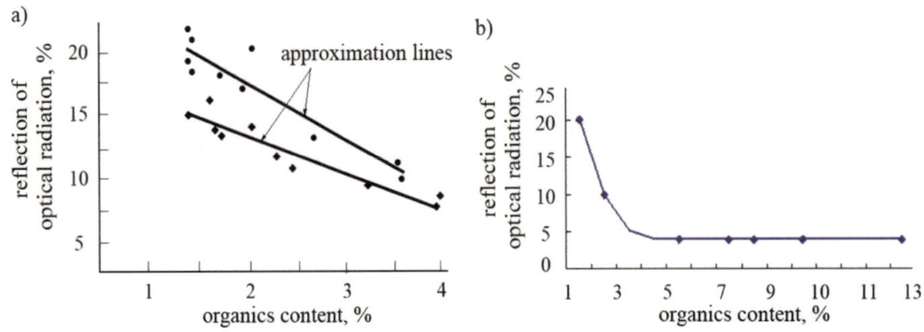


Fig. 6. Correlation of the organics content in soil and its reflection of the optical radiation: (a) well structured soil; (b) soil with a high content of sand

- using the self-learning intelligent system "ISSE" it is possible to determine the content of phosphorus and potassium in soil which is varied directly as the reflection coefficient, but the verification of an estimated model with experimental data of network outputs shows a high linear dependence.

The calculation of predictive models and special developed evaluation indicators in accordance with indexes of a soil physical state was used for the recognition of soil information patterns and for the comparison of ones with reference patterns in precision agriculture. Then algorithms of neural networks with the genetic optimization used by us enable to detect a set of basis information patterns of soil. These ones characterize not only the soil individual state (Fig. 7), but also its agrophysical state in general, increasing the level of crop yield, the quality and the biosafety of raising crops, foods, and a soil information-microbial state.

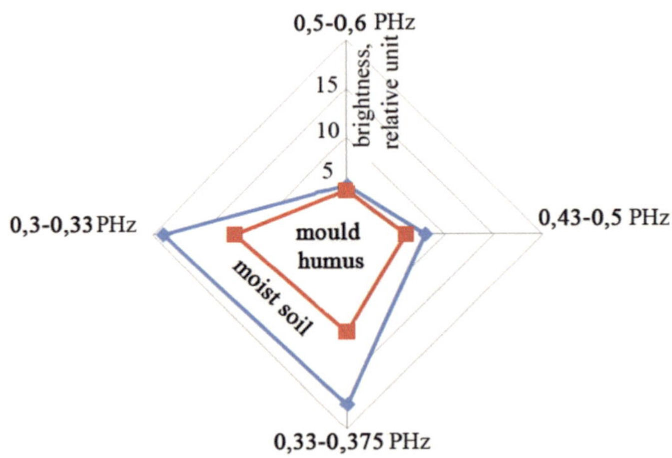


Fig. 7. Soil information patterns using "CDOT"

Sensory information processing and the control of agricultural operations in the intelligent system "CDOT" for precision agriculture is based on the self-learning ability of expert systems, e.g., by means of neural network modelling. Then the recognition of multiparameter information patterns generated by the output data transformation of sensory modules occurs on the first network level. The experimental studies of the sensory pattern recognition are fulfilled using "CDOT" for the presented light-colour technology of the soil control underlying the operation of neural networks on the first level. A complex control parameter for the technological production process of an agricultural field is formed on the second level. The neural network on the third level enables to predict the value in a spot of the field based on generalized parameter changes to a point of time when the processing machine with its actuator is located at this one. To get reference colour patterns, a special palette is developed composed of 10×10 colour cells and primary polygraphic colours of the standard CMYK (C - cyan, M - magenta, Y - yellow, K - black) system are presented in corner palette cells, but all the other colour tones of ones can be got by primary colour mixing. Advantages of the used model of reference colour patterns consists in the precise identification of palette colours and soil colour tones, respectively, but also in the application for matching colours, e.g., Pantone (R). Surfaces of reflection coefficients for every colour of the optical radiation are produced using the developed palette (Fig. 8) [1, 5]. The minimum Euclidian distance is chosen as a decision rule for the nearest reference pattern (soil colour) in accordance with soil reflection coefficients registered by the sensory system "ISSE", but soil evaluation information is stored in the database of the intelligent system "CDOT".

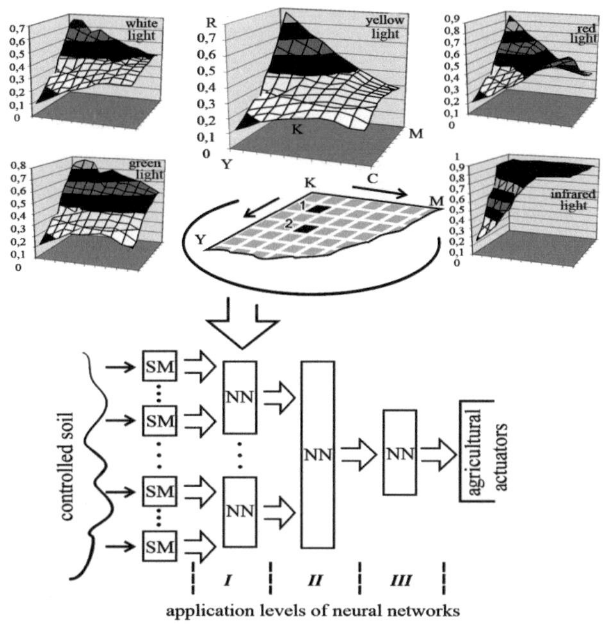


Fig. 8. Sensory modules and neural networks (NN) in precision agriculture with dependences of reflection coefficients for different wavelengths on the reference colour: 1 - dark-grey soil sample; 2 – light-grey one

### 2.4 Electronic virtual maps in precision agriculture

Having generated soil light-colour information patterns, the intelligent microsensory system "CDOT" can produce, e.g., electronic virtual maps of the fertility level of soil spots in some spectral ranges including soil electronic maps of the organics content, moisture, temperature, granulometric composition, and colour. Forming electronic maps of a mineral fertilizers distribution on fields or virtual maps of planned crop yield using imaging data to estimate growth conditions and cropping are realized by dosed applying fertilizers in soil [1, 3, 5]. The optimal strategy of the agricultural production can be fast achieved by data overlapping of electronic virtual maps but also on the basis of current information about tillage, nutrients carry-over from soil with taken crops, characteristics of used agricultural units. Then it is possible to control operations of the agricultural machinery, to keep track of information how much fuel is consumed or whether fertilizers are applied. To produce electronic maps, we used a point krinning method for the estimation of the distributed random function in an arbitrary point as the linear combination of its values in initial ones. A variogram defines a form of the optimal interpolated hypersurface in the space between reference spots of the sensory control. According to the krinning method, the estimated value of the soil quality in the known spot p from a set of k neighbouring spots is calculated as weighed mean measured values in neighbouring spots in the form:

$$\psi_p = \sum_{i=1}^{k} W_i \cdot \psi_i, \tag{6}$$

where $W_i$ – weighting coefficient of an index i of the soil quality in relation to the estimated spot p from a set of neighbouring spots.

The krinning method provides for solving a set of equations:

$$\begin{aligned} &\sum_{j=1}^{k} W_j \cdot \gamma(\xi_{ij}) + \lambda = \gamma(\xi_{ip}), \\ &\sum_{i=1}^{k} W_i = 1, \end{aligned} \tag{7}$$

where $\gamma(\xi_{ij})$, $\gamma(\xi_{ip})$ – semivariogram values for the distance $\xi_{ij}$ and $\xi_{ip}$ between a points i and estimated points j, p, $i = \overline{1,k}$; $\lambda$ – Lagrange factor.

Unknown weighting coefficients $W_i$ are computed by solving a set of equations (7), but a value of the controlled variable in the spot p is calculated using the formula (6). The semivariogram on the area boundary of spots with the different agricultural background in precision agriculture has the sharp difference in values; therefore, the considered mathematical model shows the nugget-effect. Having estimated a value of the soil quality in an agricultural spot q in accord with controlled values $k_1, k_2 \ldots k_m$ of appropriate agricultural backgrounds m, the set of krinning equations for models with the nugget-effect can be presented as:

$$\begin{aligned} &\beta_{1q} \cdot \sum_{j=1}^{k_1} W_{1j} \cdot \gamma(\xi_{ij}) + \beta_{2q} \cdot \sum_{j=1}^{k_2} W_{2j} \cdot \gamma(\xi_{ij}) + \ldots + \beta_{mq} \cdot \sum_{j=1}^{k_m} W_{mj} \cdot \gamma(\xi_{ij}) + \lambda = \gamma(\xi_{ip}), \\ &\beta_{1q} \cdot \sum_{i=1}^{k_1} W_{1i} + \beta_{2q} \cdot \sum_{i=1}^{k_2} W_{2i} + \ldots + \beta_{mq} \cdot \sum_{i=1}^{k_m} W_{mi} = 1, \end{aligned} \tag{8}$$

where $\beta_{iq} = \overline{\psi_i} / \overline{\psi_q}$, $j = \overline{1,m}$, $j \neq q$; $\overline{\psi_j}, \overline{\psi_q}$ - mean values of the soil quality in agricultural spots j, q determining a semivariogram jump $\xi_{jq}$ on their area boundary $\delta_{jq} = (\overline{\psi_j} - \overline{\psi_q})^2 / 2$.

A main advantage of modelling on the basis of the nugget-effect consists in its applicability even if a number of experimental points are scarce, so it is conditioned, e.g., by small sizes of an investigated spot of the agricultural field. Fig. 9 shows the process of generating soil electronic maps by means of the developed software "ISIDP" for data processing of the sensory control of soil and the realization of precision agriculture. The half-dispersion of distances is determined in accordance with the accepted modelling algorithm and interpolated curve fitting by the approximation of neighbouring values, bilinear, bicubic, and cubic splines is realized using the developed application and for generating maps of isolines of distributed initial data. If grid-point data are initial ones, then these ones can be presented in the form of a matrix. The visualization of every contour curve for initial data is realised after the introduction of a matrix of distributed values (Fig. 9a,b) [5]. To improve visual perception of the electronic map, spot colour filling is fulfilled according to the chosen colour legend (Fig. 9c). The isolines obtained at this stage are only precise in nodal points, so the bivariate data interpolation is used (Fig. 9d).

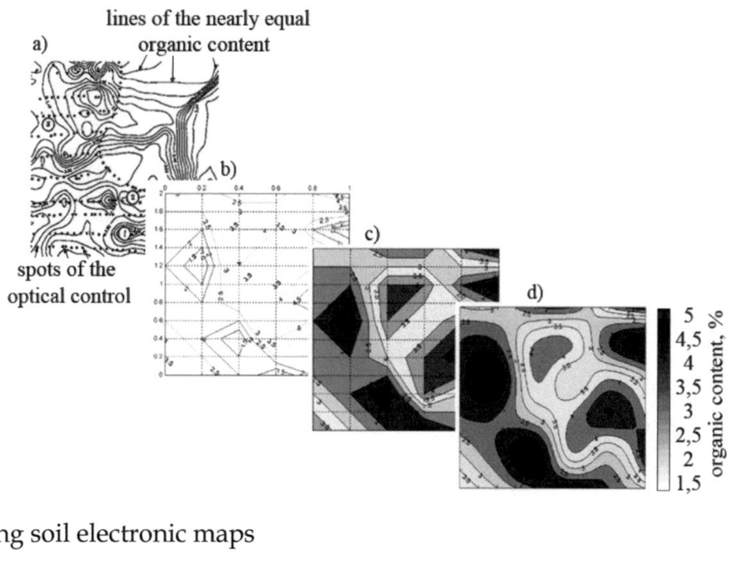


Fig. 9. Modelling soil electronic maps

The developed microsensory system "ISED" can be used for farm enterprises, individual entrepreneurs, agricultural holdings getting users exactly to know where fertilizers have to be introduced and what crops should be produced in a defined spot. "ISED" includes a multichannel sensor for the detection of organic substances in soil, a receiver of the satellite navigation system, data processing and logging controller but also a special software for this one (Fig. 10). The microsensory system "ISED" can send information automatically to a home computer or mobile devices (smartphone, communicator, iPad, etc.) of farmers, and satellite positioning enables "ISED" to be applied not with hectares, but with some hundred square metres accurate to 5 cm.

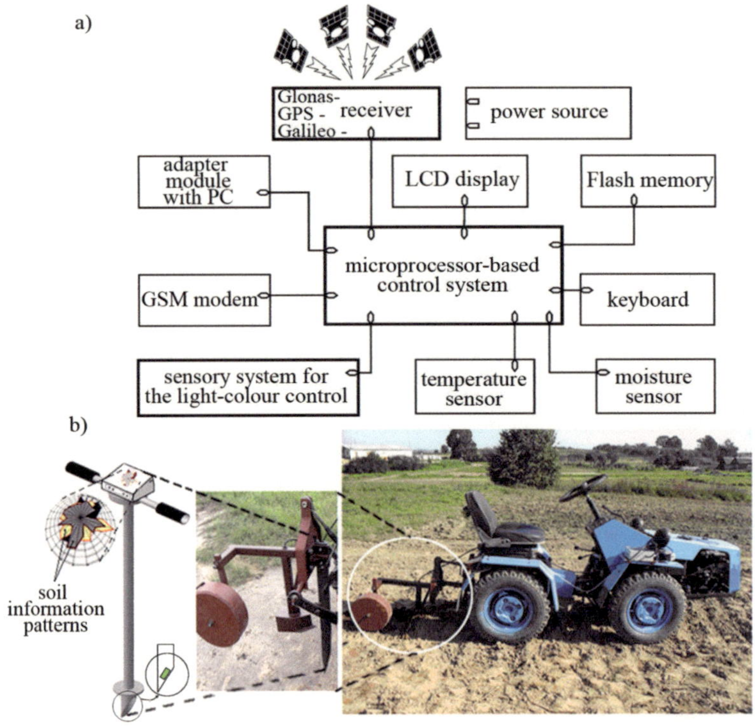


Fig. 10. (a) Structure chart of the laboratory portable multisensory system "ISED" and its design (b) for farming and individual entrepreneurs

### 2.5 Electronic intellect-maps for the maintenance of the human health and biosafety

The top priorities of society in the XXI century are striving for a maximal prolongation of life and the continuous maintenance of the human activity. An object of research of intelligent systems in precision agriculture for a personal and social biosafety is information patterns of farming cultures and foods produced from them. Genetic features, culture conditions, soil contamination, and a tilling technology generally determine the biochemical composition of food products during agrotechnical operations but also by the quality of crops for animals, intensity of the fertilizer application in soil, radiation levels, environmental ecological states, etc. However, fertilizers introduced in soil for raising the level of the crop yield contain a lot of chemical toxic substances which can be accumulated with time in plant and animal foods and cause the development of dangerous diseases and spreading of infectious ones exposing to danger the human health. Organic microelements in soil are distributed nonuniformly and accumulated in separate spots forming regions with active microbial communities. A number of microbes in soil determine the synthesis of high-molecular compounds and the storage of nutrients in soil but also the productive capacity of soil, an increase in productivity, information-microbial maps, etc. An intelligent system "ISMP" developed by us enables to generate electronic microbial maps of soil for intelligent precision agriculture and maintaining the personal and social biosafety (Fig. 11).

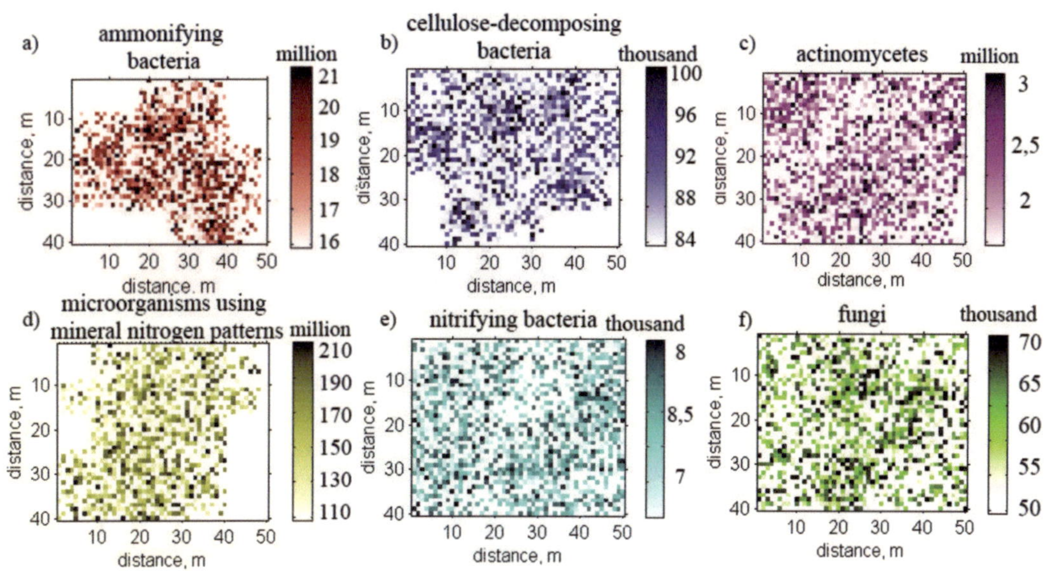


Fig. 11. Microbial maps of soil using the intelligent system "ISMP"

An increase in the number of microbial communities and their vitality in soil are determined especially by the humus level in soils, pH values and distances from pollution sources. There is a natural microbiological biosphere in soil which is not worked and used for the agricultural application. The active pesticide use in precision agriculture leads to the reduction of specified microbial communities in the next few years (Fig. 12). The pesticide application makes for the accumulation of toxic and dangerous substances in cultivated plants, animal and human organisms. There is need for using intelligent systems for the protection of human health and the control of microbial biosafety of consumed foods.

The developed intelligent system "ISLB" is intended for the control of the personal and social biosafety and the prevention of long-term general toxic influences on the human organism, e.g., of allergic, mutagenic, teratogenic or carcinogenic factors. It is quite enough even very few toxins with the concentration which is below the level of the adopted standard for the biosafety in order to bring to nonspecific changes in the human biosystem. It is necessary to use the intelligent system "ISLB" for generating electronic intellect-maps of the biosafety of farming cultures but also soil virtual information-microbial and food maps therefore.

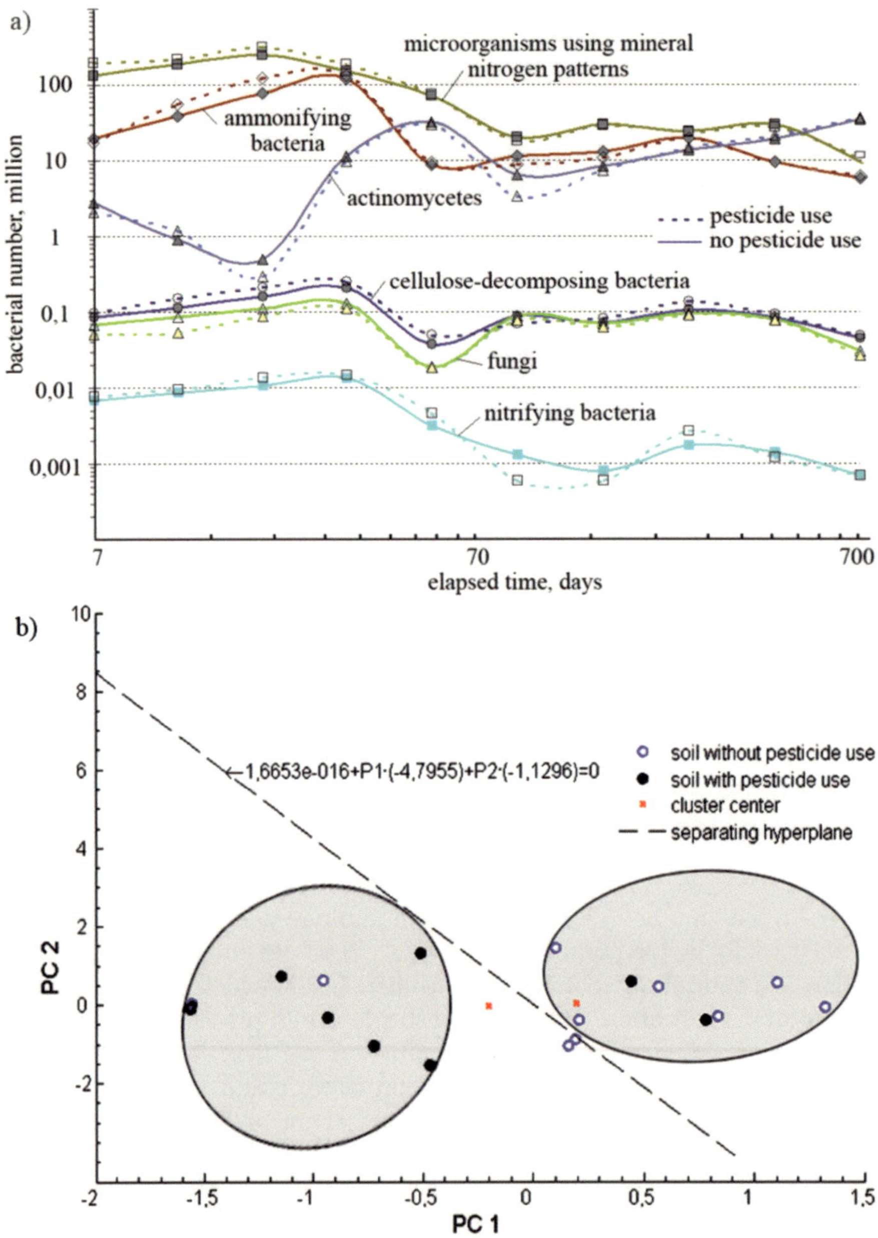


Fig. 12. (a) Changes of the number of microbial communities during some years. (b) Information patterns of soil carrying out agrotechnical methods

Sod-podzolic soils predominate in a structure of agricultural ones in the Republic of Belarus. The effective fertilizer application is possible only based on information patterns of fields with the analysis of their agrochemical data and the soil acidity. There are some results for the recognition of information patterns of soil in the Republic of Belarus in the figure 13. The high humus concentration defines the productive capacity of soil, an increased microbial amount and their enhanced vitality.

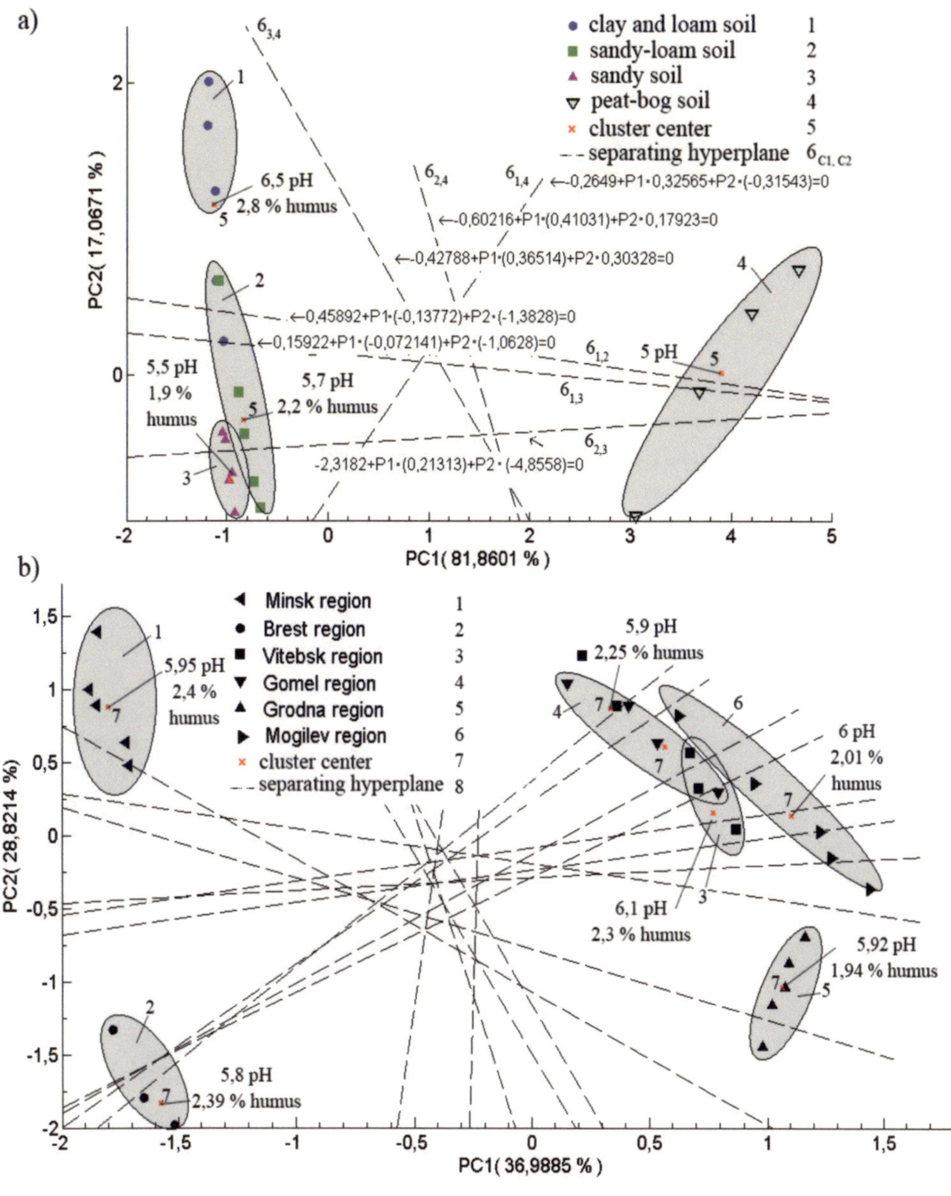


Fig. 13. (a) Information patterns of different types of soils using "ISLB". (b) Presented sensory patterns of sod-podzolic soils for main regions of the Republic of Belarus

## 3. LED technology for the analysis of biological fluids

### 3.1 Optical microtomography for the pattern recognition of biomatters

Human biological fluids (blood, saliva, sweat, urine, tears, etc.) are very sensitive to any external influences, but their information sensory pattern can be generated by means of our developed intelligent system "ISLB" with wireless mobile retransmitters. Using received sensory data of information patterns of biomatters it is possible to produce electronic virtual and intellect-maps of the quality of alimentary products or environmental conditions for the maintenance of the human health and the personal and social biosafety. The intelligent system "ISLB" can define spectral-response characteristics of biomatters, e.g., absorption, reflection, polarization factors, changes of intensity, phase, and amplitude of an electromagnetic wave in the broadband frequency range of $10^{11}$-$10^{15}$ Hz. "ISLB" is suited to be used for the individual application, e.g., in wristwatches, watch and mobile phones, smartphones, communicators, iPads, PDAs with an embedded software for the purpose of the continuous maintenance and monitoring of the human health, the prolongation of life and the improvement of the vital activity [6]. An important advantage of "ISLB" is the fast recognition of information patterns of biomatters, so there is no need for special conditions of its functioning and for a remote costly laboratory.

### 3.2 Blood

If using a mobile device (smartphone, communicator, iPad, PDA, wristwatch, watch or mobile phone, etc.) with the microsensory system "ISLB" an electromagnetic wave emitted by the microlight-emitting diode falls on the human skin surface, it is absorbed, scattered and reflected by this one. (Fig. 14) [1, 6].

The absorption of the radiation arises from the photons interaction with different chromophores, but scattering is because of changes of the reflection coefficient. There are some disturbances of the human biosystem, functioning its separate organs and biochemical processes because of the consumption of poor farming cultures, natural form foods or food products. Biochemical and spectral characteristics of blood are changed a lot and individually depending on cognitive and functional states of the human organism [6, 7]. The intelligent system "ISLB" with the developed software enables to maintain in a real time the personal and social biosafety and the human health. It is known that the hormone ghrelin is produced in stomach of a hunger man, at its maximum before eating, and then this one is reduced gradual during a meal. The satiation hormone PPY3-36 affecting hypothalamus is at its highest point after eating, and then this one is decreased in some following hours slowly [7]. The blood lipidic and carbohydrate composition is varied because of the nutritive absorption from food after a meal. An increase in the concentration of glucose in blood during eating results in ceasing neurons with sensing membrane channels to send signals and generating the hormone orexin which forces the human organism being awake, eating moderately and self-learning fast. It explains essential differences of information patterns for a man being hungry and sated (Fig. 15), excessive somnolence after a meal and the risk taking behaviour of a hunger man. In this case changes of a level of leukocytes, glucose and whole protein are defined more clearly in the table 2.

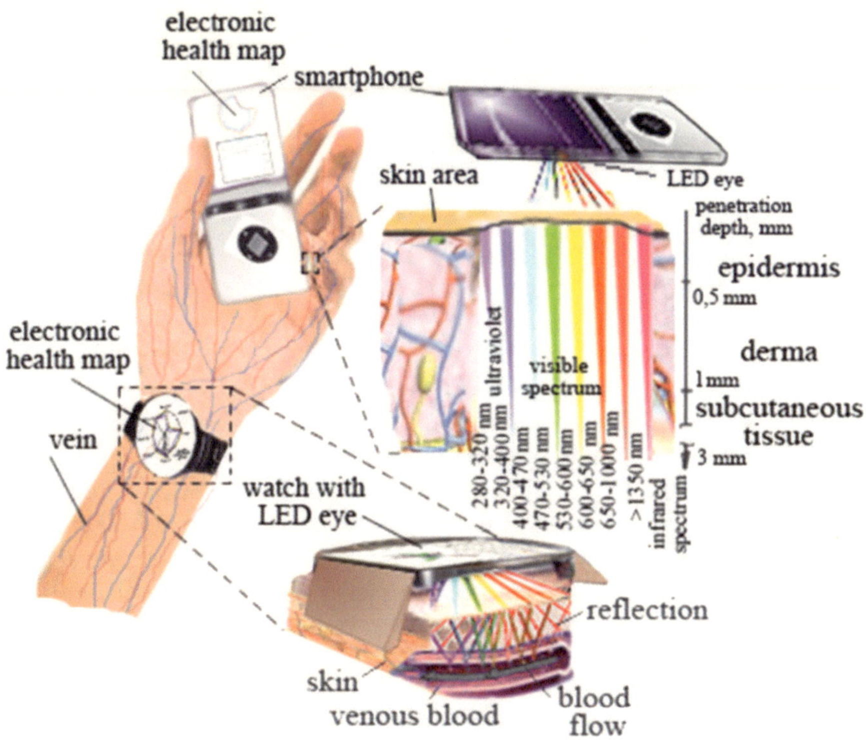


Fig. 14. Intelligent system in the wristwatch or the smartphone for non-invasive measuring

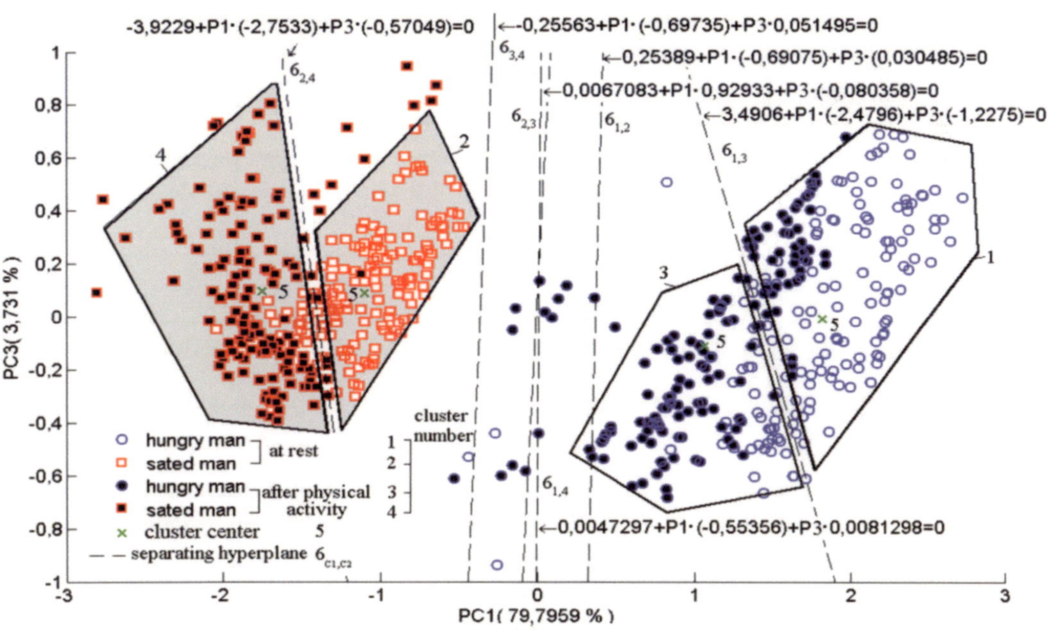


Fig. 15. Non-invasive LED analysis of blood information patterns for the hungry man and the sated one at rest and after physical activity

| Blood components | Healthy man (norm) | Hunger man | Sated man |
|---|---|---|---|
| leukocytes, $\cdot 10^9$ /l | 4-9 | 4,3-11,3 | 5,8-13,4 |
| glucose, mmole/l | 3,3-5,5 | 2,4-4,3 | 4,3-5,7 |
| whole protein, g/l | 65-85 | 56-74 | 68-80 |

Table 2. Some most variable parameters of human blood during everyday life

The intensive glycolysis in human blood and the formation of adenosine triphosphoric acids are realized during a physical activity, so a man doesn't feel its being hungry, in danger or a state of the strong mental agitation. A short-time physical activity brings about the higher blood glucose level because of the amplifying glycogen mobilization, but this one determines low glucose content in human blood over a long period of time [7]. The physical activity of subjects not going in for sports can increase the insulin activity after eating and reduce the blood glucose level. The level of lactic acid rises from 1,1-1,5 mole/l to 5-20 mole/l, and the level of haemoglobin goes up from 7,5-10 mole/l to 13-15 mole/l (Table 3). Strong changes of blood information parameters are a result of intensive physical activities, human emotional states, humoral mechanisms, nutrition, and other factors therefore [8].

| Values of blood parameters | Norm | Without physical activity | Short-timed physical activity | Long-timed physical activity |
|---|---|---|---|---|
| erythrocytes, $\cdot 10^{12}$/l | 4-5 | 4,7 | 4,4 | 4,8 |
| haemoglobin, % | 13,8-18 | 15,5 | 14,3 | 15,7 |
| hematocrit, % | 40-48 | 44,6 | 38,2 | 40,7 |
| reticulocytes, % | 2-10 | 6,7 | 3,6 | 8,1 |
| mean cell haemoglobin in erythrocyte , $\cdot 10^{-12}$g | 24-33 | 27,3 | 29,6 | 35,3 |
| mean corpuscular volume, $\mu m^3$ | 75-95 | 83,2 | 83,7 | 88 |

Table 3. Results of the clinical blood analysis during the human physical activity

There are explicit changes of blood information patterns in the right hand and the left one at rest and after clapping one's hands or stamping in the figures 16, 17.

It is connected with the variation of carbohydrate and protein metabolisms in blood, e.g., because of the increase of the lactic acid level, with the reduction of oxygen metabolism (Table 4). The lactic acid content in blood takes also place for a state of complete fatigue or unbalanced eating, for the lack of nourishment of animal proteins or vitamins. Then handclaps and stamping make it possible to improve human cognitive and motor skills, remove stress, influence positively on the blood hydrodynamic sanguimotion and enhance metabolic processes in the human organism.

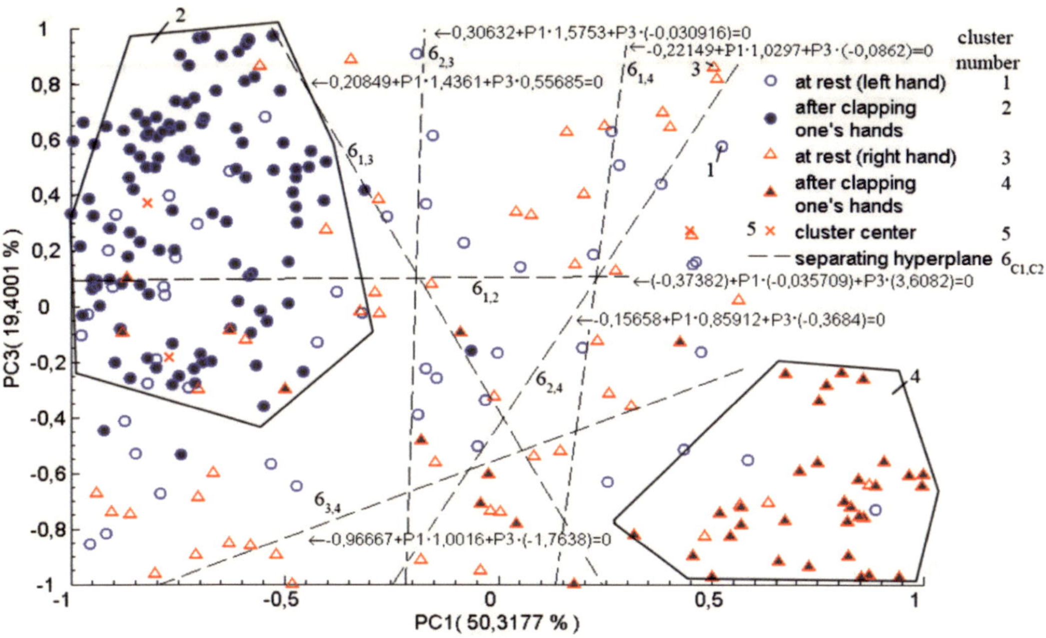


Fig. 16. Non-invasive LED analysis of blood information patterns of the right and left human hands of young men at a rest state and after making twenty handclaps

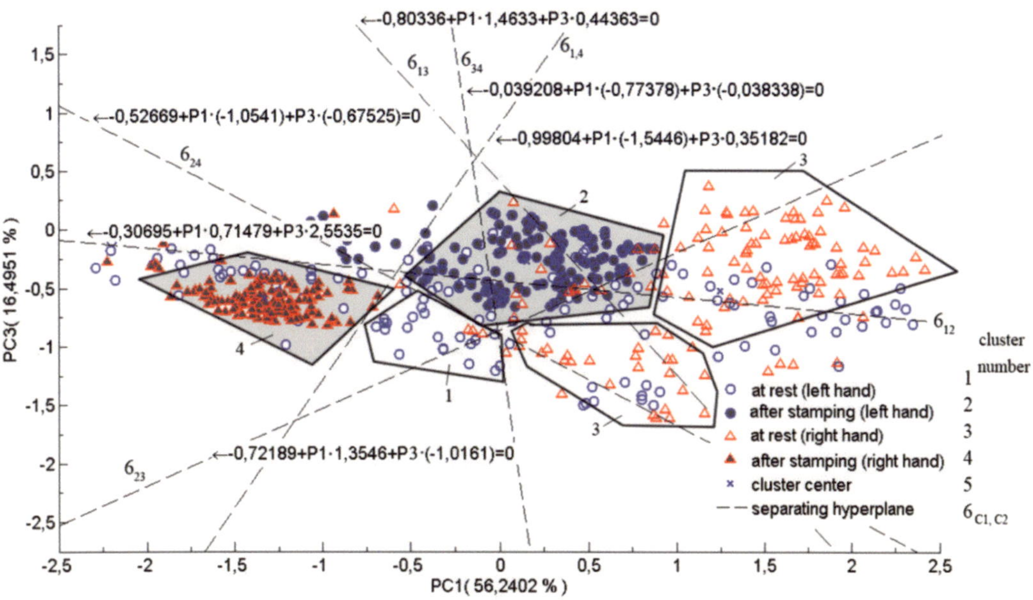


Fig. 17. Non-invasive LED analysis of blood information patterns of the right and left human hands at a rest state and after stamping during 10 sec

| Values of blood parameters | Norm | At rest | After clapping one's hands and stamping |
|---|---|---|---|
| lactic acid, mmole/l | 0,35-0,78 | 0,75 | 0,8 |
| glucose, mmole/l | 3,3-5,5 | 5,6 | 5,4 |
| kreatine, mg/l | 1-4 | 3,1 | 3,3 |
| rest nitrogen, mmole/l | 14-28 | 25 | 27 |
| blood urea, mmole/l | 2,5-8,3 | 6,5 | 6,8 |
| creatinine, mmole/l | 0,09-0,17 | 0,11 | 0,12 |
| indican, mmole/l | 0,7-5,4 | 4,1 | 4,2 |
| total lipids g/l | 3,5-8 | 4,3 | 4,5 |

Table 4. Results of the biochemical blood analysis before/after clapping and stamping

### 3.3 Saliva

The intelligent system "ISLB" can also analyse high-informative patterns of saliva for monitoring of the food, soil and human biosafety. Simplicity of saliva sampling gives an opportunity to monitor the human health and biosafety in real-time, e.g., for the recognition of physical and functional states of the human organism. There is a structure chart in the figure 18 with presented saliva basic components for intelligent monitoring systems.

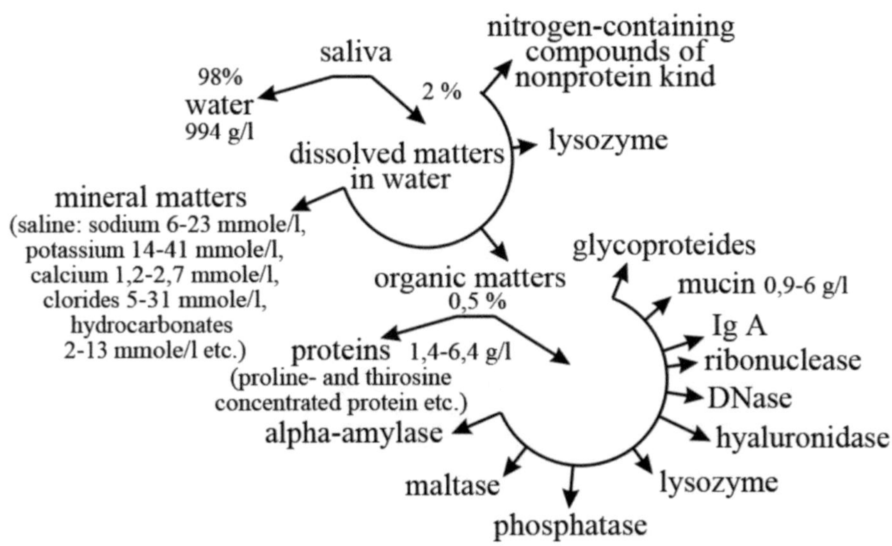


Fig. 18. Saliva structural pattern of a man

An information sensory pattern of saliva is changed under the influence of different physical activities but also depending on the state of being sated during a meal (saliva of the hungry man and the sated one) [8, 9]. Besides, a saliva pattern is changed considerable during the daily variation and defined by characteristics of the physical activity of different intensity as appears from the figure 19.

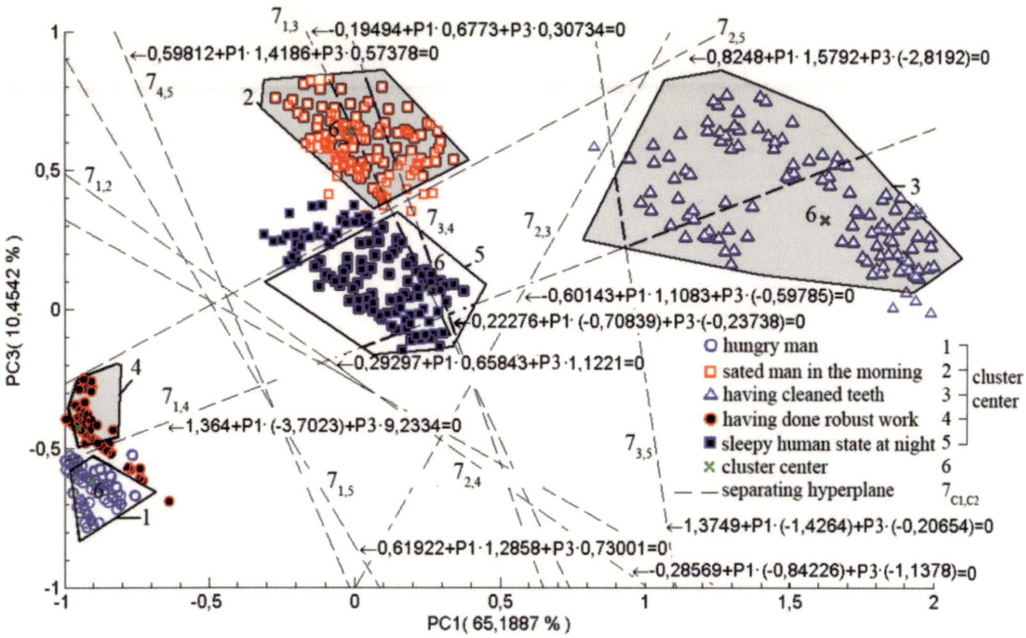


Fig. 19. Non-invasive LED analysis of saliva information patterns during the day

Ferments of the serous secretion of salivary glands suppress a microflora determining an antimicrobic function of covered coating produced by saliva of a hunger man. The saliva pH level (8,5 pH after breakfast) of a sated man exceeds greatly the saliva pH value for the hunger one (6,5-6,8 pH for awakening, 7 pH before a meal) and especially distinctly after carbonaceous eating because of the acid-produced activity of an oral cavity microflora changing saliva structural properties [9]. An information pattern after tooth brushing of toothpaste (9,4 pH) is distinctly different from other conditions of saliva taking and denotes the impossibility of immunorestoration as a result from a carbohydrate food intake (Fig. 20).

Saliva structural properties are impaired, and the application of such toothpastes will deteriorate biochemical saliva patterns in the future therefore. Toothpastes with a pH level being close to an initial saliva pattern with the normal pH level about 6-7,5 promote the recovery of saliva structural properties. Not only food, but also physical fatigue (5,5 pH) produces changes of saliva information patterns. At the same time, the saliva acidity is genetic individual for everyone and is varied according to the consumed nutrient composition. States of nervous excitement, mental or emotional strains produce an effect on saliva information patterns, so that there is the increase of a protein level in human saliva until 5 mg/ml, but its level doesn't exceed 2 mg/ml at rest.

The physical activity specifies the enhanced consumption of adenosine triphosphates in muscles, a strong oxygen need of human organism and an increase of lactic acid. A glycogen level is mainly consumed at the beginning of a physical work, but its consumption by organism is reduced during a continuous work. Saliva protein and enzymatic components characterize a human functional state during the physical activity therefore. There is the decrease in a number of antibodies depending on the physical activity, e.g., the immunoglobulin secretion (IgA) is reduced over a long period of time especially after coffee and alcohol. A simultaneous exposure to different ecological factors is known to have direct and indirect profound effects on the human organism.

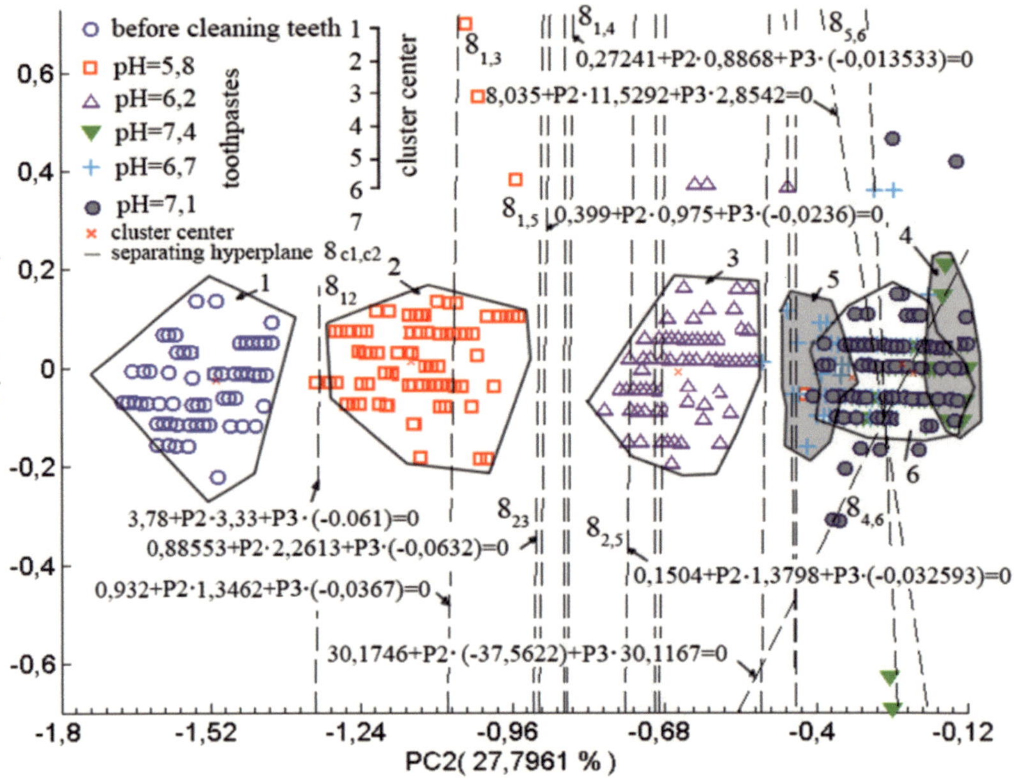


Fig. 20. Non-invasive LED analysis of saliva information patterns cleaning teeth

A geomagnetic factor connected with the Earth's magnetic field variability because of the increased solar activity has the strongest impact on the human health in particular [10]. The solar variability changes emotional and functional human states and brings to chronic diseases of nervous, circulatory and respiratory systems. There is a significant increase of the metal content (K, Mg, P, Pb, Cu, and Zn) and a reduced concentration of Na in saliva of men and women under the influence of the solar radiation exposure (Fig. 21) [10]. It means that the solar radiation taken during sunbathing enables to change saliva information patterns but also these ones for other human biomatters (blood, sweat, urine, tears, etc.).

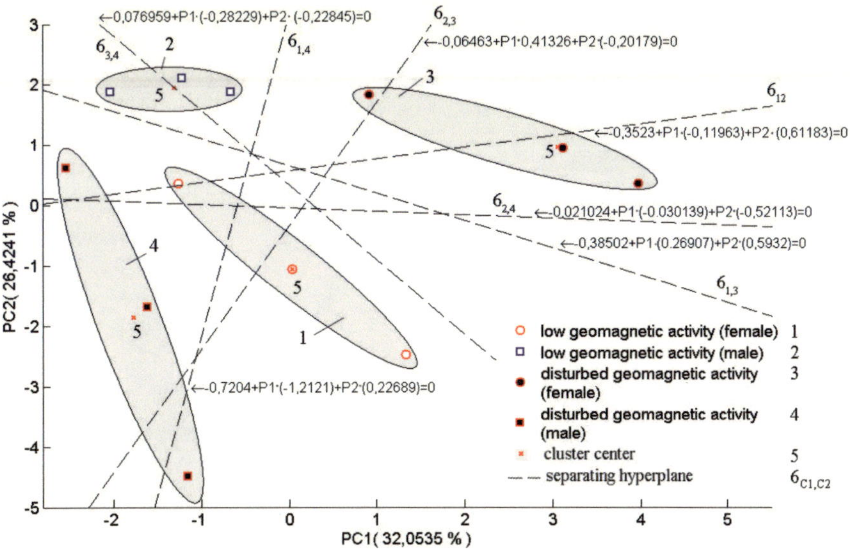


Fig. 21. Metal content in human saliva for low and disturbed geomagnetic activities

A self-learning intelligent system "ISCR" for monitoring and the recognition of a carcinoma in the broadband spectral range is developed by us which makes it possible to predict disturbances in the human organism caused by this one with the forecast precision about 80 % (Fig. 22) [8].

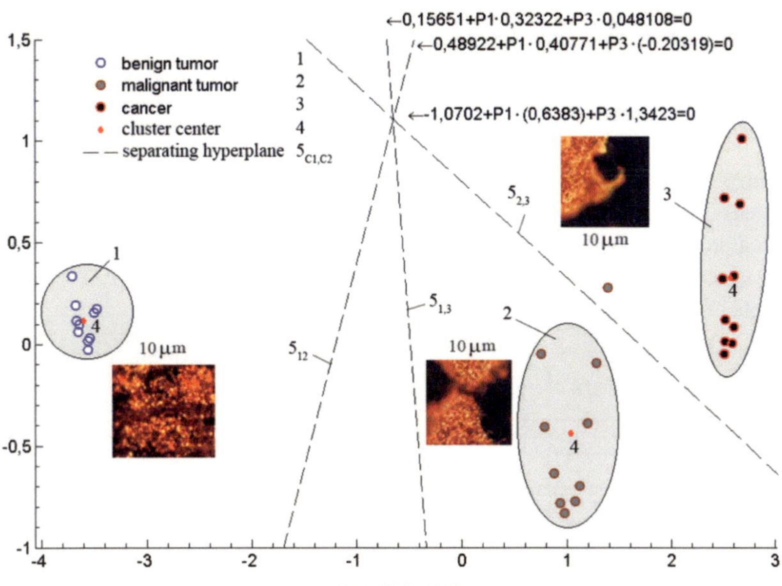


Fig. 22. Information patterns of a carcinoma using non-invasive LED eye with "ISCR"

At the same time, intelligent systems equipped with "ISCR" can transfer information to mobile devices of users (mobile and watch phones, smartphones, communicators, wristwatches,

PDAs, iPads, etc.), and after that these data are processed to produce an electronic information map of diseases for an individual subject. The use of mobile systems with "ISCR" enables non-invasive to monitor human personal and social activities therefore (Fig. 23).

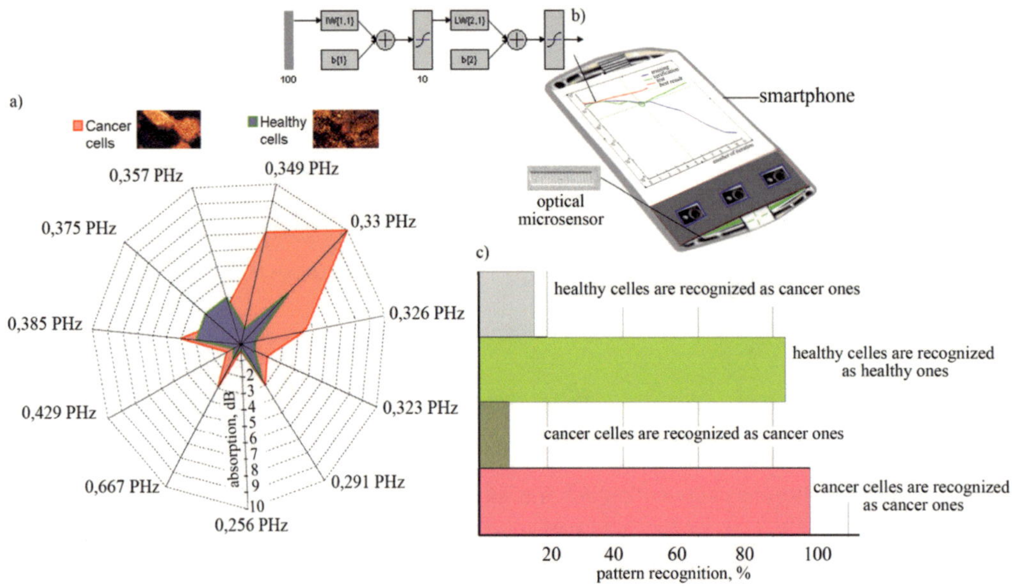


Fig. 23. Non-invasive recognition of information patterns of cells using the smartphone with LED eye

### 3.4 Sweat

The interest in sweat monitoring is increasing because of the sweat collection is convenient and non-invasive in comparison with traditional specimens (blood, urine, tears, etc.). The sweat chemical composition and the correlation of individual components depend on body perspiration (Table 5), the metabolism intensity, and the human health, emotional and functional states (Fig. 24) [11].

| Values of sweat parameters | Biochemical information pattern of sweat | |
|---|---|---|
| | before taking a shower | after taking a shower |
| whole protein, g/l | 0,8 | 0,38 |
| albumens, g/l | 0,41 | 0,11 |
| urea, mmole/l | 16,3 | 16,5 |
| creatinine, μmole/l | 52,5 | 35,9 |
| ammonia, mmole/l | 20,6 | 19,4 |
| amino acids, mg/l | 35 | 20,5 |
| glucose, mmole/l | 0,35 | 0,17 |
| pH value | 6,2 | 5,3 |

Table 5. Results of the sweat biochemical analysis in the morning

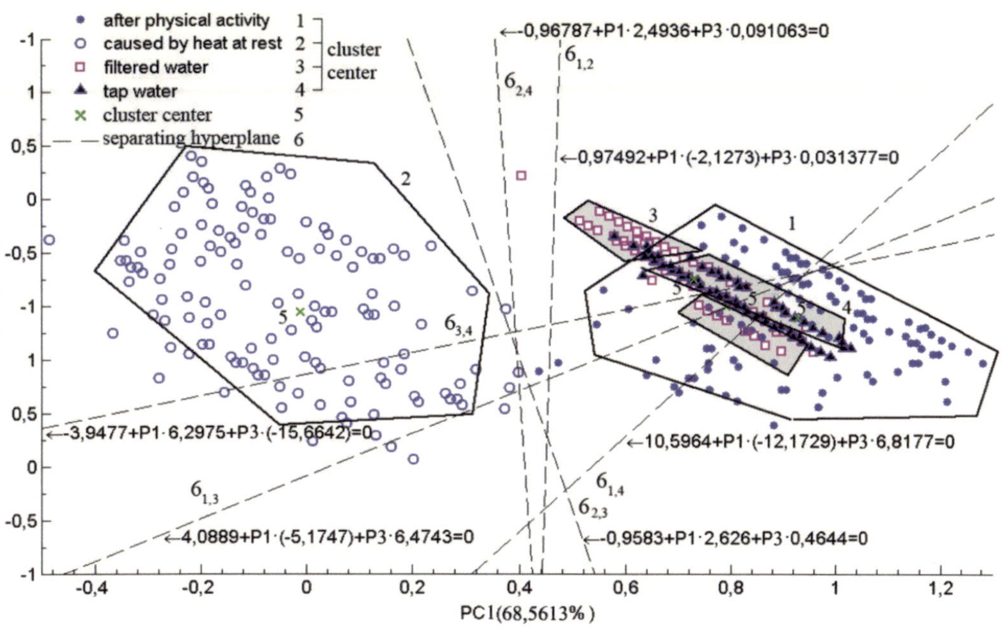


Fig. 24. Non-invasive LED analysis of sweat information patterns depending on human functional states

The intelligent system "ISLB" can analyse sweat sensory patterns to recognize harmful and dangerous substances in the human organism. There are comparative estimating fluid parameters for sweat, tap water and filtered one in the table 6 which makes clear information patterns presented in the figure 24. It makes possible to use a sweat pattern for real-time monitoring of human emotions and an improvement of the emotional self-regulation. An emotion is worried feeling which motivates, regulates and orientates our perception, thinking, activity, can be super intellectual and generates new innovative ideas. "ISLB" controls, is trained in the host response to such and such but after that recognizes on the state of health (wet skin, temperature, etc.) whether a man is in good spirits or depressed. As soon as there is clammy sweat and temperature rises to 38,5°, it is indicative of preinfarction angina or worse than this one [8]. The intelligent system "ISLB" is able to predict the state of health and the quality of human life using sweat patterns.

| Fluid parameters | Sweat (norm), mg | Tap water, mg/dm³ | Filtered water, mg/dm³ |
|---|---|---|---|
| pH | 6,2 | 7,3 (7 pH - pure water) | 7,1 |
| Cu | 0,006 | 0,006 | not defined |
| Mn | 0,006 | 0,1 | 0,1 |
| Ca | 8,7 | 56 | 1 |
| Mg, | 2,9 | 20,6 | 1,8 |
| Fe | 0,047 | 0,34 | 0,12 |
| Na | 134 | 120 | 12,72 |
| Cl | 161 | 0,7 | 0,2 |
| K | 39 | 180 | 53 |

Table 6. Comparison of a biochemical information pattern of sweat with some liquids

### 3.5 Urine

Human urine is a complex component biomatter consisting of organic components. Information patterns of urine describe general functional well-being, so urine passes through the human organism many times. Any changes of urine information patterns are connected with its pH level especially (Fig. 25). There is a low pH level (5-6,8 pH) of urine in the morning, but urine is getting neutral two hours later after eating, then alkaline (7-8,5 pH).

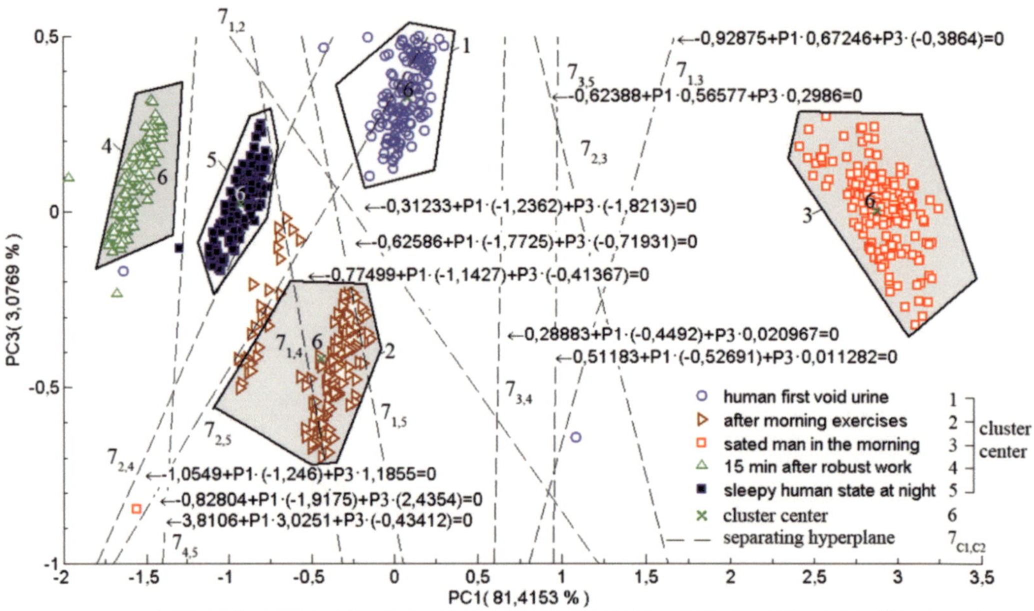


Fig. 25. Non-invasive LED analysis of information patterns of urine during the day

The pH level of urine remains to be equal to 6,6-6,8 pH by day. Ketone bodies are produced in the liver of a hunger man or after the long-term physical activity and characterize fat oxidation. There is also no glucose in urine of a healthy man, but it can be present because of the carbohydrate hypernutrition during a meal and physical activities [11, 12].

### 3.6 Tears

A lacrimal fluid is a multicomponent secreta which, e.g., total protein is a uniform dysbolism identifier in. This one is varied considerable depending on functioning states of the human health: there is total protein for a healthy man an average of 5,4 g/l but increases in case of, e.g., cornea inflammation to 7,8 g/l. The glucose content in tears correlates with its level in human blood, so that information lacrimal fluid enables to recognize patterns of emotional and functional states of the human organism. Moreover, it is possible to diagnose a human state and the health using for the analysis the alpha amylase activity in tears that catalyzes hydrolysis of starch and glycogen [13]. The concentration of amylase in a lacrimal fluid is in 4 times more than in blood. There is the amylase activity in tears of the healthy men in the range of 130-250 unit/l, but, e.g., acute pancreatitis emerges if this one is more 300 unit/l [14].

## 4. Intelligent systems in technology of biosafety

### 4.1 Intelligent system with virtual broadband polarized "electronic eye"

An intelligent mobile hardware and software microsensory system "ISPB" with a broadband polarized "electronic eye" is developed by us to recognize information patterns, e.g., of biomatters, soil, food products. The sensor intended for measuring the light polarization consists of a send-emitting module and a virtual polarizer with a self-learning software. If a polarized light penetrates, e.g., in a human biomatter (blood, saliva, sweat, urine, tears), then the plane of polarization is turned through angle depending on the concentration of individual components in a biological fluid. A refractive index of blood components strongly depends on the polarizability of protein structures in particular. The use of the virtual polarization also gives an opportunity to determine polluting and foreign surface layers on an investigated matter, produce information patterns of objects, e.g., food products for the personal and social biosafety (Fig. 26a) and for generating information patterns of the human functional state. Fig. 26b,c,d,e shows obtained average reflection factors of a scattered light and the polarized one for the investigated food products (soda, salt, water, milk) with the rotation of the plane of polarization (0°, 30°, 60°, 90°) in a direction to the plane of light incidence. If there are some surfaces with refractive indexes being different from a refractive index of an investigated matter, then the part of light is thrown back, but the rest of this one passes through the matter partially being reflected from it and after that goes out again. The reflection coefficient differs from the reflection factor of the investigated matter. Thus, the intelligent system "ISPB" makes it possible to determine refraction and reflection indexes for any light angles and any degrees of its polarization but also to carry out the research and the control of the quality of matters with impure substances, surface foreign or polluting films. "ISPB" is especially very important for the application in biotechnology, ecology, food industry, precision agriculture or for a personal and social biosafety [1, 2, 8].

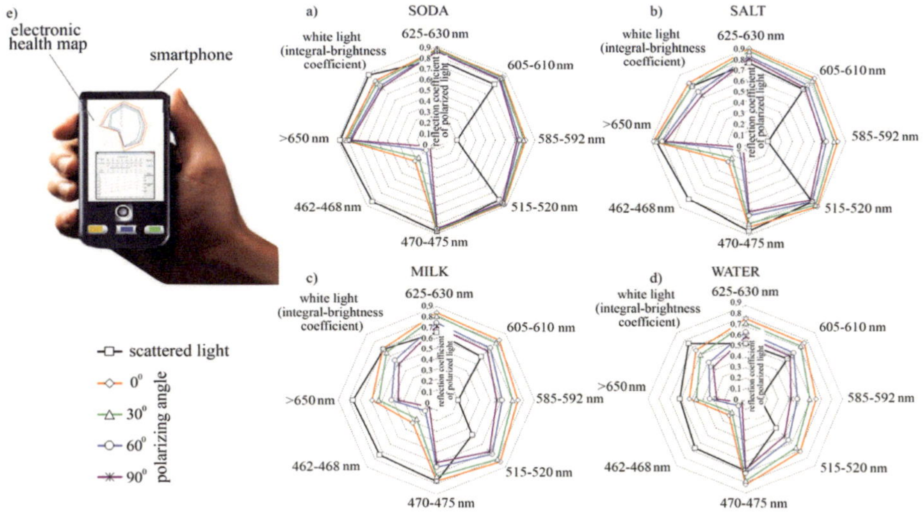


Fig. 26. Intelligent system "ISPB" with the virtual polarized "electronic eye" for the calculation of reflection coefficients of polarized light and forming information patterns

### 4.2 Recognition of food information patterns for the human biosafety

The developed intelligent system "ISSE" can be used for the recognition of information patterns of foods to maintain and control the human health and biosafety. Their physical and biochemical properties determine coefficients of the optical reflection and light scattering particularly, the quality and the biosecurity of produced food substances. There are optical reflection coefficients for light flour and dark one in the table 7. The flour is lighter, the one is more qualitative, so the reflection from lighter flour in the visible spectral range is higher for high quality one. The presented optical information patterns of different berries and foodstuffs (bread, butter, curds, flour, etc) in the figures 27, 28 can be applied as reference information for the detection of harmful or dangerous toxic components and the content of heavy metals which are accumulated in soil especially because of the nonuniform application of mineral fertilizers, microbial contamination and kept in harvested crops and produced foods [1, 3-5].

| Wavelength | Reflection coefficient | |
|---|---|---|
| | light flour | dark flour |
| 405 (violet) | 0,18 | 0,16-0,17 |
| 460 nm (blue) | 0,84 | 0,72-0,76 |
| 505, 530 nm (green) | 0,92 | 0,81-0,83 |
| 570 nm (yellow) | 0,78-0,82 | 0,7-0,6 |
| 620 nm (orange) | 0,87-0,82 | 0,81 |
| 660 nm (red) | 0,87-0,93 | 0,85 |
| 405-650 (white colour) | 0,77-0,81 | 0,7 |
| 760-2400 nm (infrared light) | 0,89 | 0,86-0,87 |

Table 7. Comparison of reflection coefficients for different kinds of flour

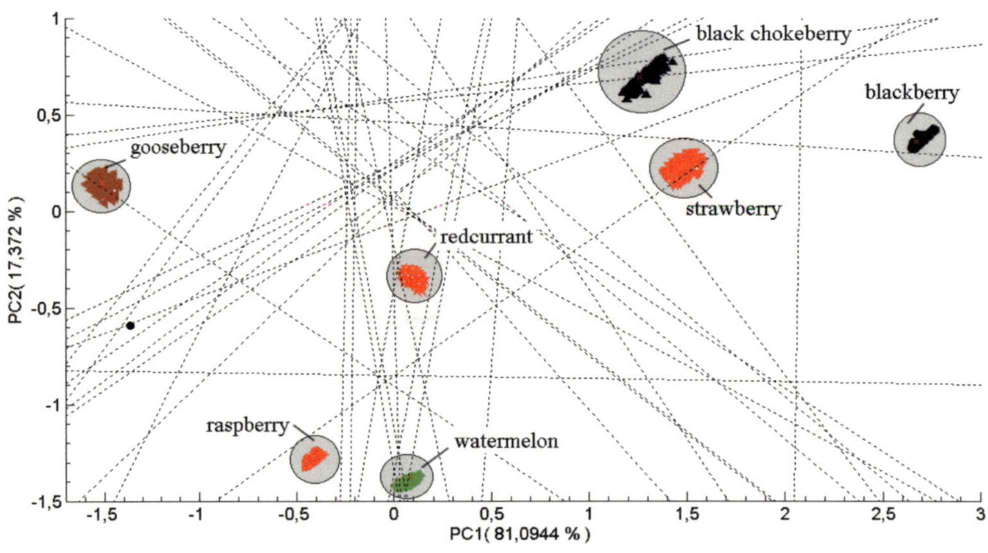


Fig. 27. Noncontact LED e-eye for measuring information patterns of berries

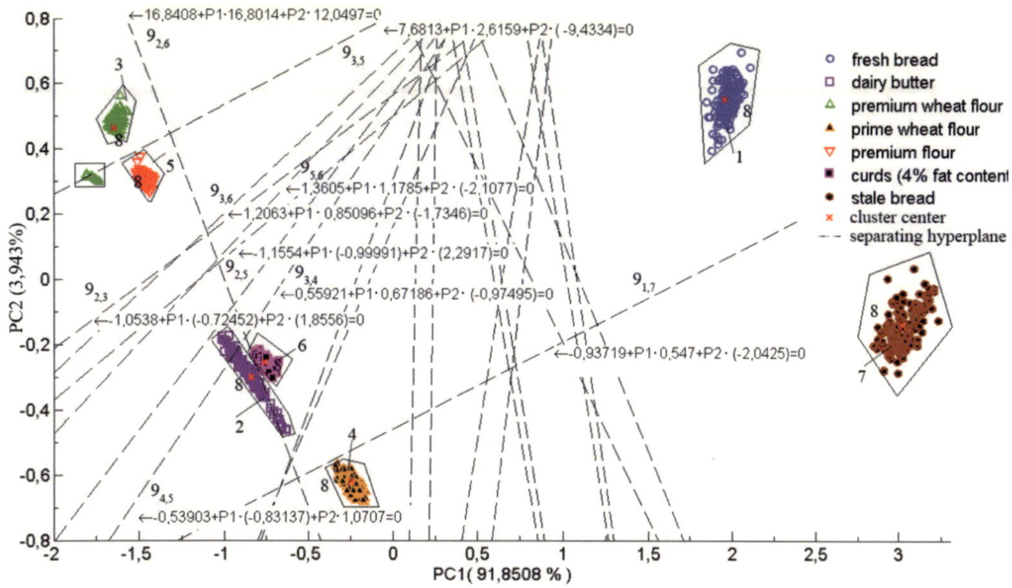


Fig. 28. Noncontact LED e-eye for measuring information patterns of foods

Up-to-date techniques for the recognition of information sensory patterns of foods are rather labour-intensive, costly, extremely time-consuming and require highly skilled specialists. The intelligent microsensory system "ISLB" represents an unique microlaboratory on a chip of the type e-eye and is intended for solving important practical problems in intelligent precision agriculture, e.g., for the control of raised farming cultures (maize) and with the generation of sensory information patterns (Fig. 29).

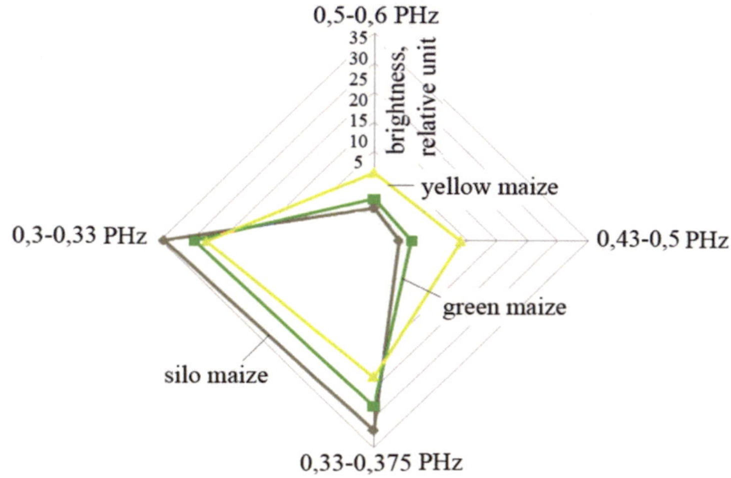


Fig. 29. Information patterns of maize using "ISLB"

Distinctive features of "ISLB" consist in the capability to function with the navigation satellite monitoring technology; therefore, "ISLB" can be presented as a mobile retransmitter and applied local with the use of pilotless vehicles or satellite mobile devices (Fig. 30) [8].

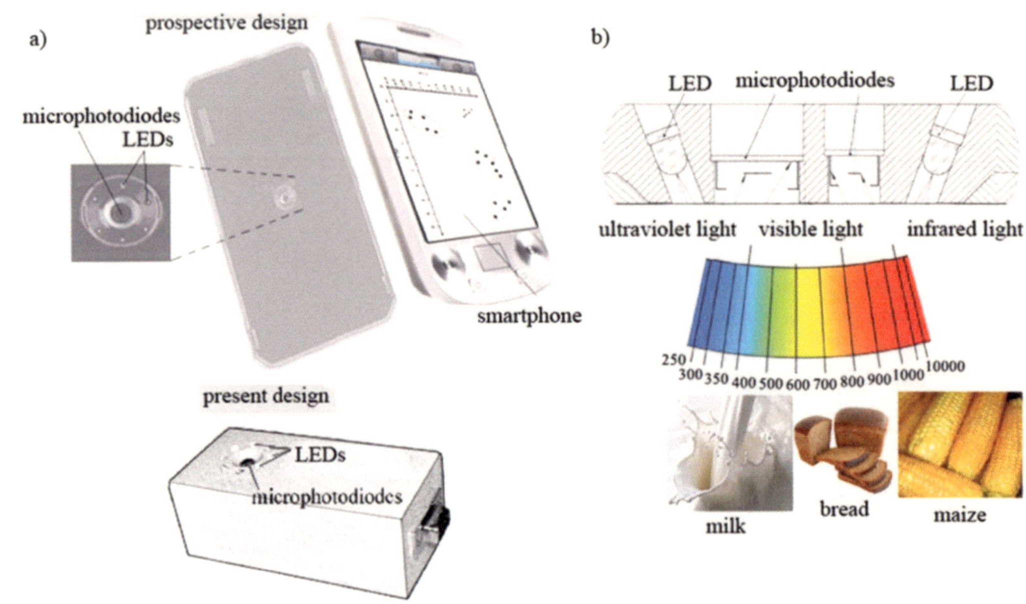


Fig. 30. (a) Design of the intelligent system "ISLB" with (b) the LED optical technology

After the registration of information patterns of biomatters (blood, saliva, sweat, urine, tears, etc.), food products or sensory patterns of soil a packet is generated, encrypted, cryptographic transformed, and antinoise encoded for the transfer to a server (Fig. 31). The transmission is realized through a socket defined at the client software or the server. Then information is conveyed to the server where the received data packet is decrypted and decoded, but data preprocessing, self-learning of the intelligent system based on expert judgements and previous obtained results are fulfilled. A high learning rate is achieved by means of the intelligent self-learning software "ISLB" based on multicore programming algorithms. Prediction results are transferred to the client software (watch and mobile phone, smartphone, communicator, iPad, PDA, wristwatch, etc.). There is displayed information on a screen with a full electronic intellect-map of functioning agricultural or farm enterprises during production steps of precision agriculture, an electronic map of the biosafety of raised cultures to control introduced fertilizers, toxic substances in soil or the level of crop yield. Moreover, an electronic virtual map of the human health with sensory information patterns of biomatters can be showed on the smartphone screen or other portable mobile devices. Intelligent client applications of Visial Studio with .NET Framework 3.5 ensure high adaptability and fast self-learning, but the data library Parallel Extensions gives an opportunity to accelerate data-handling and self-training procedures depending on a number of available system cores and SQL Server 2005 makes possible the development of Web-applications.

Owing to on-the-fly computing information patterns it is possible effective self-learning of the intelligent system "ISLB", the better opportunity to prevent the onset of human diseases at an early stage of their activity because of the consumption of poor food products or hazardous to the human health farming cultures which are raised in soils contaminated by dangerous viruses and bacteria. Thus, the scientific prognostication of the accumulation of chemical and toxigenic substances in natural plant and animal foods and food products which endanger the human health and have harmful effects on human life is very important for the recognition of offending foods and non-specific changes in a biosystem state [8, 12].

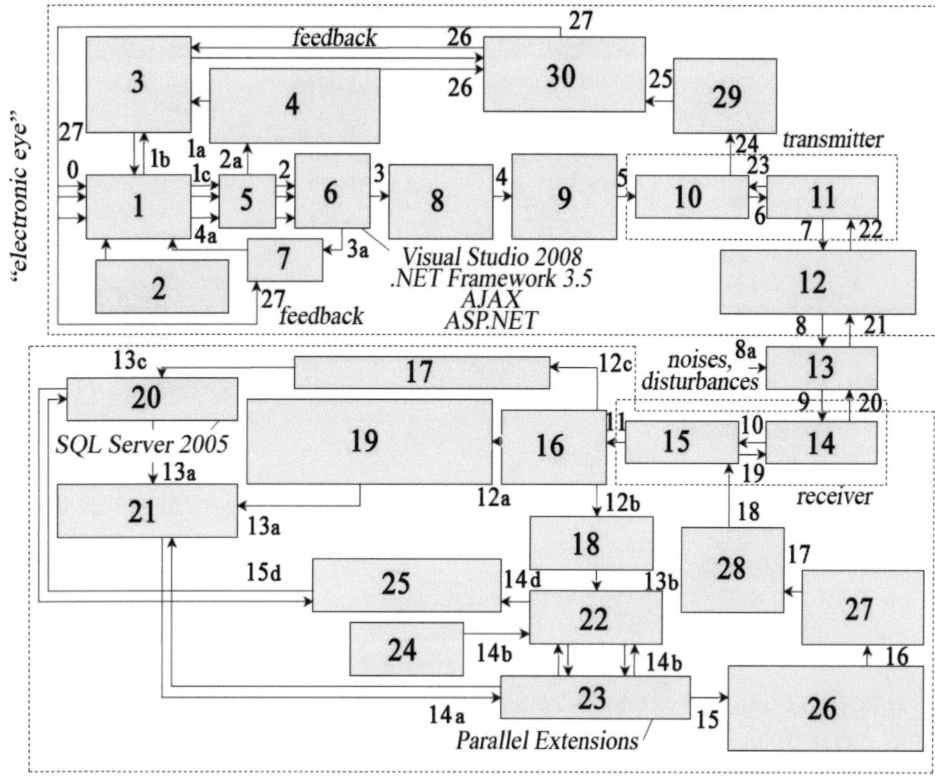


Fig. 31. Functional diagram of "ISLB": 1 - registration of information patterns; 2 -information sensory patterns of biomatters (blood, saliva, sweat, urine, tears, etc.), food products, crops or soil; 3 - authentication and identification of biometric patterns; 4 - generating biometric patterns (micro-nanostructure of investigated matters); 5 - drivers of sensory devices; 6 - sensory data acquisition; 7 - periodicity of the control; 8 - forming the data packet for the transfer to the server; 9 - encoding and cryptography of the data packet; 10 - antinoise coding; 11 - modulator; 12 - data transfer using the socket determined at the client software or the server; 13 - transmission channel; 14 - demodulator; 15 - antinoise decoding; 16 - deciphering the data packet transferred to the server; 17 - expert evaluation (statistical analysis); 18 - data pre-processing; 19 - using optimization criterions to define temporal information patterns on the basis of the minimization of intercluster centroid distances; 20 - database of stored reference patterns; 21 - calculation of distance functions in a multidimensional space; 22 - self-learning the intelligent system; 23 - multicore paralleling of data processing; 24 - neural networks, genetic algorithms; 25 - calculation of reference bioinformation patterns; 26 - generating prediction results (statistical probability, error of bioinformation pattern recognition); 27 - intelligent system of decision making for the transfer to the client software; 28 - encoding and cryptography of the data packet; 29 - deciphering the data packet transferred to the server; 30 - data transmission of decisions taken by intelligent system

### 4.3 E-eye with SAW retransmitter for wireless sensory networks

The hardware and software complex on a chip of the type "electronic eye" developed by us can be technically improved using retransmitters on surface acoustic waves (SAWs) with the RFID technology of real-time monitoring for the individual human biosafety (Fig. 32a,b) [1].

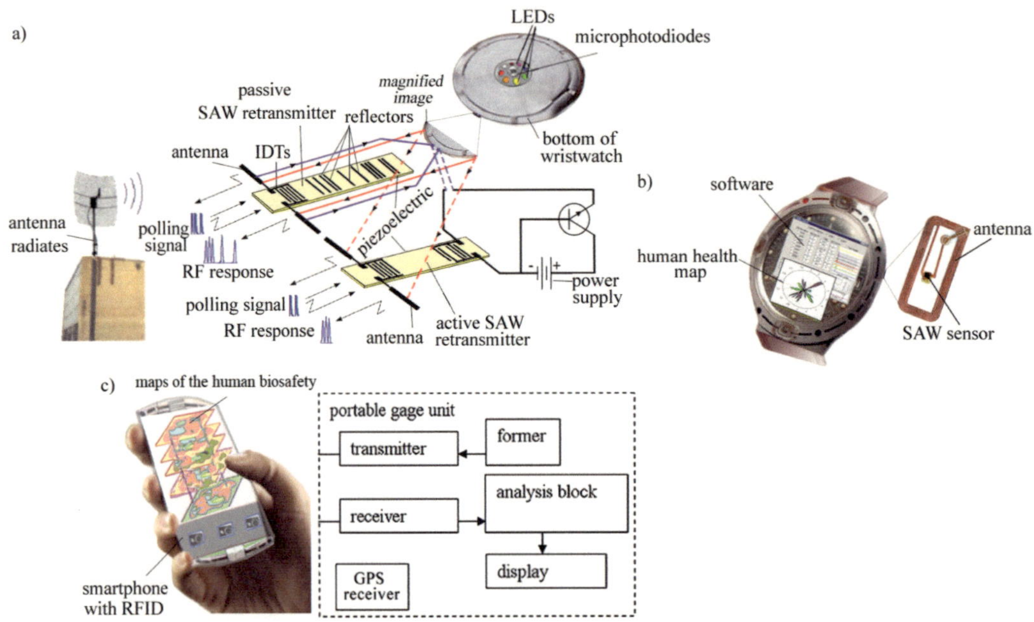


Fig. 32. (a) Wireless active (passive) SAW sensory micro-nanosystem with the LED technology e-eye. (b) Intelligent wristwatch with the RFID technology and LED e-eye. (c) Smartphone with the RFID technology for data processing from the wristwatch

The wireless SAW micro-nanosensory system consists of an antenna, interdigital transducers (IDTs) and a set of reflecting electrodes located on a piezoelectric crystal. If the antenna of the SAW sensor picks up a radio-frequency electromagnetic wave, then a received electromagnetic signal is transmitted to IDTs which are in the form of plane parallel electrodes on a substrate surface and are connected with each other through common buses and after that to a special control unit starting the optical information read-out. An outcoming time-lagged signal of spectral reflection characteristics enhances an alternating electromagnetic field which has the significant impact on an anisotropic dielectric and harmonic mechanical oscillations, tensions, strains caused by the inverse piezoelectric effect and emerged in the SAW sensor substrate. Electric charges with unlike signs are produced on the crystal surface which conditions the onset of an electric potential between IDT electrodes and the electrostatic field. There is a field with the elliptically polarized component determining an arising acoustic wave as a result of the superposition of the source field and the complementary subfield. The acoustic wave after the reflection effects on IDTs and brings to the distribution of electric charges due to the direct piezoelectric effect between IDT electrodes and to the generation of an electromagnetic signal. The SAW velocity and frequency this one are changed depending on different conditions of the propagation medium. The SAW propagates from IDTs in the direction of reflectors but then backwards to IDTs where is transformed into an electromagnetic signal emitted by the antenna to a rider. Thank to the low SAW velocity it is possible to get long time delays and prevent echo signals, but the sampling time exceeds $10^{-5}$ s, so the system can be used in driving objects (agriculture machines, portable devices of farmers, etc.). The intelligent system enables to extract the initial signal containing spectral reflection characteristics from the investigated biomatter. The principal advantages of the developed system on a chip e-eye with wireless passive SAW retransmitters are low-power consumption, high reliability and low cost and unlimited operation life. The intelligent LED microsensory system with the wireless active SAW extra has an energy source and semiconductor microcircuitries for the signal multiplication and the increase in operating distances, but the working life of such devices decreases. The identification of active SAW retransmitters can be realized by changing distances between two IDTs. The readout distance of the active SAW retransmitter with the power source (10 W) can achieve up to 50 km therefore [1, 2, 15]. The basic future tendency of mobile technologies requires the development of intelligent sensory systems and networks which are able to adapt to different conditions of real-time monitoring of the individual human biosafety flexible. If agrotechnical machines, farm enterprises with portable mobile analyzers and mobile devices are equipped with "CDOT" developed by us, then agriculture will be more precise and economic, but the food biosafety of countries will be improved (Fig. 33a,b). Information patterns of soil are presented in the form of electronic and virtual maps, e.g., an electronic map of applied nutrients and organic fertilizers, of the level of crop yield, of the yield of soil for last years or an information-microbial state of soil. The human biosafety is better controlled by intelligent systems using an electronic satellite map of field, electronic maps of the biosafety of crops, plant and animal foods along with electronic intellect-maps for precision agriculture [3, 4, 8].

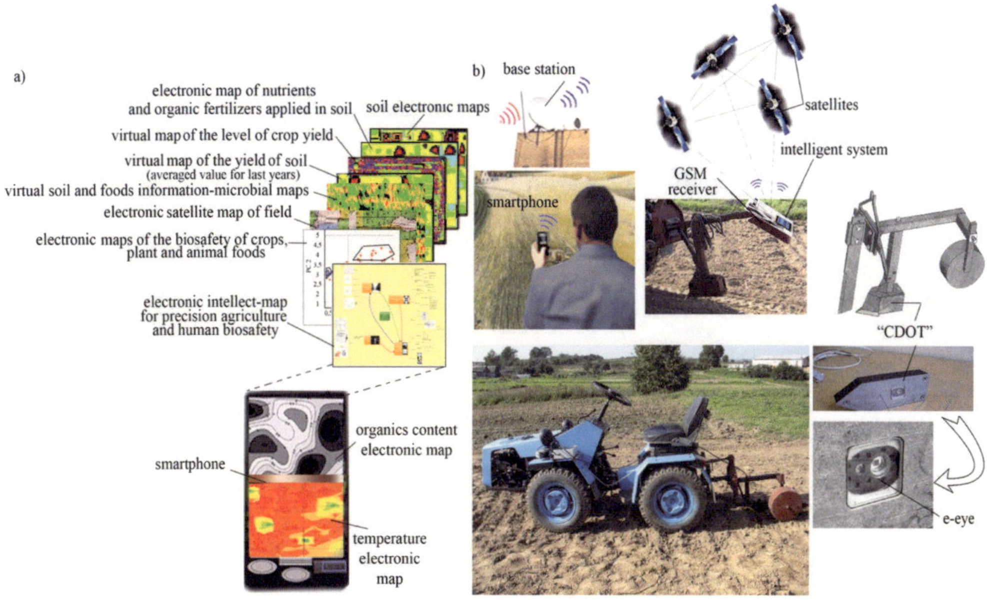


Fig. 33. (a) Intellect-map and virtual electronic ones for precison agriculture and the human biosafety. (b) Intelligent sensory system on a chip e-eye for the pattern recognition of soil

### 4.4 Data security for precision agriculture and biosafety

To ensure the confidentiality of information and the data integrity during processing and transferring in wireless self-learning intelligent sensory systems and networks, an antinoise coding, the superencryption using a private key generated from biometric data, an individual cryptographic data protection with an intelligent technique of the personal authentication superprotection patented by us are used in the sensory systems "CDOT" and "ISLB" for the recognition of the falsification, the imitation and an unauthorized use of synthetic biometric data by means of the analysis of additional micro-nanoinformation patterns of investigated biomatters (Fig. 34a,b,c) [1, 3-5, 16, 17].

A mobile application with a quick response (QR) encoding technique for mobile and watch phones, smartphones, communicators, PDAs, iPads on the Android virtual platform is developed to protect information patterns of bioobjects. A photo taken with the scanning device, e.g., with an embedded microcamera is QR encoded parallel completely, stored in a database including its QR code and divided into spectra (RGB) which are also QR encoded in a transducer separately. More precise QR code can be generated by the analysis and the comparison between the completely QR encoded pattern and the spectral ones. To read QR code, the obtained QR codes of spectral images and the base QR code of the photo are compared to produce the precise image pattern (Fig. 34).

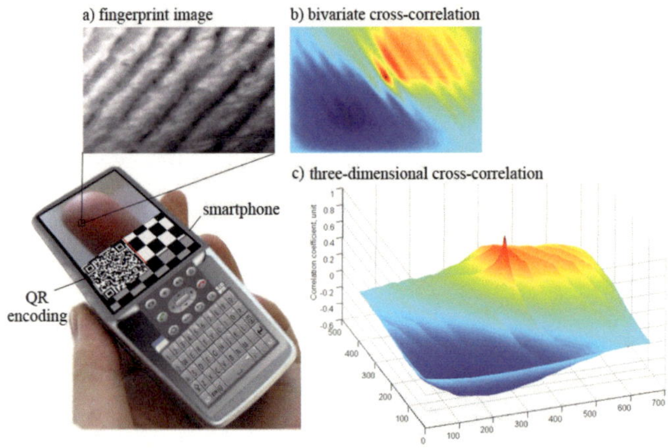


Fig. 34. Android virtual platform with QR encoding information patterns of bioobjects and the superprotection technology of biometric data: (a) nanostructure of the fingerprint; (b) bivariate / three-dimensional (c) cross-correlation function between the fingerprint and the imaged reference one

Intelligent precision agriculture requires a wide use of CIMLS-technologies for the continuous information support with an information security system at all the life-cycle stages of the agricultural production, services sectors and all the levels of personal and social activities in the process of mathematical and software modelling of perspectives and consequences of managerial and technological decision making [1, 18]. Then functioning systems are equipped with an intelligent interface and integral sensory micro-nanosystems for sensing and the adaptive control, with the wireless identification of objects, products, managerial decisions, services, etc. These principles are realized in accordance with International Standard requirements at the same time regulating an electronic data interchange with the nanotechnological biosafety and the information security. The CIMLS-technology presents distributed data storage in a network computer system including many services and subdivisions of farm enterprises. There is a unified system of rules, the data representation, storage, coding, and communication in the CIMLS-technology. A main principle of CIMLS is the fact that information generated at any stages of the life cycle is stored in CIMLS and is made accessible to every participant of this stage and other ones in concordance with available access permissions to these data. It enables to avoid duplication, unauthorized data substitution, falsification, imitation, changing, and errors of the control system, to abridge the labour, cut time and finances. Actions of government officials are opened to public scrutiny, so there is an integrated logistic control process with the intelligent system of decision-, provision-, decree-, law making. Information in the CIMLS-technology is generated, transformed, encoded, stored, and transmitted using intelligent softwares, e.g., Agro, ADAMIS, ADMOS with a "electronic description" of all the life-cycle objects, and human embellishment or information hiding is eliminated, minimized completely and identified [18].

We developed mathematical models of a controlled process of the complex agricultural production for intelligent precision agriculture, but also the intelligent system "ISAG" is developed for the control of farm enterprises. One of the important directions of precision agriculture is the improvement of control algorithms, the use of steering functions including the nonlinear constraint, the acceleration of a controlled variable, information about characteristics of the controllable system, actuators, sensors, etc.

## 5. Conclusion

The intelligent microsensory systems presented in this chapter are intended for the recognition of optical information patterns of a technology, a product or environment external conditions in the space of multidimensional sensory data on the basis of the LED technology e-eye. These ones enable to solve important practical problems in an agro-industrial complex, e.g., in intelligent precision agriculture and for the control of the biosafety of farm products, soils, plant, and animal foods. The developed intelligent system "ISLB" can inform users about probable homeostatic threats and recognize timely any changes in functioning the human organism by means of self-learning on optical data of biomatters, e.g., using systems on a chip of the type "electronic eye". The application of the intelligent systems developed by us in mobile retransmitters (smartphones, watch and mobile phones, communicators, iPads, PDAs, wristwatches, etc.) enables the fast and individual monitoring of the human biosafety, to detect whether there is the departure from the norm and quality standards in the production process, give other important information about the quality of the agricultural production and environmental conditions. At the same time, the developed microsensory systems can function not only using satellite technologies, but also local in mobile retransmitters or in pilotless vehicles. It makes possible to produce electronic and virtual maps of soil, crop yield, foods, information-microbial patterns, intellect-maps for the maintenance of intelligent precision agriculture with the CIMLS-technology. The intelligent systems with the LED e-eye can be used in micro-nanoelectronics, biotechnology, agriculture, medicine, food industry, computer and communication systems and networks.

## 6. References

[1] Koleshko V.M. (1979, 1980, 1982, 1983, 1984, 1985, 1987, 1988, 1989, 1992). *Certificate of USSR Authorship for Invention* № 491824, № 677586, № 683475, № 722449, №

780713, № 950145, № 1050511, № 1122160, № 1182939, № 1262317, № 1313292, № 1366018, № 1452423, № 1499691, № 1518985, № 1722068, № 1748575

[2] Koleshko V.M., Goidenko P.P. & Buiko L.D. (1979). *Control in Technology of Microelectronics*, Science and technology, Belarus, Minsk

[3] Koleshko V.M., Gulay A.V. & Luchenok S.A. (2006). Sensory System for Soil Express-Diagnostics in Technology of Precision Agriculture, *Proceedings of Scientific and Practical Conference on Sensory Electronics and Microsystem Technologies*, Russia, Odessa, June, 2006

[4] Koleshko V.M., Gulay A.V. & Luchenok S.A. (2006). Intelligent Sensory Systems for Technology of Precision Agriculture, *Proceedings of Scientific and Practical Conference on Scientific Innovative Activity and Entrepreneurship in Agricultural Sector: Problems of Efficiency and Management*, Belarus, Minsk, February, 2006

[5] Koleshko V.M., Gulay A.V. & Luchenok S.A. (2005). Network Technologies - a Basis for the Making of Intelligent Systems for Precision Agriculture, *Proceedings of 2nd Belarusian Space Congress*, Belarus, Minsk, October, 2005

[6] Koleshko V.M., Varabei Y.A. & Khmurovich N.A. (2010). Intelligent Sensory System for Optical Analysis of Biomatters, *Proceedings of Scientific and Practical Conference on Progressive Technologies and Development Prospects*, Russia, Tambov, November, 2010

[7] Vatansever-Ozen S., Tiryaki-Sonmez G., Bugdayci G. & Ozen G. (2011). The Effects of Exercise on Food Intake and Hunger: Relationship with Acylated Ghrelin and Leptin, *Sports Science and Medicine*, Vol. 10, pp. 283-291

[8] Koleshko V.M., Varabei Y.A. & Khmurovich N.A. (2011). *Cell Phones, Smartphones and Aging of Organism*, Belarusian National Technical University, Belarus, Minsk

[9] Papacosta E. & Nassis G.P. (2011). Saliva As a Tool for Monitoring Steroid, Peptide and Immune Markers in Sport and Exercise Science, *Science and Medicine in Sport*, Vol. 14, No. 5, pp. 424-434

[10] Khodonovich O.A. & Beljkov M.V. (2007). Influence of a Geomagnetic Factor on the Saliva Macro-and Microelemental Composition of Children, *Medical Journal*, Vol. 2, pp. 90

[11] Gleeson M. & Pyne D.B. (2000). Exercise Effects on Mucosal Immunity, *Immunology and Cell Biology*, Vol. 78, pp. 536–544

[12] Koleshko V.M., Varabei Y.A. & Khmurovich N.A. (2010). Multicore Intelligent System of Pattern Recognition, *Proceedings of International Conference on Perspective Technologies and Methods in MEMS Design (MEMSTECH-2009)*, Ukraine, Lviv, April, 2010

[13] Gupta R., Gigras P., Mohapatra H., Goswami V.K. & Chauhan B. (2003). Microbial alpha-amylases: a Biotechnological Perspective, *Process Biochemistry*, Vol. 38, No. 11, pp. 1599-1616

[14] Terehina N.A., Khlebnikov V.V. & Krivcov A.V. (2002). *Certificate of Russian Federation Authorship for Invention* № 2189044

[15] Koleshko V.M., Polynkova E.V. & Pautino, A.A. (2005). Sensory Systems with Radio Frequency Identification, *Theoretical and Applied Mechanics*, Vol. 22, pp. 51-62

[16] Koleshko V.M., Varabei Y.A., Azizov P.M. & Khudnitsky A.A. (2009). Intelligent System for Biotesting of Thoughts in Production Process. *Proceedings of the Samara Scientific Center of the Russian Academy of Sciences (Special Edition)*, Russia, Samara, April 2-3, 2009

[17] Koleshko V.M., Varabei Y.A., Azizov P.M., Khudnitsky A.A. & Snigirev S.A. (2009). *Prospective techniques of biometrical authentication and identification*, Belarusian National Technical University, Belarus, Minsk

[18] Koleshko V.M., Snigirev S.A. & Marushkevich E.V. (2010). CIMLS-technology for the control of electronic document management and flows of financial enterprises funds, *Informational systems and technologies*, pp. 513-516

# 2

# Knowledge Management in Bio-Information Systems

Kuodi Jian
*Metropolitan State University, Saint Paul, MN*
*USA*

## 1. Introduction

Knowledge management is a broad topic. For different people, it may mean different things. For business people, this phrase means the accumulated procedures/processes and experiences (organizational assets), and the way to facilitate the use, and to retain these assets within an organization. The Wikipedia website has the following definition for the knowledge management:

**"Knowledge Management (KM)** comprises a range of strategies and practices used in an organization to identify, create, represent, distribute, and enable adoption of insights and experiences. Such insights and experiences comprise knowledge, either embodied in individuals or embedded in organizational processes or practice." (Internet resource: http://en.wikipedia.org/wiki/Knowledge_management. Retrieved on 5/30/2011)

For computer science people, especially for those expert system developers, the term "knowledge management" has different meaning. We, computer science scientists, are concerned with the knowledge representation, data mining, and the knowledge structure that facilitates knowledge storage and retrieval with computers in mind. Thus, we will define the knowledge management as follows:

**Knowledge Management (KM)** comprises a wide range of methods/activities that extract information/knowledge from a body of unstructured raw data; organize the extracted information into structured form called knowledge; and design knowledge databases that are able to store and retrieve knowledge in an efficient way using computers.

In the above definition, we mentioned several terms such as raw data, information, and knowledge. What are the differences and the relationships among them? And the more fundamental question: how do we reason when faced with these entities? In the following sections, we will address these questions. First, we will outline the contributions of this document in the next section.

## 2. Contributions

In this chapter, we will introduce a computer reasoning method called "evidence theory" that is based on Bayes' theorem. We will describe relationships among raw data, knowledge, and information; we will implement a prototype of the evidence based reasoning software component in the context of the bio-information system framework. The prototype is implemented with Java language and is applied to a medical case example: colorectal cancer. The evidence based reasoning theory proposed in this chapter will have significant impact on computer reasoning and artificial intelligence research.

With the increase of raw power in computer hardware, the search for better intelligent systems never ends. The research topics cover a wide range of areas. For example, some studies focus on the emotional aspect of an intelligent system (Fujita & et al., 2010), while others use statistical reasoning method in classifying news articles (Asy'arie, A. & Pribadi, A., 2009). Compare to existing literatures and reasoning methods, our presentation on the topic of computer reasoning (evidence based reasoning) is thorough. In addition, the reasoning method we proposed is generic in nature, thus it can be used in any domain. One key feature of our method is its simple calculation. Especially when number of evidence gets large, this simplicity becomes more important. Of course, you do not get this for free. You have to do the preparation by calculating degrees for evidences. But the saving you get is well worth the effort.

## 3. Background for data, information, knowledge, and wisdom

We can view data, information, knowledge, and wisdom as hierarchical in the context of knowledge management. With the data at the bottom and the wisdom at the top, we journey through concrete to abstract, and through no relationship to strong relationship as we move from left bottom to right top. This phenomenon is shown in Figure 1.

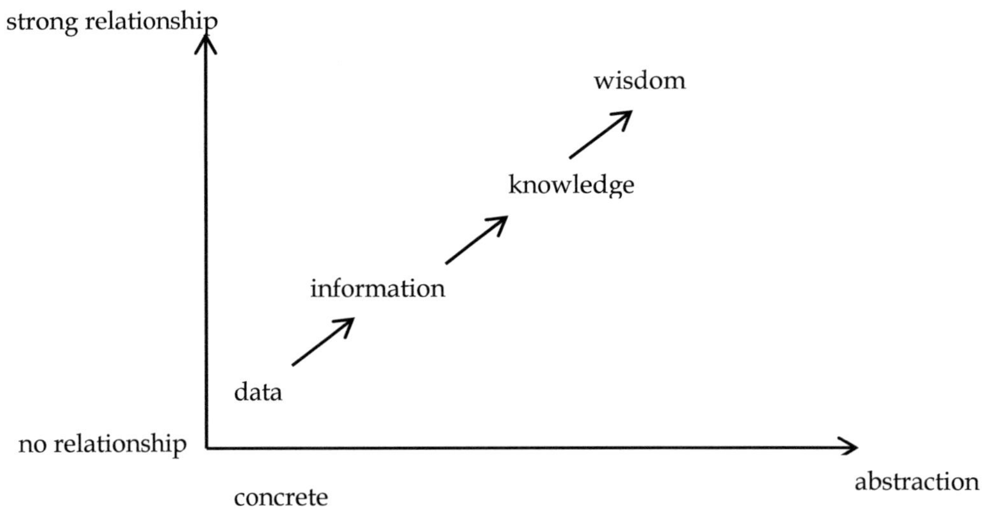


Fig. 1. Hierarchy of data to wisdom

Raw data are just meaningless points in data space. There are no references or relationships among these points. Raw data are like a phrase out of context. By themselves, they mean nothing. (referenced Bellinger, 2004)

As human, we often want to make sense out of raw data. When encountered a piece of data, we usually try to assign meaning to it, and try to find relationships for it. This is done by associating it with other things (or other data points). For example, consider the shapes in Figure 2.

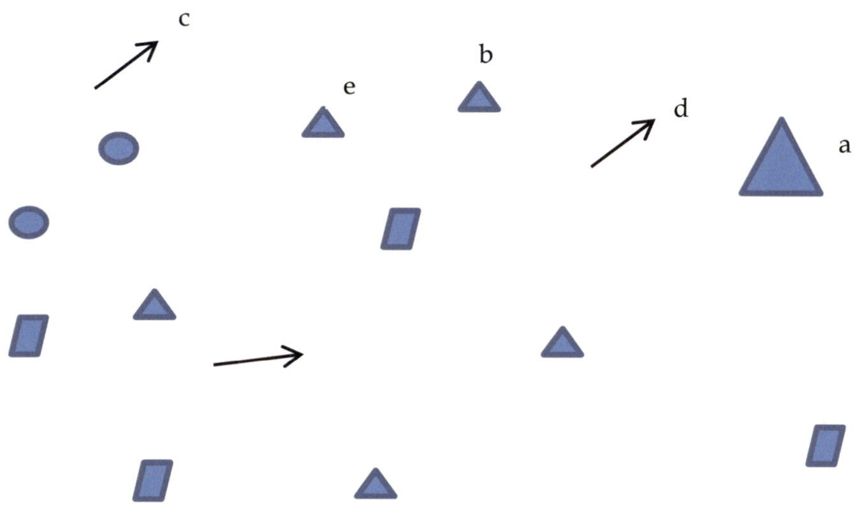


Fig. 2. Data points in data space

When seeing the items in Figure 2, we will automatically assign an "equal" relationship to item e and item b, assign the same relationship to item c and item d. We probably will assign a "similarity relationship" to item b and item a.

Take another example, if seeing the digits "3 4 5 …", most likely we will assign the meaning of "a sequence of positive integer numbers starting from 3 and extending to infinity." The point is that when there is no context, these raw data have no meaning. When we try to assign meanings to raw data, we are trying to create context for them. When raw data are put into context, some new things will happen.

The new things are information. There are some differences and relationships between raw data and information. First, information is not just a bunch of raw data piled together. Second, information is the interaction between the raw data and something we called "knowledge." Information depends on the understanding of the person perceiving the data. For example, the symbol "网 页"means nothing to an English speaker (to him, it is just raw data), but it conveys some information to a Chinese (to him, the same symbol is information and means a web page). The point is that whether some raw data represent meaningful information depends on the context. And the context is our prior experiences (often, we call these prior experiences "knowledge"). There is no guarantee that the information we extracted from raw data is correct. The correctness and usefulness of raw data depend on the knowledge of the person receiving the data. Another thing to point out is that the experiences/knowledge will have influence on the interpretation of the data. The same piece of data may carry different meanings under different contexts (knowledge).

Knowledge is our prior experience. In other words, knowledge is the accumulated relationships and patterns that a person perceives among raw data. For example, if a layman sees the blood glucose test result of 230 mg/dL, he may have no clue as what this means. But for a trained doctor's eye, it means the person had the test is diabetic. The only difference here is the pattern. In the doctor's mind, from his prior training, a series of patterns such as:

Glucose level of 230 mg/dL -> diabetic

Diabetic -> risk of blindness

Diabetic -> risk of kidney failure

exist. On the other hand, there are no such patterns in the layman's mind. In essence, knowledge is the factoring of patterns (this includes summarization, abstraction, and crystallization of patterns). In the world of knowledge management in computer science, the knowledge is accumulated and crystallized patterns and relationships; and the information is the product of the interaction between data and knowledge. In other words, when connecting the dots, you are producing information.

Wisdom is the highest form of deep patterns. Usually, we only attribute wisdom to intelligent beings. Bellinger (2004) has the following description about wisdom:

"Wisdom arises when one understands the foundational principles responsible for the patterns representing knowledge being what they are. And wisdom, even more so than knowledge, tends to create its own context. I have a preference for referring to these foundational principles as eternal truths, yet I find people have a tendency to be somewhat uncomfortable with this labeling. These foundational principles are universal and completely context independent. Of course, this last statement is sort of a redundant word game, for if the principle was context dependent, then it couldn't be universally true now could it?"

In this documentation, we will focus on data, information, and knowledge. We will leave the topic of wisdom to philosophers. Particularly, we will deal with computer reasoning and knowledge management using knowledge databases. Before presenting our methods for the knowledge representation, reasoning, and knowledge management, we need to answer the philosophical question: is there any difference between human reasoning and computer reasoning? Our answer is "Yes."

Computer reasoning and human reasoning are different. One of the biggest differences has something to do with creative ideas. Often, we see someone with so called "killer ideas." "Killer ideas" refer to those ideas that are revolutionary, creative, and not conform to the norms of the contemporary generation. For example, Sir Isaac Newton's law of gravity, Albert Einstein's theory of relativity, and the idea of ten dimensional UNIVERSE are all examples of killer ideas. How exactly these "killer ideas" are produced is still open for debate. However, we do know computers are incapable of producing these ideas (at least for the time being); because, we haven't seen any computer that can produce any meaningful killer ideas yet. Thus, we conclude that computers reasoning and human reasoning are different. With current technology, we can delegate computers to reason with low level entities (in the low-left of Figure 1) in the knowledge management hierarchy. This is because at lower levels, reasoning is more objective and concrete. The theoretical foundations of the reasoning at lower levels can be captured by the Bayes' theorem.

## 4. Theoretical foundation of computer reasoning

The insight that we get from the above discussion on raw data, information, knowledge, and wisdom tells us that reasoning at lower levels is easier than reasoning at the highest level. Since at the lower levels, we only need to deal with knowledge finding (data mining) and the application of the appropriate knowledge to some evidences. At the highest level (the killer idea level), we even do not know the mechanism that produces creative ideas; therefore, it will be much harder to reason at this level. As mentioned in the previous section, the theoretical foundation of computer is Bayes' theorem. Let's investigate what is the Bayes' theorem? Bayes' theorem can be expressed as Formula 1:

$$P(A|X) = \frac{P(X|A)*P(A)}{P(X|A)*P(A)+P(X|{\sim}A)*P({\sim}A)} \qquad \text{(Formula 1)}$$

The notation P(A | X) means the probability (or the chance) that the event A will happen given the evidence (or the observation) of X. In probability theory, this is called conditional probability. Depending on the quality of evidence X, the probability of event A happening may be heavily affected by the presence of the evidence X.

The symbol "~" means complement, that is, the opposite of what follows it. For example, if P(A) means the probability of event A will happen, then P(~A) means the probability of event A will not happen. One thing to point out is that there are three pieces in Formula 1: the reasoning about the occurrence of an event A (the left side of the equation), the evidence (X), and the causality relationship between the evidence X and the event A (embodied by P(X | A) and P(X | ~A)).

In a nutshell, Formula 1 says that if we see a piece of evidence X, we can reason about the chance of event A's occurrence given that the evidence X and the event A has a causality relationship. This is exactly the behavior that a rational person will display given a piece of evidence related to the event. Formula 1 can be extended to include two, three, ..., and many pieces of evidence. All we need to do is to apply the formula multiple times. For example, if both X and Y contribute to the occurrence of event A, we can calculate the final probability of event A by applying Formula 1 to get the probability of A given evidence X. Then, we use the result to apply Formula 1 again. Only this time, we should use the result in the first iteration to substitute the prior probability P(A), and P(~A). Actually, we can repeatedly apply Formula 1 to reason any number of evidences.

To get a better handle on how the Bayes' theorem works, let's work through a concrete example. Suppose that we have the following problem statement:

**Example 1:** "Lung cancer is the leading cause of cancer death in the United States." (Williams, 2003, p. 463) Suppose that about 0.2% of the population living in US with age above 20 has lung cancer. When doing an annual check, suppose that 85% of the people with lung cancer will show positive for the chest x-ray test. On the other hand, chest x-ray will have false alarms: 6% of the people without lung cancer will also show positive for the chest x-ray test. If a person went through the annual check and had a positive chest x-ray, what is the probability that he/she has the lung cancer? (For concreteness, you may assume that there are 10,000 people participated the annual check)

**Answer:** Most people will give the wrong answer of "the person will have 85% probability of having the lung cancer."

To get the answer right, we must first understand several important facts in statistics. The first thing is that

$$P(A \mid X) \neq P(X \mid A)$$

The reason that most people will get the incorrect answer of 85% is the confusion caused by the above inequality relationship.

The correct answer for Example 1 is 2.8%. The following is the analysis and steps showing how we get the correct answer:

1. We start out by the basic probability definition:

   P(cancer | positive x-ray) = number of people who have both cancer and positive x-ray in the annual check / total number of people with positive x-ray in the annual check (Formula 2)

   According to the meaning of conditional probability, the left side of Formula 2 is the answer we are looking for.

   **Note:** the key of the above equation is to use the number of people who have both cancer and positive x-ray as the numerator. If using people who have cancer as the numerator, the result will be wrong since there are people who have cancer but have negative x-ray test results.

2. We use concrete number. Without losing generality, we assume there are 10,000 people of age 20 and over participated in the annual check. Thus, we have the following data:

   The number of people who have lung cancer in the annual check group is 10,000*0.2% = 20.

   The number of people who are healthy in the annual check group is 10,000*99.8% = 9980.

   The number of people who have lung cancer and have positive x-ray is 20*85% = 17.

   The number of people who have lung cancer and have negative x-ray is 20*15% = 3.

   The number of people who have no lung cancer and have positive x-ray is 9980*6% = 599.

3. We use the data in step 2 and plug into the Formula 2 in step 1. We will get following answer:

   P(cancer | positive x-ray) = 17 / (17+599) = 17 / 616 = 0.028

Most people regard Bayes' theorem as statistical formula and overlook its reasoning logic. We want to point out that it is also a reasoning method that captures the essence of reasoning logic that reasons at the lower-levels. Thus, it is the theoretical foundation that underpins the computer reasoning.

## 5. Bayes' reasoning

Example 1 in previous section can also be solved by Bayes' theorem. One thing to remember in understanding Bayes' theorem is the following statistical formula:

$$P(A \& B) = P(A \mid B) * P(B) \qquad \text{(Formula 3)}$$

Or equivalently,

$$P(A \& B) = P(B \mid A) * P(A)$$

In the following, we will explain how Bayes' reasoning works and the meaning of its subparts.

### 5.1 Bayes' reasoning explained

Bayes' theorem can be viewed as the bridge that connects the reasoning to physical evidences: on the left of Formula 1 is the inference/reasoning, and on the right of Formula 1 is the physical evidence that supports the reasoning on the left. When estimating the prior probabilities (prior probability includes: the baseline probability P(A), the two conditional probabilities: P(positive x-ray | cancer) and P(positive x-ray | healthy)) on the right, we are constructing a reasoning model; when applying the Bayes' theorem, we are extracting information using the constructed model. The process of applying the theorem is the process of combining the raw data, the knowledge (context) to yield information. We can use the Bayes' theorem to solve Example 1 as follows:

1. Start with what we want to achieve: P(cancer | positive x-ray)
2. Rewrite it as following with the help of Formula 3:

$$P(\text{cancer} \mid \text{positive x-ray}) = P(\text{cancer \& positive x-ray}) \,/\, P(\text{positive x-ray})$$

3. P(positive x-ray) can be expanded to P(positive x-ray & cancer) + P(positive x-ray & ~cancer).

**Note:** this expansion captures the causality of the reasoning model. It says that the total number of people with positive x-ray in the annual check group is coming from two groups: the people with cancer and show the positive x-ray and the people with no cancer and show the positive x-ray.

4. Plug in the result from step 3 to the equation in step 2, we get

$$P(cancer|positive\ x-ray) = \frac{\mathrm{P(cancer}\ \&positive\ x{-}ray)}{\mathrm{P(positive\ x{-}ray}\ \&cancer)+P(positive\ x{-}ray\&{\sim}cancer)}$$

5. The above equation can be rewritten as following with the help of Formula 3:

$$P(cancer|positive\ x-ray) = \frac{\mathrm{P}(positive\ x-ray \mid cancer) * P(cancer)}{\mathrm{P}(positive\ x-ray \mid cancer) * P(cancer) + P(positive\ x-ray|{\sim}cancer) * P({\sim}cancer)}$$

This is exactly the same formula as in the Bayes' theorem (Formula 1). If we use the following data implied by the problem statement in Example 1:

P(cancer) = 0.2% (20 out of 10,000 have cancer) (1)

P(~cancer) = 99.8% (9980 out of 10,000 have no cancer) (2)

P(positive x-ray | cancer) = 85%

(85% of people with lung cancer have positive x-ray) (3)

P(positive x-ray | ~cancer) = 6%

(6% of people without lung cancer have positive x-ray) (4)

And plug in the above data into the above expression, we will get:

P(cancer | positive x-ray) = 85%* 0.2% / (85%*0.2%+6%*99.8%)

= 0.0017 / (0.0017+0.06)

= 0.0017 / 0.0617

= 0.028

This is exactly the same answer we got in the previous section.

Bayes' reasoning needs three pieces of information (all appear on the right of the equation at the beginning of step 5): the percentage of people with lung cancer, the percentage of people without lung cancer who have false alarms, and the percentage of people with lung cancer who show positive on the test. The first piece of information which is part of the priors is the baseline knowledge. The second and third pieces of information which also belong to the priors are the measurement of the quality of evidence. Bayes' reasoning is to use the evidence to change the belief/knowledge (shifting the baseline upwards with positive evidence or downwards with negative evidence). We will use more examples to show how this change of belief (the machine reasoning) happens. The left-side probability is the posterior probability. It is the revised view of the world in the light of evidence which is on the right-side of the equation.

To see how the first piece of information affects the Bayes' result, let's assume that the batch of people doing the annual check is high risk smokers. According to Williams (Williams, 2003, p. 464), smoker's chance of getting lung cancer is 13 times higher than non-smokers. Now, let's ask the same question: what is the probability of the person has lung cancer if he/she has the positive x-ray test given that the cancer rate in this group is 2.6% (2.6% is getting from 0.2* 13)? Sure enough, the final answer should be different. Actually, the new answer is 27.4%. The following is the analysis and steps showing how we get the correct answer:

1. We use the Bayes' theorem:

$$P(cancer|positive\ x-ray) = \frac{\mathrm{P}(positive\ x-ray \mid cancer) * P(cancer)}{\mathrm{P}(positive\ x-ray \mid cancer) * P(cancer) + P(positive\ x-ray|{\sim}cancer) * P({\sim}cancer)}$$

2. And plug in the following data:

$$P(\text{cancer}) = 2.6\% \quad \text{(260 out of 10,000 have cancer)} \tag{5}$$

$$P(\sim\text{cancer}) = 97.4\% \quad \text{(9740 out of 10,000 have no cancer)} \tag{6}$$

$$P(\text{positive x-ray} \mid \text{cancer}) = 85\%$$

$$\text{(85\% of people with lung cancer have positive x-ray)} \tag{7}$$

$$P(\text{positive x-ray} \mid \sim\text{cancer}) = 6\%$$

$$\text{(6\% of people without lung cancer have positive x-ray)} \tag{8}$$

3. And plug in the above data into the above Bayes' theorem, we will get:

$$\begin{aligned} P(\text{cancer} \mid \text{positive x-ray}) &= 85\%* 2.6\% \;/\; (85\%*2.6\%+6\%*97.4\%) \\ &= 0.0221 \;/\; (0.0221+0.0584) \\ &= 0.0221 \;/\; 0.0805 \\ &= 0.274 \end{aligned}$$

As you can see, comparing to the non-risky population (the probability of having cancer 0.028), the probability value of 0.274 of a person in the risky group is much higher. This makes sense since the prior probability of getting lung cancer is higher in this high risk group. In this new example, the quality of the x-ray equipment does not change. The only thing changed is the prior cancer rate, from 0.2% to 2.6%. At first look to the new problem, most people will give the same wrong answer of 85%. But Bayes' reasoning gives us more objective and correct answer. Here is an example that computer reasoning can be better than a human!

Bayes' reasoning can be used in situations that have multiple evidences. Let's use Example 2, which is the extension of Example 1, to illustrate how this is done.

**Example 2:** "Lung cancer is the leading cause of cancer death in the United States." (Williams, 2003, p. 463) Suppose that about 0.2% of the population living in US with age above 20 has lung cancer. When doing an annual check, assume that 85% of the people with lung cancer will show positive for the chest x-ray test. On the other hand, chest x-ray will have false alarms: 6% of the people without lung cancer will also show positive for the chest x-ray test. Suppose that a hospital will do two lung cancer screen tests for each annual check patient (assume the two tests are independent). The second test called CT scan is done to improve the accuracy of diagnosis. Suppose that the CT scan has the following characteristics: it returns positive for 85% of the people with lung cancer; it has a lower false rate than the x-ray test and will return false positive for one out of one thousand people without lung cancer. If a person went through the annual check and had positives on both the chest x-ray and the CT scan, what is the probability that he/she has the lung cancer?

**Answer:** We can solve this problem by using the Bayes' theorem twice. We already know that the probability of a person has cancer given that he has positive x-ray is 2.8%; the probability of a person has no cancer given that he has positive x-ray is 97.2%. We can use this result and continue to solve the problem as follows:

1. We use the Bayes' theorem:

$$P(cancer \mid positive\ x-ray\ \&positive\ CT\ scan)$$
$$= \frac{P(positive\ CT\ scan \mid cancer) * P(cancer\ new\ proir)}{P(positive\ CT\ scan \mid cancer) * P(cancer\ new\ prior) + P(positive\ CT\ scan|{\sim}cancer) * P({\sim}cancer\ new\ prior)}$$

2. And plug in the following data:

P(cancer new prior) = 2.8% (the poster probability of ) (9)

P(~cancer new prior) = 97.2% (the complement of equation (9)) (10)

P(positive CT scan | cancer) = 85%
(85% of people with lung cancer have positive CT scan) (11)

P(positive CT scan | ~cancer) = 0.1%
(0.1% of people without lung cancer have positive CT scan) (12)

3. And plug in the above data into the above Bayes' theorem, we will get:

P(cancer | positive x-ray & positive CT scan) =

85%* 2.8% / (85%*2.8%+0.1%*97.2%)
= 0.0238 / (0.0238+0.00097)
= 0.0238 / 0.02477
= 0.96

As you can see, the person's probability of having lung cancer is very high in this instance. In this example, each application of the Bayes' theorem can be viewed as a mapping from one statistical sample space to another statistical sample space and there are two such mappings as shown in Figure 3.

In Figure 3, P(xp&c) means the probability of a person who has lung cancer and is x-ray positive; P(xp&CTp&c) means the probability of a person who has lung cancer and is both x-ray positive and CT scan positive. Similarly, P(xp&CTp&h) means the probability of a person who is healthy and is both x-ray positive and CT scan positive. To help our understanding of what's going on, we list some calculated data below (assume total of 10,000 people):

Prior probability P(cancer) = 0.2% number of cancer people=20
Prior probability P(healthy) = 99.8% number of healthy people=9980
conditional probability P(positive x-ray | cancer) = 85%
number of people having cancer and positive=P(p | c)*#cancer=17
conditional probability P(positive x-ray | healthy) = 6%
number of people who are healthy and positive=P(p | h)*#healthy=599

P(cancer | positive x-ray) = #people having cancer&positive / total#people having positive
= 17 / (17 + 599) = 0.028

posterior probability (our answer)

As shown in Figure 3, the application of Bayes' theorem is the mapping from one space to another space. In the initial world, the probability of a person in the sample is healthy is 99.8% while the probability of having the lung cancer is 0.2%. The first application of the Bayes' theorem has two distortions: one distorts the probability of having cancer, P(cancer), to the probability of both having cancer and being positive for x-ray test, P(positive x-ray & cancer), (the distorting leverage/filter is the conditional probability P(positive x-ray | cancer)), the other distorts the probability of being healthy, P(healthy), to the probability of being positive for x-ray and being healthy, P(positive x-ray & healthy), (the distorting leverage/filter is the conditional probability P(positive x-ray | healthy)). In the new alternate universe, though the number of people who have cancer to be included is almost the same as in the initial world (from 20 in the initial world to 17 in the first mapped world), the number of people who are healthy to be included is greatly reduced (from 9980 in the initial world to 599 in the first mapped world). Thus, when we try to answer the question of "the probability of a person having lung cancer given that he has a positive x-ray" by dividing the number of people with cancer by the total number of people with positive x-ray, we will get a much higher probability. In other words, the mapping altered our assessment. The mapping reflects the effect of the evidence "positive x-ray" in shifting our judgment of deciding whether a person has lung cancer.

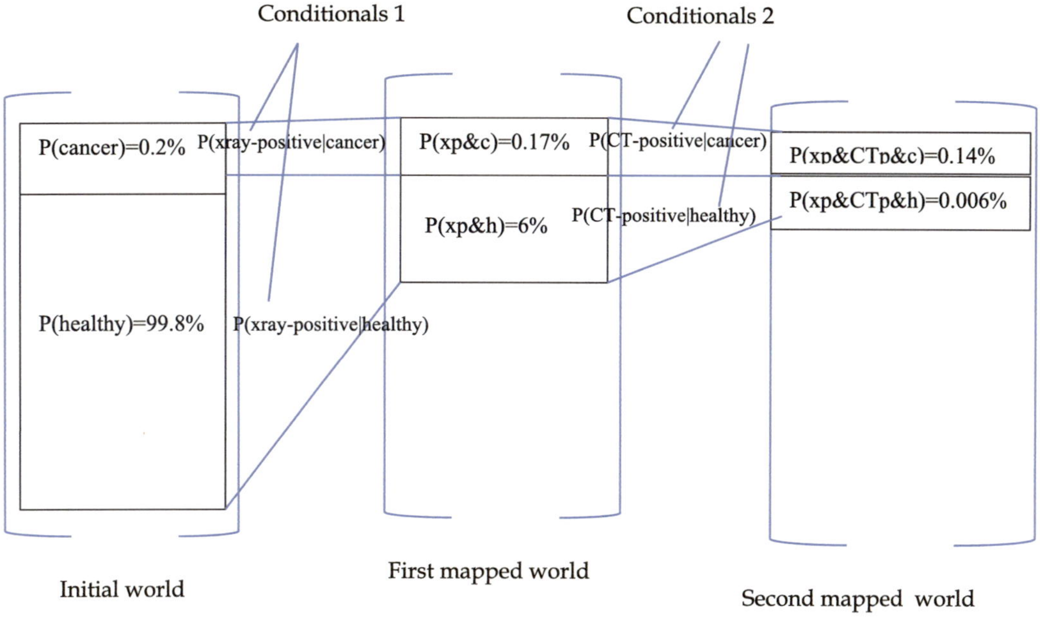


Fig. 3. We apply Bayes' theorem twice for two tests; each application of Bayes' theorem can be viewed as a mapping

One thing to point out, the x-ray test will not affect the actual probability of a person has cancer (otherwise no one will take the test). However, the test will affect our beliefs. A positive x-ray is a membership test. If the test is positive, it will eliminate many more people without lung cancer than people with the cancer. The number of people without cancer is reduced by a factor of more than 16, from 9980 to 599, while the number of people with cancer is reduced only from 20 to 17. Thus, the proportion of 17 within 616 (the total number of people with positive x-ray) is much larger than the proportion of 20 within 10,000.

### 5.2 Conditional probabilities play the role as shifters

From Example 2, you may have already seen the role played by the two conditional probabilities: P(positive x-ray | cancer) and P(positive x-ray | healthy). They are the shifters: P(positive x-ray | cancer) shifts our view positively and P(positive x-ray | healthy) shifts our view negatively. In other words, large value of P(positive x-ray | cancer) will increase our confidence in predicting a person has cancer given that he has a positive test. On the other hand, small value of P(positive x-ray | healthy) will increase our confidence in predicting a person has cancer given that he has a positive test. The quality measurement of a test in altering our view to the world is the inter-play of these two conditional probabilities. They map the number of cancerous people and the number of healthy people in one world into another world. Their ratio can be used as a measurement of effectiveness for a test to be evidence.

We will show later that for a test to be effective, its positive conditional probability cannot have the same value as its negative conditional probability. Otherwise, the test will shift our view to the same amount and the net effect is nil.

The second application of the Bayes' theorem alters the ratio of number of healthy people to the number of cancer people in the universe even further. In the second mapped world, the number of people who have cancer to be included is 14, and the number of people who are healthy to be included is 0.6. In the second new world, seeing both positive evidences (a positive x-ray and a positive CT scan) is convincing evidence that the person has lung cancer (96% probability).

Bayes' theorem is important in understanding the basic statistical reasoning mechanism. In its original form, it is not easy to use, especially in the face of multiple evidences. In the next section, we will introduce a computer reasoning theory: evidence theory that is based on the Bayes' theory.

## 6. The evidence theory of computer reasoning

In this section, we are going to present a computer reasoning method called evidence theory that is more convenient and easier to use than the Bayes' theorem. To help our presentation, we will define some terms and use some mathematical formulas along the way.

If we take an abstract view, the computer reasoning can be summarized as: capture the causality relationships from raw data, build a knowledge database using these relationships, and make a judgment (or inference) on pieces of evidence based on existing knowledge database. The essence of the summary is shown in Figure 4.

The computer reasoning mechanism shown in Figure 4 can be explained as having two stages: the knowledge/pattern building and the application of knowledge to the new evidence. In the first stage (indicated by arrows from the Raw data to the Knowledge database), knowledge is produced either by data mining from raw data or by direct human insertion; in the second stage (indicated by arrows from the Knowledge database to the

Solution), the reasoning occurs by applying the knowledge from the Knowledge database to the evidence.

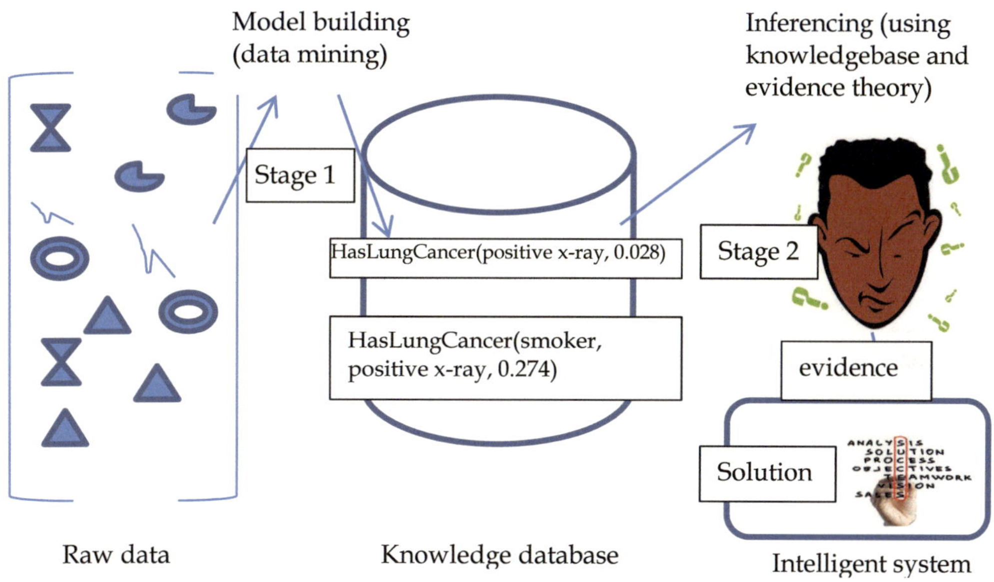


Fig. 4. Abstract view on computer reasoning

One of the important components in Figure 4 is evidence. In computer reasoning, evidence is the main factor that influences a computer's judgment. One of the important characteristics of evidence is its quality. In this abstract view, reasoning is persuaded by the presence of evidence. For example, without any evidence, our view of the initial world about the probability of a person with lung cancer is 0.2%, with the presence of first piece of evidence, the positive result of x-ray test, our view of the modified world about the probability of a person with lung cancer is 2.8%, with the presence of two pieces of evidence, the positive result of x-ray and the positive result of CT scan, our view of the new world about the probability of a person with lung cancer is changed again to 96%.

### 6.1 The properties and the definition of evidence (or a test)

The main role of a piece of evidence is its influence on a rational mind. To see how this influence is realized, we need to investigate the properties about evidence. In this section, we will give definition of evidence; and will describe properties of evidence. These definition and properties are given in the following highlight box.

**Evidence Theory and Evidence Properties**

**The Main Interest:** Suppose that A represents an event of interest; E represents the a piece of envidence. The main interest of the evidence theory is to calculate the probability:

$$P(A \mid E) \qquad \text{(Formula 4)}$$

**Definition of Evidence:** we define evidence (or a test) E as a piece of information that has the ability to change the value of probability defined in Formula 4. The underlining reason for this ability is the causality relationship existed between the event A and the evidence E.

**Assumption about Event A:** in the absence of any evidence, we will assume that the probability of event A occurring is the same as the probability of its not occurring. That is, P(A) = 50%.

**Properties of Evidence:** evidence has following three properties:

**Property 1:** if evidence E increases the probability of event A, then the evidence E is positive evidence relative to event A.
**Property 2:** if evidence E decreases the probability of event A, then the evidence E is negative evidence relative to event A.
**Property 3:** the quality of evidence E is measured in terms of evidence strength (which will be defined in the next section).

## 6.2 The quality of evidence (evidence strength)

As mentioned before, one important function of a piece of evidence is its influence on a rational mind. Thus, the quality measurement of a piece of evidence should also be based on its ability to influence. For example, if evidence A convinced us an event (or goal achievability) will happen with 80 percent certainty while evidence B convinced us the same event will happen with 90 percent certainty, then we would say evidence B is better. We can quantify the quality of evidence by introducing the concept of evidence strength. With this measurement criterion in mind, try to answer the following question:

**Question 1:** With regard to the two tests mentioned in Example 2: the x-ray test, and the CT scan test, which one is better in swaying us to believe that the person in question has lung cancer?

Here is the repeat of some statistics for the two evidences (a medical test can be regarded as evidence from Bayes' theorem's point of view):

- X-ray test: 85% of the people with lung cancer will show positive; 6% of the people without lung cancer will also show positive.
- CT scan test: 85% of the people with lung cancer will show positive; 0.1% of the people without lung cancer will also show positive.

Before answering the above question, let's define some terms. In the following, "Posi | Cause" means that the existence of "Cause" causes the evidence "Posi" to appear; "Posi | ~Cause" means that the absence of "Cause" causes the evidence "Posi" to appear. Now, we will define the strength of evidence as follows:

**Definition of evidence strength:** we define strength of evidence (or a test) as the probability that the evidence gives true positive divided by the probability that the evidence gives a false positive. In other words, it can be represented as the following formula:

strength(evidence) = P(Posi | Cause) / P(Posi | ~Cause) (Formula 5)

One thing to point out is that the summation of the probability of P(Posi | Cause) and the probability of P(Posi | ~Cause) is not necessarily 1. Once defined evidence strength, we can divide evidence two categories: positive evidence and negative evidence. When the value of strength is greater than 1, the evidence will shift our belief in the positive way, thus we name it positive evidence; on the other hand, when the value of strength is smaller than 1, the evidence has the effect of shift our belief in the negative way, thus we name it negative evidence.

The probability P(Posi | Cause) on the right side of Formula 5 captures the causality relationship in the real world. It means the probability of something causes the evidence (test) to be positive. In our Example 1, it will take the form: P(positive x-ray | cancer), and it means that the probability of lung cancer causes the x-ray to be positive; and P(positive x-ray | ~cancer) means the probability of a false alarm.

Now, let's give some observations about evidence. First, as mentioned before, to be effective evidence, the value of a test's positive conditional probability cannot have the same value as its negative conditional probability. Thus, in terms of strength, we have the following observation:

**Observation 1:** when the evidence strength is 1, it is not good evidence. Using the above definition, the effectiveness of a test (or a piece of evidence) is measured in terms of its strength. If the value of strength is 1, then the test is useless as a piece of evidence (it is neutral). When the value of strength is greater than 1, it is positive evidence (seeing the evidence will shift our view regarding the trueness of the event "Cause" to the positive side); when the value of strength is smaller than 1 and greater than 0, it is negative evidence (diminishes our view about the trueness of the "Cause").

For example, if we are asked whether flipping a fair coin is a good test for predicting a person has lung cancer (assume that a head means the person has cancer and a tail means the person has no cancer)? We can proceed like the following:

1. First, we calculate the strength of flipping a coin as a test and it will be:

   strength(flipping a coin) = P(head | cancer) / P(head | ~cancer) = 0.5 / 0.5 = 1

**Note:** the reason that P(head | cancer) = 0.5 is the fact that the information of a patient has cancer has nothing to do with the outcome of flipping a coin. The chance of getting a head is still governed by its old chance of 50%. We will have the same argument for the probability P(head | ~ cancer).

2. Based on our evidence theory, we know it shifts our belief to the same distance for positive and negative direction. Thus, we conclude that it's not a good test.

With regard to the cause of strong evidence, we have the following observation:

**Observation 2:** strong evince is not caused by a very high probability of cause leads to the positive test, rather it is caused by a very low probability of not-cause could have led to the positive test.

For example, if it is raining, the grass in my front yard (there is no roof) is likely to be wet. But seeing the grass wet does not necessarily mean that it is raining (maybe it is caused by the sprinkler). In other words, when seeing the evidence of wet grass, we cannot reason that it is raining with certainty. This is a case of high probability of cause-effect but week evidence.

On the hand, if we are watching an area there is no sprinkler. Then, seeing the wet grass would always mean that it is raining, even though we assume that there is a weak causation link such as the rain will cause the grass wet only 60% of times. This is a case of low probability of cause-effect but strong evidence.

Now, let's answer the Question 1. We will use the evidence strength value to help us make the conclusion. For x-ray test, we have the following:

$$\text{strength(x-ray test)} = P(\text{positive x-ray} \mid \text{cancer}) / P(\text{positive x-ray} \mid \sim\text{cancer})$$

$$= 0.85 / 0.06 = 14.17$$

For CT scan, we have:

$$\text{strength(CT scan test)} = P(\text{positive CT scan} \mid \text{cancer}) / P(\text{positive CT scan} \mid \sim\text{cancer})$$

$$= 0.85 / 0.001 = 850$$

Since the value 850 is greater than 14.17, we conclude that CT scan test is a better evidence in convincing us that the patient in question has lung cancer.

### 6.3 The relationship between the evidence strength and its influence power

The discussion above gives us some insights about evidence. In this section, we will investigate the relationship between the evidence strength and its power to influence the outcome of an event. Specifically, we want to see how the existence of a piece of evidence will shift our belief (its direction and its amount (may be rough estimation)). Based on the intuition we have about the evidence, we make the following claim.

**Claim 1:** the influence power of a given piece of evidence is proportional to the value of evidence strength. For positive evidence, the larger evidence strength value, the stronger the influence power; for negative evidence, the smaller evidence strength value, the stronger the influence power.

We will use the following example to give some insight about our Claim 1:

**Example 3:** Using the data in Example 2, calculate the strength for x-ray test and the strength for the CT scan test. Then, calculate the distance that each test moves our belief (including the direction) in terms of percentage change. We repeat the main points and data in the following:

1. About 0.2% of the population living in US with age above 20 has lung cancer.

2. When doing an annual check, assume that 85% of the people with lung cancer will show positive for the chest x-ray test. About 6% of the people without lung cancer will also show positive for the chest x-ray test.
3. The second test called CT scan is done independently. It returns positive for 85% of the people with lung cancer; its false rate is 0.1%.

**Answer:** For first part of the question, we can use the result in the previous section. Here is the repeat: For x-ray test, we have the following:

strength(x-ray test) = P(positive x-ray | cancer) / P(positive x-ray | ~cancer)

= 0.85 / 0.06 = 14.17

For CT scan, we have:

strength(CT scan test) = P(positive CT scan | cancer) / P(positive CT scan | ~cancer)

= 0.85 / 0.001 = 850

For the second part of the problem (the distance each test sways our beliefs), we will proceed as follows:

We started in the initial world with following probabilities:

P(cancer) = 0.2%, P(healthy) = 99.8%

For a person in this initial world, the probability of having lung cancer is 0.2% (pretty low). If we use the x-ray as a membership test, then the probability become following (already calculated in previous sections):

P(cancer | positive x-ray) = 2.8%, P(healthy | positive x-ray) = 97.2%

The x-ray test shifted our view from P(cancer) = 0.2% to P(cancer | positive x-ray) = 2.8%. It is a positive evidence. The percentage increase is 2.6%.

Now, let's see how much the CT scan test will shift our view. Starting from the initial world, if we use the CT scan as a membership test, then the probability can be calculated as following:

We use the Bayes' theorem:

$$P(cancer|positive\ CT\ scan) = \frac{\mathrm{P}(positive\ CT\ scan \mid cancer) * P(cancer)}{\mathrm{P}(positive\ CT\ scan \mid cancer) * P(cancer) + P(positive\ CT\ scan|{\sim}cancer) * P({\sim}cancer)}$$

And plug in the following data:

P(cancer) = 0.2% (20 out of 10,000 have cancer)

P(~cancer) = 99.8% (9980 out of 10,000 have no cancer)

P(positive CT scan | cancer) = 85%

(85% of people with lung cancer have positive CT scan)

P(positive CT scan | ~cancer) = 0.1%

(0.1% of people without lung cancer have positive CT scan)

And plug in the above data into the above Bayes' theorem, we will get:

P(cancer | positive CT scan) = 85%* 0.2% / (85%*0.2%+0.1%*99.8%)

= 0.0017 / (0.0017+0.001)

= 0.0017 / 0.0027

= 0.63

This result tells use that the CT scan test will shift our belief in positive direction, The percentage increase is 62.8%. These results support our claim 1.

Note that the x-ray test and CT scan test have the same positive cause-effect probability rate but different false alarm rate. In x-ray test, the false alarm probability P(positive x-ray | ~cancer) is 6%, while in CT scan test, the false alarm probability P(positive CT scan | ~cancer) is only 0.1%. Here is an example that the **low false alarm probability is the dominate factor** in deciding the strength of evidence.

### 6.4 The logarithmical representation of evidence degrees

In the previous section, we used the ratio of two conditional probabilities as the strength measurement. Under our abstract view of reasoning model in Figure 4, evidences are used to distort the world space. As indicated in that figure, reasoning is the process of make a judgment using the knowledge (embedded in the conditionals) based on the evidence (the right side of " | " on the left side of Formula 1) presented. One thing to point out is that our abstract reasoning model can be applied to multiple evidences.

To capture the essence of the low-level reasoning in situations with multiple evidences, we can use a tool in mathematics called ratio and the concept in statistics called odds. Also, the use of these tools will make reasoning in situations that have multiple evidences easier. Odds can capture the same information as probability. In statistics, odds are defined as the ratio of the probability of an event's occurring to the probability of its not occurring. The reasoning of solving the problem in Example 2 using the odds concept will be like this: in the initial world, the lung cancer rate is 0.2%. Thus, 2 out of 1000 people have lung cancer, and 998 people out of 1000 people do not have lung cancer. Using odds, we define the event of interest as a person has lung cancer vs. a person has no cancer. So the 0.2% cancer rate can be expressed as the following odds:

2:998

And the evidence strengths of the two tests x-ray, and CT scan can be expressed in odds notation as:

14.17:1 (get from 0.85/0.06)

850:1 (get from 0.85/0.001)

To get the answer for low level reasoning, we calculate the odds for a person with cancer who score positive on the two tests, versus a person without cancer who score positive on the two tests. Using the basic principles in algebra, the above odds can be calculated as following

2*14.17*850:998*1*1 =

24089:998

Once get the final odds, we can get probability of a person having lung cancer given that he score both tests positive as following:

P(cancer | positive x-ray & positive CT scan) = 24089 / (24089+998)

= 24089 / 25087

= 96%

This is the same answer as we get using Bayes' theorem in section 5.

As you can see, using the ratio and the odds tool is simpler than using the Bayes' theorem directly. We can simplify our calculation even further by using another tool called logarithm in mathematics. Before we can take the advantage of logarithm, we need to give a new definition on evidence called evidence degree.

**Definition of evidence degree:** we define evidence degree of a test as the as the following formula:

$$\text{degree(test)} = 10 \log_{10} \text{strength (test)} \qquad \text{(Formula 6)}$$

To get the strength from the degree, we use the following formula:

$$\text{strength(test)} = 10^{\text{degree(test)} / 10} \qquad \text{(Formula 7)}$$

Once represented in logarithmic format (degree of evidence), the aggregated effect of evidence toward a goal can be obtained by simple adding instead of multiplying.

### 6.5 The evidence based reasoning

As mentioned before, at low-level reasoning, the logic employed by a human is the same as the Bayes' theorem. In this section, we will show how to reason using the evidence expressed in the form of degree. As the topic suggested, the focus of our reasoning method is on evidence. The reasoning method addresses the question of the following type:

**Question Type:** Given a set of evidences and prior probability of an event A, we want to reason about the posterior probability of A (here, the event of interest can be anything, such as the survival chance of a disease, the goal in a planning problem, etc.). In other words, we want to figure out the left side of the following equation:

P(A | seen evidences x, y, z, ...) = ?

The assumption of this method is that each piece of evidence is independent. Because of the strength of Bayes' theorem, this assumption works even for evidences that are not independent. Studies show that systems based on Bayes' theorem with the same assumption such as Hidden Naïve Bayes (Jin & et al., 2007) are robust because of the model constructing can accommodate minor factors easily. The reason for this robustness stems from the fact that the model itself has already captured the main causality. Any other accuracy consideration does not improve too much. In a sense, it only adds the complexity.

Our reasoning method can be represented as the following algorithm:

**EvidenceBasedReasoning Algorithm: Inputs: raw data, input question of probability of an event of interest; Output: posterior probability information (answer to the input question)**

Step 1: constructing models (or knowledge) from raw data.
Step 2: calculate the quality of evidence related to the input question in terms of evidence degree with the help of Formulas 6 and 7.
Step 3: calculate the overall evidence degree.
Step 4: interpret the information by converting the overall evidence degree back to the probability (using Formulas 6 and 7 again).

We have the following comments about the degree of evidence:

1. The critical point for the degree of evidence is 0. 0 means the evidence is neutral; the probability of positive conditional is equal to the probability of negative conditional. It does not add anything in shifting our view to the world.
2. If the evidence's degree is greater than 0, then it will shift our view toward believing event A is true; if the evidence's degree is less than 0, then it will shift our view toward believing event A is not true;
3. Degree is measured in terms of order of degree. If evidence A's degree is 10 and evidence B's degree is 20, then evidence B is ten order of magnitude (100 times) stronger than evidence A in persuasion power.

Now, let's use an example to illustrate how our EvidenceBasedReasoning works.

**Example 4:** Solve the problem in Example 2 again using the EvidenceBasedReasoning algorithm. We repeat the main points and assumptions in the following:

1. About 0.2% of the population living in US with age above 20 has lung cancer.
2. When doing an annual check, assume that 85% of the people with lung cancer will show positive for the chest x-ray test. About 6% of the people without lung cancer will also show positive for the chest x-ray test.
3. The second test called CT scan is done independently. It returns positive for 85% of the people with lung cancer; its false rate is 0.1%.
4. If a person went through the annual check and had positives on both the chest x-ray and the CT scan, what is the probability that he/she has the lung cancer?

**Answer:** We will solve this problem using the EvidenceBasedReasoning algorithm. Using Bayes' theorem, we already solved the problem and knew the correct answer for that question is

$$P(\text{cancer} \mid \text{positive x-ray \& positive CT scan}) = 0.96$$

Here, we are going to show you that our new framework of reasoning will help us to get the result easier. The following is the analysis and steps of finding the answer:

First, we decide what is the question: after read the problem statement, we know the question is: P(cancer | positive x-ray & positive CT scan) = ?

Second, we calculate the degree for the prior probability (having cancer in a population) and the degrees for the two tests (x-ray and CT scan):

$$\begin{array}{llll} \text{degree(prior)} & = 10 \log_{10} (0.002) & = -27 & \text{(get from 2:998)} \\ \text{degree(x-ray)} & = 10 \log_{10} (14.17) & = 11.5 & \text{(get from 0.85/0.06)} \\ \text{degree(CT scan)} & = 10 \log_{10} (850) & = 29.3 & \text{(get from 0.85/0.001)} \end{array}$$

Third, we get the overall degree by adding all above degree values:

$$\text{degree(answer)} = 13.8$$

Fourth, we extract the answer in terms of probability by using Formula 7:

$$\begin{aligned} \text{strength(answer)} &= 10^{\text{degree(answer)} / 10} \\ &= 10^{13.8 / 10} \\ &= 23.99 \end{aligned}$$

Convert to probability, it equals P = 23.99 / (23.99 + 1) = 0.96

Thus the final answer is:

$$P(\text{cancer} \mid \text{positive x-ray \& positive CT scan}) = 0.96$$

(same value as the one got in Example 2)

As you can see, our evidence based reasoning is easier than the original Bayes' theorem in dealing with many evidences. One thing to point out is that our evidence based reasoning can be used in many areas. For example, in bioinformatics, data mining, category classification, etc., just to name a few.

## 7. Knowledge management in bio-information system architecture

We described the fundamentals of computer reasoning and proposed an EvidenceBasedReasoning algorithm. In this section, we will introduce a framework of knowledge management in the context of bio-information system architectures. Based on this framework, we will introduce a prototype implementation of the Bio-information knowledge management system.

### 7.1 Knowledge management framework

In a typical knowledge management system, there are many components. Figure 5 shows an information system architecture upon which we base our reasoning framework and knowledge management methods.

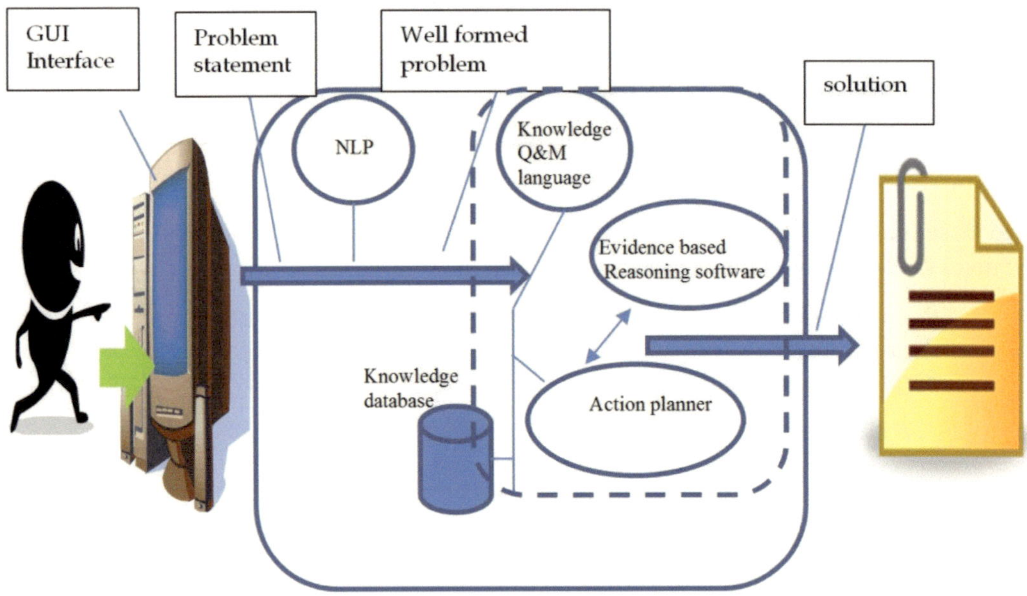


Fig. 5. A bio-information knowledge management framework

In Figure 5, the NLP stands for the natural language processor. NLP is used to translate a problem written in natural language such as English or Chinese into a well formed problem statement that is understood by reasoning engine which is enclosed inside the dotted region in Figure 5. The reasoning engine consists of Knowledge Query and Manipulation Language (KQML), the Evidence based reasoning software, and the Action planner. KQML is used to manage data stored in the knowledge database. Its role in an expert system is much like the role that the SQL language played in a database management system. Action planner is the component that drives the system. One thing to point out is that the reasoning engine works with the help of the knowledge database.

### 7.2 The evidence based reasoning software

As you can see from Figure 5, the complete system of a bio-information knowledge management system has both software and hardware. In this presentation, we will focus on the software side. In particular, we will focus on one software component: the evidence based reasoning software (expert Software). We will assume that other components are already implemented and working.

### 7.3 The potential areas of using the evidence based reasoning system

One of the application areas of our evidence reasoning system is the terminal patient consulting bio-information system. When a patient is diagnosed with terminal illness, his first reaction is disbelieving. Then, he probably will ask questions like: what is the prognosis such as how long he can live; what is its etiology such as the cause of the disease; and whether it is hereditary. These questions are usually being answered by doctors or nurses. Often, answers that a patient got are generic based on average cases. Also, because of tight schedules of doctors and nurses, sometimes the patient is not able to get answers in a timely manner. Here, we will develop a prototype system that will answer most of the questions that a terminal patient will have. Also, the answers from our system will be tailored to individual patients. Ideally, our system should be able to relieve a lot of burdens from doctors and nurses.

### 7.4 The evidence based reasoning software design ideas

We are going to develop a prototype of the evidence based reasoning software component. In the following, we will outline our design ideas.

**Main design ideas:** we strive the following:

1. The component should have a Graphic User Interface (GUI) to facilitate the use of the system. Figure 6 is a screen capture of the user interface.
2. It should be interactive. Based on the information in the knowledge data base, it may ask patient questions.
3. The component should be developed in such a way that it can be used to query different terminal illnesses, in other words, it should be generic.
4. There should be default values for those fields that a user does not input specific information.
5. The knowledge database should be separated from this component for the benefit of less coupling.

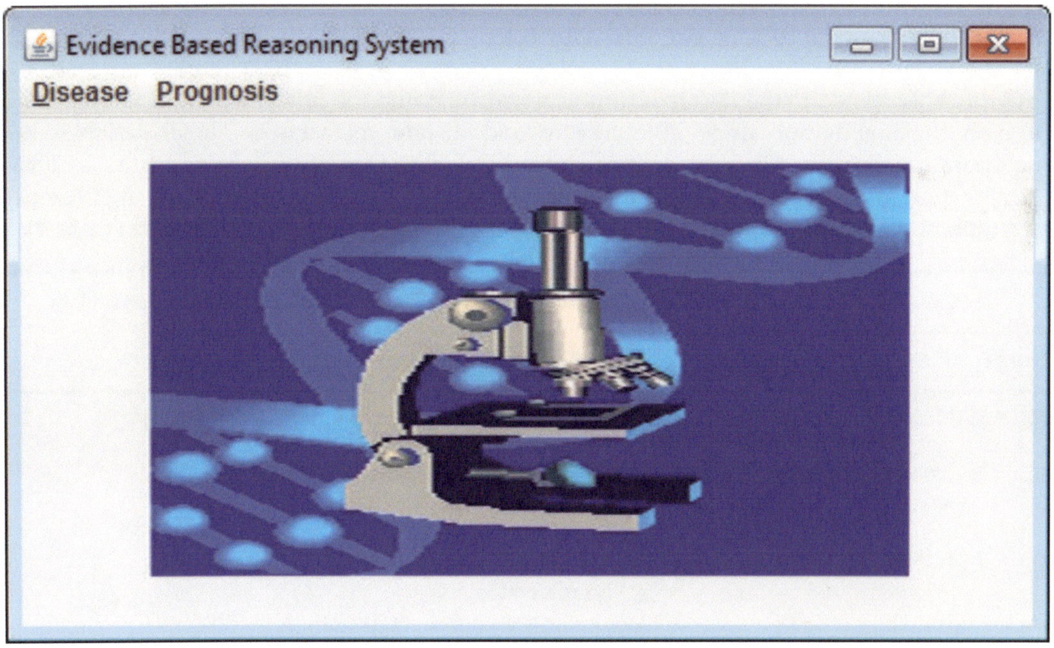


Fig. 6. A screen capture of the uesr interface for the evidence based reasoning system

With the above design ideas in mind, we will set the boundaries and make assumptions for the system. The following is the assumptions that we made.

**Assumption:** we assume the following:

1. All other components shown in Figure 5 are developed and working. The only component that we are focusing on is the evidence based reasoning software.
2. The diagnosis of the illness is already known.
3. The component will answer only predefined set of questions (most important to a patient) such as the cause of the disease (etiology), once diagnosed, how long a person can live (prognosis), etc.

To emphasize the main point, our implementation uses a simple design. Without losing generality, we loaded data from a file instead of asking the user to input them from a keyboard. We also watered down some features for the sake of simplicity. For example, the whole knowledge database is substituted by hard-coded logic.

### 7.5 A case example: Colorectal cancer

To help our presentation, we will use a medical case example to illustrate some features of our evidence based reasoning system. The medical case used is the colorectal cancer. And we will use the most common form of the colorectal cancer: the hereditary nonpolyposis colon cancer (HNPCC). This form of cancer is also called *Lynch syndrome*. The following is some facts related to this disease:

**Some facts of colorectal cancer:** "Cancer of the large bowel is second only to lung cancer as a cause of cancer death in the United States; 146,940 new cases occurred in 2004, and 56,730 deaths were due to colorectal cancer." (Kasper, 2005, p. 527) This disease has hereditary factors. "As many as 25% of patients with colorectal cancer have a family history of the disease, suggesting a hereditary predisposition." (Kasper, 2005, p. 527) Once diagnosed, the prognosis "is related to the depth of tumor penetration into the bowel wall and the presence of both regional lymph node involvement and distant metastases. These variables are incorporated into the staging system introduced by Dukes and applied to a TNM classification method, in which T represents the depth of tumor penetration, N the presence of lymph node involvement, and M the presence or absence of distant metastases (Table 1).

| Stage | | | | Approximate 5-yr survival, % |
|---|---|---|---|---|
| Dukes | TNM | Numerical | Pathologic Description | |
| A | T1N0M0 | I | Cancer limited to mucosa and submucosa | >90 |
| $B_1$ | T2N0M0 | I | Cancer extends into muscularis | 85 |
| $B_2$ | T3N0M0 | II | Cancer extends into or through serosa | 70-80 |
| C | TxN1M0 | III | Cancer involves regional lymph nodes | 35-65 |
| D | TxNxM1 | IV | Distant metastases (i.e., liver, lung) | 5 |

"

Table 1. Staging of and Prognosis for Colorectal Cancer (Kasper, 2005, p. 529-530)

The prevalent belief of the cause of the disease is the interplay between the environment and the cancer suppressing genes. The reason why we have colorectal cancers (in fact, any type of cancers) is because our body lost control to the cell growth. For normal cells, their growth is controlled by the information in their DNA. These cells know when to stop. On the other hand, for a cancer cell (either caused by spontaneous mutation or by hereditary predisposition), this control is lost. Thus, it will grow unchecked and with misshape. Environment factors such as high animal fat diet, radiation exposure, Streptococcus bacterial infection (bacteremia), inflammatory bowel disease, etc. make a person susceptible to colorectal cancers. But these factors do not mean a person has cancer. Cells in our body have innate ability to fight cancers. This ability is rested on the fact that normal cells have cancer suppressing genes. For example, "the long arm of chromosome 5 (including the APC gene)" is responsible for the suppression of one type of colon cancer (polyposis coli) development. "The loss of this genetic material (i.e., allelic loss) results in the absence of tumor-suppressor genes whose protein products would normally inhibit neoplastic growth." (Kasper, 2005, p. 528) Thus, when we see a cancer, it is the result of both the presence of the environmental risk factors and the absence of the cancer fighting genes.

### 7.6 Sample runs of the evidence based reasoning software

In this section, we will apply our prototype reasoning software to the case example introduced in the previous section. To show the effect of evidence, we will show two outputs: one with specific personal information and one without. The case information for the one that has no specific personal information is the following:

**Case 1: we use the following general information (with no specific personal information):**

> Suppose that the patient (Michael Dodd) is diagnosed with (HNPCC) colon cancer stage III.
> The information stored in the knowledge database is contained in Table 1.

Using the input information in case 1, we will get the default 5-year survival chance. Figure 7 is the output screen capture for case 1.

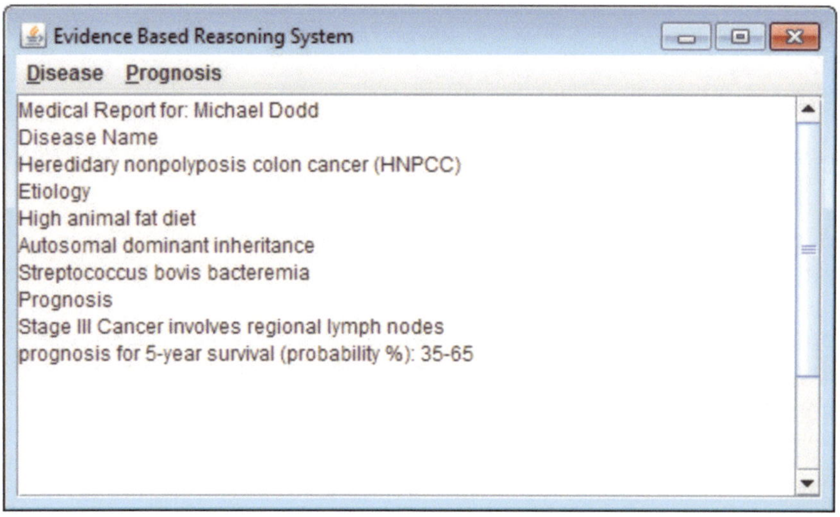


Fig. 7. A screen capture of the general 5-year survival probability for a person with colon cancer of stage III

The case information for the second run that has specific personal information is the following:

**Case 2: we use the following specific information (with personal information):**

> Suppose that the patient (Michael Dodd) is diagnosed with (HNPCC) colon cancer stage III.
> Michael's father had colon cancer, the time between the diagnosis and the death was 3 years.
> Michael's older sister had colon cancer, the time between the diagnosis and the death was 4 years.
> The information stored in the knowledge database is contained in Table 1.

Using the input information in case 2, we are able to get the revised 5-year survival chance. Figure 8 is the output screen capture for case 2.

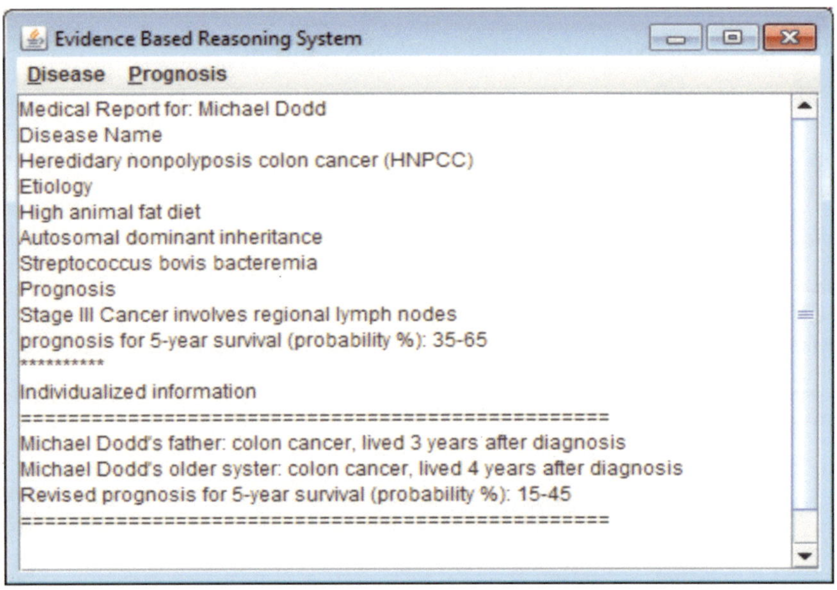


Fig. 8. A screen capture of the individualized 5-year survival probability for a person with colon cancer of stage III

As you can see from the output in Figure 8, the 5-year survival probability is revised down words. Since in this case, we have more information (patient's father's cancer history; patient's older sister's cancer history), the evidence based reasoning software takes the new information into account and produces more accurate output. With regard to the event of 5-year survival, these evidences reduce the probability. Thus, they are negative evidences according to our evidence theory. Specifically, the 5-year survival probability is revised from 35-65% down to 15-45%. The following is the rationale and steps to get this new result.

1. We first calculate the degree of prior probability (in this case, take the data from Table 1 (< 65%)) as follows:

$$\text{degree(prior)} \quad = 10 \log_{10} (0.65) \quad = - 1.9$$

2. We rate the evidence E1 as follows: Michael's father lived 3 years after diagnosis as negative relative to the event of interesting: Michael is able to live 5 years. Considering Michael's father is his direct relative, we assign a degree(father's condition->Michael 5-year survival) = -1.
3. Similarly, we rate the evidence E2 as follows: Michael's older sister lived 4 years after diagnosis as negative relative to the event of interesting: Michael is able to live 5 years. Considering Michael's sister is his direct relative and the year 4 is pretty close to 5, we assign half degree(older sister's condition->Michael 5-year survival) = -.5.
4. Calculate the overall degree: FinalDegree = -1 + (-.5) + (-1.9) = -3.4.
5. Convert the degree to the final strength:

$$\text{strength(answer)} = 10^{\text{degree(answer)} / 10}$$

$$= 10^{-3.4 / 10}$$

$$= 1 / 2.2 = 0.45$$

6. Thus, the revised range will be: 15-45%.

**Note:** our assignments of degrees to the two evidences (in step 2, 3) are arbitrary in a sense that it is not verified. In real situation, we should determine these values by clinical trials.

As a consequence of these reasoning steps, the evidence reasoning software produces the revised survival probability as shown in Figure 8.

### 7.7 Java code for the reasoning software

The screen captures in the previous section are produced by Java code. We implemented the prototype using popular Java language. List 1 shows the code that produces the output screens.

List 1: Java code to produce the output screens

```
=========================================================================
import java.awt.event.*;
import java.awt.*;
import javax.swing.*;
import java.io.*;
import java.util.Scanner;

public class EvidenceBasedReasoningSystemApp extends JFrame implements ActionListener{
    private JMenuItem   diseaseMenuItem, closeMenuItem, prognosisMenuItem;
    private JTextArea contents;
    JLabel imageLabel;

    public static void main(String args[]) {
        EvidenceBasedReasoningSystemApp  frame = new EvidenceBasedReasoningSystemApp();
    }

    public EvidenceBasedReasoningSystemApp() {
        java.net.URL bkpic = getClass().getResource("genetics.jpg");
        ImageIcon bkpicture = new ImageIcon(bkpic);
```

```
    imageLabel = new JLabel (bkpicture);
    JMenuBar  menuBar = new JMenuBar();
    JMenu  diseaseMenu = new JMenu("Disease");
    diseaseMenuItem = new JMenuItem("Load Disease File");
    closeMenuItem = new JMenuItem("Close");
    diseaseMenu.add(diseaseMenuItem);
    diseaseMenu.add(closeMenuItem);
    JMenu  prognosisMenu = new JMenu("Prognosis");
    prognosisMenuItem = new JMenuItem("Display Prognosis");
    prognosisMenu.add(prognosisMenuItem);
    diseaseMenu.setMnemonic('D');
    prognosisMenu.setMnemonic('P');
    setJMenuBar(menuBar); //add menu bar to current frame
    menuBar.add(diseaseMenu);
    menuBar.add(prognosisMenu);
    add(imageLabel, BorderLayout.CENTER); //add background image
    contents = new JTextArea(20, 40);
    diseaseMenuItem.addActionListener(this); //subscribe events
    prognosisMenuItem.addActionListener(this);
    closeMenuItem.addActionListener(this);
    setSize(500, 300); //set the size of the frame
    setTitle("Evidence Based Reasoning System");
    setVisible(true);
    addWindowListener(new WindowAdapter()
    {
        public void windowClosing(WindowEvent event)
            {shutDown();}
        }
    );
}

public void actionPerformed(ActionEvent e) {
    Object sourceObject = e.getSource();
    String string, tmp;

    if (sourceObject == diseaseMenuItem) {
        JFileChooser fileChooser = new JFileChooser(System.getProperty("user.dir"));
        String lineSeparator = System.getProperty("line.separator");
        JScrollPane scrollPane = new JScrollPane(contents);
        int result = fileChooser.showOpenDialog(this);

        if (result == JFileChooser.APPROVE_OPTION) {
            File file = fileChooser.getSelectedFile();
            try {
                Scanner fileScan = new Scanner(file);
                contents.setText("Medical Report for: ");
                string = fileScan.nextLine();
                contents.append(string + lineSeparator);
                while (fileScan.hasNext()) {
                    string = fileScan.nextLine();
                    Scanner fieldScan = new Scanner(string);
                    fieldScan.useDelimiter("/");
                    while (fieldScan.hasNext()) {
```

```
                        tmp = fieldScan.next();
                        contents.append(tmp + lineSeparator);
                    }
                }
                imageLabel.setVisible(false);
                add(scrollPane, BorderLayout.CENTER);
            } catch(IOException ioe) {
                ioe.printStackTrace();
                return;
            }
        }
    }
    else if (sourceObject == prognosisMenuItem) {
        JFileChooser fileChooser = new JFileChooser(System.getProperty("user.dir"));
        String lineSeparator = System.getProperty("line.separator");
        JScrollPane scrollPane = new JScrollPane(contents);
        int result = fileChooser.showOpenDialog(this);

        if (result == JFileChooser.APPROVE_OPTION) {
            File file = fileChooser.getSelectedFile();
            try {
                Scanner fileScan = new Scanner(file);
                contents.setText("Medical Report for: ");
                string = fileScan.nextLine();
                contents.append(string + lineSeparator);
                while (fileScan.hasNext()) {
                    string = fileScan.nextLine();
                    Scanner fieldScan = new Scanner(string);
                    fieldScan.useDelimiter("/");
                    while (fieldScan.hasNext()) {
                        tmp = fieldScan.next();
                        contents.append(tmp + lineSeparator);
                    }
                }
                imageLabel.setVisible(false);
                add(scrollPane, BorderLayout.CENTER);
            } catch(IOException ioe) {
                ioe.printStackTrace();
                return;
            }
        }
    }
    else if (sourceObject == closeMenuItem) {
        shutDown();
    }
  }

  public void shutDown() {
      System.exit(0);
  }
}
```

==================================================================

## 8. Conclusion

In this chapter, we described the relationships among data, knowledge, and intelligence. We proposed one reasoning theory: evidence based reasoning theory. We gave the Java code for the implementation of a prototype. The future work includes more detailed mapping between the evidence strength value and its percentage change; the implementation of missing components such as the knowledge database, the beef up of the watered down features.

## 9. Acknowledgement

I want to give thanks to my family for their support for this book writing project: Enlu Peng, Yuqing Peng, and Daniel Jian.

## 10. References

Asy'arie, A., & Pribadi, A. (2009). Automatic News Articles Classification in Indonesian Language by Using Naive Bayes Classifier method, *In Proceedings of iiWAS2009*, Kuala Lumpur, Malaysia, 2009

Bellinger, G. (2004). Knowledge Management—Emerging Perspectives, (Internet resouce: http://www.systems-thinking.org/kmgmt/kmgmt.htm. Retrieved on 5/30/2011)

Fujita, H.; and et al. (2010). Virtual Doctor System (VDS): Medical Decision Reasoning Based On Physical and Mental Ontologies, *In Proceedings of IEA/AIE'10 Proceedings of the 23rd international conference on Industrial engineering and other applications of applied intelligent systems*, Volume Part III, 2010

Jin, X.; and et al. (2007). Automatic Web Pages Categorization with ReliefF and Hidden Naive Bayes, *In Proceedings of SAC 2007*, pp. 617-621, Seoul, Korea, March, 2007

Kasper, D.; and et al. (2005). *Harrison's Principles of Internal Medicine* (Sixteenth Edition), McGraw-Hill Companies, Inc., ISBN 0-07-139140-1, USA

Williams, L. & Hopper, P. (2003). *Understaning Medical Surgical Nursing* (2nd Edition), F. A. Davis Company, ISBN 0-8036-1037-8, Philadelphia, PA, USA

3

# Efficiency of Knowledge Transfer by Hearing a Conversation While Doing Something

Eiko Yamamoto and Hitoshi Isahara
*Gifu Shotoku Gakuen University, Toyohashi University of Technology*
*Japan*

## 1. Introduction

One of the most common means of acquiring useful knowledge is reading suitable documents and websites. However, this is time-consuming and cannot be done in parallel with other tasks. Is there a way to acquire knowledge when we cannot read written texts, such as while driving a car, walking around or doing housework? It is not easy to remember the contents of a document simply by listening to its reading aloud from the top, even if we concentrate while listening. In contrast, it is sometimes easier to remember words heard on the radio or television even if we are not concentrating on them.

While we are doing something, listening to conversation is better than listening to a precise reading out of a draft or summary for memorizing the contents and turning them into knowledge. We are therefore trying to improve the efficiency of knowledge transfer[1] by "hearing a conversation while doing something."

In order to support knowledge acquisition by humans, we aim to develop a system which provides people with useful knowledge while they are doing something or not concentrating on listening. We did not try to edit notes to be read out, or to summarize documents; rather, we aimed to develop a way of transferring knowledge. Specifically, in order to provide knowledge efficiently with computers, we consider how to turn the content into a dialogue that is easily remembered, and develop a system to produce dialogue by which one can easily acquire knowledge.

In the next section of this article, we explain our prototype system named "Sophisticated Eliza" (Isahara et al., 2005) Then, we discuss the idea of "Efficient knowledge transfer by hearing a conversation while doing something"(Yamamoto & Isahara, 2008).

---

1 In this paper, "(knowledge) transfer" is a movement of knowledge/information from a knowledge source, including a human, to a human recipient. That is to say, the term "knowledge transfer" means not only transferring knowledge between people but also transferring knowledge from computers to human. "Acquisition" is a process of understanding/memorizing knowledge by the human recipient. We focus on the process of synthesizing conversation being uttered for knowledge transfer, which relates to the "externalization" in SECI model (Nonaka & Takeuchi, 1995), in order to realize efficient knowledge acquisition by the recipient, which relates to the "combination" in the model.

In section 4, we evaluate the effectiveness of knowledge transfer via listening to conversation, comparing it with listening to monologues. We firstly choose several topics and select suitable documents on the topic. Then we extract informative sentences from the document and form conversation by splitting a sentence into conversational fragments. In order to verify our hypothesis, we conduct evaluation on the usefulness of listening conversation formed by the fragments with human subjects. We will also get the suggestion from the experiments how to select suitable domain for our system.

In section 5, we introduce our prototype system and present some examples of the conversations extracted by the system. As for the information transfer system, although our final target is to handle topics which are practically useful such as knowledge from newspapers, encyclopedia and Wikipedia, as a first step we tried to compile rules for small procedural domains such as cooking recipes.

## 2. Sophisticated Eliza

Recently, thanks to the improvement of natural language processing (NLP) technology, development of high-performance computers and the availability of huge amounts of stored linguistic data, there are now useful NLP-based systems. There are also practical speech synthesis tools for reading out documents and tools for summarizing documents. These tools do not necessarily use state-of-the-art technologies to achieve deep and accurate language understanding, but are based on huge amounts of linguistic resources that used not to be available. Although current computer systems can collect huge amounts of knowledge from real examples, it is not obvious how to transfer knowledge more naturally between such powerful computer systems and humans. We need to develop a novel way to transfer knowledge from computers to humans.

We believe that, based on large amounts of text data, it is possible to devise a system which can generate dialogue by a simple mechanism to give people the impression that two intelligent persons are talking. We verified this approach by implementing a system named Sophisticated Eliza which can simulate conversation between two persons on a computer. Sophisticated Eliza is not a Human-Computer Interaction system; instead, it simulates conversation by two people and users acquire information by listening to the conversation generated by the system. Concretely, using an encyclopedia in Japanese (Kodansha International, 1998) as a knowledge base, we develop rules to extract information from the knowledge base and create fragments of conversation. We extract rules with syntactic patterns to make a conversation, for example, "What is A?" "It's B." from "A is B." The system extracts candidate fragments of conversation using these simple scripts and two voices then read the conversation aloud. This system cannot generate long conversations as humans do on one topic, but it can simulate short conversations from stored linguistic resources and continue conversations while changing topics.

Figure 1 shows a screenshot of Sophisticated Eliza and Figure 2 shows its system flow. Figure 3 is examples of conversation generated by the system.

The encyclopedia utilized here contains all about Japan, e.g., history, culture, economy and politics. All sentences in the encyclopedia are analyzed syntactically using a Japanese parser

Fig. 1. Screenshot of Sophisticated Eliza

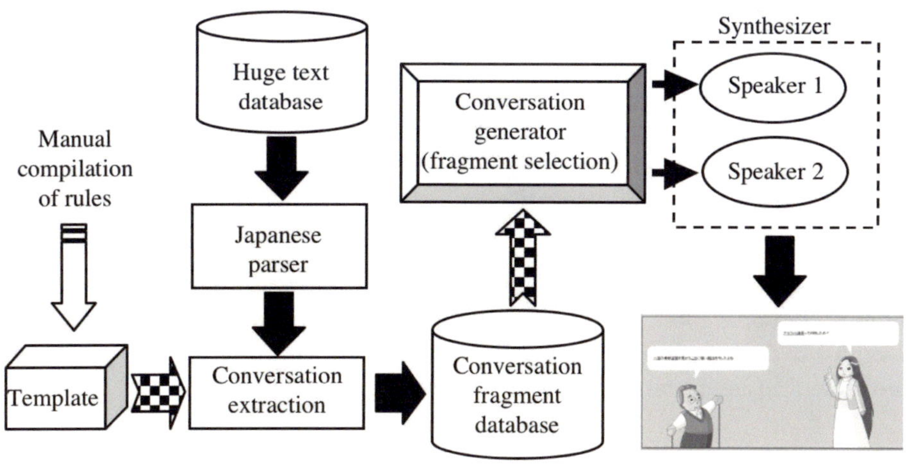


Fig. 2. System Flow of Sophisticated Eliza

and we use rules to extract the fragments of conversation using information in the encyclopedia. As for the manual compilation of rules, we carefully analyzed the output of the Japanese parser and found useful patterns to extract knowledge from the encyclopedia.

The terms extracted during the syntactic analysis are stored in the keyword table and are used for selection of topics and words during the conversation synthesis.

Example 1

| |
|---|
| Original text in knowledge base |
| Osaka Castle was a castle in Osaka prefecture from 15th century to 17th century. |
| Extracted fragment of conversation |
| A: What is Osaka Castle? |
| B: It is a castle in Osaka prefecture from 15th century to 17th century. |

Example 2

| |
|---|
| Extracted fragment of conversation |
| A: Japanese government reinforces bi-relation with African countries and appeals Japanese policy of foreign affairs, aiming to establish environment to solve problems at United Nations. |
| B: What activities are done under the supporting program for Africa? |

Fig. 3. Examples of Generated Conversation

Note that in our current system, we use Japanese documents as the input. Because we are using only syntactic information output by the Japanese parser, our mechanism is also applicable to other languages such as English. We use a rather simple mechanism to generate actual conversations in the system, which includes rules to select fragments containing similar words and rules to change topics. The contents in the encyclopedia are divided into seven categories, i.e. geography, history, politics, economy, society, culture and life. When the topic in a conversation moves from one topic to another, the system generates utterance showing such move. As for the speech synthesis part, we use the synthesizer "Polluxstar" developed by Oki Electric Industry Co. Ltd., Japan. The two authors of this paper, one male and one female, recorded 400 sentences each and the two characters in the system talk to each other by impersonating our voices. The images of the two characters are also based on the authors.

Because this system uses simple template-like knowledge, it cannot generate semantically deep conversation on a topic by considering context or by compiling highly precise rules to extract script-like information from text. Thus, the mechanism used in this system has room for improvement to create conversations for knowledge transfer.

## 3. Efficiency of hearing a conversation comparing with hearing a monologue

In the daily transfer of knowledge, such as in a cooking program on TV, there are not only the reading aloud of recipes by the presenter but also conversation between the cook and assistant. Through such conversations, information which viewers want to know and which they should memorize is transferred to them naturally.

To verify above mentioned fact, we conducted experiments with human subject.

### 3.1 Settings

We utilized the speech synthesizer "Polluxstar" by Oki Electric Co. Ltd., which enables speech synthesis with one's own voice. We input information of voice of authors of this paper (one male and one female).

We prepared three materials to be synthesized for the experiments. Two are about recipes and another is about sports news. For recipes, we chose them from one of recipes sites with movies in Japan (http://recipe.gnavi.co.jp/movie/sweetkitchen/). One is about cooking rice bowl with chicken and eggs, and the other is about cooking gratin. This site contains a short movie with chef and assistant, and contains written recipes for each dish. For dialogue example, we transcribed all conversation between chef and assistant and made speech synthesizer read it aloud. For monologue example, we simply made speech synthesizer read it aloud with one of two voices in the system. As for news article, we chose a news article about women's soccer games in the newspaper in Japan. For its monologue, we made speech synthesizer read it aloud with one of two voices in the system. For its dialogue, we added inquiries manually about some of the point of the news, and made speech synthesizer read it aloud.

We gathered participants of our experience among students of Toyohashi University of Technology, Japan. We had 33 participants and additional 4 male student participants. Because the main topic of the experience is recipe, we gathered mainly woman students. The participants were requested to listen to all six synthesized speeches, i.e. two dialogues for cooking, two monologues for cooking, one dialogue of news, and one monologue of news, and fill questionnaire when one finished each speech.

The items which are asked in the questionnaire are as follows;

1. Recipe
   1a: whether you can make the dish or not
   1b: ingredients
   1c: cooking procedure
   1d: important points for the procedure
   1e: comparison between monologue and dialogue
2. News
   2a: impression of monologue
   2b: impression of dialogue
   2c: comparison between monologue and dialogue
3. Over all comparison

### 3.2 Results

#### 3.2.1 Recipe

The objective features extracted from the questionnaire are as follows;

For rice ball recipe;

Number of ingredients

Dialogue: 8.1 items (111)
Monologue: 7.3 items (100)
Number of words for cooking procedure
Dialogue: 99 words (96)
Monologue: 103 words (100)
Number of word for the important points for the procedure
Dialogue: 61 words (124)
Monologue: 49 words (100)

It seems that dialogue is slightly better than monologue. However, the experiment about gratin recipe shows different result, i.e., monologue is better than dialogue. We checked the result carefully and found the followings;

A group which listened to Gratin dialogue listened to it at the beginning of the experiment. But another group which listened to Gratin monologue listened to Riceball speech before they listen to Gratin monologue. Therefore each participant who listened to Gratin monologue already knows what kind of inquiries they will be asked. They can concentrate to grasp such points. We did additional experiments with smaller participant where each participant listened to the Gratin dialogue after listening to the Riceball speech. Then, the results became closer to the Riceball case. Actually, Gratin dialogue can not be such worse than its monologue. In the free answer opinion in the questionnaire, more participants wrote that they prefer dialogue to monologue than the reverse.

This situation also occurred for Riceball case, i.e., Riceball monogolue was heard after Gratin speech. The difference between Dialogue and Monologue for riceball recipe can be bigger than the figures above.

### 3.2.2 News

We asked participant which you prefer between monologue and dialogue. Then more than two third of participants explicitly wrote that they prefer dialogue to monologue.

### 3.2.3 Discussion

As for recipe listening, dialogue seems slightly better than monologue. However, there are several factors in our experiment which affect the result in favor of monologue. We utilized written text on the web as a text for monologue. The important points of the recipe are listed at the end of the texts, therefore it will be memorable to listeners. If we make text for dialogue from written text, the result will be better than the one in our current settings.

As for news listening, the second speaker inserted only several inquiries about topics talked next. This is not a conversation but something like an interview. Some participants strongly prefer this situation. We should establish the way to generate dialogues properly from texts.

Our hypothesis is that dialogue is more useful to get information while doing something. However, in this experiment, participants were asked to listen to monologue and dialogue and answer questionnaire. This situation is different from our original settings. We should make more suitable way to verify our hypothesis.

## 4. Efficient knowledge transfer by hearing a conversation while doing something

We started to develop a mechanism to achieve natural knowledge acquisition for humans by turning information that is written in documents into conversational text. Efficient methods of acquiring knowledge include not only "reading documents" and "listening to passages read aloud," but also "hearing a conversation while doing something," provided that information is appropriately embedded into the conversation. We believe that we can verify that this "conversation hearing" can assist knowledge acquisition by developing a system for synthesizing conversations by collecting fragments of conversation and conducting experiments by using the system.

As a means to transfer information, contents conveyed by an interpretive reading with pronounced intonation are better retained in memory than if read monotonously from a document or summary. Furthermore, by turning contents into conversation style, even someone who is not concentrating on listening may become interested in the topic and acquire the contents naturally. This suggests that several factors in conversations, such as throwing in words of agreement, pauses and questions, which may appear to decrease the density of information, are actually effective means of transferring information matching humans' ability to acquire knowledge with limited concentration. Based on this idea, we propose a novel mechanism of an information transfer system by considering the way of transferring knowledge from computers to humans.

Various dialogue systems have already been developed as communication tools between humans and computers (Waizenbaum, 1966; Matsusaka et al., 1999). However, in our novel approach, the dialogue system regards the user as an outsider, presents conversation by two speakers in the computer which is of interest to the outside user, and thus provides the user with useful knowledge.

There are dialogue systems (Nadamoto & Tanaka, 2004; ALICE; UZURA) which can join in a conversation between a human and a computer, but they simply create fragments of conversation and so do not sound like an intelligent human speaker. One reason is that they do not aim to provide knowledge or transfer information to humans, and few theoretical evaluations have been done in this field. In this research, we consider a way to transfer knowledge and develop a conversation system which generates dialogue by which humans can acquire knowledge from dialogue conducted by two speakers in the computer. We analyze the way to transfer knowledge to humans with this system. This kind of research is beneficial not only from an engineering viewpoint but also cognitive science and cognitive linguistics. Furthermore, a speech synthesis system in which two participants conduct spoken conversation automatically is rare. In this research, we develop an original information-providing system by assigning conversation to two speakers in the computer in order to transfer knowledge to humans.

## 5. System implementation

The principle of Sophisticated Eliza is that because a large amount of text data is available, even if the recall of information extraction is low, we can obtain sufficient information to generate short conversations. However, the rules still need to be improved by careful analysis of input texts.

As for the information transfer system, although our final target is to handle topics which are practically useful such as knowledge from newspapers, encyclopedia and Wikipedia, as a first step we are trying to compile rules for small procedural domains such as cooking recipes. Concretely, we are developing the new system via the following five steps repeatedly.

1. Enlargement of conversational script and template in order to generate sentences in natural conversation
   We have already compiled simple templates for extracting fragments of conversation as a part of Sophisticated Eliza. We are now enlarging the set of templates to handle wider contexts, domain-specific knowledge and insertion of words. This enlargement is basically being done manually. Here, domain-specific knowledge includes domain documents in a specific format, such as recipes. Insertion of words includes words of agreement and encouragement for the other speaker, part of which is already introduced in Sophisticated Eliza. An example of synthesized conversation is shown in Figure 4.
2. Implementation of system in which two speakers (agents/characters) make conversation in a computer considering dialogue and document contexts
   Using the conversational templates extracted based on the contexts, the system continues conversation with two speakers. Fundamental functions of this kind have already been developed for Sophisticated Eliza.
   Here, there are two types of "context." One is the context in the documents, i.e. knowledge-base. For the recipe example, cooking heavily depends on the order of each process and on the result of each process. The other type is the context in the conversation.

A: Let's make boiled scallop with lettuce and cream.
B: It is 244 Kcal for one person.
A: What kinds of materials are needed?
B: Lettuce and scallop.
For four persons, four peaces of tomatoes and ……
……………
A: How will we cook lettuce?
B: Pour off the hot water after boiling it. Then cool it.
A: How about tomatoes?
B: Remove seeds and dice them.

Fig. 4. Example conversation

If all subevents included in an event are explicitly uttered in conversation, it would be very dull and makes understanding obstruct. For example, "Make hot water in a pan. Peel potatoes and boil them" is enough and it is not necessary to say "boil peeled potatoes in the hot water in a pan." Appropriate use of ellipsis and anaphoric representation based on the context in the conversation are useful tools for easy understanding.
Though speech synthesis itself is out of the scope of our research, pauses in utterances are also important in natural communication.

3. Mechanism to extract (fragment of) knowledge from text
   Sophisticated Eliza outputs informative short conversations, but the content of the conversation is not consistent as a whole. In this research, we are developing a system to provide people with some useful knowledge. We have to recognize the useful part of the knowledge base and to place great importance on the extracted useful part of the text. We previously reported how to extract an informative set of words using a measure of inclusive relations (Yamamoto et al., 2005), and will apply a similar method to this conversation system.
4. Improvement of conversation script and template considering "fragment of knowledge"
   By considering the useful part of information written in the knowledge base, we modify the templates to extract conversational text. Contextual information such as ellipsis and anaphora is also treated in this part. As a first step, we will handle anaphora resolution in a specific domain, such as cooking, considering factors described at 2). We will use domain knowledge about cooking such as cookware, cookery and ingredient.
5. Evaluation
   We will conduct tests with participants to evaluate our methodology and verify the effectiveness of our method for transferring knowledge. So far, we are reported by some small number of participants that it is rather easy to listen to the voice of the system, however, objective evaluation is still our future work.

## 6. Conclusion

We introduced an approach for developing an information-providing system in order to support knowledge acquisition. The system can transfer knowledge to humans even while the person is doing something or is not concentrating on listening to the voice. Our approach does not create a summary of the key points of what is being read out, but focuses on the knowledge transferring method. Specifically, to provide knowledge efficiently, we consider what kinds of conversation are naturally retained in the brain, as such conversations may enable people to obtain knowledge more easily. We aim to construct an intelligent system which can create such conversations by applying natural language processing techniques.

## 7. Acknowledgment

We would like to thank Mr. Satoshi Watanabe of WANT Co. Ltd. for his support on tuning speech synthesizer to our voice and generate all speech data for our experiments.

## 8. References

A.L.I.C.E. The Artificial Linguistic Internet Computer Entity, http://alice.pandorabots.com

Artificial non-Intelligence UZURA, http://www.din.or.jp/~ohzaki/uzura.htm

Isahara, H.; Yamamoto, E.; Ikeno, A. & Hamaguchi, Y. (2005). Eliza's daughter. *Annual Meeting of Association for Natural Language Processing of Japan*, Japan

Kodansha International (1998). *The Kodansha Bilingual Encyclopedia about Japan* (in Japanese and English), Kodansha International Ltd., ISBN 978-477-0021-30-4, Tokyo, Japan

Matsusaka, Y.; Tojo, T.; Kuota, S.; Furukawa, K. Tamiya, D.; Hayata, K.; Nakano, Y. & Kobayashi, T. (1999). Multi-person Conversation via Multimodal Interface -A Robot who Communicate with Multi-user-, *Proceedings of 6th European Conference on Speech Communication Technology* (*EUROSPEECH-99*), Vol.4, pp.1723-1726, Budapest, Hungary, September, 1999

Nadamoto, A. & Tanaka, K. (2004). Passive viewing of Web contents based on automatic generation of conversational sentences *Japanese Society of Information Processing*, 2004-DBS-134(1), pp.183-190, Japan

Nonaka, I. & Takeuchi, H. (1995). *The Knowledge-Creating Company*, Oxford University Press, ISBN 978-019-5092-69-1, USA

Waizenbaum, J. (1966). ELIZA—A Computer Program For the Study of Natural Language Communication Between Man And Machine, *Communications of the ACM*, Vol.9, No.1, pp.36-45, NY, USA

Yamamoto, E.; Kanzaki, K. & Isahara, H. (2005). Extraction of hierarchies based on inclusion of co-occurring words with frequency information, *Proceedings of the 19th International Joint Conference on Artificial Intelligence*, pp.1166-1172, ISBN 0-938075-94-2, Edinburgh, Scotland, UK, August, 2005

Yamamoto, E. & Isahara, H. (2008). Efficient Knowledge Transfer by Hearing a Conversation While Doing Something, *Collection of New Directions in Intelligent Interactive Multimedia*, pp.231-238

# 4

# Algorithm Selection: From Meta-Learning to Hyper-Heuristics

Laura Cruz-Reyes[1], Claudia Gómez-Santillán[1], Joaquín Pérez-Ortega[2], Vanesa Landero[3], Marcela Quiroz[1] and Alberto Ochoa[4]
[1]*Instituto Tecnológico de Cd. Madero*
[2]*Centro Nacional de Investigación y Desarrollo Tecnológico*
[3]*Universidad Politécnica de Nuevo León*
[4]*Universidad de Ciudad Juárez*
*México*

## 1. Introduction

In order for a company to be competitive, an indispensable requirement is the efficient management of its resources. As a result derives a lot of complex optimization problems that need to be solved with high-performance computing tools. In addition, due to the complexity of these problems, it is considered that the most promising approach is the solution with approximate algorithms; highlighting the heuristic optimizers. Within this category are the basic heuristics that are experience-based techniques and the metaheuristic algorithms that are inspired by natural or artificial optimization processes.

A variety of approximate algorithms, which had shown satisfactory performance in optimization problems, had been proposed in the literature. However, there is not an algorithm that performs better for all possible situations, given the amount of available strategies, is necessary to select the one who adapts better to the problem. An important point is to know which strategy is the best for the problem and why it is better.

The chapter begins with the formal definition of the Algorithm Selection Problem (ASP), since its initial formulation. The following section describes examples of "Intelligent Systems" that use a strategy of algorithm selection. After that, we present a review of the literature related to the ASP solution. Section four presents the proposals of our research group for the ASP solution; they are based on machine learning, neural network and hyper-heuristics. Besides, the section presents experimental results in order to conclude about the advantages and disadvantages of each approach. Due to a fully automated solution to ASP is an undecidable problem, Section Five reviews other less rigid approach which combines intelligently different strategies: The Hybrid Systems of Metaheuristics.

## 2. The Algorithm Selection Problem (ASP)

Many optimization problems can be solved by multiple algorithms, with different performance for different problem characteristics. Although some algorithms are better than others on average, there is not a best algorithm for all the possible instances of a given problem. This phenomenon is most pronounced among algorithms for solving NP-Hard problems, because runtimes for these algorithms are often highly variable from instance to instance of a problem (Leyton-Brown et al., 2003). In fact, it has long been recognized that there is no single algorithm or system that will achieve the best performance in all cases (Wolpert & Macready, 1997). Instead we are likely to attain better results, on average, across many different classes of a problem, if we tailor the selection of an algorithm to the characteristics of the problem instance (Smith-Miles et al., 2009). To address this concern, in the last decades researches has developed technology to automatically choose an appropriate optimization algorithm to solve a given instance of a problem, in order to obtain the best performance.

Recent work has focused on creating algorithm portfolios, which contain a selection of state of the art algorithms. To solve a particular problem with this portfolio, a pre-processing step is run where the suitability of each algorithm in the portfolio for the problem at hand is assessed. This step often involves some kind of machine learning, as the actual performance of each algorithm on the given, unseen problem is unknown (Kotthoff et al., 2011).

The Algorithm Selection Problem (ASP) was first described by John R. Rice in 1976 (Rice, 1976) he defined this problem as: learning a mapping from feature space to algorithm performance space, and acknowledged the importance of selecting the right features to characterize the hardness of problem instances (Smith-Miles & Lopes, 2012). This definition includes tree important characteristics (Rice, 1976):

a. *Problem Space*: The set of all possible instance of the problem. There are a big number of independent characteristics that describe the different instances which are important for the algorithm selection and performance. Some of these characteristics and their influences on algorithm performance are usually unknown.
b. *Algorithm Space*: The set of all possible algorithms that can be used to solve the problem. The dimension of this set could be unimaginable, and the influence of the algorithm characteristics is uncertain.
c. *Performance Measure*: The criteria used to measure the performance of a particular algorithm for a particular problem and see how difficult to solve (hard) is the instance. There is considerable uncertainly in the use and interpretation of these measures (e. g. some prefer fast execution, others effectiveness, others simplicity).

Rice proposed a basic model for this problem, which seeks to predict which algorithm from a subset of the algorithm space is likely to perform best based on measurable features of a collection of the problem space: Given a problem subset of the problem space $P$, a subset of the algorithm space $A$, a mapping from $P$ to $A$ and the performance space $Y$. The Algorithm Selection Problem can be formally defined as: for a particular problem instance $p \in P$, find the selection mapping $S(p)$ into the algorithm space $A$, such that the selected algorithm $a \in A$ maximizes the performance measure $||y||$ for $y(a,p) \in Y$. This basic abstract model is illustrated in Figure 1 (Rice, 1976; Smith-Miles & Lopes, 2012).

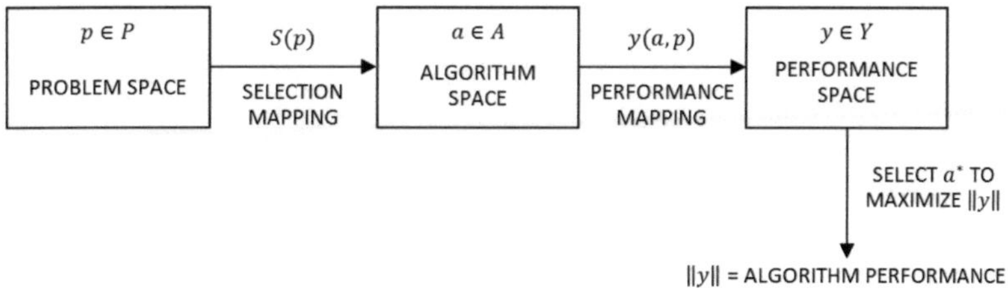


Fig. 1. The Algorithm Selection Problem (ASP)

The Figure 2 shows the dimensions of ASP and allows see a higher level of abstraction scope. There are three dimensions: 1) in the $x$-axis expresses a set of algorithms of solution $\{s, t, w, y, z\}$, 2) $z$-axis shows a set of instances of the problem $\{a, b, c, d\}$, and a new instance $e$ to solve, 3) in the $y$-axis the set of values of the results of applying the algorithms to each of the instances is represented by vertical lines. As shown in figure, to solve the instance $a$ and $b$ the algorithms have different performances, it is noteworthy that no algorithm is superior to others in solving all instances. Moreover, as shown in figure the algorithm $s$ has a different performance by solving each of the instances. Finally the problem to be solved is to select for the new instance $e$ the algorithm that will solve better.

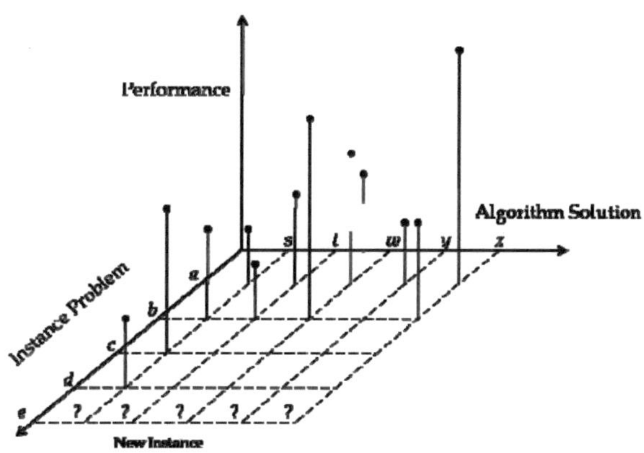


Fig. 2. Dimensions of algorithm selection problem

As we can see in the definition of the Algorithm Selection Problem there are three principal aspects that must be tackled in order to solve the problem:

a. The *selection of the set features of the problem* that might be indicative of the performance of the algorithms.
b. The *selection of the set of algorithms* that together allow to solve the largest number of instances of the problem with the highest performance.
c. The *selection of an efficient mapping mechanism* that permits to select the best algorithm to maximize the performance measure.

Some studies have been focused in construct a suitable set of features that adequately measure the relative difficulty of the instances of the problem (Smith-Miles et al., 2009; Messelis et al., 2009; Madani et al., 2009; Quiroz, 2009; Smith-Miles & Lopes, 2012). Generally there are two main approaches used to characterize the instances: the first is to identify problem dependent features based on domain knowledge of what makes a particular instance challenging or easy to solve; the second is a more general set of features derived from landscape analysis (Schiavinotto & Stützle, 2007; Czogalla & Fink, 2009). To define the set of features that describe the characteristics of the instances is a difficult task that requires expert domain knowledge of the problem. The indices of characterization should be carefully chosen, so as to permit a correct discrimination of the difficulty of the instances to explain the algorithms performance. There is little that will be learned via a knowledge discovery process if the features selected to characterize the instances do not have any differentiation power (Smith-Miles et al., 2009).

On the other hand, portfolio creation and algorithm selection has received a lot of attention in areas that deal with solving computationally hard problems (Leyton-Brown et al., 2003; O'Mahony et al., 2008). The current state of the art is such that often there are many algorithms and systems for solving the same kind of problem; each with its own performance on a particular problem. Machine learning is an established method of addressing ASP (Lobjois & Lemâitre, 1998; Fink, 1998). Given the performance of each algorithm on a set of training problems, we try to predict the performance on unseen problems (Kotthoff et al., 2011). There have been many studies in the area of algorithm performance prediction, which is strongly related to algorithm selection in the sense that supervised learning or regression models are used to predict the performance ranking of a set of algorithms, given a set of features of the instances (Smith-Miles & Lopes, 2012).

In the selection of the efficient mapping mechanism a challenging research goal is to design a run-time system that can repeatedly execute a program, learning over time to make decisions that maximize the performance measure. Since the right decisions may depend on the problem size and parameters, the machine characteristics and load, the data distribution, and other uncertain factors, this can be quite challenging. Some works treats algorithms in a black-box manner: each time a single algorithm is selected and applied to the given instance then a regression analysis or machine learning techniques are used to build a predictive model of the performance of the algorithms given the features of the instances (Lobjois & Lemâitre, 1998; Fink, 1998; Leyton-Brown et al., 2003; Ali & Smith, 2006). Other works focus on dynamic selection of algorithm components while the instance is being solved. In that sense, each instance is solved by a mixture of algorithms formed dynamically at run-time (Lagoudakis & Littman, 2000; Samulowitz & Memisevic, 2007; Streeter et al., 2007). The use of efficient mapping mechanism in intelligent systems is described in the next section.

## 3. Applications of algorithm selection to real world and theorists problems

The principles applied to ASP can be used in a wide range of applications in the real world and theoretical. Generally an application that solves a real problem is an extended version of parameters and constraints in another application that solves a theoretical problem. The nature of the algorithm selection problem is dynamic because it must incorporate new knowledge periodically, in order to preserve the efficacy of selection strategies. This section describes some applications to real-world complex problems, such as knowledge discovery and data mining, bioinformatics and Web services. It also describes some applications to solve complex theoretical problems; some examples are NP-hard problems, also called combinatorial optimization problems.

### 3.1 Bioinformatics

In (Nascimento et al., 2009) the authors investigate the performance of clustering algorithms on gene expression data, by extracting rules that relate the characteristics of the data sets of gene expression to the performance achieved by the algorithms. This represents a first attempt to solve the problem of choosing the best cluster algorithm with independence of gene expression data. In general, the choice of algorithms is basically driven by the familiarity of biological experts to the algorithm, rather than the characteristics of the algorithms themselves and of the data. In particular, the bioinformatics community has not reached consensus on which method should be preferably used. This work is directly derived from the Meta-Learning framework, originally proposed to support algorithm selection for classification and regression problems. However, Meta-Learning has been extended to other domains of application, e.g. to select algorithms for time series forecasting, to support the design of planning systems, to analyze the performance of meta-heuristics for optimization problems. Meta-Learning can be defined by considering four aspects: (a) the problem space, P, (b) the meta-feature space, F, (c) the algorithm space, A and (d) a performance metric, Y. As final remark, authors demonstrated that the rule-based ensemble classifier presented the most accuracy rates in predicting the best clustering algorithms for gene expression data sets. Besides, the set of extracted rules for the selection of clustering algorithms, using an inductive decision tree algorithm, gave some interesting guidelines for choosing the right method.

### 3.2 WEB services

In recent years, many studies have focused on developing feasible mechanisms to select appropriate services from service systems in order to improve performance and efficiency. However, these traditional methods do not provide effective guidance to users and, with regard to ubiquitous computing, the services need to be context-aware. In consequence, the work achieved by (Cai et al., 2009) proposed a novel service selection algorithm based on Artificial Neural Network (ANN) for ubiquitous computing environment. This method can exactly choose a most appropriate service from many service providers, due to the earlier information of the cooperation between the devices. Among the elements that exist in the definition of a service, Z represents the evaluation value of respective service providers' service quality, and its value is calculated with a function that involves the time and the conditions of current context environment, e.g. user context, computing context, physical context, with a division into static and dynamical information.

Among the advantages of using ANN to solve the service selection problem, is that, the method can easily adapt the evaluation process to the varying context information, and hence, it can provide effective guidance so that lots of invalid selecting processes can be avoided. The neural network selected was Back Propagation (BP) because is the most commonly used; however, this algorithm was improved with a three-term approach: learning rate, momentum factor and proportional factor. The efficiency of such algorithm was obtained because adding the proportional factor enhanced the convergence speed and stability. In conclusion, the authors claim, that this novel service selection outperforms the traditional service selection scheme.

### 3.3 Learning systems

In (Bradzil et al., 2003) is described a meta-learning method to support selection of candidate learning algorithms. Bradzil et al. use the Instance-Based Learning (IBL) approach because IBL has the advantage that the system is extensible; once a new experimental result becomes available, it can be easily integrated into the existing results without the need to reinitiate complex re-learning. In this work a k-Nearest Neighbor (k-NN) algorithm to identify the datasets that are most similar to the one is used. The distance between datasets is assessed using a relatively small set of data characteristics, which was selected to represent properties that affect algorithm performance; it is used to generate a recommendation to the user in the form of a ranking. The prediction, is constructed by aggregating performance information for the given candidate algorithms on the selected datasets. They use a ranking method based on the relative performance between pairs of algorithms. This work shown how can be exploited meta-learning to pre-select and recommend one or more classification algorithms to the user. They claimed that choosing adequate methods in a multistrategy learning system might significantly improve its overall performance. Also it was shown that meta-learning with k-NN improves the quality of rankings methods in general.

### 3.4 Knowledge discovery and data mining

In (Hilario & Kaousis, 2000) is addressed the model selection problem in knowledge discovery systems, defined as the problem of selecting the most appropriate learning model or algorithm for a given application task. In this work they propose framework for characterizing learning algorithms for classification as well as their underlying models, using learning algorithm profiles. These profiles consist of metalevel feature-value vectors, which describe learning algorithms from the point of view of their representation and functionality, efficiency, resilience, and practicality. Values for these features are assigned on the basis of author specifications, expert consensus or previous empirical studies. Authors review past evaluations of the better known learning algorithms and suggest an experimental strategy for building algorithm profiles on more quantitative grounds. The scope of this paper is limited to learning algorithms for classification tasks, but it can be applied to learning models for other tasks such as regression or association.

In (Kalousis & Theoharis, 1999) is presented an Intelligent Assistant called NOEMON, which by inducing helpful suggestion from background information can reduce the effort in classifier selection task. For each registered classifier, NOEMON measures its performance in order to collect datasets for constituting a morphologic space. For suggest the most appropriate classifier, NOEMON decides on the basis of morphological similarity between the new dataset and the existing collection. Rules are induced from those measurements and accommodated in a knowledge database. Finally, the suggestions on the most appropriate classifier for a dataset are based on those rules. The purpose of NOEMON is to supply the expert with suggestions based on its knowledge on the performance of the models and algorithms for related problems. This knowledge is being accumulated in a knowledge base end is updated as new problems as are being processed.

### 3.5 Scheduling problem

In (Kadioglu et al., 2011) the main idea is taken from an algorithm selector called Boolean Satisfiability (SAT) based on nearest neighbor classifier. On one hand, authors presented two extensions to it; one of them is based on the concept of distance-based weighting, where they assign larger weights to instances that are closer to the test instance. The second extension, is based on clustering-based adaptive neighborhood size, where authors adapt the size of the neighborhood based on the properties of the given test instance. These two extensions show moderate but consistent performance improvements to the algorithm selection using Nearest-Neighbor Classification (Malitsky et al., 2011). On the other hand, authors developed a new hybrid portfolio that combines algorithm selection and algorithm scheduling, in static and dynamic ways. For static schedules the problem can be formulated as an integer program, more precisely, as a resource constrained set covering problem, where the goal is to select a number of solver-runtime pairs that together "cover" (i.e., solve) as many training instances as possible. Regarding dynamic schedules, the column generation approach works fast enough when yielding potentially sub-optimal but usually high quality solutions. This allows us to embed the idea of dynamic schedules in the previously developed nearest-neighbor approach, which selects optimal neighborhood sizes by random sub-sampling validation. With SAT as the testbed, experimentation demonstrated that author's approach can handle highly diverse benchmarks, in particular a mix of random, crafted, and industrial SAT instances, even when deliberately removed entire families of instances from the training set. As a conclusion, authors presented a heuristic method for computing solver schedules efficiently, which O'Mahony (O'Mahony et al., 2008) identified as an open problem. In addition, they showed that a completely new way of solver scheduling consisting of a combination of static schedules and solver selection is able to achieve significantly better results than plain algorithm selection.

### 3.6 Traveling salesman problem

In (Kanda et al., 2011), the work is focused in the selection of optimization algorithms for solving TSP instances; this paper proposes a meta-learning approach to recommend optimization algorithms for new TSP instances. Each instance is described by meta-features of the TSP that influences the efficiency of the optimization algorithms. When more than one algorithm reaches the best solution, the multi-label classification problem is addressed applying three steps: 1) decomposition of multi-label instances into several single-label instances, 2) elimination of multi-label instances, and 3) binary representation, in order to transform multi-label instances into several binary classification problems. Features were represented as a graph. The success of this meta-learning approach depended on the correct identification of the meta-features that best relate the main aspects of a problem to the performances of the used algorithms. Finally the authors claimed that it is necessary to define and expand the set of metafeatures, which are important to characterize datasets in order to improve the performance of the selection models.

### 3.7 Satisfiability problem

In (Xu et al., 2009) is described an algorithm for constructing per-instance algorithm portfolios for SAT. It has been widely observed that there is no single "dominant" SAT solver; instead, different solvers perform best on different instances. SATzilla is an automated approach for constructing per-instance algorithm portfolios for SAT that use so-called empirical hardness models to choose among their constituent solvers. This approach takes as input a distribution of problem instances and a set of component solvers, and constructs a portfolio optimizing a given objective function (such as mean runtime, percent of instances solved, or score in a competition). The algorithm selection approach is based on the idea of building an approximate runtime predictor, which can be seen as a heuristic approximation to a perfect oracle. Specifically, they use machine learning techniques to build an empirical hardness model, a computationally inexpensive predictor of an algorithm's runtime on a given problem instance based on features of the instance and the algorithm's past performance. By modeling several algorithms and, at runtime, choosing the algorithm predicted to have the best performance; empirical hardness models can serve as the basis for an algorithm portfolio that solves the algorithm selection problem automatically.

### 3.8 Vehicle routing problem

In (Ruiz-Vanoye et al., 2008) the main contribution of this paper is to propose statistical complexity indicators applied to the Vehicle Routing Problem with Time Windows (VRPTW) instances in order that it allows to select appropriately the algorithm that better solves a VRPTW instance. In order to verify the proposed indicators, they used the discriminant analysis contained in SPSS software, such as a machine learning method to find the relation between the characteristics of the problem and the performance of algorithms (Perez et al., 2004), as well as the execution of 3 variants of the genetic algorithms and the random search algorithm. The results obtained in this work showed a good percentage of prediction taking into account that this based on statistical techniques and not on data-mining techniques. By means of the experimentation, authors conclude that it is possible to create indicators applied to VRPTW that help appropriately to predict the algorithm that better solves the instances of the VRPTW.

## 4. Related work on automatic algorithm selection

In this section some examples of related works of the reviewed literature are classified by Methods or methodologies utilized for establishing the relation between the problems and algorithms, and solve the algorithm selection problem. 2.1. Solution Environments, where the algorithm selection problem is boarded, are described in section 2.2.

### 4.1 Simple statistical tests

The most common method to compare experimentally algorithms consists in the complementary use of a set of simple well-known statistical tests: The Sign, Wilcoxon and Friedman tests, among others. The tests are based on the determination of the differences in the average performance, which is observed experimentally: if the differences among the algorithms are significant statistically, the algorithm with the best results is considered as superior (Lawler 1985). Reeves comments that a heuristic with good averaged performance, but with high dispersion, has a very high risk to show a poor or low performance in many instances (Reeves 1993). He suggests as alternative to formulate for each algorithm, a utility function adjusted to a gamma distribution, whose parameters permit to compare the heuristics on a range of risk value.

### 4.2 Regression analysis

Gent and Walsh make an empirical study of the GSAT algorithm, it is an approximation algorithm for SAT, and they apply regression analysis to model the growth of the cost of obtaining the solution with the problem size (Gent 1997).

In (Cruz 1999), Pérez and Cruz present a statistical method to build algorithm performance models, using polynomial functions, which relate the performance with the problem size. This method first generates a representative sample of the algorithms performance, and then the performance functions are determined by regression analysis, which finally are incorporated in an algorithm selection mechanism. The polynomial functions are used to predict the best algorithm that satisfies the user requirements.

The performance of local search algorithms Novelty and SAPS for solving instances of the SAT problem were analyzed by (Hutter 2006). The authors used linear regression with linear and quadratic basis functions to build prediction models. Firstly, they built a prediction model, using problem features and algorithm performance, to predict the algorithm run time. Secondly, they build another prediction model, using problem features, algorithm parameter settings and algorithm performance. This model is used to automatically adjust the algorithm's parameters on a per instance basis in order to optimize its performance.

### 4.3 Functions of probability distribution

Frost finds that the performance of the algorithms to solve CSP instances can be approximated by two standard families of functions of continuous probability distribution (Frost 1997). The resoluble instances can be modeled by the Weibull distribution and the instances that are not resoluble by the lognormal distribution. He utilizes four parameters to generate instances: number of constraints, number of prohibited value pairs per constraint, the probability of a constraint existing between any pair of variables, the probability each constraint is statistically independent of the others, and the probability that a value in the domain of one variable in a constraint will be incompatible with a value in the domain of the other variable in the constraint.

Hoos and Stuzle present a similar work to Frost. They find that the performance of algorithms that solve the SAT instances can be characterized by an exponential distribution (Hoos 2000). The execution time distribution is determined by the execution of $k$ times of an algorithm over a set of instances of the same family, using a high time as stop criteria and storing for each successful run the execution time required to find the solution. The empirical distribution of the execution time is the accumulated distribution associated with these observations, and it allows projecting the execution time $t$ (given by the user) to the probability of finding a solution in this time. A family is a set of instances with the same value of the parameters that are considered critical for the performance.

An algorithm portfolio architecture was proposed in (Silverthorn 2010). This architecture employs three core components: a portfolio of algorithms; a generative model, which is fit to data on those algorithms past performance, then used to predict their future performance; and a policy for action selection, which repeatedly chooses algorithms based on those predictions. Portfolio operation begins with offline training, in which a) training tasks are drawn from the task distribution, b) each solver is run many times on each training task, and c) a model is fit to the outcomes observed in training. In the test phase that follows, repeatedly, (1) a test task is drawn from the same task distribution, (2) the model predicts the likely outcomes of each solver, (3) the portfolio selects and runs a solver for some duration, (4) the run's outcome conditions later predictions, and (5) the process continues from (2) until a time limit expires.

The models of solver behavior are two latent class models: a multinomial mixture that captures the basic correlations between solvers, runs, and problem instances, and a mixture of Dirichlet compound multinomial distributions that also captures the tendency of solver outcomes to recur. Each model was embedded in a portfolio of diverse SAT solvers and evaluated on competition benchmarks. Both models support effective problem solving, and the DCM-based portfolio is competitive with the most prominent modern portfolio method for SAT (Xu 2009).

### 4.4 Functions of heuristic rules

Rice introduced the poly-algorithm concept (Rice 1968) in the context of parallel numeric software. He proposes the use of functions that can select, from a set of algorithms, the best to solve a given situation. After the Rice work, other researchers have formulated different functions that are presented in (Li 1997, Brewer 1995). The majority of the proposed functions are simple heuristic rules about structural features of the parameters of the instance that is being solved, or about the computational environment. The definition of the rules requires of the human experience.

The objective of the proposed methodology in (Beck 2004) is to find the best solution to a new instance, when a total limit time T is given. Firstly, the selection strategies for a set of algorithms A were formulated and denominated as prediction rules, these are: Selection is based on the cost of the best solution found by each algorithm; Selection is based on the change in the cost of the best solutions found at 10 second intervals; Selection is based on the extrapolation of the current cost and slope to a predicted cost at T.

These rules are applied for the training dataset and the optimal sampling time t* (required time to select the algorithm with the less solution error) is identified for each of them. After, when a new instance is given, each prediction rule is utilized to find the algorithm with the best found solution in a time $tp = |A| \times t^*$, and it is executed in the remaining time $tr = T - tp$. One of the advantages is that the methodology can be applied to different problems and algorithms. Nevertheless, the new dataset must have similarity with the training dataset.

### 4.5 Machine learning

The algorithm selection problem is focused by Lagoudakis and Littam in (Lagoudakis 2000) as a minimization problem of execution total time, which is solved with a Reinforced Learning algorithm (RL). Two classical problems were focused: selecting and ordering. A function that predicts the best algorithm for a new instance using its problem size is determined by means of training. The learned function permits to combine several recursive algorithms to improve its performance: the actual problem is divided in subproblems in each recursive step, and the most adequate algorithm in size is used for each of them. This work is extended to backtracking algorithms to SAT problem in (Lagoudakis 2001).

A system (PHYTHIA-II) to select the most appropriated software to solve a scientific problem is proposed in (Houstis 2002). The user introduces the problem features (operators of the equation, its domain, values of the variables, etc.) and time requirements and allowed error. The principal components of PHYTHIA-II are the statistical analysis, pattern extraction module and inference engine. The first consists in ranking the algorithms performance data by means of Friedman rank sums (Hollander 1973). The second utilizes different machine learning methods to extract performance patterns and represent them with decision and logic rules. The third is the process to correspond the features of a new problem with the produced rules; the objective is to predict the best algorithm and the most appropriated parameters to solve the problem.

The METAL research group proposed a method to select the most appropriate classification algorithm for a set of similar instances (Soares 2003). They used a K-nearest neighborhood algorithm to identify the group of instances from a historical registry that exhibit similar features to those of a new instance group. The algorithm performance on instances of historical registry is known and is used to predict the best algorithms for the new instance group. The similarity among instances groups is obtained considering three types of problem features: general, statistical and derived from information theory.

A Bayesian approach is proposed in (Guo, 2004) to construct an algorithm selection system which is applied to the Sorting and Most Probable Explanation (MPE) problems. From a set of training instances, their features and the run time of the best algorithm that solves each instance are utilized to build the Bayesian network. Guo proposed four representative indexes from the Sorting problem features: the size of the input permutation and three presortedness measures. For the MPE problem he utilizes general features of the problem and several statistical indexes of the Bayesian network that represents the problem.

A methodology for instance based selection of solver's policies that solves instances of the SAT problem was proposed by (Nikolic 2009). The policies are heuristics that guide the search process. Different configurations of these policies are solution strategies. The problem structure of all instances was characterized by indices. The problem instances were grouped by the values of these indices, forming instances families. All problem instances were solved by all solution strategies. The best solution strategy for each family is selected. The k-nearest neighbor algorithm selects the solution strategy for a new input instance. The results of the performance of the algorithm ARGOSmart, that performs the proposed methodology, were superior to ARGOSAT algorithm.

## 5. Approaches to building algorithm selectors

In this chapter we solve ASP with two approaches: meta-learning and hyper-heuristics. The meta-learning approach is oriented to learning about classification using machine learning methods; three methods are explored to solve an optimization problem: Discriminant Analysis (Pérez, 2004), C4.5 and the Self-Organising Neural Network. The hyper-heuristic approach is oriented to automatically produce an adequate combination of available low-level heuristics in order to effectively solve a given instance (Burke et al., 2010); a hyper-heuristic strategy is incorporated in an ant colony algorithm to select the heuristic that best adjust one of its control parameter.

### 5.1 Selection of metaheuristics using meta-learning

In this section a methodology based on Meta-Learning is presented for characterizing algorithm performance from past experience data. The characterization is used to select the best algorithm for a new instance of a given problem. The phases of the methodology are described and exemplified with the well known one-dimensional Bin-Packing problem.

#### 5.1.1 Algorithms for the solution of the Bin Packing Problem

The Bin Packing Problem (BPP) is an NP-hard combinatorial optimization problem, in which the objective is to determine the smallest number of bins to pack a set of objects. For obtaining suboptimal solutions of BPP, with less computational effort, we used deterministic and non-deterministic algorithms. The algorithm performance is evaluated with the optimal deviation percentage and the processing time (Quiroz, 2009).

The deterministic algorithms always follow the same path to arrive at the same solution. The First Fit Decreasing (FFD) algorithm places the items in the first bin that can hold them. The Best Fit Decreasing (BFD) places the items in the best-filled bin that can hold them. The Match to First Fit (MFF) algorithm is a variation of FFD, wich uses complementary bins for holding temporarily items. The Match to Best Fit (MBF) algorithm is a variation of BFD and, like MFF uses complementary bins. The Modified Best Fit Decreasing (MBFD) partially pack the bins in order to find a "good fit" item combination.

The Non-Deterministic Algorithms do not obtain the same solution in different executions, but in many cases they are faster than deterministic algorithms. The Ant Colony Optimization (ACO) algorithm builds a solution with each ant: it starts with an empty bin; next, each new bin is filled with "selected items" until no remaining item fits in it; finally, a "selected item" is chosen stochastically using mainly a pheromone trail (Ducatelle, 2001). In the Threshold Accepting (TA) algorithm, a new feasible solution is accepted if the difference with the previous solution is within a threshold temperature; the value of the temperature is decreased each time until a thermal equilibrium is reached (Pérez, 2002).

#### 5.1.2 Methodology

The methodology proposed for performance characterization and its application to algorithm selection consists of three consecutive phases: Initial Training, Prediction and Training with Feedback. Figure 3 depicts these phases.

In the *Initial Training Phase,* two internal processes build a past experience database: the Problem Characterization Process obtains statistical indices to measure the computational complexity of a problem instance and, the Algorithm characterization Process solves instances with the available algorithms to obtain performance indices. The Training Process finally builds a knowledge base using the Problem and Algorithms Database. This knowledge is represented through a learning model, which relates the algorithms performance and the problem characteristics. In the *Prediction Phase,* The relationship learned is used to predict the best algorithm for a new given instance. In the *Training with*

*Feedback phase,* the new solved instances are incorporated into the characterization process for increasing the selection quality. The relationship learned in the knowledge base is improved with a new set of solved instances and is used again in the prediction phase.

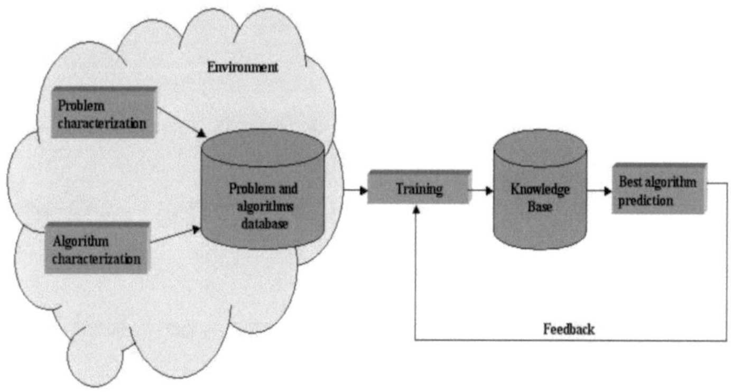


Fig. 3. Phases of the algorithm selection methodology

**Initial training phase**

The steps of this phase are shown in Figure 4 In step 1 (Characteristics Modeling) indices are derived for measuring the influence of problem characteristics on algorithm performance (see Equations 1 to 5). In step 2 (Statistical Sampling) a set of representative instances are generated with stratified sampling and a sample size derived from survey sampling. In step 3 (Characteristics Measurement) the parameter values of each instance are transformed into indices. In step 4 (Instances Solution) instances are solved using a set of heuristic algorithms. In Step 5 (Clustering) groups are integrated in such a way that they are constituted by instances with similar characteristics, and for which an algorithm outperformed the others. Finally, in step 6 (Classification) the identified grouping is learned into formal classifiers.

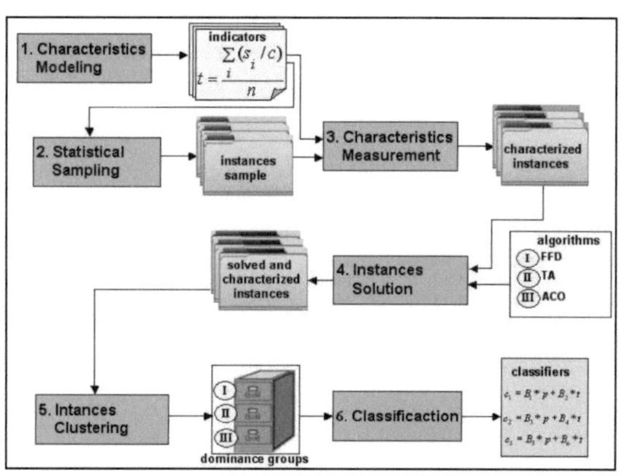


Fig. 4. Steps of the initial training phase

We propose five indices to characterize the instances of BPP:

*Instance size* $p$ expresses a relationship between instance size and the maximum size solved, where, $n$ is the number of items, $maxn$ is the maximum size solved

$$p = \frac{n}{maxn} \tag{1}$$

a. *Constrained capacity* $t$ expresses a relationship between the average item size and the bin size. The size of item $i$ is $s_i$ and the bin size is $c$.

$$t = \frac{\sum_i (s_i / c)}{n} \qquad 1 \le i \le n \tag{2}$$

b. *Item dispersion* $d$ expresses the dispersion degree of the item size values.

$$d = \sigma\ (t) \tag{3}$$

c. *Number of factors* $f$ expresses the proportion of items whose sizes are factors of the bin capacity.

$$f = \frac{\sum_i factor(c, s_i)}{n} \qquad 1 \le i \le n \tag{4}$$

d. *Bin usage* $b$ expresses the proportion of the total size that can fit in a bin of capacity $c$.

$$b = \begin{cases} 1 & \text{if } \ c \ge \sum_i s_i \\ \dfrac{c}{\sum_i s_i} & \text{otherwise} \end{cases} \qquad 1 \le i \le n \tag{5}$$

**Prediction phase**

The steps of this phase are shown in Figure 5. For a new instance, step 7 (Characteristics Measurement) calculates its characteristic values using indices. Step 8 uses the learned classifiers to determine, from the characteristics of the new instance, which group it belongs to. The algorithm associated to this group is the expected best algorithm for the instance.

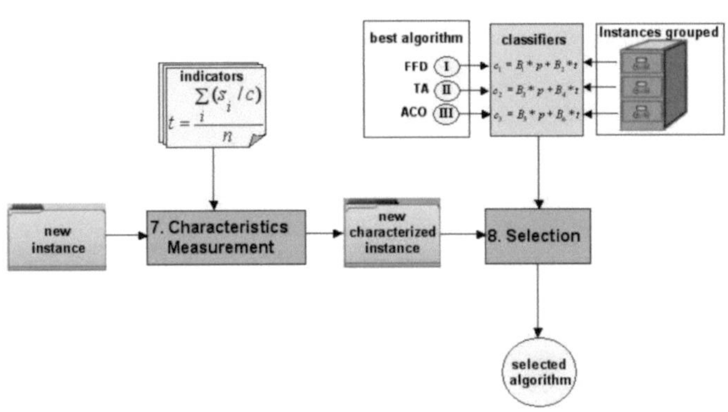


Fig. 5. Steps of the prediction phase

**Training and FeedBack phase**

The steps of this phase are shown in Figure 6. The objective is to feedback the system in order to maintain it in a continuous training. For each new solved and characterized instance, step 9 (Instance Solution) obtains the real best algorithm. Afterwards, step 10 (Patterns Verification) compares the result, if the prediction is wrong and the average accuracy is beyond an specified threshold, then the classifiers are rebuilt using the old and new dataset; otherwise the new instance is stored and the process ends.

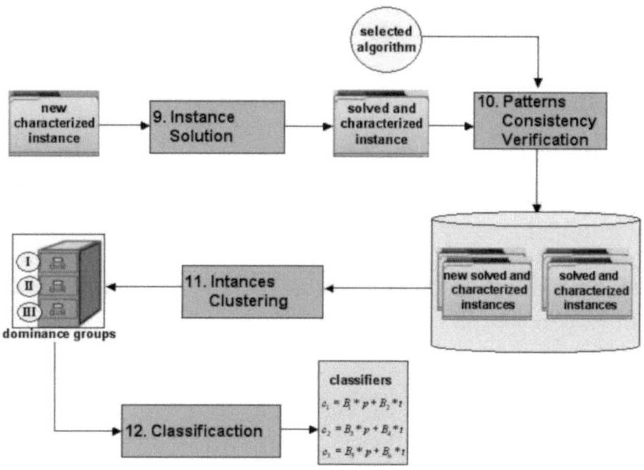


Fig. 6. Steps of the training with feedback phase

### 5.1.3 Experimentation

For test purposes 2,430 random instances of the Bin-Packing problem were generated, characterized and solved using the seven heuristic algorithms described in Section 5.1.1. Table 1 shows a small instance set, which were selected from the sample.

| Instance | Problem characteristic indices | | | | | Real best algorithms |
|---|---|---|---|---|---|---|
| | $p$ | $b$ | $t$ | $f$ | $d$ | |
| E1i10.txt | 0.078 | 0.427 | 0.029 | 0.000 | 0.003 | FFD,TA |
| E50i10.txt | 0.556 | 0.003 | 0.679 | 0.048 | 0.199 | BFD,ACO |
| E147i10.txt | 0.900 | 0.002 | 0.530 | 0.000 | 0.033 | TA |

Table 1. Example of random intances with their characteristics and the best algorithms

The K-means clustering method was used to create similar instance groups. Four groups were obtained; each group was associated with a similar instances set and an algorithm with the best performance for it. Three algorithms had poor performance and were outperformed by the other four algorithms. The Discriminant Analysis (DA) and C4.5 classification methods were used to build the algorithm selector. We use the machine learning methods available in SPSS version 11.5 and Weka 3.4.2, respectively. Afterwards, for validating the system, 1,369 standard instances were collected [Ross 2002]. In the selection of the best algorithm for all standard instances, the experimental results showed an accuracy of 76% with DA and 81% with C4.5. This accuracy was compared with a random selection from the seven algorithms: 14.2%. For the instances of the remaining percentage (100-76%), the selected algorithms generate a solution close to the optimal.

The selection system with feedback was implemented using a neural network, particularly the Self-Organizing Map (SOM) of Kohonen available in Matlab 7.0. The best results were obtained with only two problem characteristic indices (*p,t*) in a multi-network. The accuracy increased from 78.8% in 100 epochs up to 100% in 20,000 epochs. These percentages correspond to the network with initial-training and training-with-feedback, respectively. The SOM was gradually feedback with all the available instances. Using all indices (*p,b,t,f,d*) the SOM only reached 76.6% even with feedback.

### 5.2 Selection of heuristics in a hyper-heuristic framework

A hyper-heuristic is an automated methodology for selecting heuristics to solve hard computational search problems (Burke et al., 2009; Burke et al., 2010; Duarte et al., 2007). Its methodology is form by a high-level algorithm that, given a particular problem instance and a number of low-level heuristics or metaheuristic, can select and apply an appropriate low-level heuristic or metaheuristic at each decision step. These procedures on their way to work raise the generality at which search strategy can operate. General scheme for design a hyper-heuristic is shown in Figure 7.

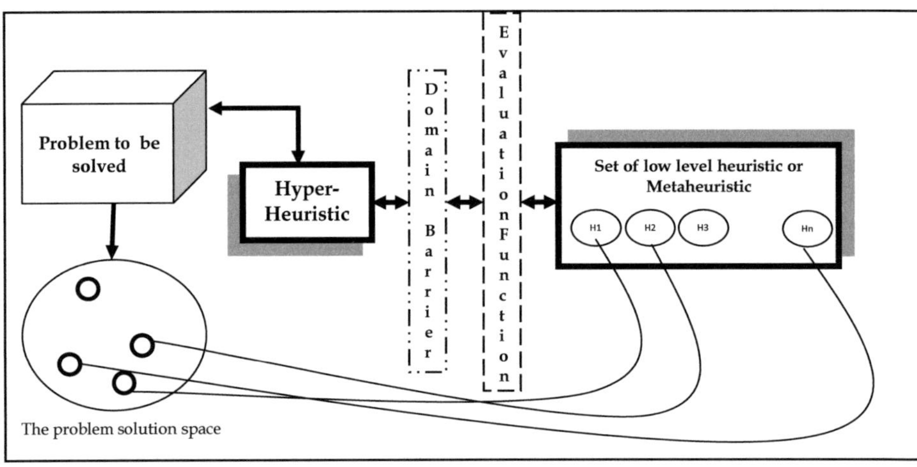


Fig. 7. Hyper-heuristic Elements

The first low-level algorithms build a solution incrementally; starting with an empty solution with the goal is to intelligently select the next construction heuristics or metaheuristic to gradually build a complete solution (Garrido, & Castro, 2009).

#### 5.2.1 Representative examples

SQRP is the problem of locating information in a network based on a query formed by keywords. The goal of SQRP is to determine the shortest paths from a node that issues a query to nodes that can appropriately answer it (by providing the requested information). Each query traverses the network, moving from the initiating node to a neighboring node and then to a neighbor of a neighbor and so forth, until it locates the requested resource or gives up in its absence. Due to its complexity (Michlmayr, 2007) solutions proposed to SQRP typically limit to special cases.

Hyper-Heuristic_AdaNAS (HH_AdaNAS) is an adaptive metaheuristic algorithm, which resolves SQRP (Hernandez, 2010). This algorithm was created from AdaNAS (Gómez et al., 2010). The *high-level algorithm* is formed by HH_AdaNAS, which use as solution algorithm AdaNAS, that is inspired by an ant colony and the set of *low-level heuristics* are included in the algorithm called HH_TTL. The goal of hyperheuristic HH_TTL is to define by itself in real time, the most adequate values for time to live (TTL) parameter during the execution of the algorithm. The main difference between AdaNAS and HH_AdaNAS are: when applying the modification of the TTL and the calculation of the amount of TTL to be allocated. In the Figure 8 we show HH_AdaNAS is form by AdaNAS + HH_TTL.

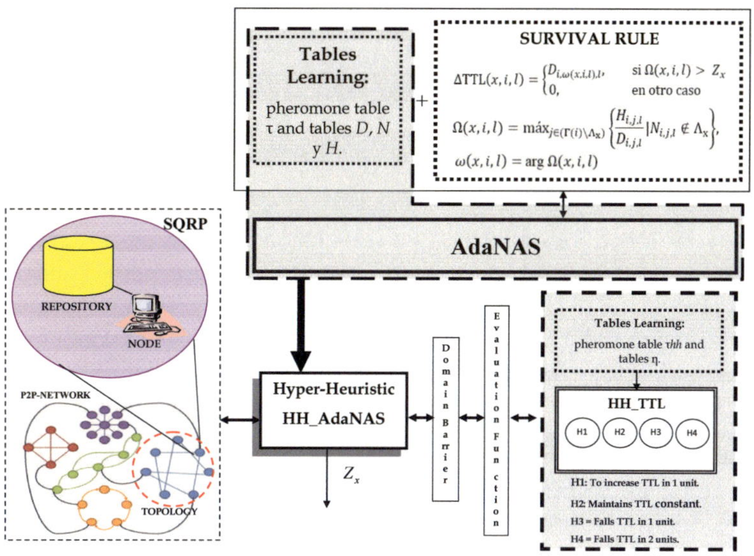


Fig. 8. HH_AdaNAS is form by AdaNAS + HH_TTL.

**Data structures of HH_AdaNAS**

HH_AdaNAS inherited some data structures of AdaNAS, as the pheromone table τ and the tables *H, D* and *N*. Besides the data structures of the high level metaheuristics, are the structures that help to select the low-level heuristic these are the pheromone table τ*hh* and the table hiperheuristic visibility states η. All the tables stored heuristic information or gained experience in the past. The relationship of these structures is shown in Figure 9.

When HH_AdaNAS searches for the next node, in the routing process of the query, is based on the pheromone table τ and tables *D, N* y *H;* these tables are intended to give information on distant *D, H* is a table that records the successes of past queries and number of documents *N* which are the closest nodes that can satisfy the query. In the same way, when HH_TTL chooses the following low level heuristic, through data structures τ*hh* and η. The memory is composed of two data structures that store information of prior consultations. The first of these memories is the pheromone table τ*hh* which has three dimensions, and the other memory structure is the table hiper-heuristic visibility states η, which allows the hiperheuristic know in what state is SQRP. Is to say, if is necessary to add more TTL, because the amount of resources found are few and decreases the lifetime.

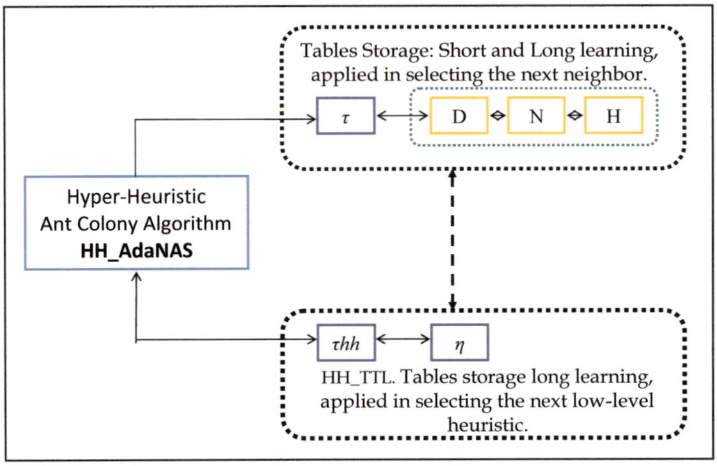


Fig. 9. Storage structures of HH_AdaNAS.

The pheromone table τ is divided into $n$ two-dimensional tables, one corresponding to each node $i$ of the network. These tables contain only entries for a node fixed $i$, therefore, its dimensions are at most $|L| \times |\Gamma(i)|$, where $L$ is the dictionary, which defines the keywords allowed for consultation and $\Gamma(i)$ is the set of neighboring nodes of $i$. Each in turn contains a two-dimensional table $|m| \times |h|$, where $m$ is the states visibility set of the problem and $h$ is the available heuristics set. The pheromone table is also called learning structure long.

The visibility state table η expresses the weight of the relation between SQRP-states and TTL-heuristics and was inspired by the deterministic survival rule designed by Rivera (Rivera G. 2009). Table η is formed by the combination of $|m| \times |h|$, where a visibility state $m_i$ is identified mainly by α, which depends on the node selected by AdaNAS to route the query SQRP. The variable α in Equation 6 contributes to ensure that the node selected by HH_AdaNAS, in the future, not decreases the performance of the algorithm. A TTL-heuristic is intelligently selected according with the past performance given by its pheromone value, and its visibility value, given by an expert. The Figure 10 shows the visibility state table used in this work.

| | $h_1$ | $h_2$ | $h_3$ | $h_4$ |
|---|---|---|---|---|
| $m_1$ | 1 | 0.75 | 0.5 | 0.25 |
| $m_2$ | 0.75 | 1 | 0.5 | 0.5 |
| $m_3$ | 0.5 | 0.5 | 1 | 0.75 |
| $m_4$ | 0.25 | 0.5 | 0.75 | 1 |

Fig. 10. Visibility state table

$$\alpha=(H_{i,j,l} \,/\, D_{i,j,l}) \,/\, Z_x \qquad (6)$$

Where $H_{i,j,l}$ indicates the number of documents consistent with the query $l$, $D_{i,j,l}$ indicates the length of the route to obtain the documents, $i$ represented the current node and $j$ is the node chosen, and $Z_x$ is a measure of current performance. In this work the visibility states are: $m_1 = (\alpha > 1)\&(TTL < D)\&(TTL != 1)$, $m_2 = (\alpha > 1)\&(TTL < D)\&(TTL = 1)$, $m_3 = (H = 0) \mid\mid ((\alpha > 1)\&(TTL \geq D)) \mid\mid ((\alpha \leq 1)\&(TTL = 1))$ and $m_4 = (\alpha \leq 1)\&(TTL > 1)$. All the visibility states are calculated to identify which heuristic will be applied to TTL.

### 5.2.2 Experimentation

The experimental environment used during experiments, and the results obtained are presented in this section. **Software:** Microsoft Windows 7 Home Premium; Java programming language, Java Platform, JDK 1.6; and integrated development, Eclipse 3.4. **Hardware:** Computer equipment with processor Intel (R) Core (TM) i5 CPU M430 2.27 GHz and RAM memory of 4 GB. **Instances:** It has 90 different SQRP instances; each of them consists of three files that represent the topology, queries and repositories. The description of the features can be found in (Cruz et al. 2008).

The average performance was studied by computing three performance measures of each 100 queries: **Average hops**, defined as the average amount of links traveled by a Forward Ant until its death that is, reaching either the maximum amount of results required or running out of TTL. **Average hits**, defined as the average number of resources found by each Forward Ant until its death, and **Average efficiency**, defined as the average of resources found per traversed edge (hits/hops). The initial Configuration of HH_AdaNAS is shown in Table 2. The parameter values were based on values suggested of the literature as (Dorigo & Stützle, 2004; Michlmayr, 2007; Aguirre, 2008 and Rivera, 2009).

In this section we show experimentally that HH_AdaNAS algorithm outperforms the AdaNAS algorithm. Also HH_AdaNAS outperforms NAS (Aguirre, 2008), SemAnt (Michlmayr, 2007) and random walk algorithms (Cruz et al., 2008), this was reported in (Gómez et al., 2010), so HH_AdaNAS algorithm is positioned as the best of them.

| Parameter | Description | Value |
|---|---|---|
| $\tau_0$ | Pheromone table initialization | 0.009 |
| $D_0$ | Distance table initialization | 999 |
| $\rho$ | Local pheromone evaporation factor | 0.35 |
| $\beta_1$ | Intensification of local measurements (degree and distance) | 2.0 |
| $\beta_2$ | Intensification of pheromone trail | 1.0 |
| $q$ | Relative importance between exploration and Exploitation | 0.65 |
| $W_h$ | Relative importance of the hits and hops in the increment rule | 0.5 |
| $W_{deg}$ | Degree's influence in the selection the next node | 2.0 |
| $W_{dist}$ | Distance's influence in the selection the next node | 1.0 |
| $TTL_{inic}$ | Initial Time To Live of the Forward Ants | 10 |

Table 2. Shows the assignment of values for each HH_AdaNAS parameter.

In this experiment, we compare the HH_AdaNAS and AdaNAS algorithms. The performance achieved is measured by the rate of found documents and the experiments were conducted under equal conditions, so each algorithm was run 30 times per instance and used the same configuration parameters for the two algorithms, which is described in Table 2.

The Figure 11 shows the average efficiency performed during a set of queries with HH_AdaNAS and AdaNAS algorithms; for the two algorithms the behavior is approximately the same. The algorithm HH_AdaNAS at the beginning the efficiency is around 2.38 hits per hop in the first 100 queries and the algorithm AdaNAS start approximately at 2.37 hits per query also in the top 100 queries. Analyzing at another example of the experiment, after processing the 11 000 queries at the end the efficiency increases around 3.31 hits per hop for the algorithm HH_AdaNAS and the algorithm AdaNAS at 3.21 hits per query. Finally, due to the result we conclude that HH_AdaNAS achieves a final improvement in performance of 28.09%, while AdaNAS reaches an improvement of 26.16%.

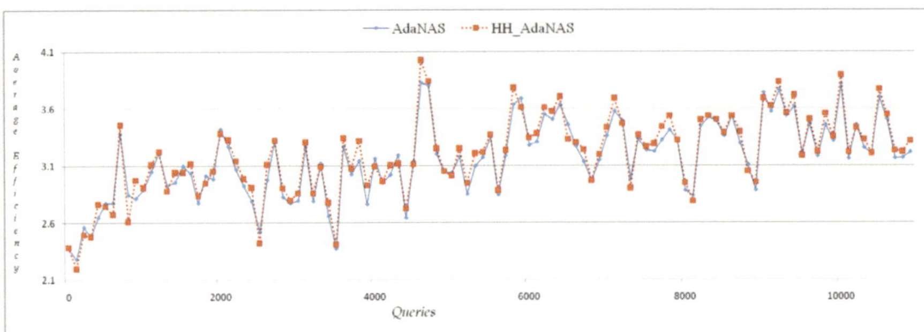


Fig. 11. The average efficiency performed during 11,000 queries with two algorithms.

## 6. Hybrid systems of metaheuristics: an approximate solution of ASP

The majority of problems related with ASP have a high level of complexity, according to application domains. An alternative solution is the use of Hybrid Systems based on Heuristics and Metaheuristics. Algorithm selection has attracted the attention of some research in hybrid intelligent systems, for which many algorithms and large datasets are available. Hybrid Intelligent Systems seek to take advantage of the synergy between various intelligent techniques in solving real problems (Ludermir et al., 2011).

### 6.1 Relation of meta-learning and hybridization

Although some algorithms based on Hybrid Systems of Metaheuristics are better than others on average, there is rarely a best algorithm for a given problem according to the complexity and application domain related with the proposal solution. Instead, it is often the case that different algorithms perform well on different problem instances. This condition is most accentuated among algorithms for solving NP-Hard problems, because runtimes of these algorithms are often highly variable from instance to instance.

When algorithms present high runtime variability, one is faced with the problem of deciding which algorithm to use. Rice called this the "algorithm selection problem" (Rice, 1976). The algorithm selection has not received widespread attention. The most common approach to algorithm selection has been to measure the performance of different algorithms on a given instances set with certain distribution, and then select the algorithm with the lowest average runtime.

This "winner-take-all" approach has produced recent and important advances in algorithm design and refinement, but has caused the rejection of many algorithms that has an excellent performance on an specific cases, but result uncompetitive on average. The following two questions emerge from the literature (Leyton-Brown, 2003). How to perform an algorithm selection for a given instance? How to evaluate novel hybrid algorithms?

a. Algorithms with high average running times can be combined to form a hybrid algorithm more robust and with low average running time when the algorithm inputs are sufficiently easy and uncorrelated.
b. New hybrid algorithm design should find more robust solution and focus on problems on which a single algorithm performs poorly.
c. A portfolio of algorithms can also be integrated through the use of hybrid algorithms because the solutions are considering more innovative.

In previous section we use machine learning algorithms to automatically acquire knowledge for algorithm selection, leading to a reduced need for experts and a potential improvement of performance. In general, the algorithm selection problem can be treated via meta-learning approaches. The results of this approach can cause an important impact on hybridization. In order to clarify this point, is important to speculate about how the empirical results of meta-learning can be analyzed from a theoretical perspective with different intentions:

a. Confirm the sense of the selection rules
b. Generate insights into algorithm behavior that can be used to refine the algorithms.

The acquired knowledge is confirmed when the performance of the refined algorithms is evaluated. The knowledge can be used to integrate complementary strategies in a hybrid algorithm.

### 6.2 Use of hybridization to solve ASP in social domains

The principal advanced in the reduction of Complexity is related with the amalgam of different perspectives established on different techniques which to demonstrate their efficiency in different application domains with good results.

Hybridization of Algorithms is one of the most adequate ways to try to improve and solve different ASP related with the optimization of time. Many applied ASP´s have an impact on social domains specially to solve dynamic and complex models related with human behavior. In (Araiza, 2011) is possible analyze with a Multiagents System the concept of "Social Isolation", featuring this behavior on the time according with interchanges related with a minority and the associated health effects, when this occurs.

In addition, is possible specify the deep and impact of a viral marketing campaign using a Social Model related with Online Social Networking. In (Azpeitia, 2011), an adequate ASP determines the way on the future of this campaign and permits analyze the track of this to understand their best features.

### 6.3 Future trends on the resolution of ASP using a hybrid system of metaheuristics

We expected that the future trends for solving ASP with hybridization will be based on models that tend to perform activities according to a selection framework and a dynamic contextual area. The decision of the most appropriate actions requires advanced Artificial Intelligence Technique to satisfy a plethora of application domains in which interaction and conclusive results are needed. This only is possible with Intelligent Systems equipped with high processing speed, knowledge bases and an innovative model for designing experiments, something will happen in this decade.

## 7. Conclusions

Many real world problems belong to a special class of problems called NP-hard, which means that there are no known efficient algorithms to solve them exactly in the worst case. The specialized literature offers a variety of heuristic algorithms, which have shown satisfactory performance. However, despite the efforts of the scientific community in developing new strategies, to date, there is no an algorithm that is the best for all possible situations. The design of appropriate algorithms to specific conditions is often the best option. In consequence, several approaches have emerged to deal with the algorithm selection problem. We review hyper-heuristics and meta-learning; both related and promising approaches.

Meta-learning, through machine learning methods like clustering and classification, is a well-established approach of selecting algorithms, particularity to solve hard optimization problems. Despite this, comparisons and evaluations of machine learning methods to build algorithm selector is not a common practice. We compared three machine learning techniques for algorithm selection on standard data sets. The experimental results revealed in general, a high performance with respect to a random algorithm selector, but low perform with respect to other classification tasks. We identified that the Self-Organising Neural Network is a promising method for selection; it could reaches 100% of accuracy when feedback was incorporated and the number of problem characteristics was the minimum.

On the other hand, hyper-heuristics offers a general framework to design algorithms that ideally can select and generate heuristics adapted to a particular problem instance. We use this approach to automatically select, among basic-heuristics, the most promising to adjust a parameter control of an Ant Colony Optimization algorithm for routing messages. The adaptive parameter tuning with hyper-heuristics is a recent open research.

In order to get a bigger picture of the algorithm performance we need to know them in depth. However, most of the algorithmic performance studies have focused exclusively on identifying sets of instances of different degrees of difficulty; in reducing the time needed to resolve these cases and reduce the solution errors; in many cases following the strategy "the -winner takes-all". Although these are important goals, most approaches have been quite particular. In that sense, statistical methods and machine learning will be an important element to build performance models for understanding the relationship between the characteristics of optimization problems, the search space that defines the behavior of algorithms that solve, and the final performance achieved by these algorithms. We envision that the knowledge gained, in addition to supporting the growth of the area, will be useful to automate the selection of algorithms and refine algorithms; hiper-heuristics, hybridization, and meta-learning go in the same direction and can complement each other.

## 8. Acknowledgment

This research was supported in part by CONACYT and DGEST

## 9. References

Ali, S. & Smith, K. (2006). On learning algorithm selection for classification. *Applied Soft Computing*, Vol. 6, No. 2, (January 2006), pp. 119-38.

Aguirre, M. (2008). *Algoritmo de Búsqueda Semántica para Redes P2P Complejas*. Master's thesis, Divisi6n de Estudio de Posgrado e Investigaci6n del Instituto Tecnol6gico de Ciudad Madero, Tamaulipas, México.

Azpeitia, D. (2011). Critical Factors for Success of a Viral Marketing Campaign of Real-Estate Sector at Facebook: The strength of weak learnability. *Proceedings of the HIS Workshop at MICAI*

Beck, J. & Freuder, E. (2004). Simple Rules for Low-Knowledge Algorithm Selection. *Proceedings of the 1st International Conference on Integration of IA and OR Techniques in Constraint Programming for Combinatorial Optimization Problems*, Nice, France, April 2004, J. Regin and M. Rueher (Ed.). Springer-Verlag Vol. 3011, pp. 50-64.

Brazdil, P. B., Soares C., & Pinto, D. C. J. (2003). Ranking Learning Algorithms: Using IBL and Meta-Learning on Accuracy and Time Results. *Machine Learning*, Vol. 50, No. 3, pp. 251–277, ISSN: 08856125

Brewer, E. (1995). High-Level Optimization Via Automated Statistical Modeling. *Proceedings of Principles and Practice of Parallel Programming*, Santa Barbara, CA, July 1995, ACM Press, New York, USA, pp. 80-91

Burke, E., Hyde, M., Kendall, G., Ochoa, G., Özcan, E. & Woodward, J. (2009). Exploring hyper-heuristic methodologies with genetic programming. In: *Computational Intelligence*: Collaboration, Fusion and Emergence, Intelligent Systems Reference Library

Burke, K., Hyde, M., Kendall, G., Ochoa, G., Özcan, E. & Woodward, R. (2010). A Classification of Hyper-heuristic Approaches, In: *International Series in Operations Research & Management Science*, Gendreau, M. and Potvin, J.Y. pp.(449). Springer Science+Business Media, ISBN 978-1-4419-1663-1, NY, USA

Cai, H., Hu X., Lü Q., & Cao, Q. (2009). A novel intelligent service selection algorithm and application for ubiquitous web services environment. *Expert Systems with Applications*, Vol. 36, No. 2, Part 1, pp. 2200-2212, ISSN: 09574174

Cruz, L. (1999). *Automatización del Diseño de la Fragmentación Vertical y Ubicación en Bases de Datos Distribuidas usando Métodos Heurísticos y Exactos*. Master's thesis, Instituto Tecnol6gico y de Estudios Superiores de Monterrey, México.

Cruz, L., G6mez, C., Aguirre, M., Schaeffer, S., Turrubiates, T., Ortega, R. & Fraire,H.(2008). NAS algorithm for semantic query routing systems in complex networks. In: *International Symposium on Distributed Computing and Artificial Intelligence 2008/ Advances in Soft Computing 2009*. Corchado J., Rodríguez S., Llinas J. & Molina J., pp. (284-292), Springer, Berlin /Heidelberg, ISBN 978-3-540-85862-1, DOI 10.1007/978-3-540-85863-8

Czogalla, J. & Fink, A. (2009). Fitness Landscape Analysis for the Resource Constrained Project Scheduling Problem. *Lecture Notes in Computer Science, Learning and Intelligent Optimization*, Vol. 5851, pp. 104-118

Dorigo, M. & Stützle, T. (2004). *Ant Colony Optimization*. MIT Press, Cambridge, MA., ISBN 0-262-04219-3, EUA

Duarte, A., Pantrigo, J., Gallego, M. (2007). *Metaheurísticas,* Ed. Dykinson S.L. España

Ducatelle, F., & Levine, J. (2001). Ant Colony Optimisation for Bin Packing and Cutting Stock Problems. *Proceedings* of the UK Workshop on Computational Intelligence, Edinburgh

Fink, E. (1998). How to solve it automatically: Selection among Problem-Solving methods. *Proceedings of ICAPS 1998*, pp. 128–136

Frost, D.; Rish, I. & Vila, L. (1997). Summarizing CSP hardness with continuous probability distributions. *Proceedings of the 14th National Conference on AI*, American Association for Artificial Intelligence, pp. 327-333

Garrido, P. & Castro C. (2009). Stable solving of cvrps using hyperheuristics. *Proceedings of the 11th Annual conference on Genetic and evolutionary computation (GECCO'09)*, ACM, Montreal, Canada, July 2009

Gent, I.; Macintyre, E.; Prosser, P. & Walsh, T. (1997). The Scaling of Search Cost. In: *Proceedings of the fourteenth national conference on artificial intelligence and ninth conference on Innovative applications of artificial intelligence,* pp. 315-320, AAI Press, Retrieved from: https://www.aaai.org/Papers/AAAI/1997/AAAI97-049.pdf

Gómez, C.G., Cruz, L., Meza, E., Schaeffer, E. & Castilla, G.(2010). A Self-Adaptive Ant Colony System for Semantic Query Routing Problem in P2P Networks. *Computación y Sistemas* Vol. 13, No. 4, pp (433-448), ISSN 1405-5546

Guo, H. & Hsu, W. (2004). A Learning-based Algorithm Selection Meta-reasoner for the Real-time MPE Problem. *Proceedings of the 17th Australian Joint Conference on Artificial Intelligence,* Cairns, Australian, Dec 2004, G. I. Webb and Xinghuo Yu (Ed.), Springer-Verlag Vol. 3339, pp. 307-318

Hernández P. (2010). *Método Adaptativo para el Ajuste de Parámetros de un Algoritmo Evolutivo Hiperheurístico.* Master's thesis, División de Estudio de Posgrado e Investigación del Instituto Tecnológico de Ciudad Madero, Tamaulipas, México

Hilario, M., & Kalousis, A. (2000). Building algorithm profiles for prior model selection in knowledge discovery systems. *International Journal of Engineering Intelligent Systems for Electrical Engineering and Communications*, Vol. 8, No. 2, 2000, pp. 77-88, ISSN: 09691170

Hollander, M. & Wolfe, D. (1973). *Non-parametric Statistical Methods.* John Wiley and Sons. New York, USA

Hoos, H. & Stutzle, T. (2000). Systematic vs. Local Search for SAT. *Journal of Automated Reasoning*, Vol. 24, pp. 421-481

Houstis, E.; Catlin, A. & Rice, J. (2002). PYTHIA-II: A Knowledge/Database System for Managing Performance Data and Recommending Scientific Software, ACM Transactions on Mathematical Software (TOMS) - Special issue in honor of John Rice's 65th birthday, Vol. 26, No. 2, (June 2000)

Hutter, F.; Hamadi, Y.; Hoos, H. & Leyton-Brown, K. (2006). Performance prediction and automated tuning of randomized and parametric algorithms. *Lecture Notes in Computer Science, Principles and Practice of Constraint Programming,* Vol. 4204, pp. 213-228

Kadioglu, S., Malitsky, Y., Sabharwal, A., Samulowitz, H., & Sellmann, M. (2011). Algorithm Selection and Scheduling, *Proceedings of the 17th International Conference on Principles and Practice of Constraint Programming (CP2011)*, Italy, September 2011

Kalousis, A., & Theoharis, T. (1999). NOEMON: Design, implementation and performance results of an intelligent assistant for classifier selection, *Intelligent Data Analysis,* Vol. 3, No. 5, pp. 319-337, ISSN: 1088467X

Kotthoff, L.; Gent, I. & Miguel I. (2011). A Preliminary Evaluation of Machine Learning in Algorithm Selection for Search Problems. In: *AAAI Publications, Fourth International Symposium on Combinatorial Search (SoCS)*, Borrajo, Daniel and Likhachev, Maxim and López, Carlos Linare, pp. 84-91, AAAI Press, Retrieved from: http://www.aaai.org/ocs/index.php/SOCS/SOCS11/paper/view/4006

Lagoudakis, M. & Littman, M. (2000). Algorithm Selection Using Reinforcement Learning. *Proceedings of the Sixteenth International Conference on Machine Learning*. P. Langley (Ed.), AAAI Press, pp. 511–518

Lagoudakis, M. & Littman, M. (2001). Learning to select branching rules in the dpll procedure for satisfiability. *Electronic Notes in Discrete Mathematics*, Vol. 9, (June 2001), pp. 344-359

Lawler, E.; Lenstra, J.; Rinnooy, K. & Schmoys, D. (1985). *The Traveling Salesman Problem: A Guided Tour of Combinatorial Optimization*. John Wiley & Sons, New York, USA

Leyton-Brown, K.; Nudelman, E.; Andrew, G.; McFadden, J. & Shoham, Y. (2003). A portfolio approach to algorithm selection. *Proceedings of International joint conference on artificial intelligence*, Vol. 18, pp. 1542-3

Li, J.; Skjellum, A. & Falgout, R. (1997). A Poly-Algorithm for Parallel Dense Matrix Multiplication on Two-Dimensional Process Grid Topologies. *Concurrency, Practice and Experience*, Vol. 9, No. 5, pp. 345-389

Lobjois, L. & Lemâitre, M. (1998). Branch and bound algorithm selection by performance prediction. In: *AAAI '98/IAAI '98 Proceedings of the fifteenth national/tenth conference on Artificial intelligence/Innovative applications of artificial intelligence*, Jack Mostow, Charles Rich, Bruce Buchanan, pp. 353-358, AAAI Press, Retrieved from: http://www.aaai.org/Papers/AAAI/1998/AAAI98-050.pdf

Ludermir, T.B.; Ricardo B. C. Prudêncio, R.B.C; Zanchettin, C. (2011). Feature and algorithm selection with Hybrid Intelligent Techniques. *International Journal Hybrid Intelligent Systems* ,Vol. 8, No. 3, pp. 115-116

Madani, O.; Raghavan, H. & Jones, R. (2009). On the Empirical Complexity of Text Classification Problems. *SRI AI Center Technical Report*

Malitsky, Y., Sabharwal, A., Samulowitz, H., & Sellmann M. (2011). Non-Model-Based Algorithm Portfolios for SAT, *Proceedings of the 14th international conference on Theory and Applications of Satisfiability Testing*, Ann Arbor, June 2011

Messelis, T.; Haspeslagh, S.; Bilgin, B.; De Causmaecker, P. & Vanden Berghe, G. (2009). Towards prediction of algorithm performance in real world optimization problems. *Proceedings of the 21st Benelux Conference on Artificial Intelligence*, BNAIC, Eindhoven, pp. 177-183

Michlmayr, E. (2007). *Ant Algorithms for Self-Organization in Social Networks*. PhD thesis, Women's Postgraduate College for Internet Technologies (WIT), Vienna, Austria

Nascimento, A. C. A., Prudencio, R. B. C., Costa, I. G., & de Souto, M. C. P. (2009). Mining rules for the automatic selection process of clustering methods applied to cancer gene expression data, *Proceedings of 19th International Conference on Artificial Neural Networks (ICANN)*, Cyprus, September 2009

Nikolić, M.; Marić, F. & Janičić, P. (2009). Instance-Based Selection of Policies for SAT Solvers. *Lecture Notes in Computer Science, Theory and Applications of Satisfiability Testing*, Vol. 5584, pp. 326-340

O'Mahony, E., Hebrard, E., Holland, A., Nugent, C., & O'Sullivan, B. (2009). Using Case-based Reasoning in an Algorithm Portfolio for Constraint Solving. (2008).

*Proceedings of The 19th Irish Conference on Artificial Intelligence and Cognitive Science*, Ireland, August 2008

Pérez, O.J., Pazos, R.A., Frausto, J., Rodríguez, G., Romero, D., Cruz, L. (2004). A Statistical Approach for Algorithm Selection. *Lectures Notes in Computer Science*, Vol. 3059, (May 2004) pp. 417-431, ISSN: 0302-9743

Pérez, J., Pazos, R.A., Vélez, L. Rodríguez, G. (2002). Automatic Generation of Control Parameters for the Threshold Accepting Algorithm. *Lectures Notes in Computer Science*, Vol. 2313, pp. 119-127

Quiroz, M. (2009). *Caracterización de Factores de Desempeño de Algoritmos de Solución de BPP*. Master´s thesis, Instituto Tecnológico de Cd. Madero, Tamaulipas, México

Reeves, C. (1993). *Modern heuristic techniques for combinatorial problems*. John Wiley & Sons, ISBN: 0-470-22079-1, New York, USA

Rice, J. R. (1976). The algorithm selection problem. *Advances in Computers*, Vol. 15, pp. 65-118

Rice, J.R. (1968). On the Construction of Poly-algorithms for Automatic Numerical Analysis. *Interactive System for Experimental Applied Mathematics*, M. Klerer & J. Reinfelds, (Ed.) Academic Press, Burlington, MA, pp. 301-313

Ruiz-Vanoye, J. A., Pérez, J., Pazos, R. A., Zarate, J. A., Díaz-Parra, O., & Zavala-Díaz, J. C. (2009). Statistical Complexity Indicators Applied to the Vehicle Routing Problem with Time Windows for Discriminate Appropriately the Best Algorithm, *Journal of Computer Science and Software Technology*, Vol. 2, No. 2, ISSN: 0974-3898

Samulowitz, H. & Memisevic, R. (2007). Learning to solve QBF. In: *AAAI-07*, pp. 255-260, retrieved from: https://www.aaai.org/Papers/AAAI/2007/AAAI07-039.pdf

Schiavinotto, T. & Stützle, T. (2007). A review of metrics on permutations for search landscape analysis. *Computers & Operations Research*, Vol. 34, No. 10, (October 2007), pp. 3143-3153

Silverthorn, B. & Miikkulainen, R. (2010). Latent Class Models for Algorithm Portfolio Methods. *Proceedings of the Twenty-Fourth AAAI Conference on Artificial Intelligence*

Smith-Miles, K. & Lopes, L. (2012). Measuring instance difficulty for combinatorial optimization problems. *Computers & Operations Research*, in press (accepted 6/7/11)

Smith-Miles, K.; James, R.; Giffin, J. & Tu, Y. (2009). Understanding the relationship between scheduling problem structure and heuristic performance using knowledge discovery. In: *Learning and Intelligent Optimization*, LION-3, Vol. 3, Available from: lion.disi.unitn.it/intelligent-optimization/LION3/online_proceedings/35.pdf

Soares, C. & Pinto, J. (2003). Ranking Learning Algorithms: Using IBL and Meta-Learning on Accuracy and Time Results. *Machine Learning*, Vol. 50, No. 3, pp. 251-277

Streeter, M; Golovin, D. & Smith, S. F. (2007). Combining multiple heuristics online. In: *AAAI 2007, Proceedings of the 22nd national conference on Artificial intelligence*, Vol. 22, Anthony Cohn, pp. 1197-1203, AAAI Press, Retrieved from: http://www.aaai.org/Papers/AAAI/2007/AAAI07-190.pdf

Wolpert, D. H. & Macready, W. G. (1997). No free lunch theorems for optimization. *IEEE Transactions on Evolutionary Computation*, Vol. 1, No. 1, pp. 67–82

Xu, L.; Hutter, F.; Hoos, H. & Leyton-Brown, K. (2009). SATzilla2009: An automatic algorithm portfolio for SAT. In: *Solver description, 2009 SAT Competition*

# 5

# Experiences and Obstacles in Industrial Applications of Intelligent Systems

Leonardo M. Reyneri[1] and Valentina Colla[2]
[1]*Politecnico di Torino, Dipartimento di Elettronica e Telecomunicazioni, Torino,*
[2]*Scuola Superiore Sant'Anna, TeCIP Institute, PERCRO, Pisa,*
*Italy*

## 1. Introduction

*Neural networks* and *fuzzy systems* are well known soft computing techniques, which date back several decades since the preliminary work of McCulloch and Pitts, Grossberg, Zadeh, and dozens of other precursors. At first, the neural network was believed to be "simple and workable solution" for all the difficult problems can be dealt with, and then gave rise to a broad interest in research around the world and garnered a lot of funding. During this preliminary period, many theories have been developed, analyzed and applied.

Later, the domain of neural networks and fuzzy systems has broadened and also many other algorithms and methods have been collected under the term of *Soft Computing* and, more general, *Intelligent Systems*. These include, among others, neural networks, fuzzy logic, wavelet networks, genetic algorithms, expert systems, etc... It was then discovered that several simple problems (the so-called "toy problems") actually found very simple solutions using intelligent systems. On the other hand, difficult problems (for example, handwriting recognition and most problems of industrial relevance), still could not be completely resolved, even if intelligent systems could contribute to simplify their solution.

Today, after several decades of alternating interest of the scientific and industrial community, after the publication of tens of thousands of theoretical and practical papers, and after several attempts to apply them in a large number of application domains, intelligent systems are now reaching a rather *mature phase*. People have begun to understand the real capabilities, potentials, limitations and disadvantages, so they are on the right path towards a widespread adoption, without excessive and inappropriate enthusiasm, but also, more importantly, with a good rationale for their use.

This chapter attempts to analyze the actual level of maturity and acceptance achieved by intelligent systems and attempts to assess how, where and why they are (or can be) accepted in the industry. Note that, although the focus is on *industrial applications*, this term generally applies also to several other real-world applications such as agronomy, economics, mathematics, weather forecasting, etc.

## 2. Maturity level of intelligent systems

As mentioned in the introduction, all soft computing and intelligent systems techniques suffered alternating periods of *acceptance* (due to the novelty and the promising preliminary results) and *rejection* (due to the acquired awareness of limits). Hundreds of algorithms, topologies, training rules have been: i) *conceived* and *developed;* ii) *tested, evaluated, tuned* and *optimized;* iii) *temporarily or partially abandoned* (>>90%); iv) *accepted* and *applied* to real problems (<<10%).

Most of the original theories have been nearly abandoned (like, for instance, *Hopfield networks* and *Boltzmann machines, glass spin theories, stochastic networks*, etc.) either because they could not offer reasonable performance or because they were too cumbersome to use. Other theories (like, for instance, *perceptrons, radial basis functions* and *fuzzy systems*) eventually reached widespread acceptance, since they are more viable.

What is then at present the level of maturity of intelligent systems? This can be evaluated from a series of clues such as:

- how many theories and paradigms *have been developed altogether*. This number should be as high as possible, to ensure that no option has been forgotten;
- how many paradigms *have survived after maybe ten years*. This should be low, to minimize the knowledge one needs to learn (see section 2.2);
- the *level of acquaintance* a typical engineer has with these techniques. This should be high and it should be achieved quickly (see section 2.1);
- the *count of accepted industrial applications* should be significant (see sections 3, 4, 5).

Due to the maturity level they reached in about half a century from the preliminary works, intelligent systems now deserve to be in the *knowledge briefcase* of each engineer, economist, agronomist, scientist, etc. *together with, and at the same acceptance level of* several other basic techniques like algebra, statistics, geometry, etc.

A way to reach a widespread industrial acceptance is to avoid using statements like:

*I have used/developed a neural network for...*

but, instead:

*I have just developed a complex system with interacting signal pre-processor, neural network, user interface, a differential equation solver, a post processor, some sensor and actuator interface, etc.*

The major difference between the two approaches is which element(s) of a system receive(s) more attention by the designer. In the former statement, attention (therefore the design effort) is stressed on the presence of a neural network, which therefore improperly becomes the most relevant block. In the latter statement, the neural network takes its proper place, that is, at the same level as all the other system elements. In many cases, the blocks surrounding intelligent subsystem are the most complex to design and use.

An example for this is in the field of image processing and handwriting recognition, where a successful application relies much more on a proper image pre-processing (filtering, contrast enhancement, segmentation, labelling, skeletonization, etc.) than on the neurofuzzy processing itself.

Despite the level of maturity they reached, intelligent systems still experience a lot of difficulties to be *accepted* by the industrial community, which still sees them as *academic experiments* or *bizarre techniques* and not as a powerful tool to solve their problems. Thus, *what still misses to a complete industrial maturity?* This will be analyzed in the following.

### 2.1 Availability of expertise and training personnel

Knowledge and expertise on intelligent systems cannot easily be found in the industrial domain, at least in decision-making people (namely: *decision staff, businessmen* and *engineers*), except perhaps in the newest generation (these are still too few and not yet high enough in the decision-making stair). Decision-making people are the key actors for having intelligent systems accepted in the industry. On the other hand, the real experts in intelligent systems are those who have been trained for long time in the area of soft computing, but these often have *too little knowledge of the specific problem they are faced with,* therefore they might not tackle the problem in the most appropriate or efficient way.

Personnel training is rather time consuming, therefore costly, for industry and it can seldom be afforded unless there is a reasonable guarantee to get appropriate returns. It must be remembered that adopting *any* novel method *may* offer advantages, but it *surely* costs money. The lack of good expertise, together with people laziness often leads to using oversized networks, oversized training sets, conservative choices for paradigms and learning coefficients, etc. Altogether, more complex (therefore more costly) networks, longer design and training time, less advantages; in conclusion, *less chance of acceptance.*

### 2.2 The apparent diversity of neurofuzzy paradigms

At the beginning, neural networks, fuzzy systems and other soft computing techniques like wavelet networks, Bayesian classifiers, clustering methods, etc., were believed to be independent, although complementary, methods, which had to be analyzed and studied independently of each other. This caused an excessive effort to study, analyze, get familiar with a huge variety of methods and therefore to train personnel consequently. It was also believed that each paradigm had its characteristics and preferred application domains, such that a lot of experience was required to choose the best architecture for any application.

On the contrary, Reyneri (Reyneri, 1999) proved that most soft computing techniques are nothing but different *languages* for a few basic paradigms. For instance, he proved that Perceptrons, Adaline, Wavelet networks, linear transforms, and adaptive linear filters are equivalent to each other. Also Fuzzy logic, Radial Basis, Bayesian classifiers, Gaussian regressors, Kernel methods, Kohonen maps and fuzzy/hard c-means are equivalent methods, as well as Local-global networks, TKS fuzzy systems and gain scheduling controllers which are also equivalent.

With a good use of such *neurofuzzy unification,* the number of independent paradigms reduces to as few as four. All known topologies for neural, fuzzy, wavelet, Bayesian, clustering paradigms, etc. and supervised or unsupervised training algorithms are, in practice, just particular implementations and interconnections of four elementary blocks, namely: i) *computing elements;* ii) *computing layers;* iii) *normalization layers* and iv) *sensitivity layers.* All traditional neurofuzzy paradigms are then nothing else than specific *languages,* each one being more appropriate to any given application.

The efficient use of *neurofuzzy unification* would simplify personnel training, since: i) it helps the practitioner to quickly learn and get familiar with the very few basic paradigms; ii) it augments flexibility and performance of intelligent systems; iii) it therefore increases the economical return and iv) reducing the corresponding risks. Nevertheless, neurofuzzy unification is still far from being widely applied, for several historical reasons. The permanence of tens of apparently different paradigms often still creates *confusion, noise, disaffection*; it increases *personnel training costs* and reduces *advantages*; altogether it significantly reduces the *appeal of neurofuzzy systems*.

## 3. Relevant characteristics for industry

In this section, we try to analyze here some of the reasons why intelligent systems still experience difficulties in being accepted as an industrial standard.

### 3.1 Crypticity

Many intelligent systems are often felt to be rather *cryptic*, in the sense that nobody can really understand why and how a trained network solves a given problem. Apart from the many theoretical proofs that an intelligent system is capable of solving a large variety of problems, the real industrially-relevant question is that all the knowledge of a trained network is hidden within a chunk of numbers, usually arranged into *weight* or *centre matrices* or *genomes*. There is usually no clue on how to interpret such "magic numbers", thus engineers are often sceptical in regards to their correctness, reliability or robustness.

In practice, correctness of weights is based on a successful training, although it is often difficult to either guarantee or feel that training has properly succeeded. Quality of training is measured on the amount of a residual *error measure*, but there is often no indication on which is an appropriate value for this error, especially when *sum-of-errors measures* are used, as in several commercial simulation tools. The user cannot reliably argue that a trained model is really representative of the desired system/function.

Furthermore, most training processes are often based on some amount of *randomness*, which is seldom appreciated in the industrial domain. On the other hand, traditional design methods (namely, those not using intelligent systems) are based on some predictable analytical or empirical model which is *chosen by the designer*, together with its parameters. Designer's *knowledge and experience* usually provide enough information to properly solve a problem, even though seldom in an optimal way. Nothing is apparently left to randomness.

In reality, the process of empirical adaptation of a given analytical or empirical model to a given system resembles the approach of training/adapting a soft computing system (which is nothing but a highly generic parametric model) based on a set of training data. Yet everybody considers the former as normal and straightforward, while most designers are still sceptical when facing the latter. Why is that so?

One of the reasons is that traditional (namely, non-intelligent) parametric models currently used in practice are much less generic than any soft computing models; therefore they are always under total control of the engineer, who is capable of properly interpreting parameters and values.

For instance, the model of an *electric motor* can model nothing else than an *electric motor*, and its parameters represent, for instance, winding resistance and inductance, rotor inertia, friction, etc. which are directly measurable and for which the designer can feel if they assume reasonable values or not. By appropriately varying these parameters, the model will be adapted to either *large or small motors*, either *fast or slow*, but it will never be able to model, for instance, a *chemical process*. The designer can easily become aware that, for instance, an improperly tuned model has a too large or too narrow winding resistance in comparison with the size of the motor under examination. He can therefore immediately be aware of improper tuning or of some motor fault or damage and behave accordingly.

On the other hand, intelligent systems are so generic that they can adapt to virtually any system, either electrical or chemical or economical or mechanical or agronomic, etc. The same parameters can therefore mean anything, depending on the actual use of the network (e.g. pollution of a chemical process, yield of a manufacturing process, winding resistance of a motor, rate of infection in an agricultural plant, etc.); in addition, parameters are interchangeable and there is no clue to understand what a given parameter really represents in practice. Further, nobody will ever be aware that training has not been done correctly and whether the model really represents a given system or not.

### 3.2 How to avoid crypticity

The use of modern unification paradigms (Reyneri, 1999) allows to easily convert neural and wavelet networks into fuzzy systems and viceversa, with several advantages, among which, for instance:

- a given neuro/wavelet network can be converted into fuzzy language, thus interpreted linguistically by experts, who are then able to "validate" and consequently "accept" an otherwise cryptic neuro/wavelet model;
- human experience, usually expressed as a set of fuzzy rules, can be converted into a neural network and then empirically tuned by means of an appropriate training set. Fuzzy (or expert systems) rules are usually understandable by an expert, such as he/she can understand the "concept" which lays behind them. An appropriate neural training of the rules therefore allows to fine tune the expert's knowledge based on the available empirical evidence.

It is therefore mandatory to abandon all the older approaches who were more like "magic formulae" than real engineering methods and concentrate on modern approaches that consider neural, wavelet, fuzzy, Bayesian, regressor, clustering techniques, etc. as *interchangeable paradigms*. The ever lasting fight among neural- and fuzzy-people is so detrimental, as it helps to maintain the level of crypticity high, therefore preventing a widespread acceptance of intelligent systems.

The choice between, for instance, *neural networks* and *fuzzy logic* should therefore be converted into a more appropriate selection between a *neural* and a *fuzzy language*, which should be chosen depending on: i) the available knowledge from human experts; ii) the size of available training set; iii) the availability of other piece of information on the problem; iv) the level of crypticity which is accepted; v) if and how the model has to be interpreted by humans or processed by computers.

### 3.3 Gathering data for network training

Many intelligent systems (mostly, those based on *neural languages*) rely on the availability of *empirical data*, which is usually gathered into large *training sets*. Unfortunately, these are often too expensive to obtain, as each data point is usually an appropriate *measurement* of a mechanical or chemical or biological or economical process. Several processes are so slow that each point may require up to several days to be acquired. In some cases, if an accurate numerical model is available, computer simulations can substitute direct measurements.

Some soft computing techniques (in particular, those based on *fuzzy* and *Bayesian languages*) may require much smaller training sets, as they rely on a predefined model, described in *linguistic terms* according to *previous human experience*. This is the main reason why fuzzy logic has been accepted more quickly and extensively by industry than neural systems.

An industrial manager has to consider attentively the trade-off between the cost of gathering a large training set and the reliability of the trained neurofuzzy network. As already said, this trade-off often pushes towards the use of *fuzzy languages* whenever possible and bounds the use of *neural languages* to applications which have enough (historical) data available.

### 3.4 Analytical vs. empirical methods

As already said, one of the advantages of intelligent systems is that a given analytical/ empirical model is by definition specific and cannot be tailored to a different problem, while neural networks are. Furthermore an analytical/empirical model usually comes after years of improvements, while neural networks are trained in a short time. Yet, a purely analytical model can be developed without any field measurement, while an empirical model requires a limited amount of field measurement. Instead most intelligent systems always require a huge amount of field measurements which, in several cases, can take years to gather.

Last but not least, the amount of field measurements which is required (that is roughly the development time) is a function of the reliability which is asked to the model. A large training set is in fact mandatory in industry to offer an adequately high reliability, while reliability of analytical models is often independent of field measurements but relies on designer's experience.

### 3.5 Performance is always optimistic...

Virtually any paper published in literature shows that, for a "wide range of applications, neural networks and fuzzy systems offer tremendously good performance".

Unfortunately, more than 90% of them do not even try to afford a fair performance comparison with other *state-of-the-art* techniques and it becomes difficult to feel how good such performance really is. Just as an example, a paper (not cited) claimed that *the proposed neural model of a biochemical process is 90% accurate* and the author was *enthusiast* of that *incredible result*. Since the reviewer had little experience on modelling that specific process, he could not do anything else than blindly accept author's statement. But, when the paper was read by an experienced colleague, he pointed out that state of the art had already achieved about 95% since a few years, making those results useless for industry. It is quite sure that the author was really convinced of the optimality of his result, due perhaps to his limited experience on the specific application domain, which was not enough to judge.

What the author surely did was to try a number of different topologies, paradigms, network sizes, training algorithms and found that his own network was offering the very best performance among all those tests. All tests were neural and no test was performed according to the state-of-the-art using traditional approaches. This method is (partially) correct to *optimize the performance of a novel intelligent system* (namely, to find which are the best choices to get the best out of is, among all possible intelligent systems), but **not** to evaluate the *appropriateness of an intelligent system for the given application*, compared against a standard one.

What was true for that specific problem, was that the proposed hybrid empirical/analytical model developed by a team of experienced engineers and biologists offered a much better performance than the best existing neural network, even for a comparable computation complexity, not considering the possible performance of the state-of-the-art. The reason for that (which happens much more frequently than one can even imagine) is that human experience, knowledge and mental capacities, which are used to develop a given "non-intelligent" model, boost so much the overall performance of a given system than even an optimal intelligent system, trained in the best way but without using the available human knowledge, cannot compensate ignoring human knowledge during its development.

### 3.6 How to avoid optimism…

An important step towards acceptance is to avoid unnecessary and inapplicable optimism. Any development, comparison or selection has to be *fair* and based on *real and well proven data*; never on *hypotheses*. Optimism usually tends to push the designer towards a solution which then proves less performing than originally expected, therefore convincing even more the decision-making people that intelligent systems are not yet a viable solution to their problem.

### 3.7 Tools and support

An important step towards industrial acceptance (as for many other industrially relevant items) is the availability of an appropriate support to the development, use, integration, conduction and maintenance of the system.

An excellent intelligent system will never be applied until its use is straightforward and user-friendly. The only chance to have an intelligent system applied is therefore the development, around the intelligent system itself together with its surrounding elements (e.g. pre-processors, postprocessors, data mining, etc.), of an appropriate user interface and development tool which supports, in the order:

- the decision-making process in helping to choose the intelligent systems instead of any other traditional system
- the preparation phase (e.g. data collection, training, tuning and testing)
- the conduction phase, namely the nominal operation of the intelligent system, when applied to the industrial process under interest
- maintenance, to overcome any problem might occur during conduction.

## 4. Case studies

This chapter will present a number of real industrial applications where all the aspects described and commented in the previous sections have been applied. Most of them come from our personal experience, as acquiring enough, reliable and trustable details from other people is usually difficult.

### 4.1 Prediction of Jominy profiles of steels

The *Jominy profile* of a steel is a curve obtained in a test, where a small cylindrical specimen of steel is kept at a very high temperature (usually more than 1500 °C) and one end of the specimen is cooled by quenching it for at least 10 min. in a water stream, while the other specimen end is cooled in air. This treatment causes a cooling rate gradient to develop over the length of the specimen, with the highest cooling rate corresponding to the quenched end. This procedure affects the steel micro-structure along the length of the specimen and, as a consequence, the steel hardness in the diverse portions of the test bar. The Jominy profile is built by measuring the specimen hardness values $h_i$ on the Rockwell C scale at increasing distances $d_i$ from the quenched end. Several studies investigated the correlation between the shape of such curve and the steel chemistry (Doane & Kirkaldy, 1978) and some of them applied neural networks to this purpose, such as (Vermeulen et al., 1996).

In particular Colla et al. (Colla et al., 2000) propose a parametric characterization of the profile, namely the approximation of the generic profile with a parametric curve, and then predict the shape of each profile through a neural network which links the steel chemistry to the curve parameters.

This approach proved to be successful when the "shape" of the profile is constant (which happens, for instance, when dealing with the same steel grades produced by one single manufacturer). On the other hand, when facing the prediction of the Jominy curve of many different steel grades manufactured by different steel producers, the actual shape of the curve might considerably vary and the parametric approach is no more successful.

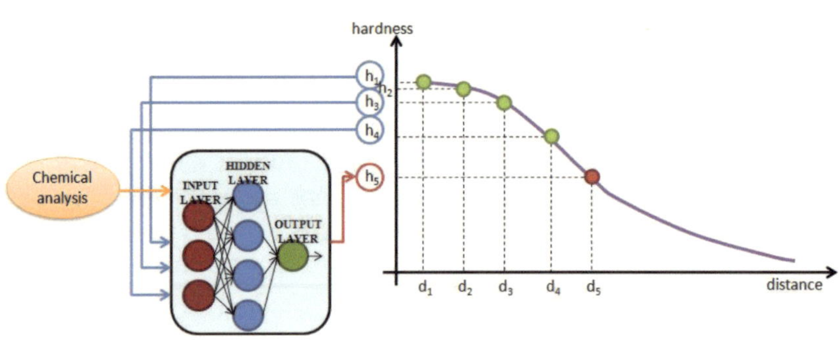


Fig. 1. Conceptual scheme of the sequential predictor of Jominy curves.

In fact, a different approach to the same problem has been proposed by Marin et al. (Marin et al. 2007), where a neural sequential predictor has been proposed: here, apart from the first two points of the curve (i.e. the ones corresponding to the lowest distance values from the quenched end), each single point of the Jominy profile is singularly predicted by a neural network having as inputs the contents of some chemical elements and some of the previously predicted hardenability values, according to the schematic description provided in Fig. 1.

*This application proved to be successful because: i) results were accurate and accuracy could easily be measured; ii) the intelligent systems (a neural network in both cases) was very simple, with few weights, and these could easily be interpreted by the technician; iii) the neural predictor has been coupled with a user-friendly software interface allowing not only to run the model, but also to collect data and re-train all the neural networks with new data provided by the user, so that each steel company can progressively "specialise" the predictor on its own steel grades; iv) training time for using the software tool which was developed was very short. It is worth noting that, as pointed out at the beginning, the neural network itself is just a small element of the whole system (software tool, pre-processing, data collection, result presentation, etc.*

### 4.2 Prediction of malfunctioning during steel casting

In the standard steelmaking practice, during continuous casting, the liquid material produced in the blast furnace is cast, after some manufacture, into the ladle and, subsequently, into the tundish (see Fig. 2). On the bottom of the tundish, some nozzles are located, through which the liquid steel passes into the mould or strip casters. The section of such nozzles is far smaller with respect to the tundish dimensions. When particular steel grades are produced, some alumina precipitation on the entry and on the lateral surface of these nozzles can partially or even totally block the flow of the liquid steel. This phenomenon is commonly known as *clogging* and is highly detrimental to casting reliability and quality of the cast products.

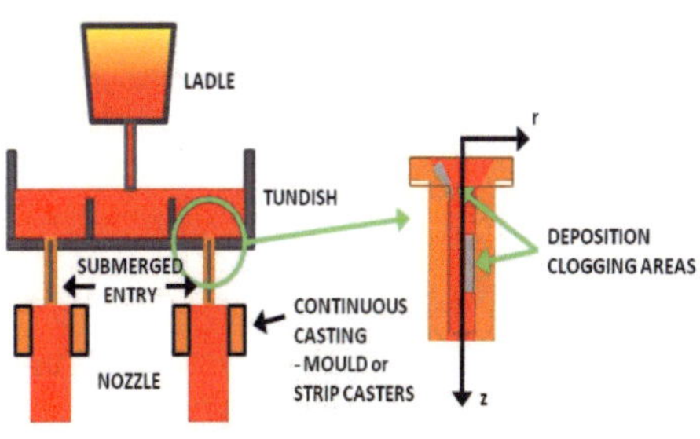

a)

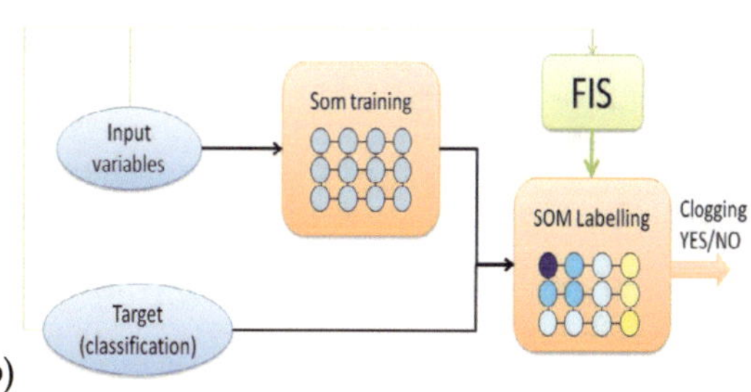

b)

Fig. 2. a) Location of the nozzles that can be occluded; b) Schematic description of the labelled SOM-based classifier.

The clogging phenomenon is still not deeply understood (Heesom 1988), due to the very high number of chemical and process factors affecting the occurrence of the precipitation of the materials on the nozzle internal surface as well as to the impossibility of installing complex systems of probes and sensors in order to closely observe the phenomenon itself.

For this reason, some attempts have been performed to apply intelligent systems for the prediction of clogging occurrence on the basis of the steel chemical composition and on the process parameters. In particular, such as it can be frequently found in fault diagnosis applications, the prediction of clogging has been faced as a binary classification problem where one of the two classes to be distinguished (i.e. the one corresponding to malfunctioning) is far less frequent than the other one. Firstly Self Organising Maps (SOM) have been applied (Colla et al., 2006) in order to predict the clogging occurrence, in parallel with a physical model that takes into account some basic mechanism of the alumina precipitation and the geometry of the nozzles, but is not capable to explain all the complex relationships between process and chemical variables.

*The performance of the overall system are acceptable (this is also a key element in industry: the aim is seldom to optimize but often to achieve any performance better than a given threshold in a limited time) and the system has been successfully applied in the industrial context, mainly because: i) after a short testing, the prediction accuracy was proven to be higher; ii) risk was little as the traditional approach could be used to crosscheck the predictions of the intelligent system; iii) the availability of a simplified end-user interface reduced personnel training to the minimum, allowing the operator to input the relevant process parameters and obtain immediate indication of the actual danger of clogging occurrence and the potential countermeasure to adopt (i.e. Calcium Oxide addition to the liquid steel) (Fera et al. 2005).*

Improvements are also possible, by taking into account the different importance of misclassification errors. In fact the erroneous classification of a faulty situation as a normal one (sometimes called *missed detection*) prevents the operators to develop suitable countermeasures to avoid the clogging, with potential heavier consequences with respect to the opposite case, when a potential unnecessary warning message is raised in a standard condition (the so-called *false alarm*). Actually standard classifiers are not always capable of providing excellent results when dealing with imbalanced datasets: therefore in (Vannucci & Colla 2011) a classified has been applied, which is explicitly designed to cope with imbalanced datasets and exploits the labelled SOMs, according to the scheme depicted in Fig. 2.b. Once trained, each neuron of the SOM is labelled as corresponding to the frequent or infrequent class through a procedure that exploits a Fuzzy Inference System in order to find a suitable compromise between missed detection and false alarms rates.

### 4.3 Prediction of the end-point in the converter

In the integrated steelmaking cycle, where steel is produced from primary raw materials, the Blast Oxygen Furnace (BOF) is the plant where steel is produced from pig iron, scrap and lime, by blowing oxygen to burn off the carbon. In the BOF, the sublance device that measures carbon content and temperature rapidly before the late period of blowing is the most important tool for BOF process control. The use of such sublance has been an important step for controlling the BOF steel making processes. Sublance is basically used to take sample at the end of blow usually 3-4 minutes before end of blow for analysis of sample and also measures temperature of the bath. Since the introduction of sublance, the accuracy of the end point prediction (hit rate) at most of steel plants has gradually increased from approximately 60% to 90%. In (Valentini et al. 2004) a neural network has been applied to predict the final Carbon content *[C]* for an OBM (from the German *Oxygen Bodenblasen Maxhuette*) converter in steel making industry by exploiting the estimates of the Oxygen content *[O]*and of the temperature *T*. These three variables are usually linked by the following approximate mathematical equation:

$$Log\frac{P_c}{[C]^n[O]} = \frac{A}{T} + B \qquad (1)$$

where $P_c$ is a constant pressure value in the range [1, 1.5] atm, $A$ and $B$ are constants whose nominal values are respectively, $A=1895$ °K and $B=1.6$ and $n$ is commonly assumed to be unitary, but some literature results provide $n \approx 0.5$ for $[C]<0.08\%$ and $n \approx 1$ otherwise.

Equation (1) can easily be inverted in order to predict *[C]* from *[O]* and *T*, but the prediction obtained using the nominal values of the constant parameters is not very reliable compared to the *[C]* measurements contained in a dataset provided by the steel manufacturer for the steel grades of interest. A reliable prediction of the final Carbon content at the end of the refining process is very important, as it allows to evaluate the process parameters (such as the amount of inflated Oxygen and the duration of the refining process) required to achieve the desired results optimizing the time and cost of the production process. By adopting a simple two-layer MLP with 3 neurons in the hidden layer, the prediction error has been reduced of 64% with respect to the prediction obtained through eq.(1).

*This system presents the following advantages: i) the performance is acceptable, ii) the neural network is very simple; iii) the training time is negligible. However the neural model has been not very well perceived by the end-users mainly because it is difficult to attribute a precise physical meaning and interpretation to the network parameters, such as it happens for the parameters of the formula (1).*

Therefore the alternative solution of a fine tuning of the physical parameters around the nominal values has finally been preferred.

### 4.4 Prediction of the time required by each stage of hot rolling mills

The efficiency and productivity of steel hot rolling mills is heavily affected by the possibility of precisely estimating when the different manufacturing stages are completed, as this avoids bottlenecks and provides important time and energy savings. For this reason, several Mill Pacing Control (MPC) systems have been realised and implemented, which allow optimising the production flow starting from the reheating furnaces, where slabs are heated at a temperature between 1100°C and 1300°C for optimal workability before being rolled. Hot steel rolling mills are usually composed of two main stages, namely the *roughing mill*, where the slab is firstly compressed, and the *finishing* mill, where the aimed thickness of the hot rolled coil is reached. A further rolling stage can be afterwards required, named *cold rolling*, which is pursued at far lower temperatures in order to produce flat products, such as plate, sheets or coils of various thicknesses.

MPC systems allow shorten the discharging interval between two subsequent slabs avoiding collisions. To this aim, schedule systems are developed and simulations are performed in order to test new strategies without affecting the production cycle.

Colla et al. (Colla et al., 2010) applied neural networks to solve a particular mill pacing problem, different from the usual one, namely the prediction of the total roughing time and of the time required for passing the first gauge of the finishing mill. This investigation has been pursued in order to increase the rolling efficiency and decrease the total rolling time. The slabs that are subsequently rolled can differ in steel grade and other features, thus the related rolling processes can require different times and energy amounts. The time required for the roughing process is in average (but not always) smaller than the finishing time. Thus a slab can be output by the roughing mill while the rolling of the previous coil is being completed: this fact may cause a collision or may force the second slab to remain stuck while its temperature decreases, which makes its successive rolling more difficult. On the other hand, the time between the input of two successive slabs to the roughing time cannot be excessive, in order to keep productivity and avoid energy losses. Ideally, a slab should be input to roughing mill exactly at a time instant that will allow it to arrive at the entrance of the finishing mill when the rolling of the previous coil is just terminated. (Colla et al. 2010) applied various neural networks-based approaches to predict the time $\square_i$ *(1≤i≤6)* required by the slab to pass each one of the 6 stages that form the roughing mill (see Fig. 3).

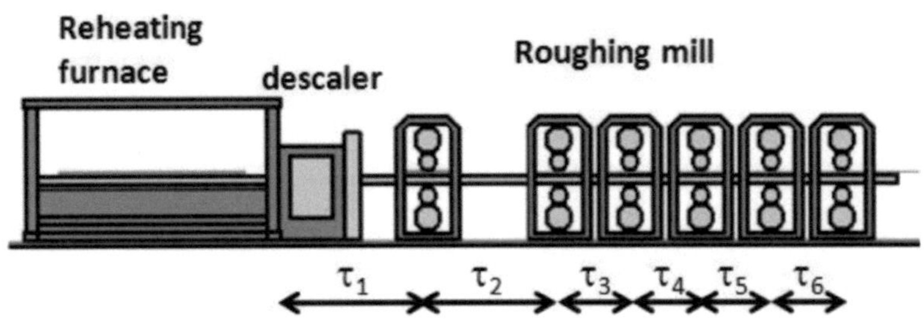


Fig. 3. Scheme of the first stages of a steel hot rolling mill.

In particular, the most successful solution performs a sequential prediction, namely bases the prediction of $\square_i$ (for *i>1*) not only on product and process parameters, but also on the prediction of the times required to pass the previous stages, i.e. $\tau_k$ with *1≤k≤i*. Moreover, neural networks have been applied also to predict the time required for passing the finishing mill.

*In this case, the application of neural networks were actually advantageous for the following main reasons: i) neural networks proved to outperform more traditional approaches; ii) the neural system is naturally adaptable to the changing operating conditions thanks to its capability of self-learning from data. However the on-site real-time implementation has not been easy and required considerable efforts because it has been difficult to interface the system with the control system of the mill.*

### 4.5 Estimate of train position and speed from wheels velocity measurements

Within an Automatic Train Protection (ATP) system, two subsystems are usually included: a ground subsystem, which provides updated information on the train position and the line gradient by exploiting fixed balises or another source of absolute information (e.g. GPS), and an on-board subsystem, which estimates the actual train position and speed, according to the scheme depicted in Fig.4.

The ground subsystem communicates to the on-board one the distance from the next reference point on the line, the gradient of the line and the allowed speed at the next reference point. The on-board subsystem then evaluates the distances from the next information point and the minimum distance that allow compliance with the speed limit at the next reference point. If it turns out that the train cannot meet the target speed at the next reference point (as the residual breaking resources of the train are not sufficient), the on-board subsystem actuates suitable countermeasures, such as emergency breaking. The evaluation of the above-mentioned distance values requires the knowledge of the breaking parameters and of the actual train speed: a correct estimate of this last variable even in poor adhesion conditions (i.e. when one or more train wheels are sliding on the rails and, thus, the axle angular velocity is not proportional to the train speed) is crucial.

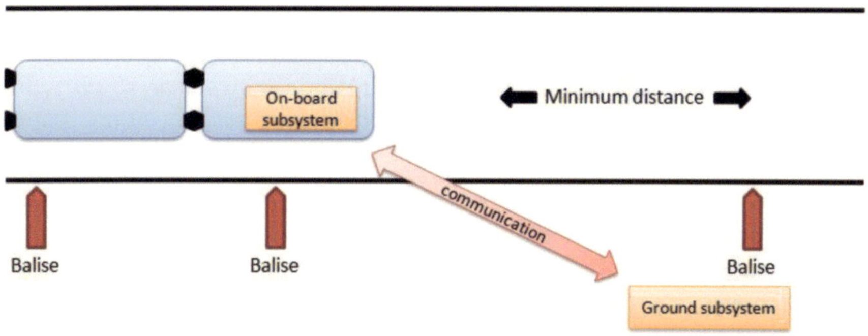


Fig. 4. Working principle of an ATP

Allotta et al. (Allotta et al 2001, Allotta et al 2002) developed a series of algorithms for estimating the actual train speed on the basis of the information collected concerning two axles of the locomotor. A first set of such algorithms have been developed according to expert personnel specifications and following the traditional "crisp" reasoning, which exploits different simple deterministic formulas for calculating the train speed depending on the condition of adhesion of the wheels to the rails. In fact, among a huge number of state variables that are considered in the procedure, there are two binary variables indicating the adhesion condition of each axle. The technical personnel of the train society formalised the reasoning that leads the human operators to a correct determination of the adhesion conditions. Then two identical fuzzy systems have been developed, which take two inputs each, namely the difference between the velocities of the two controlled axles and the acceleration of the axle whose adhesion condition is estimated, and return the degree of adhesion of one axle. The design of two fuzzy systems have been refined by means of a training procedure exploiting a great quantity of the available data and, finally, they have been merely substituted to the old crisp algorithm for adhesion condition estimation, by leaving the rest of the speed estimation procedure unchanged. As an alternative, the standard rule-based system merely implementing the human operators' reasoning has been implemented and its own parameters (such as thresholds) have been tuned by means of Genetic Algorithms (GA) exploiting the available experimental data and adopting as fitness function to minimise the error between the actual and estimated train speed. A second set of algorithms that have been tested for this application perform a direct estimate of the train velocity taking as inputs some of the available state variables (in particular axles velocities, accelerations and acceleration variations). Both neural networks and fuzzy inference systems have been tested to this purpose.

*From a comparison among all the tested approaches it turned out that the algorithms purely based on AI techniques (and, in particular, the neural network (Colla et al. 2003)) outperform the rule-based ones and have also a simpler structure. However, these systems also present the following non negligible disadvantages: i) a difficult physical interpretation of fuzzy rules or of the neural network;*

*ii) a difficult implementation of the specification requirements; iii) the FIS-based methods are also computationally less efficient; iv) when testing the more frequent fault conditions, all the developed algorithms present an acceptable degree of reliability and robustness, but the crisp algorithm, which is actually adherent to the specifications provided by the expert personnel of the train society, provides the best guarantee of estimated speed values lying within acceptable limits; v) with respect the merely crisp algorithm and to its improved version, where some parameters have been optimized through GA, the soft computing-based algorithms provide less control over the internal parameters of the estimator, which increase in number but loose in physical meaning (this is especially true for the neural predictor, which has been applied as a black-box parametric estimator); vi) soft computing-based procedures, and especially the ones which exploit neural networks, do not guarantee that a particular input pattern (or series of input patterns) will lead to unacceptable velocity estimates.*

Thus finally the rule-based algorithm tuned through GA has been preferred to all the other approaches for the final implementation.

### 4.6 Optimisation of the logistic in an automatic warehouse of steel tubes

Optimisation of logistic is one of the fields where intelligent systems have most successfully been applied. Colla et al. (Colla et al., 2010) tested several AI-based techniques for the optimisation of products allocation in an automatic warehouse of steel tubes. The warehouse has been designed to stock a large variety of typologies of steel tubes, differing in quality of the steel, in the length as well as in the shape and dimensions of the section. As soon as the tubes are produced, they are grouped in packs and automatically transferred to a stocking area, where they are located in piles that must be composed by the same typology of tubes. A non optimal allocation strategy can cause the available space in the warehouse not to be fully exploited, such as, for instance, the case in which many short (i.e. composed by a few packs) piles are present in place of a few higher ones. To this aim, firstly some Key Performance Indicators (KPIs) have been defined in order to derive objective functions to be optimised by the different allocation strategies. Afterwards, an optimisation problem has been formulated, for which an analytical model of the problem was really too complex to define and implement, due to the variability of the workload and to the interaction between the automatic tube conveyors, as traffic control is only partially centralised (for instance collision avoidance is managed at local level through suitable sensing and communicating devices mounted on each conveyor). Traditional derivative-based optimisation models cannot be applied, while GAs are a very suitable solution for the optimisation problem, as they allow a decoupling between the problem formulation and the search procedure. The destination of each tubes pack has been suitably codified in a chromosome and GAs have been applied in order to minimise a fitness function obtained from a composition of the above-defined KPIs. Different ways to aggregate the selected KPIs have been tested, from a simple weighted sum up to a Fuzzy Inference System implementing a complex combination according to rules derived from the knowledge of the technical personnel working on the plant. However, this application is intrinsically a Multi-Objective Optimization (MOO) problem, as the KPIs represent requirements that are often in contrast to each other. Any kind of aggregation of the KPIs simplifies it to a Single Objective Optimization problem, but surely the most suitable way to cope with this problem is by exploiting GA-based MOO algorithms. The Strength Pareto Evolutionary Algorithm (Zitzler & Thiele 1999) has been successfully applied to this problem and outperforms all the other approaches.

*The success of this applications of intelligent systems with respect to the previous system which was based on heuristics depends on the following reasons: i) a the correct formalisation of the MOO problem; ii) a suitable simulation system of the automatic warehouse (Colla & Nastasi 2010) that has been realised in order to reproduce the monitoring system of the warehouse itself and can be fed with the same data files that are used by the real system; iii) the possibility (as a consequence of point ii) to easily test the different strategies in a realistic way without affecting the normal operations of the warehouse; iv) the possibility (as a consequence of point ii) of performing an easy and user-friendly comparison of the standard and simulated situation of the warehouse obtained through the previous and improved strategies is possible, which can be of help for the technical personnel in order to evaluate the advantages of a new strategy; v) the easiness of collecting training data, which are no more than standard system data; vi) the modularity of the software for simulation and for the implementation of the allocation strategy, which makes the substitution of the new code within the control system of the warehouse straightforward.*

## 5. Conclusion

According to authors' personal experience, it *cannot* be stated that intelligent systems are so advantageous with respect to traditional techniques to be *universally* accepted for industrial applications. Or better, advantages exist but they are often too limited when compared with the additional risks, training costs, design time, and documentation/maintenance effort. There are surely applications were they provide advantages, especially in tough problems, but these are rather limited, therefore they do not justify a universal acceptance.

**Unfortunately, in most industrial applications that we have encountered so far, very few intelligent system offered such better performance with respect to other techniques to really convince the sceptical user. Of course the comparison is made between the *best* intelligent system and the correspondingly *best* non-intelligent technique.**

### 5.1 A global advantage of intelligent system

There is perhaps a major advantage which makes intelligent systems attractive in a wider range of applications. In practice, intelligent systems are:

*generic approximation and modelling techniques which allow accurate system modelling/ forecasting/approximation/classification/etc. without any specific experience of the designer.*

In practice anybody without any experience in a specific subject can afford solving a problem which could otherwise (namely, with traditional techniques) be afforded only by an expert (or a team of experts) in that field. It is likely that an expert, with appropriate knowledge of the problem and of a bunch of more specific methods would achieve a better result, but this would be far more expensive for an industry, both because of the higher cost of the expert and for the longer development time. This is a rather interesting advantage, even when intelligent systems are suboptimal, as it significantly reduces training costs of inexperienced personnel.

### 5.2 How to help industry accepting intelligent systems

The authors personally believe that industry strongly needs to be helped to accept intelligent systems and this should be a major role for universities and research institutions.

Yet this has to be done in the most appropriate way, that is, by showing industry *unambiguously if, where and when* intelligent systems offer significant advantages or, more realistically, more advantages than drawbacks and associating the intelligent system with an appropriate *development environment* and enough *supporting tools*, which is often the most time consuming element to be developed.

This is one of the major reasons for the several Special Sessions on Industrial Applications of Intelligent Systems which have been held in the last decade. Authors are usually requested to present their ideas on intelligent systems but, more important, to prove that they are either comparable or significantly better than other standard techniques. *Such a comparison has to be as fair as possible, as it is not normally the case.* In practice, in most papers, intelligent systems are usually compared among themselves. The expert reader is left with the question:

*Are you sure that other techniques would not be even better or simpler?*

Or, when a comparison is attempted with standard techniques, these are usually much older, that is, the paper demonstrates, for instance, that an *up-to-date neurofuzzy network* is much better than an *older-than-my-father standard technique*, which is rather obvious, as technology keeps improving, independent of intelligent system.

One of the major reasons for this lack of fair comparisons is that comparing an intelligent system against an *up-to-date standard method* requires developing by scratch an appropriate demonstrator, which often requires either a lot of specific experience or a lot of time, and usually nobody wants to afford it.

*Only those research groups who tightly cooperate with an industrial group can merge industrial and academic experiences, to develop both techniques appropriately, although these are seldom done together, due to unaffordable additional costs.*

### 5.3 A critical question

So far very few applications of intelligent systems provided such better performance with respect to other techniques to really convince even the most sceptical user. In most cases, they can either offer a slightly better performance (when compared with an alternative well-designed method) with a shorter design time but, on the other hand, design risks are often so critical that they definitely impair the advantages. It is therefore time for a critical question:

*In which applications are neural networks have fuzzy logic a higher chance of being accepted?*

We think that, at present, the most promising areas are, for instance:

- *data mining, knowledge based systems*, where information, data, knowledge and models are *valuable items*, but they are often *hidden* in a huge amount of noise, ambiguous, contradicting data. Data is so wide, contradicting, ambiguous, that no method can be accurate and predictable, therefore neural networks may provide advantages, without the need to be 100% correct;
- *prediction/classification of partially random processes*, like *time-series prediction, forecasting, complex pattern classification, semantic Web*, etc., where the randomness of the

process/patterns prevents a 100% prediction accuracy, therefore the errors of the intelligent systems can be accepted at no cost;

- *modelling of complex systems*, where any other modelling technique would be as incomprehensible as a neurofuzzy model;
- *consumer applications* where the appeal of the "fuzzy label" increases the market of an appliance.

## 6. References


Allotta, B; Malvezzi, M.; Toni, P.; Colla, V. (2001). Train speed and position evaluation using wheel velocity measurements, *Proceedings of the 2001 IEEE/ASME International Conference on Advanced Intelligent Mechatronics AIM'01*, Como, Italy.

Allotta, B; Colla, V.; Malvezzi, M. (2002). Train Position And Speed Estimation Using Wheel Velocity Measurements *Journal of Rail and Rapid Transit Proceedings of the Institution of Mechanical Engineers Part F*, Vol. 216, No. 3, pp. 207-225.

Colla, V.; Reyneri, L.M.; Sgarbi, M. (2000). Parametric Characterization of Jominy Profiles in Steel Industry, *Integrated Computer-Aided Engineering*, Vol. 7, pp. 217-228.

Colla, V.; Vannucci, M.; Allotta, B.; Malvezzi, M. (2003). Comparison of traditional and neural system for train speed estimation, *Proceedings of the 11th European Symposium on Artificial Neural Networks ESANN 2003*, Brugges, Belgium, 23-25 April.

Colla, V.; Vannucci, M.; Fera, S.; Valentini, R. (2006). Ca-treatment of Al-Killed steels: inclusion modification and application of Artificial Neural Networks for the prediction of clogging, *Proceedings of the 5th European Oxygen Steelmaking Conference EOSC'06*, 26-28 June 2006, Aachen, Germany, pp. 387-394.

Colla, V.; Vannucci, M.; Valentini, R. (2010). Neural network based prediction of roughing and finishing times in a hot strip mill, *Revista de Metalurgia*, Vol. 46, No 1, pp. 15-21.

Colla, V.; Nastasi, G. (2010). Modelling and Simulation of an Automated Warehouse for the Comparison of Storage Strategies, Chap.21 in *Modelling, Simulation and Optimization*, INTECH pp. 471-486 (ISBN 978-953-7619-36-7).

Colla, V.; Nastasi, G.; Matarese, N.; Reyneri L.M. (2010). GA-Based Solutions Comparison for Storage Strategies Optimization for an Automated Warehouse" *Journal of Hybrid Intelligent Systems*, Vol. 7 pp. 283–297.

Doane, D.V.; Kirkaldy, J.S. (1978). Hardenability Concepts with Applications to Steel, *TMS-AIME*, Warrendale.

Fera, S.; Harloff, A.; Roedl, S.; Mavrommatis, K.; Colla, V.; Santisteban, V.; Roessler S. (2005). Development of a model predicting inclusions precipitation in nozzles based on chemical composition and process parameters such as casting rate, liquid temperature, nozzle design and slag composition, *European Commission Ed.* Technical Report EUR 21442.

Haykin, S. (1994), Neural Networks: A Comprehensive Foundation, *Mc Millan College Publishing Company*, New York, 1994.

Heesom, M.J. (1988). 'Physical and chemical aspects of nozzle blockage during continuous casting, *Proceedings of the 1st Int. Calcium Treatment Symposium*, London (UK).

Marin, B.; Bell, A.; Idoyaga, Z.; Colla, V.; Fernàndez, L.M. (2007). Optimization of the influence of Boron on the properties of steels, *European Commission Ed.* Technical Report EUR 22446.

Reyneri, L.M. (1999) Unification of Neural and Wavelet Networks and Fuzzy Systems, *IEEE Trans. on Neural Networks*, Vol. 10(4), pp. 801-814.

Valentini, R.; Colla, V.; Vannucci, M. (2004). Neural predictor of the end point in a converter", *Revista de Metalurgia*, Vol 40, No. 6, pp. 416-419.

Vannucci, M.; Colla, V. (2011). Novel classification methods for sensitive problems and uneven datasets based on neural networks and fuzzy logic, *Applied Soft Computing*, Vol. 11, pp. 2383-2390.

Vermeulen, W.G.; Van Der Wolk, P.J.; De Weijer, A.P.; Van Der Zwaag, S. (1996). Prediction of Jominy Hardness Profiles of Steels Using Artificial Neural Networks," *Journal of Materials Engineering and Performances*, Vol. 5, No. 1, pp. 57-63.

Zhang, Q. (1997) Using Wavelet Network in Non-parametric Estimation, *IEEE Transactions on Neural Networks*}, Vol. 8(2), pp. 227-236.

Zitzler, E.; Thiele, L. (1999) Multiobjective Evolutionary Algorithms: A Comparative Case Study and the Strength Pareto Evolutionary Algorithm, *IEEE Transactions on Evolutionary Computation*, Vol. 3 (4), pp. 257-271.

6

# Intelligent Problem Solvers in Education: Design Method and Applications

Nhon Van Do
*University of Information Technology*
*Vietnam*

## 1. Introduction

In this chapter we present the method for designing intelligent problem solvers (IPS), especially those in education. An IPS, which is an intelligent system, can consist of AI-components such as theorem provers, inference engines, search engines, learning programs, classification tools, statistical tools, question-answering systems, machine-translation systems, knowledge acquisition tools, etc (Sowa, John F. 2002). An IPS in education (IPSE) considered here must have suitable knowledge base used by the inference engine to solve problems in certain knowledge domain, and the system not only give human readable solutions but also present solutions as the way teachers and students usually write them. Knowledge representation methods used to design the knowledge base should be convenient for studying of users and for using by inference engine. Besides, problems need to be modeled so that we can design algorithms for solving problems automatically and propose a simple language for specifying them. The system can solve problems in general forms. Users only declare hypothesis and goal of problems base on a simple language but strong enough for specifying problems. The hypothesis can consist of objects, relations between objects or between attributes. It can also contain formulas, determination properties of some attributes or their values. The goal can be to compute an attribute, to determine an object, a relation or a formula. After specifying a problem, users can request the program to solve it automatically or to give instructions that help them to solve it themselves. The second function of the system is "Search for Knowledge". This function helps users to find out necessary knowledge quickly. They can search for concepts, definitions, properties, related theorems or formulas, and problem patterns. By the cross-reference systems of menus, users can easily get knowledge they need.

Knowledge representation has a very important role in designing the knowledge base and the inference engine of the system. There are many various models and methods for knowledge representation which have already been suggested and applied in many fields of science. Many popular methods for knowledge representation such as logic, frames, classes, semantic networks, conceptual graphs, rules of inference, and ontologies can be found in George F. Luger (2008), Stuart Russell & Peter Norvig (2010), or in Sowa, John F. (2000). These methods are very useful in many applications. However, they are not enough and not easy to use for constructing an IPSE in practice. Knowledge representation should be convenient for studying of users and for using by inference engine. Besides, problems need to be modeled so that we can design algorithms for solving problems automatically and propose a simple language for specifying them. Practical intelligent systems expect more powerful and useful models for knowledge representation. The *Computational Object Knowledge Base* model (COKB) presented in Nhon Van Do (2010) will be used to design the system. This model can be used to represent the total knowledge and to design the knowledge base component of systems. Next, computational networks (Com-Net) and networks of computational objects (CO-Net) in Nhon Van Do (2009) and Nhon Van Do (2010) can be used for modeling problems in knowledge domains. These models are tools for designing inference engine of systems.

We used COKB model, CO-Net and Com-Net in constructing some practical IPSE such as the program for studying and solving problems in plane geometry presented in Nhon Van Do (2000) and Nhon Do & Hoai P. Truong & Trong T. Tran (2010), the system that supports studying knowledge and solving of analytic geometry problems, the system for solving algebraic problems in Nhon Do & Hien Nguyen (2011), the program for solving problems in electricity, in inorganic chemistry, etc. The applications have been implemented by using programming tools and computer algebra systems such as C++, C#, JAVA, and MAPLE. They are very easy to use for students in studying knowledge, to solve automatically problems and give human readable solutions agree with those written by teachers and students.

The chapter will be organized as follows: In Section 2, the system architecture and the design process will be presented. In Section 3, models for knowledge representation are discussed. Designing the knowledge base and the inference engine of an IPSE will be presented in Section 4. Some applications will be introduced in section 5. Conclusions and future works are drawn in Section 6.

## 2. System architecture and the design process

The structure of an IPSE are considered here consists of the components such as knowledge base, inference engine, interface, explanation component, working memory and knowledge manager. In this setion, these components will be studied together with relationships between them; we will also study and discuss how an IPSE runs, and present a process to construct the system together with methods and techniques can be used in each phase of the process.

### 2.1 Components of the system

An IPSE is also a knowledge base system, which supports searching, querying and solving problems based on knowledge bases; it has the structure of an expert system. We can design the system which consists of following components:

- The knowledge base.
- The inference engine.
- The explanation component.
- The working memory.

- The knowledge manager.
- The interface.

Knowledge Bases contain the knowledge for solving some problems in a specific knowledge domain. It must be stored in the computer-readable form so that the inference engine can use it in the procedure of automated deductive reasoning to solve problems stated in general forms. They can contain concepts and objects, relations, operators and functions, facts and rules.

The Inference engine will use the knowledge stored in knowledge bases to solve problems, to search or to answer for the query. It is the "brain" that systems use to reason about the information in the knowledge base for the ultimate purpose of formulating new conclusions. It must identify problems and use suitable deductive strategies to find out right rules and facts for solving the problem. In an IPSE, the inference engine also have to produce solutions as human reading, thinking, and writing.

The working memory contains the data that is received from the user during operation of the system. Consequents from rules in the knowledge base may create new values in working memory, update old values, or remove existing values. It also stores data, facts and rules in the process of searching and deduction of the inference engine.

The explanation component supports to explain the phases, concepts in the process of solving the problem. It presents the method by which the system reaches a conclusion may not be obvious to a human user, and explains the reasoning process that lead to the final answer of the system.

The knowledge manager aims to support updating knowledge into knowledge base. It also supports to search the knowledge and test consistence of knowledge.

The user interface is the means of communication between a user and the system problem-solving processes. An effective interface has to be able to accept the queries, instructions or problems in a form that the user enters and translate them into working problems in the form for the rest of the system. It also has to be able to translate the answers, produced by the system, into a form that the user can understand. The interface component of the system is required to have a specification language for communication between the system and learners, between the system and instructors as well.

The figure 1 below shows the structure of the system.

The main process for problem solving: From the user, a problem in a form that the user enter is input into the system, and the problem written by specification language is created; then it is translated so that the system receives the working problem in the form for the inference engine, and this is placed in the working memory. After analyzing the problem, the inference engine generates a possible solution for the problem by doing some automated reasoning strategies such as forward chaining reasoning method, backward chaining reasoning method, reasoning with heuristics. Next, The first solution is analyzed and from this the inference engine produces a good solution for the interface component. Based on the good solution found, the answer solution in human-readable form will be created for output to the user.

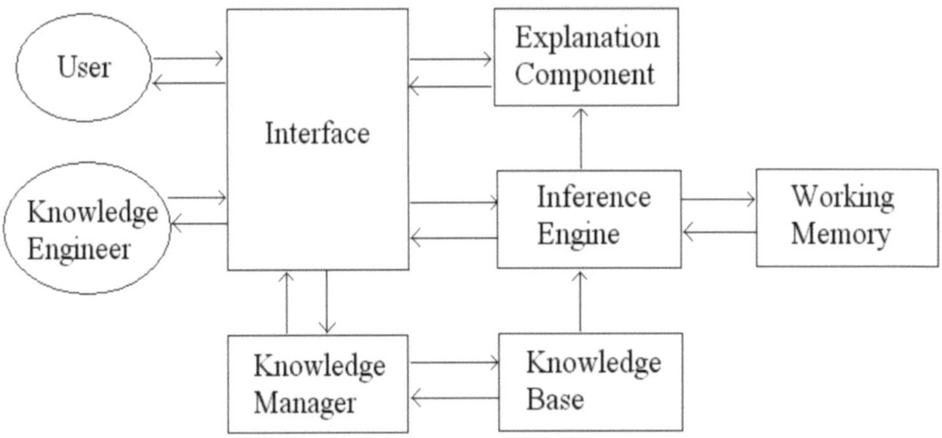


Fig. 1. Structure of a system

### 2.2 Design process

The process of analysis and design the components of the systems consists of the following stages.

**Stage 1:** Determine the knowledge domain and scope; then do collecting real knowledge consisting of data, concepts and objects, relations, operators and functions, facts and rules, etc. The knowledge can be classified according to some ways such as chapters, topics or subjects; and this classification help us to collect problems appropriately and easily. Problems are also classified by some methods such as frame-based problems, general forms of problems.

**Stage 2:** Knowledge representation or modeling for knowledge to obtain knowledge base model of the system. This is an important base for designing the knowledge base. Classes of problem are also modeled as well to obtain initial problem models.

The above stages can be done by using the COKB model, Com-Nets, CO-Nets, and their extensions. These models will be presented in section 3.

**Stage 3:** Establishing knowledge base organization for the system based on COKB model and its specification language. Knowledge base can be organized by structured text files. They include the files below.

- Files stores names of concepts, and structures of concepts.
- A file stores information of the Hasse diagram representing the component H of COKB model.
- Files store the specification of relations (the component R of COKB model).
- Files store the specification of operators (the component Ops of COKB model).
- Files store the specification of functions (the component Funcs of COKB model).
- A file stores the definition of kinds of facts.
- A file stores deductive rules.
- Files store certain objects and facts.

**Stage 4:** Modeling of problems and designing algorithms for automated reasoning. General problems can be represented by using Com-Nets, CO-Nets, and their extensions. The CO-Net problem model consists of three parts:

$$O = \{O_1, O_2, \ldots, O_n\},\ F = \{f_1, f_2, \ldots, f_m\},$$

$$Goal = [\ g_1, g_2, \ldots, g_m\ ].$$

In the above model the set O consists of n Com-objects, F is the set of facts given on the objects, and Goal is a list, which consists of goals.

The design of deductive reasoning algorithms for solving problems and the design of interface of the system can be developed by three steps for modeling:

**Step 1.** Classify problems such as problems as frames, problems of a determination or a proof of a fact, problems of finding objects or facts, etc…

**Step 2.** Classify facts and representing them based on the kinds of facts of COKB model.

**Step 3.** Modeling kinds of problems from classifying in step 1 and 2. From models of each kind, we can construct a general model for problems, which are given to the system for solving them.

The basic technique for designing deductive algorithms is the unification of facts. Based on the kinds of facts and their structures, there will be criteria for unification proposed. Then it produces algorithms to check the unification of two facts.

The next important work is doing research on strategies for deduction to solve problems on computer. The most difficult thing is modeling for experience, sensible reaction and intuitional human to find heuristic rules, which were able to imitate the human thinking for solving problems.

**Stage 5**: Creating a query language for the models. The language helps to design the communication between the system and users by words.

**Stage 6**: Designing the interface of the system and coding to produce the application. Intelligent applications for solving problems in education of mathematic, physic, chemistry have been implemented by using programming tools and computer algebra systems such as Visual Basic.NET or C#, SQL Server, Maple. They are very easy to use for students, to search, query and solve problems.

**Stage 7**: Testing, maintaining and developing the application. This stage is similar as in other computer systems.

The main models for knowledge representation used in the above process will be presented in the next section.

## 3. Knowledge representation models

In artificial intelligence science, models and methods for knowledge representation play an important role in designing knowledge base systems and expert systems, especially intelligent problem solvers. Nowadays there are many various knowledge models which have already been suggested and applied. In the books of Sowa (2002), George F. Luger

(2008), Michel Chein & Marie-Laure Mugnier (2009) and Frank van Harmelem & Vladimir & Bruce (2008) we have found popular methods for knowledge representation. They include predicate logic, semantic nets, frames, deductive rules, conceptual graphs. The above methods are very useful for designing intelligent systems, especially intelligent problem solvers. However, they are not suitable to represent knowledge in the domains of reality applications in many cases, especially the systems that can solve problems in practice based on knowledge bases. There have been new models proposed such as computational networks, networks of computational objects in Nhon Van Do (2009) and model for knowledge bases of computational objects (COKB) in Nhon Van Do (2010). The COKB model can be used to represent the total knowledge and to design the knowledge base component of practical intelligent systems. Networks of computational objects can be used for modeling problems in knowledge domains. These models are tools for designing inference engine of systems. The models have been used in designing some intelligent problem solvers in education (IPSE) such as the program for studying and solving problems in Plane Geometry in Nhon (2000), the program for solving problems about alternating current in physics. These applications are very easy to use for students in studying knowledge, to solve automatically problems and give human readable solutions agree with those written by teachers and students. In this section, the COKB model and computational networks, that are used for designing IPSE will be presented in details.

### 3.1 COKB model

The model for knowledge bases of computational objects (COKB) has been established from Object-Oriented approach to represent knowledge together with programming techniques for symbolic computation. There have been many results and tools for Object-Oriented methods, and some principles as well as techniques were presented in Mike (2005). This way also gives us a method to model problems and to design algorithms. The models are very useful for constructing components and the whole knowledge base of intelligent system in practice of knowledge domains.

#### 3.1.1 Computational objects

In many problems we usually meet many different kinds of objects. Each object has attributes and internal relations between them. They also have basic behaviors for solving problems on its attributes.

**Definition 3.1:** A computational object (or Com-object) has the following characteristics:

1. It has valued attributes. The set consists of all attributes of the object O will be denoted by **M(O)**.
2. There are internal computational relations between attributes of a Com-object O. These are manifested in the following features of the object:
   - Given a subset A of M(O). The object O can show us the attributes that can be determined from A.
   - The object O will give the value of an attribute.
   - It can also show the internal process of determining the attributes.

The structure computational objects can be modeled by (*Attrs, F, Facts, Rules*). *Attrs* is a set of attributes, *F* is a set of equations called computation relations, *Facts* is a set of properties or events of objects, and *Rules* is a set of deductive rules on facts. For example, knowledge about a triangle consists of elements (angles, edges, etc) together with formulas and some properties on them can be modeled as a class of C-objects whose sets are as follows:

*Attrs* = {A, B, C, a, b, c, R, S, p, ...} is the set of all attributes of a triangle,

*F* = {A+B+C = π; a/sin(A) = 2R; b/sin(B) = 2R; c/sin(C) = 2R; a/sin(A) = b/sin(B); ... },

*Facts* = {a+b>c; a+c>b; b+c>a ; …},

*Rules* = { {a>b} ⇔ {A>B}; {b>c} ⇔ {B>C}; {c>a} ⇔ {C>A}; {a=b} ⇔ {A=B};
{a^2= b^2+c^2} ⇒ {A=pi/2}; {A=pi/2} ⇒ {a^2 = b^2+c^2, b ⊥ c}; ...}.

An object also has basic behaviors for solving problems on its attributes. Objects are equipped abilities to solve problems such as:

1. Determines the closure of a set of attributes.
2. Executes deduction and gives answers for questions about problems of the form: determine some attributes from some other attributes.
3. Executes computations
4. Suggests completing the hypothesis if needed.

*For example,* when a triangle object is requested to give a solution for problem {a, B, C} ⇒ S, it will give a solution consists of three following steps:

Step 1: determine A, by A = π -B-C;
Step 2: determine b, by b = a.sin(B)/sin(A);
Step 3: determine S, by S = a.b.sin(C)/2;

### 3.1.2 Components of COKB model

**Definition 3.2:** The model for knowledge bases of computational objects (COKB model) consists of six components:

(C, H, R, Ops, Funcs, Rules)

The meanings of the components are as follows:

- C is a set of concepts of computational objects. Each concept in C is a class of Com-objects.
- **H** is a set of hierarchy relation on the concepts.
- **R** is a set of relations on the concepts.
- **Ops** is a set of operators.
- **Funcs** is a set of functions.
- **Rules** is a set of rules.

There are relations represent specializations between concepts in the set **C**; **H** represents these special relations on **C**. This relation is an ordered relation on the set **C**, and **H** can be considered as the Hasse diagram for that relation.

**R** is a set of other relations on **C**, and in case a relation r is a binary relation it may have properties such as reflexivity, symmetry, etc. In plane geometry and analytic geometry, there are many such relations: relation "belongs to" of a point and a line, relation "central point" of a point and a line segment, relation "parallel" between two line segments, relation "perpendicular" between two line segments, the equality relation between triangles, etc.

The set **Ops** consists of operators on **C**. This component represents a part of knowledge about operations on the objects. Almost knowledge domains have a component consisting of operators. In analytic geometry there are vector operators such as addition, multiplication of a vector by a scalar, cross product, vector product; in linear algebra there are operations on matrices. The COKB model helps to organize this kind of knowledge in knowledge domains as a component in the knowledge base of intelligent systems.

The set **Funcs** consists of functions on Com-objects. Knowledge about functions is also a popular kind of knowledge in almost knowledge domains in practice, especially fields of natural sciences such as fields of mathematics, fields of physics. In analytic geometry we have the functions: distance between two points, distance from a point to a line or a plane, projection of a point or a line onto a plane, etc. The determinant of a square matrix is also a function on square matrices in linear algebra.

The set **Rules** represents for deductive rules. The set of rules is certain part of knowledge bases. The rules represent for statements, theorems, principles, formulas, and so forth. Almost rules can be written as the form "if <facts> then <facts>". In the structure of a deductive rule, <facts> is a set of facts with certain classification. Therefore, we use deductive rules in the COKB model. Facts must be classified so that the component **Rules** can be specified and processed in the inference engine of knowledge base system or intelligent systems.

### 3.1.3 Facts in COKB model

In the COKB model there are 11 kinds of facts accepted. These kinds of facts have been proposed from the researching on real requirements and problems in different domains of knowledge. The kinds of facts are as follows:

- **Fact of kind 1**: information about object kind. Some examples are ABC is a right triangle, ABCD is a parallelogram, matrix A is a square matrix.
- **Fact of kind 2**: a determination of an object or an attribute of an object. The following problem in analytic geometry gives some examples for facts of kind 2.

Problem: Given the points E and F, and the line (d). Suppose E, F, and (d) are determined. (P) is the plane satisfying the relations: E $\in$ (P), F $\in$ (P), and (d) // (P). Find the general equation of (P).

In this problem we have three facts of kind 3: (1) point E is determined or we have already known the coordinates of E, (2) point F is determined, (3) line (d) is determined or we have already known the equation of (d).

- **Fact of kind 3**: a determination of an object or an attribute of an object by a value or a constant expression. These are some examples in plane geometry and in analytic geometry: in the triangle ABC, suppose that the length of edge BC = 5; the plane (P) has the equation 2x + 3y – z + 6 = 0, and the point M has the coordinate (1, 2, 3).

- **Fact of kind 4**: equality on objects or attributes of objects. This kind of facts is also popular, and there are many problems related to it on the knowledge base. The following problem in plane geometry gives some examples for facts of kind 4.

Problem: Given the parallelogram ABCD. Suppose M and N are two points of segment AC such that AM = CN. Prove that two triangles ABM and CDN are equal.

In the problem we have to determine equality between two C-objects, a fact of kind 4.

- **Fact of kind 5**: a dependence of an object on other objects by a general equation. An example in geometry for this kind of fact is that w = 2*u + 3*v; here u, v and w are vectors.
- **Fact of kind 6**: a relation on objects or attributes of the objects. In almost problems there are facts of kind 6 such as the parallel of two lines, a line is perpendicular to a plane, a point belongs to a line segment.
- **Fact of kind 7**: a determination of a function.
- **Fact of kind 8**: a determination of a function by a value or a constant expression.
- **Fact of kind 9**: equality between an object and a function.
- **Fact of kind 10**: equality between a function and another function.
- **Fact of kind 11**: a dependence of a function on other functions or other objects by an equation.

The last five kinds of facts are related to knowledge about functions, the component **Funcs** in the COKB model. The problem below gives some examples for facts related to functions.

Problem: Let d be the line with the equation 3x + 4y - 12 = 0. P and Q are intersection points of d and the axes Ox, Oy.

a. Find the central point of PQ
b. Find the projection of O onto the line d.

For each line segment, there exists one and only one point which is the central point of that segment. Therefore, there is a function MIDPOINT(A, B) that outputs the central point M of the line segment AB. Part (a) of the above problem can be represented as to find the point I such that I = MIDPOINT(P,Q), a fact of kind 9. The projection can also be represented by the function PROJECTION(M, d) that outputs the projection point N of point M onto line d. Part (b) of the above problem can be represented as to find the point A such that A = PROJECTION(O,d), which is also a fact of kind 9.

Unification algorithms of facts were designed and used in different applications such as the system that supports studying knowledge and solving analytic geometry problems, the program for studying and solving problems in Plane Geometry, the knowledge system in linear algebra.

### 3.1.4 Specification language for COKB model

The language for the COKB model is constructed to specify knowledge bases with knowledge of the form COKB model. This language includes the following:

- A set of characters: letter, number, special letter.
- Vocabulary: keywords, names.
- Data types: basic types and structured types.
- Expressions and sentences.
- Statements.
- Syntax for specifying the components of COKB model.

The followings are some structures of definitions for expressions, Com-Objects, relations, facts, and functions.

**Definitions of expressions:**

| | | |
|---|---|---|
| expr | ::= | expr \| rel-expr \| logic-expr |
| expr | ::= | expr add-operator term \| term |
| term | ::= | term mul-operator factor \| factor |
| factor | ::= | **-** factor \| element **^** factor \| element |
| element | ::= | **(** expr **)** \| name \| number \| function-call |
| rel-expr | ::= | expr rel-operator expr |
| logic-expr | ::= | logic-expr **OR** logic-term \| logic-expr **IMPLIES** logic-term \| **NOT** logic-term \| logic-term |
| logic-term | ::= | logic-term **AND** logic-primary \| logic-primary |
| logic-primary | ::= | expr \| rel-expr \| function-call \| quantify-expr \| **TRUE** \| **FALSE** |
| quantify-expr | ::= | **FORALL(**name <, name>***),** logic-expr \| **EXISTS(**name**),** logic-expr |

**Definitions of Com-object type:**

cobject-type ::= **COBJECT** name;

[isa]
[hasa]
[constructs]
[attributes]
[constraints]
[crelations]
[facts]
[rules]

**ENDCOBJECT;**

**Definitions of computational relations:**

**crelations** ::= **CREATION:**
**crelation-def+**
**ENDCRELATION;**

crelation-def ::= **CR** name;
**MF**: name <, name>*;
**MFEXP**: equation;
**ENDCR;**

equation ::= expr = expr

**Definitions of special relations:**

| | | |
|---|---|---|
| isa | ::= | ISA: name <, name>*; |
| hasa | ::= | HASA: [fact-def] |

**Definitions of facts:**

| | | |
|---|---|---|
| facts | ::= | **FACT**: fact-def+ |
| fact-def | ::= | object-type \| attribute \| name \| equation \| relation \| expression |
| object-type | ::= | cobject-type **(**name**)** \| cobject-type **(**name <, name>* **)** |
| relation | ::= | relation **(** name <, name>+ **)** |

**Definitions of relations based on facts:**

| | | |
|---|---|---|
| relation-def | ::= | **RELATION** name; |
| | | **ARGUMENT**: argument-def+ |
| | | [facts] |
| | | **ENDRELATION**; |
| argument-def | ::= | name <, name>*: type; |

**Definitions of functions – form 1:**

| | | |
|---|---|---|
| function-def | ::= | **FUNCTION** name; |
| | | **ARGUMENT**: argument-def+ |
| | | **RETURN**: return-def; |
| | | [constraint] |
| | | [facts] |
| | | **ENDFUNCTION**; |
| return-def | ::= | name: type; |

**Definitions of functions – form 2:**

| | | |
|---|---|---|
| function-def | ::= | **FUNCTION** name; |
| | | **ARGUMENT**: argument-def+ |
| | | **RETURN**: return-def; |
| | | [constraint] |
| | | [variables] |
| | | [statements] |
| | | **ENDFUNCTION**; |
| statements | ::= | statement-def+ |
| statement-def | ::= | assign-stmt \| if-stmt \| for-stmt |
| asign-stmt | ::= | name := expr; |
| if-stmt | ::= | **IF** logic-expr **THEN** statements+ **ENDIF**; \| |
| | | **IF** logic-expr **THEN** statements+ **ELSE** statements+ **ENDIF**; |
| for-stmt | ::= | **FOR** name **IN [**range**] DO** statements+ **ENDFOR**; |

### 3.2 Computational networks

In this section, we present the models computational networks with simple valued variables and networks of computational objects. They have been used to represent knowledge in many domains of knowledge. The methods and techniques for solving the problems on the networks will be useful tool for design intelligent systems, especially IPSE.

### 3.2.1 Computational networks with simple valued variables

In this part a simple model of computational networks will be presented together related problems and techniques for solving them. Although this model is not very complicated, but it is a very useful tool for designing many knowledge base systems in practice.

**Definition 3.3:** A *computational network (Com-Net) with simple valued variables* is a pair (M, F), in which $M = \{x_1, x_2, ..., x_n\}$ is a set of variables with simple values (or unstructured values), and $F = \{f_1, f_2, ..., f_m\}$ is a set of computational relations over the variables in the set M. Each computational relation $f \in F$ has the following form:

i. An equation over some variables in M, or
ii. Deductive rule $f : u(f) \rightarrow v(f)$, with $u(f) \subseteq M$, $v(f) \subseteq M$, and there are corresponding formulas to determine (or to compute) variables in v(f) from variables in u(f).We also define the set $M(f) = u(f) \cup v(f)$.

Remark: In many applications equations can be represented as deduction rules.

**Problems:** Given a computational net (M, F). The popular problem arising from reality applications is that to find a solution to determine a set $H \subseteq M$ from a set $G \subseteq M$. This problem is denoted by the symbol $H \rightarrow G$, H is the hypothesis and G is the goal of the problem. To solve the problem we have to answer two questions below:

Q1: Is the problem solvable based on the knowledge K = (M, F)?

Q2: How to obtain the goal G from the hypothesis H based on the knowledge K = (M, F) in case the problem is solvable?

**Definition 3.4:** Given a computational net K = (M, F).

i. For each $A \subseteq M$ and $f \in F$, denote $f(A) = A \cup M(f)$ be the set obtained from A by applying f. Let $S = [f_1, f_2, ..., f_k]$ be a list consisting relations in F, the notation $S(A) = f_k(f_{k-1}(\ldots f_2(f_1(A)) \ldots ))$ is used to denote the set of variables obtained from A by applying relations in S.
ii. The list $S = [f_1, f_2, ..., f_k]$ is called a *solution* of the problem $H \rightarrow G$ if $S(H) \supseteq G$. Solution S is called a good solution if there is not a proper sublist S′ of S such that S′ is also a solution of the problem. The problem is *solvable* if there is a solution to solve it.

**Definition 3.5:** Given a computational net K = (M, F). Let A be a subset of M. It is easy to verify that there exists a unique set $\overline{A} \subseteq M$ such that the problem $A \rightarrow \overline{A}$ is solvable; the set $\overline{A}$ is called the closure of A.

The following are some algorithms and results that show methods and techniques for solving the above problems on computational nets.

**Theorem 3.1:** Given a computational net K = (M, F). The following statements are equivalent.

i. Problem $H \rightarrow G$ is solvable.
ii. $\overline{H} \supseteq G$.
iii. There exists a list of relations S such that $S(H) \supseteq G$.

**Algorithm 3.1:** Find a solution of the problem $H \rightarrow G$.

```
Step 1: Solution ← empty;
Step 2: if G ⊆ H then        begin Solution_found ← true; goto step 4; end
              else Solution_found ← false;
Step 3: Repeat
                    Hold ← H;
                    Select f ∈ F;
                    while not Solution_found and (f found) do begin
                              if (applying f from H produces new facts)
                              then begin
                                        H ← H ∪ M(f); Add f to Solution;
                                        end;
                              if G ⊆ H then
                                        Solution_found ← true;
                              Select new f ∈ F;
                              end;      { while }
          Until Solution_found or (H = Hold);
Step 4: if not Solution_found then
                    There is no solution found;
              else
                    Solution is a solution of the problem;
```

**Algorithm 3.2:** Find a good solution from a solution $S = [f_1, f_2, ..., f_k]$ of the problem $H \rightarrow G$ on computational net (M, F).

```
Step 1: NewS ← []; V ← G;
Step 2: for i := k downto 1 do
          If v(f_k) ∩ V ≠ ∅ the Begin
            Insert f_k at the beginning of NewS;
            V ← (V - v(f_k)) ∪ (u(f_k) - H);
            End
Step 3: NewS is a good solution.
```

On a computational net (M, F), in many cases the problem $H \rightarrow G$ has a solution S in which there are relations producing some redundancy variables. At those situations, we must determine necessary variables of each step in the problem solving process. The following theorem shows the way to analyze the solution to determine necessary variables to compute at each step.

**Theorem 3.2:** Given a computational net K = (M, F). Let $[f_1, f_2, ..., f_m]$ be a good solution of the problem $H \rightarrow G$. denote $A_0 = H$, $A_i = [f_1, f_2, ..., f_i](H)$, with i=1, ..., m. Then there exists a list $[B_0, B_1, ..., B_{m-1}, B_m]$ satisfying the following conditions:

1. $B_m = G$,
2. $B_i \subseteq A_i$, with i=0, 1, ..., m.
3. For i=1,...,m, $[f_i]$ is a solution of the problem $B_{i-1} \rightarrow B_i$ but not to be a solution of the problem $B \rightarrow B_i$, with B is any proper subset B of $B_{i-1}$.

### 3.2.2 Networks of computational objects

In many problems we usually meet many different kinds of objects. Each object has attributes and internal relations between them. Therefore, it is necessary to consider an extension of computational nets in which each variable is a computational object.

**Definition 3.6:** A computational object (or Com-object) has the following characteristics:

1. It has valued attributes. The set consists of all attributes of the object O will be denoted by M(O).
2. There are internal computational relations between attributes of a Com-object O. These are manifested in the following features of the object:
   - Given a subset A of M(O). The object O can show us the attributes that can be determined from A.
   - The object O will give the value of an attribute.
   - It can also show the internal process of determining the attributes.

Example 3.1: A triangle with some knowledge (formulas, theorems, etc ...) is an object. The attributes of a "triangle" object are 3 edges, 3 angles, etc. A "triangle" object can also answer some questions such as "Is there a solution for the problem that to compute the surface from one edge and two angles?".

**Definition 3.7:** A computational relation f between attributes or objects is called a *relation between the objects*. A network of Com-objects will consists of a set of Com-objects $O = \{O_1, O_2, ..., O_n\}$ and a set of computational relations $F = \{f_1, f_2, ... , f_m\}$. This network of Com-objects is denoted by (O, F).

On the network of Com-objects (O, F), we consider the problem that to determine (or compute) attributes in set G from given attributes in set H. The problem will be denoted by $H \rightarrow G$.

Example 3.2: In figure 2 below, suppose that AB = AC, the values of the angle A and the edge BC are given (hypothesis). ABDE and ACFG are squares. Compute EG.

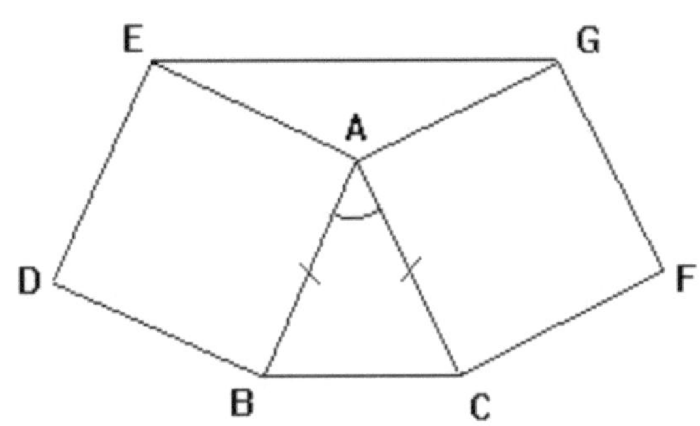


Fig. 2. A problem in geometry

The problem can be considered on the network of Com-objects (O, F) as follows:

O = {$O_1$: triangle ABC with AB = AC, $O_2$ : triangle AEG, $O_3$ : square ABDE, $O_4$ : square ACFG }, and F = {$f_1$, $f_2$, $f_3$, $f_4$, $f_5$} consists of the following relations
$f_1$ : $O_1.c = O_3.a$ {the edge c of triangle ABC = the edge of the square ABDE}
$f_2$ : $O_1.b = O_4.a$ {the edge b of triangle ABC = the edge of the square ACFG}
$f_3$ : $O_2.b = O_4.a$ {the edge b of triangle AEG = the edge of the square ACFG}
$f_4$ : $O_2.c = O_3.a$ {the edge c of triangle AEG = the edge of the square ABDE}
$f_5$ : $O_1.A + O_2.A = \pi$.

**Definition 3.8:** Let (O, F) be a network of Com-objects, and M be a set of concerned attributes. Suppose A is a subset of M.

a. For each f ∈ F, denote f(A) is the union of the set A and the set consists of all attributes in M deduced from A by f. Similarly, for each Com-object $O_i \in O$, $O_i(A)$ is the union of the set A and the set consists of all attributes (in M) that the object $O_i$ can determine from attributes in A.
b. Suppose D = [$t_1, t_2, ..., t_m$] is a list of elements in $F \cup O$. Denote $A_0 = A$, $A_1 = t_1(A_0)$, . . ., $A_m = t_m(A_{m-1})$, and $D(A) = A_m$.

We have $A_0 \subseteq A_1 \subseteq . . . \subseteq A_m = D(A) \subseteq M$. Problem H→G is called *solvable* if there is a list $D \subseteq F \cup O$ such that $D(A) \supseteq B$. In this case, we say that D is a *solution* of the problem.

Technically the above theorems and algorithms can be developed to obtain the new ones for solving the problem H→G on network of Com-objects (O,F). They will be omitted here except the algorithm to find a solution of the problem. The worthy of note is that the objects may participate in solutions as computational relations.

**Algorithm 3.3:** Find a solution of the problem H→G on a network of Com-objects.

```
Step 1: Solution ← empty;
Step 2: if G ⊆ H then      begin Solution_found ← true; goto step 5; end
            Else Solution_found ← false;
Step 3: Repeat
                  Hold ← H;
                  Select f ∈ F;
                  while not Solution_found and (f found) do begin
                        if (applying f from H produces new facts) then begin
                              H ← H ∪ M(f); Add f to Solution;
                              end;
                        if G ⊆ H then Solution_found ← true;
                        Select new f ∈ F;
                        end;      { while }
         Until Solution_found or (H = Hold);
Step 4: if not Solution_found then begin
                  Select Oi ∈ O such that Oi(H) ≠ H;
                  if (the selection is successful) then begin
                        H ← Oi(H); Add Oi to Solution;
                        if (G ⊆ H) then begin
```

```
                    Solution_found ← true; goto step 5;
                    end;
            else
                    goto step 3;
            end;
    end;
Step 5: if not Solution_found then There is no solution found;
        else Solution is a solution of the problem;
```

Example 3.3: Consider the network (O, F) in example 3.2, and the problem $H \rightarrow G$, where

$$H = \{O_1.a, O_1.A\}, \text{ and } G = \{O_2.a\}.$$

Here we have: $M(f_1) = \{ O_1.c , O_3.a \}$, $M(f_2) = \{ O_1.b , O_4.a \}$, $M(f_3) = \{ O_2.b , O_4.a \}$,

$$M(f_4) = \{ O_2.c , O_3.a \}, M(f_5) = \{ O_1.\alpha , O_2.\alpha \},$$

$$M = \{ O_1.a, O_1.b, O_1.c, O_1.A, O_2.b, O_2.c, O_2.A , O_2.a, O_3.a, O_4.a \}.$$

The above algorithms will produce the solution $D = \{ f_5, O_1, f_1, f_2, f_3, f_4, O_2\}$, and the process of extending the set of attributes as follows:

$$A_0 \xrightarrow{f_5} A_1 \xrightarrow{O_1} A_2 \xrightarrow{f_1} A_3 \xrightarrow{f_2} A_4 \xrightarrow{f_3} A_5 \xrightarrow{f_4} A_6 \xrightarrow{O_2} A_7$$

with $A_0 = A = \{O_1.a , O_1.A\}$,
$A_1 = \{O_1.a , O_1.A, O_2.A\}$,
$A_2 = \{ O_1.a , O_1.A, O_2.A, O_1.b, O_1.c \}$,
$A_3 = \{O_1.a , O_1.A, O_2.A, O_1.b, O_1.c, O_3.a\}$,
$A_4 = \{O_1.a , O_1.A, O_2.A, O_1.b, O_1.c, O_3.a, O_4.a\}$,
$A_5 = \{O_1.a , O_1.A, O_2.A, O_1.b, O_1.c, O_3.a, O_4.a, O_2.b\}$,
$A_6 = \{O_1.a , O_1.A, O_2.A, O_1.b, O_1.c, O_3.a, O_4.a, O_2.b, O_2.c\}$,
$A_7 = \{O_1.a , O_1.A, O_2.A, O_1.b, O_1.c, O_3.a, O_4.a, O_2.b, O_2.c, O_2.a\}$.

### 3.2.3 Extensions of computational networks

Computational Networks with simple valued variables and networks of computational objects can be used to represent knowledge in many domains of knowledge. The basic components of knowledge consist of a set of simple valued variables and a set of computational relations over the variables. However, there are domains of knowledge based on a set of elements, in which each element can be a simple valued variables or a function. For example, in the knowledge of alternating current the alternating current intensity i(t) and the alternating potential u(t) are functions. It requires considering some extensions of computational networks such as *extensive computational networks* and *extensive computational objects networks* that are defined below.

**Definition 3.9:** An *extensive computational network* is a structure (M,R) consisting of two following sets:

- $M = M_v \cup M_f$ is a set of attributes or elements, with simple valued or functional valued.$M_v = \{x_{v1}, x_{v2}, \ldots, x_{vk}\}$ is the set of simple valued variables. $M_f = \{x_{f1}, x_{f2}, \ldots x_{fm}\}$ is the set of functional valued elements.
- $R = R_{vv} \cup R_{fv} \cup R_{vf} \cup R_{fvf}$ is the set of deduction rules, and R is the union of four subsets of rules $R_{vv}$, $R_{fv}$, $R_{vf}$, $R_{fvf}$. Each rule r has the form r: $u(r) \rightarrow v(r)$, with u(r) is the hypotheses of r and v(r) is the conclusion of r. A rule is also one of the four cases below.

Case 1: $r \in R_{vv}$. For this case, $u(r) \subseteq M_v$ and $v(r) \subseteq M_v$.
Case 2: $r \in R_{fv}$. For this case, $u(r) \subseteq M_f$ and $v(r) \subseteq M_v$.
Case 3: $r \in R_{vf}$. For this case, $u(r) \subseteq M_v$ and $v(r) \subseteq M_f$.
Case 4: $r \in R_{fvf}$. For this case, $u(r) \subseteq M$, $u(r) \cap M_f \neq \varnothing$, $u(r) \cap M_v \neq \varnothing$, and $v(r) \subseteq M_f$.

Each rule in R has the corresponding computational relation in $F = F_{vv} \cup F_{fv} \cup F_{vf} \cup F_{fvf}$.

**Definition 3.10:** An *extensive computational Object* (ECom-Object) is an object O has structure including:

- A set of attributes $Attr(O) = M_v \cup M_f$, with $M_v$ is a set of simple valued variables; $M_f$ is a set of functional variables. Between the variables (or attributes) there are internal relations, that are deduction rules or the computational relations.
- The object O has behaviors of reasoning and computing on attributes of objects or facts such as: find the closure of a set $A \subset Attr(O)$; find a solution of problems which has the form $A \rightarrow B$, with $A \subseteq Attr(O)$ and $B \subseteq Attr(O)$; perform computations; consider determination of objects or facts.

**Definition 3.11:** An *extensive computational objects network* is a model **(O, M, F, T)** that has the components below.

- $O = \{O_1, O_2, \ldots, O_n\}$ is the set of extensive computational objects.
- M is a set of object attributes. We will use the following notations: $M_v(O_i)$ is the set of simple valued attributes of the object $O_i$, $M_f(O_i)$ is the set of functional attributes of $O_i$, $M(O_i) = M_v(O_i) \cup M_f(O_i)$, $M(O) = M(O_1) \cup M(O_2) \cup \ldots \cup M(O_n)$, and $M \subseteq M(O)$.
- $F = F(O)$ is the set of the computational relations on attributes in M and on objects in O.
- $T=\{t_1, t_2, \ldots, t_k\}$ is set of operators on objects.

On the structure (O,T), there are expressions of objects. Each expression of objects has its attributes as if it is an object.

## 4. Design of main components

The main components of an IPSE are considered here consists of the knowledge base, the inference engine. Design of these components will be discussed and presented in this section.

### 4.1 Design of knowledge base

The design process of the system presented in section 2 consists of seven stages. After stage 1 for collecting real knowledge, the knowledge base design includes stage 2 and stage 3. It includes the following tasks.

- The knowledge domain collected, which is denoted by K, will be represented or modeled base on the knowledge model COKB, Com-Net, CO-Net and their extensions or restrictions known. Some restrictions of COKB model were used to design knowledge bases are the model COKB lacking operator component (C, H, R, Funcs, Rules), the model COKB without function component (C, H, R, Ops, Rules), and the simple COKB sub-model (C, H, R, Rules). From Studying and analyzing the whole of knowledge in the domain, It is not difficult to determine known forms of knowledge presenting, together with relationships between them. In case that knowledge K has the known form such as COKB model, we can use this model for representing knowledge K directly. Otherwise, the knowledge K can be partitioned into knowledge sub-domains $K_i$ (i = 1, 2, …, n) with lower complexity and certain relationships, and each $K_i$ has the form known. The relationships between knowledge sub-domains must be clear so that we can integrate knowledge models of the knowledge sub-domains later.
- Each knowledge sub-domain $K_i$ will be modeled by using the above knowledge models, so a knowledge model $M(K_i)$ of knowledge $K_i$ will be established. The relationships on $\{K_i\}$ are also specified or represented. The models $\{M(K_i)\}$ together with their relationships are integrated to produce a model M(K) of the knowledge K. Then we obtain a knowledge model M(K) for the whole knowledge K of the application.
- Next, it is needed to construct a specification language for the knowledge base of the system. The COKB model and CO-Nets have their specification language used to specify knowledge bases of these form. A restriction or extension model of those models also have suitable specification language. Therefore, we can easily construct a specification language L(K) for the knowledge K. This language gives us to specify components of knowledge K in the organization of the knowledge base.
- From the model M(K) and the specification language L(K), the knowledge base organization of the system will be established. It consists of structured text files that stores the components concepts, hierarchical relation, relations, operators, functions, rules, facts and objects; and their specification. The knowledge base is stored by the system of files listed below,

- File CONCEPTS.txt stores names of concepts, and it has the following structure:
  **begin_concepts**
  <concept name 1>
  < concept name 2>
  …
  **end_concepts**
  For each concept, we have the corresponding file with the file name <concept name>.txt, which contains the specification of this concept. This file has the following structure:
  **begin_concept**: <concept name>[based objects]
  specification of based objects
  **begin_variables**
  <attribute name> : <attribute type>;
  …
  **end_variables**

**begin_constraints**
specification of constraints
**end_constraints**
**begin_properties**
specification of internal facts
**end_properties**
**begin_computation_relations**
**begin_relation**
specification of a relation
**end_relation**
...
**end_computation_relations**
**begin_rules**
**begin_rule**
kind_rule = "<kind of rule>";
**hypothesis_part:**
{ facts}
**goal_part:**
{ facts}
**end_rule**
...
**end_rules**
**end_concept**

- File HIERARCHY.txt stores information of the Hasse diagram representing the component H of COKB model. It has the following structure:
  **begin_Hierarchy**
  [<concept name 1>, <concept name 2>]
  ...
  **end_Hierarchy**
- Files RELATIONS.txt and RELATIONS_DEF.txt are structured text files that store the specification of relations. The structure of file RELATIONS.txt is as follows
  **begin_Relations**
  [<relation name>, <concept>, <concept>, ... ], {<property>, <property>, ...};
  [<relation name>, <concept>, <concept>, ... ], {<property>, <property>, ...};
  ...
  **end_Relations**
- Files OPERATORS.txt and OPERATORS_DEF.txt are structured text files that store the specification of operators (the component Ops of KBCO model). The structure of file OPERATORS.txt is as follows
  **begin_Operators**
  [<operator symbol>, <list of concepts>, <result concept>], {<property>, <property>, ...};
  [<operator symbol>, <list of concepts>, <result concept>], {<property>, <property>, ...};
  ...
  **end_Operators**

- Files FUNCTIONS.txt and FUNCTIONS_DEF.txt are structured text files that store the specification of functions (the component Funcs of KBCO model). The structure of file FUNCTIONS.txt is as follows

  **begin_Functions**
  <result concept> <function name>(sequence of concepts);
  <result concept> <function name>(sequence of concepts);
  ...
  **end_Functions**

- File FACT_KINDS.txt is the structured text file that stores the definition of kinds of facts. Its structure is as follows

  **begin_Factkinds**
  1, <fact structure>, <fact structure>, ...;
  2, <fact structure>, <fact structure>, ...;
  ...
  **end_Factkinds**

- File RULES.txt is the structured text file that stores deductive rules. Its structure is as follows

  **begin_Rules**
  **begin_rule**
  kind_rule = "<rule kind>";
  <object> : <concept>;
  ...
  **hypothesis_part:**
  <set of facts>
  **goal_part:**
  <set of facts>
  **end_rule**
  ...
  **end_Rules**

- Files OBJECTS.txt and FACTS.txt are the structured text files that store certain objects and facts. The structure of file OBJECTS.txt is as follows

  **begin_objects**
  <object name> : <concept>;
  <object name> : <concept>;
  ...
  **end_objects**

### 4.2 Design the inference engine

Design the inference engine is stage 4 of the design process. The inference engine design includes the following tasks:

- From the collection of problems obtained in stage 1 with an initial classification, we can determine classes of problems base on known models such as Com-Net, CO-Net, and their extensions. This task helps us to model classes of problems as frame-based problem models, or as Com-Nets and CO-Nets for general forms of problems. Techniques for modeling problems are presented in the stage 4 of the design process.

Problems modeled by using CO-Net has the form (O, F, Goal), in which O is a set of Com-objects, F is a set of facts on objects, and Goal is a set consisting of goals.

- The basic technique for designing deductive algorithms is the unification of facts. Based on the kinds of facts and their structures, there will be criteria for unification proposed. Then it produces algorithms to check the unification of two facts. For instance, when we have two facts *fact1* and *fact2* of kinds 1-6, the unification definition of them is as follows: fact1 and fact2 are unified they satisfy the following conditions
  1. *fact1* and *fact2* have the same kind k, and
  2. *fact1* = *fact2* if k = 1, 2, 6.
     [*fact1*[1], {*fact1*[2..nops(*fact1*)]}] = [*fact2*[1], {*fact2*[2..nops(*fact2*)]}] if k = 6 and the relation in *fact1* is symmetric.
     lhs(*fact1*) = lhs(*fact2*) and compute(rhs(*fact1*)) = compute(rhs(*fact2*)) if k =3.
     ( lhs(*fact1*) = lhs(*fact2*) and rhs(*fact1*) = rhs(*fact2*)) or
     ( lhs(*fact1*) = rhs(*fact2*) and rhs(*fact1*) = lhs(*fact2*)) if k = 4.
     evalb(simplify(expand(lhs(*fact1*)-rhs(*fact1*)- lhs(*fact2*)+rhs(*fact2*))) = 0) or
     evalb(simplify(expand(lhs(*fact1*)-rhs(*fact1*)+ lhs(*fact2*)-rhs(*fact2*))) = 0) if k = 5.
- To design the algorithms for reasoning methods to solve classes of problems, the forward chaining strategy can be used with artificial intelligent techniques such as deductive method with heuristics, deductive method with sample problems, deductive method based on organization of solving methods for classes of frame-based problems. To classes of frame-based problems, designing reasoning algorithms for solving them is not very difficult. To classes of general problems, the most difficult thing is modeling for experience, sensible reaction and intuitional human to find heuristic rules, which were able to imitate the human thinking for solving problems. We can use Com-Nets, CO-Nets, and their extensions to model problems; and use artificial intelligent techniques to design algorithms for automated reasoning. For instance, a reasoning algorithm for COKB model with sample problems can be briefly presented below.

**Definition 4.1**: Given knowledge domain K = (C, H, R, Ops, Funcs, Rules), knowledge sub-domain of knowledge K is knowledge domain which was represented by COKB model, it consists of components as follows

$$K_P = (C_P, H_P, R_P, Ops_P, Funcs_P, Rules_P)$$

where, $C_P \subset C$, $H_P \subset H$, $R_P \subset R$, $Ops_P \subset Ops$, $Funcs_P \subset Funcs$, $Rules_P \subset Rules$.

Knowledge domain $K_P$ is a restriction of knowledge K.

**Definition 4.2**: Given knowledge sub-domain $K_P$, Sample Problem (SP) is a problem which was represented by networks of Com-Objects on knowledge $K_P$, it consists of three components ($O_P$, $F_P$, $Goal_P$); $O_P$ and $F_P$ contain objects and facts were specificated on knowledge $K_P$.

**Definition 4.3**: A model of Computational Object Knowledge Base with Sample Problems (COKB-SP) consists of 7 components: (C, H, R, Ops, Funcs, Rules, Sample); in which, (C, H, R, Ops, Funcs, Rules) is knowledge domain which presented by COKB model, the Sample component is a set of Sample Problems of this knowledge domain.

**Algorithm 4.1**: To find a solution of problem P modelled by (O,F,Goal) on knowledge K of the form COKB-SP.

**Step 1.** Record the elements in hypothesis part and goal part.
**Step 2.** Find *the Sample Problem* can be applied.
**Step 3.** Check goal G. If G is obtained then goto step 8.
**Step 4.** Using heuristic rules to select a rule for producing new facts or new objects.
**Step 5.** If selection in step 3 fails then search for any rule which can be used to deduce new facts or new objects.
**Step 6.** If there is a rule found in step 3 or in step 4 then record the information about the rule, new facts in Solution, and new situation (previous objects and facts together with new facts and new objects), and goto step 2.
**Step 7.** Else {search for a rule fails} Conclusion: Solution not found, and stop.
**Step 8.** Reduce the solution found by excluding redundant rules and information in the solution.

**Algorithm 4.2**: To find sample problems.

Given problem P = (O, F, Goal) on on knowledge K of the form COKB-SP. The Sample Problem can be applied on P has been found by the following procedure:

```
Step 1: H ← O ∪ F
Step 2: SP ← Sample
        Sample_found← false
Step 3: Repeat
        Select S in SP
  if facts of  H can be applied in (S.Op and S.Fp)  then
          begin
            if kind of S.Goalp = kind of Goal then
                Sample_found  ← true
            Else  if S.Goalp ⊆ H then
                Sample_found  ← true
          end
        SP ← (SP - S)
    Until SP = {} or Sample_found
Step 3: if Sample_found then
            S is a sample problem of the problem;
        else
            There is no sample problem found;
```

This algorithm simulates a part of human mind when to find SP that relate to practical problem. Thereby, the inference of system has been more quickly and effectively. Moreover, the solution of problem is natural and precise.

## 5. Applications

The design method for IPS and IPSE presented in previous sections have been used to produce many applycations such as program for studying and solving problems in Plane Geometry, program for studying and solving problems in analytic geometry, program for solving problems about alternating current in physics, program for solving problems in inorganic chemistry, program for solving algebraic problems, etc. In this section, we introduce some applications and examples about solutions of problems produced by computer programs.

- The system that supports studying knowledge and solving analytic geometry problems. The system consists of three components: the interface, the knowledge base, the knowledge processing modules or the inference engine. The program has menus for users searching knowledge they need and they can access knowledge base. Besides, there are windows for inputting problems. Users are supported a simple language for specifying problems. There are also windows in which the program shows solutions of problems and figures.
- The program for studying and solving problems in plane geometry. It can solve problems in general forms. Users only declare hypothesis and goal of problems base on a simple language but strong enough for specifying problems. The hypothesis can consist of objects, relations between objects or between attributes. It can also contain formulas, determination properties of some attributes or their values. The goal can be to compute an attribute, to determine an object, a relation or a formula. After specifying a problem, users can request the program to solve it automatically or to give instructions that help them to solve it themselves. The program also gives a human readable solution, which is easy to read and agree with the way of thinking and writing by students and teachers. The second function of the program is "Search for Knowledge". This function helps users to find out necessary knowledge quickly. They can search for concepts, definitions, properties, related theorems or formulas, and problem patterns.

Examples below illustrate the functions of a system for solving problems of analytic geometry, a system for solving problems in plane geometry, and a system for solving algebraic problems. The systems were implemented using C#, JAVA and MAPLE. Each example presents the problem in natural language, specifies the problem in specification language to input into the system, and a solution produced from the system.

**Example 5.1**: Let d be the line with the equation 3x + 4y - 12 = 0. P and Q are intersection points of d and the axes Ox, Oy.

a. Find the midpoint of PQ
b. Find the projection of O on the line d.

Specification of the problem:

Objects = {[d,line], [P,point], [Q,point]}.
Hypothesis = { d.f = (3*x+4*y-12 = 0), Ox.f = (y = 0), O = [0, 0], P = INTERSECT(Ox, d), Q = INTERSECT (Oy, d), H = PROJECTION(O, d), Oy . f = (x = 0) }.
Goal = { MIDPOINT(P, Q), H }.

Solution found by the system:

Step 1: {d.f = (3*x+4*y-12 = 0), Ox.f = (y = 0), Oy.f = (x = 0)} → {d.f, Ox.f , Oy.f }.

Step 2: {Ox.f, Oy.f, d.f} → {Ox, Oy, d}.
Step 3: {P = INTERSECT(Ox,d), d, Ox} →{P = [4, 0]}.
Step 4: {d, Oy, Q = INTERSECT(Oy,d)} → {Q = [0, 3]}.
Step 5: {P = [4, 0], Q = [0, 3]} → {P, Q}.
Step 6: {P, Q} → {MIDPOINT(P,Q) = [2, 3/2]}.
Step 7: {d, H = PROJECTION(O,d), O} →{ H = [36/25, 48/25]}.
Step 8: {H = [36/25, 48/25]} → {H}.

**Example 5.2**: Given two points P(2, 5) and Q(5,1). Suppose d is a line that contains the point P, and the distance between Q and d is 3. Find the equation of line d.

Specification of the problem:

Objects = {[P, point], [Q, point], [d, line]}.
Hypothesis = {DISTANCE(Q, d) = 3, P = [2, 5], Q = [5, 1], ["BELONG", P, d]}.
Goal = [d.f ].

Solution found by the system:

Step 1: {P = [2, 5]} → {P}.
Step 2: {DISTANCE(Q, d) = 3} → {DISTANCE(Q, d)}.
Step 3: {d, P} → {2d[1]+5d[2]+d[3] = 0}.
Step 4: {DISTANCE(Q, d) = 3}

$$\rightarrow \Rightarrow \frac{|5d[1]+d[2]+d[3]|}{\sqrt{d[1]^2 + d[2]^2}} = 3.$$

Step 5: $\left\{ d[1]=1,\ 2d[1]+5d[2]+d[3]=0, \frac{|5d[1]+d[2]+d[3]|}{\sqrt{d[1]^2 + d[2]^2}} = 3 \right\}$

$$\Rightarrow \left\{ d.f=(x+\frac{24}{7}y-\frac{134}{7}=0), d.f=(x-2=0) \right\}$$

Step 6: $\left\{ d.f=(x+\frac{24}{7}y-\frac{134}{7}=0), d.f=(x-2=0) \right\}$

$$\Rightarrow \{\ d.f\ \}$$

**Example 5.3**: Given the parallelogram ABCD. Suppose M and N are two points of segment AC such that AM = CN. Prove that two triangles ABM and CDN are equal.

Specification of the problem:

Objects = {[A, POINT], [B, POINT], [C, POINT], [D, POINT], [M, POINT], [N, POINT],
[O1, PARALLELOGRAM[A, B, C, D], [O2, TRIANGLE[A, B, M]],
[O3, TRIANGLE [C, D, N]]}.
Hypothesis = { [« BELONG », M, SEGMENT[A, C]],

[« BELONG », N, SEGMENT[A, C]], SEGMENT[A, M] = SEGMENT[C, N] }.
Goal = { O2 = O3}.

Solution found by the system:

Step 1: Hypothesis
→ { O2.SEGMENT[A, M] = O3. SEGMENT[C, N],
O2.SEGMENT[A, B] = O1. SEGMENT[A, B],
O3.SEGMENT[C, D] = O1.SEGMENT[C, D]}.
Step 2: Produce new objects related to O2, O3, and O1
→ {[O4, TRIANGLE[A, B, C]], [O5, TRIANGLE[C, D, A]]}.
Step 3: {[O1, PARALLELOGRAM[A, B, C, D]}
→{O4 = O5, SEGMENT[A, B] = SEGMENT[C, D]}.
Step 4: { O2.SEGMENT[A, B] = O1.SEGMENT[A, B],
O3.SEGMENT[C, D] = O1.SEGMENT[C, D],
SEGMENT[A, B] = SEGMENT[C, D]}
→{O2.SEGMENT[A, B] = O3.SEGMENT[C, D]}.
Step 5: {[« BELONG », M, SEGMENT[A, C]]}
→ {O4.angle_A = O2.angle_A}.
Step 6: {[« BELONG », N, SEGMENT[A, C]]}
→ { O5.angle_A = O3.angle_A }.
Step 7: {O4 = O5 }
→ {O4.angle_A = O5.angle_A}.
Step 8: { O4.angle_A = O2.angle_A ,
O5.angle_A = O3.angle_A ,
O4.angle_A = O5.angle_A }
→{ O2.angle_A = O3.angle_A}.
Step 9: { O2.SEGMENT[A, M] = O3. SEGMENT[C, N],
O2.SEGMENT[A, B] = O3.SEGMENT[C, D],
O2.angle_A = O3.angle_A }
→ {O2 = O3}.

**Example 5.4**: Let the equation, with m is a parameter, and x is a variable:

$$\left(m^2 - 4\right)x + 2 = m$$

Solve this equation by m.

Solution found by the system:

Solve the equation:

$$\left(m^2 - 4\right)x + 2 = m$$

$$\left(m^2 - 4\right)x = -2 + m$$

The coefficient of x has a set of roots:

$$\{-2 \ , \ 2\}$$

+ if parameter $m = -2$, then:

"This equation has no root"

+ if parameter $m = 2$, then:

"This equation has set of roots is the set of real numbers "

+ if parameter $m \notin \{-2 , 2\}$, then:

$$x = \frac{-2+m}{m^2-4} = \frac{1}{m+2}$$

## 6. Conclusions and future work

In this chapter, we proposed a method for designing intelligent problem solvers (IPS), especially those in education (IPSE). These systems have suitable knowledge base used by the inference engine to solve problems in certain knowledge domain, they not only give human readable solutions of problems but also present solutions as the way instructors and learners usually write them. Knowledge bases contain concepts of computational objects (Com-Objects), relations, operators, functions, facts and rules. The *Computational Object Knowledge Base* model (COKB) and its specification language can be used for knowledge modeling, for designing and implementing knowledge bases. The COKB model has been established from Object-Oriented approach for knowledge representation together with programming techniques for symbolic computation. The design of inference engine requires to model problems and to design reasoning algorithms with heuristics and sample problems. Computational networks (Com-Net) and networks of computational objects (CO-Net) can be used effectively for modeling problems and construction of reasoning algorithms in practical knowledge domains. These models are tools for designing inference engine of systems.

The proposed design method has been used to produce applycations in many fields such as mathematics, physics and chemistry. They support studying knowledge and solving problems automatically based on knowledge bases. Users only declare hypothesis and goal of problems base on a simple language but strong enough for specifying problems. The programs produce a human readable solution, which is easy to read and agree with the way of thinking and writing by students and instructors.

Designing an intelligent problem solver in education is a very challenging task, as domain knowledge and human thinking are very complicated and abstract. There are domains of knowledge with functional attributes such as knowledge of alternating current in physics. This motivates another extensions of COKB model, Com-Net and CO-Net, and develops design techniques. They will accept simple valued variables and also functional variables.

On the network of computational objects, operators will be considered. Such future works our models more powerful for representing knowledge in practice. Besides, To have a user-interface using natural language we have to develop methods for translating problems in natural language to specification language, and vice versa.

## 7. References

Chitta Baral (2003). Knowledge Representation, Reasoning and Declarative Problem Solving. Cambridge University Press, ISBN 0 521 81802 8.

Fatos X.; Leonard B. & Petraq J. P. (2010). Complex intellgent systems and their applications. *Springer Science+Business Media, LLC.* ISBN 978-1-4419-1635-8

Frank van Harmelem, Vladimir & Bruce (2008). Handbook of Knowledge Representation. *Elsevier*, ISBN: 978-0-444-52211-5.

George F. Luger (2008). Artificial Intelligence: Structures And Strategies For Complex Problem Solving. Addison Wesley Longman

Johns M. Tim (2008). Artificial Intelligence - A System Approach. *Infinity Science Press LLC*, ISBN: 978-0-9778582-3-1

Michel Chein & Marie-Laure Mugnier (2009). Graph-based Knowledge representation: Computational foundations of Conceptual Graphs. *Springer-Verlag London Limited.* ISBN: 978-1-84800-285-2.

Mike O'Docherty (2005). Object-oriented analysis and design: understanding system development with UML 2.0. *John Wiley & Sons Ltd*, ISBN-13 978-0-470-09240-8.

Nhon Do & Hien Nguyen (2011). A Reasoning Method on Computational Network and Its Applications. *Proceedings of the International MultiConference of Engineers and Computer Scientists* 2011 (ICAIA'11), pp. 137-141

Nhon Do & Hoai P. Truong & Trong T. Tran (2010). An Approach for Translating Mathematics Problems in Natural Language to Specification Language COKB of Intelligent Education Software. *Proceedings of 2010 International Conference on Artificial Intelligence and Education*, Hangzhou, China. 10-2010

Nhon Van Do (2010). Model for Knowledge Bases of Computational Objects. *International Journal of Computer Science Issues*, Vol. 7, Issue 3, No 8, pp. 11-20

Nhon Van Do (2009). Computational Networks for Knowledge Representation. *Proceedings of World Academy of Science, Engineering and Technology*, Volume 56, pp. 266-270

Nhon Do (2008). An ontology for knowledge representation And Applications. *Proceedings of World Academy of Science, Engineering and Technology*, Volumn 32, pp. 23-31, ISSN 2070-3740

Nhon Van Do (2000). A Program for studying and Solving problems in Plane Geometry. *Proceedings of International on Artificial Intelligence 2000*, Las Vegas, USA, 2000, pp. 1441-1447

Sowa, John F. (2002). Architectures for Intelligent Systems. *IBM Systems Journal*, vol. 41, no.3, pp. 331-349

Sowa, John F. (2000). Knowledge Representation: Logical, Philosophical and Computational Foundations. *Brooks/Cole Thomson Learning*, ISBN 0 534-94965-7

Stuart Russell & Peter Norvig (2010). Artificial Intelligence - A modern approach (Third edition). *Prentice Hall*, by Pearson Education, Inc.

7

# Logic of Integrity, Fuzzy Logic and Knowledge Modeling for Machine Education

Fatma Khanum Bunyatova
*Intellect School, Baku, Azerbaijan*

## 1. Introduction

Fast development of ICT clearly shows how training is behind this development. Quick modification of process devices leaves far behind it hard on the modernization of education. Though new directions in teaching how to e- learning, m-learning, online learning, machine learning etc. were formed by ICT technical means, but these means are not yet in a position to influence the fundamental change in education. The reason is that educational principles existing more than 300 years of memory oriented traditional teaching didactics were invested into these technical means. Knowledge was memorized through the transfer of private, unsystematically, non-logically constructed knowledge. But as we know, besides human memory there is human cognition, whose reserves are used no more than 2-3% (Gordon D., Jannette Voz 2000). Learning can be changed qualitatively and made accessible to all, if we make a shift from memorization and quantitative accumulation of knowledge to the organization of reasoning activities of students on knowledge for understanding. Learning in the mainstream of intellectual activity allows increasing the use of these resources several times and adequately raising the quality of education of all students. Cognitive activity - the activity of the intellect, is the area of psychology, the subject matter of its study.

Didactics – is the science about learning ways of a student, a science that seeks in more and more sophisticated ways to teach the students certain knowledge. Psychology of intelligence states that the knowledge that students receive is a reflection of what they have heard or read, in the best case, it is a converted form of information. The present knowledge should be built with the understanding of students on the basis of their previous experiences. New knowledge must be combined, divided, associated with previous and subsequent knowledge. Each student on the basis of his/her design of understanding constructs proposed knowledge in his/her understanding. In practice, it actually looks this way, but it is apparently only on the condition that a learner designs the structure of knowledge, structure of mental activity and structure of learning activities. Furthermore, these structures must be identical to the structures of intelligence. Under these conditions, a student regardless of learning forms, based on the capabilities of his/her internal understanding enters an active cognitive activity. Engaging in active learning activities, students gain active knowledge to expand their **understanding**. Knowledge, while at work, in such learning process destroys its traditional vertical structure of construction and it is logically arranged in a horizontal structure of thinking. That is, according to Piaget, Swiss psychologist "alogism of learning" is destroyed. Each new structure of knowledge, entering into logical operation with the old ones or adequate structures of the following knowledge builds them in the scheme of integrity of structures of knowledge. By taking advantage of high-tech, relying on psycho-pedagogy it is possible to model the contents of subject knowledge of isomorphic structures of intelligence. In this model, the following transfer and alignment occur:

Conversion:

a. The traditional concept of didactic unit of knowledge will be understood as the structure of knowledge;
b. Knowledge structures will be considered as the logical structures of knowledge of Bunyatova;
c. Traditional learning exercises will be completed by logical operations of thinking;
d. The logical structures of knowledge will be considered as the nanostructures of knowledge.

These conversions origin from the juncture of three sciences: pedagogy, psychology and high technology, which develop a new direction in the science of **nanopsychopedagogy** (F.Bunyatova 2009).

## 2. Necessary fundamental changes in education

To rotate learning from the position of memorization to the position of cognitive activity and for organization of learning without a student, it is needed to make the following fundamental changes in education:

a. Changing the way of learning

it is necessary to shift from the position of the transfer of knowledge to the position of the construction of the educational process, in which each student builds the knowledge based on his/her competence (Ф.Бунятова 2007). This means the transition from private practices to technology of training. In this case, the technology of constructive teaching by Bunyatova is applied (Ф.Бунятова 2009).

b. Modeling of structures of knowledge

The structures of subject knowledge should be modeled. This model should be constructed similar to models of natural and artificial intelligence brain (Лотфи Заде 1976).

c. Model of natural intelligence

The model of natural intelligence was constructed by Piaget and of artificial intelligence was constructed by Zadeh. Logic integrity of J. Piaget or the work of reasoning at an operational level that is at the formal-logical level is the work of human brain (Р.Алиев 1999) .

d. Model of artificial Intelligence by Zadeh

Zadeh had created an SC, which provided joint use of such numerical new approaches as fuzzy logic, neural networks, evolutionary computing, etc. These technologies are important for data compression and system design with high MIG and the best model of SC is human brain as noted by Zadeh (Р.Алиев 1999).

e. Building of holistic logic and fuzzy logic models of knowledge on the basis of these two theories

On the basis of these two theories, holistic logic and fuzzy logic models of knowledge are built F.Bunyatova (2009). This model can be a psychopedagogical and technologically constructed model for subject knowledge of not only machine learning in all its directions, but for learning in a whole. This model is constructed from the perspective of pedagogy, psychology, and high technology.

These three principles as a result, change not only the form and method of learning, but also the structure of contents of learning. Students here do not gain knowledge. They, relying on their experience construct them by means of logically constructed structures of knowledge. These structures of knowledge are built by isomorphic structures of intelligence.

**Creative learning technology by Bunyatova - CT by Bunyatova**

Change of the way of training means shift from private practices to the technology of training. In this case, technology of constructive teaching by Bunyatova is proposed. This technology is based on the cognitive theory by Piaget. Constructive teaching technology aims to develop structures of intelligence of students and organize their reasoning activities over knowledge.

Constructive teaching is a creative, activity-and operational learning, which provides an opportunity for each student to build new knowledge, based on his/her experience and available knowledge. The philosophy of constructive teaching is a synthesis of Eastern and Western philosophy of learning; this is a shift from private knowledge to the integrity of knowledge or the vice versa from the integrity of knowledge to the private. The constructive teaching is aimed to change the form of activities of learning and a student in the learning process, which in the end leads not only to the change of learning process, but all its relevant components.

CT by Bunyatova takes its origins from the psychology schools of Piaget and Vigotsky; it contains the co-operative structure of the educational activities of the American psychologist Spencer Kagan. While establishment of machine learning classes, the CT principles do not change principally, they just bear an individual character of learning, enriching the methods of individual learning.

**Principles of constructive teaching by Bunyatova**

**Principle 1. Searching meaning of the topic**

The lesson in a constructive teaching starts with searching the **theme of the lesson**, that is determines the real understanding of entity of the study. The teacher poses questions for discussion. Answers of students generate new questions and new discussions. Students, by discussing, actively adapt their knowledge and attitudes to these logically designed questions. In this process, they may make mistakes, go the wrong way, go back and start again. By scientific definition of meaning, they come from the definition of that meaning with their personal terms. In the interaction of ideas, in online education, these personal definitions, by self-correcting, self-regulating and self-enriching transform into a new structure of knowledge.

**Principle 2. Integrity scheme of knowledge structure**

Structures of knowledge in constructive teaching are provided for studying in the scheme of integrity. Knowledge is divided into invariant and variable (example: in language studies invariants - are parts of speech, in mathematics – they are figures; variables - are the rules of language, and in math they are mathematical operations and etc.). For example, if we study the numeral, then the scheme of integrity will be constructed as follows: the numeral in the middle, to the left of previous knowledge - adjective, noun, and to the right following pronoun, verb and adverb. In the end, it will be as follows: a noun, adjective, numeral, pronoun, verb and adverb. At the end, the scheme will be the following: noun, adjective, numeral, pronoun, verb and adverb. In this scheme of integrity, the numeral is studied in depth in a combination of relations, connections and interdependence with a noun, adjective, pronoun and verb in the system of integrity of the language.

**Principle 3. Logical structures of knowledge by Bunyatova – LSK by Bunyatova**

Using the tools of integrity logic by J. Piaget in the contents of subject studies have been identified following logical connections, relationships and dependencies among the structures of knowledge (Ф.Бунятова.2001)

- Agreed structures

Two structures of knowledge, agreeing with common relationships are connected and form a new structure of knowledge.

- Reversible structures

United by common relationships, structures of knowledge are reversible and transformed.

- Associated structures

Thinking always retains the ability to rejection and finding other variants of solution. The result obtained in various ways, in all cases is the same.

- Annulled structures

The structure of knowledge is annulled, disappears, canceled if it is multiplied by zero.

- Identical structures

Two identical structures can be combined into one complex structure.

The logical structure of knowledge (LSk) identified in knowledge, are the load bearing parts of constructive teaching.

**Principle 4. Logical operations of thinking**

In the analysis of tasks to the subject in the traditional way of learning it is revealed that most of the tasks are included in the exercises, that is repeating same actions in order to assimilate it, which consist of finding, underlining, determination, etc. These tasks are performed on one or two of the structures of knowledge and are aimed to determine the level of knowledge and skills.

In constructive teaching besides this on the structures of knowledge are performed logical operations of thinking. These operations allow students to integrate structures of knowledge into groups to clarify their interrelationship and relationship, classify, enrich, or replace them with other structures. A student, performing thinking activities of such operations on the structures of knowledge adequately builds the structure of his/her thinking and logical structure of his/her knowledge. Logical operations on the structures of knowledge are performed by commands or setting of a student.

1. The operation of classification

With the assistance of this operation, students acquire intellectual skills of the partition of the set into subsets according to certain criteria.

2. The operation of seriation

Performing the logical operation of seriation on structures of knowledge, students form intellectual skills of grouping structures of knowledge according to their combining criteria or for only one criterion.

3. The operation of substitution

By this operation structures are replaced by others (for example, in mathematics, numbers replaced by letters $(6 + 7) = (a + b)$; replacement of signs $5 \times 5 = 5^2$, etc.). This is very basic logical operation on the structures of knowledge and intellectually important skill that qualitatively transforms knowledge. This operation destroys the vertical structure of knowledge and develops in students the ability to arrange them into thinking in a horizontal structure [6].

4. The operation of enrichment

In carrying out this operation on the structures of knowledge, students who have knowledge enriched their knowledge with new structures of knowledge and turn it into new knowledge. The operation of enrichment, as the operation of substitution, generates future knowledge from the acquired knowledge.

5. Multiplicative operations

This operation is used simultaneously on multiple structures of knowledge that have common relations or communications (example: in a linguistic knowledge it is the change of some parts of speech - on cases, by the numbers.

**Principle 5. Mental models of students**

According to psychology of intelligence by Piaget, a child from birth to 8 years old goes through a pre logical operations; from 8 to 12 years, the stage of concrete operations, and from 12 to the end of youth stage of formal operations. Each stage of development corresponds to its settings, its commands. Under pre logical operations stage students typically argue based on their life experiences, and try as much as possible to extend it with such tasks that are set for them. In the bowels of pre logical operations students in a logical setting ask teacher questions generated by the makings of concrete operations, which are expanded, enriched, balanced and smoothly go to transition to the stage of concrete operations. In the frequent repetition of the same commands, units of the structures of knowledge, students gain not only stable knowledge, but also reveal their relationship and communication with other structures of knowledge. The concretization of knowledge and its consideration in relations and connections, allow the student to generate knowledge based on previous knowledge, or by identifying stable relationship, connections among the structures of knowledge, he/she formalizes them and moves to the stage of formal operations. It can be said that knowledge of every student in a constructive teaching goes through three stages: intuitive, concrete and formal. Quantity of previous knowledge through these stages is the result of intelligence, its richness, its diversity.

**Principle 6. Lesson structure**

The lesson in constructive teaching is designed structurally. The learner designs logical structures of knowledge, structures of mental activity and structure of the learning activities of students.

*The structure of mental activity*

Construction of thinking and cooperative structure activities are designed in isomorphic stages of intellectual development of students. Over the logical structures of knowledge students perform mental operations. This intellectual activity of students individually or in co-operation builds, destroys, strengthens and develops structures of intelligence of each separately helps a student to build his/her own individual way of thinking, understanding, which he/she later turns into personal tool of knowledge.

*Structure of educational activities*

Learning activities of students can be individual or interactive. For organization of an interactive activity students use cooperative learning structures of American scientist Spencer Kagan. Interaction of students in these structures leads to reflection, which is one of the major factors in construction of knowledge. Social skills acquired in the structures of interactive activities are combined with the intellectual skills that are generated by thinking activity.

Each lesson in constructive teaching is designed by the teacher in advance. For design of the lesson of constructive teaching 7 elements are used.

**Seven elements of constructive teaching**

While establishing a lesson, the CT uses the following elements:

## 2.1 Search

The teacher poses questions to the subject, to determine what students know about the topic what they will do, what decisions will be taken and what conclusions they will come. Search is to identify the essence of the meaning of the theme, determine its place in the system of knowledge; search - it is a motivation of cognitive activities of a student and understanding of given tasks from his/her pyramids of knowledge. Search - it is a concept for a teacher, how well students understand and explain the topic. Search - it is definition by the teacher zone of knowledge of students about the given subject and the prospect of its extension and application. Search - are statements by teachers to bring students on the track, which he has drawn.

## 2.2 Structures

In constructive teaching, as mentioned above, the lesson is built structurally:

1. It is a structure of knowledge. Based on the content of the topic, the teacher finds the goal in subject knowledge of logical structure of knowledge, that is, he/she can logically combine and separate one structure of knowledge from other structures; each structure of knowledge beyond that may be associated, coincide with another, or generally, after the actions on it, eliminated.
2. Having identified the logical structures, the student determines for himself/herself what mental operations students will perform over the logical structures of knowledge.
3. It is a structure of educational activity. A teacher, making the design of the lesson, determines which determines in which structures of activity students will work in pairs or in teams.

## 2.3 Logical operations of thinking

In a traditional approach to education work on exercises, examples, tasks are usually expressed as assignments: underline, find, agree, put in the required form, solve, run, etc. All these tasks are aimed at numerous varying repeat of learned and its application to one or two structures of knowledge. In contrast to this approach in constructive teaching several logically built mental activities, that is, operations are performed over the knowledge. Mental operations, or operations of thinking - they are commands, setups, expressed in verb, for example, isolate and connect the appropriate, replace one another, and convert and explain the outcome, express in a different form and create a new, etc. Students by regularly performing tasks over these settings, then in the follow up these settings gradually turn to their instrument of knowledge.

## 2.4 Connection

This element serves for connecting a structure of knowledge with others. In constructive teaching, knowledge is represented in the scheme of integrity. In this scheme of integrity it is clearly visible not only structural connection inside of the subject of knowledge, but also interdisciplinary communications. This communication allows for considering the subject matter under scrutiny from different viewpoints, identify among them the similarities and differences, determine its compatibility, identify options and make replacement of certain knowledge with others.

## 2.5 Questions

In a constructive teaching, the learner by making lesson design should determine with what question he will start the lesson and with what question he will finalize it. The questions posed by training, help him determine what students know about the topic, how they imagine it, how they by arguing explain their vision. Responses of students may be correct and not correct, complete, or short, and the whole spectrum of responses of students which were received by the training gives him an opportunity with the help of same training go to the right answer, that is to the point of knowledge to which he moved purposefully.

### 2.6 Adjunction and connections

This element of the lesson serves as communication of knowledge under study with past and future knowledge. Addition of a student in this communication of knowledge often changes them qualitatively and that knowledge of high school by moving down becomes knowledge of junior classes. This means the integration of knowledge horizontally, that is, integrity of knowledge is built, which creates a large space for the flight of thought.

### 2.7 Reflection or rejection (Presentation or a reflection of the students accumulated)

Presentation is the last element in the design of the lesson of constructive teaching. Teacher, in constructive teaching, prepares worksheets in advance for both individually and gives tasks on the basis of its set goal. Tasks and settings should cover work done in classes; they must start from easy and smoothly move to a more complex, which includes not only understanding, but also a deep comprehension and the transition of this meaning to a higher level, to the level of generation of new knowledge.

## 3. Modeling knowledge structure

In a traditional training, the structures of knowledge are established vertically and students get a comprehensive knowledge through the educational years. In the example of Russian, we can say that, at the primary school, students do not get holistic knowledge of a language. A student accomplishes this holistic knowledge in only 6$^{th}$ year of education. Such a set of knowledge leads to fragmentary and non-systematic knowledge. This knowledge as a whole can only be kept by memorizing. Therefore, it becomes difficult to students to find ties, relations, adequacy, and etc between knowledge. Logic modeling of the structures of knowledge allows building a structure of subjective knowledge in the scheme of integrity. Study of the structures in this scheme allows the students to build his knowledge adequately and hold them in a manner of the logic operation of thinking.

## 4. Building a formal logic model of a language on the basis of the logic of integrity by Piaget

The model of natural intelligence was established by Piaget. The logic integrity of J. Piaget or the work of sense, at an operational level, that is the level of formal logic, is the work of human brain.

Piaget developed this model in a natural language. Hence, we can say that if the cognitive logic is established in a natural language, then this natural language itself can be adequately and logically structured. Building of a fuzzy-logic language model will be constructed on the basis of Russian by the logic of integrity.

1. By terms of **"groups"** and **"grouping"**, Piaget define a certain equilibrium form of intellectual operations, that is, actions interiorized and organized in the **structure of integrity** (Ж.Пиаже 2001).

The **structure of integrity** of Russian comprises of 10 parts of speech.

**Note: In Russian,** 6 of the parts of speech are independent and 4 of them are supportive. Independent parts of speech are the noun, the adjective, the numeral, the pronoun, the verb and the adverb, and the support parts of speech are the proposition, the conjunction, the interjection and the determiners.

The act of intelligence organized in the holistic structure is transferred by holistic structures of Russian. In this case, these actions are transferred by the holistic structure of Russian.

2. Piaget established 4 stipulations for the "groups" of mathematical order and 5 stipulations for "groupings" of quality orders.

According to a psychological theory of Piaget, **"groups" and "groupings"** definitions compare the following definitions of the Grammar of Russian:

"Groups" and "groupings" fall in the framework of integrity. Within the framework of integrity, there are 10 parts of speech in the language. Piaget consecutively compares the psychological definition of "groups" with the parts of speech in Russian (at the same time, in any language).

Hence, the operational "groups" of the natural language will be 10. Encoding these groups or the parts of speech, that is, altering the logical operation, we get the following holistic structure of the language:

1 -Noun; 2 – Adjective; 3 – Numeral; 4 – Pronoun; 5 – Verb; 6 – Adverb; 7 – Proposition; 8 – Conjunction; 9 – Interjection; and 10 – Determiner

**1 ----2----3----4----5----6----7----8----9----10**

We will consider **"the groupings" in this holistic structure of the language** as word groups bearing common features. For example: *2* **----***3* **----***4***----***5***---**, *6* **–** are grouped as words approached to an object;

Groupings *7----8----9----10* are supportive words, which are not used independently. At the same time, in these "groupings", the parts of speech can be combined with each other in terms of relations and features, that is, within the framework of the holistic system in a new arrangement, related to quality.

For example: **1 ----2; 3 ----4; 1 ----5; 5 ----6; 3 ----4; 4 ----5,** etc.

**Note:** 1 ----2; 3 ----4; 4 ----5 coincide with each other in terms of gender, quantity and the cases of noun).

3. The way of "grouping"

**How are these psychological rules of Piaget interpreted and compared with the language rules?**

- Two of the elements of "Grouping" may coincide with each other and as a result, may form a new element or a new unit of knowledge.

From the point of a language, it is understood like this:

For example: **new - 2; home – 1.** Combination of 1 – noun (**home**) and 2 – adjective (**new)** forms a new element of knowledge – phrase of **new home;**

*Two* relations A >B> C may be A >C, where they exist.

For example, 1 - *egg* 5 - ***broils*** 6 – ***light***: can also be expressed like this: ***1 – light 6 – egg light egg.***

***Note:*** *Although the verb defines the action of an object and the adjective defines the character of the action, the adverb defines the character of the noun.*

- All forms of transformation are available. For example, new home; if we separate these phrases, we can get the followings: 2 – new; 1 – home;
- The composition of the operations is "associated". A physical definition of composition is commented as consideration of the roles of "groupings", that is, the parts of speech from the points of morphology and syntax.

For example: A strong wind started to blow in the morning. In this sentence, from the point of point morphology, ***strong*** *– is a supportive pat of the speech and* ***wind*** *is a key part.* From the point of syntax, *the phrase of strong wind* is a sequence, that is? These words coincide in terms of gender, quantity and case of noun.

- An operation united with its repeated operation, it is cancelled, for example:

***Home (noun in singular) + home (noun in singular) = homes (noun in plural) repeated operation - homes = home (noun in singular).***

- Identical operation – In the knowledge of language, it reconciles the combination of two simple sentences or words in a complex sentence or phrase.

For example: **The sky suddenly got darkened. It started raining strongly. Suddenly the sky got darkened and it started raining strongly ...**

## 5. Forming of groupings or the parts of speech

The system of "groupings" is formed through, so-called, logical operations. The logical operations of thinking are understood in the context of language meanings as logical units for conversion or consecutive exercises.

Such operations are implemented as follows:

- A present cluster of words are classified and are subjected to seriation:

***книга, стол, дом, земля, девочка, тетрадь, ученик,юноша, знамя, соня, лошадь, поле, окно, время, солнце. день, конь.***

***book, table, house, girl, copybook, school-child, youth, flag, dormouse, horse, field, window, time, sun, day, foal.***

1. the first operation is the operation of classification, that is, classification of words in terms of gender.

**Note:** In Russian, the nouns are divided into three genders or three categories in terms of their endings:

The feminine gender includes the words with endings of **–а, -я, -ья** and **–ь**. The masculine gender includes the words with no ending, with ending of **ь,** and in some words, with endings of **–а** and **–я**. The neuter gender includes the nouns with endings of **-о -е , -ье,** and in 10 words, with **–мя.**

Class 1: the words of feminine gender:

книга, земля, девочка, соня
book, land, girl, dormouse

Class 2: the words of masculine gender:

стол, ученик, юноша
table, student, youth

Class 3: the words of neuter gender:

знамя, поле, окно, время, солнце
flag, field, window, time, sun

Class 4: the words having two ways

конь, лошадь, мышь
foal, horse, mouse

**Note:** Identification of the gender of the words subject to Class 4 is performed through transformation, that is, by changing of these words in terms of cases of the noun.

*нет коня* (masculine gender) ***нет лошади*** – feminine gender
There is no foal. ***There is no horse.***

Class 5: It includes the words with ending of *–мя;* these words are declined as *nouns of neuter gender*

At the present case, the operation of classification coincides with division of nouns into gender.

2. **The second "grouping" is formed though the operation of seriation** of appropriate endings. The operation of seriation coincides with declination.

**Note:** There are three forms of declination in the grammar of Russian:

Form 1 includes the words with endings of **-а** , **-я** and **ья;**
Form 2 includes the words with no endings and endings of **-ь;**
Form 3 includes the words with endings of **-о, -е** and **–ье.**

Serial 1:

words with endings of *-а,-я* (книга (book) -feminine; земля (land) –feminine, девочка (girl) -feminine, юноша (youth) - masculine, соня (dormouse) – feminine and masculine)

The words of this serial includes the nouns of feminine gender and some words of masculine gender, with endings of –а and –я

Serial 2:

The words with no endings of the masculine gender and the words of the neuter gender with endings of –о , -е, and -ье.

стол,ученик, поле, окно, солнце.

table, student, field, window, sun

These words are transformed, that is, declined in a same manner

Serial 3:

This serial includes the words of the feminine gender with ending of **-ь** (лошадь - horse, мышь - mouse, дочь - daughter)

Serial 4:

Words with ending of –мя. There are only 10 words with such an ending in this language and they are exceptions.

The operation of seriation in Russian is subject to declination of nouns. So, Serial 1 is subject to the first declination; Serial 2 to the second declination; and Serial 3 to the second declination. Serial 4 is an exception.

The operations of classification and seriation form "groups" and "groupings". And with the remaining operations are used to form "sub-groups" and "sub-groupings".

3. **The third major operation is the operation of alteration. It replaces a definition or a word with another one. In the Russian grammar, it is equal to definitions of synonyms, antonyms and homonyms.**
4. **The fourth operation is the operation of enrichment. It has relationship uniting elements of one or another class, that is, equivalence.**

For example: *1* – школа (school), 2-новая (new); 1-- school), 3- одна (alone); 1—школа (school), 4 моя (my) 1 -школа (school); 1- школа (school) 5—строится (to be built); 5—строится (to be built) 6--- быстро (rapidly).

5. **Multiple operations** are those that are included to more than one system at a given period.

**Note:** For example: A category of declination, the number covers 1 --- 2 --- 3 ---4; and the category of number covers 1---2---3—4---5.

As said above, the structures of knowledge are divided into invariant and variable ones.

Invariant structures of knowledge are the parts of speech or the "groups".

Variable structures are categorical structures of knowledge.

**Note:** There are 10 categories of language in Russian.

While modeling subject knowledge, the invariant structures are placed in horizontals of coordinate planes, but the variable ones are placed vertically. In this coordinate plate, the parts of speech of 1,2,.....9,10 will be placed horizontally and1.2,3,.......10 language categories will be placed vertically.

While the study process, the structures of the knowledge of formal logic model of a language are subjected to logical operations of thinking.

Exactly these two important points - logical construction of knowledge and logical operations transform these separate structures of knowledge into a logical model, which is adequate to the way of building of thinking.

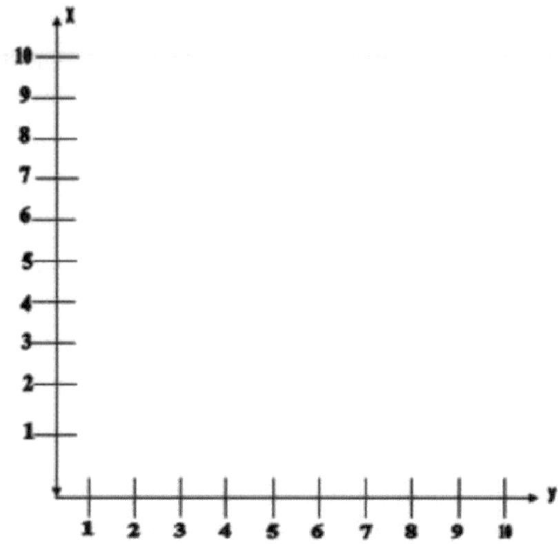


Sxem №1

## 6. Definition of Zadeh's fuzzy logic theory

Mathematical theory of fuzzy sets by *Zadeh* has allowed since more than a quarter of a century ago up to now to describe fuzzy definitions and knowledge and operate with this knowledge as well as make fuzzy outputs. (Пивкин , Бакулин и др)

The universal set is indicated by – E

Elements of a set are indicated by -- X

**R** - Indicates several properties, and *x* – indicates element **E**.

Ordinary (certain) Sub-set **A** of Universal Set **E**, whose elements

content the Property R, is indicated as the set of Ordered Pairs **A** = {$m_A$ ($x$)/$x$}, where $m_A(x)$ – *is a characteristic function,* accepting

Value 1, if *x* contents Property **R,** and vice versa **0**.

Difference of a fuzzy sub-set from a certain one is that there is not a single valued answer "yes-no" for the elements of *x* of E, regarding Property **R**.

In this respect, Fuzzy set A of Universal set **E** is indicated as the set of Ordered Pairs **A** = {$m_A$($x$ of Sub-set **A** of Universal Set **E**.

## 7. Comparison of psychological theories by Piaget with mathematical theories of Zadeh

Let us understand the term "a universal set" by Zadeh as "groups" and "groupings" or the vocabulary of a language and sign it though – E. Then, the "elements of a set" by Zadeh and "groups" by Piaget will be considered as the parts of speech. Let us sign these elements by x.

As we mentioned above, there are 10 parts of speech in Russian. Let us sign each part of speech by - x. Then x1 will be a noun, x2 - a adjective, x3 - a numeral, x4 - a pronoun, x5 - a verb, x6 - an adverb, x7 - conjunction, x8 - proposition, x9 - determiner, and x10 - interjection. Hence, Universal Set E has 10 elements x1, x2, ... x10. If we note the element of Universal Set E by 0, 1, as marks of a set, then 0,1 - the word indicates an object; 0,2 - a property of the object; 0,3 - the quantity of the object; and 0,4 points out the object; 0,5 - indicates action of the object; and 0,6 indicates a sign of the action. 0,7 is a conjunction; 0,8 is a proposition; 0,9 is a determiner; and 1 is an interjection.

The parts of speech of Russian, according to the psychological concepts by Piaget, are "groups", and according to mathematical concepts by Zadeh are "elements of a set".

**Parts of speech - "groups" - "elements of a set"**
**X - an element of Set E**
**Let us sign the properties of this element by - R**

**Note.** Each part of speech has its own properties - internal rules, which have relationship with rules of other particles of the speech, that is, elements of a set.

The **"fuzzy set"** may be presented in a form of a language vocabulary.

Then, under functions of properties of the "fuzzy set", the words will be interpreted in a direct lexical meaning. For example: *дом (house), стол (table), берег (coast), океан (ocean), and etc.*

Proceeding from concepts of linguistic variable by Zadeh , the membership function corresponds to two rules:

1. syntactical, which is set in the form of a grammar that generates the title variable in the form of language categories.
2. semantic, which determines the procedure to compute the meaning of algorithmic each value.

Then, *Y*- will indicate the grammatical rules of the language, and *X*- the parts of speech, which also have their own rules.

Rule *X* will comply with Rule *Y*, as Rule *Y* complies with Rule *X*.

Then, in this property function:

*x1*- is a noun;
*x2*- is an adjective;
*x3*- is a numeral;
*x4*- is a pronoun;
*x5* -is a verb;
*x6* - is an adverb;
x7- is a conjunction;
x8 - is a proposition;
x9 - is a determiner; and
x10 - is an interjection.
Y - are categories of a language: -
y1 - is the category of quantity - singular and plural

y2 - are the categories of gender - feminine gender (1), masculine gender (2), and neuter gender (3);
y3 - is the category of case (1-6) ;
y4 -are the categories of person;
y5 - is the category of person;
y6 - is the category of tense;
y7 - is the category of type;
y8 - is the category of declination;
y9
y10

## 8. Replacing the formal logic model of the language with the concepts of linguistic logic by Zadeh the model of formal-fuzzy logic at the example of Russian lanqiaqe

Replacing the concepts of formal logic by Piaget with the linguistic logic by Zadeh, we get the following fuzzy model of the language: (F.Bunyatova 2009]

(a) If we replace the definition of "groups" with the definition of "elements of a set", then under "set" we will consider "groups" and" groupings" within the framework of holistic.

*X1, x2,;x3....x10* will be elements of Set E

Under the "groups" will turn the whole vocabulary of the language, and Universal Set *E* - will consist of the vocabulary of Russian.

*The variable and invariant concepts will be replaced with the concepts of linguistic variable.*

*The variable concepts – are grammatical categories of the language and they will be indicated by Y.*

We can indicate the invariant concepts with X.

*The Scheme of Fuzzy Model of Language*

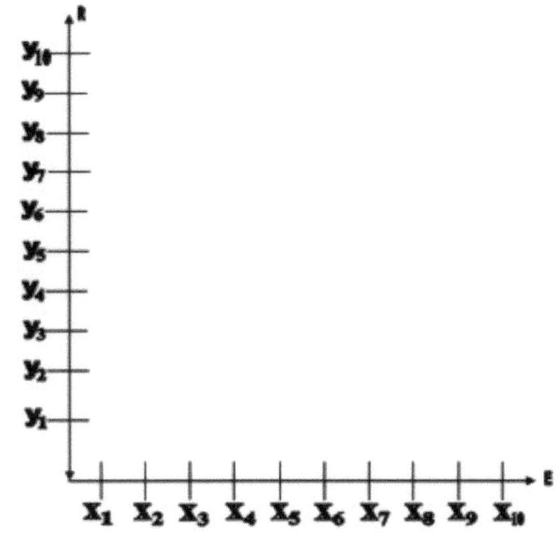


Sxem №2

**This fuzzy model of a natural language, treating** the conversion of the definition tool of the logic by Zadeh, gets the following form:

1. Fuzzy set may have an end or may be endless; as a part of speech it has an end, but as a vocabulary of a language it is endless. X = (x1, x2... – x10)
2. Fuzzy set A may be characterized by a set of pairs (composition according to the logic by Piaget): A= E *x*

For example: *x3- x1* --один мальчик (one boy) , *x2- x1* -- высокий мальчик (a tall boy) ; x1-x4 мой друг (my firend), etc.

3. Fuzzy set A may be presented in the following form:

(We present the noun in the form of A =*0,1 – игра (game): 0,1□+ 0,2-сильная игра (a strong game); 0,1+ +0,3;-*

*одна игра (a game); 0,1+ 0,4;- моя игра (my game); etc.*

4. The operation of unification

Unification of two fuzzy sets *A* and *B* will be specified as the following: if *A –1-is a noun,* and *B – 2 is an adjective,* then the function of property y*1* and y2 belongs to *A* and *B*.

*Based on the abovementioned conversion, the sentence: "На улице стоял сильный мороз" (There was heavy snow on the street) will be indicated as signs like the followings:*

x7- x1y2 y3/6 - x5y2y5-x2y1y2y3 – x1y1y2y3.

*If we present this sentence in a coordinate plane, this sentence graphically may be indicated as spots in that coordinate plane:*

x7- x1y2 y3/6 - x5y2y5-x2y1y2y3 – x1y1y2y3.

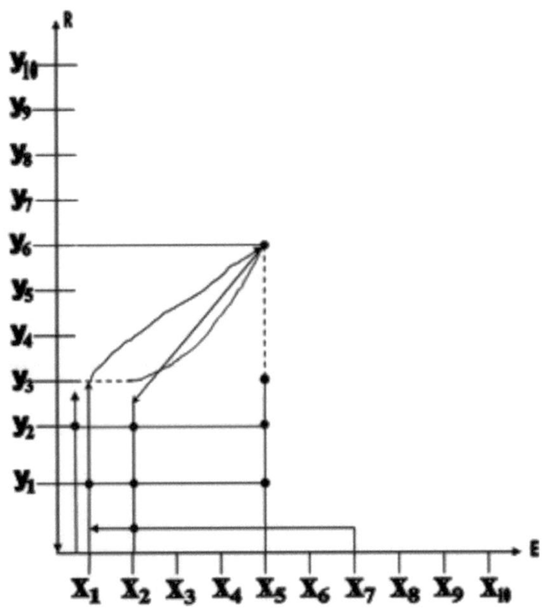

## 9. How is a model of subject knowledge built for machine learning?

In order to build a model of subject knowledge for machine learning without a teacher, the following needs to be done:

1. Divide structures of knowledge into variables that is into linguistic variables and invariant variables namely, into a universal set.
2. Invariant knowledge or universal set of knowledge is denoted by X.
3. This knowledge is classified divided into classes or elements of the set and is build on the horizontal. The resulting classes of invariant knowledge or elements of the set are denoted by x 0.1 ... x0, 9. Invariant knowledge or the set of knowledge can be finite or infinite according to the classification of the classes themselves.
4. Variable, categorical knowledge or linguistic variable are located vertically and denoted by U. They are also classified and denoted by 0.1; 0.2 and etc [3]. In work [Nordhausen and Langley, 1990] it was noted that formation of categories - is the basis of a unified theory of scientific research. Denoting classes and groups of the set, as well as categorical knowledge of a linguistic variable in number, we can present this knowledge with their properties. Each property takes a serial number. So the sentence "The day was sunny" can be defined on a coordinate plane as points: xa, 1,1 y a, 1, x a, 5, y, a 4 / 1 xa, 2 ya1 / 5. Each element of the set, for example, x0,1 is characterized by its own linguistic variable - y0,. Numerical parameters x0,1,1 by the rules of Russian grammar mean masculine noun, y0, 1 mean a single number, etc. Analogous to these characters, a set of proposals on the basis of available knowledge can be constructed. This property can be one of the justifications for machine learning without a teacher as it was derived from an example of the natural language. Each class of knowledge or element of the set is at the same time, a cluster of the structure of knowledge. They have their own rules and laws. Structures of knowledge clusters can be combined, divided, associated and canceled according to logical settings of rules of a linguistic variable. Belonging of the linguistic variable into elements of the set or the logical structures of clusters is determined by logical operations such as operation of substitution, enrichment, identical and multiplicative operations. That is, in this case as the rules of linguistic variable and the rules of elements of the set are in mobile motion all the time, by combining according to the given settings around the logical structure of knowledge or elements of the set become nanostructures of knowledge.

## 10. What innovations can bring this knowledge model in education?

1. Knowledge is considered in the scheme of integrity. Since language is a means of communication and expression of ideas, then, certainly, the conditions of integrity scheme and logic of Zadeh can be in any scientific knowledge and the rules of logic of Piaget and fuzzy logic can be applied to them.
2. Structures of knowledge will be divided into invariant and variable or into syntactic and semantic. Numeric designation of categorical and invariant properties of knowledge makes it possible to build coordinates of knowledge on the basis of which the process of knowledge construction will go.
3. Operationality of thinking enables to collect structures of knowledge into clusters, figure out their interrelationship and attitudes, classify them, enrich, or replace with the other structures. These logical operations gather as a magnet around the structures of

knowledge relating to them relevant knowledge and turn them into a nanostructure of knowledge.

4. The logic of integrity by Piaget and fuzzy logic by Zadeh break down the traditional vertical construction of structures of knowledge and arrange them into a horizontal structure (Ф.Бунятова 1990) Such construction of knowledge based on psychology, pedagogy, and high technology, in its turn makes nanopsychopedagogical approach to training (F.Bunyatova 2009)].

## 11. References

Gordon Dryden&DR.Jannette Voz (2000) The learning revolution. The learning web.

F.Bunyatova IETC(2009) Ankara, Turkey Constructive teaching technology and perspectives of nanopsychopedagogy. Ankara, Turkey

Ф. Д. Бунятова. (01.07.02).Baku Применение нечётной логики в образовательных технологиях CopyrightAgency of the Azerbaijan Republic № 328

Ф.Д.Бунятова (2007) Педагогическая технология. Конструктивное обучение. URLwww. Eidos-internet-magazine.

Ф.Д. Бунятова. AICT-2009 Baku . Логика целостности, нечетка логика и моделирование содержания предметных знаний.

Ф. Д. Бунятова. (1990) Баку Логический способ обучения. Альтернативное образование.Баку 1990 Маариф

Жан Пиаже. ( 2001) Москва. Избранные труды.

В. Я. Пивкин, Е. П. Бакулин, Д. И. Кореньковa Нечеткие множества в системах управления. URL www. allmath.ru/appliedmath

Лотфи Аскер Заде. (1976). Москва. Мир.Понятие лингвистической переменной и его применение к принятию приближенных решений

F. C. Bunyatova, (2008) Bakı Konstruktiv təlim. Mahiyyəti, prinsip, vəzifələr və dərslərdən numunələr

Р. А. Алиев, (1999) Баку Soft computering. Баку. АзДНА.

Ф. Д. Бунятова. (2001) Жан Пиаже в школе. Elmi axtarışlar. Bakı.

Nordhausen and Langley, 1990 URL.www.filosof.historic.ru/books

# 8

# Morphosyntactic Linguistic Wavelets for Knowledge Management

Daniela López De Luise
*Universidad de Palermo*
*Argentina*

## 1. Introduction

Morphosyntactics studies grammatical categories and linguistic units that have both morphological and syntactic properties. In its proscriptive form, morphosyntactics describes the set of rules that govern linguistic units whose properties are definable by both morphological and syntactic paradigms.

Thus, morphosyntactics establishes a commons framework for oral and written language that guides the process of externally encoding ideas produced in the mind. Speech is an important vehicle for exchanging thoughts, and phonetics also has a significant influence on oral communication. Hearing deficiency causes a leveling and distortion of phonetic processes and hinders morphosyntactic development, particularly when present during the second and third years of life (Kampen, 2005).

Fundamental semantic and ontologic elements of speech become apparent though word usage. For example, the distance between successive occurrences of a word has a distinctive Poisson distribution that is well characterized by a stretched exponential scaling (Altmann, 2004). The variance in this analysis depends strongly on semantic type, a measure of the abstractness of each word, and only weakly on frequency.

Distribution characteristics are related to the semantics and functions of words. The use of words provides a uniquely precise and powerful lens into human thought and activity (Altmann, 2004). As a consequence, word usage is likely to affect other manifestations of collective human dynamics.

### 1.1 Words may follow Zipf's empirical law

Zipf's empirical law was formulated using mathematical statistics. It refers to the fact that many types of data studied in the physical and social sciences can be approximated with a Zipfian distribution, one of a family of related discrete power law probability distributions (Figure 1)[1] (Wolfram, 2011).

---

[1] In the English language, the probability of encountering the $r^{th}$ most common word is given roughly by $P(r)=0.1/r$ ($r>1000$).

There is no theoretical proof that Zipf's law applies to most languages (Brillouin, 2004), but Wentian Li (Li, 1992) demonstrated empirical evidence supporting the validity of Zipf's law in the domain of language. Li generated a document by choosing each character at random from a uniform distribution including letters and the space character. Its words follow the general trend of Zipf's law. Some experts explain this linguistic phenomenon as a natural conservation of effort in which speakers and hearers minimize the work needed to reach understanding, resulting in an approximately equal distribution of effort consistent with the observed Zipf distribution (Ferrer, 2003).

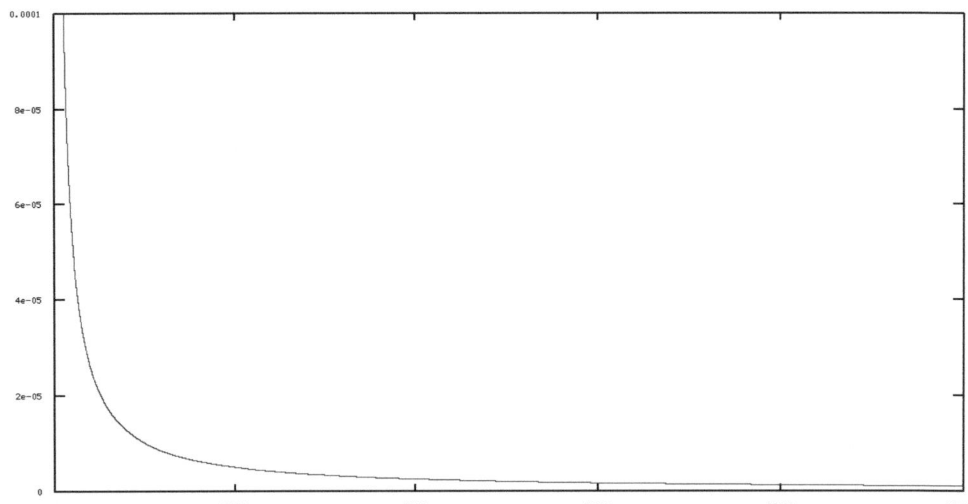


Fig. 1. Zipf's law for English

Whatever the underlying cause of this behavior, word distribution has established correspondences between social activities and natural and biological phenomena. As language is a natural instrument for representation and communication (Altmann, 2004), it becomes a particularly interesting and promising domain for exploration and indirect analysis of social activity, and it offers a way to understand how humans perform conceptualization. Word meaning is directly related to its distribution and location in context. A word's position is also related to its thematic importance and its usefulness as a keyword (López De Luise, 2008b, 2008c). This kind of information (recurrence, distribution and position) is strongly correlated with morphosyntactic analysis and strongly supports "views of human conceptual structure" in which all concepts, no matter how abstract, directly or indirectly engage contextually specific experience tracing language in the ever larger digital databases of human communications can be a most promising tool for tracing human and social dynamics". Thus, morphosyntactic analysis offers a new and promising tool for the study of dynamic social interaction. (Altmann, 2004).

### 1.2 Why morphosyntactic wavelets?

The evidence that wavelets offer the best description of such morphosyntactic decomposition is revealed by comparing the details of both traditional and morphosyntactical analyses.

| ID | Topic | Traditional wavelet | MLW |
|---|---|---|---|
| 1 | application | just for signals[I] | any text[II] |
| 2 | type of transformation | mathematical | heuristic/statistical |
| 3 | goal | highlight, reinforce and obtain further information that is not readily available in the raw signal | extraction of information that highlights and reinforce knowledge that is not readily available in the raw text |
| 4 | time-domain signals | measured as a function of time. They have not undergone any transformation | they are analogous to the knowledge structure model (Hisgen, 2010). The sequence of the sentences is essential for contextualizing spoken/written words |
| 5 | frequency-domain signals | processed to transform then into a useful representation | are the $E_{ci}$, that represent sentence content and retain its main features |
| 6 | unit | Frequency: the number of the oscillations per seconds in a signal, measured in Hertz (Hz, cycles per second) | $E_{ci}$ symbolizes morphosyntactic representations of sentences |
| 7 | domain | any type of data, even with sharp discontinuities[III] | any text |
| 8 | type of information | can represent signal in both the frequency and time domains[III] | also represents the time and frequency dimensions[IV] |
| 9 | scaling role | important. Can process at different scales and resolutions | represents knowledge at different levels of abstraction and detail |
| 10 | data decomposition result | decompose data x(t) into a two-dimensional function of time and frequency | decompose data into $E_{ci}$ (representation of concrete/specific knowledge) and $E_{ce}$ (abstract knowledge)[V] |
| 11 | data decomposition procedure | decompose x(t) using a "mother" wavelet W(x) | decompose using morphosyntactic rules and "mother sequence" of filters |

I. Detectable physical quantity or impulse by which information may be sent
II. Although this theory is explained in general, it has only been proved in Spanish
III. This is an advantage over the FFT alternative
IV. This is true within the MLW context, given the statements in rows 4 and 5
V. The knowledge derived from the filtering processing is called $E_{ce}$ in the MLW context

Table 1. Traditional wavelets versus MLW

Figure 2 shows a graphical comparison between a signal and its FFT. Figure 3 is a linguistic version: $E_{ci}$ and ER. The graphics in Figure 2 represent the original signal (time-domain) and the resulting FFT decomposition (Lahm, 2002). The images in Figure 3 represent a translated original Spanish text (content from wikipedia.org, topic Topacio) transformed into an $E_{ci}$ (López De Luise, 2007) that models dialog knowledge. (Hisgen, 2010) Statistical modeling of knowledge is beyond the scope of this chapter, but additional information is available in (López De Luise, 2005, 2008, 2008b, 2008c, 2007b, 2007c).

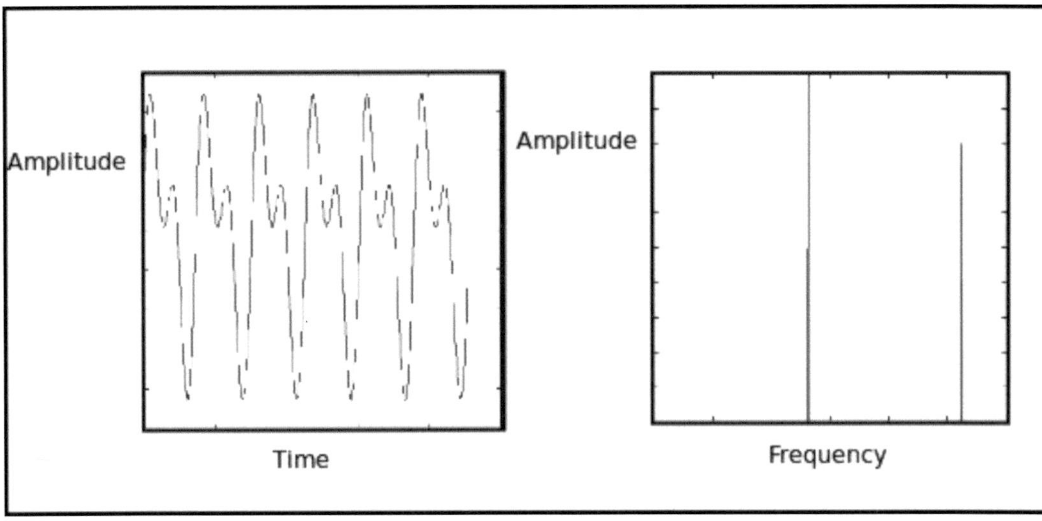


Fig. 2. Signal and frequency decomposition

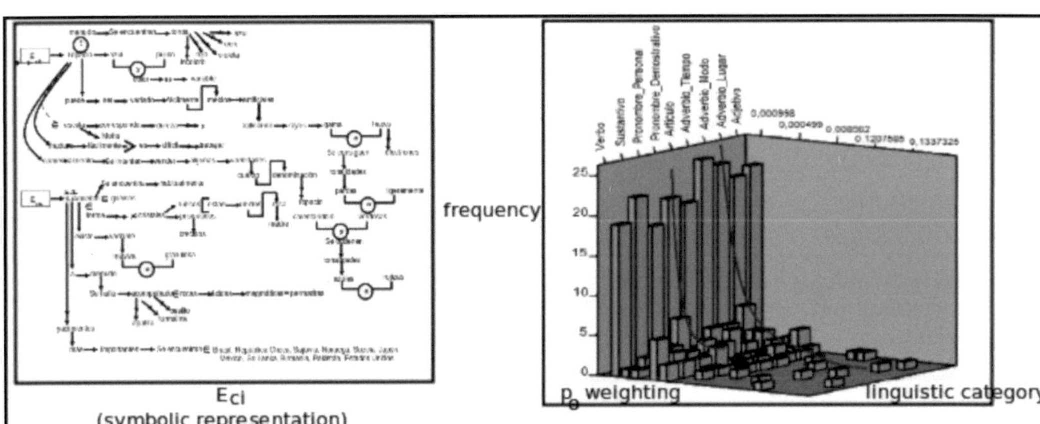


Fig. 3. Original text and knowledge structure model

Figure 4 shows a sample wavelet decomposition. It is a signature decomposition using a Daubechies wavelet, a wavelet specially suited for this type of image. Figure 5 shows a MLW decomposition of a generic text. There, $C_i$, and $C_{j,k}$ stand for abstract knowledge and $F_m$ represents filters. This Figure will be described further in the final section.

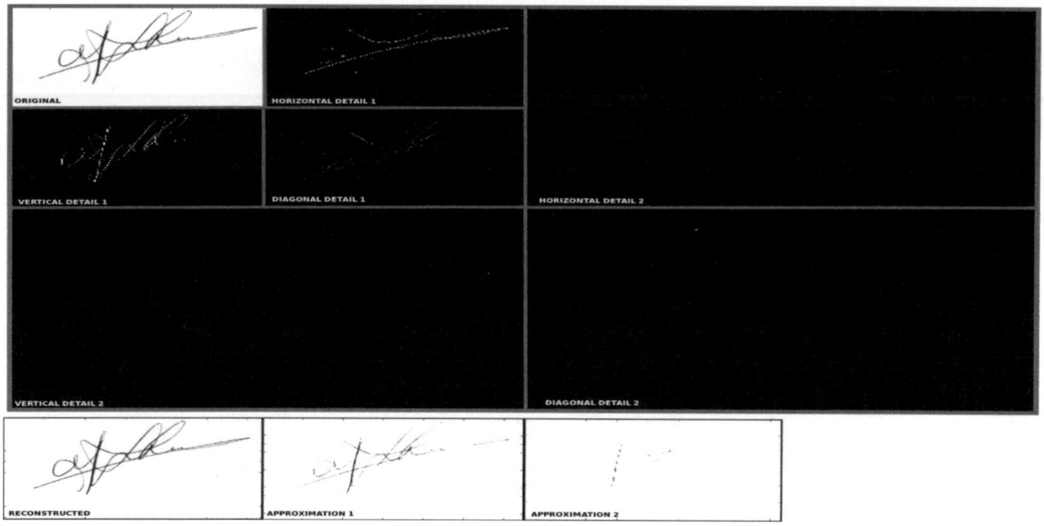


Fig. 4. Traditional wavelet decomposition

## 2. Technical overview

### 2.1 Wavelets

Wavelets are mathematical tools that are used to decompose/transform data into different components (coefficients) that describe different levels of detail (Lahm, 2002). Thus, they can extract the main features of a signal while simultaneously and independently analyzing details.

These tools have been applied to several problems, including the challenges of linguistic information retrieval. For example, wavelets have been used to build a Fuzzy Wavelet Neural Network (FWNN) for decision making over multiple criteria (Chen, 2008). In that analysis, custom built linguistic labels were used to represent information about events and situations and were processed with the FWNN.

Wavelets are sometimes used to replace linguistic analysis. For example, Tolba (Tolba, 2005) used consonant and vowel segmentation to develop automatic speech recognition for Arabic speech without linguistic information. Segmentation was performed with a combination of wavelet transformation and spectral analysis.

Hui and Wanglu combined the Linguistic Cloud Model (LCM) with wavelets to produce Advanced Synthetic Aperture Radar (ASAR) image target detection (Hui, 2008). This approach first solves image segmentation, avoids noise and recovers errors. Then, it uses LCM to solve the uncertainty of pixels. Representation using LCM bridges the gap between qualitative knowledge and quantitative knowledge, and it is thus used to map linguistic terms with contextually specific meaning to numeric processing.

### 2.2 Comparison between MLW and traditional wavelets

To demonstrate the concept of MLW and its relationship to its traditional counterpart, this table summarizes the main characteristics that unite or distinguish them:

| characteristic | morphosyntactic | traditional wavelet |
|---|---|---|
| goal | content description and classification with granularities | scaled decomposition |
| scaling | concept abstraction and ontology classification | reduced and representative signal |
| Uses | Extract the main concept of a signal | extract the main features of a signal |
| | summarization | compression |
| | manage spelling and some grammatical errors | De-noising |
| | Complement knowledge | Reconstruct portions of a corrupted signal |
| Types of wavelets | Depends on the specific sequence of filters | depends on the functions used as mother function |
| | auto-fitting | Must be manually detected according to results |

Table 2. Characteristics of traditional wavelets and MLW

### 2.3 Linguistic cloud model and MLW

LCM models linguistic knowledge (Li, 2000) using a set of predefined, customized fuzzy linguistic variables. These variables are generated in accordance with two rules:

1. *The atom generation rule* specifies the manner in which a linguistic "atom" may be generated. An atom is a variable that cannot be sliced into smaller parts.
2. *The semantic rule* specifies the procedure by which composite linguistic terms are computed from linguistic atoms. In addition, there are connecting operators ("and" "or", etc.), modifiers ("very" "quite", etc.) and negatives that are treated as soft operators that modify an operand's (atom's) meaning to produce linguistic "terms".

The MSW and the LCM share a common goal. However, the MSW replaces the manual procedure used to obtain linguistic atoms with automated processing that determines an atom's linguistic category (e.g., noun or verb) (López De Luise, 2007d, 2008c). The result is not an atom or a term but is a structure named $E_{ci}$ (an acronym from the Spanish, Estructura de Composición Interna). The $E_{ci}$ is used to model the morphosyntactic configuration within sentences (López De Luise, 2007; Hisgen, 2010). Thus, the core processing is based on $E_{ci}$ structures instead of linguistic variables. An $E_{ci}$ is a plastic representation that can evolve to reflect more detailed information regarding the represented portion of text. While atoms cannot be sliced, any $E_{ci}$ can be partitioned as required during the learning process. Further differences between the LCM and the MSW are shown in Table 3.

### 2.4 Morphosyntactics as a goal

Most morphological and syntactical processing is intended for information retrieval, while alignment supports automatic translation. Those approaches are mainly descriptive and are defined by cross-classifying different varieties of features (Harley, 1994) such as number and person. When morphological operations are an autonomous subpart of the derivation, they acquire a status beyond descriptive convenience. They become linguistic primitives, manipulated by the rules of word formation.

| | LCM | MSW |
|---|---|---|
| Basis | Atom | $E_{ci}$ |
| Characteristics of the unit of processing | Cannot be sliced | Can be sliced |
| | Represents the meaning of a word | Represents morphosyntactic characteristics of a sentence |
| | Fixed | Can evolve |
| | Hand made | Automatically extracted |
| Rules | Atom generation rule | Morphosyntactic rules |
| | Semantic rules | Clustering filters |
| Semantic | Directly manipulated by term definitions | Indirectly manipulated by clustering filtering and morphosyntactic context |

Table 3. Comparison Between the LCM and the MSW

In many approaches, they are manipulated as an undifferentiated bundle divided only into nominal and verbal atoms. The following section describes elements of the morphosyntactic approach.

### 2.4.1 Detecting language tendencies

Language tendencies denote cultural characteristics, which are represented as dialects and regional practices. Noyer (Noyer, 1992) described a hierarchical tree organization defined by applying manually predefined morphological feature filters to manage morphological contrasts. They used this organization as an indicator of linguistic tendencies in language usage. Extensions of this approach attempt to derive the geometry of morphological features[2] (Harley, 1994, 1998), with the goal of classifying features into subgroups based on an universal geometry while accounting for universals in feature distribution and realization. In MLW, the structure of the information is organized in a general oriented graph ($E_{ci}$ structure) for only the smallest unit of processing (a sentence), and a hierarchy is defined by a chained sequence of clustering filters (Hisgen, 2010). Language tendencies are therefore visible in the configuration of a current graph.

### 2.4.2 Sentence generation

Morphosyntax has also been used to implement a language sentence generator. In an earlier study (Martínez López, 2007), Spanish adverbial phrases were analyzed to extract the reusable structures and discard the remainder, with the goal of using the reusable subset to generate new phrases. Interestingly, the shortest, simplest structures presented the most productive patterns and represented 45% of the corpus.

Another study (López De Luise, 2007) suggested translating Spanish text, represented by sets of $E_{ci}$, into a graphic representing the main structure of the content. This structure was

[2] This is a well-known method that is used to model phonological features (Clements, 1985) (Sagey, 1986)

tested with 44 subjects (López De Luise, 2005). The results showed that this treatment, even without directly managing semantics, could communicate the original content. Volunteers were able to reconstruct the original text content successfully in 100% of the cases. As MLW is based on $E_{ci}$ structure, it follows that it:

- represents keywording well.
- performs well independent of an individual's knowledge on a specific subject.
- performs well independent of an individual's knowledge of informatics.

### 2.4.3 Language comprehension detection

As language is an expression of mind and its processes, it becomes also the expression of meaning (or lack of meaning) in general. This fact is also true when the subject is the language itself. A recent study focused on the most frequently recurrent morphosyntactic uses in a group of students who study Spanish as a foreign language (González Negrón, 2011) revealed a peculiar distribution of nouns and personal pronouns. These parts of speech were present at a higher frequency than in the speech of native speakers, probably to guarantee the reader comprehension of the text. Other findings included preposition repetition and a significant number of misplaced prepositions. Thus, morphosyntactic statistics detect deficient language understanding. A similar study was performed in (Konopka, 2008) with Mexican subjects living in Chicago (USA). In the case of MLW, the $E_{ci}$ and $E_{ce}$ structures will shape irregular language usage and make detection of incorrect language practices easy.

### 2.4.4 Semantics detection

Morphosyntactics can be used to detect certain types of semantics in a text. An analysis of vowel formant structure and vowel space dispersion revealed overall spectral reduction for certain talkers. These findings suggest an interaction between semantic and indexing factors in vowel reduction processes (Cloppera, 2008).

Two morphosyntactic experimental studies of numeral quantifiers in English (*more than* k, *at least* k, *at most* k, and *fewer than* k) (Koster-Moeller, 2008) showed that Generalized Quantifier Theory (GQT)[3] must be extant to manage morphosyntactic differences between denotationally equivalent quantifiers. The formal semantic is focused on the correct set of entailment patterns of expressions but is not concerned with deep comprehension or real-time verification. However, certain systematic distinctions occur during real-time comprehension. The degree of compromise implicit in a semantic theory depends on the types of semantic primitives it assumes, and this also influences its ability to treat these phenomena. In (López De Luise, 2008b), sentences were processed to automatically obtain specific semantic interpretations. The shape of the statistics performed over the $E_{ci}$'s internal weighting value (named $p_o$) is strongly biased by the semantics behind sentence content.

---

[3] Generalized Quantifier Theory is a logical semantic theory that studies the interpretation of noun phrases and determinants. The formal theory of generalized quantifiers already existed as a part of mathematical logic (Mostowski, 1957), and it was implicit in Montague Grammar (Montague, 1974). It has been fully developed by Barwise & Cooper (1981) and Keenan & Stavi (Barwise, 1981) as a framework for investigating universal constraints on quantification and inferential patterns concerning quantifiers.

### 2.4.5 Improvement of translation quality/performance

Automatic translation has an important evolution. Translation quality depends on proper pairing or alignment of sources and on appropriate targeting of languages. This sensible processing be improved using morphosyntactic tools.

Hwang used morphosyntactics intensively for three kinds of language (Hwang, 2005). The pairs were matched on the basis of morphosyntactical similarities or differences. They investigated the effects of morphosyntactical information such as base form, part-of-speech, and the relative positional information of a word in a statistical machine translation framework. They built word and class-based language models by manipulating morphological and relative positional information.

They used the language pairs Japanese-Korean (languages with same word order and high inflection/agglutination[4]), English-Korean (a highly inflecting and agglutinating language with partial free word order and an inflecting language with rigid word order), and Chinese-Korean, (a highly inflecting and agglutinating language with partially free word order and a non-inflectional language with rigid word order).

According to the language pairing and the direction of translation, different combinations of morphosyntactic information most strongly improve translation quality. In all cases, however, using morphosyntactic information in the target language optimized translation efficacy. Language models based on morphosyntactic information effectively improved performance. $E_{ci}$ is an important part of the MLW, and it has inbuilt morphophonemic descriptors that contribute significantly to this task.

### 2.4.6 Speech recognition

Speech recognition requires real-time speech detection. This is problematic when modeling languages that are highly inflectional but can be achieved by decomposing words into stems and endings and storing these word subunits (morphemes) separately in the vocabulary. An enhanced morpheme-based language model has been designed for the inflectional Dravidian language Tamil (Saraswathi, 2007). This enhanced, morpheme-based language model was trained on the decomposed corpus. The results were compared with word-based bi-gram and trigram language models, a distance-based language model, a dependency-based language model and a class-based language model. The proposed model improves the performance of the Tamil speech recognition system relative to the word-based language models. The MLW approach is based on a similar decomposition into stems and endings, but it includes additional morphosyntactical features that are processed with the same importance as full words (for more information, see the last sections). Thus, we expect that this approach will be suitable for processing highly inflectional languages.

---

[4] This term was introduced by Wilhelm von Humboldt in 1836 to classify languages from a morphological point of view. An agglutinative language is a language that uses agglutination extensively: most words are formed by joining morphemes together. A morpheme is the smallest component of a word or other linguistic unit that has semantic meaning.

## 3. Morphosyntactic linguistic wavelet approach

### 3.1 A sequential approach to wavelets

Because language is complex, soft decomposition into a set of base functions (as in traditional wavelets) is a multi-step process with several components.

Developing numeric wavelets usually includes the following steps:

1. Take the original signal sample
2. Apply filtering (decomposition using the mother wavelet)
3. Analyze coefficients defined by the basis function
4. If the granularity and details are inadequate for the current problem, repeat from step 2
5. Take the resulting coefficients as a current representation of the signal

Language requires additional steps, which are described in more detail in the following section. In brief, these steps are:

1. Take the original text sample
2. Compress and translate text into an oriented graph ($E_{ci}$) preserving most morphosyntactic properties
3. Apply filtering using the most suitable approach
4. If abstraction granularity and details are insufficient for the current problem
   4.1 Insert a new filter, $E_{ce}$, in the knowledge organization
   4.2 Repeat from step 3
5. Take the resulting sequence of filtering as a current representation of the knowledge about and ontology of the text
6. Take the resulting $E_{ci}$ as the internal representation of the new text event

A short description of the MLW steps is presented below, with an example in the Use case.

### 3.2 Details of the MLW process

Further details of the MLW process are provided in this section, with the considerations relevant to each step included.

#### 3.2.1 Take the original text sample

Text can be extracted from Spanish dialogs, Web pages, documents, speech transcriptions, and other documents. The case study in the section 4 uses dialogs, transcriptions, and other documents. Several references mentioned in this chapter were based on Web pages.

#### 3.2.2 Compress and translate text into an oriented graph (Called $E_{ci}$) preserving most morphosyntactic properties

Original text is processed using predefined and static tables. The main components of this step are as follows:

- Filter useless morphemes[5] using reference tables.

[5] Syntagm (linguistics) is any sequenced combination of morphologic elements that is considered a unit, has stability and is commonly accepted by native speakers.

- Extract morphosyntactic descriptors (numeric values automatically extracted, such as the number of vowels) for each word processed. Words were previously represented by Porter's Stemming, but this tool does not have enough classification power for use as a sole instrument. Morphosyntactic descriptors are required to process text with sufficient confidence levels (López De Luise, 2007d).
- Collapse syntagmas into a condensed internal representation (usually, selected morphemes[6]). The resulting representation is called EBH (Estructura Básica Homogénea, uniform basic structure). EBHs are linked with specific connectors.
- Calculate and set the morphosyntactic weighting $p_o$ for $E_{ci}$.

More details of each of these steps are outside of the scope of this chapter (but see (López De Luise, 2008c) and (López De Luise, 2008)).

### 3.2.3 Apply filtering using the most suitable approach

Since knowledge management depends on previous language experiences, filtering is dynamic process that adapts itself to current cognitive capabilities. Furthermore, as shown in the Case Study section, filtering is a very sensitive step in the MLW transformation.

Filtering is a process composed of several filters. The current paper includes the following three clustering algorithms: Simple K-means, Farthest First and Expectation Maximization (Witten, 2005). They are applied sequentially for each new $E_{ce}$. When an $E_{ce}$ is "mature", the filter no longer changes.

The distance used to evaluate clustering is based on the similarity between the descriptor values and the internal morphosyntactic metric, $p_o$, that weights EBH (representing morphemes). It has been shown that clusters generated with $p_o$ represent consistent word agglomerations (López De Luise, 2008, 2008b). Although this chapter does not use fuzzy clustering algorithms, it is important to note that such filters require a specific adaptation for distance using the categorical metrics defined in (López De Luise, 2007e).

### 3.2.4 If "Abstraction" granularity and details are inadequate for the current problem

Granularity is determined by the ability to discriminate the topic and by the degree of detail required to represent the $E_{ci}$. In the MLW context it is the logic distance between the current $E_{ci}$ and the $E_{ce}$ partitions[7] (see Figure 5). This distance depends on the desired learning approach. In the example included herein (Section 4), it is the number of elements in the $E_{ci}$ that fall within each $E_{ce}$ partition. The distribution of EBHs determines whether a new $E_{ce}$ is a necessary. When the EBHs are too irregular, a new $E_{ce}$ is built per step 3.2.4.1. Otherwise the new $E_{ci}$ is added to the partition that is the best match.

#### 3.2.4.1 Insert a new filter, $E_{ce}$, in the knowledge organization

The current $E_{ce}$ is cleaned so that it keeps all the $E_{ci}$s that best match its partitions, and a new $E_{ce}$ that includes all the $E_{ci}$s that are not well represented is created and linked.

[6] A meaningful linguistic unit that cannot be divided into smaller meaningful parts.
[7] Partition in this context is a cluster obtained after the filtering process.

**3.2.4.2 Repeat from step 3.2.3**

### 3.2.5 Take the resulting sequence of filtering as a current representation of the knowledge about and ontology of the text

The learned $E_{ci}$'s ontology is distributed along the chain of $E_{ce}$s.

### 3.2.6 Take the resulting $E_{ci}$ as the internal representation of the new text event

The specific acquired, concrete knowledge is now condensed in the $E_{ci}$. This provides a good representation of the original text and its keywording (López De Luise, 2005).

Real texts include contradictions and ambiguities. As previously shown (López De Luise, 2007b), they are processed and handled despite potentially inadequate contextual information. The algorithm does not include detailed clause analysis of or encode linguistic knowledge about the context because these components complicate the process and make it less automatic.

Furthermore, using the $p_o$ metric can distinguish the following Writing Profiles: general document, Web forum, Web index and blogs. This metric is therefore independent of document size and mentioned text styles (López De Luise, 2007c). Consequently, it is useful to define the quality of the text that is being learned and to decide whether to accept it as a source of knowledge.

## 3.3 Gelernter's perspective on reasoning

Section 3.2.3. defines that the clustering algorithms must be used first hard clusterings and afterwards fuzzy. It is not a trivial restriction. Its goal is to organize learning across a range from specific concrete data to abstract and fuzzy information. The filters are therefore organized as a sequence from simple k-means clustering to fuzzy clustering. This approach is compatible with Gelernter's belief that thinking is not a static algorithm that applies to every situation. Thinking requires a set of diverse algorithms that are not limited to reasoning. Some of these algorithms are sharp and deep, allowing clear manipulation of concrete objects, but there are other algorithms with different properties.

David Gelernter Theory (Gelernter, 2010) states that thinking is not the same as reasoning. When your mind wanders, you are still thinking. Your mind is still at work. This free association is an important part of human thought. No computer will be able to think like a man unless it can perform free association.

People have three common misconceptions:

### 3.3.1 The belief that "thinking" is the same as "reasoning"

There are several activities in the mind that are not reasoning. The brain keeps working even when the mind is wandering.

### 3.3.2 The belief that reality and thoughts are different and separated things

Reality is conceptualized as external while the mental landscape created by thoughts is seen as internal and mental. According to Gelernter, both are essentially the same although the attentional focus varies.

### 3.3.3 The separation of the thinker and the thought

Thinking is not a PowerPoint presentation in which the thinker watches the stream of his thoughts. When a person is dreaming or hallucinating, the thinker and his thought-stream are not separate. They are blended together. The thinker inhabits his thoughts.

Gelernter describes thinking as a spectrum of many methods that alternate depending on the current attentional focus. When the focus is high, the method is analytic and sharp. When the brain is not sharply focused, emotions are more involved and objects become fuzzy. That description is analogous to the filtering restriction: define sharp clustering first and leave fuzzy clustering approaches for the final steps. As Gelernter writes, "No computer will be creative unless it can simulate all the nuances of human emotion."

## 4. Case study

This section presents a sample case to illustrate the MLW procedure. The database is a set of ten Web pages with the topic "Orchids". From more than 4200 original symbols and morphemes in the original pages, 3292 words were extracted; 67 of them were automatically selected for the example. This section shows the sequential MLW decomposition. Table 4 shows the filtering results for the first six $E_{ci}$s.

### 4.1 Build $E_{ci}1$

Because the algorithm has no initial information about the text, we start with a transition state and set the d parameter to 20%. This parameter assesses the difference in the number of elements between the most and least populated partitions.

### 4.2 Apply filters to $E_{ci}1$

The K-means clustering, in the following KM, is used as the first filter with settings N= 5 clusters, seed 10. Diff=16%<d. Keep KM as the filter.

### 4.3 Apply filters to $E_{ci}2$

Filter using KM with the same settings, and the current Diff=11%<d. Keep KM as the filter.

### 4.4 Apply filters to $E_{ci}3$

Filter using KM with the same settings, and the current Diff=10%<d. Keep KM as the filter and exit the transition state.

### 4.5 Apply filters to $E_{ci}4$

Filter using KM with d=10% for steady state. This process will indicate whether to change the filter or build a new $E_{ce}$. Clustering settings are the same, and the current Diff=20%>d. Change to Farthest First (FF) as the filter.

### 4.6 Apply filters to $E_{ci}5$

Filter using FF with clustering settings N=5 clusters, seed 1. The current Diff=45%>d. Change to Expectation Maximization (EM) as the next filter.

### 4.7 Apply filters to $E_{ci}6$

Filter using EM. The clustering settings are min stdDev :1.0E-6, num clusters: -1 (automatic), seed: 100. The current Diff=13%>d, Log likelihood: -18.04546. Split $E_{ce}$ and filter the more cohesive[8] subset of $E_{ci}$s using EM. Log likelihood: -17.99898, diff=8.

| Cluster | $E_{ci}1$ | $E_{ci}2$ | $E_{ci}3$ | $E_{ci}4$ | $E_{ci}5$ | $E_{ci}6$ | $E_{ci}6^*$ |
|---|---|---|---|---|---|---|---|
| 0 | 1 ( 17%) | 3 ( 33%) | 3 ( 20%) | 3 ( 20%) | 2 ( 6%) | 13 ( 29%) | 8 ( 18%) |
| 1 | 1 ( 17%) | 1 ( 11%) | 5 ( 33%) | 5 ( 33%) | 4 ( 11%) | 7 ( 16%) | 8 ( 18%) |
| 2 | 1 ( 17%) | 2 ( 22%) | 2 ( 13%) | 2 ( 13%) | 9 ( 26%) | 11 ( 24%) | 12 ( 26%) |
| 3 | 2 ( 33%) | 2 ( 22%) | 3 ( 20%) | 3 ( 20%) | 18 ( 51%) | 14 ( 31%) | 8 ( 18%) |
| 4 | 1 ( 17%) | 1 ( 11%) | 2 ( 13%) | 2 ( 13%) | 2 ( 6%) | | 9 ( 20%) |
| diff | 16,00% | 11,00% | 10,00% | 20,00% | 45,00% | 13,00% | 8,00% |

*This is the result of EM to define the splitting of $E_{ce}1$.

Table 4. Filtering results for each $E_{ci}$

### 4.8 Build $E_{ce}2$ to $E_{ci}6$

Keep all the individuals as $E_{ci}1$, and put in $E_{ce}2$ the individuals in cluster 1 (one of the three less cohesive, with lower $p_o$). This procedure is shown in Figure 6.

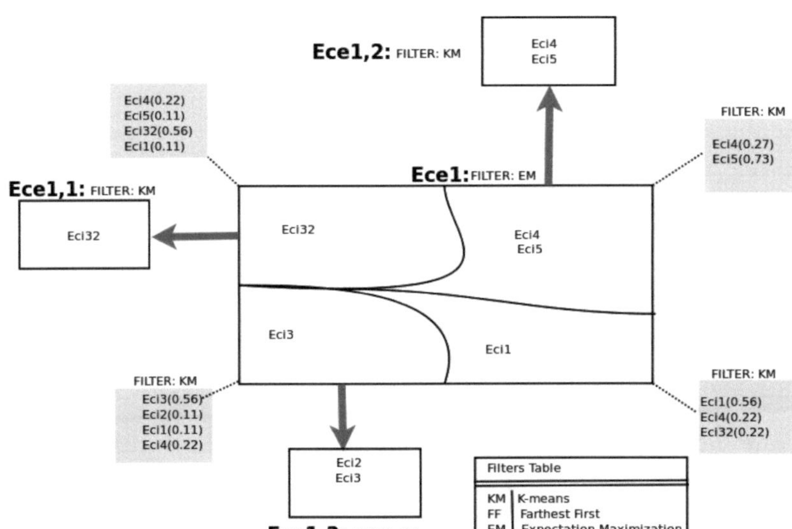


Fig. 6. $E_{ce}1$ after cleaning up the less cohesive $E_{ci}$s

[8] Cohesiveness is defined according to MLW as distance and sequence of filters. In this case it is implemented using EM forcing 5 clusters, and selecting the four clusters with more elements.

### 4.9 Apply filters to $E_{ci}7$

Detect the $E_{ce}1$ partition that best suits $E_{ci}7$ using cohesiveness criteria. The result shows that the partition that holds $E_{ci}6$ is the best. $E_{ci}7$ now hangs from this partition as indicated in Figure 7.

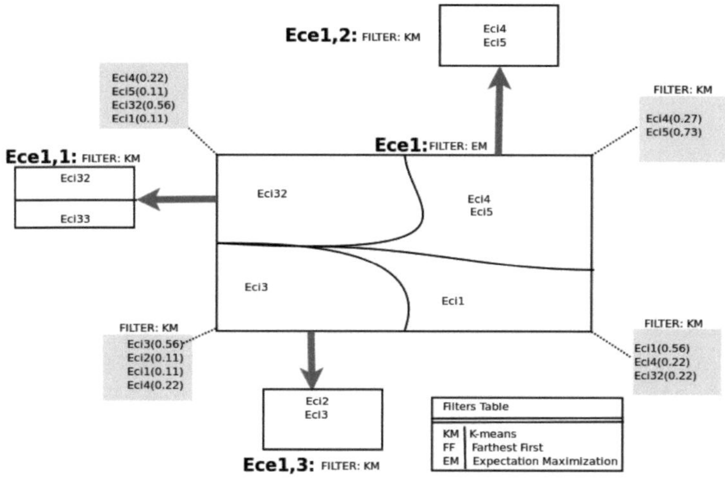


Fig. 7. $E_{ce}1,1$ hanging from $E_{ce}1$

### 4.10 Apply filters to $E_{ci}8$

Detect the $E_{ce}1$ partition that best suits $E_{ci}8$ using the same cohesiveness criteria. The partition that holds $E_{ci}5$ is the best. $E_{ce}1,1$ now contains $E_{ci}4$, $E_{ci}5$ and $E_{ci}6$. Filter $E_{ce}1,1$ using KM with clustering settings of N= 5 clusters, seed 10. The value of Diff=20%>d. Change to Farthest First (FF) as the next filter.

Now the $E_{ce}$ sequence is as indicated in Figure 8.

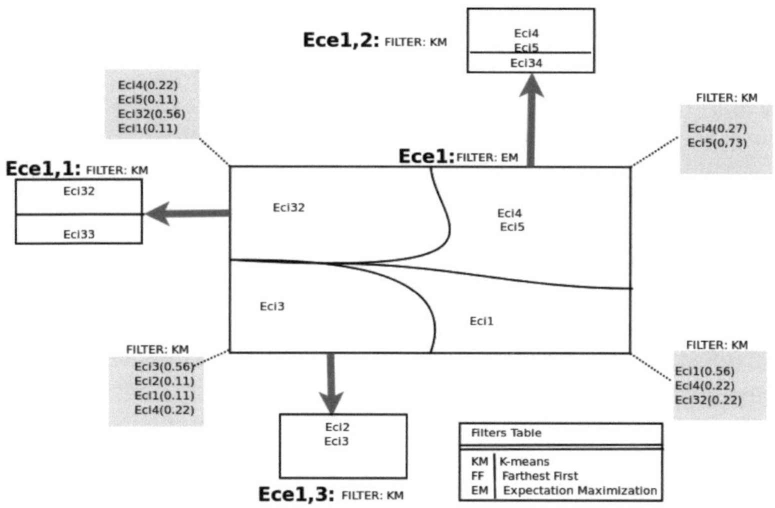


Fig. 8. $E_{ce}1$ and $E_{ce}1,1$ after learning $E_{ci}8$

### 4.11 The representation in MLW

We do not expect $E_{ce}$ content to be understood from the human point of view, but it should be considered a tool to condense and potentially regenerate knowledge from textual sources. This is a first step in the study of this type of tool that uses mathematical and statistical extraction of knowledge to automatically decompose text and represent it in a self-organizational approach.

For instance, the following sentence from the dataset,

"Dactylorhiza incarnata es orquídea de especies Europeas"
(Dactylorhiza incarnata is an European orchid species)

corresponds to the EBH number 04, and can be found (after MLW) as the sequence $E_{ce}1$-$E_{ce}1,2$-$E_{ci}4$.

If there is an interest in understanding the topic, the main entry of the set of $E_{ci}$s in the cluster can be used as a brief description. To regenerate the concepts saved in the structure for human understanding, it is only necessary to use the symbolic representation of the $E_{ci}$ (López De Luise, 2007).

## 5. Conclusion

MLW is a new approach that attempts to model natural language automatically, without the use of dictionaries, special languages, tagging, external information, adaptation for new changes in the languages, or other supports. It differs from traditional wavelets in that it depends on previous usage, but it does not require human activities to produce definitions or provide specific adaptations to regional settings. In addition, it compresses the original text into the final $E_{ci}$. However, the long-term results require further testing, both to further evaluate MLW and to evaluate the correspondence between human ontology and conceptualization and the $E_{ce}$s sequence .

This approach can be completed with the use of a $p_o$ weighting to filter the results of any query or browsing activity according to quality and to detect additional source types automatically.

It will also be important to test the use of categorical metrics for fuzzy filters and to evaluate MLW with alternate distances, filter sequences and cohesiveness parameters.

## 6. References

(Altmann,2004) E.G. Altmann, J.B. Pierrehumbert & A.E. Motter. Beyond word frequency: Bursts, lulls, and scaling in the temporal distributions of words. *PLoS ONE* 4(11): e7678. ISSN 1932-6203.

(Brillouin, 2004) L. Brillouin. La science et la théorie de l'information. Masson, Paris. *Open Library.* ISBN 10-2876470365.

(Chen, 2008) K. Chen, J. Li. Research on Fuzzy MCDM Method based on Wavelet Neural Network Model. *Information Sci. And Eng.* ISISE'08. 2008. ISBN: 978-0-7695-3494-7.

(Clements, 1985) G.N. Clements. The Geometry of Phonological Features. *Phonology Yearbook* 2. pp. 225 - 252. ISBN 9780521332323 . USA.

(Cloppera, 2008) C. G. Cloppera & J. B. Pierrehumbert. Effects of semantic predictability and regional dialect on vowel space reduction. *Journal of the Acoustical Society of America*, 124, 1682-1688. ISSN: 0001-4966. USA.

(Ferrer, 2003) R. Ferrer & R.V. Sole. Least effort and the origins of scaling in human language. *Proc. of the National Academy of Sciences* of the United States of America 100 (3): 788–791.*ISSN* 0027-8424. USA.

(Gelernter, 2010) D. Gelernter. Dream-logic, the internet and artificial thought. *EDGE*. Available in: www.edge.org

(González Negrón, 2011) N. González Negrón. Usos morfosintácticos en una muestra de exámenes de estudiantes que cursan el español como idioma extranjero. *ELENET*. N. 1. ISBN: 2-9524532-0-9. Spain.

(Harley, 1994) H. Harley. Hug a tree: deriving the morphosyntactic feature hierarchy. *MIT Working Papers in Linguistics* 21, 289-320. ISBN: 9780262561211. USA.

(Harley, 1998) H. Harley & E. Ritter. Meaning in Morphology: motivating a feature-geometric analysis of person and number. *Ms. University of Calgary & University of Pennsylvania*.

(Hisgen, 2010) D. Hisgen & D. López De Luise. Dialog Structure Automatic Modeling. *MICAI*. *ISBN* 978-3-642-16772-0. Mexico.

(Hui, 2008) H. Hui & P. Wanglu. ASAR Image target recognition based on the combined wavelet transformation. *ISPRS Congress*. Beijing, Proceedings of Commission VII. ISBN:0-7803-9051-2. South Korea.

(Hwang, 2005) Y. Hwang, T. Watanabe & Y. Sasaki. Empirical Study of Utilizing Morph-Syntactic Information in SMT. *2nd IJCNLP*. ISBN 3-540-29172-5. Korea.

(Kampen, 2005) J. Van Kampen. Morph-syntactic development and the effects on the lexicon (A comparison between normal hearing children and children with a temporary hearing deficiency. Poster. *ELA2005*. *ISBN* 9780387345871. France.

(Koster-Moeller, 2008) J. Koster-Moeller, J. Varvoutis & M. Hackl. Verification Procedures for Modified Numeral Quantifiers. *Proc. of the 27th WCCFL*. ISBN 978-1-57473-428-7. USA.

(Konopka, 2008) K. Konopka. Vowels in Contact: Mexican Heritage English in Chicago. Salsa XVI- *Texas Linguistic Forum*. 52: 94–103. *ISSN* 1615-3014. Germany.

(Lahm, 2002) Z. Lahm. Wavelets: A tutorial. University of Otago. In: Dep. Of Computer Science (2011). Available from www.cs.otago.ac.nz.

(Li, 1992) W. Li. Random Texts Exhibit Zipf's-Law-Like Word Frequency Distribution. *IEEE Trans. on Information Theory*. 38 (6): 1842–1845. ISSN: 0018-9448. USA.

(Li, 2000) D. Li, K. Di, D. Li & X. Shi. Mining Association Rules With Linguistic Cloud Models. *Journal of Software*,Vol.11, No. 2, pp.143-158.

(López De Luise, 2005) D. López De Luise. A Morphosyntactical Complementary Structure for Searching and Browsing. *CISSE 2005*. Pp. 283 - 290.*ISBN* 1-4020-5262-6. USA.

(López De Luise, 2007) D. López De Luise. Una representación alternativa para textos (Alternate representation for [Spanish] texts). *J. Ciencia y Tecnología*. Vol 6. ISSN 1850 0870. Argentina.

(López De Luise, 2007b) D. López De Luise. Ambiguity and Contradiction From a Morpho-Syntactic Prototype Perspective. *CISSE*. Bridgeport. *ISBN* 978-1-4020-8740-0. USA.

(López De Luise, 2007c) D. López De Luise. A Metric for Automatic Word categorization. *SCSS*. Bridgeport. ISBN 978-1-4020-8740-0. USA.

(López De Luise, 2007d) D. López De Luise & J. Ale. Induction Trees for automatic Word Classification. *CACIC*.

(López De Luise, 2007e) D. López De Luise. Aplicación de Métricas Categóricas en Sistemas Difusos. *IEEE LATIN AMERICA*. ISSN: 1548-0992. Brasil.

(López De Luise, 2008) D. López De Luise, M. Soffer. Modelización automática de textos en castellano. *ANDESCON*. ISBN 978-603-45345-0-6. Peru.

(López De Luise, 2008b) D. López De Luise & M. Soffer. Automatic Text processing for Spanish Texts. *CERMA 2008*. ISBN: 978-0-7695-3320. Mexico.

(López De Luise, 2008c) D. López De Luise. Mejoras en la usabilidad de la Web a través de una estructura complementaria. PhD thesis. Universidad Nacional de La Plata. Argentine.

(Martínez López, 2007) J. A. Martínez López. Patrones e índice de frecuencia en algunas locuciones adverbiales. *Forma funcion*, Bogotá. v 20. pp 59-78. ISSN 0120-338X. Colombia.

(Montague, 1974) R. Montague. *Formal Philosophy. Yale University Press*. ISBN: 0300015275. USA.

(Barwise, 1981) J. Barwise & R. Cooper. Generalized Quantifiers and Natural Language. *Linguistics and Philosophy* 4, pp. 159-219. ISBN 978-94-007-2268-2. USA.

(Mostowski, 1957) A. Mostowski. A generalization of Quantifiers. *Fundamenta Mathematicae*. vol 44. pp. 12 - 36. ISSN : 0016-2736. Polish.

(Noyer, 1992) R. Noyer. Features, Positions and Affixes in Autonomous Morphological Structure. MIT PhD dissertation. Cambridge MITWPL. USA.

(Sagey, 1986) E. Sagey. The representation of Features and Relations in Non-Linear Phonology. PhD dissertation. MIT. MITWPL. USA.

(Saraswathi, 2007) S. Saraswathi & T.V. Geetha. Comparison of Performance of Enhanced Morpheme-Based Language Model with Different Word-based Language Models for Improving the Performance of Tamil Speech Recognition System. *ACM Trans. Asian Lang. Information*. V. 6, N. 3, Article 9. ISBN: 978-1-4503-0475-7. USA.

(Tolba, 2005) M. F. Tolba, T. Nazmy, A. A. Abdelhamid & M. E. Gadallah. A novel method for Arabic consonant/vowel segmentation using wavelet transform. *IJICIS*, Vol. 5, No. 1. ISBN: 978-960-474-064-2. USA.

(Witten, 2005) I.H. Witten & E. Frank. Data Mining - *Practical Machine Learning Tools And Techniques*, 2Nd Edition. Elsevier. *ISBN*: 978-0-12-374856-0. New Zeland.

(Wolfram,2011) Zipf's Law. (2011), Wolfram Research, Inc. In: *Wolfram MathWorld*, 2011, Available from http://mathworld.wolfram.com/ZipfsLaw.html

# 9

# Intelligent Distributed eLearning Architecture

S. Stoyanov[1], H. Zedan[2], E. Doychev[1], V. Valkanov[1],
I. Popchev[1], G. Cholakov[1] and M. Sandalski[1]
[1]*University of Plovdiv,*
[2]*de Montfort University - Leicester Country*
[1]*Bulgaria*
[2]*UK*

## 1. Introduction

One of the main characteristics of the eLearning systems today is the 'anytime-anywhere-anyhow' delivery of electronic content, personalized and customized for each individual user. To satisfy this requirement new types of context-aware and adaptive software architectures are needed, which are enabled to sense aspects of the environment and use this information to adapt their behavior in response to changing situation. In conformity with [Dey,2000], a context is any information that can be used to characterize the situation of an entity. An entity may be a person, a place, or an object that is considered relevant to the interaction between a user and an application, including the user and the application themselves.

Development of context-aware and adaptive architectures can be benefited from some ideas and approaches of pervasive computing. Pervasive computing is a new paradigm for next-generation distributed systems where computers disappear in the background of the users' everyday activities. In such a paradigm computation is performed on a multitude of small devices interconnected through a wireless network. Fundamental to pervasive computing is that any component (including user, hardware and software) can be mobile and that computations are context-aware. As a result, mobility and context-awareness are important features of any design framework for pervasive computing applications. Context-awareness requires applications to be able to sense aspects of the environment and use this information to adapt their behaviours in response to changing situations.

One of the main goals of the Distributed eLearning Centre (DeLC) project [Ganchev, 2005] is the development of such an architecture and corresponding software that could be used efficiently for on-line eLearning distance education. The approach adopted for the design and development of the system architecture is focused on the development of a service-oriented and agent-based intelligent system architecture providing wireless and fixed access to electronic services and electronic content. This chapter provides a general description of the architecture for two types of access - mobile and fixed.

Furthermore, we present the Calculus of Context-aware Ambients (CCA in short) for the modelling and verification of mobile systems that are context-aware. This process calculus is built upon the calculus of mobile ambient and introduces new constructs to enable ambients and processes to be aware of the environment in which they are being executed. This results in a powerful calculus where both mobility and context-awareness are first-class citizens. We present the syntax and a formal semantics of the calculus. We also present a new theory of equivalence of processes which allows the identification of systems that have the same context aware behaviours. We prove that CCA encodes the Pi-calculus which is known to be a universal model of computation.

We have used our CCA to specify DeLC in its entirety, hence achieving its correctness. Such a dynamic system must enforce complex policies to cope with security, mobility and context-awareness. We show how these policies can be formalised and verified using CCA. In particular an important liveness property of the mLearning system is proved using the reduction semantics of CCA.

## 2. DeLC overview

Distributed eLearning Center (DeLC) is a reference architecture, supporting a reactive, proactive and personalized provision of education services and electronic content. The DeLC architecture is modeled as a network (Fig.1.), which consists of separate nodes, called eLearning Nodes (eLNs). Nodes model real units (laboratories, departments, faculties, colleges, and universities), which offer a complete or partial educational cycle. Each eLearning Node is an autonomous host of a set of electronic services. The configuration of the network edges is such as to enable the access, incorporation, use and integration of electronic services located on the different eLNs.

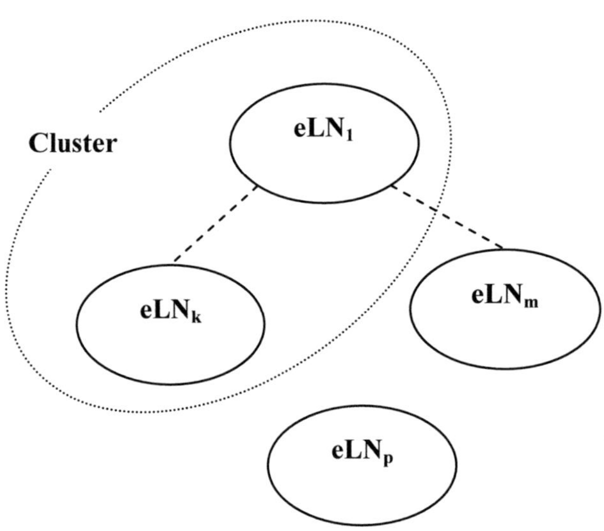


Fig. 1. DeLC Network Model

The eLearning Nodes can be isolated ($eLN_p$) or integrated in more complex virtual structures, called clusters. Remote eService activation and integration is possible only within a cluster. In the network model we can easily create new clusters, reorganize or remove existing clusters (the reorganization is done on a virtual level, it does not affect the real organization). For example, the reorganization of an existing cluster can be made not by removing a node but by denying the access to the offered by it services. The reorganization does not disturb the function of other nodes (as nodes are autonomous self-sufficient educational units providing one or more integral educational services).

An important feature of the eLearning Nodes is the access to supported services and electronic content. In relation to the access there are two kinds of nodes:

- Mobile eLearning Node and
- Fixed eLearning Node.

For both nodes individual reference architectures are proposed within DeLC.

The current version of DeLC (Fig.2), two standardized architecture supporting fixed and mobile access to the eLearning services and teaching contend have been implemented. The fixed access architecture is adapted for the following domains implemented as particular nodes:

- Education portal supporting blended learning in the secondary school;
- Specialized node for electronic testing (DeLC Test Center);
- Specialized node for education in software engineering (eLSE);
- Specialized nod for examination of creative thinking and handling of students (CA). The node adapts the Creativity Assistant environment [Zedan,2008];

Intelligent agents that support the eLearning services provided by the DeLC portal (AV). The Agent Village will be presented in this chapter in more detail.

## 3. Mobile eLearning node

A distinguishable feature of contemporary mobile eLearning (mLearning) systems is the anywhere-anytime-anyhow aspect of delivery of electronic content, which is personalised and customised to suit a particular mobile user [Barker,2000], [Maurer,2001]. In addition, mobile service content is expected to be delivered to users always in the best possible way through the most appropriate connection type according to the always best connected and best served communication paradigm [O'Droma,2007], [Passas,2006]. In the light of these trends, the goal is to develop an intelligent mobile eLearning node which uses an InfoStation-based communication environment with distributed control [Frenkiel,1996], [Ganchev,2007]. The InfoStation paradigm is an extension of the wireless Internet, where mobile clients interact directly with Web service providers (i.e. InfoStations). By their mobile devices the users request services from the nearest InfoStation utilizing Bluetooth or WiFi wireless communication.

### 3.1 InfoStation-based network architecture

The continuing evolution in the capabilities and resources available within modern mobile devices has precipitated an evolution in the realm of eLearning. The architecture presented here attempts to harness the communicative potential of these devices in order to present learners with a more pervasive learning experience, which can be dynamically altered and

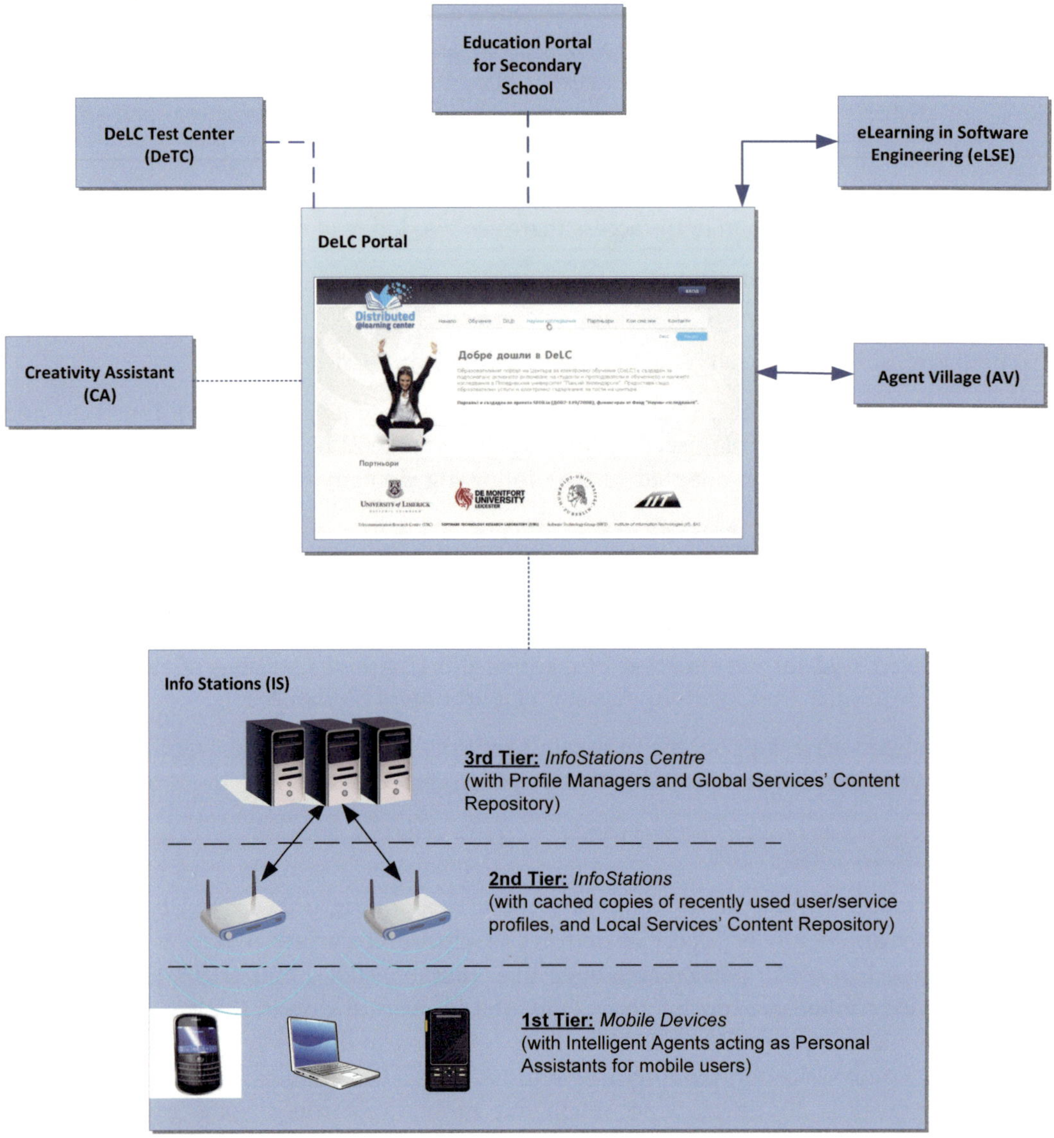


Fig. 2. Distributed eLearning Center

tailored to suit them. The following network architecture enables mobile users to access various mLearning services, via a set of intelligent wireless access points, or InfoStations, deployed in key points across the University Campus. The InfoStation-based network consists of three tiers as shown in Figure 3.

The first tier encompass the user mobile devices (cell phones, laptops, PDAs), equipped with intelligent agents acting as Personal Assistants to users. The Personal Assistant gathers information about the operating environment onboard the mobile device, as well as soliciting information about the user. Supplied with this information, the InfoStation can make better decisions on applicable services and content to deliver to the Personal Assistant.

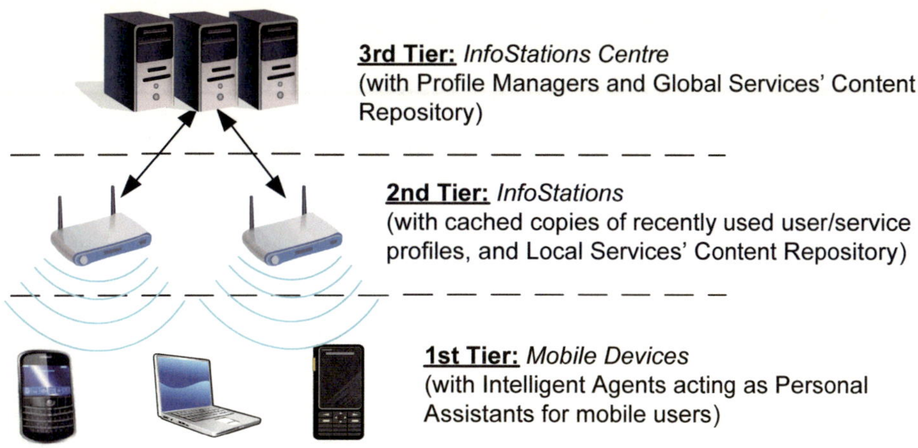


Fig. 3. The 3-tier InfoStation-based network architecture

The second tier consists of InfoStations, satisfying the users' requests for services through Bluetooth and/or WiFi wireless mobile connections. The InfoStations maintain connections with mobile devices, create and manage user sessions, provide interface to global services offered by the InfoStation Centre, and host local services. The implementation of these local services is an important aspect of this system. By implementing particular services within specific localised regions throughout the University campus, we can enrich the service users experience within these localities. A prime example of how this type of local service can enrich a learners experience, is the deployment of library-based services [Ganchev,2008a]. Within the library domain, library users experience can be greatly enhanced through the facilitation of services offering resource location capabilities or indeed account notifications. The division of global and local services allows for a reduction of the workload placed on the InfoStation Centre. In the original InfoStation architecture, the InfoStations operated only as mediators between the user mobile devices and a centre, on which a variety of electronic services are deployed and executed. The InfoStations within this architecture do not only occupy the role of mediators, they also act as the primary service providing nodes.

The third tier is the InfoStation Centre concerned with controlling the InfoStations, and overall updating and synchronisation of information across the system. The InfoStation Centre also acts as the host for global services.

### 3.2 Context-aware service provision

In order to ensure a context-aware service provision we propose that an application is built as an integration of two components [Stoyanov,2008]:

- A standardized **middleware**, which is able to detect the dynamic changes in the environment during the processing of user requests for services *(contex-awareness)* and correspondingly to ensure their efficient and non-problematic execution (*adaptability*);
- A set of **electronic services** realizing the functionality of the application area (education), which could be activated and controlled by the middleware.

As the middleware is concerned with the context-awareness and adaptability aspects, it is important to clarify these concepts. Within our development approach, Dey's definition [Dey,2000] was adopted, according to which "context is any information that can be used to characterize the situation at an entity". An entity could be a person, place, or object that is considered relevant to the interaction between a user and an application, including the user and applications themselves. Context could be of different type, e.g. location, identity, activity, time.

Dey's definition is utilized here as a basis for further discussions. In order to elaborate on this definition a working one for the creation of the desired middleware architecture, we first solidify the definition as presented further in the chapter. We want clearly to differentiate context-awareness from the adaptability. Context-awareness is the middleware's ability to identify the changes in the environment/context as regards:

- Mobile device's location (*device mobility*) - in some cases this mobility leads to changing the serving InfoStation. This is especially important due to the inherent mobility within the system, as users move throughout the University campus. This information has a bearing on the local services deployed within a particular area i.e. within the University Library;
- User device (*user mobility*) - this mobility offers different options for the delivery of the service request's results back to the user. What is important here is to know the capabilities of the new device activated by the user, so as to adapt the service content accordingly;
- Communication type - depending on the current prevailing wireless network conditions/constraints, the user may avail of different communications possibilities (e.g. Bluetooth or WiFi);
- User preferences - service personalisation may be needed as to reflect the changes made by users in their preferences, e.g., the way the service content is visualised to them, etc.;
- Goal-driven sequencing of tasks engaged in by the user;
- Environmental context issues such as classmates and/or learner/educator interactions.

The goal of adaptability is to ensure trouble-free, transparent and adequate fulfilment of user requests for services by taking into account the various aspects of the context mentioned above. In other words, after identifying a particular change in the service environment, the middleware must be able to take compensating actions (counter-measures) such as handover of user service sessions from one InfoStation to another, re-formatting/transcoding of service content due to a change of mobile device (varying device capabilities), service personalisation, etc.

To ensure adequate support for user mobility and device mobility (the first two aspects of the context change), the following four main communications scenarios are identified for support in our middleware architecture [Ganchev,2008b]:

- '*No change*' - a mLearning service is provided within the range of the same InfoStation and without changing the user mobile device;
- '*Change of user mobile device*' - due to the inherent mobility, it is entirely possible that during an mLearning service session, the user may shift to another mobile device, e.g. with greater capabilities, in order to experience a much richer service environment and utilize a wider range of resources;

- '*Change of InfoStation*' - within the InfoStation paradigm, the connection between the InfoStations themselves and the user mobile devices is by definition geographically intermittent. With a number of InfoStations positioned around a University campus, the users may pass through a number of InfoStation serving areas during the service session. This transition between InfoStation areas must be completely transparent to the user, ensuring the user has continuous access to the service;
- '*Change of InfoStation and user mobile device*' - most complicated scenario whereby the user may change the device simultaneously with the change of the InfoStation.

To support the third aspect of the context change (different communication type), the development of an intelligent component (agent) working within the communication layer (c.f. Figure 4) is envisaged. This component operates with the capability to define and choose the optimal mode of communication, depending on the current prevailing access network conditions (e.g. congestion level, number of active users, average data rate available to each active user, etc.). The user identification and corresponding service personalisation is subject to a middleware adaptation for use in the particular application area. In the case of eLearning, the architecture is extended to support the three fundamental eLearning models - the educational domain model, the user/learner model, and the pedagogical model [Stoyanov,2005],[ Ganchev,2008c].

### 3.3 Layered system architecture

The layered system architecture (Figure 4) is a distributed architecture, meaning that its functional entities are deployed across the different tiers/nodes, i.e. on mobile devices, InfoStations, and InfoStation Centre. In this architecture the role of the InfoStations is expanded, enabling them to act (besides the mediation role) as hosts for the local mLearning services (LmS) and for preparation, adaptation, and conclusive delivery of global mLearning services (GmS). This way the service provision is efficiently distributed across the whole architecture. Each of the system network nodes have a different structure depending on their functioning within the system. However, each node is built upon a Communication Layer whose main task is to initialize, control and maintain communications between different nodes. This layer is also concerned with choosing the most appropriate mode of communication between a mobile device and an InfoStation - whether that be Bluetooth or WiFi, or indeed as the platform evolves perhaps WiMAX in the future. The software architecture of the InfoStations and InfoStation Centre includes a Service Layer on the top. The main task of this layer is to prepare the execution of the users' service requests, to activate and receive the results of the execution of different services (local and global).

The InfoStations' middle layer is responsible for the execution of scenarios and control of user sessions. It is at this layer where the user service requests are mainly processed by taking into account all contex-aware aspects and applying corresponding adaptive actions. The middle layer of the InfoStation Centre ensures the needed synchronisation during particular scenarios (c.f. Section 8). In addition, different business supporting components, e.g. for user accounting, charging and billing, may operate here.

The software architecture of the user mobile devices contains two other layers:

- Personal Assistant - its task is to help the user in specifying the service requests sent to the system, accomplish the communication with the InfoStations' software, receive and visualise the service requests' results to the user, etc. Moreover the assistant can provide information needed for the personalisation of services (based on information stored in the user profile) and/or for the synchronisation of scenario execution;
- Graphical User Interface (GUI) - its task is to prepare and present the forms for setting up the service requests, and visualise the corresponding results received back from the system.

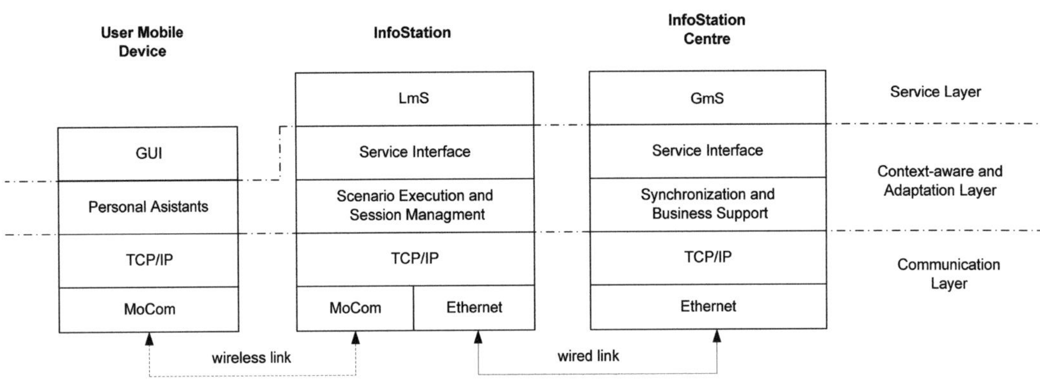


Fig. 4. The layered system architecture

### 3.4 Agent-oriented middleware architecture

The main implementation challenges within this system are related to the support of distributed control, as the system should be capable of detecting all relevant changes in the environment (context-awareness) and according to these changes, facilitate the service offerings in the most flexible and efficient manner (adaptability). The system architecture presented in the previous section is implemented as a set of cooperating intelligent agents. An agent oriented approach has been adopted in the development of this architecture in order to:

- Model adequately the real distributed infrastructure;
- Allow for realisation of distributed models of control;
- Ensure pro-active middleware behaviour which is quite beneficial in many situations;
- Use more efficiently the information resources spread over different InfoStations.

Moreover, the agent-oriented architecture can easily be extended with new agents (where required) that cooperate with the existing ones and communicate by means of a standardized protocol (in this case the FIPA -Agent Communication Language (ACL) [FIPA,2002]). Indeed the InfoStations and InfoStation Centre exist as networks of interoperating agents and services, with the agents fulfilling various essential roles necessary for system management. Within each of these platforms, agents take responsibility for selecting and establishing a client-server cross-platform connection, conveyance of context information and the delivery of adapted and personalised service content. This multi-agent approach differs from the classic multi-tier architectures in which the relationships between the components at a particular tier are much stronger.

Conceptually we define different layers in the system architecture in order to present the functionality of the middleware that is being developed in a more systematic fashion. Implementation-wise, the middleware architecture is considered as a set of interacting intelligent agents. Communication between the user mobile devices and the serving InfoStations could be realized in two ways:

- An agent operating within the InfoStation discovers all new devices entering the range and subsequently initiates communication with them; or
- Personal Assistant agents on the user mobile devices are the active part in communication, and initiate the connection with the InfoStation.

In the current implementation of the prototype architecture, the former approach is used for Bluetooth communication, whereas the latter applies for WiFi communication.

Figure 4 highlights the main components necessary to ensure continuity to the service provision, i.e. support for the continuous provision of services and user sessions in the case of scenario change or resource deficiency. The agents which handle the connection and session establishment perform different actions, such as:

- Searching for and finding mobile devices within the range of an InfoStation;
- Creating a list of services required by mobile devices;
- Initiation of a wireless connection with mobile devices;
- Data transfer to- and from mobile devices.

Also illustrated within Figure 5 are the components which serve to facilitate a level of context sensitivity and personalisation to the presented services. A short description of the various agents (for Bluetooth communication) within the architecture is presented below.

The first step in the delivery of the services involves the Scanner agent, which continuously searches for mobile devices/Personal Assistant agents within the service area of the InfoStation. In addition, this agent retrieves a list of services required by users (registered on their mobile devices upon installation of the client part of the application), as well as the profile information, detailing the context (i.e. device capability and user preference information. The Scanner agent receives this information in the form of an XML file, which itself is extracted from the content of an ACL message. The contents of this XML file are then passed on via the Connection Advisor agent, to the Profile Processor agent, which parses the received profile and extracts meaningful information. This information can in turn be utilized to perform the requisite alterations to services and service content.

The information is also very important in relation to the tasks undertaken by the Scenario Manager agent. The role of this agent is to monitor and respond to changes in the operating environment, within which the services are operating (i.e. change of mobile device). In the event of a significant change of service environment, this agent gathers the new capability and preference information (CPI) via the Scanner agent. Then, in conjunction with the Query Manager agent and the Content Adaptation agent, facilitates the dynamic adaptation of the service content to meet the new service context.

The main duty of the Connection Adviser agent is to filter the list (received from the Scanner agent) of mobile devices as well as requested services. The filtration is carried out with respect to a given (usually heuristic) criterion. Information needed for the filtration is stored in a local database. The Connection Adviser agent sends the filtered list to the Connection Initiator agent, who takes on the task of initiating a connection with the Personal Assistant onboard the mobile device. This agent generates the so-called Connection Object, through which a communication with the mobile device is established via Bluetooth connection. Once this connection has been established, the Connection Initiator generates an agent to which it hands over the control of the connection, called a Connection agent.

From this point on, all communications between the InfoStation and the Personal Assistant are directed by the Connection agent. The internal architecture of the Connection agent contains three threads: an agent thread used for communication with the Query Manager agent, and a Send thread and Receive thread, which look after each direction of the wireless communication with the mobile device.

The Query Manager performs one of the most crucial tasks within the InfoStation architecture. It determines where information received from the mobile device is to be directed, e.g. directly to simple services, or via Interface agents to sophisticated services. It also transforms messages coming from the Connection agent into messages of the correct protocols to be understood by the relevant services, i.e. for simple services - UDDI or SOAP, or for increasingly sophisticated services by using more complicated, semantic-oriented protocols (e.g. OWL-S [OWL-S,2010]). The Query Manager agent also interacts with the Content Adaptation agent in order to facilitate the Personal Assistant with increasingly contextualised service content. This Content Adaptation agent, operating under the remit of the Query Manager agent, essentially performs the role of an adaptation engine, which takes in the profile information provided by the Profile Processor agent, and executes the requisite adaptation operations on the service content (e.g. file compression, image resizing etc.)

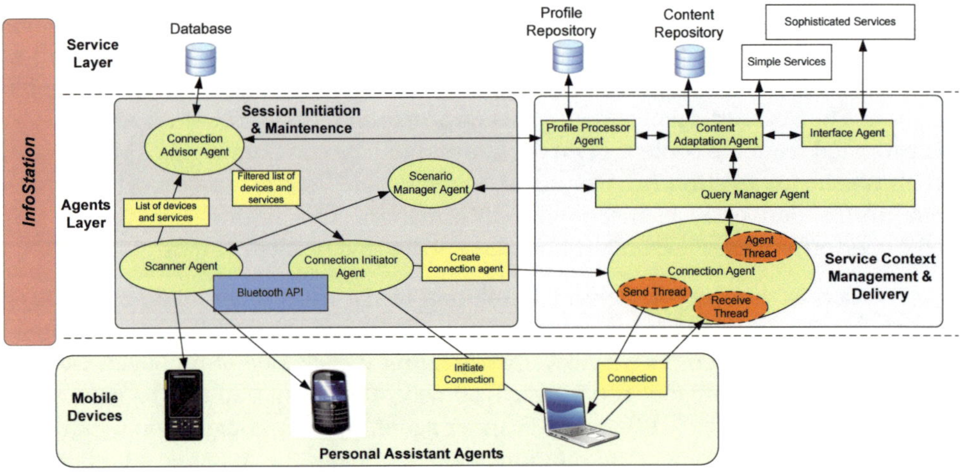


Fig. 5. The Agent-Oriented Middleware Architecture

The Query Manager agent receives user service requests via the Connection agent, and may communicate with various services. Once it has passed the request on to the services, all service content is passed back to the Query Manager via the Content Adaptation agent. The Profile Processor agent parses and validates received profiles (XML files) and creates a Document Object Model (DOM) tree [W3C,2010]. Using this DOM tree the XML information may be operated on, to discern the information most pertinent to the adaptation of service content. The Content Adaptation agent receives requests-responses from the services, queries the Profile Processor agent regarding the required context, and then either selects a pre-packaged service content package which closely meets the requirements of the mobile device, or applies a full transformation to the service content to meet the constraints of the operating environment of the device.

The tasks undertaken by the Content Adaptation agent, the Scenario Manager agent and the Profile Processor agent, enable the system to dynamically adapt to changing service environments, even during a particular service session. Once the connection to a particular service has been initialized and the service content adapted to the requisite format, the Connection agent facilitates the transfer of the information to the user mobile device.

## 4. Fixed eLearning node

The fixed nodes of the DeLC are implemented as education portals, which provides personalized educational services and teaching material. A standardized portal architecture is described in this section, which is used as generic framework for implementation of particular education portals for university and secondary school. The architecture has been extended by intelligent components (agents, called assistants) in order to enhance the flexibility, reactivity and pro-activeness of the portals.

### 4.1 Education portal architecture

The architecture of the educational portal is service-oriented and multi-layered, consisting of three logical layers (Figure 6): user interface, e-services and digital libraries.

The user interface supports the connection between the users and the portal. Through it the users can register in the system and create their own personalized educational environment. The user interface visualizes and provides access for the user to services, depending on their role, assigned during the registration.

Two kinds of e-services are located in the middle layer - system services and eLearning services. The system services, called 'engines', are transparent for the users and their basic purpose is to assist in the processing of the eLearning services. Using the information, contained in the meta-objects, they can effectively support the activation, execution and finalization of the eLearning services. In the current portal architecture the next engines are implemented:

- SCORM Engine;
- Exams Engine;
- Events and Remainders Engine;
- Integration Engine;
- User Profiling.

SCORM Engine is implemented in the portal architecture for delivering an interpreter of the electronic content, developed in accordance with the SCORM 2004 standard. The Test Engine assists in performing electronic testing using the portal. It processes basically the meta objects, which describe the questions and the patterns of the tests. The Event Engine supports a model for event management, enabling the users to see and create events and also be notified for them in advance. The events in the system reflect important moments for the users, such as a lecture, examination, test, national holiday, birthday, etc. One event is characterized by attributes, such as a name, start and end date and time, details, and information if it is a recurring one, as well as rules for its recurrence. The Event Engine supports yearly, monthly and weekly recurring. The User Profiling implements the user model of the portal. The profiles could be classified by roles, user groups, communities, and organizations. The standard user profile consists of three main groups of attributes:

- Standard attributes - necessary for user identification through username, password, e-mail, and others;
- Extended attributes - addresses, phone numbers, Internet pages, IM, social networks contacts, and others;
- DeLC custom attributes - other user identifications. Thus, for example, for users with role "student" these can be faculty number, subject, faculty, and course.

The portal gives an opportunity for extending the user profile with some additional attributes. The users' profiles contain the whole information needed for personalization of the provided by DeLC portal services, educational content and user interface. The profile is created automatically during the first user's log in, through a call to the university's database, filling in the standard and custom attributes. The integration with the university database and with ?nother external components is supported by the Integration Engine. Extended attributes are filled by the user. During each next user's log in in the portal the information in their profile is synchronized, as eventual updates in the university's database are automatically migrated in the user's profile, for example passage in the upper course or changing the subject.

Educational services serve all stages in one educational process. Supported by the portal, services are grouped in three categories:

- Services for training, organizing and planning of the educational process;
- Services for conduction and management of the education process - examples of these services are electronic lectures, electronic testing, online and offline consultations;
- Services for recording and documenting the educational process - these services support automated generation of the documents recording the educational process (examination protocols, student books, teachers' personal notebooks and archives).

The third layer contains electronic content in the form of repositories, known as digital libraries. In the current version are supported lecture courses digital library, questionary library, test templates library, course projects library and diploma theses library. The supported portal services work directly with the digital libraries. The digital libraries content can be navigated by help of a generalized catalog.

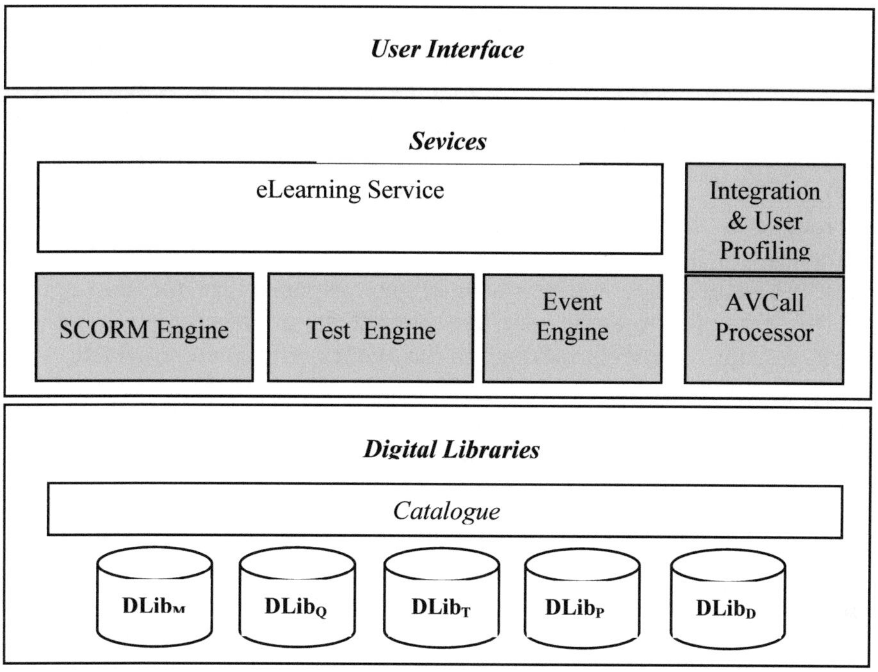


Fig. 6. Standarised Architecture of the portal

### 4.2 Education cluster

In order to provide more effective and personalized user support, we need to enhance the flexibility, reactivity and pro-activeness of the portal including intelligent components into the architecture. The pro-activity improves the usability and friendliness of the system to the users. Pro-activity means that the software can operate "on behalf" of the user" and "activate itself" when it "estimates" that its intervention is necessary. Two approaches are available:

- Direct integration of intelligent components in the currently existing architecture - in this way we extend the existing portal architecture;
- Building an education cluster.

The litter approach is preferable because it match with DeLC philosophy for building of more complex structures. Moreover, the former approach involves difficulties in the integration of two environments with different characteristics - portal frame and agent-oriented environment.

The education cluster consists of two nodes - the existing portal and a new node, called Agent Village (AV), where the "assistants" will "live in" (Figure 7). Three basic problems have to be solve in order to create the cluster:

- Architecture of the AV node;
- Interaction between the portal and AV;
- What kind of intelligent assistance for the portal services.

AV node is implemented as an agent-oriented server, by help of JADE environment [Bellifemine,2007].

The connection of the educational portal and the AV node is made through the middle layer of the portal architecture, where the electronic services are located. Depending on the direction of the asked assistance we distinguish reactive and proactive behavior of the architecture. In the reactive behavior the interaction between the two nodes is initiated by the portal. This is necessary in the cases when a user request is processed and a service needs an "expert" assistance. The service addresses the corresponding agent, located in the AV. The problem is that, in their nature, the services are passive and static software modules, intended mainly for the convenient realization and integration of some business functionality. Therefore they must "transfer" the responsibility for the activation and support of the connection to an active component of the architecture, as agents do. To do this, the service sends a concrete message to the agent's environment, which, on its behalf, identifies the change of the environment and reacts by interpreting the message. Depending on the identified need of assistance the agent activates the necessary actions. The reactive behavior of the architecture could be implemented using a:

- Synchronous model - this model is analogous to calling subroutines in programming languages. In this model the service sends a message to AV and waits for the result from the corresponding agent before continuing its execution.
- Asynchronous model - in the asynchronous model the interaction is accomplished through some kind of a mechanism for sending and receiving messages.

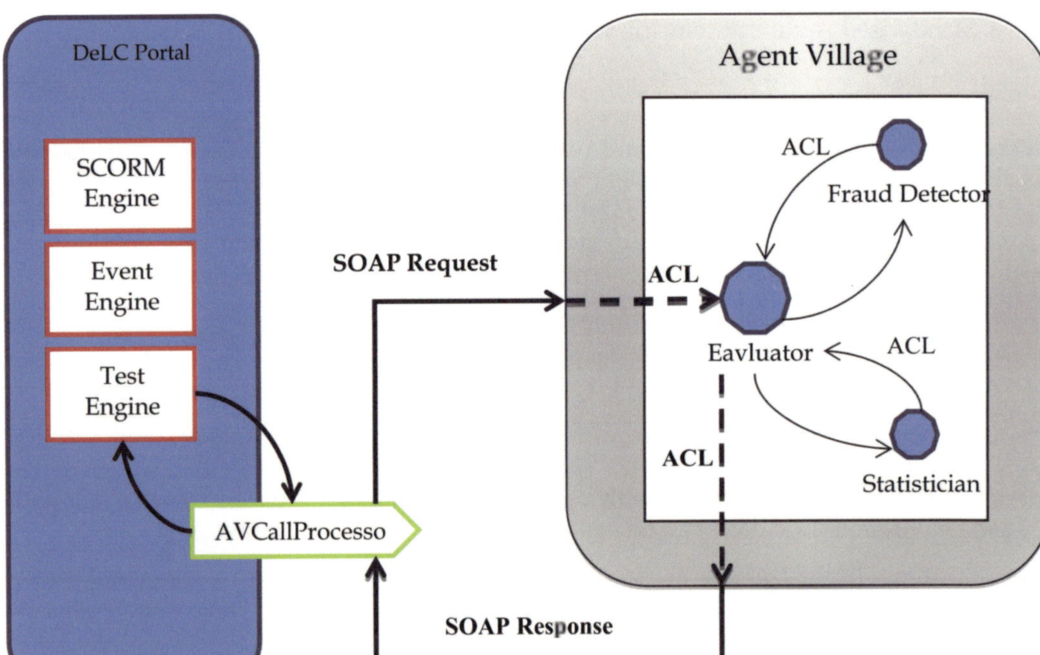


Fig. 7. Cluster architecture

In the proactive behavior (agents work "on behalf of the user"), an agent from the AV can determine that in its environment "something is happening", that would be interesting for the user, who is assisted by that agent. The agent activates and it can perform certain actions to satisfy the preferences (wishes) of the user. The agent can inform the user of its actions through the educational portal.

The difficulties, associated with the management of the pro-activity of our architecture, result from the fact that the portal is designed for reaction of the user's requests. Therefore the pro-activity can be managed only asynchronously and for this purpose we provide development of a specialized service, which is to check a "mailbox" periodically for incoming messages from AV.

According our architecture, the reactivity and the pro-activity are possible if the environment of the agents (Agent Village) remains not more passive. In order to be identified, the agents need a wrapper (the environment), which "masks" it as a web service for the portal. In such a way the portal send the request to this service (masked environment), which in its turn transform the request into an ACL message, understandable for the agents. In a similar manner the active environment transform ACL messages into SOAP responses, which can be process from the portal services.

The next assistants are developing in the first version of the AV node:

- Evaluator Assistant (EA);
- FraudDetector;
- Statistician;
- Intelbos

The Evaluator Assistant (EA) provides expert assistance to the teacher in assessment of the electronic tests. In the Exam Engine a service is built for automated assessment of "choice like" questions. In the standard version of the architecture questions of the "free text" type are assessed by the teacher and the ratings are entered manually in the service to prepare the final assessment of the test. In the cluster the Exam Engine calls the assistant (an intelligent agent), which makes an "external" assessment of the "free text" type questions. In the surrounding environment of the EA, the received SOAP Request messages are transformed into ACL messages, understandable for the agent. Some of the basic parameters of the messages are:

- Text, which is an answer of a "free text" type question.
- Parameters for the used estimation method.
- Maximum number of points for this answer.

The EA plans the processing of the request. In the current version of the assistant two methods are available for estimation:

- **Word Matching (WM)** method - counts "exact hits" of the keywords in the answer. The minimum threshold of percentage match (i.e. a keyword to be considered as "guessed"), which is laid in the experiments, is between 70% and 80%. Intentionally, the method does not look for 100% match, in order to give a chance to words with some minor typos also to be recognized. To calculate the points, offered by this method, a coefficient is formed in the following way: the number of hits is divided by the number of keywords. The actual number of points for the answer is calculated as the maximum number of points is multiplied by this coefficient;

- **Optimistic Percentage (OP)** method - makes an optimistic estimation of the points for the answer. Its essence is to iterate over the keywords list and summarize their percentage matches. Thus, the calculated amount of rates for each keyword, divided by the maximum possible match (in %), gives the reduction coefficient. The actual number of points for the answer is calculated by multiplying the maximum number of points by the coefficient of the reduction. This method is more "tolerant" to allowing spelling mistakes in the answers, because low percentage matches are not ignored (unlike the first method) and are included in the formation of the final amount of points.

When the calculations finish, the EA generates an answer as an ACL message, which then is transformed by the environment into a SOAP Response message (a result from a web service call). In the answer there is a parameter, representing the calculated amount of points, extracted afterwards by the Exam Engine. A comparison of the scores, given by the two methods and by the teacher, are presented in Figure 8.

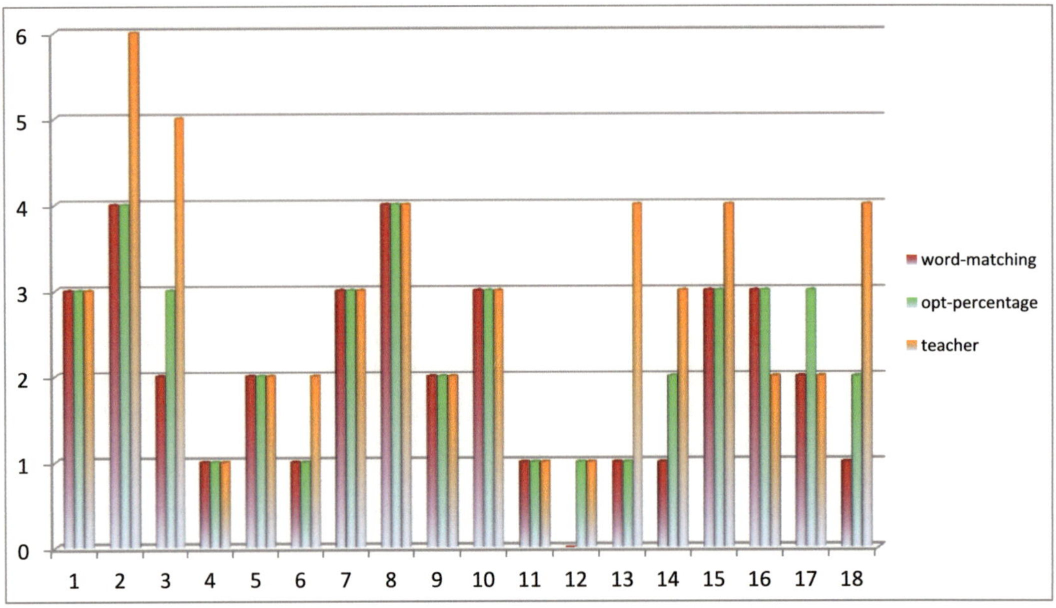


Fig. 8. Comparison of WM, OP and the teacher for 18 tests

The FraudDetector will try to recognize any attempts to cheat in the answer given by the student. Such attempts would be to guess the keywords or copy/paste results from Internet search engines. This assistant cooperates with the Evaluator agent and if its receptors detect a probability of a cheating attempt, it informs the Evaluator agent, which for its part informs the assessing teacher that this answer requires a special attention, because it is a suspicious one. The Statistician stores information about all processed answers with a full history of the details from all calculating methods used by the Evaluator agent. This assistant needs a feedback how many points are finally given by the teacher for each answer. Thus it accumulates a knowledge base for each teacher and is able to decide which of the methods best suits the assessment style of the current assessing teacher. Upon returning the results of the Evaluator assistant, information by this agent determines which results from each method will be presented to the teacher as main result, and the results of the other methods will be presented as an alternative. Another feature of this agent will be also to provide actual statistics on the performance of each of the calculating methods, as the "weakest" of them goes out of service until new and better performing methods are added to the Evaluator agent. This monitoring of the methods' behavior becomes really significant when the so-called genetic algorithms are added, which we are still working on - as it is known, they can be "trained" and thus their effectiveness can change. In this process a knowledge base is developing for each specific subject, which supports the methods in their work.

## 5. Calculus of context aware systems - CCA

Context-awareness requires applications to be able to adapt themselves to the environment in which they are being used such as user, location, nearby people and devices, and user's social situations. In this section we use small examples to illustrate the ability of CCA to model applications that are contextaware.

### 5.1 Syntax of processes and capabilities

This section introduces the syntax of the language of CCA. Like in the $\pi$-calculus [Milner,1999], [Sangiorgi,2001], the simplest entities of the calculus are *names*. These areused to name for example ambients, locations, resources and sensors data. We assume a countably-infnite set of names, elements of which are written in lower-case letters, e.g. $n$, $x$ and $y$. We let $\tilde{y}$ denote a list of names and $|\tilde{y}|$ the arity of such a list. We sometimes use $\tilde{y}$ as a set of names where it is appropriate. We distinguish three main syntactic categories: processes $P$, capabilities $M$ and context expressions $\kappa$.

The syntax of processes and capabilities is given in Table 1 where $P$, $Q$ and $R$ stand for processes, and $M$ for capabilities. The first five process primitives (inactivity, parallel composition, name restriction, ambient and replication) are inherited from MA [Cardelli,2000]. The process $0$ does nothing and terminates immediately. The process $P \mid Q$ denotes the process $P$ and the process $Q$ running in parallel. The process $(\upsilon n)\ P$ states that the scope of the name $n$ is limited to the process $P$. The replication $!P$ denotes a process which can always create a new copy of $P$. Replication was first introduced by Milner in the $\pi$-calculus [Milner,1999]. The process $n[P]$ denotes an ambient named $n$ whose behaviours are described by the process $P$. The pair of square brackets `[' and `]' outlines the boundary of that ambient. This is the textual representation of an ambient. The graphical representation of that ambient is:

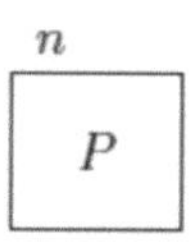


The graphical representation highlights the nested structure of ambients.

CCA departs from MA and other processes calculi such as [Zimmer,2005], [Bucur,2008], [Bugliesi,2004] with the notion of *context-guarded capabilities*, whereby a capability is guarded by a context-expression which specifes the condition that must be met by the environment of the executing process. A process prefxed with a context-guarded capability is called a *context-guarded prefix* and it has the form $\kappa?\,M.P$. Such a process waits until the environment satisfies the context expression $\kappa$, then performs the capability $M$ and continues like the process $P$. The process learns about its context (i.e. its environment) by evaluating the guard. The use of context-guarded capabilities is one of the two main mechanisms for context acquisition in CCA (the second mechanism for context acquisition is the call to a process abstraction as discussed below). The syntax and the semantics of context expressions are given below. We let $M.P$ denote the process **True**?$M.P$, where **True** is a context expression satisfied by all context.

| | |
|---|---|
| $\boldsymbol{P, Q, R}$ ::= | **Process** |
| 0 | inactivity |
| P \| Q | parallel composition |
| (υn) P | name restriction |
| n[P] | ambient |
| ! P | repliaction |
| κ! M. P | context-guarder action |
| x ⊳ (ỹ). P | process abstraction |
| **α** ::= | **Locations** |
| ↑ | any parent |
| n ↑ | parent n |
| ↓ | any child |
| n ↓ | child n |
| :: | any sibling |
| n :: | sibling n |
| ϵ | locally |
| **M** ::= | **Capabilities** |
| del n | delete n |
| in n | move in n |
| out | move out |
| α x⟨z̃⟩ | process call |
| α (ỹ) | input |
| α ⟨ỹ⟩ | output |

Table 1. Syntax of CCA processes and capabilities

A process abstraction $x \rhd (\tilde{y}).P$ denotes the linking of the name $x$ to the process $P$ where $\tilde{y}$ is a list of *formal parameters*. This linking is local to the ambient where the process abstraction is defined. So a name $x$ can be linked to a process $P$ in one ambient and to a diferent process $Q$ in another ambient. A call to a process abstraction named $x$ is done by a capability of the form $\alpha\, x\langle\tilde{z}\rangle$ where $\alpha$ specifies the location where the process abstraction is defined and $\tilde{z}$ is the list of *actual parameters*. There must be as many actual parameters as there are formal parameters to the process abstraction being called. The location $\alpha$ can be '$\uparrow$' for any parent, '$n\uparrow$' for a specifc parent $n$, '$\downarrow$' for any child, '$n\downarrow$' for a specific child $n$, '$::$' for any sibling, '$n$ ::'for a specific sibling $n$, or $\epsilon$ (empty string) for the calling ambient itself. A process call

$\alpha\ x\langle\tilde{z}\rangle$ behaves like the process linked to $x$ at location $\alpha$, in which each actual parameter in $\tilde{z}$ is substituted for each occurrence of the corresponding formal parameter. A process call can only take place if the corresponding process abstraction is available at the specified location.

In CCA, an ambient provides context by (re)defining process abstractions to account for its specific functionality. Ambients can interact with each other by making process calls. Because ambients are mobile, the same process call, e.g. $\uparrow x\langle\tilde{z}\rangle$, may lead to different behaviours depending on the location of the calling ambient. So process abstraction is used as a mechanism for context provision while process call is a mechanism for context acquisition.

Ambients exchange messages using the capability $\alpha\ \langle\tilde{z}\rangle$ to send a list of names $\tilde{z}$ to a location $\alpha$, and the capability $\alpha\ (\tilde{y})$ to receive a list of names from a location $\alpha$. Similarly to a process call, an ambient can send message to any parent, i.e. $\uparrow\langle\tilde{z}\rangle$; a specific parent $n$, i.e. $n \uparrow \langle\tilde{z}\rangle$; any child, i.e. $\downarrow\langle\tilde{z}\rangle$; a specific child $n$, i.e. $n \downarrow \langle\tilde{z}\rangle$; any sibling, i.e. $::\langle\tilde{z}\rangle$; a specific sibling $n$, i.e. $n :: \langle\tilde{z}\rangle$; or itself, i.e. $\langle\tilde{z}\rangle$.

An *input prefix* is a process of the form $\alpha(\tilde{y}).P$ , where $\tilde{y}$ is a list of variable symbols and $P$ is a continuation process. It receives a list of names $\tilde{z}$ from the location $\alpha$ and continues like the process $P\{\tilde{y} \leftarrow \tilde{z}\}$, where $P\{\tilde{y} \leftarrow \tilde{z}\}$ is the process $P$ in which each name in the list $\tilde{z}$ is substituted for each occurrence of the corresponding variable symbol in the list $\tilde{y}$.

The mobility capabilities in and out are defined as in MA [Cardelli,2000] with the exception that the capability out has no explicit parameter in CCA, the implicit parameter being the current parent (if any) of the ambient performing the action. An ambient that performs the capability in $n$ moves into the sibling ambient $n$. The capability out moves the ambient that performs it out of that ambient parent. Obviously, a root ambient, i.e. an ambient with no parents, cannot perform the capability out. The capability del $n$ deletes an ambient of the form $n[0]$ situated at the same level as that capability, i.e. the process del $n.P|n[0]$ reduces to $P$. The capability del acts as a garbage collector that deletes ambients which have completed their computations. It is a constrained version of the capability open used in MA to unleash the content of an ambient. As mentioned in [Bugliesi,2004], the open capability brings about serious security concerns in distributed applications, e.g. it might open an ambient that contains a malicious code. Unlike the capability open, the capability del is secure because it only opens ambients that are empty, so no risk of opening a virus or a malicious ambient.

### 5.2 Context model

In CCA the notion of ambient, inherited from MA, is the basic structure used to model entities of a context-aware system such as: a user, a location, a computing device, a software agent or a sensor. As described in Table 1, an ambient has a name, a boundary, a collection of local processes and can contain other ambients. Meanwhile, an ambient can move from one location to another by performing the mobility capabilities in and out. So the structure of a CCA process, at any time, is a hierarchy of nested ambients. This hierarchical structure changes as the process executes. In such a structure, the context of a sub-process is obtained by replacing in the structure that sub-process by a placeholder '$\odot$'. For example, suppose a system is modelled by the process $P|n[Q|m[R|S]]$. So, the context of the process $R$ in that system is $P|n[Q|m[\odot|S]]$, and that of ambient $m$ is $P|n[Q|\odot]$. Following are examples of contexts in the smart phone system described in Sect. 5.3. The following context is the context of the smart phone carried by Bob when Bob is inside the conference room with Alice:

$$e_1 \triangleq conf[P \mid bob[\odot] \mid alice[Q]],$$

where $P$ models the remaining part of the internal context of the conference room and $Q$ the internal context of the ambient alice. We assume that there is only one ambient named *alice* in the conference room.

If Bob is inside the conference room while Alice is outside that room, the context of the smart phone carried by Bob can be described as follows:

$$e_2 \triangleq alice[Q] \mid conf\ [P \mid bob[\odot]].$$

Bob might carry with him another device, a PDA say, while inside the conference room. In this case the context of the smart phone can be modelled as:

$$e_3 \triangleq conf[P' \mid bob[\odot] \mid pda[R]],$$

where $P'$ models the remaining part of the internal context of the conference room, $pda$ is the name of the ambient modelling the PDA device and $R$ specifies the functionality of the PDA.

Our context model is depicted by the grammar in Table 2, where the symbol $E$ stands for context (environment), $n$ ranges over names and $P$ ranges over processes (as defined in Table 1). The context 0 is the empty context, also called the *nil* context. It contains no context information. The position of a process in that process' context is denoted by the symbol $\odot$. This is a special context called the *hole context*. The context $(vn)\ E$ means that the scope of the name n is limited to the context$E$. The context $n[E]$ means that the internal environment of the ambient $n$ is described by the context $E$. The context $E|P$ says that the process $P$ runs in parallel with the context $E$, and so $E$ is part of process $P$'s context.

**Ground context.** A ground context is a context containing no holes.

Note that a context contains zero or one hole; and that a ground context is a process. We do not allow multi-hole contexts because they are not suitable to our purpose.

| **E** ::= | | **Context** |
|---|---|---|
| | 0 | nil |
| | $\odot$ | hole |
| | $n[E]$ | location |
| | $(vn)\ E$ | restriction |

Table 2. Syntax contexts

**Context evaluation.** Let $E_1$ and $E_2$ be contexts. The evaluation of the context $E_1$ at the context $E_2$, denoted by$E_1(E_2)$, is the context obtained by replacing the hole in $E_1$ (if any) by $E_2$, viz

$$E_1(E_2) = \begin{cases} E_1 & \textit{if } E_1 \textit{ is a ground context} \\ E_1\{\odot \leftarrow E_2\} & \textit{otherwise.} \end{cases}$$

where $E_1\{\odot \leftarrow E_2\}$ is the substitution of $E_2$ for $\odot$ in $E_1$.

The hole $\odot$ plays an important role in our context model. In fact a context $E$ containing a single hole represents the environment of a process $P$ in the process $E(P)$. A process modelling Bob using a smart phone in the conference room with Alice can be specified as:

$$e_1(phone[S]) \triangleq conf\left[P \mid bob[phone[S]] \mid alice[Q]\right],$$

where $e_1$ is the context specified in Example 5.2 and $S$ is the specification of the smart phone.

A process modelling Bob using a PDA in the conference room can be specified as:

$$e_3(0) \triangleq conf\left[P' \mid bob[pda[R]]\right],$$

where $e_3$ is the context specified in Example 5.2. The syntax of CEs is given in Table 3 where $\kappa$ ranges over CEs, $n$ ranges over names and $x$ is a variable symbol which also ranges over names.

| $\kappa$ ::= | | **Context Expressions** |
|---|---|---|
| | **True** | true |
| | $n = m$ | name match |
| | $\bullet$ | hole |
| | $\neg\kappa$ | negation |
| | $k_1 \mid k_2$ | parallel composition |
| | $k_1 \wedge k_2$ | conjunction |
| | $n[\kappa]$ | location |
| | $\mathrm{new}(n, k)$ | relevation |
| | $\oplus\kappa$ | spatial next modality |
| | $\diamond\, \kappa$ | somewhere modality |
| | $\exists x.\kappa$ | existential quantification |

Table 3. Syntax context expressions

### 5.3 A simple example

This example illustrates the use of process abstraction and process call as a mechanism for context provision and context acquisition, respectively. A process abstraction can be thought of as the declaration of a procedure in procedural programming languages and a process call as the invocation of a procedure.

A process abstraction links a name $x$ to a process $P$ using the following syntax:

$$x \rhd (\tilde{y}).P$$

where $\tilde{y}$ is the list of formal parameters. A process call to this process abstraction has the following syntax:

$$x\langle\tilde{z}\rangle$$

where $\tilde{z}$ is the list of the actual parameters. This process call behaves exactly like the process $P$ where each actual parameter in $\tilde{z}$ is substituted for each occurrence of the corresponding formal parameter in $\tilde{y}$. In the smart phone example presented above, switchto is a process abstraction.

Suppose a software agent $agt$ (here modelled as an ambient) is willing to edit a text file *foo*. This is done by calling a process abstraction named edit say, as follows:

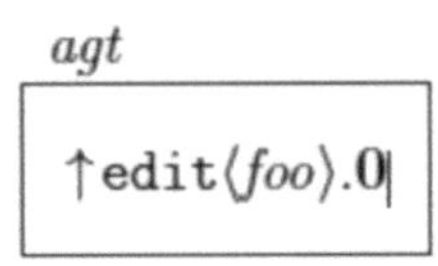


where the symbol ↑ indicates that the edit process called here is the one that is defined in the parent ambient of the calling ambient *agt*. Now suppose agent *agt* has migrated to a computing device win running Microsoft Windows operating system:

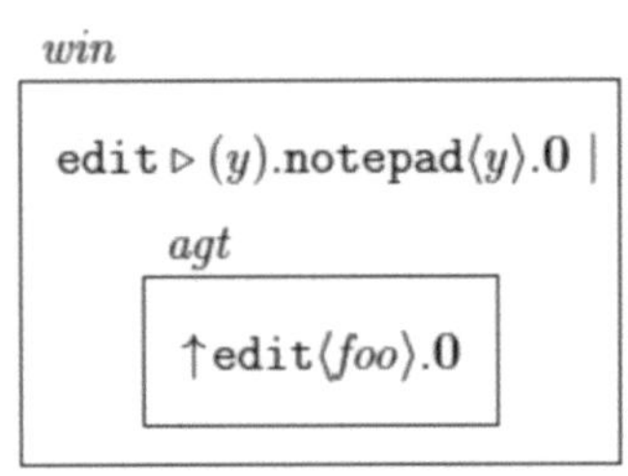


On this machine, the process abstraction edit is defined to launch the text editor notepad as follows:

$$\text{edit} \triangleright (y).\text{notepad}\langle y\rangle.0.$$

So the request of the agent *agt* to edit the fille *foo* on this machine will open that file in notepad according to the following reduction:

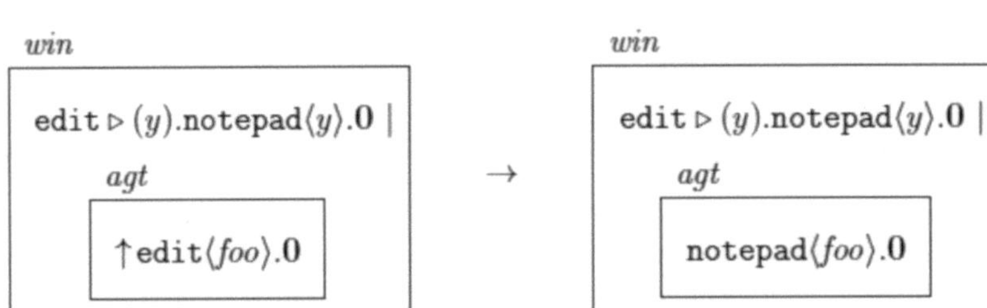


Note that the command notepad has replaced the command edit in the calling ambient *agt*.

Now assume the agent *agt* first moved to a computer *lin* running linux operating system:

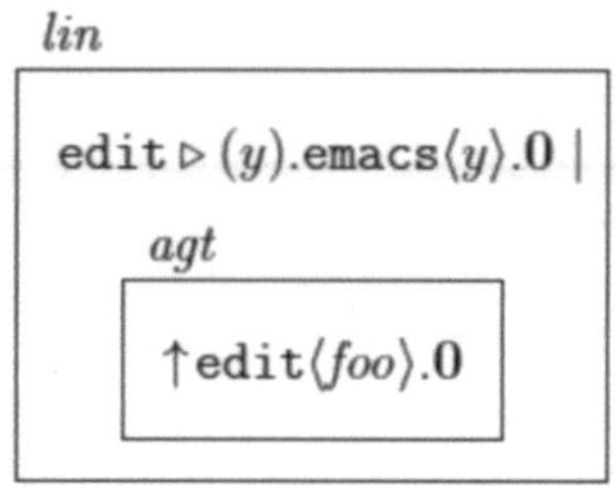


On this computer, the command edit is configured to launch emacs. So in this context, the file *foo* will be opened in emacs as illustrated by the following reduction:

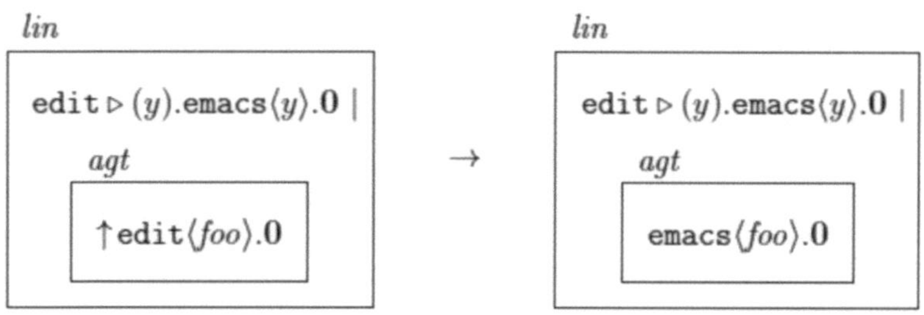


Our agent *agt* might have even moved to a site where the command edit is not *available* because no process abstraction of that name is defined. In this case the agent *agt* will not be able to edit the file *foo* at this site and might consider moving to a nearby computer to do so.

## 6. InfoStation-based mLearning system

As we have mentioned earlier that eLearning is becoming an authentic possible alternative educational approach as the technologies regarding that area are developing so fast, and there is a recognisable growth of a great variety of wide-band telecommunication delivery technologies. The infostation paradigm first proposed by Frenkiel et al. [Frenkiel,1996] and used in [Ganchev,2007] to devise an infostation-based mlearning system which allows mobile devices such as cellular phones, laptops and personal digital assistants (PDAs) to communicate to each other and to a number of services within a university campus. This mLearning system provides a number of services among which are: mLecture, mTutorial, mTest and communication services (private chat, intelligent message notification and phone calls). This section presents the architecture of the infostation-based mLearning system and describes the policies of the mLecture service.

### 6.1 mServices

This section introduces at glance each of the mServices provided by the infostation-based mLearning system.

- *AAA*: in order for any user to use any mService in the system, the user device should be registered. The AAA service (Authentication, Authorisation and Accounting) allows the users to register their devices with the system to gain the ability of using the mLearning services offered by the system.

- *mLecture*: this service allows the users to gain access to the lecture material through their mobile devices. The users can request a specific lecture, which is adapted according to the capabilities of the user devices and then delivered to their mobile devices.
- *mTest*: this service is crucial to the learning process. The mTest service allows the users to gain access to test materials that provide means of an evaluating process. A user can request, like the mLecture service, a specific test, which is also adapted to the capabilities of the user device then delivered to the user mobile device. The mTest service may only runs individually on a user device and unaccompanied with any other service whatsoever.
- *mTutorial* : this service allows the users to gain access to a self-assessment test. It is a combination between the mLecture and the mTest services. A user can request a self-assessment test in a similar way as requesting a mLecture. After the user submits their answers, he receives a feedback on his performance and the correct answers to the questions he got wrong.
- *Intelligent Message Notification (IMN in short)*: this service allows the users to communicate with each other by exchanging messages via their mobile devices.
- *VoIP*: this service allows the users to communicate with each other via phone calls throughout the infostation-based mLearning system.

## 6.2 Policies

The InforStationCentre (ISC) provides the User Authentication, Authorisation and Accounting (AAA) service which identifies each mobile user and provides him with a list of services the user is authorised to access. This service is regulated by the following policies:

- When a user is within the range of an IS, the intelligent agent (PA) of the user's device and the IS mutually discover each other. The PA sends a request to the IS for user Authorisation, Authentication and Accounting (AAA). This request also includes a description of the mobile device currently being used and any updates of user pro_le and user service profile.
- The IS forwards this AAA request to the ISC along with the profile updates. If the user is successfully authenticated and authorised to utilise the services by the AAA module within the ISC, a new account record is created for the user and a positive acknowledgement is sent back to the IS. Then the IS compiles a list of applicable services and sends this to the PA along with the acknowledgement. The PA displays the information regarding these services to the user who then makes a request for the service he wishes to use.

If the user chooses the mLecture service, then the following policies of the mLecture service apply:

- The PA forwards the mLecture service request to the InfoStation, which instantiates the service. If the IS is unable to satisfy fully the user service request it is forwarded to the ISC, which is better equipped to deal with it. In either case, the lecture is adapted and customised to suit the capabilities of the user devices and the user own preferences, and then delivered to their mobile devices.

- During the execution of the service, the user is free to move into a different infostation, to switch between devices or to do both.
- A user cannot use the mLecture and mTest services simultaneously. The mTest service should operate unaccompanied at all occasions.

This section presents the formalisation of the policies of the infostation-based context-aware mLearning system using . We first introduce some naming conventions (sect. 6.2.1) which are used in the specification of the system. Then we give the specification of two mServices which are AAA and the *mLecture* services (sect. 6.3).

### 6.2.1 Notations

The following naming conventions are used to differentiate between variables' names and constants. A variable name begins with a lowercase letter while a constant begins with a number or a uppercase letter. The list of the constant names that are used in the formalisation process is given in Table 4. And the list of variable names is given in Table 5.

| Notations | Descriptions |
|---|---|
| $ISC$ | the InfoStation Centre |
| $IS_i$ | the i-th InfoStation |
| $Phone$ | a phone |
| $PDA$ | a PDA |
| $PC$ | a PC |
| $SLIST$ | list of mServices |
| $ACK$ | an acknowledgement |
| NULL | empty message |
| DENIED | request denied |

Table 4. Constants

### 6.3 A Model of the InfoStation-based mLearning system

The system consists mainly of one central ISC, multiple ISs and multiple user devices. Each component of the system is modelled as an ambient. That is, the ISC, each IS and each user device is modelled as an ambient. In particular, a device, *PC* say, being used by a user, *303* say, is modelled by an ambient named *PC303*. The ISC ambient runs in parallel with the IS ambients, and all the user devices within the range of an IS are child ambients of that IS ambient.

| | |
|---|---|
| *uid*<br>301, 302, 303 | a user's ID |
| *dtype*<br>Phone, PDA, PC | a user's device type |
| *aname*<br>Phone301, PC303 | an ambient's name |
| *lect*<br>Lect001 | a lecture's ID |
| *reply*<br>OK, DENIED, content | a reply to a request |
| *content*<br>CONTENT | lecture's content |
| *slist*<br>SLIST | list of services |
| *ack*<br>ACK | acknowledgement |

Table 5. Variabbles

This is textually represented by the following process:

$$\begin{aligned} ISC[P_{ISC}] \ \mid \ & IS1[PDA303[P_{PDA303}] \mid PC401[P_{PC401}] \\ & \mid P_{IS1}] \\ \mid \ & IS2[PDA301[P_{PDA301}] \\ & \mid Phone402[P_{Phone402}] \mid P_{IS2}] \\ \mid \ & IS3[Phone300[P_{Phone300}] \mid P_{IS3}] \\ & \mid IS4[Phone403[P_{Phone403}] \mid PC302[P_{PC302}] \\ & \mid P_{IS4}] \end{aligned} \tag{1}$$

where each $P_x$ is a process modelling the behaviour of the corresponding ambient $x$.

Now we give the formal specification of the ISC and the ISs below.

**InfoStation** An abstract model of an infostation $IS_i$ (for some integer $i$) has the following main components are the AAA request ambient $AAAreq_i$, the lecture ambient $Lectreq_i$ and the cache ambient $Cache_i$.

The InfoStation is a parent to the inside ambients which are siblings to each other. The specification of each of these ambients is as follows:

$\boldsymbol{AAAreq_i}$ This ambient is responsible for handling AAA requests sent by user devices willing to register with the InfoStation $IS_i$. The $AAAreq_i$ ambient receives a request from a device and, immediately, forwards it to the InfoStation, then receives a reply from the InfoStation and again, forwards it to the user's device. This behaviour is modelled by the following process:

$$P_{A_i} \triangleq ! :: (uid, dtype, aname). IS_i \uparrow \langle uid, dtype, aname \rangle. IS_i \uparrow (ack, aname, slist). aname :: \langle aname, slist \rangle. 0$$

where *uid* is the user ID, *dtype* is the device type and *aname* is the name of the ambient sending the request.

The InfoStation accordingly receives a request from the $AAreq_i$ ambient, forwards it to the InfoStation Centre, and after receiving the reply from the InfoStation Centre it forwards it to the $AAreq_i$ ambient. This behaviour is modelled as:

$$\left( \begin{array}{l} !AAreq_i \downarrow (uid, dtype, aname).ISC :: \langle AAreq, uid, \\ dtype, aname, IS_i \rangle.\mathbf{0} \mid \\ !ISC :: (ack, aname, slist).(\mathbf{has}(aname))? \\ AAreqi \downarrow \langle ack, aname, slist \rangle.\mathbf{0} \end{array} \right) \quad (2)$$

***Lectreq$_i$*** This ambient handles all the mLecture service requests sent by the user devices. It receives a lecture request from a user device and forwards it to the infostation $IS_i$, i.e.

$$! :: (lectid, uid, dtype, aname). IS_i \uparrow \langle lectid, uid, dtype, aname \rangle. 0 \quad (3)$$

Then it gets the reply from that infostation and forwards it to the user device which initiated the request, i.e.

$$! :: (lectid, reply, aname). aname :: \langle lectid, reply \rangle. 0 \quad (4)$$

So the whole behaviour of the $Lectreq_i$ ambient is

$$P_{L_i} \triangleq Eq.(3) | \; Eq.(4) \quad (5)$$

We show how the InfoStation handles a request from the $Lectreq_i$ ambient after we have specified the $Cache_i$ ambient.

***Cache$_i$*** This is the ambient where the InfoStation stores copies of requested lectures for future rapid access. It models a cache memory. A lecture is stored as an ambient (named after that lecture's id) which contains three persistent memory, each containing a version of the lecture suitable to a specific type of device (phone, PDA or PC). When an InfoStation receives a mLecture service request from a device, it checks for the requested material in its cache first rather than getting it from the InfoStation Centre directly. The process of checking the availability of a lecture inside the cache is done by sending a request to the $Cache_i$ ambient which then checks whether it has the ambient of the requested lecture or not. If the requested lecture is available the cache ambient retrieves it and sends it back to the InfoStation, otherwise, it replies immediately to the InfoStation that this lecture does not exist. The behaviour of the $Cache_i$ ambient is modelled by the following process:

$$P_{C_i} \mathrel{\widehat{=}} !\uparrow(lectid, uid, dtype, aname).\left(\begin{array}{l}\mathbf{has}(lectid)?lectid\downarrow\langle dtype, aname\rangle.\\ lectid\downarrow(reply, aname).\\ \uparrow\langle lectid, uid, dtype, reply, aname\rangle.\mathbf{0} \mid \\ \neg\mathbf{has}(lectid)?\uparrow\langle lectid, uid, dtype,\\ NULL, aname\rangle.\uparrow(lectid, content, dtype).\\ lectid\downarrow\langle content, dtype\rangle.lectid\downarrow(ack).\uparrow\langle ack\rangle.\mathbf{0}\end{array}\right) \tag{6}$$

The behaviour of each lecture ambient (named after the lecture's id *lectid*) in the cache is modelled by the following process:

$$P_{lectid} \mathrel{\widehat{=}} !\uparrow(dtype, aname).\left(\begin{array}{l}\mathbf{has}(dtype)?dtype\downarrow\langle\rangle.\ dtype\downarrow(reply).\\ \uparrow\langle reply, aname\rangle.\ \mathbf{0} \mid \\ \neg\mathbf{has}(dtype)?\uparrow\langle NULL, aname\rangle.\\ \uparrow(content, dtype).dtype\downarrow\langle content\rangle.dtype\downarrow().\\ \uparrow\langle ACK\rangle.\mathbf{0}\end{array}\right) \tag{7}$$

The InfoStation will act as follows. First, it receives a request from $Lectreq_i$, then it checks the availability of the lecture in its cache by sending a request to the $Cache_i$ ambient, i.e.

$$!Lectreq_i \downarrow (lectid, uid, dtype, aname).Cache_i \downarrow \langle lectid, uid, dtype, aname\rangle.0 \tag{8}$$

If the cache replies with the content of the lecture, it will send a request to the InfoStation Centre with a flag set to 1 (meaning that the requested lecture exists in its cache) asking whether the user is currently taking a mTest. If the user is taking a mTest, then the mLecture service request must be denied. If the cache did reply with NULL as lecture's content, then the infostation will send a request to the InfoStation Centre with the flag set to 0 (meaning that the lecture does not exist in its cache) asking for both the requested lecture and to check whether the user is taking a mTest. This behaviour of the IS is modelled as:

$$!Cache_i\downarrow(lectid, uid, dtype, creply, aname).\left(\begin{array}{l}\neg(creply = NULL)?\ ISC :: \langle lectid, uid, dtype,\\ aname, 1\rangle.\mathbf{C} \mid \\ (creply = NULL)?\ ISC :: \langle lectid, uid, dtype,\\ aname, 0\rangle.\mathbf{N}\end{array}\right) \tag{9}$$

where C and N are de_ned as follows:

$$\mathbf{C} \mathrel{\widehat{=}} ISC :: (lectid, reply, aname).\left(\begin{array}{l}(reply = OK \wedge \mathbf{has}(aname))?\\ Lectreq_i\downarrow\langle lectid, creply, aname\rangle.\mathbf{0} \mid \\ (reply = OK \wedge \neg\mathbf{has}(aname))?\\ ISC :: \langle lectid, uid, dtype, aname, 0\rangle.\mathbf{0} \mid \\ (reply = DENIED \wedge \mathbf{has}(aname))?\\ Lectreq_i\downarrow\langle lectid, reply, aname\rangle.\mathbf{0}\end{array}\right)$$

and

$$\mathbf{N} \mathrel{\hat{=}} ISC :: (lectid, aname, reply). \begin{pmatrix} (\neg(reply = DENIED) \wedge \mathbf{has}(aname))? \\ Cache_i\downarrow\langle lectid, reply, dtype\rangle.Lectreq_i\downarrow\langle lectid, \\ reply, aname\rangle.\ Cache_i\downarrow(ack).\mathbf{0} \mid \\ (\neg(reply = DENIED) \wedge \neg\mathbf{has}(aname))? \\ Cache_i\downarrow\langle lectid, reply, dtype\rangle.ISC :: \langle lectid, uid, \\ dtype, aname, 0\rangle.\ Cache_i\downarrow(ack).\mathbf{0} \mid \\ (reply = DENIED \wedge \mathbf{has}(aname))? \\ Lectreq_i\downarrow\langle lectid, reply, aname\rangle.\mathbf{0} \end{pmatrix}$$

Thus, the whole behaviour of an infostation $IS_i$ is modelled as

$$P_{IS_i} \triangleq Eq.(2) \mid Eq.(8) \mid Eq.(9) \tag{10}$$

### 6.3.1 InfoStation centre

A model of the ISC encompasses ambients modelling users' accounts and named after the users' IDs; an ambient named *Lectures* that contains all the lecture ambients, each named after the corresponding lecture ID Each lecture ambient contains three persistent memory cells named *Phone, PDA* and *PC;* each storing the lecture's version suitable for the corresponding type of device. The mTest service is not represented as we are only dealing with the mLecture service in this paper. These components of the ISC are formalised below.

**Users' accounts** An ambient modelling a user's account contains two ambients named *Loc* and *Utest*. Each of these two ambients models a persistent memory cell which stores, at any time, the current location of that user (for the former) or a Boolean indicating whether that user is taking a mTest or not (for the latter). We understand by location of a user the IS the user is registered with. The behaviour of the *Loc* ambient and the *Utest* ambient are specified exactly with appropriate initial values. The ISC requests the value of any of these cells by sending the name *Loc* or *Utest* to the user's account ambient (see Eq. (14)) which then can *get* (i.e. read) the value of the corresponding child ambient as follows, where the parameter $x$ is the corresponding child ambient name:

$$!ISC \uparrow (x).x \downarrow \langle\rangle.x \downarrow (y).ISC \uparrow \langle y\rangle.0 \tag{11}$$

The user's account ambient can also put (i.e. write) a value in any of its child ambients as follows, where the parameter $x$ is the corresponding child ambient name and the parameter $n$ is that value:

$$!ISC \uparrow (x,n).x \downarrow \langle n\rangle.x \downarrow (\,).ISC \uparrow \langle x, ACK\rangle.0 \tag{12}$$

So the whole behaviour of a user's account ambient named uid is specified as:

$$P_{uid} \triangleq Eq.(11) \mid Eq.(12)$$

**Lectures** As mentioned above, this ambient contains all the lectures that are available in the mLecture service. Each lecture has a unique ID and the corresponding ambient is named after that ID. The behaviour of a lecture ambient is specified in Eq. (7). The *Lectures* ambient behaves exactly as the cache ambient specified in Eq. (6).

**Infostation centre** We now formalise the behaviour of the ISC when it receives a request from an IS. We are interested in two types of request in this paper: an AAA request and a lecture request.

When the ISC receives an AAA request from an IS, it updates the user's account with its new location and then replies to that IS with an acknowledge along with a list of available services. For the sake of simplicity, the service list is represented by the name '*SLIST*'. This is modelled by the following process:

$$!IS_i :: (aaareq, uid, dtype, aname).uid \downarrow \langle IS_i \rangle.uid \downarrow (ack). \tag{13}$$

$$IS_i :: \langle ack, aname, SLIST \rangle.0$$

After receiving a lecture request, the ISC checks whether the user requesting the service is currently taking a mTest. This is done by it sending a message to the corresponding user's account ambient. That user's account ambient reply with 0 for 'No' and 1 for 'Yes'. If the reply is 'Yes' then the ISC fetches the current location of the user and forward a 'DENIED' message to that location. If the reply is 'No' and the flag is set to 1, a 'OK' message is forwarded to the current user location; otherwise (i.e. reply is 'No' and the flag is set to 0), the ISC fetches the appropriate lecture version for the user device and sends it to the current user location. This behaviour is represented by the following process:

$$!IS_i :: (lectid, uid, dtype, aname, flag).uid \downarrow \langle Utest \rangle.uid \downarrow (y).(P_{ISC_1} \mid P_{ISC_2}) \tag{14}$$

where

$$P_{ISC_1} \triangleq (y = 1)?uid \downarrow \langle Loc \rangle.uid \downarrow (z).z :: \langle lectid, DENIED, aname \rangle.0$$

and

$$P_{ISC2} \triangleq \begin{pmatrix} (y = 0 \wedge flag = 1)?uid\downarrow\langle Loc\rangle.uid\downarrow(z). \\ z :: \langle lectid, OK, aname\rangle.\mathbf{0} \mid \\ (y = 0 \wedge flag = 0)?Lectures\downarrow\langle lectid, uid, \\ dtype, aname\rangle.Lectures\downarrow(lectid, uid, \\ dtype, reply, aname).uid\downarrow\langle Loc\rangle.uid\downarrow(z). \\ z :: \langle lectid, reply, aname\rangle.\mathbf{0} \end{pmatrix}$$

So the whole behaviour of the ISC is modelled by the following process:

$$P_{ISC} \triangleq Eq.(13) \mid Eq.(14)$$

## 7. Validation

Now that a formal model of the infostation-based mLearning system has been presented, we show how this model can be used to validate the properties of the mLearning system. Lamport proposed two main classes of system's properties: *safety properties*, which state that 'nothing bad will happen'; and *liveness properties*, which assert that 'something good will happen, eventually'. In the light of this classification, we wish to establish the liveness property that every lecture request from a user is eventually replied to by the system, provided that the user does not become infinitely unavailable after that request has been made.

**Theorem 7.1** *Every user's lecture request will eventually get a reply, provided that the user stays long enough in the system.*

The proof of this theorem is based on the reduction semantics of given by a congruence relation '≡' defined in Table 9 and a reduction relation '→' defined in Table 10.

In this proof we will assume, without loss of generality, that the user is using a laptop (PC) to access the system from an infostation $IS_i$. Given that the user is mobile, the following cases must be considered:

1. the user sends the request and waits for the reply in the same infostation $IS_i$ (i.e. the user may move around within the range of the infostation)
2. the user sends the request and move into a different infostation $IS_j, j \neq i$.

In Case 1, the user behaviours can be modelled by the following ambient:

$$PC303[Lectreq_i :: \langle Lect001, 303, PC, PC303\rangle . Lectreq_i :: (lectid, reply).0] \qquad (15)$$

This ambient sends a lecture request to the $Lectreq_i$ ambient and waits for a reply from that ambient, and then terminates. The lecture request contains the following information: (i) the lecture ID, *Lect001* ; (ii) the user ID, *303;* (iii) the device type, *PC;* and (iv) the name of the ambient to reply to, *PC303.*

The behaviours of the $Lectreq_i$ ambient is modelled by the process $P_{L_i}$ in Eq. (5), which basically receives a lecture request from a sibling ambient (e.g. a user device), forward the request to the infostation$IS_i$, get the reply from that infostation and forwards it to the very ambient which initiated the request. How the infostation $IS_i$ interacts with the $Lectreq_i$ ambient is specified in Eq. (8). These interactions between a user device, the $Lectreq_i$ ambient and the infostation $IS_i$ can be expressed as a sequence of derivations using the reduction relation →. Because of the space limit, we cannot give the full sequence of derivations in this paper. For illustration, the following sequence of derivations describes how a lecture request sent by the user gets to the infostation to be processed:

$$
\begin{array}{ll}
 & \text{Eq. (8)} \mid \text{Eq. (15)} \mid Lectreq_i[P_{L_i}] \\
\rightarrow & \{\text{Rule (Red Com S2) in Table 10; the request is sent to the } Lectreq_i \text{ ambient}\} \\
 & \text{Eq. (8)} \mid PC303[Lectreq_i :: (lectid, reply).\mathbf{0}] \mid \\
 & Lectreq_i \left[ \begin{array}{l} IS_i \uparrow \langle Lect001, 303, PC, PC303\rangle.\mathbf{0} \mid \\ ! :: (lectid, uid, dtype, aname). \\ IS_i \uparrow \langle lectid, uid, dtype, aname\rangle.\mathbf{0} \mid \\ !IS_i \uparrow (lectid, reply, aname). \\ aname :: \langle lectid, reply\rangle.\mathbf{0} \end{array} \right]
\end{array}
$$

$$\rightarrow \{\text{Rule (Red Com R6) in Table 10; the } \mathit{Lectreq}_i \text{ ambient forwards the request to the infostation}\}$$

$$\text{Eq. (8)} \mid \mathit{Cache}_i\!\downarrow\!\langle \mathit{Lect001}, \mathit{303}, \mathit{PC}, \mathit{PC303}\rangle.\mathbf{0} \mid \mathit{PC303}[\mathit{Lectreq}_i :: (\mathit{lectid}, \mathit{reply}).\mathbf{0}] \mid \mathit{Lectreq}_i \left[\begin{array}{l} ! :: (\mathit{lectid}, \mathit{uid}, \mathit{dtype}, \mathit{aname}). \\ IS_i \uparrow \langle \mathit{lectid}, \mathit{uid}, \mathit{dtype}, \mathit{aname}\rangle.\mathbf{0} \mid \\ !IS_i \uparrow (\mathit{lectid}, \mathit{reply}, \mathit{aname}). \\ \mathit{aname} :: \langle \mathit{lectid}, \mathit{reply}\rangle.\mathbf{0} \end{array}\right]$$

At this stage, the infostation $IS_i$ has received a lecture request from the $Lectreq_i$ ambient and is willing to check with the $Cache_i$ ambient whether it has the requested lecture for the specified type of device. The behaviour of the $Cache_i$ ambient is specified by the process $P_{C_i}$ in Eq. (6). If the requested lecture *Lect001* exists in the cache for the specified type of device, then the $Cache_i$ ambient gets a copy of the lecture for the specified type of device by interacting with the child ambient named *Lect001* whose behaviour is specified by the process $P_{Lect001}$ as in Eq. (7). It can also be seen from Eq. (6) and Eq. (7) that if the requested lecture *Lect001* does not exist in the cache for the specified type of device, then a reply message 'NULL' is forwarded to the infostation $IS_i$. So in either situation, the infostation $IS_i$ receives a reply from the cache.

Once a reply is received from the $Cache_i$ ambient, the infostation $IS_i$ contacts the infostation centre *ISC* as specified by the process in Eq. (9). How the *ISC* reacts is modelled by Eq. (14); it replies with a 'DENIED' message if the user requesting the lecture is currently using a mTest service, otherwise it replies with a 'OK' message and possibly a copy of the requested lecture if it is not available locally in $IS_i$'s cache. How each of these types of reply is handled by the $IS_i$ is modelled by the component C and N in Eq. (9). One can see that for every case where the user is still in the range of the infostation $IS_i$ (i.e. the context expression 'has(*aname*)' holds), the infostation $IS_i$ sends a reply to the $Lectreq_i$ ambient which subsequently forwards the reply to the user device as specified in Eq. (4). This completes the proof of Case 1.

The proof of Case 2 can be done in a similar manner as in Case 1, with the user behaviours specified as in Eq. (16), where $i \neq j$, i.e. the request is sent from one infostation and the reply to that request is received after the user has moved to a different infostation.

$$\mathit{PC303}\left[\begin{array}{l} \mathit{Lectreq}_i :: \langle \mathit{Lect001}, 303, \mathit{PC}, \mathit{PC303}\rangle.\mathtt{out}. \\ \mathtt{in}\ IS_j.\mathit{AAAreq}_j :: \langle 303, \mathit{PC}, \mathit{PC303}\rangle.\mathbf{0} \mid \\ \mathtt{at}(IS_j)?\mathit{AAAreq}_j :: (\mathit{ack}, \mathit{slist}). \\ \mathit{Lectreq}_j :: (\mathit{lectid}, \mathit{reply}).\mathbf{0} \end{array}\right] \quad (7)$$

This ambient sends a lecture request from the infostation $IS_i$, moves to a different infostation $IS_j$ , registers with this infostation by sending an AAA request then waits for the acknowledgement of its registration. Once its registration has been confirmed, it then prompts to receive the reply to the lecture request and then terminates.

## 8. Acknowledgment

The authors wish to acknowledge the support of the National Science Fund (Research Project Ref. No. DO02-149/2008) and the Science Fund of the University of Plovdiv "Paisij Hilendarski" (Research Project Ref. No. NI11-FMI-004).

## 9. References

[Barker,2000] P. Barker, Designing Teaching Webs: Advantages, Problems and Pitfalls, in Proc. of ED-MEDIA 2001 World Conference on Educational Multimedia, Hypermedia Telecommunication, Association for the Advancement of Computing in Education, Charlottesville, VA, 2000, pp. 54-59.

[Bellifemine,2007] F. Bellifemine, G. Caire, D. Greenwood, Developing Multi-Agent Systems with JADE, John Wiley & Sons Ltd., 2007.

[Bucur,2008] D. Bucur, M. Nielsen, Secure Data Flow in a Calculus for Context Awareness, in: Concurrency, Graphs and Models, Vol. 5065 of Lecture Notes in Computer Science, Springer, 2008, pp. 439-456.

[Bugliesi,2004] M. Bugliesi, G. Castagna, S. Crafa, Access Control for Mobile Agents: The Calculus of Boxed Ambients, ACM Trans. on Programming Languages and Systems, 26 (1), 2004, 57-124.

[Cardelli,2000] L. Cardelli, A. Gordon, Mobile Ambients, Theoretical Computer Science 240, 2000, 177-213.

[Dey,2000] Dey, A.K., Abowd, G.D.Towards a better understanding of context and context-awareness. Proceedings of the Workshop on the What, Who, Where, When and How of Context-Awareness, New York, ACM Press, 2000.

[FIPA,2002] FIPA, ACL Message Structure Specification, Foundation for Intelligent Physical Agents, Geneva, Switzerland SC00061G, 3rd December 2002.

[Frenkiel,1996] R. Frenkiel and T. Imielinski, Infostations: The joy of `many-time, many-where' communications, WINLAB Technical Report,1996.

[Ganchev, 2005] Ganchev, I., S. Stojanov, M. O'Droma. Mobile Distributed e-Learning Center. In Proc. of the 5th IEEE International Conference on Advanced Learning Technologies (IEEE ICALT'05), pp. 593-594, Kaohsiung, Taiwan. DOI 10.1109/ICALT.2005.199. ISBN 0-7695-2338-2. 5-8 July 2005.

[Ganchev,2007] I. Ganchev, et al., An InfoStation-Based Multi-Agent System Supporting Intelligent Mobile Services Across a University Campus, Journal of Computers, vol. 2, pp. 21-33, May 2007.

[Ganchev,2008a] I. Ganchev, et al., On InfoStation-Based Mobile Services Support for Library Information Systems, in 8th IEEE International Conference on Advanced Learning Technologies (IEEE ICALT-08), Santander, Cantabria, Spain, 2008, pp. 679 - 668.

[Ganchev,2008b] I. Ganchev, et al., InfoStation-Based Adaptable Provision of m-Learning Services: Main Scenarios, International Journal Information Technologies and Knowledge (IJ ITK), vol. 2, pp. 475-482, 2008.

[Ganchev,2008c] I. Ganchev, et al., InfoStation-based mLearning System Architectures: Some Development Aspects, in 8th IEEE International Conference on Advanced Learning Technologies, (ICALT'08), Santander, Spain, 2008, pp. 504-505.

[Maurer,2001] H. Maurer and M. Sapper, E-Learning Has to be Seen as Part of General Knowledge Management, in Proc. of ED-MEDIA 2001 World Conference on Educational Multimedia, Hypermedia Telecommunications, Tampere, AACE, Chalottesville, VA, 2001, pp. 1249-1253.

[Milner,1999] R. Milner. Communication and Mobile Systems: The π-Calculus. Cambridge University Press, 1999.

[O'Droma,2007] M. O'Droma and I. Ganchev, Toward a Ubiquitous Consumer Wireless World, IEEE Wireless Communications, vol. 14, pp. 52-63, February 2007.

[OWL-S,2010] OWL-S: Semantic Markup for Web Services. [Online]. Available - http://www.w3.org/Submission/OWL-S/ [Accessed: Mar 3, 2010].

[Passas,2006] N. Passas, et al., Enabling technologies for the 'always best connected' concept: Research Articles, Wirel. Commun. Mob. Comput., vol. 6, pp. 523-540, 2006.

[Sangiorgi,2001] D. Sangiorgi and D. Walker. The π-calculus: A Theory of Mobile Processes. Cambridge University Press, 2001.

[Stoyanov,2005] S. Stoyanov, et al., From CBT to e-Learning, Journal Information Technologies and Control, vol. 4, pp. 2-10, 2005.

[Stoyanov,2008] S. Stoyanov, et al., An Approach for the Development of InfoStation-Based eLearning Architectures Compt. Rend. Acad. Bulg. Sci., vol.61, pp. 1189-1198, 2008.

[W3C,2010] W3C, Document Object Model (DOM) [online]. Available - http://www.w3.org/DOM/. [Accessed Mar 03, 2010].

[Zedan,2008] H. Zedan, A. Cau, K. Buss, S. Westendorf, A. Hugill, S. Thomas, Mapping Human Creativity, STRL Internal Monograph, STRL-2008-09, De Montfort University, Leicester, 2008,UK.

[Zimmer,2005] P. Zimmer, A Calculus for Context-awareness, Tech. rep., BRICS, 2005.

# 10

# Analysis of Fuzzy Logic Models

Beloslav Riečan
*M. Bel University, Banská Bystrica,*
*Matematický Ústav SAV, Bratislava*
*Slovakia*

## 1. Introduction

One of the most important results of mathematics in the 20th century is the Kolmogorov model of probability and statistics. It gave many impulses for research and develop so in theoretical area as well as in applications in a large scale of subjects.

It is reasonable to ask why the Kolmogorov approach played so important role in the probability theory and in mathematical statistics. In disciplines which have been very successfull for many centuries.

Of course, Kolmogorov stated probability and statistics on a new and very effective foundation - set theory. For the first time in the history basic notions of probability theory have been defined precisely but simply. So a random event has been defined as a subset of a space, a random variable as a measurable function and its mean value as an integral. More precisely, abstract Lebesgue integral. It is hopeful to wait some new stimuls from the fuzzy generalization of the classical set theory. The aim of the chapter is a presentation of some results of the type.

## 2. Fuzzy systems and their algebraizations

Any subset $A$ of a given space $\Omega$ can be identified with its characteristic function

$$\chi_A : \Omega \to \{0,1\}$$

where

$$\chi_A(\omega) = 1,$$

if $\omega \in A$,

$$\chi_A(\omega) = 0,$$

if $\omega \notin A$. From the mathematical point of view a fuzzy set is a natural generalization of $\chi_A$(see [73]). It is a function

$$\varphi_A : \Omega \to [0,1].$$

Evidently any set (i.e. two-valued function on $\Omega, \chi_A \to \{0,1\}$) is a special case of a fuzzy set (multi-valued function), $\varphi_A : \Omega \to [0,1]$.

There are many possibilities for characterizations of operations with sets (union $A \cup B$ and intersection $A \cap B$). We shall use so called Lukasiewicz characterization:

$$\chi_{A \cup B} = (\chi_A + \chi_B) \wedge 1,$$

$$\chi_{A \cap B} = (\chi_A + \chi_B - 1) \vee 0.$$

(Here $(f \vee g)(\omega) = \max(f(\omega), g(\omega)), (f \wedge g)(\omega) = \min(f(\omega), g(\omega))$.) Hence if $\varphi_A, \varphi_B : \Omega \to [0,1]$ are fuzzy sets, then the union (disjunction $\varphi_A$ or $\varphi_B$ of corresponding assertions) can be defined by the formula

$$\varphi_A \oplus \varphi_B = (\varphi_A + \varphi_B - 1) \wedge 1,$$

the intersection (conjunction $\varphi_A$ and $\varphi_B$ of corresponding assertions) can be defined by the formula

$$\varphi_A \odot \varphi_B = (\varphi_A + \varphi_B - 1) \vee 0.$$

In the chapter we shall work with a natural generalization of the notion of fuzzy set so-called IF-set (see [1], [2]), what is a pair

$$A = (\mu_A, \nu_A) : \Omega \to [0,1] \times [0,1]$$

of fuzzy sets $\mu_A, \nu_A : \Omega \to [0,1]$, where

$$\mu_A + \mu_A \leq 1.$$

Evidently a fuzzy set $\varphi_A : \Omega \to [0,1]$ can be considered as an IF-set, where

$$\mu_A = \varphi_A : \Omega \to [0,1], \nu_A = 1 - \varphi_A : \Omega \to [0,1].$$

Here we have

$$\mu_A + \nu_A = 1,$$

while generally it can be $\mu_A(\omega) + \nu_A(\omega) < 1$ for some $\omega \in \Omega$. Geometrically an IF-set can be regarded as a function $A : \Omega \to \Delta$ to the triangle

$$\Delta = \{(u,v) \in R^2 : 0 \leq u, 0 \leq v, u + v \leq 1\}.$$

Fuzzy set can be considered as a mapping $\varphi_A : \Omega \to D$ to the segment

$$D = \{(u,v) \in R^2; u + v = 1, 0 \leq u \leq 1\}$$

and the classical set as a mapping $\psi : \Omega \to D_0$ from $\Omega$ to two-point set

$$D_0 = \{(0,1), (1,0)\}.$$

In the next definition we again use the Lukasiewicz operations.

**Definition 1.1.** By an IF subset of a set $\Omega$ a pair $A = (\mu_A, \nu_A)$ of functions

$$\mu_A : \Omega \to [0,1], \nu_A; \Omega \to [0,1]$$

is considered such that

$$\mu_A + \nu_A \leq 1.$$

We call $\mu_A$ the membership function, $\nu_A$ the non membership function and

$$A \leq B \Longleftrightarrow \mu_A \leq \mu_B, \nu_A \geq \nu_B.$$

If $A = (\mu_A, \nu_A), B = (\mu_B, \nu_B)$ are two IF-sets, then we define

$$A \oplus B = ((\mu_A + \mu_B) \wedge 1, (\nu_A + \nu_B - 1) \vee 0),$$

$$A \odot B = ((\mu_A + \mu_B - 1) \vee 0, (\nu_A + \nu_B) \wedge 1),$$

$$\neg A = (1 - \mu_A, 1 - \nu_A).$$

Denote by $\mathcal{F}$ a family of IF sets such that

$$A, B \in \mathcal{F} \Longrightarrow A \oplus B \in \mathcal{F}, A \odot B \in \mathcal{F}, \neg A \in \mathcal{F}.$$

**Example 1.1.** Let $\mathcal{F}$ be the set of all fuzzy subsets of a set $\Omega$. If $f : \Omega \to [0,1]$ then we define

$$A = (f, 1 - f),$$

i.e. $\nu_A = 1 - \mu_A$.

**Example 1.2.** Let $(\Omega, \mathcal{S})$ be a measurable space, $\mathcal{S}$ a $\sigma$-algebra, $\mathcal{F}$ the family of all pairs such that $\mu_A : \Omega \to [0,1], \nu_A : \Omega \to [0,1]$ are measurable. Then $\mathcal{F}$ is closed under the operations $\oplus, \odot, \neg$.

**Example 1.3.** Let $(\Omega, \mathcal{T})$ be a topological space, $\mathcal{F}$ the family of all pairs such that $\mu_A : \Omega \to [0,1], \nu_A : \Omega \to [0,1]$ are continuous. Then $\mathcal{F}$ is closed under the operations$\oplus, \odot, \neg$.

**Remark.** Of course, in any case $A \oplus B, A \odot B, \neg A$ are IF-sets, if $A, B$ are IF-sets. E.g.

$$A \oplus B = ((\mu_A + \mu_B) \wedge 1, (\nu_A + \nu_B - 1) \vee 0),$$

hence

$$\begin{aligned}
&(\mu_A + \mu_B) \wedge 1 + (\nu_A + \nu_B - 1) \vee 0 = \\
&= ((\mu_A + \mu_B) \wedge 1 + (\nu_A + \nu_B - 1)) \vee ((\mu_A + \mu_B) \wedge 1) = \\
&= ((\mu_A + \mu_B + \nu_A + \nu_B - 1) \wedge (1 + \nu_A + \nu_B - 1)) \vee ((\mu_A + \mu_B) \wedge 1) \leq \\
&\leq ((1 + 1 - 1) \wedge (\nu_A + \nu_B)) \vee ((\mu_A + \mu_B) \wedge 1) = \\
&= (1 \wedge (\nu_A + \nu_B)) \vee ((\mu_A + \mu_B) \wedge 1) \leq \\
&\leq 1 \vee 1 = 1.
\end{aligned}$$

Probably the most important algebraic model of multi-valued logic is an MV-algebra ([48],[49]). MV-algebras play in multi-valued logic a role analogous to the role of Boolean algebras in two-valued logic. Therefore we shall present a short information about MV-alegras and after it we shall prove the main result of the section: a possibility to embed the family of IF-sets to a suitable MV-algebra.

Let us start with a simple example.

**Example 1.4.** Consider the unit interval $[0,1]$ in the set $R$ of all real numbers. It will stay an MV-algebra, if we shall define two binary operations $\oplus, \odot$ on $[0,1]$, one unary operation $\neg$ and the usual ordering $\leq$ by the following way:

$$a \oplus b = \min(a+b,1),$$

$$a \odot b = \max(a+b-1,0),$$

$$\neg a = 1-a.$$

It is easy to imagine that $a \oplus b$ corresponds to the disjunction of the assertions $a, b$, $a \odot b$ to the conjunction of $a, b$ and $\neg a$ to the negation of $a$.

By the Mundici theorem ([48])any MV-algebra can be defined similarly as in Example 1.4, only the group $R$ must be substitute by an arbitrary $l$-group.

**Definition 1.2.** By an $l$-group we consider an algebraic system $(G,+,\leq)$ such that

(i) $(G,+)$ is an Abelian group,

(ii) $(G,\leq)$ is a lattice,

(iii) $a \leq b \Longrightarrow a+c \leq b+c$.

**Definition 1.3.** By an $MV$-algebra we consider an algebraic system $(M,0,u,\oplus,\odot)$ such that $M=[0,u] \subset G$, where $(G,+,\leq)$ is an $l$-group, 0 its neutral element, $u$ a positive element, and

$a \oplus b = (a+b) \wedge u,$

$a \odot b = (a+b-u) \vee 0,$

$\neg a = u-a.$

**Example 1.5.** Let $(\Omega, \mathcal{S})$ be a measurable space, $\mathcal{S}$ a $\sigma$-algebra,

$G = \{A = (\mu_A, \nu_A); \mu_A, \nu_A : \Omega \to R\},$

$A+B = (\mu_A+\mu_B, \nu_A+\nu_B-1) = (\mu_A+\mu_B, 1-(1-\nu_A+1-\nu_B)),$

$A \leq B \Longleftrightarrow \mu_A \leq \mu_B, \nu_A \geq \nu_B.$

Then $(G,+,\leq)$ is an $l$-group with the neutral element $\mathbf{0} = (0,1)$, $A-B = (\mu_A-\mu_B, \nu_A-\nu_B+1)$, and the lattice operations

$A \vee B = (\mu_A \vee \mu_B, \upsilon_A \wedge \nu_B),$

$A \wedge B = (\mu_A \wedge \mu_B, \nu_A \vee \nu_B).$

Put $u=(1,0)$ and define the MV-algebra

$M = \{A \in G; (0,1) = \mathbf{0} \leq \mathrm{A} \leq \mathrm{u} = (1,0)\},$

$A \oplus B = (A+B) \wedge u =$

$= (\mu_A+\mu_B, \nu_A+\nu_B-1) \wedge (1,0) =$

$= ((\mu_A+\mu_B) \wedge 1, (\nu_A+\nu_B-1) \vee 0,$

$A \odot B = (A+B-u) \vee (0,1) =$

$= ((\mu_A + \mu_B, \nu_A + \nu_B - 1) - (1,0)) \vee (0,1) =$

$= (\mu_A + \mu_B - 1, \nu_A + \nu_B - 1 - 0 + 1) \vee (0,1) =$

$= ((\mu_A + \mu_B - 1) \vee 0, (\nu_A + \nu_B) \wedge 1),$

$\neg A = (1,0) - (\mu_A, \nu_A) =$

$= (1 - \mu_A, 0 - \nu_A + 1) =$

$= (1 - \mu_A, 1 - \nu_A).$

Connections with the family of IF-sets (Definition 1.1) is evident. Hence we can formulate the main result of the section.

**Theorem 1.1.** Let $(\Omega, \mathcal{S})$ be a measurable space, $\mathcal{F}$ the family of all IF-sets $A = (\mu_A, \nu_A)$ be such that $\mu_A, \nu_A$ are $\mathcal{S}$-measurable. Then there exists an MV-algebra $\mathcal{M}$ such that $\mathcal{F} \subset \mathcal{M}$, the operations $\oplus, \odot$ are extensions of operations on $\mathcal{F}$ and the ordering $\leq$ is an extension of the ordering in $\mathcal{F}$.

Proof. Consider MV-algebra $\mathcal{M}$ constructed in Example 1.5. If $A, B \in \mathcal{F}$, then the operations on $\mathcal{M}$ coincide with the operations on $\mathcal{F}$. The ordering $\leq$ is the same.

Theorem 1.1 enables us in the space of IF-sets to use some results of the well developed probability theory on MV-algebras ([66 - 68]). Of course, some methods of the theory can be generalized in so-called D-posets ([28]). The system $(D \leq, -, 0, 1)$ is called D-poset, if $(D, \leq)$ is partially ordered set with the smallest element 0 and the largest element 1, $-$ is a partially binary operation satisfying the following statements:

1. $b - a$ is defined if and only if $a \leq b$.

2. $a \leq b$ implies $b - a \leq b$ and $b - (b - a) = a$.

3. $a \leq b \leq c$ implies $c - b \leq c - a$ and $(c - a) - (c - b) = b - a$.

## 3. Probability on IF-events

In IF-events theory an original terminology is used. The main notion is the notion of a state ([21], [22],[57], [58], [61][, [62]). It is an analogue of the notion of probability in the Kolmogorov classical theory. As before $\mathcal{F}$ is the family of all IF-sets $A = (\mu_A, \nu_A)$ such that $\mu_A, \nu_A : (\Omega, \mathcal{S}) \to [0,1]$ are $\mathcal{S}$-measurable.

**Definition 2.1.** A mapping $m : \mathcal{F} \to [0,1]$ is called a state if the following properties are satisfied:

(i) $m(1_\Omega, 0_\Omega) = 1, m(0_\Omega, 1_\Omega) = 0,$

(ii) $A \odot B = (0_\Omega, 1_\Omega) \Longrightarrow m((A \oplus B)) = m(A) + m(B),$

(iii) $A_n \nearrow A \Longrightarrow m(A_n) \nearrow m(A).$

Of course, also the notion with the name probability has been introduced in IF-events theory.

**Definition 2.2.** Let $\mathcal{J}$ be the family of all compact intervals in the real line, $\mathcal{J} = \{[a,b]; a, b \in R, a \leq b\}$. Probability is a mapping $P : \mathcal{F} \to \mathcal{J}$ satisfying the following conditions:

(i) $P(1_\Omega, 0_\Omega) = [1,1], P(0_\Omega, 1_\Omega) = [0,0]$,

(ii) $A \odot B = (0_\Omega, 1_\Omega) \Longrightarrow P((A \oplus B)) = P(A) + P(B)$,

(iii) $A_n \nearrow A \Longrightarrow P(A_n) \nearrow P(A)$.

It is easy to see that the following property holds.

**Proposition 2.1.** Let $P : \mathcal{F} \to \mathcal{J}, P(A) = [P^\flat(A), P^\sharp(A)]$. Then $P$ is a probability if and only if $P^\flat, P^\sharp : \mathcal{F} \to [0,1]$ are states.

Hence it is sufficient to characterize only the states ([4], [5], [54]).

**Theorem 2.1.** For any state $m : \mathcal{F} \to [0,1]$ there exist probability measures $P, Q : \mathcal{S} \to [0,1]$ and $\alpha \in [0,1]$ such that

$$m((\mu_A, \nu_A)) = \int_\Omega \mu_A dP + \alpha(1 - \int_\Omega (\mu_A + \nu_A) dQ).$$

Proof. The main instrument in our investigation is the following implication, a corollary of (ii):

$$f, g \in \mathcal{F}, f + g \leq 1 \Longrightarrow m(f,g) = m(f, 1-f) + m(0, f+g). \quad (1)$$

We shall define the mapping $P : \mathcal{S} \to [0,1]$ by the formula $P(A) = m(\chi_A, 1 - \chi_A)$. Let $A, B \in \mathcal{S}, A \cap B = \emptyset$. Then $\chi_A + \chi_B \leq 1$, hence $(\chi_A, 1 - \chi_A) \odot (\chi_B, 1 - \chi_B) = (0,1)$. Therefore

$P(A) + P(B) = m(\chi_A, 1 - \chi_A) + m(\chi_B, 1 - \chi_B) =$

$= m((\chi_A, 1 - \chi_A) \oplus (\chi_B, 1 - \chi_B)) =$

$= m(\chi_A + \chi_B, 1 - \chi_A - \chi_B) = m(\chi_{A \cup B}, 1 - \chi_{A \cup B} = P(A \cup B)$.

Let $A_n \in \mathcal{S}(n = 1, 2, ...), A_n \nearrow A$. Then

$$\chi_{A_n} \nearrow \chi_A, 1 - \chi_{A_n} \searrow 1 - \chi_A,$$

hence by (iii)

$$P(A_n) = m(\chi_{A_n}, 1 - \chi_{A_n}) \nearrow m(\chi_A, 1 - \chi_A) = P(A).$$

Evidently $P(\Omega) = m(\chi_\Omega, 1 - \chi_\Omega) = m((1,0)) = 1$, hence $P : \mathcal{S} \to [0,1]$ is a probability measure.

Now we prove two identities. First the implication:

$$A_1, ..., A_n \in \mathcal{S}, \alpha_1, ..., \alpha_n \in [0,1], A_i \cap A_j = \emptyset (i \neq j) \Longrightarrow$$

$$m(\sum_{i=1}^n \alpha_i \chi_{A_i}, 1 - \sum_{i=1}^n \alpha_i \chi_{A_i}) = \sum_{i=1}^n m(\alpha_i \chi_{A_i}, 1 - \alpha_i \chi_{A_i}). \quad (2)$$

It can be proved by induction. The second identity is the following

$$0 \leq \alpha, \beta \leq 1 \Longrightarrow m(\alpha\beta\chi_A, 1 - \alpha\beta\chi_A) = \alpha m(\beta\chi_A, 1 - \beta\chi_A). \quad (3)$$

First it can be proved by induction the equality

$$qm(\frac{1}{q}\beta\chi_A, 1 - \frac{1}{q}\beta\chi_A) = m(\beta\chi_A, 1 - \beta\chi_A)$$

holding for every $q \in N$. Therefore

$$m(\frac{1}{q}\beta\chi_A, 1 - \frac{1}{q}\beta\chi_A) = \frac{1}{q}m(\beta\chi_A, 1 - \beta\chi_A)$$

$$m(\frac{p}{q}\beta\chi_A, 1 - \frac{p}{q}\beta\chi_A) = \frac{p}{q}m(\beta\chi_A, 1 - \beta\chi_A),$$

hence (3) holds for every rational $\alpha$. Let $\alpha \in R, \alpha \in [0,1]$. Take $\alpha_n \in Q, \alpha_n \nearrow \alpha$. Then

$$\alpha_n\chi_A \nearrow \alpha\chi_A, 1 - \alpha_n\chi_A \searrow 1 - \alpha\chi_A.$$

Therefore

$$m(\alpha\beta\chi_A, 1 - \alpha\beta\chi_A) = \lim_{n\to\infty} m(\alpha_n\beta\chi_A, 1 - \alpha_n\beta\chi_A) =$$

$$= \lim_{n\to\infty} \alpha_n m(\beta\chi_A, 1 - \beta\chi_A) = \alpha m(\beta\chi_A, 1 - \beta\chi_A),$$

hence, (3) is proved, too. Particularly, if we give $\beta = 1$, then

$$m(\alpha\chi_A, 1 - \alpha\chi_A) = \alpha m(\chi_A, 1 - \chi_A).$$

Let $f : \Omega \to [0,1]$ be simple, $\mathcal{S}$-measurable, i.e.

$$f = \sum_{i=1}^{n} \alpha_i\chi_{A_i}, A_i \in \mathcal{S}(i = 1,.,,,n), A_i \cap A_j = \emptyset(i \neq j).$$

Combining (2), (3), and the definition of $P$ we obtain

$$m(f, 1 - f) = \sum_{i=1}^{n} m(\alpha_i\chi_{A_i}, 1 - \alpha_i\chi_{A_i}) =$$

$$= \sum_{i=1}^{n} \alpha_i m(\chi_{A_i}, 1 - \chi_{A_i}) =$$

$$= \sum_{i=1}^{n} \alpha_i P(A_i) = \int_\Omega f dP,$$

hence

$$m(f, 1 - f) = \int_\Omega f dP,$$

for any $f : \Omega \to [0,1]$simple. If $f : \Omega \to [0,1]$ is an arbitrary $\mathcal{S}$-measurable function, then there exists a sequence $(f_n)$ of simple measurable functions such that $f_n \nearrow f$. Evidently, $1 - f_n \searrow 1 - f$. Therefore

$$m(f, 1 - f) = \lim_{n\to\infty} m(f_n, 1 - f_n) = \lim_{n\to\infty} \int_\Omega f_n dP = \int_\Omega f dP,$$

hence

$$m(f, 1-f) = \int_{\Omega} dP, \qquad (4)$$

for any measurable $f : \Omega \to [0,1]$.

Now take our attention to the second term $m(0, f+g)$ in the right side of the equality (1). First define $M : \mathcal{S} \to [0,1]$ by the formula

$$M(A) = m(0, 1-\chi_A).$$

As before it is possible to prove that $M$ is a measure. Of course,

$$M(\Omega) = m(0,0) = \alpha \in [0,1].$$

Define $Q : \mathcal{S} \to [0,1]$ by the formula

$$m(0, 1-\chi_A) = \alpha Q(A).$$

As before, it is possible to prove

$$m(0, 1-f) = \alpha \int_{\Omega} f dQ,$$

for any $f : \Omega \to [0,1]$ measurable, or

$$m(0, h) = \alpha \int_{\Omega} (1-h) dQ, \qquad (5)$$

for any $h : \Omega \to [0,1]$, $\mathcal{S}$-measurable. Combining (1), (4), and (5) we obtain

$$m(A) = m((\mu_A, \nu_A) = m((\mu_A, 1-\mu_A)) + m((0, \mu_A + \nu_A))$$

$$= \int_{\Omega} \mu_A dP + \alpha(1 - \int_{\Omega} (\mu_A + \nu_A) dQ).$$

A simple consequence of the representation theorem is the following property of the mapping $P - \alpha Q : \mathcal{S} \to R$.

**Proposition 2.2.** Let $P, Q : \mathcal{S} \to [0,1]$ be the probabilities mentioned in Theorem 2.1, $\alpha$ is the corresponding constant. Then

$$P(A) - \alpha Q(A) \geq 0$$

for any $A \in \mathcal{S}$.

Proof. Put $B = (0,0), C = (\chi_A, 0)$. Then $B \leq C$, hence $m(0,0) \leq m(\chi_A, 0)$. Therefore

$$\alpha = m(0,0) \leq m(\chi_A, 0) = P(A) + \alpha(1 - Q(A)).$$

Theorem 1.1 is an embedding theorem stating that every IF-events algebra $\mathcal{F}$ can be embedded to and MV-algebra $\mathcal{M}$. Now we shall prove that any state $m : \mathcal{F} \to [0,1]$ can be extended to a state $\overline{m} : \mathcal{M} \to [0,1]$ ([63]).

**Theorem 2.2.** Let $\mathcal{M} \supset \mathcal{F}$ be the MV-algebra constructed in Theorem 1.1. Then every state $m : \mathcal{F} \to [0,1]$ can be extended to a state $\overline{m} : \mathcal{M} \to [0,1]$.

Proof. It is easy to see that any element $(\mu_A, \nu_A) \in \mathcal{M}$ can be presented in the form

$$(\mu_A, \nu_A) \odot (0, 1 - \nu_A) = (0, 1),$$

$$(\mu_A, 0) = (\mu_A, \nu_A) \oplus (0, 1 - \nu_A).$$

If $(\mu_A, \nu_A) \in \mathcal{F}$, then

$$m((\mu_A, 0)) = m((\mu_A \nu_A)) + m((0, 1 - \nu_A)).$$

Generally, we can define $\overline{m} : \mathcal{M} \to [0, 1]$ by the formula

$$\overline{m}((\mu_A, \nu_A)) = m((\mu_A, 0)) - m((0, 1 - \nu_A)),$$

so that $\overline{m}$ is an extension of $m$. Of course, we must prove that $\overline{m}$ is a state. First we prove that $\overline{m}$ is additive.

Let $A = (\mu_A, \nu_A) \in \mathcal{M}, B = (\mu_B, \nu_B) \in \mathcal{M}, A \odot B = (0, 1)$, hence

$$((\mu_A + \mu_B - 1) \vee 0, (\nu_A + \nu_B) \wedge 1) = (0, 1),$$

$$\mu_A + \mu_B \leq 1, 1 - \nu_A + 1 - \nu_B \leq 1.$$

Therefore

$$\overline{m}(A) + \overline{m}(B) = \overline{m}(\mu_A, \nu_A) + \overline{m}(\mu_B, \nu_B)$$
$$= m(\mu_A, 0) - m(0, 1 - \nu_A) + m(\mu_B, 0) - m(0, 1 - \nu_B) =$$
$$= m(\mu_A + \mu_B, 0) - m(0, 1 - \nu_A - \nu_B) =$$
$$= m(\mu_A + \mu_B, \nu_A + \nu_B) = \overline{m}(A \oplus B).$$

Before the continuity of $\overline{m}$ we shall prove its monotonicity. Let $A \leq B$, i.e. $\mu_A \leq \mu_A, \nu_A \geq \nu_B$. Then by Theorem 2.1

$$\overline{m}(A) = m(\mu_A, 0) - m(0, 1 - \nu_A) =$$
$$= \int_\Omega \mu_A dP + \alpha(1 - \int_\Omega (\mu_A + 0) dQ - \int_\Omega 0 dP - \alpha(1 - \int_\Omega (0 + 1 - \nu_A) dQ) =$$
$$= \int_\Omega \mu_A dP + \alpha(1 - \int_\Omega (\mu_A + \nu_A) dQ).$$

Therefore

$$\overline{m}(B) - \overline{m}(A) = \int_\Omega \mu_B dP + \alpha - \alpha \int_\Omega \mu_B dQ - \alpha \int_\Omega \nu_B dQ -$$
$$-(\int_\Omega \mu_A dP + \alpha - \alpha \int_\Omega \mu_A dQ - \alpha \int_\Omega \nu_A dQ) =$$
$$= \int_\Omega (\mu_B - \mu_A) dP - \alpha \int_\Omega (\mu_B - \mu_A) dQ + \alpha \int_\Omega (\nu_A - \nu_B) dQ.$$

Of course, as an easy consequence o Proposition 2.1 we obtain the inequality

$$\int_\Omega f dP - \alpha \int_\Omega f dQ \geq 0$$

for any non-negative measurable $f : \Omega \to R$. Therefore

$$\overline{m}(B) - \overline{m}(A) = \int_\Omega f dP - \alpha \int_\Omega f dQ + \alpha \int_\Omega (\nu_A - \mu_B) dQ \geq 0.$$

Finally let $A_n = (\mu_{A_n}, \nu_{A_n}) \in \mathcal{M}, A = (\mu_A, \nu_A) \in \mathcal{M}, A_n \nearrow A$, i.e. $\mu_{A_n} \nearrow \mu_A, \nu_{A_n} \searrow \nu_A$. We have

$$\overline{m}(A_n) = \int_\Omega \mu_{A_n} dP - \alpha \int_\Omega \mu_{A_n} dQ + \alpha - \alpha \int_\Omega \nu_{A_n} dQ \nearrow$$
$$\nearrow \int_\Omega \mu_A dP - \alpha \int_\Omega \mu_A dQ + \alpha - \alpha \int_\Omega \nu_A dQ = \overline{m}(A).$$

## 4. Observables

In the classical probability there are three main notions:

probability = measure

random variable = measurable function

mean value = integral.

The first notion has been studied in the previous section. Now we shall define the second two notions.

Classically a random variable is such function $\xi : (\Omega, \mathcal{S}) \to R$ that $\xi^{-1}(A) \in \mathcal{S}$ for any Borel set $A \in \mathcal{B}(R)$ (here $\mathcal{B}(R) = \sigma(\mathcal{J})$ is the $\sigma$-algebra generated by the family $\mathcal{J}$ of all intervals). Now instead of a $\sigma$-algebra $\mathcal{S}$ we have the family $\mathcal{F}$ of all IF-events, hence we must give to any Borel set $A$ an element of $\mathcal{F}$. Of course, instead of random variable we shall use the term observable ([15], [16], [18], [32], [35]).

**Definition 3.1.** An observable is a mapping

$$x : \sigma(\mathcal{J}) \to \mathcal{F}$$

satisfying the following conditions:

(i)
$$x(R) = (1,0), x(\emptyset) = (0,1),$$

(ii)
$$A \cap B = \emptyset \Longrightarrow x(A) \odot x(B) = (0,1), x(A \cup B) = x(A) \oplus x(B),$$

(iii)
$$A_n \nearrow A \Longrightarrow x(A_n) \nearrow x(A).$$

**Proposition 3.1.** If $x : \sigma(\mathcal{J}) \to \mathcal{F}$ is an observable, and $m : \mathcal{F} \to [0,1]$ is a state, then

$$m_x = m \circ x : \sigma(\mathcal{J}) \to [0,1]$$

defined by

$$m_x(A) = m(x(A))$$

is a probability measure.

Proof. First

$$m_x(R) = m(x(R)) = m((1,0)) = 1.$$

If $A \cap B = \emptyset$, then $x(A) \odot x(B) = (0,1)$, hence

$$m_x(A \cup B) = m(x(A \cup B)) = m((x(A) \oplus x(B)) =$$

$$= m(x(A)) + m(x(B)) = m_x(A) + m_x(B).$$

Finally, $A_n \nearrow A$ implies $x(A_n) \nearrow x(A)$, hence

$$m_x(A_n) = m(x(A_n)) \nearrow m(x(A)) = m_x(A).$$

**Proposition 3.2.** Let $x : \sigma(\mathcal{J}) \to \mathcal{F}$ be an observable, $m : \mathcal{F} \to [0,1]$ be a state. Define $F : R \to [0,1]$ by the formula

$$F(u) = m(x((-\infty, u))).$$

Then $F$ is non-decreasing, left continuous in any point $u \in R$,

$$\lim_{u\to\infty} F(u) = 1, \lim_{u\to-\infty} F(u) = 0.$$

Proof. If $u < v$, then

$$x((-\infty, v)) = x((-\infty, u)) \oplus x((u, v)) \geq x((-\infty, u)),$$

hence

$$F(v) = m((-\infty, v)) \geq m(x((-\infty, u))) = F(u),$$

F is non decreasing. If $u_n \nearrow u$, then

$$x((-\infty, u_n)) \nearrow x((-\infty, u)),$$

hence

$$F(u_n) = m(x((-\infty, u_n))) \nearrow m(x((-\infty, u))) = F(u),$$

F is left continuous in any $u \in R$. Similarly $u_n \nearrow \infty$ implies

$$x((-\infty, u_n)) \nearrow x((-\infty, \infty)) = (1,0).$$

Therefore

$$F(u_n) = m(x((-\infty, u_n))) \nearrow m((1,0))) = 1$$

for every $u_n \nearrow \infty$, hence $\lim_{u\to\infty} F(u) = 1$. Similarly we obtain

$$u_n \searrow -\infty \Longrightarrow -u_n \nearrow \infty,$$

hence

$$m(x((u_n, -u_n))) \nearrow m(x(R)) = 1.$$

Now

$$1 = \lim_{n\to\infty} F(-u_n) = \lim_{n\to\infty} m(x((u_n, -u_n))) + \lim_{n\to\infty} F(u_n) =$$

$$= 1 + \lim_{n\to\infty} F(u_n),$$

hence $\lim_{n\to\infty} F(u_n) = 0$ for any $u_n \searrow -\infty$.

Of course, we must describe also the random vector $T = (\xi, \eta) : \Omega \to R^2$. We have

$$T^{-1}(C \times D) = \xi^{-1}(C) \cap \eta^{-1}(D).$$

In the IF case we shall use product of functions instead of intersection of sets ([47], [56], [68]).

**Definition 3.2.** The product $A.B$ of two IF-events $A = (\mu_A, \nu_A), B = (\mu_B, \nu_B)$ is the IF set

$$A.B = (\mu_A.\mu_B, 1 - (1-\nu_A).(1-\nu_B)) = (\mu_A.\mu_B, \nu_A + \nu_B - \nu_A.\nu_B).$$

**Definition 3.3.** Let $x_1, ..., x_n : \sigma(\mathcal{J}) \to \mathcal{F}$ be observables. By the joint observable of $x_1, ..., x_n$ we consider a mapping $h : \sigma(\mathcal{J}^n) \to \mathcal{F}(\mathcal{J}^n$ being the set of all intervals of $R^n$) satisfying the following conditions:

(i) $h(R^n) = (1, 0)$

(ii) $A \cap B = \emptyset \Longrightarrow h(A) \odot h(B) = (0, 1)$, and $h(A \cup B) = h(A) \oplus h(B)$,

(iii) $A_n \nearrow A \Longrightarrow h(A_n \nearrow h(A)$,

(iv) $h(C_1 \times C_2 \times ... \times C_n) = x_1(C_1).x_2(C_2).....x_n(C_n)$, for any $C_1, C_2, ..., C_n \in \mathcal{J}$.

**Theorem 3.1.** ([63]) For any observables $x_1, ..., x_n : \sigma(\mathcal{J}) \to \mathcal{F}$ there exists their joint observable $h : \sigma(\mathcal{J}^n) \to \mathcal{F}$.

Proof. We shall prove it for $n = 2$. Consider two observables $x, y : \sigma(\mathcal{J}) \to \mathcal{F}$. Since $x(A) \in \mathcal{F}$, we shall write

$$x(A) = (x^\flat(A), 1 - x^\sharp(A))$$

and similarly

$$y(B) = (y^\flat(B), 1 - y^\sharp(B)).$$

By the definition of product we obtain

$$x(C).y(D) = (x^\flat(C).y^\flat(D), 1 - x^\sharp(C).y^\sharp(D)).$$

Therefore, we shall construct similarly

$$h(K) = (h^\flat(K), 1 - h^\sharp(K))$$

Fix $\omega \in \Omega$ and define $\mu, \nu : \sigma(\mathcal{J}) \to [0, 1]$ by

$$\mu(A) = x^\flat(A)(\omega), \nu(B) = y^\flat(B)(\omega).$$

Let $\mu \times \nu$ be the product of the probability measures $\mu, \nu$. Put

$$h^\flat(K)(\omega) = \mu \times \nu(K).$$

Then

$$h^\flat(C \times D)(\omega) = \mu(C).\nu(D) = x^\flat(C).y^\flat(D)(\omega)$$

hence

$$h^\flat(C \times D) = x^\flat(C).y^\flat(D).$$

Analogously

$$h^\sharp(C \times D) = x^\sharp(C).y^\sharp(D).$$

If we define

$$h(A) = (h^\flat(A), 1 - h^\sharp(A)), A \in \sigma(\mathcal{J}^2),$$

then

$$h(C \times D) = (x^\flat(C).y^\flat(D), 1 - x^\sharp(C).y^\sharp(D)) = x(C).y(D).$$

Now we shall present two applications of the notion of the joint observable. The first is the definition of function of a finite sequence of observables, e.g. their sum. In the classical case

$$\xi + \eta = g \circ T : \Omega \to R$$

where $g(u,v) = u + v, T(\omega) = (\xi(\omega), \eta(\omega))$. Hence $\xi + \eta$ can be defined by the help of pre-images:

$$(\xi + \eta)^{-1} = T^{-1} \circ g^{-1} : \mathcal{B}(R) \to \mathcal{S}.$$

**Definition 3.4.** Let $x_1, ..., x_n : \mathcal{B}(R) \to \mathcal{F}$ be observables, $g : R_n \to R$ be a measurable function. Then we define

$$g(x_1, ..., x_n) : \mathcal{B}(R) \to \mathcal{F}$$

by the formula

$$g(x_1, ..., x_n)(C) = h(g^{-1}(C)), C \in \mathcal{B}(R),$$

where $h : \mathcal{B}(R^n) \to \mathcal{F}$ is the joint observable of the observables $x_1, ..., x_n$.

**Example 3.1.** $x_1 + ... + x_n : \mathcal{B}(R) \to \mathcal{F}$ is the observable defined by the formula $(x_1 + ... + x_n)(C) = h(g^{-1}(C))$, where $h : \mathcal{B}(R^n) \to \mathcal{F}$ is the joint observable of $x_1, ..., x_n$, and $g : R^n \to R$ is defined by the equality $g(u_1, ..., u_n) = u_1 + ... + u_n$.

The second application of the joint observable is in the formulation of the independency.

**Definition 3.5.** Let $m : \mathcal{F} \to [0,1]$ be a state, $(x_n)_{n=1}^\infty$ be a sequence of observables, $h_n : \sigma(\mathcal{J}^n) \to \mathcal{F}$ be the joint observable of $x_1, ..., x_n (n = 1, 2, ...)$. Then $(x_n)_{n=1}^\infty$ is called independent, if

$$m(h_n(C_1 \times C_2 \times ... \times C_n)) = m(x_1(C_1)).m(x_2(C_2)).....m(x_n(C_n))$$

for any $n \in N$ and any $C_1, ..., C_n \in \sigma(\mathcal{J})$.

Now let us return to the notion of mean value of an observable. In the classical case

$$E(g \circ \xi) = \int_\Omega g \circ \xi dP = \int_R g dF$$

where $F$ is the distribution function of $\xi$.

**Definition 3.6.** Let $x : \mathcal{B}(R) \to \mathcal{F}$ be an observable, $m : \mathcal{F} \to [0,1]$ be a state, $g : R \to R$ be a measurable function, $F$ be the distribution function of $x$ $(F(t) = m(x((-\infty, t))))$. Then we define the mean value $E(g \circ x)$ by the formula

$$E(g \circ x) = \int_R g dF$$

if the integral exists.

**Example 3.2.** Let $x$ be discrete, i.e. there exist $x_i \in R, p_i \in (0,1], i = 1, ..., k$ such that

$$F(t) = \sum_{x_i < t} p_i.$$

Then

$$E(x) = \int_R t dF(t) = \sum_{i=1}^{k} x_i p_i.$$

The second classical case is the continuous distribution, where

$$F(t) = \int_{-\infty}^{t} \varphi(u) du.$$

Then

$$E(x) = \int_R t dF(t) = \int_{-\infty}^{\infty} t\varphi(t) dt.$$

**Example 3.3.** Let us compute the dispersion

$$\sigma^2(x) = E(g \circ x),$$

where

$$g(u) = (u - a)^2, a = E(x).$$

Here we have two possibilities. The first

$$\sigma^2 = \int_R (t - a)^2 dF(t)$$

i.e.

$$\sigma^2(x) = \sum_{i=1}^{k} (x_i - a)^2 p_i$$

in the discrete case, and

$$\sigma^2(x) = \int_{-\infty}^{\infty} (t - a)^2 \varphi(t) dt$$

in the continuous case. The second possibility is the equality

$$\sigma^2(x) = E((x - a)^2) = E(x^2) - 2aE(x) + E(a^2) =$$

$$= E(x^2) - a^2, a = E(x).$$

Since $a = E(x)$ is known, it is sufficient to compute $E(x^2)$. In the case we have $g(t) = t^2$, hence

$$E(x^2) = \int_R g(t) dF(t) = \int_R t^2 dF(t).$$

In the discrete case we have

$$E(x^2) = \sum_{1=i}^{k} x_i^2 p_i,$$

in the continuous case we obtain

$$E(x^2) = \int_{-\infty}^{\infty} t^2 \varphi(t) dt.$$

## 5. Sequences

In the section we want to present a method for studying of limit properties of some sequences $(x_n)_n, x_n : \mathcal{B}(R) \to \mathcal{F}$ of observables ([7], [25], [31], [32], [49]). The main idea is a representation of the given sequence by a sequence of random variables $(\xi_n)_n, \xi_n : (\Omega, \mathcal{S}, P) \to R$. Of course, the space $(\Omega, \mathcal{S})$ depends on a concrete sequence $(x_n)_n$, for different sequences various spaces $(\Omega, \mathcal{S}, P)$ can be obtained.

The main instrument is the Kolmogorov consistency theorem ([67]). It starts with a sequence of probability measures $(\mu_n)_n, \mu_n : \sigma(\mathcal{J}_n) \to [0,1]$ such that

$$\mu_{n+1} | \sigma(\mathcal{J}_n) \times R = \mu_n$$

i. e. $\mu_{n+1}(A \times R) = \mu_n(A)$ for any $A \in \sigma(\mathcal{J}_n)$ (consistency condition). Let $\mathcal{C}$ be the family of all cylinders in the space $R^N$, i. e. such sets $A \subset R^N$ that

$$A = \{(t_n)_n; (t_1, ..., t_k) \in B\},$$

where $k \in N, B \in \mathcal{B}(R^k) = \sigma(\mathcal{J}^k)$. Then by the Kolmogorov consistency theorem there exists exactly one probability measure

$$P : \sigma(\mathcal{C}) \to [0,1]$$

such that

$$P(A) = \mu_k(B). \tag{6}$$

If we denote by $\pi_n$ the projection $\pi_n : R^N \to R^n$,

$$\pi_n((t_i)_{i=1}^{\infty}) = (t_1, t_2, ..., t_n),$$

then we can formulate the assertion (6) by the equality

$$P(\pi_n^{-1}(B)) = \mu_n(B), \tag{7}$$

for any $B \in \mathcal{C}$.

**Theorem 4.1.** Let $m$ be a state on a space $\mathcal{F}$ of all IF-events. Let $(x_n)_n$ be a sequence of observables, $x_n : \mathcal{B}(R) \to \mathcal{F}$, and let $h_n : \mathcal{B}(R^n) \to \mathcal{F}$ be the joint observable of $x_1, ..., x_n, n = 1, 2, ....$ If we define $\mu_n : \mathcal{B}(R^n) \to [0,1]$ by the equality

$$\mu_n = m \circ h_n,$$

then $(\mu_n)_n$ satisfies the consistency condition

$$\mu_{n+1} | (\sigma(\mathcal{J}_n) \times R) = \mu_n.$$

Proof. Let $C_1, C_2, ..., C_n \in \mathcal{B}(R)$. Then by Definition 3.3. and Definition 3.1

$$\mu_{n+1}(C_1 \times C_2 \times ... \times C_n \times R) = m(x_1(C_1)).x_2(C_2).....x_n(C_n).x_{n+1}(R)) =$$

$$= m(x_1(C_1)).x_2(C_2).....x_n(C_n).(1,0)) =$$
$$= m(x_1(C_1)).x_2(C_2).....x_n(C_n)) =$$
$$= \mu_n(C_1 \times C_2 \times ... \times C_n),$$

hence $\mu_{n+1}|(\mathcal{J}_n \times R) = \mu_n|\mathcal{J}_n$. Of course, if two measures coincide on $\mathcal{J}_n$ then they coincide on $\sigma(\mathcal{J}_n)$, too.

Now we shall formulate a translation formula between sequences of observables in $(\mathcal{F}, m)$ and corresponding random variables in $(R^N, \sigma(\mathcal{C}), P)$ ([67]).

**Theorem 4.2.** Let the assumptions of Theorem 4.1 be satisfied. Let $g_n : R^n \to R$ be Borel measurable functions $n = 1, 2, ....$ Let $\mathcal{C}$ be the family of all cylinders in $R^N, \xi_n : R^N \to R$ be defined by the formula $\xi_n((t_i)_i) = t_n$,

$$\eta_n : R^N \to R, \eta_n = g_n(\xi_1., ..., \xi_n),$$

$$y_n : \mathcal{B}(R^n) \to \mathcal{F}, y_n = h_n \circ g_n^{-1}.$$

Then

$$P(\eta_n^{-1}(B)) = m(y_n(B))$$

for any $B \in \mathcal{B}(R)$.

Proof. Put $A = g_n^{-1}(B)$. By Theorem 4.1.

$$m(y_n(B)) = m(h_n(g_n^{-1}(B))) = P(\pi_n^{-1}(g_n^{-1}(B))) =$$

$$= P((g_n \circ \pi_n)^{-1}(B)) = P(\eta_n^{-1}(B)).$$

As an easy corollary of Theorem 4.2 we obtain a variant of central limit theorem. In the classical case

$$\lim_{n\to\infty} P(\{\omega; \frac{\frac{1}{n}\sum_{i=1}^n \xi_i(\omega) - a}{\frac{\sigma}{\sqrt{n}}} < t\}) = \frac{1}{\sqrt{2\pi}} \int_{-\infty}^{t} e^{-\frac{u^2}{2}} du$$

Of course, we must define for observables the element

$$(\frac{\sqrt{n}}{\sigma}\sum_{i=1}^{n} x_i - a)(-\infty, t)$$

It is sufficient to put

$$g_n(u_1, ..., u_n) = \frac{\sqrt{n}}{\sigma}\sum_{i=1}^{n} u_i - a$$

**Theorem 4.3.** Let $(x_n)_n$ be a sequence of square integrable, equally distributed, independent observables, $E(x_n) = a, \sigma^2(x_n) = \sigma^2 (n = 1, 2, ...)$. Then

$$\lim_{n\to\infty} m(\frac{\frac{1}{n}\sum_{i=1}^n x_i - a}{\frac{\sigma}{\sqrt{n}}}(-\infty, t) = \frac{1}{\sqrt{2\pi}} \int_{-\infty}^{t} e^{-\frac{u^2}{2}} du$$

Proof. We shall use the notation from the last two theorems. Then for $C \in \sigma(\mathcal{J})$

$$m(x_n(C)) = m(h_n(R \times ... \times R \times C) = P(\pi_n^{-1}(R \times ... \times R \times C)) = P(\xi_n^{-1}(C)),$$

hence

$$E(\xi_n) = \int_{-\infty}^{\infty} t dP_{\xi_n}(t) = \int_{-\infty}^{\infty} t dm_{x_n}(t) = E(x_n) = a,$$

and

$$\sigma^2(\xi_n) = \sigma^2(x_n) = \sigma^2.$$

Moreover,

$$P(\xi_1^{-1}(C_1) \cap ... \cap \xi_n^{-1}(C_n)) = P(\pi_n^{-1}(C_1 \times ... \times C_n)) =$$

$$= m(h_n(C_1 \times ... \times C_n) = m(x_1(C_1)).....m(x_n(C_n)) = P(\xi_1^{-1}(C_1)).....P(\xi_n^{-1}(C_n)),$$

hence $\xi_1, ..., \xi_n$ are independent for every $n$. Put $g_n(u_1, ..., u_n) = \frac{\sqrt{n}}{\sigma} \sum_{i=1}^n u_i - a$. By Theorem 4.2. we have

$$m(\frac{\sqrt{n}}{\sigma}(\sum_{i=1}^n x_i - a)((-\infty, t)) = m(h_n(g_n^{-1}(-\infty, t))) = m(y_n((-\infty, t)) =$$

$$= P(\eta_n^{-1}((-\infty, t))) = P(\{(\omega); \frac{\sqrt{n}}{\sigma} \sum_{i=1}^n \xi_i(\omega) - a < t\}).$$

Therefore by the classical central limit theorem

$$\lim_{n \to \infty} m(\frac{\frac{1}{n} \sum_{i=1}^n x_i - a}{\frac{\sigma}{\sqrt{n}}}(-\infty, t)) = \frac{1}{\sqrt{2\pi}} \int_{-\infty}^{t} e^{-\frac{u^2}{2}} du$$

Let us have a look to the previous theorem from another point of view, say, categorial. We had

$$\lim_{n \to \infty} P(\eta_n^{-1}((-\infty, t)) = \phi(t)$$

We can say that $(\eta_n)_n$ converges to $\phi$ in distribution. Of course, there are important possibilities of convergencies, at least in measure and almost everywhere.

A sequence $(\eta_n)_n$ of random variables (= measurable functions) converges to 0 in measure $\mu : \mathcal{S} \to [0, 1]$, if

$$\lim_{n \to \infty} \mu(\eta^{-1}(-\varepsilon, \varepsilon)) = 0$$

for every $\varepsilon > 0$. And the sequence converges to 0 almost everywhere, if

$$\lim_{n \to \infty} P(\cap_{p=1}^{\infty} \cup_{k=1}^{\infty} \cap_{n=k}^{\infty} \eta_n^{-1}((-\frac{1}{p}, \frac{1}{p})) = 1$$

Certainly, if $\eta_n(\omega) \to 0$,then

$$\forall \varepsilon > 0 \exists k \forall n > k : -\varepsilon < \eta(\omega) < \varepsilon$$

If we instead of $\varepsilon$ use $\frac{1}{p}, p \in N$, then $\eta_n(\omega) \to 0$ if and only if

$$\forall p \exists k \forall n > k : \omega \in \eta_n^{-1}((-\frac{1}{p}, \frac{1}{p})).$$

And $\eta_n \to 0$ almost everywhere, if the set $\{\omega; \eta(\omega) \to 0\}$ has measure 1.

**Definition 4.1.** A sequence $(y_n)_n$ of observables

(i) converges in distribution to a function $F : R \to R$, if

$$\lim_{n\to\infty} m(y_n((-\infty, t)) = F(t)$$

for every $t \in R$;

(ii) it converges to 0 in state $m : \mathcal{F} \to [0,1]$, if

$$\lim_{n\to\infty} m(y_n((-\varepsilon, \varepsilon))) = 0$$

for every $\varepsilon > 0$;

(iii) it converges to 0 $m$-almost everywhere, if

$$\lim_{p\to\infty} \lim_{k\to\infty} \lim_{i\to\infty} m(\wedge_{n=k}^{k+i} y_n(-\frac{1}{p}, \frac{1}{p})) = 0.$$

**Theorem 4.4.** Let $(y_n)_n$ be a sequence of observables, $(\eta_n)_n$ be the sequence of corresponding random variables. Then

(i) $(y_n)_n$ converges to $F : R \to R$ in distribution if and only if $(\eta_n)_n$ converges to $F$;

(ii) $y_n)_n$ converges to 0 in state $m : \mathcal{F} \to [0,1]$ if and only if $(\eta_n)_n$ converges to 0 in measure $P : \mathcal{S} \to [0,1]$

(iii) if $(\eta_n)_n$ converges $P$-almost everywhere to 0, then $(y_n)_n$ $m$-almost everywhere converges to 0.

The details can be found in [66]. Many applications of the method has been described in [25], [31], [35], [37], [39] , [52].

## 6. Conditional probability

Conditional entropy (of $A$ with respect to $B$) is the real number $P(A|B)$ such that

$$P(A \cap B) = P(B)P(A|B).$$

When $A, B$ are independent, then $P(A|B) = P(A)$, the event $A$ does not depend on the ocuring of event $B$. Another point of view:

$$P(A \cap B) = \int_B P(A|B)dP.$$

The number $P(A|B)$ can be regarded as a constant function, Constant functions are measurable with respect to the $\sigma$-algebra $\mathcal{S}_0 = \{\emptyset, \Omega\}$.

Generally $P(A|\mathcal{S}_0)$ can be defined for any $\sigma$-algebra $\mathcal{S}_0 \subset \mathcal{S}$, as an $\mathcal{S}_0$-measurable function such that

$$P(A \cap C) = \int_C P(A|\mathcal{S}_0)dP, C \in \mathcal{S}_o.$$

If $\mathcal{S}_0 = \mathcal{S}$, then we can put $P(A|\mathcal{S}_0) = \chi_A$, since $\chi_A$ is $\mathcal{S}_0$-measurable, and

$$\int_C \chi_A dP = P(A \cap C).$$

An important example of $\mathcal{S}_0$ is the family of all pre-images of a random variable $\xi : \Omega \to R$

$$\mathcal{S}_0 = \{\xi^{-1}(B); B \in \sigma(\mathcal{J})\}.$$

In this case we shall write $P(A|\mathcal{S}_0) = P(A|\xi)$, hence

$$\int_C (P(A|\xi)dP = P(A \cap C), C = \xi^{-1}(B), B \in \sigma(\mathcal{J}).$$

By the transformation formula

$$P(A \cap \xi^{-1}(B)) = \int_{\xi^{-1}(B)} g \circ \xi dP = \int_B g dP_\xi, B \in \sigma(\mathcal{J})$$

And exactly this formulation will be used in our $IF$-case,

$$m(A.x(B)) = \int_B p(A|x)dm_x = \int_B p(A|x)dF.$$

Of course, we must first prove the existence of such a mapping $p(A|x) : R \to R$ ([34], [70], [72]). Recall that the product of $IF$-events is defined by the formula

$$K.L = (\mu_K.\mu_L, \nu_K + \nu_L - \nu_K.\nu_L).$$

**Theorem 5.1.** Let $x : \sigma(\mathcal{J}) \to \mathcal{F}$ be an observable, $m : \mathcal{F} \to [0,1]$ be a state, and let $A \in \mathcal{F}$. Define $\nu : \sigma(\mathcal{J}) \to [0,1]$ by the equality

$$\nu(B) = m(A.x(B)).$$

Then $\nu$ is a measure.

Proof. Let $B \cap C = \emptyset, B, C \in \mathcal{B}(R) = \sigma(\mathcal{J})$. Then $x(B).x(C) = (0,1)$, hence

$$A.(x(B) \oplus x(C)) = (A.x(B)) \oplus (A.x(C)),$$

and therefore

$$\nu(B \cup C) = m(A.x(B \cup C)) = m(A.(x(B) \oplus x(C)) = m((A.x(B)) \oplus (A.x(C))) =$$

$$= m(A.x(B)) + m(A.x(C)) = \nu(B) + \nu(C).$$

Let $B_n \nearrow B$. Then $x(B_n) \nearrow x(B)$, hence $A.x(B_n) \nearrow A.x(B)$. Therefore

$$\nu(B_n) = m(A.x(B_n)) \nearrow m(A.x(B)) = \nu(B).$$

**Theorem 5.2.** Let $x : \sigma(\mathcal{J}) \to \mathcal{F}$ be an observable, $m : \mathcal{F} \to [0,.1]$ be a state, and let $A \in \mathcal{F}$. Then there exists a Borel measurable function $f : R \to R$ (i. e. $B \in \sigma(\mathcal{J}) \Longrightarrow f^{-1}(B) \in \sigma(\mathcal{J})$) such that

$$m(A.x(B)) = \int_B f dm_x$$

for any $B \in \sigma(\mathcal{J})$. If $g$ is another such a function, then

$$m_x(\{u \in R; f(x) \neq g(x)\}) = 0.$$

Proof. Define $\mu, \nu : \sigma(\mathcal{J}) \to [0,1]$ by the formulas

$$\mu(B) = m_x(B) = m(x(B)), \nu(B) = m(A.x(B)).$$

Then $\mu, \nu : \sigma(\mathcal{J}) \to [0,1]$ are measures, and $\nu \leq \mu$.

By the Radon - Nikodym theorem there exists exactly one function $f : R \to R$ (with respect to the equality $\mu$- almost everywhere) such that

$$m(A.x(B)) = \nu(B) = \int_B f d\mu = \int_B f dm_x, B \in \sigma(\mathcal{J}).$$

**Definition 5.1.** Let $x : \sigma(\mathcal{J}) \to \mathcal{F}$ be an observable $A \in \mathcal{F}$. Then the conditional probability $p(A|x) = f$ is a Borel measurable function (i. e. $B \in \mathcal{J} \Longrightarrow f^{-1}(B) \in \sigma(\mathcal{J})$) such that

$$\int_B p(A|x) dm_x = m(A.x(B))$$

for any $B \in \sigma(\mathcal{J})$.

## 7. Algebraic world

At the end of our communication we shall present two ideas. The first one is in some algebraizations of the product

$$A.B = (\mu_A.\mu_B, \nu_A + \nu_B - \nu_A.\nu_B).$$

The second idea is a presentation of a dual notion to the notion of $IF$-event.

In MV-algebras the product was introduced independently in [56] and [47]. Let us return to Definition 1.3 and Example 1.5.

**Definition 6.1.** An MV-algebra with product is a pair $(M, .)$, where $M$ is an MV-algebra, and . is a commutative and associative binary operation on $M$ satisfying the following conditions:

(i) $1.a = a$

(ii) $a.(b \odot \neg c) = (a.b) \odot \neg(a.c)$.

**Example 6.1.** Let $\mathcal{M} \supset \mathcal{F}$ be the MV-algebra defined in Theorem 1.1 (Example1.5). Then $\mathcal{M}$ with the product $A.B = (\mu_A\mu_B, \nu_A + \nu_B - \nu_A\nu_B)$ is an MV-algebra with product. Indeed,

$$(1,0).(\mu_A, \nu_A) = (1.\mu_A, 0 + \nu_A - 0.\nu_A) = (\mu_A, \nu_A).$$

Moreover

$$(\mu_A, \nu_A).((\mu_B, \nu_B) \odot (1 - \mu_C, 1 - \nu_C)) =$$
$$= (\mu_A((\mu_B - \mu_C) \vee 0), \nu_A + (\nu_B - \nu_C + 1) \wedge 1 - \nu_A((\nu_B + 1 - \nu_C) \wedge 1)).$$

On the other hand

$$((\mu_A, \nu_A).(\mu_B, \nu_B)) \odot (\neg(\mu_A, \nu_A).(\mu_C, \nu_C)) =$$
$$((\mu_A(\mu_B - \mu_C)) \vee 0, (\nu_A + (\nu_B - \nu_C + 1) - \nu_A(\nu_B + 1 - \nu_C)) \wedge 1).$$

Denote

$$\nu_B - \nu_C + 1 = k.$$

If $1 \leq k$, then

$$\nu_A + k \wedge 1 - \nu_A(k \wedge 1) = \nu_A + 1 - \nu_A = 1,$$
$$(\nu_A + k - \nu_A k) \wedge 1 = (\nu_A + k(1 - \nu_A)) \wedge 1 = 1.$$

If $k < 1$, then

$$\nu_A + k \wedge 1 - \nu_A k \wedge 1 = \nu_A + k - \nu_A k,$$
$$(\nu_A + k - \nu_A k) \wedge 1 = \nu_A + k - \nu_A k,$$

hence actually

$$A.(B \odot \neg C) = (A.B) \odot (\neg(A.C)).$$

Similarly as in Section 1 we can define a product in D-posets, we shall name such D-posets Kôpka D-posets.

**Definition 6.2.** A Kôpka D-poset is a pair $(D, *)$, where D is a D-poset, and $*$ is a commutative and associative operation on D satisfying the following conditions:

1. $\forall a \in D : a * 1 = a;$

2. $\forall a, b \in D, a \leq b, \forall c \in D : a * c \leq b * c;$

3. $\forall a, b \in D : a - (a * b) \leq 1 - b;$

4. $\forall (a_n)_n \subset D, a_n \nearrow a, \forall b \in D : a_n * b \nearrow a * b.$

Evidently every IF-family $\mathcal{F}$ can be embedded to an MV-algebra with product and it is a special case of a Kôpka D-poset, hence any result from the Kôpka D-poset theory can be applied to our IF-events theory ([26], [64]).

Now let us consider a theory dual to the IF-events theory, theory of IV-events. A prerequisity of IV-theory is in the fact that it considers natural ordering and operations of vectors. On the other hand the IV-theory is isomorphic to the IF-theory ([65],[43]).

**Definition 6.3.** Let $(\Omega, \mathcal{S})$ be a measurable space, $\mathcal{S}$ be a $\sigma$-algebra. By an IV-event a pair $\overline{A} = (\overline{\mu}_A, \overline{\nu}_A) : \Omega \to [0,1]^2$ is considered such that

$$\overline{A} \leq \overline{B} \Longleftrightarrow \overline{\mu}_A \leq \overline{\mu}_B, \overline{\nu}_A \leq \overline{\nu}_B;$$

$$\overline{A} \boxplus \overline{B} = ((\overline{\mu}_A + \overline{\mu}_B) \wedge 1, (\overline{\nu}_A + \overline{\nu}_B) \wedge 1);$$
$$\overline{A} \boxdot \overline{B} = ((\overline{\mu}_A + \overline{\mu}_B - 1) \vee 0, (\overline{\nu}_A + \overline{\nu}_B - 1) \vee 0).$$

Denote by $\mathcal{V}$ the family of all IV-events. By an IV-state a map $\overline{m} : \mathcal{V} \to [0,1]$ is considered such that the following properties are satisfied:

(i) $\overline{m}((0,0)) = 0, \overline{m}((1,1)) = 1;$

(ii) $\overline{A} \boxdot \overline{B} = (0,0) \Longrightarrow \overline{m}(\overline{A} \boxplus \overline{B}) = \overline{m}(\overline{A}) + \overline{m}(\overline{B});$

(iii)$\overline{A}_n \nearrow \overline{A} \Longrightarrow \overline{m}(\overline{A}_n) \nearrow \overline{m}(\overline{A}).$

**Theorem 6.1.** Let $\mathcal{V}$ be the family of all IV-events (with respect to $\Omega, \mathcal{S})), \overline{m} : \to [0,1]$ be an IV-state. Define

$$\mathcal{F} = \{(\overline{\mu}_A, 1 - \overline{\nu}_A); (\overline{\mu}_A, \overline{\nu}_A) \in \mathcal{V}\},$$
$$m : \mathcal{F} \to [0,1], m((\mu_A, \nu_A)) = 1 - \overline{m}(\mu_A, 1 - \nu_A)),$$
$$\varphi : \mathcal{V} \to \mathcal{F}, \varphi((\overline{\mu}_A, \overline{\nu}_A)) = (\overline{\mu}_A, 1 - \overline{\nu}_A).$$

Then $\mathcal{F}$ is the family of all IF-events (with respect to $(\Omega, \mathcal{S})$, $m$ is an IF-state and $\varphi$ is an isomorphism such that

$\varphi((0,0)) = (0,1), \varphi((1,0)) = (1,1),$

$\varphi(\overline{A} \boxdot \overline{B}) = \varphi(\overline{A}) \odot \varphi(\overline{B}),$

$\varphi(\overline{A} \boxplus \overline{B}) = \varphi(\overline{A}) \oplus \varphi(\overline{B}),$

$\varphi(\neg \overline{A}) = \neg \varphi(\overline{A}),$

$\overline{m}(\overline{A})) = m(\varphi(\overline{A})), \overline{A} \in \mathcal{V}.$

Proof. It is almost straightforward. Of course, the using of the family $\mathcal{V}$ is more natural and the results can be applied immediately to probability theory on $\mathcal{F}$.

## 8. Conclusion

The structures studied in this chapter have two aspects: the first one is practical, the second theoretical one. Fuzzy sets and their generalization - Atanassov intuitionistic fuzzy sets - in both directions new possibilities give.

From the practical point of view we can recommend e. g. [1], [9], [69]. Of course, the whole IF - theory can be motivated by practical problems and applications (see[10],[44 - 46], [53]).

The main contribution of the presented theory is a new point of view on human thinking and creation. We consider algebraic models for multi valued logic: IF-events, and more generally MV-algebras, D-posets, and effect algebras. They are important for many valued logic as Boolean algebras for two valued logic. Of course, we presented also some results about entropy ([11], [12], [40 - 42], [59]), or inclusion - exclusion principle ([6], [26], [30])for an illustration. But the more important idea is in building the probability theory on IF-events.

The theoretical description of uncertainty has two parts in the present time : objective - probability and statistics, and subjective - fuzzy sets. We show that both parts can be considered together.

## 9. Acknowledgement

This work was partially supported by the Agency of Slovak Ministry of Education for the structural Funds of the EU, uder project ITMS 26220120007 and the Agency VEGA 1/0621/11

## 10. References

[1] Atanassov: Intuitionistic Fuzzy Sets: Theory and Applications. Studies in Fuzziness and Soft Computing. PhysicaVerlag, Heidelberg, 1999.

[2] Atanassov K.T. and Riečan B.: On two new types of probability on IF-events. Notes on IFS, 2007.

[3] Cignoli L., D'Ottaviano M., Mundici D.: Algebraic Foundations of Many-valued Reasoning. Kluwer, Dordrecht, 2000.

[4] Ciungu L., Riečan, B.: General form of probabilities on IF-sets. In: Fuzzy Logic and Applications. Proc. WILF Palermo, 2009, 101 - 107.

[5] Ciungu L., Riečan B.: Representation theorem for probabilities on IFS-events. Information Sciences 180, 2010, 793 - 798.

[6] Ciungu L., Riečan B.: The inclusion - exclusion principle for IF-states. Information sciences (to appear).

[7] Čunderlíková K.: The individual ergodic theorem on the IF-events. Soft Computing - A Fusion of Foundations, Methodologies and Applications, Vol. 14, Number 3, Springer 2010, 229 - 234.

[8] Čunderlíková K., Riečan B.: The probability on B-structures. Developments in Fuzzy Sets, Intuitionistic Fuzzy Sets, Generalized Nets and related Topics Vol I. EXIT, Warsaw 2008, 33 - 60.

[9] De S.K., Biswas R., Roy A.R.: An application of intuitionistic fuzzy sets in medical diagnosis. Fuzzy Sets and Systems 117, 2001, 209 - 213.

[10] Deschrijver G., Kerre E.E.: On the relationship between some extensions of fuzzy set theory. Fuzzy Sets and Systems133, 227 - 235.

[11] Di Nola A., Dvurečenskij A., Hyčko M., and Manara C.: Entropy of efect algebras with the Riesz decomposition property I: Basic properties. Kybernetika 41, 143-160, 2005.

[12] Di Nola A., Dvurečenskij A., Hyčko M., and Manara C.: Entropy of efect algebras with the Riesz decomposition property II: MV-algebras. Kybernetika 41, 2005, 161-176.

[13] Drygas P.: Problem of monotonicity for decomposable operations. Recent Advances in Fuzzy Sets, Intuitionistic Fuzzy Sets, Generalized Nets and related Topics I, IBS PAN SRI PAS Warsaw 2011, 79 - 88.

[14] Ďurica M.: Hudetz entropy on IF-events. Developments in Fuzzy Sets, Intuitionistic Fuzzy Sets, Generalized Nets and related Topics Vol I., IBS PAN SRI PAS Warsaw 2010,73 - 86.

[15] Dvurečenskij A. and Pulmannová S.: New Trends in Quantum Structures. Kluwer, Dordrecht, 2000.

[16] Dvurečenskij A. and Rachunek : Riečan and Bosbach states for bounded non-commutative RI-monoids. Math. Slovaca 56, 2006, 487-500.

[17] Dvurečenskij A. and Riečan B.: Weakly divisible MV-algebras and product. J. Math. Anal. Appl. 234, 1999, 208-222.

[18] Dvurečenskij A. and Riečan B.: On states on BL-algebras and related structures. In: Tributes 10, 2009, Essays in honour of Petr Hajek (P. Cintula et al. eds.), 287 - 302.

[19] Foulis D. and Bennett M.: Effect algebras and unsharp quantum logics. Found. Phys. 24, 1994, 1325-1346.
[20] Georgescu G.: Bosbach states on fuzzy structures. Soft Computing 8, 2004, 217-230.
[21] Gerstenkorn T., Manko J.: Probabilities of intuitionistic fuzzy events. In: Issues in Intelligent Systems: Paradigms, (O.Hryniewicz et al. eds.), Intuitionistic fuzzy probability theory 45 2005, 63-58.
[22] Grzegorzewski P. and Mrowka E.: Probability of intuistionistic fuzzy events. In: Soft Metods in Probability, Statistics and Data Analysis, (P. Grzegorzewski et al.eds),2002, 105-115.
[23] Hájek P.: Metamathematics of Fuzzy Logic. Kluwer, Dordrecht, 1998.
[24] Hanesová R.: Statistical estimation on MV-algebras. Proc. of the Eleventh International Workshop on Generalized Nets and the Second International Workshop on Generalized Nets, Intuitionistic Fuzzy Sets and Knowledge Engineering, London 9 July 2010, 66 - 70.
[25] Jurečková, M.: The addition to ergodic theorem on probability MV-algebras with product. Soft Computing 7, 2003, 105 - 115.
[26] Kelemenová,J.: The inclusion-exclusion principle in semigroups. Recent Advances in Fuzzy Sets, Intuitionistic Fuzzy Sets, Generalized Nets and related Topics, Vol.I IBS PAN SRI PAS Warsaw 2011, 87- 94.
[27] Klement E., Mesiar R., and Pap E.: Triangular Norms. Kluwer, Dordrecht, 2000.
[28] Kôpka F., Chovanec F.: D-posets. Math. Slovaca 44, 1994, 21-34.
[29] Krachounov M.: Intuitionistic probability and intuitionistic fuzzy sets. In: First Intern. Workshop on IFS, (El-Darzi et al. eds.), 2006, 714-717.
[30] Kuková M.: The inclusion-exclusion principle on some algebraic structures. Recent Advances in Fuzzy Sets, Intuitionistic Fuzzy Sets, Generalized Nets and related Topics, Vol.I IBS PAN SRI PAS Warsaw 2011, 123 - 126.
[31] Lašová L.: The individual ergodic theorem on IF-events. Developments in Fuzzy Sets, Intuitionistic Fuzzy Sets, Generalized Nets and related Topics, Vol.I IBS PAN SRI PAS Warsaw 2010, 131 - 140.
[32] Lendelová K.: Convergence of IF-observables. In: Issues in the Representation and Processing of Uncertain and Imprecise Information - Fuzzy Sets, Intuitionistic Fuzzy Sets, Generalized nets, and Related Topics. EXIT, Warsaw 2005, 232 - 240.
[33] Lendelová K.: IF-probability on MV-algebras. Notes on Intuitionistic Fuzzy Sets 11, 2005, 66-72.
[34] Lendelová K.: Conditional IF-probability. In: Advances in Soft Computing: Soft Methods for Integrated Uncertainty Modelling, 2006, 275-283.
[35] Lendelová K., Petrovičová J.: Representation of IF-probability for MV- algebras. Soft Computing (A Fusion of Fundations, Metodologies and Applications 10, 2006, 564-566.
[36] Lendelová K., Riečan B.: Weak law of large numbers for IF-events. In: Current Issues in Data and Knowledge Engineering,(Bernard De Baets et al. eds.), 2004, 309-314.
[37] Lendelová K., Riečan B.: Probability on triangle and square. In: Proceedings of the Eleventh International Conference IPMU 2006, July, 2-7, 2006, Paris, 977 - 982.
[38] Lendelová K., Riečan B.: Strong law of large numbers for IF-events. In: Proceedings of the Eleventh International Conference IPMU 2006, July, 2-7, 2006, Paris 2006, 2363-2366.
[39] Markechová D.: The conjugation of fuzzy probability spaces to the unit interval. Fuzzy Sets and Systems 47, 1992, 87 - 92.
[40] Markechová D.: F-quantum spaces and their dynamics. Fuzzy Sets and Systems 50, 1992, 79- 88.

[41] Markechová D.: Entropy of complete fuzzy partitions. Mathematica Slovaca 43, 1993, 1 - 10.
[42] Markechová D.: A note on the Kolmogorov - Sinaj entropy of fuzzy dynamical systems. Fuzzy Sets and Systems 64, 1994, 87 - 90.
[43] Mesiar R., Komorníková M.: Probability measures on interval-valued fuzzy events. Acta Univ. M. Belii,Math. 19(2011), 5 - 10.
[44] Michalíková A.: Outer measure on IF-sets. First International Workshop on Intuitionistic Fuzzy Sets, Generalized Nets and Knowledge Engineering. Univ. Westminster London, 6 - 7 September 2006, 39 - 44.
[45] Michalíková A.: A measure extension theorem in l-groups. Proc. IPMU'08 Torremoklinos Malaga, Spain, 22 - 27 June 2008, 1666 - 1670.
[46] Michalíková A.: The differential calculus on IF sets. FUZZ-IEEE 2009 Korea 2009, 1393 - 1395.
[47] Montagna, F.: An algebraic approach to propositional fuzzy logic. J. Logic Lang. Inf. (D. Mundici et al. eds.), Special issue on Logics of Uncertainty 9, 2000, 91 - 124.
[48] Mundici D.: Interpretation of AFC⋆ algebras in Lukasiewicz sentential calculus. J. Funct. Anal. 56 (1986), 889 - 894.
[49] Mundici D.: Advanced Lukasiewicz calculus and MV-algebras. Springer,Dordrecht 2011.
[50] Potocký R.: On random variables having values in a vector lattice. Math.Slovaca 27, 1977, 267 - 276.
[51] Potocký R.: On the expected value of vector lattice - valued random variables. Math. Slovaca 36, 1986, 401 - 405.
[52] Renčová, M.: A generalization of probability theory on MV-algebras to IF-events. Fuzzy Sets and Systems 161, 2010, 1726 - 1739.
[53] Renčová, M.: General form of strongly additive phi-probabilities. In: Proc. IPMU'08 (L. Magdalena et al. eds.) Torremolinos (Malaga), Spainm 2008, 1671 - 1674.
[54] Renčová M.: State - preserving mappings on IF-events. Developments in Fuzzy Sets, Intuitionistic Fuzzy Sets, Generalized Nets and related Topics, Vol.I, EXIT Warsaw 2008, 313 - 318.
[55] Renčová M., Riečan B.:Probability on IF-sets: an elementary approach. In: First Int. Workshop on IFS, Generalized Nets and Knowledge Engineering, 2006, 8 - 17.
[56] Riečan, B.: On the product MV-algebras. Tatra Mt. Math. Publ. 16, 1999, 143 - 149.
[57] Riečan B.: A descriptive definition of the probability on intuitionistic fuzzy sets. In: EUSFLAT '2003 ( M. Wagenecht, R. Hampet eds.) 2003, 263 -266.
[58] Riečan B. : Representation of probabilities on IFS events. In: Soft Methodology and Random Information Systems, (Lopez-Diaz et al. eds)., 2004, 243 - 248.
[59] Riečan B. :Kolmogorov - Sinaj entropy on MV-algebras. Int. J. Theor. Physics, 44, 2005, 1041 - 1052.
[60] Riečan B. : On the probability on IF-sets and MV-algebras. Notes on IFS, 11, 2005, 21 - 25.
[61] Riečan B. : On a problem of Radko Mesiar: general form of IF-probabilities. Fuzzy Sets and Systems, 152, 2006, 1485 - 1490.
[62] Riečan B.: On the probability and random variables on IF events. In: Applied Artificial Intelligence, Proc. 7th FLINS Conf. Genova ( D. Ruan et al. eds.), 2006, 138 - 145.
[63] Riečan B.: Probability theory on intuitionistic fuzzy events. In: Algebraic and Proof theoretic Aspects of Non-classical Logic (S. Aguzzoli et. al., eds.) Papers in honour of Daniele Mundici's 60th birthday. Lecture Notes in Computer Science, Springer, Berlin 2007, 290 - 308.

[64] Riečan, B., Lašová. L.: On the probability on the Kôpka D-posets. In: Developments in Fuzzy Sets, Intuitionistic Fuzzy Sets, Generalized Nets and related Topics I (K. Atanassov et al. eds.), Warsaw 2010, 167 - 176.
[65] Riečan, B., Kráľ, P.: Probability on interval valued events. Proc. of the Eleventh International Workshop on Generalized Nets and the Second International Workshop on Generalized Nets, Intuitionistic Fuzzy Sets and Knowledge Engineering, London 9 July 2010, 66 - 70.
[66] Riečan B. and Mundici D.: Probability in MV-algebras. Handbook of Measure Theory II ( E. Pap ed.) Elsevier, Heidelberg, 2002, 869 - 910.
[67] Riečan B. and Neubrunn T.: Integral, Measure and Ordering. Kluwer, Dordrecht, 1997.
[68] Riečan, B., Petrovičová J.: On the Lukasiewicz probability theory on IF-sets. Tatra Mt. Math. Publ. 46, 2010, 125 - 146.
[69] Szmidt, E., Kacprzyk, J.: Intuitionistic fuzzy sets in some medical applications. Notes IFS 7, 2001, No 4, 58 - 64.
[70] Valenčáková, V.: A note on the conditional probability on IF-events. Math. Slovaca 59, 2009, 251 - 260.
[71] Vrábel P.: Integration on MV - algebras. Tatra Mt. Math. Publ. 12, 1997, 21 - 25.
[72] Vrábelová, M.: On the conditional probability in product MV-algebras. Soft Computing 4, 2000, 58 - 61.
[73] Zadeh L. A.: Fuzzy sets.Inform.and Control 8, 1965, 338 - 358.

11

# Recognition and Resolution of "Comprehension Uncertainty" in *AI*

Sukanto Bhattacharya[1,*] and Kuldeep Kumar[2]
[1]*Deakin Graduate School of Business, Deakin University,*
[2]*School of Business, Bond University,*
*Australia*

## 1. Introduction

### 1.1 Uncertainty resolution as an integral characteristic of intelligent systems

Handling uncertainty is an important component of most intelligent behaviour - so uncertainty resolution is a key step in the design of an artificially intelligent decision system (Clark, 1990). Like other aspects of intelligent systems design, the aspect of uncertainty resolution is also typically sought to be handled by emulating natural intelligence (Halpern, 2003; Ball and Christensen, 2009). In this regard, a number of computational uncertainty resolution approaches have been proposed and tested by Artificial Intelligence (*AI*) researchers over the past several decades since birth of *AI* as a scientific discipline in early 1950s post- publication of Alan Turing's landmark paper (Turing, 1950).

The following chart categorizes various forms of uncertainty whose resolution ought to be a pertinent consideration in the design an artificial decision system that emulates natural intelligence:

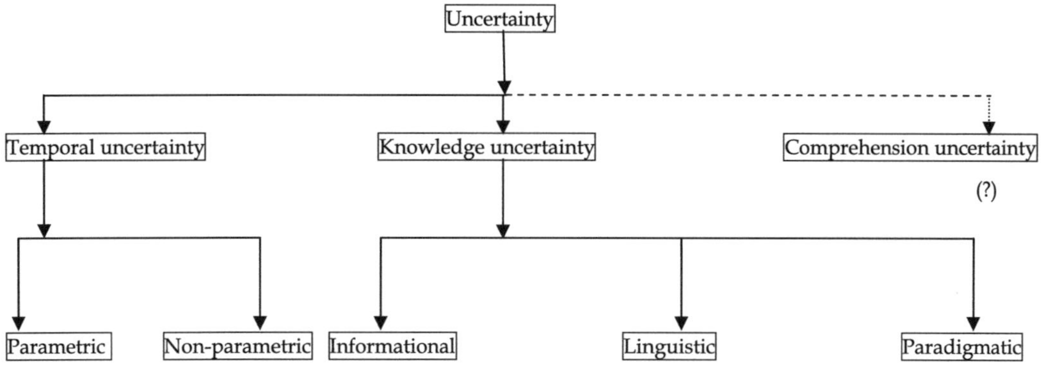


Fig. 1. Broad classifications of "uncertainty" that intelligent systems are expected to resolve

* Corresponding author

Temporal uncertainty, as the name suggests, arises out of *imperfect foresight* – i.e. it concerns the general problem of determining the future decision state of a dynamic system the current and past decision states of which are known. As a sub-category of temporal uncertainty, parametric uncertainty is that form of uncertainty the resolution of which wholly depends on estimating a set of underlying parameters that determine a future decision state of a system given its current and/or past decision states. The fundamental premise is that there exist parameters, which if estimated accurately, would fully explain the temporal transition from current to a future decision state. In most practical *AI* applications it is handled by embedding an efficient parameter estimation *kernel* e.g. an asset price prediction kernel that is embedded within an intelligent financial trading system (Huang, Pasquier and Quek, 2009). On the other hand non-parametric uncertainty is that form of temporal uncertainty the resolution of which is either wholly or substantially independent of any parameters that can be statistically estimated from the current or past decision states of the system. That is, in resolving non-parametric uncertainty one cannot assume that there is a set of parameters whose accurate estimation can fully explain the dynamic system's time-path (Kosut, Lau and Boyd, 1992). To resolve non-parametric uncertainty, *AI* models are usually equipped with some feedback/learning mechanism coupled with a *performance measure index* that indicates when optimal learning has occurred so that predictive utility isn't lost on account of *overtraining* when predicting a future state using the current/past states as the *inputs* (Yang et al, 2010).

Knowledge uncertainty, again as the name suggests, arises out of *imperfect understanding* – i.e. it concerns the general problem of determining the future decision state of a dynamic system the knowledge about whose current and/or past states are either *incomplete, ill-defined* or *inconsistent*. If there is incomplete information available about the current decision state of the system then the sub-category of knowledge uncertainty it would be categorized under is informational uncertainty. A common way of dealing with informational uncertainty is to try and *enhance* the current level of information by applying an appropriate information theoretic tool e.g. Ding *et al* (2008) applied rough sets theory coupled with a self-adaptive algorithm to separately "mine" consistent and inconsistent decision rules; along with experimental validation for large incomplete information systems. If the information available about the current decision state of the system is ill-defined i.e. it is subject to *interpretational ambiguity* then it would come under the sub-category of linguistic uncertainty. A large part of interpretational ambiguity arises as a direct result of statements made in natural language (Walley and Cooman, 2001). Lotfi Zadeh, the proponent of *fuzzy logic*, contended that *possibility measures* are best used to resolve linguistic uncertainty in decision systems (Zadeh, 1965). If the information available about the current decision state of the system is inconsistent i.e. it is fundamentally dependent on the origin, then the resulting uncertainty would come under the sub-category of paradigmatic uncertainty. If available information is dependent on its origin then it can be expected to materially change if one chooses a different source for the same information. For example, software agents have to reason and act on a domain in which the universe of possible scenarios is fundamentally prescribed by the available metadata records. But these metadata records can sometimes be found to be mutually inconsistent when compared. The paradigmatic uncertainty resulting from the inconsistency and imprecision is best addressed by building in enough flexibility in the system so that the cogency of information related to the current (and past) decision states gleaned from different sources is a *set-valued* rather than *point-valued* feature (Sicilia, 2006).

A three-valued extension of classical (i.e. binary) fuzzy logic was proposed by Smarandache (2002) when he coined the term "neutrosophic logic" as a generalization of fuzzy logic to such situations where it is impossible to *de-fuzzify* the original fuzzy-valued variables via some tractable membership function into either of set $T$ or its complement $T^C$ where both $T$ and $T^C$ are considered crisp sets. In these cases one has to allow for the possibility of a third unresolved state intermediate between $T$ and $T^C$. As an example one may cite the well known "thought experiment" in quantum metaphysics of *Schrödinger's cat* (Schrödinger, 1935) - the cat in a closed box is in limbo between two states "dead" and "alive" and it is impossible to tell which unless one opens the box at which point the effect of observer participation is said to intervene and cause that indeterminate state to collapse into a classical state of either a dead or an alive cat to be observed in the box. But as long as observer participation is completely absent one cannot in any way *disentangle* these two crisp sets!

This brings us to the final form of uncertainty that an artificially intelligent decision system ought to be able to resolve - something which we christened here as "comprehension uncertainty". While some elements of "comprehension uncertainty" is sought to be handled (often unknowingly) by the designers of intelligent systems by using one or more tools targeted to resolve either temporal or knowledge uncertainty, the concept of "comprehension uncertainty" has not yet been adequately described and addressed in contemporary *AI* literature. That is the reason we decided to depict this form of uncertainty using a *dashed rather than continuous connector* in the above chart. Also the question mark in the chart denotes the fact that there is no known repository of theoretical knowledge (not necessarily limited to the discipline of *AI*) that addresses such a form of uncertainty. The purpose of this chapter is to therefore posit a scientific theory of "comprehension uncertainty".

## 2. The meaning of "comprehension uncertainty"

While all the other forms of uncertainty as discussed above necessarily *originates from and deals with the contents/specification of an elementary set of interest,* which is a subset of the universal set, by the term "comprehension uncertainty" we mean and include any form of uncertainty that *originates from and deals with the contents/specification of the universal set itself.* If the stock of our entire knowledge about a problem is *universal* (i.e. there is absolutely nothing else that is 'fundamentally unknown' about that problem) only then we can claim to fully comprehend the problem so that no "comprehension uncertainty" would then exist. There is a need here to distinguish between "complete knowledge" and "universal knowledge". The knowledge about a problem can be said to be complete if it consists of the *entire stock of current knowledge* that is pertinent to that particular problem. However the current stock of knowledge, even in its entirety, may not be the universal knowledge simply because ways of adding to that current stock of knowledge could be beyond the current limits of comprehension i.e. *the universal set could itself be ill-defined.* If intelligent systems are primarily intended to emulate natural intelligence and treat "functional comparability" with natural intelligence as the most desirable outcome, then the limits to comprehension for natural intelligence should translate to similar limits for such systems as well.

### 2.1 How does natural intelligence resolve "comprehension uncertainty" in decision-making?

As highly evolved, intelligent beings, humans have become adept at continually taking decisions based on information that is subject to various forms of uncertainty. We can negotiate a busy sidewalk more often than not without colliding with other pedestrians and can cross a road safely (again most of the times) without being flattened by a car although we have at best a very imprecise idea of the speed of an oncoming car. Human brain, as the highest seat of natural intelligence, has evolved unique ways of working with various uncertainties including "comprehension uncertainty". Humans are also dealing with "comprehension uncertainty", for example when designing an unmanned, deep-space probe. We design the space probe using our current stock of knowledge in astrophysics; thermodynamics etc., identifying, assessing and resolving the pertinent temporal and knowledge uncertainties. At the same time we are also cognisant of a *gap* in our knowledge. This is not because we haven't been able to fully utilize our current stock of knowledge; rather it is the gap that exists between our current knowledge of deep space etc. and the *universal* knowledge which is outside of our "limits" of comprehension i.e. primarily originating from an ill-defined universal set.

Artificially intelligent decision systems are typically programmed to inexorably seek a 'global' optimum while in reality, the presence of "comprehension uncertainty" will always negate that prospect. What an intelligent system returns as a 'global' optimum is thus at best only such within its current domain knowledge and not a "universal" optimum. But an artificially intelligent system will always terminate its search once it attains what it perceives as the "global" optimum; based on the underlying premise that its current stock of domain-specific knowledge is in fact the universal one! On the other hand, naturally intelligent beings recognize the fundamental gap between current and universal knowledge and so will endeavour to keep expanding their "limits of comprehension".

An artificially intelligent decision system ought to be designed to 'realize' that its current stock of knowledge may not be the universal knowledge pertinent to a decision problem it is invoked to work out. Emulating natural intelligence, *AI models* should aim to be 'auto-cognisant' of any fundamental knowledge gaps and therefore be able to reconcile any deviations of the "global" from the "universal" optimum. A first step towards that is *effective operationalization* of the "comprehension uncertainty" concept. In the following section we posit and develop a formal conceptualization of the "comprehension uncertainty" concept. This basically involves an extension of classical probability theory to a realm of *higher-order probabilities* in a manner that is computationally tractable and fully reconcilable with the classical theory. Finally we posit and defend a logical framework justifying the due consideration of "comprehension uncertainty" in the context of designing artificially intelligent systems for practical applications in business, industry and society.

## 3. Developing some necessary theoretical groundwork

The primary objective of our work here is to simply posit the logically conceivable underpinnings of a probability theory extended to formalize comprehension uncertainty – we believe that our main purpose here is to merely open the proverbial Pandora's Box and thereby spawn a healthy stream of new research along both philosophical as well as mathematical lines. In that desired direction, we firstly posit and prove a fundamental theorem necessary for such an extension to the theory of probability. Subsequently we show some computational 'tests' to illustrate the posited framework.

### 3.1 A foray into higher order probabilities

It is well known that much of modern theory of probability rests upon the three fundamental *Kolmogorov axioms* (Kolmogorov, 1956) which are conventionally stated as follows:

1st axiom: The probability of any event is a non-negative real number i.e. $P(E) \geq 0 \quad \forall E \in U$

2nd axiom: The probability of any one of the elementary events in the whole event space occurring is 1 i.e. $P(U)=1$

3rd axiom: Any countable sequence of pair-wise *non-overlapping* events $E_1, E_2, \ldots E_n$ satisfies the following relation: $P(E_1 \cup E_2 \cup \ldots \cup E_n) = \sum_i P(E_i)$; $i = 1, 2, \ldots, n$.

It is basically Kolmogorov's second and third axioms as noted above that render any extensions of the probability concept to higher orders (i.e. "probability of probability") superfluous as the information content of any such higher order probability can be satisfactorily transmuted via existing set-theoretic constructs. So, extending to a higher order would arguably yield trivial information. However the Kolmogorov axioms by themselves are also open to 'extensions' – for instance there is previous research that has revisited the proofs of the well-known Bell inequality based on underlying assumptions of separability and non-contextuality and constructed a model of generalized "non-contextual contrapositive conditional probabilities" consistent with the results of the famous Aspect experiment showing in general such probabilities are not necessarily all positive (Atkinson, 2000). By themselves the Kolmogorov axioms do not unequivocally rule out an extension of the definition of the universal set U itself so as to make U possess a *time-dynamic* rather than a *time-static* nature. So; in effect this means that if we were to consider a time-dynamic version of the universal set; then one would suddenly find that the information content of higher order probability no longer remains trivial i.e. an extension of the probability concept to higher orders (i.e. "probability of probability") is no longer superfluous – in fact it is logical! The good thing is that no new probability calculus needs to be formulated to describe such a theory of higher-order probabilities and this extended theory could still rest on the Kolmogorov axioms and could still draw fundamentally from the standard set-theoretic approach (as we will be demonstrating shortly); by merely using an extended definition of the universal set U which would now denote not merely an event space but a broader concept, which we christen as *event-spacetime*, i.e. an event space that can *evolve* over a time dimension.

Perhaps the only academic work preceding ours to have alluded that a higher-order probability theory is justifiable by an event space evolving over time was that by Haddawy and others (Haddawy, 1996; Lehner, Laskey and Dubois, 1996), where they provided "a logic that incorporates and integrates the concepts of subjective probability, objective probability, time and causality" (Lehner, Laskey and Dubois, 1996). We take a similar philosophical stance but go on to explicitly develop a logically tenable higher-order probability concept in discrete time. We have no doubt that an extension in continuous time is also attainable but it's left for later.

**Lemma 1**

*The probability that any one of the elementary events contained within the event space-time will occur between two successive time points $t_0$ and $t_1$ given that the contents/contours of the event space remains unchanged from $t_0$ to $t_1$ is unity i.e.* $P(U_0 \mid U_0 = U_1) = 1$. *By extension,* $P(U_t \mid U_t = U_{t+1}) = 1$ *for all* $t = 0, 1, 2, 3, \ldots$

**Proof**

Lemma 1 results from a natural extension of Kolmogorov's second axiom if we allow the event space to be of a time-dynamic nature i.e. if U is allowed to evolve through time in discrete intervals.

*QED*

**Lemma 2**

*If the classical probability of occurrence of a specific elementary event E contained within the event space-time is defined as P(E), then the first-order probability of occurrence of such event E becomes* $P\{P(E)\} = P^1(E) = P\{E \mid (U_0 = U_1)\} = P(E).[P\{(U_0 = U_1) \mid E\}/P(U_0 = U_1)]$

**Proof**

Applying the fundamental law of conditional probability we can write as follows:

$$P\{E \mid (U_0 = U_1)\} = P\{E \cap (U_0 = U_1)\} / P(U_0 = U_1)$$

$$P\{E \cap (U_0 = U_1)\} = P\{(U_0 = U_1) \cap E\} = P(E).P\{(U_0 = U_1) \mid E\};$$ and thus the result follows.

*QED*

**Lemma 3**

*Given the first-order probability of occurrence of elementary event E and assuming that* $(U_t = U_{t+1})$ *and* $(U_{t+1} = U_{t+2})$ *are independent for all* $t = 0, 1, 2, 3, \ldots$, *the second-order probability of occurrence of E becomes* $P^2(E) = P(E) . P^1(E). [P\{(U_1 = U_2) \mid E\}/P(U_1 = U_2)]$.

**Proof**

By definition, $P^2(E) = P\{P^1(E)\} = P[\{E \mid (U_0 = U_1)\} \cap \{E \mid (U_1 = U_2)\}]$

Since $(U_t = U_{t+1})$ and $(U_{t+1} = U_{t+2})$ are assumed independent for $t = 0, 1, 2, 3, \ldots$, we can write:

$$P[\{E \mid (U_0 = U_1)\} \cap \{E \mid (U_1 = U_2)\}] = P\{E \mid (U_0 = U_1)\} . P\{E \mid (U_1 = U_2)\}.$$

Substituting $P\{E \mid (U_0 = U_1)\}$ with $P^1(E)$ and then applying the fundamental law of conditional probability; the result follows.

*QED*

Thus, given the first-order probability of occurrence of an elementary event E, the second-order probability is obtained as a "probability of the first-order probability" and is necessarily *either equal to or less than* the first-order probability, as is suggested by common intuition. This logic could then be extended to each of the subsequent higher order probability terms. Based on lemmas 1 - 3, we next propose and prove a fundamental theorem of higher order (hereafter *H-O*) probabilities.

**A fundamental theorem of higher order probabilities (in discrete time)**

*If we set* $P^0(E) \equiv P(E)$, *then* $P^t(E) = P(E).\ P^{t-1}(E).[P\{(U_{t-1}= U_t) \mid E\}/P(U_{t-1}= U_t)]$ *for* $t = 1, 2, 3, \ldots, n$

**Proof**

$$P^1(E) = P\{P^0(E)\} = P(E).\ [P\{(U_0 = U_1) \mid E\}/P(U_0 = U_1)] \qquad \textit{from lemma 2}$$

$$P^2(E) = P\{P^1(E)\} = P(E)\ .\ P^1(E)\ .\ [P\{(U_1 = U_2) \mid E\}/P(U_1 = U_2)] \qquad ..\textit{from lemma 3}$$

$$P^3(E) = P[\{E \mid (U_0 = U_1)\} \cap \{E \mid (U_1 = U_2)\} \cap \{E \mid (U_2 = U_3)\}]$$

$$= P[[\{E \mid (U_0 = U_1)\} \cap \{E \mid (U_1 = U_2)\}] \cap \{E \mid (U_2 = U_3)\}]$$

$$= P^2(E)\ .\ P\{E \mid (U_2 = U_3)\}$$

$$= P(E).\ P^2(E).[P\{(U_2 = U_3) \mid E\}/P(U_2 = U_3)$$

$$P^4(E) = P[\{E \mid (U_0 = U_1)\} \cap \{E \mid (U_1 = U_2)\} \cap \{E \mid (U_2 = U_3)\} \cap \{E \mid (U_3 = U_4)\}]$$

$$= P[[\{E \mid (U_0 = U_1)\} \cap \{E \mid (U_1 = U_2)\} \cap \{E \mid (U_2 = U_3)\}] \cap \{E \mid (U_3 = U_4)\}]$$

$$= P^3(E)\ .\ P\{E \mid (U_3 = U_4)\}$$

$$= P(E).\ P^3(E).[P\{(U_3 = U_4) \mid E\}/P(U_3 = U_4)]$$

Extending to the (t-1)-th term, we can therefore write:

$$P^{t-1}(E) = P(E).\ P^{t-2}(E).[P\{(U_{t-2}= U_{t-1}) \mid E\}/P(U_{t-2}= U_{t-1}) \qquad (1)$$

The expression for the t-th term is derived from (1) as follows:

$$P^t(E) = P(E).\ P^{(t-2)+1}(E).[P\{(U_{(t-2)+1}=U_t) \mid E\}/P(U_{(t-2)+1} = U_t)$$

$$= P(E).P^{t-1}(E).[P\{(U_{t-1}=U_t) \mid E\}/P(U_{t-1}=U_t) \qquad (2)$$

However we may also write:

$$P^t(E)=P[\{E \mid (U_0 = U_1)\}\cap\{E \mid (U_1 = U_2)\}\cap\{E \mid (U_2 = U_3)\}\cap\{E \mid (U_3 = U_4)\}\cap\ldots\cap\{E \mid (U_{t-1} = U_t)\}]$$

$$=P[[\{E \mid (U_0=U_1)\}\cap\{E \mid (U_1=U_2)\}\cap\{E \mid (U_2=U_3)\}\cap\{E \mid (U_3=U_4)\}\cap\ldots\cap\{E \mid (U_{t-2} =U_{t-1})]\cap\{E \mid (U_{t-1}= U_t)\}]$$

$$= P^{t-1}(E)\ .\ P\{E \mid (U_{t-1} = U_t)\}$$

$$= P^{t-1}(E).\ P(E).\ [P\{(U_{t-1}=U_t) \mid E\}/P(U_{t-1}=U_t)] \qquad (3)$$

As (2) is identical to (3); by *principle of mathematical induction* the general case is proved for t= n.

*QED*

Obviously then, if $P(U_{t-1}=U_t) = P\{(U_{t-1}=U_t) \mid E\}$, for all t = 1, 2, 3, ..., n; we will end up with $P^n(E) =[P(E)]^n$ which makes this approach to *H-O* probability fully consistent with classical probability theory and in fact a very natural extension thereof if one sees the fundamentally time-dynamic characteristic of U.

### 3.2 Simple computational 'tests' to better illustrate the above-posited concept of *H-O* probability

To provide a simple illustration of how the *H-O* probabilities would pan out in discrete event-spacetime we have done a series of computations the results of which are graphically represented below. The graphs show the temporal evolution of the event-spacetime in discrete "time steps" and the resulting $P^t(E)$ values for t = 1, 2, ..., 5. We assume three temporal evolution forms - "*expanding event-spacetime*", "*contracting event-spacetime*" and "*oscillating event-spacetime*" and plot the $P^t(E)$ values for each of these three forms starting with a pervading assumption that $P(U_{t-1} = U_t) = 1$. This assumption simplifies a lot of the computations as $P^t(E)$ then depends totally on $P\{(U_{t-1} = U_t)/E\}$. When $P\{(U_{t-1} = U_t)/E\} = 1$, we see that $P^t(E)$ converges to $P(E)^t$ for all values of t. On the other hand, when $P\{(U_{t-1} = U_t)/E\} = 0$, $P^t(E)$ converges to zero for all values of t. So, holding $P(E) = 0.10$, in an "expanding event-spacetime", $P^1(E) = P(E) = 0.10$, $p^2(E) = 0.10^2 = 0.01$ and so on for $P\{(U_{t-1}=U_t)/E\} = 1$. For $P\{(U_{t-1}=U_t)/E\} = 0$, $P^1(E) = p^2(E) = P^3(E) = p^4(E) = P^5(E) = 0$, while $P^t(E)$ values are seen to oscillate for $P\{(U_{t-1}=U_t)/E\}$ values randomly oscillating about 0.50 - the degree of oscillation decreasing with increasing order of probability i.e. $P^1(E)$ oscillates more than $P^2(E)$, $P^2(E)$ more than $P^3(E)$ and so on.

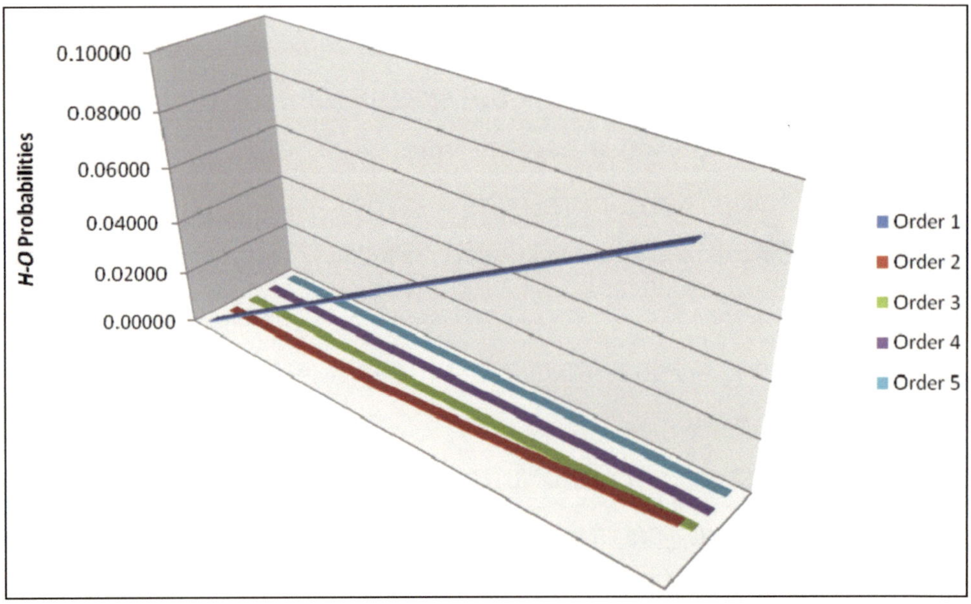


Fig. 2. Expanding Event-Spacetime, $[P(E) = 0.10]$
Plot of $P^t(E)$; t = 1, 2, ..., 5 for $P\{(U_{t-1} = U_t)/E\}$ increasing from 0 to 1 in steps of 0.05

The expanding event-spacetime represents the situation where, with passage of time and evolution of the current stock of domain knowledge, there is a steadily increasing "probability of probability" of the occurrence of the elementary event of interest. The contracting event-spacetime represents the situation where, with passage of time and evolution of the current stock of domain knowledge, there is a steadily decreasing "probability of probability" of the occurrence of the elementary event of interest. The oscillating event-spacetime represents the situation where, with passage of time and evolution of the current stock of domain knowledge, there is an erratic pattern in the "probability of probability" of the occurrence of the elementary event of interest because of the fact that some old knowledge that were 'replaced' by new knowledge make comebacks following newer discoveries.

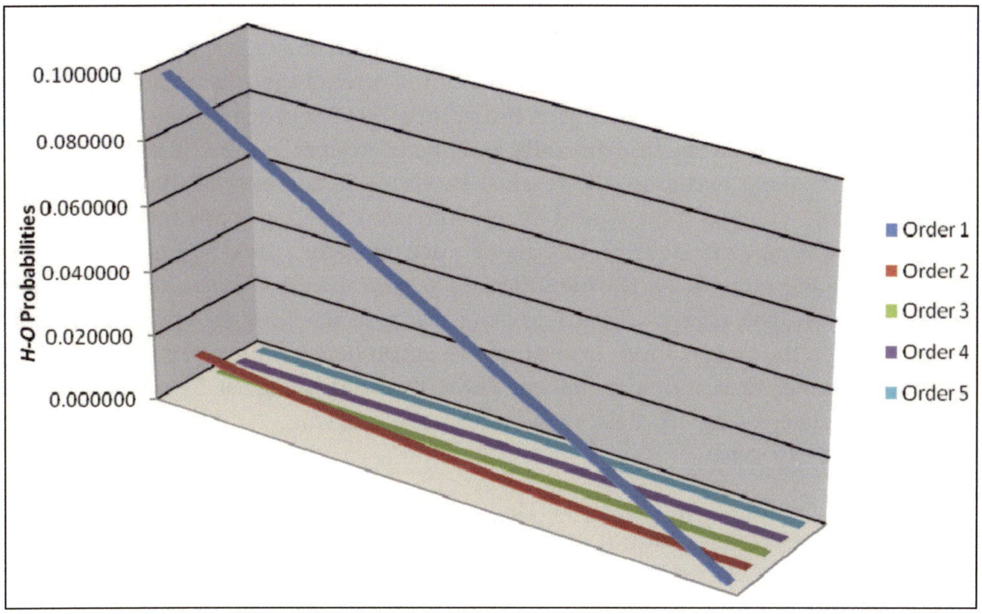


Fig. 3. Contracting Event-Spacetime, [P($E$) = 0.10]
Plot of $P^t(E)$; t = 1, 2, ..., 5 for $P\{(U_{t-1} = U_t)/E\}$ decreasing from 1 to 0 in steps of 0.05

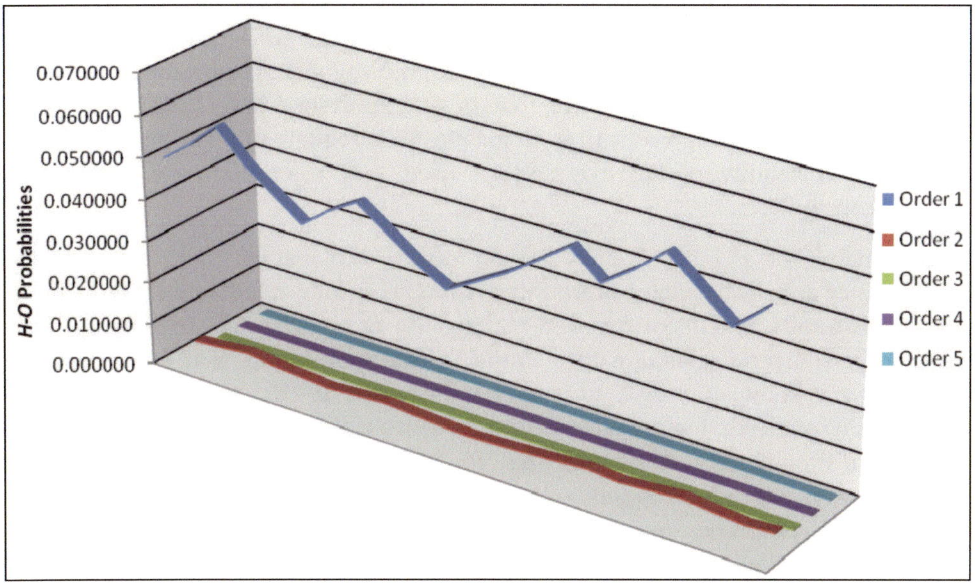


Fig. 4. Oscillating Event-Spacetime, [P($E$) = 0.10]
Plot of $P^t(E)$; t = 1, 2, ..., 5 for $P\{(U_{t-1} = U_t)/E\}$ allowed to randomly oscillate about 0.50

### 3.3 *H-O* probability implications for intelligent resolution of comprehension uncertainty

Although we do not mathematically compute *H-O* probabilities while taking decisions (or for that matter even ordinary probabilities), human intelligence does enough 'background processing' of fringe information (mostly even without knowing) to 'see' a bigger picture of the likely scenarios. Going back to the example of crossing a busy road, we are continuously processing information (often unknowingly) from the environment in terms of the rapidly changing pertinent event space. As long as the pertinent event space is 'pre-populated' with likely forms of road hazards, an artificially intelligent system can be 'trained' to emulate human decision-making and cross the road. It is when the contents of the pertinent event space dynamically changes that would throw off even the most advanced of AI-based systems given the current state of design of such systems. This is pretty much what Bhattacharya, Wang and Xu (2010) identified as a 'gap' in the current state of design of intelligent systems. The current design paradigm is overwhelmingly concerned with the "how" rather than the "why" - and resolution of comprehension uncertainty involves more of the "why". Rather than trying to answer "how to avoid being hit by a vehicle or some other hazard while crossing" *AI* designers ought to be focusing on "why are we vulnerable while crossing a busy road".

As soon as the focus of the design shifts to the "why", the link with comprehension uncertainty becomes a very natural extension thereof. Then we are simply asking *why* a particular event space is a pertinent one for the problem at hand? The natural answer is that in a specified time window, it contains all the elementary events out of which one or a few are conducive for the desired outcome. Then the question naturally progresses to what would happen outside that specified time window? If we are pre-populating the pertinent event space and then assuming that it would hold good for all times, it would be at the cost of ignoring comprehension uncertainty which can defeat the AI design. At this point it is perhaps useful to again remind readers that it is not the vagueness or imprecision associated with some contents of an event space that is of importance here (existing uncertainty resolution methods like rough sets, fuzzy logic etc. are adequate for dealing with those) - it is a temporal instability of the event space itself that is crux of the comprehension uncertainty concept.

The mathematics of *H-O* probabilities then offers a plausible route towards formal incorporation of comprehension uncertainty within artificially intelligent systems designed to replicate naturally intelligent decision-making. As naturally intelligent beings, humans are capable of somehow grasping the "limits to comprehension" that result from a gap between current knowledge and universal knowledge. If this was not the case then 'research' as an intellectual endeavour would have ceased! In the current design paradigm the focus is on training *AI* models to 'search' for global optimality while, ideally, the focus ought to be on training such models to do 'research' rather than 'search'! Recognition and incorporation of comprehension uncertainty in their learning framework would at least allow future *AI* models to 'grasp' the limits to comprehension so as not to invariably terminate as soon as a 'globally optimal' decision point has been reached using the current domain knowledge.

## 4. Conclusion: "comprehending the incomprehensible" – the future of *AI* systems design

In its current state, the design of artificially intelligent systems is pre-occupied with solving the "how" problems and as such do not quite recognize the need for resolving comprehension uncertainty. In fact, the concept of comprehension uncertainty was not even formally posited prior to this work by us although there have been a few takes on the mathematics of *H-O* probabilities. Earlier researchers mainly found the concept of *H-O* probabilities superfluous because they failed to view it in the context of formalizing comprehension uncertainty like we have done in this article.

However, given that the exact emulation of human intelligence continues to remain the Holy Grail for *AI* researchers, they have to grapple with comprehension uncertainty at some point or the other. The reason for this is simple - a hallmark of human intelligence is that it recognizes the limitations of the current stock of knowledge from which it draws. Thus any artificial system that ultimately seeks to emulate that intelligence must also necessarily see the limitations in current domain knowledge and allow for the fact that the current domain knowledge can evolve over time so that the global optimum attained with the current stock of knowledge may not remain the same at a future time. Once an artificially intelligent system is hardwired to recognize the *time-dynamic* aspect of the relevant event space within which it has to calculate the probabilities of certain outcomes and take a decision so as to maximize the expected value of the most desirable outcome, it will not terminate its search as soon as global optimality is reached in terms of the contents/contours of the current event space. It would rather go into a 'dormant' mode and continue to monitor the evolution of the event space and 're-engage' in its search as soon as $P\{(U_{t-1}=U_t)/E\} > 0$ at any subsequent time point.

With the formal hardwiring of comprehension uncertainty within the core design of an artificially intelligent system it can be trained to transcend from simply answering the "how" to ultimately formulating the "why" - firstly; why is the current body of knowledge an exhaustive source to draw from for finding the optimal solution to a particular problem and secondly; why that current body of knowledge may not be continue to remain an exhaustive source to draw from for all time in future. When it has been trained to formulate these "why" questions, only then can we expect an artificially intelligent system to take that significant leap towards finally gaining parity with natural intelligence.

## 5. References

Atkinson, D. (2000). Bell's Inequalities and Kolmogorov's Axioms, *Pramana – Journal of Physics*, Vol. 54, pp. 1–15

Ball, L. J. and B. T. Christensen (2009). Analogical reasoning and mental simulation in design: two strategies linked to uncertainty resolution, *Design Studies*, Vol. 30, No. 2, pp. 169–186

Bhattacharya, S., Y. Wang and D. Xu (2010). Beyond Simon's Means-Ends Analysis: Natural Creativity and the Unanswered 'Why' in the Design of Intelligent Systems for Decision-Making, *Minds and Machines*, Vol. 20, No. 3, pp.327–347

Clark, D. A. (1990). Numerical and symbolic approaches to uncertainty management in AI, *Artificial Intelligence Review*, Vol. 4, pp. 109–146

Ding, Z., X. Zhu, J. Zhao and H. Xu (2008). New knowledge acquisition method in incomplete information system based on rough set and self-adaptive genetic algorithm, In: *Proceedings of IEEE International Conference on Granular Computing*, Hangzhou, China (26th-28th August), pp. 196–200

Haddawy, P. (1996). Believing change and changing belief, *IEEE Transactions on Systems, Man and Cybernetics, Part A: Systems and Humans*, Vol. 26, No. 3, pp.385–396

Halpern, J. Y. (2003). *Reasoning about uncertainty*, Cambridge, MA, and London: MIT Press

Huang, H., M. Pasquier and C. Quek (2009). Financial Market Trading System with a Hierarchical Co evolutionary Fuzzy Predictive Model, *IEEE Transactions on Evolutionary Computation*, Vol. 13, No. 1, pp. 56–70

Kolmogorov, A. N. (1956). *Foundations of the Theory of Probability*, Second Ed. (English), Chelsea Publishing Company, NY

Kosut, R. L., M. K. Lau and S. P. Boyd (1992). Set-Membership Identification of Systems with Parametric and Nonparametric Uncertainty, *IEEE Transactions on Automatic Control*, Vol. 37, No. 7, pp. 929–941

Lehner, P. E., K. B. Laskey and D. Dubois (1996). An introduction to issues in higher order uncertainty, *IEEE Transactions on Systems, Man and Cybernetics, Part A: Systems and Humans*, Vol. 26, No. 3, pp.289–293

Schrödinger, E. (1935). Die gegenwärtige Situation in der Quantenmechanik (The present situation in quantum mechanics), *Naturwissenschaften*, Vol. 23, pp. 807–849

Smarandache, F. (2002). Preface: An Introduction to Neutrosophy, Neutrosophic Logic, Neutrosophic Set, and Neutrosophic Probability and Statistics, In: F. Smarandache (Ed.) *Proceedings of the First International Conference on Neutrosophy, Neutrosophic Logic, Neutrosophic Set, and Neutrosophic Probability and Statistics*, Xiquan, Phoenix, AZ

Sicilia, M-A. (2006). On Some Problems of Decision-Making under Uncertainty in the Semantic Web, *Studies in Fuzziness and Soft Computing*, Vol. 204, pp. 231–246

Turing, A. M. (1950). Computing machinery and intelligence, *Mind*, Vol. 59, pp. 433–460

Walley, P. and G. de Cooman (2001). A behavioral model for linguistic uncertainty, *Information Sciences*, Vol. 134, pp. 1–37

Yang, Z., S. C. P. Yam, L. K. Li and Y. Wang (2010). Universal Repetitive Learning Control for Nonparametric Uncertainty and Unknown State-Dependent Control Direction Matrix, *IEEE Transactions on Automatic Control*, Vol. 55, No. 7, pp. 1710 - 1715

Zadeh, L. A. (1965). Fuzzy sets, *Information and Control*, Vol. 8, pp. 338–353

# 12

# Intelligent Systems in Cartography

Zdena Dobesova and Jan Brus
*Palacký University in Olomouc*
*Czech Republic*

## 1. Introduction

According to the recent progress and technical development in Geographic Information Science (GIScience) [Kraak, MacEachren, 1999], and in information technology we can trace the progressive significance of the role of maps, images, and computer graphics as mediators of collaboration - in a range of contexts including environmental and urban planning, resource management, scientific inquiry, and education [Brewer et al., 2000]. Maps became a tool for sharing knowledge around people. They are comprehended as a unique expression tool used for a variety of purposes that can be broadly grouped around two main roles: maps as tools for analysis, problem solving and decision making "visual thinking", [MacEachren, Kraak, 1997], and maps as tools for communication of ideas between people. Although the communicative role of maps seems to fully comply with the cartographic tradition, it should be borne in mind that the concept of cartographic communication has recently extended [Andrienko, Andrienko, Voss, 2002]. Maps are unique means for communication of adequate amount of spatial information. Visualizing allows us to grasp and retain larger amount of information compared to the usage of words. Without the visual image, recalling the same information would require memorizing a long list of area descriptions [O'Looney, 2000].

If the maps are processed correctly, they transmit spatial information accurately and quickly. If some of the rules of cartography are violated, communication of spatial information is inaccurate. The communication of spatial information is sometimes completely wrong. Subsequently, the map-reader can be significantly affected by the result of representation of information. From the other point of view, badly understood map may have fatal consequences in crisis management when transferring of the right information between collaborating people is necessary. In this context, map plays the role of symbolic operator able to act in such a decision making, characterized by urgency and criticality.

Thus, the good knowledge of all the rules for maps making is expected from the map maker. Knowledge of design principles can help the user create a highly specialized view on the data. Customized and right visualized data can help viewers identify patterns, which can be lost when using the un-adequate method [O'Looney, 2000].

Map making process can be done in two main ways. Firstly, the users make map from some datasets using adequate software. The opposite situation requires map server as end tool for visualizing of datasets. In both cases is necessary build-in acquired cartographical knowledge into these systems. There is a need for implementation of cartographic rules directly into the programs for the map making especially into GIS software.

The usage of intelligent systems has been enabled by the development in the field of artificial intelligence. Therefore, these systems find application in many sectors of cartography. Real cartographer can be partly substituted by the utilization of knowledge system (intelligent system).

## 2. Cartography and intelligent systems

Computer-assisted thematic cartography has been highlighted in the forefront of interest by the following development in the field of GIS and map making but also thanks to the expansion of improper map-making. Usage of different methods in thematic cartography is very dependent on the specific type of map, user and the resulting information. Cartographer accesses very often at this stage and determines what is appropriate and what is not. The possibility of intelligent system usage can be found in that stage.

Quantity of used thematic cartography methods, different types and quality of input data and other factors, however, can cause problems. The creating of a high-quality and comprehensive system for thematic cartography is extremely complex task. The main idea of designing the decision-making support system in thematic mapping is using all kinds of technologies and methods. The aim is to solve the decision-making problems in thematic mapping in order to make a perfect map through operating intelligent system by users [Quo, 1993]. Key decision-making issues referred to the thematic map design should be analyzed clearly at the beginning of designing a good intelligent system. Nevertheless, corresponding decision-making models and reasoning methods should be proposed according to different problems.

In order to transfer map information effectively, it must reduce the noise hidden behind the map information and prevent over much map information. In thematic cartography, there are more than 10 commonly known thematic map types, namely point diagram maps, linear diagram maps, chorochromatic mosaic maps, isoline maps, stereoscopic perspective methods, nominal point symbol maps, proportional symbol maps, dot methods (dot mapping), classification ratio method (choropleth maps), statistical maps (areal diagram methods), cartographic arrowhead methods, triangle charts law [Quo, Ren, 2003].

Various geographic data have a different structure of data. Every method should be corresponding to geographic data characteristics. Moreover, only some specific types of map graphics express specific geographic phenomena (Population Pyramid). This is the very important part of thematic cartography. Different methods will emphasize differently on different map data characteristics. Furthermore, some data characteristics can be only expressed by particular methods. When we can distinguish type of data and their structure, we will be able to know which method to choose [Andrienko, Andrienko, Voss, 2002]. We can select a different map representation according to the spatial distribution of quality, quantity, grade combined, compared, direction and temporal options.

Producers of GIS software try to incorporate sub-expert cartographic knowledge as part of the program functionality. For example, we can consider the offer of color scale as a specific program codified cartographic knowledge in ArcGIS software. A program shows appropriate scales according to visualization qualitative or quantitative data. When a quantity type of data is selected than the predefined color scales of tones based on one color with different saturation will be automatically offered in ArcGIS. This offer is cartographically correct. However, the user can make mistakes here because bad choice scales are also offered. This mistake of choosing wrong color ramp for expression quality or quantity is represented on Fig 1. This map visualizes the different six weeks of the student vacation in the Czech Republic. This qualitative phenomenon is correctly expressed with different tone of the color (yellow, orange, light blue, green, dark blue and violet) for every week on the upper map. Wrong usage of color for expression of six weeks by graduated color ramp (colours from yellow to brown) is in the map on top in Fig. 1. This graduated color ramp can be used only for quantitative data. Light color (yellow) expresses small value, dark color (brown) expresses big value. The week of vacation is not small or big value.

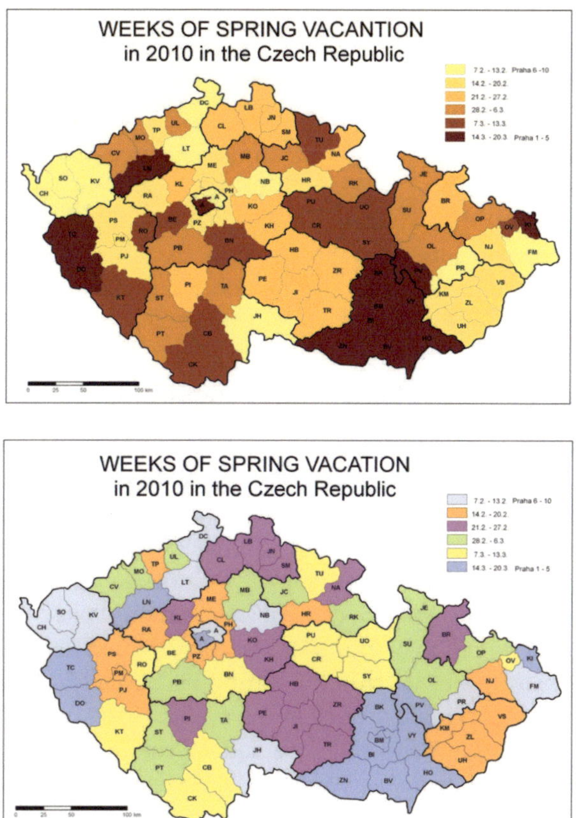


Fig. 1. Example of bad use of color ramp for qualitative data - wrong map (up) and correct map (bottom)

In developing an intelligent system, there are two related sets of problems. Transformation of existing cartographic practice into rule-based knowledge stands the first and the second is to guide the system through the map-making task. The knowledge in the domain is encoded in the form of rules, which constitute the building blocks of the knowledge base. The application logic and the procedural information of the system are described by rules and operated on objects, classes and slots [Stefanakis, Tsoulos 2005]. The structure and organization of the knowledge base is critical for efficiency and the overall performance of the system. Only features referred to the usage of a map can be presented and, on the other hand, only important elements can be shown when there are too many features [Hua, 1991].

That is why it is necessary to include all the potential factors to the database when designing such a system, or it is necessary to focus only on some issues in a map-making process.

In disrespect of the basic rules, there may be restrictions of expressing the ability of the map or the cartographic expression becomes unreadable. Intelligent system can assist to the correct selection of colour in accordance with the rules of cartography. E.g. conservation principle of conventionality (blue colour for waters, brown colour for contour lines), conservation principle of associativity (green forests for topographic maps), the right choice of colours for the qualitative data or the correct shade of colour for expressing the intensity of the phenomenon. They can take into consideration the type of imaging methods and the people suffering from daltonism etc. There is also an art to displaying information visually, and sometimes principles contradict each other [Andrienko, Andrienko, Voss, 2002].

The basic principle of the intelligent system is to divide the whole process into subsections, which affect the result. The resulting proposed system must be coherent and comprehensive. Good comprehensive intelligent system for thematic cartography should be able to propose appropriate solutions of the problem. Excellent intelligent system should be even able to offer not only one possible solution but also give the explanation and justification to the user.

## 3. Cartographic intelligent systems with a specific knowledge

With the development of digital cartography and transfer maps to digital form there is an increasing need to vectorize and generalize properly. Both processes are widely used in the last decade. This process, however, requires the presence of expert and correction of the process. Software that directly vectorize scanned image maps can be divided into automatic and semi-automatic, depending on the modes of information processing [Hori, Tanigawa, 1993], [Eikvil, Aas, Koren, 1995]. Most of current automatic vectorial systems apply the same method for all maps and do not take into consideration their different nature. It is expected from the user as the most accurate manual setting as possible, which presupposes good knowledge of the problems and knowledge of the system used [Hori, Tanigawa, 1993]. One option is to use the knowledge base and thus reduce the overall demand of cartographic literacy of the users and facilitate the whole process of vectorization. In conjunction with the knowledge base we get a system that is able to give results very similar to the of outputs highly sophisticated manual digitization. In addition, it provides more agreeable user interface which allows the selection of appropriate parameters in accordance with the visual information contained in the original map.

Even generalizing algorithms of existing systems often ignore the role of maps or fuzzy logic to optimize the process. There are thus not able to extract hidden information. The specific knowledge, which is not taken into account in so far known algorithms, is required

[Meng, 2003]. Generalization entails a number of different rules that must be correctly applied in a certain sequence. Different roles have different rules and different knowledge base. This compilation of a dynamic system is a possible solution to the automatic generalization. In the context of digital cartography and expert systems is therefore very necessary to examine and interpret the processes at manual generalization. The overwriting the procedure of the cartographer into a sequence of a procedure of very well defined processes is a key objective in creating a successful expert system [Lee, 1994].

Implementation of the knowledge of experts to the programs for work with a map can greatly specify and simplify the whole process. Automatic generalization is interesting example. These intelligent guides can be found in different software such as ArcGIS, DynaGen and LaserScan. The development of intelligent systems is a major commercial application of artificial intelligence (AI) which is proposed to increase the quality and availability of knowledge for automated decision-making [Boss, 1991].

For common users it is much more preferable to use freely available software resources. These resources can help with the creation of maps. In the following text, there are some of these applications. The "MapBrewer" system is named after the researcher and cartographer Cynthia Brewer. It is a new type of a system developed to encourage the creation of maps. It helps the user always with only one particular aspect in the production of maps.

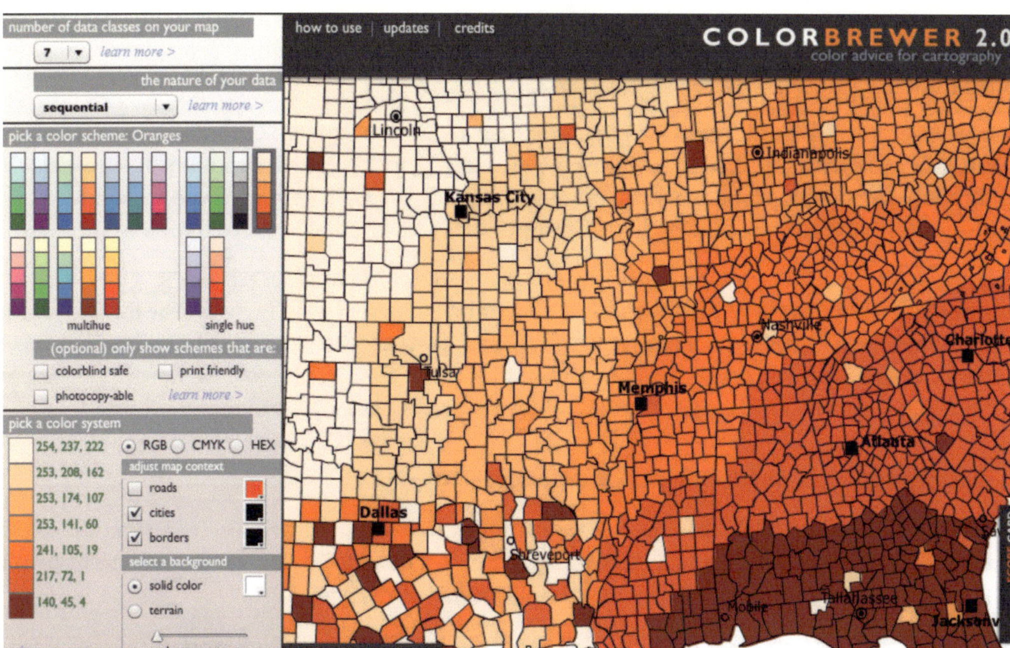


Fig. 2. ColorBrewer 2.0 - Color advice for cartography

Three versions, namely ColourBrewer [Harrower, Brewer, 2003] instrument for the correct choice of colour composition, SymbolBrewer [Schnabel, 2005] for the selection of appropriate map symbols, and TypeBrewer [Sheesley, 2006] to the appropriate font, are now available. These described systems can be rather referred as "digital teaching assistants".

They offer important theoretical background, but also user-specialist can find out solutions in them. They differ from other forms of online assistance such as wizards, tutorials, guides, forums, and others. They do not effort the user only one solution and they do not work for him without an explanation. They rather propose a user the range of possible correct solutions and seek to encourage users to think of the problem as an expert does. This activity is similar to that offered by the expert consultation. Another system belonging to a group of research applications is the expert system developed in China for decision support in thematic cartography [Zhang, Guo, Jiao, 2008]. It is the kind of a geographic information system, which helps users with the process of creating thematic maps. The system has a single interface. Through this system, you can choose the thematic elements and then it is possible to create automatically thematic maps according to the type and characteristics of their elements. User can modify the design parameters of various charts and through the interface obtain satisfactory results. This system is the unique solution of a complex expert system in thematic cartography. Special distributed solution was developed in Switzerland [Iosifescu-Enescu, Hugentobler, Hurni, 2010]. QGIS mapserver is an open source WMS (Web Map Service) (1.3.0 and 1.1.1) implementation. In addition, it implements advanced cartographic features as specified in the Map and Diagram Service specifications. With QGIS mapserver the content of vector and raster data sources (e.g. shapefiles, gml, postgis, wfs, geotiff) can be visualized according to cartographic rules (specified as request parameters). The generated map is sent back to the client over the internet. The cartographic rules handle advanced filtering and symbolisation of features. For improved cartographic representation, the data should be enriched with attributes to control rotation, scale, size or even transparency.

As a cartographical guide we can consider also a knowledge-based software component, called task support guide, that proposes the users appropriate interactive techniques for accomplishing specific data analysis tasks and explains how to apply these techniques. The guide is integrated in mapping system CommonGIS [Andrienko, Andrienko, Voss, 2002].

In addition, there is a large number of systems as an outcome of research work. These systems come from number of the world's research places but they are mostly aimed at the individual field cartography. These systems also often end just as the output of research or as a springboard for further research. From most important we can choose, MAPAID [Robinson, Jackson, 1985], MAPKEY [Su, 1992], ACES [Pfefferkorn et al., 1985] and many others.

### 3.1 Cartographical knowledge and their acquiring

The first part of construction of cartographic intelligent system is transfer of expert knowledge from various sources to computer form. The sources in the area of cartography are cartographers - experts, cartographic books, maps and atlases.

Knowledge acquisition and building knowledge base is a complex and time-consuming stage of intelligent system development which is indispensable without collaborating between experts (cartographers) and knowledge engineers. An effectively deployed system must do more than embody expertise. Its rule base must be complete, non-contradictory, and reasonable. Knowledge engineers employ a variety of techniques for eliciting information from the expert in order to construct a complete and consistent rule base [Balch, Schrader, Ruan, 2007].

The cooperation with cartographers is considerable in some ways [Návrat et al., 2002]:

- oriented interview - obtaining of facts,
- structural interview - obtaining of terms and models,
- free association - obtaining of relation between knowledge,
- monitoring - obtaining of global strategy,
- comment of steps - obtaining of derived strategy,
- dialogue of expert with users – results are interaction between knowledge and way of communication of user.

The knowledge engineer should be aware that expert knowledge is more than one kind and not all this knowledge can be acquired from one person. An interview with only one expert-cartographer can avoid some fail in expert system. Interview with group of cartographers is better. The suitable way of interview is brainstorming. There is necessary more punctually prepare interview and carefully lead interview with group of experts. There is also danger of conflicts between experts.

Process of building expert system in cartography can involve certain steps. Knowledge acquisition step which involve individual expert interviews, the knowledge representation step which involve the creation of the knowledge base, knowledge validation occurred during the testing and fine-tuning of the final knowledge base.

Possible and appropriate method how to collect data can be usage of a modified Delphi method. The Delphi method [Okoli, Pawlowski, 2004] is a structured and iterative approach to collecting expert knowledge involving a series of interviews or questionnaires. As basement for building can be used ontologies. The plan for acquiring the knowledge and building the knowledge base had the following steps:

- have initial free-form interviews with experts;
- based on the results of the free-form interviews, develop a questionnaire to collect knowledge from a larger group of experts;
- use the data collected from the questionnaires to create a preliminary knowledge base to store and represent knowledge;
- distribute the preliminary knowledge base through the experts to fine-tune it, repeating this process if necessary;
- use available data and statistical tools to further refine the knowledge base.

The first step in developing the cartographical knowledge base should be to contact experts with experience in cartography (mostly cartographers). Since this kind of work often involves a time commitment, it is important to develop a means of motivating experts to participate in this work [Booker, Meyer, 2001]. Motivation for the experts' participation in this work is necessary to use the results in the beta testing phase.

Once their expertise is collected, it should be implemented into a draft of knowledge base rules and stored in an if-then format. This draft should be after fine-tuned by being passed back to the cartographers for further review. From collected results should be build final knowledge base and it is necessary to test whole knowledge base for errors after finalization.

There are also other methods which can be used. The best way is using cartographical literature and combined these results with interview methods. Methods strictly depend on the size of knowledge base and type of acquired cartographical knowledge. One intelligent system is not possible due to amount of rules and facts, which should be involved into database.

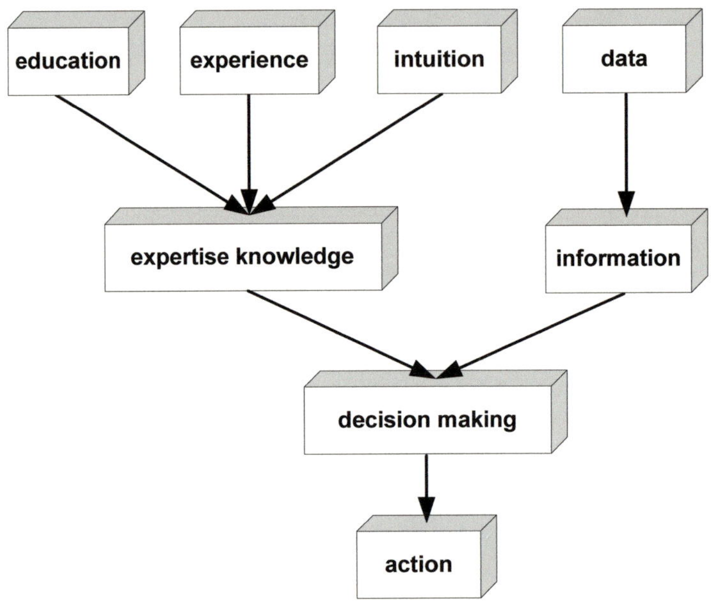


Fig. 3. The bases of expertise knowledge and expert decision making

### 3.2 Evaluation of cartographic functionality in GIS software

Starting point for design intelligent system was previous research at Palacký University in 2009 (Brus et al., 2010). This research compared possibilities of creation thematic map in various GIS software. Research was carried out to search the conditions and the possibilities of map making process in GIS software. The special evaluation method named "CartoEvaluation" has been proposed for finding out the GIS software cartography potential. New evaluation method is based on Goal-Question-Metric method. More than 13 GIS software of commercial production and Open Source Software (Czech and world-wide) were evaluated under this method. The evaluation results are summarized into complex tables and accessible at web pages of the scientific project (Dobesova, 2009).

| 5 | G: Color schemes (ramps) (max. 40 %) | | | | | |
|---|---|---|---|---|---|---|
| | M1–5: 0 – no<br>1 – yes | Q1: Are there predefined qualitative (categorical) color schemes (various colors)? | 1 | 0,50 | 0,50 | |
| | | Q2: Are there predefined sequential color schemes? | 1 | 0,50 | 0,50 | |
| | | Q3: Are there predefined bipolar (diverging) color schemes? | 1 | 0,50 | 0,50 | |
| | | Q4: Are there predefined color hypsometric ramps (tint)? | 1 | 0,50 | 0,50 | |
| | | Q5: Can you create your own color schemes and save them for reuse? | 1 | 0,40 | 0,40 | |
| Total | | | | | 6,00 | |

Fig. 4. The part of evaluation table for evaluation of color scheme in GIS software

The results of the evaluation confirm that most of the programs achieved satisfactory basic cartographic functions. Nine programs achieved more than 50 from the maximum possible score (100%). Tested programs were ArcGIS, MapInfo, Geomedia, GRASS, TopoL, AutoCAD Map, Kristýna GIS, MISYS and OCAD. Commercial programs are among the best because they are being developed for a long time, and thus have the chance to meet the requirements of expert cartographic outputs. The ArcGIS program was the bets in evaluation.

Evaluation of programs also revealed some weak or missing cartographic functions. They are missing of some compound line (motivated line) and point symbol in symbol libraries. Programs also have insufficiencies in creating point and area diagram map (chart diagrams). Multi-parameters totalizing diagrams, comparative diagrams and dynamic diagrams are missing. Cartograms methods (anamorphosis) are very seldom implemented.

Functionality of setting colours is acceptable. It is possible to select the color from a palette in different color models (RGB, HSV). Some color schemes (ramps) are, however, missing, in particular bipolar, gradation or hypsometric color schemes. Possibility to create, save and re-use custom color schemes is very rare.

GIS software is not only aimed for creation of cartographic outputs. Cartographic outputs are in the end of GIS analyses. The overlay analyses of spatial data (spatial clip, symmetrical difference, spatial union etc.) bring new results and new spatial data e.g. for urban planning (Dobesova, Krivka, 2011). Another example of spatial analysis is the field of the spreading of diseases (Absalon, Slesak, 2011). The results of analyses are necessary correctly express in the map. The process of analyzing and cartographic outputs can be automated by data flow diagrams or by programming language (Dobesova, 2011 a, b).

## 4. Cartographical ontology

In fact, there is significant convergence of artificial intelligence and geographic information systems recently (Vozenilek, 2009). Artificial Intelligence (AI) takes many forms such as expert systems (ES), fuzzy logic, and neural networks (Ham, 1996). Two artificial intelligence methods are widely used in GIS - artificial neural networks and fuzzy logic. The position of cartographic expert system in computer science is on Fig. 5.

The development of intelligent (expert) system needs formalization of cartographical knowledge for computers "to understand" the map making process. Humans understand intuitively. On the contrary, computers need explicit coding. A design of ontology is way for coding the formal cartographic knowledge. Ontology is a formal specification of a shared understanding of a knowledge domain that facilitates accurate and effective communication meaning (Gruber 1993).

Ontologies are defined for purposes of sharing and re-use of knowledge across information systems. Specialized ontologies are aimed to design a common conceptual system - thesaurus. Similarly, the cartographic ontology defines the basic conceptual system (conceptualization) for the cartography. Cartographic concepts (classes) are formed as a hierarchy of classes with simple constraints. The cartographic ontology had to capture also the context and constraints of classes using description logic. The final target was not only the creating of cartographical thesaurus but the usefulness of cartographic knowledge in the process of machine inference. Protégé program is often used for building of ontology. Protégé allows the definition in the language OWL-DL. This language is currently the most commonly used ontological language. The cartography is a very extensiveness discipline. From that fact, two methods were chosen from thematic cartography - choropleth method (area quantitative method) and diagram maps (cartodiagram) for the pilot stage of scientific research. Built ontology was created the necessary basis for an intelligent system that supported the users in the creation of the cartography correct maps.

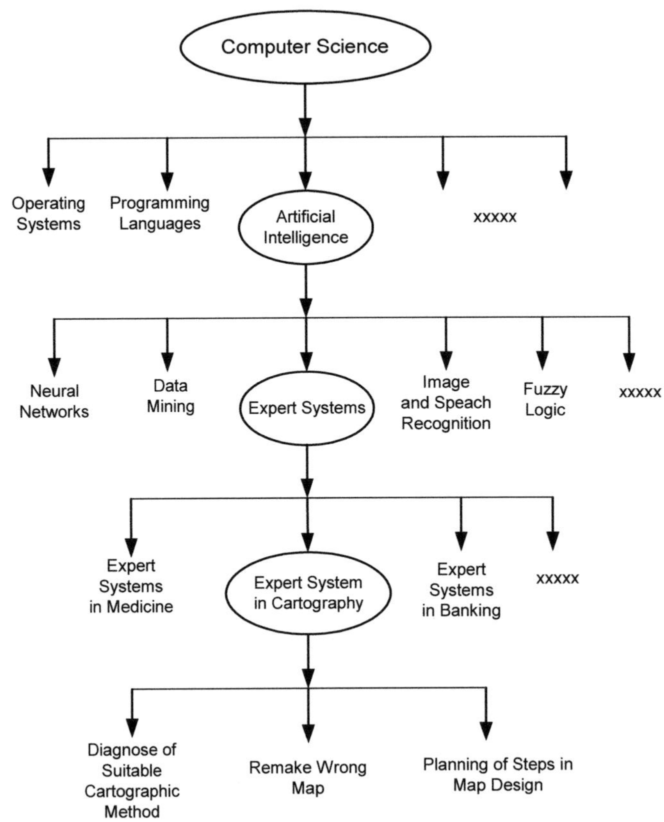


Fig. 5. The position of cartographic expert system in computer science

### 4.1 Current state of the cartographical ontologies

Well-known ontology can be found in literature and on websites for various fields of study, e.g. Protégé Ontologies Library. As a starting point, we tried to find some related works for cartography, geography, GIS and related sciences. Main concepts found in related works in the field of ontology for GIS data operability (Stanimirovic, 2010). GeoSpatial semantic web and geo-ontology should be also taken into consideration when designing a cartographical ontology.

After examination of accessible ontologies on the web and other ontological repository, we came to this conclusion: Only a few particular examples of domain ontology exist in the related field. There is no complex ontology which takes into consideration all aspects of cartographical knowledge. There exist some attempts to design a comprehensive ontology. This effort nevertheless collides with different cartographical schools and nomenclatures.

E. Pantaleáo (2003) presented a simple proposal of cartographic ontology in her dissertation work. This ontology concerns only basic class as map symbols, variables of symbols, shape of features and category of attribute data (nominal, ordinal and numeric). There are no classes about cartographic methods (graduated point method, choropleth method) and about main components (elements) of maps (map title, map area, legend, north arrow, scale, and imprint).

Interesting results in cartographical ontology development can be found in the Institute of Cartography, EHT Zurich (Enescu & Hurni, 2007). Their cartographic ontology is centered on map concepts, graphic elements, visual variables and symbols. Furthermore, their cartographic domain ontology also focuses on the complexity of map semiotics because of the fact that different types of thematic maps (choropleth maps, graduated symbol maps, multi-variable graduated symbol maps, dot density maps, etc.) can be defined. Some details of the domain ontology such as thematic point symbols like diagrams (bar charts, pie charts, ring charts ...) as well as some of their properties (divergent, divided, polar, proportional ...) and some additional concepts - are arranged in the logical hierarchy. All these aspects were included in their proposed ontology. The latest research at the field of cartographical ontology can be traced at University of Georgia (Smith, 2010). The basic concept is similar to our CartoExpert ontology; however, there are several aspects which differ.

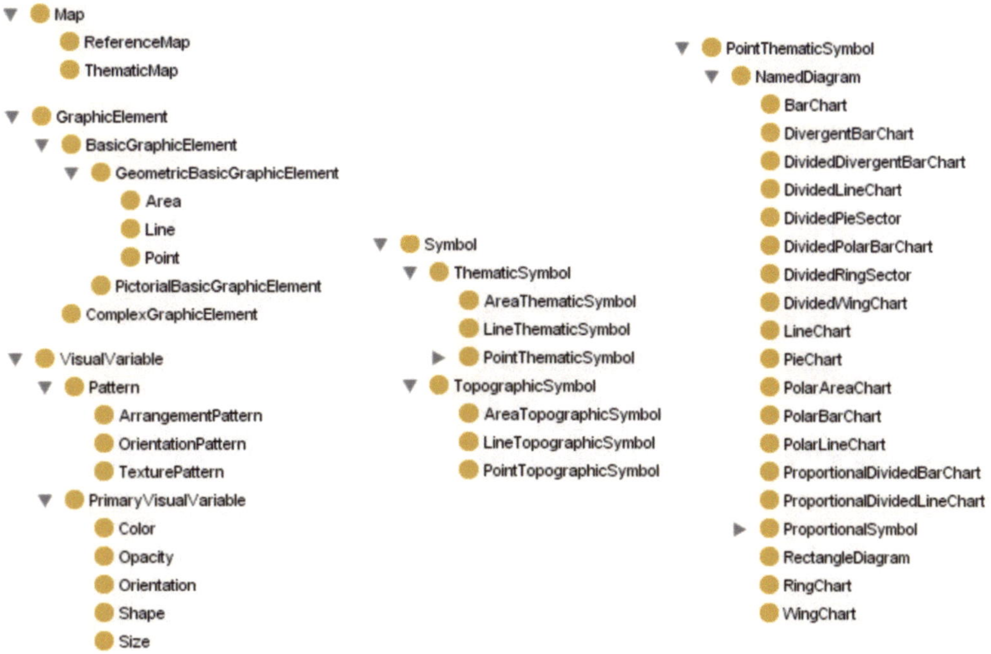

Fig. 6. Detail of domain ontology from the Institute of Cartography, Zurich

### 4.2 Ontology CartoExpert

Our research team decided to create new cartographic ontology CartoExpert in 2010. Basic terms of the conceptualization of cartographic knowledge can be found in cartographical books. There are several important books that deal with cartography like "Thematic Cartography and Geographic Visualization" by Slocum et al. (2004), "Cartography, Visualization of Geospatial Data" by Kraak and Ormeling (2003) and "Elements of Cartography" by Robinson et al. (1995). Other resources are e.g. "How maps work? Representation, Visualization and Design" by MacEachren (2004) and "Mapping It Out: Expository Cartography for the Humanities and Social Sciences" by Monmonier (1993).

Some different cartographical concepts and methods exist in Central Europe. Other authors and their books like "Methods of map expression" by Pravda (2006), "Application of Cartography and Thematic Maps" by Vozenilek (2004) and "Quantitative method in cartography" by Kanok (1992) were also considered. All terms, rules and recommendations were collected from these books. Subsequently, they were used in the phase of ontology building and knowledge base design.

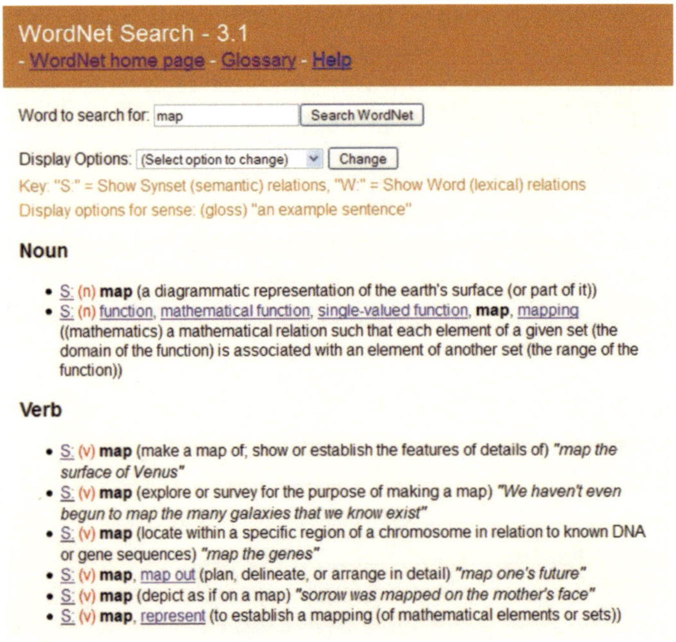


Fig. 7. The result of search for word "map" at the WordNet ontology

Maps are divided according to cartography to two main groups. There are thematic maps and topographic maps. Every thematic map contains a simple topographic base map. Thematic maps represent the distribution of one or more particular phenomena (Kraak, Ormeling, 2003). Census and statistical data are very often depicted on thematic maps. Data are divided into two types: qualitative and quantitative data. Quantitative data have absolute or relative value. Absolute and relative values are expressed by different cartographic methods in maps. Absolute values, which have a non-area related ratio, are expressed by diagrams in maps. All methods use cartographic symbols (point, line, area).

The creation of a thematic map, use of symbols and the use of cartographic methods are under theoretical principals. Additionally, creation of thematic maps also respects practical experience (Vozenilkek, 2004).

The basic terms were also compared with terminological world lexical ontology WordNet. The term as cartography, map, symbol, sign, choropleth map are included there.

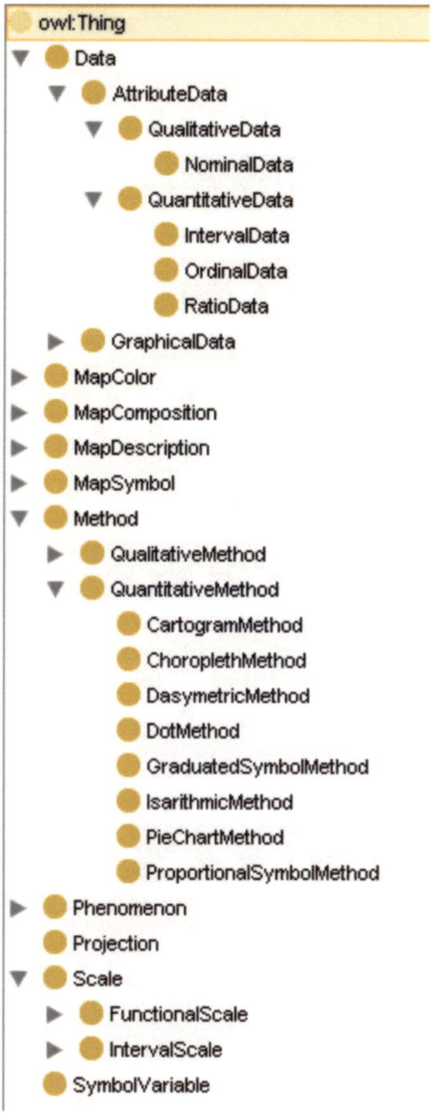


Fig. 8. The classes in CartoExpert ontology in Protégé

The base for the cartographical ontology was thesaurus - lexicon of cartographical terms. The lexicon also contained a list of synonyms. In the dictionary pruning stage, a pair wise comparison between the cartographic terms and their descriptions result to lexicon set. Synonyms of terms were grouped together. As a result, one description was chosen to represent all the synonym terms. The differences between the Central Europe and the English cartographic school were solved by the decision to design two ontologies - the Czech ontology and the English ontology. This chapter and figures describes only the English ontology for the better readability. The main classes are Data, MapColor, MapComposition, MapDescription, MapSymbol, Method, Phenomenon, Projection, SymbolVariables and Scale. These cartographic terms are expressed by **classes** in ontology in OWL language.

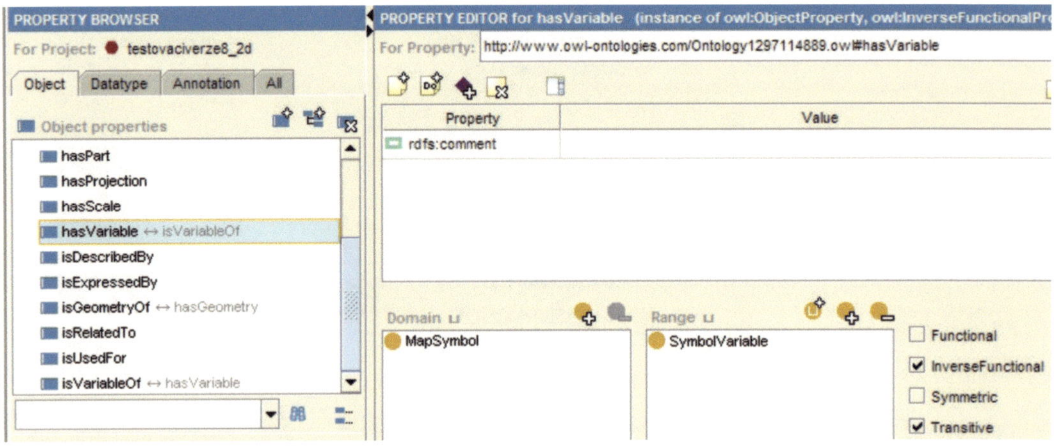


Fig. 9. List of object properties in Protégé (properties "hasVariable")

Very carefully was designed the **hierarchy** of classes. The relation of two classes is expressed by *subsumption, equivalence* or *disjunction.* The example of subsumption is upper class *AttributeData* and two sub class *QualitativeData* and *QuantitativeData.* The disjunction is also defined for these two classes. When data have qualitative value they can not have quantitative value. The terms isoline, isopleth and isochor are the example of equivalence (synonyms) (Penaz, 2010).

The important part of ontology is also the definition of **properties**. The property constructs relation between classes or individuals. The name of the property contains verb

**is** or **has**. The relation is set as Domain *D(f)* and Range *H(f)*. The fig. 9 shows the relation between class MapSymbol and class SymbolVariable. The name of property is "hasVariable".

The main cartographic terms were necessary for the pilot project that concern only to two cartographic methods for thematic maps based on Quantitative data. The Choroplets map methods and Chart map methods are aimed. The system of the class hierarchy was designed more detailed for them than other part of the ontology. The names and division of these methods differ in the Czech and English version of the ontology. The last important class for method based on quantitative data is class Scale. This class expresses the **scale of values** (not scale of the map). This call contents two subclasses FunctionalScale and IntervalScale.

The definition of hierarchy of classes and definition of properties represent the collection of stored knowledge for the domain of cartography. Ontology gathers mainly declarative knowledge. **Declarative knowledge** is the set of definitions of terms from the specific domain - cartography. The set is not only list of terms (thesaurus) but important is grouping terms to joint classes and creation of taxonomy. **Procedural knowledge** is the second type of knowledge. Procedural knowledge describes activities and processes in map creation. This type procedural knowledge can not be introduced to ontology. They can be record as rules and such some mathematical equations.

## 5. Conclusion

Intelligent systems have already covered a range of usages, the growing trend can be traced in their development especially in recent years. The possibility of their usage is increasing with the increasing power of computer technology. It is commendable that some attempts of creation of intelligent system to force GIS have occurred recently.

Within the development, it is necessary to require the presence of thematic cartographer in the role of the knowledge expert and equally important expert - the knowledge engineer who is able to incorporate this information into the intelligent system. Knowledge acquisition and building knowledge base is a complex and time-consuming stage of intelligent system development which is indispensable without collaborating between experts (cartographers) and knowledge engineers. An effectively deployed intelligent system must do more than embody expertise. Its rule base must be complete, non-contradictory, and reasonable. Knowledge engineers employ a variety of techniques for eliciting information from the expert in order to construct a complete and consistent rule base.

The situation in the field of professional software is still insufficient. Even the world's largest producers of GIS software do not implement tools that should increasingly guide the process of map-making in the accordance with the cartographical rules in their products. It is still necessary to have at least basic cartographic knowledge to visualize maps properly.

So far, there has been no comprehensive tool, which can easily deal with the problem of thematic cartography completely. The main reason is the complexity and comprehensiveness of a map-making process. To build a hierarchy of rules, affect all types of maps and the appropriate methods of thematic cartography in a single system, requires more than a comprehensive approach. Higher demands are put on the user's knowledge because he must be able to select correctly from the proposed system of options.

Despite the complexity of a map-making process the knowledge base of expert system is a solution how to help primarily non-cartographers in the production of maps according with the rules of thematic cartography towards to better decisions based on map output.

A great problem for those who tries to develop up-to-date knowledge-based software for computer mapping is the absence of systematized knowledge concerning building and use of interactive, dynamic maps. Replacing the human expert by a comprehensive intelligent system is a highly efficient objective for cartography as a whole. Not only reaching correct map, but also helping people to make right decisions is a main aim of whole cartography. Main objective will be to create a user-friendly expert system, simple and so comprehensive that will allow you to create the correct cartographic map without the need of combining more software. This software will become a popular tool for the broadest range of users. The educational potential of intelligent systems allows the extension of expertise among a large group of non-cartographers. Another advantage of intelligent system is the gradual insertion of further new expert knowledge of cartography into the knowledge base of expert system. This will quickly transfer expert knowledge between non-cartographers in the future. The elimination of the future inexpert and inaccurate maps will be achieved.

## 6. Acknowledgment

The research was supported by the project of the Czech Grant Science Foundation No. 205/09/1159 „Intelligent system for interactive support of thematic map creation".

## 7. References

Absalon D., Slesak B. (2011). The importance of time of exposure to harmful anthropogenic factors as an element of cancer risk assessment in children. *Ecotoxicology and Environmental Safety* 74, pp. 967 - 973, Elsevier

Andrienko, G., Andrienko, N., Voss, H. (2002) Computer cartography and cartographic knowledge. Proceedings: *Intercarto 8,* International Conference, Saint-Petersburg, Russia. St. Petersburg, pp. 114-117

Balch S. R., Schrader S. M., Ruan T. (2007) Collection, storage and application of human knowledge in expert system development, Expert Systems, 24 no. 5, pp. 346-355

Booker, J.,M., Meyer, M. (2001) Eliciting and Analyzing Expert Judgment: A practical guide, ASA-SIAM Series on Statistics and Applied Probability, 459 p. ISBN: 0-89871-474-5

Boss, R., W. (1991) What Is an Expert System? ERIC Digest. ERIC Clearing House on Information Resources, Syracuse, NY, 1-3.

Borst, W. N. (1997). Construction of engineering ontologies for knowledge sparing and reuse. [Ph.D. thesis]. University of Twente, Enschede, 243 p.

Brus, J., Dobesova, Z., Kanok, J., Pechanec, V. (2010) Design of intelligent system in cartography. In Brad, R. (ed.): *Proceedings. 9 RoEduNet IEEE International Conference.* Sibiu, University of Sibiu, pp. 112-117 ISSN 2068-1038. ISBN 978-1-4244-7335-9

Brus J., Dobesova Z., Kanok J. (2009). Utilization of expert systems in thematic cartography *International Conference on Intelligent Networking and Collaborative Systems, INCoS,* Barcelona

Brus J, Kanok, J. Dobesova, Z. (2010). Assisted cartography, vision or reality? [Asistovaná kartografie: vize nebo realita?], *Proceedings o 18th congress of Czech geographical society,* University of Ostrava, Ostrava, pp. 255-258, ISBN 978-80-7368-903-2 (in Czech)

Brewer, I., MacEachren, A. M., Abdo, H., Gundrumand, J., Otto, G. (2000) Collaborative geographic visualization: Enabling shared understanding of environmental processes. In: IEEE Information Visualization Symposium, Salt Lake City, Utah, pp. 137-141.

Dhaliwal, J. S., & Benbasat, I. (1996). The use and effects of knowledge-based system explanations: theoretical foundations and a framework for empirical evaluation. *Information Systems Research,* 7, pp. 342–362.

Dobesova, Z., Brus, J. (2011). Coping with cartographical ontology. *Conference Proceedings SGEM 2011, 11th International Multidisciplinary Scientific GeoConfrence.* STEF92 Technology Ltd., Sofia, Bulgaria, pp. 377-384 ISSN 1314-2704, DOI:10.5593/ sgem2011

Dobesova, Z. (2011a). Visual programming language in geographic information systems, *Recent Researches in Applied Informatics,* Proceedings of the 2nd International Conference on Applied Informatics and Computing Theory, AICT `11, Prague, WSEAS Press, pp. 276-280 , ISBN 978-1-61804-034-3

Dobesova, Z. (2011b). Programming Language Python for Data Processing, *Proceedings of 2nd International Conference on Electrical and Control Engineering ICECE 2011,* Yichang, China, Volume 6, Institute of Electrical and Electronic Engineers (IEEE), pp. 4866-4869, ISBN 978-1-4244-8163-7

Dobesova, Z, Krivka, T. (2011). Walkability index in the urban planning: A case study in Olomouc city, *Urban Planning,* InTech, ISBN 979-953-307-412-1

Dobesova, Z. (2009). *Evaluation of Cartographic Functionality in Geographic Information Systems.* Hodnoceni kartografické funkcionality geografických informačních systémů. Publishing house Palacký University, Olomouc, 132 p., ISBN 978-80-244-2353-1

Eikvil, L., Aas, K., Koren, H. (1995) Tools for interactive map conversion and vectorization. In: Third International Conference on Document Analysis and Recognition: 927-930.

Enescu, I. I., Hurni, L. (2007). Towards cartographic ontologies or how computers learn cartography, In: *Proceedings of the 23rd International Cartographic Conference,* Moscow, Russia.

Gruber, T. R. (1993). Toward Principles for the Design of Ontologies Used for Knowledge Sharing. *International Journal Human-Computer Studies* 43: pp. 907-928.

Ham, J. (1996). Artificial intelligence: building on expert knowledge, InTech, 43 (3), 52-55 pp.

Harrower, M., Brewer C. (2003). ColourBrewer.org: An Online Tool for Selecting Colour Schemes for Maps. Cartographic Journal 40 (1): 27-37.

Hori, O., Tanigawa, S. (1993). Raster-to-vector conversion by line based on contours and skeletons. In: Second International Conference on Document Analysis and Recognition. Tsukuba, Japan, 353-358.

Hua, Y., (1991) Determine the map symbol type of map element with expert system technology. Journal of the People's Liberation Army Institute of Surveying and Mapping, Vol. 3: 43-47.

Iosifescu-Enescu,I., Hugentobler, M., Hurni, L., (2010) Web cartography with open standards - A solution to cartographic challenges of environmental management, Environmental Modelling & Software, Volume 25, Issue 9, pp. 988-999,

Kaňok, J. (1992). *Kvantitativní metody v kartografii*, [Quantitative method in cartography] Ostravská univerzita, Ostrava (in Czech)

Karvaš, P. (2011). Design of knowledge base for expert system in the realative data expresion, [diploma thesis], department of Geoinformatics, Palacky University in Olomouc, 67 p., (in Czech)

Kraak, M., J., MacEachren, A., M., (1999) Visualization for exploration of spatial data. International Journal of Geographical Information Science 13:285-287.

Kraak, M., J., Ormeling, F. (2003) *Cartography, Visualization of Geospatial data*, Second Edition, Prentice Hall, London

Kasturi, R., Bow, S.T., Masri, W.E., Shah, J., Gattiker, J.R., Mokate, U.B. (1990). A system for interpretation of line drawings. IEEE Transactions on Pattern Analysis and Machine Intelligence 12 (10): 973-992.

Lee D. (1994). "Knowledge Acquisition of Digital Cartographic Generalization". EGIS, 1-20.

MacEachren, A.M., Kraak, M. J., (1997) Exploratory cartographic visualization: advancing the agenda. Computers & Geosciences, 23(4): 335-343.

MacEachren A., M. (2004) *How maps work: representation, visualization, and design*, The Guilford Press

Meng L. (2003)."Cognitive Modelling of Cartographic Generalization". Strategies on Automated Generalization of Cartographic Data, Project Report.

Monmonier, M. (1993) *Mapping It Out: Expository Cartography for the Humanities and Social Sciences*, The Univesity of Chicago Press

Návrat, P. Bieliková, M., Beňušková, L., Kapustník, I., Unger, M. (2002): Umelá inteligencia, Vydavateľstvo STU, Bratislava, 396 p. ISBN 80-227-1645-6

O'Looney, J. (2000) Beyond maps: GIS and decision making in local government. Redlands, California: ESRI Press.

Okoli, C. & Pawlowski, S. D. (2004). The Delphi method as a research tool: an example, design considerations and applications. Information & Management, 42, 15-29.

Pantaleáo, E. (2003) Aplicacáo de técnicas de sistemas baseados em conhecimento em projeto cartográfico temático (Application of techniques for knowledge based systems in thematic cartography), disertation thesis, Universidade Federal de Paraná, Curitiba, Brasil.

Penaz, T. (2010) An Ontological Model Building for Application Use of Knowledge in Thematic Cartography Domain, Proceedings o 18th congress of Czech geographical society, University of Ostrava, pp. 259-265, ISBN 978-80-7368-903-2 (in Czech)

Pravda, J. (2006) Metódy mapového vyjadrovania, Klasifikácia a ukážky, [Methods of map expression, Classification and examples], Geographia Slovaca 21, Slovak academy of sciences, Geographical institute, Bratislava, 127 p. (in Slovak)

Protégé Ontologies Library. http://protege.stanford.edu/ontologies/ontologies.html.

Guo Q. (1993) Design a decision-making support system of thematic mapping. Journal of Wuhan University of Science and Technology Mapping, 1993, Vol.18 additional: 91-9.

Guo Q, Ren, X. (2003) Intelligent geographic information processing. Wuhan University Press.

Robinson, A. Morrison, J., Muehrcke, P., Kimerling, A., Guptill, S. (1995) *Elements of Cartography*, John Wiley & Sons, INC., USA

Robinson, G., Jackson, M. (1985). Expert Systems in map design. Proceedings Auto Carto 7, Washington D.C.

Schnabel, O. (2005). Map Symbol Brewer—A New Approach for a Cartographic Map Symbol Generator. Paper read at 22nd International Cartographic Conference, 9-16 July, at Coruña, Spain

Slocum T., McMaster, R., Kesseler, F., Howard, H. (2004). *Thematic Cartography and geographic Visualization*, Prentice Hall, 518 p.

Smith, A. R. (2010). Designing a cartographic ontology for use with expert systems. A special joint symposium of ISPRS Technical Commission IV & AutoCarto in conjuction with ASPRS/CaGIS 2010. Orlando, Florida.

Stanimirovic, A., Bogdanovic, M. et al. (2010) Mapping Ontologies to Object-Oriented Representation in Geonis Framework for Gis Interoperability. 10th International Multidisciplinary Scientific Geoconference: Sgem 2010, Vol I: 1127-1134

Stefanakis, K., Tsoulos, L. (2005) Structure and Development of a Knowledge. Base for Cartographic Composition, Proceedings of International Cartographic Conference, La Coruna, Spain.

Su, B. (1992) Expert System in the application of cartographic. Journal of Geomatics, Vol. 1: 31-35

Vozenilek, V. (2004). *Aplikovaná kartografie I., Tematické mapy*, [Application of cartography, Thematic maps], Publishing house of Palacký University, Olomouc, ISBN 80-224-0270-X (In Czech)

Vozenilek V. (2009). Artificial intelligence and GIS: Mutual meeting and passing. *International Conference on Intelligent Networking and Collaborative Systems*, INCoS 2009, Spain, pp. 279-284.

WordNet. http://wordnetweb.princeton.edu/perl/webwn

Zhang, L., Guo, Q., Jiao, L. (2008). Design and Implementation of Decision-making Support System for Thematic Map Cartography. The international archives of the photogrammetry, remote sensing and spatial information science. Volume XXXVII. Bejing China.

# 13

# Intelligent Expert System for Protection Optimization Purposes in Electric Power Distribution Systems

Ivan N. da Silva et al.*
*University of São Paulo (USP), São Carlos, SP*
*Brazil*

## 1. Introduction

The objective of this chapter consists of presenting an expert system that assists the procedures involved with the protection specification of transformers and equipments against atmospheric discharges, allowing also to analyze in a detailed and systematic way the behavior of the respective voltage transients that are generated at the supplying area.

For such purpose, the expert system developed makes efficient integration of approaches and techniques that take into account the characteristic aspects of the atmospheric discharges, the experimental analyses that represent the phenomenon and the mathematical models that allow to map the process involved with the formation of the lightning.

The results obtained from the experimental application of the expert system have contributed in a substantial way to optimize the processes involved with the efficient specification of protection devices associated with the transformers and equipments of the distribution system.

The decision process taken into account by the expert system is based on information provided by the software "SimSurto", which was especially developed to simulate the voltage transients caused by atmospheric discharges in distribution lines, and its objective is the computation of several parameters related to the respective transients, considering the equipments already installed, the geographical location of the distribution line and the respective incidence of atmospheric discharges in the distribution system.

The use of the developed tool has allowed the optimized specification for protection devices of equipments and transformers belonging to distribution system, enabling that differentiated protection strategies can be applied according to the particularities of each

* Nerivaldo R. Santos[2], Lucca Zamboni[2], Leandro N. Soares[3], José A. C. Ulson[4], Rogério A. Flauzino[1], Danilo H. Spatti[1], Ricardo A. S. Fernandes[1], Marcos M. Otsuji[2] and Edison A. Goes
[1]*University of São Paulo (USP), São Carlos, SP, Brazil*
[2]*EDP Bandeirante, São Paulo, SP, Brazil*
[3]*EDP ESCELSA, Vitória, ES, Brazil*
[4]*São Paulo State University, Bauru, SP, Brazil*

region, contributing then for value aggregation to services provided by the distribution company, since the available tools proportionate more optimized analyses in relation to the procedures involved with the protection specification.

Therefore, in this chapter, the particularities for estimation of induced voltages in real distribution networks, such as the network discontinuity, the phase conductor arrangement, the intrinsic characteristics of the incident atmospheric discharges in each region of the considered distribution system, are taken into account by the expert system. Performance evaluations indicate that the expert system provides coherent results and its practical application contributes to optimize the processes involved with parameters specification related to the protection of equipments and transformers.

For such purpose, this paper is organized as follows. In Section 2, a brief summary about induced voltage estimation techniques are presented. In Section 3, the achieved modifications in relation to the conventional techniques are introduced in order to produce a greater accuracy when compared to the results obtained from real situations. The expert system for protection specification against atmospheric discharges, named by Protection Plus, is briefly described in Section 4. The expert system for optimized design of grounding systems is presented in Section 5. Finally, in Section 6, the key issues raised in the paper are summarized and conclusions are drawn.

## 2. Rusck's conventional model for induced voltage estimation in overhead distribution lines

In this section the main aspects concerning to Rusck's methodology for induced voltage estimation in distribution lines caused by atmospheric discharges are presented.

Therefore, it is achieved a general study regarding induced voltage estimation in distribution lines through use of conventional methods discussed in the technical literature.

Although the methodology originally developed in Rusck (1957) has some limitations to areas with soil resistivity less than 100 Ωm, it is still widely used for induced voltage estimation in overhead distribution and transmission lines generated from indirect atmospheric discharges occurred near to the respective line.

The induced voltage estimation methodology presented in Rusck (1957) has as start point the modeling of the return current imposed by the atmospheric discharge in the distribution line. Rusck's method calculates the electric field generated by this return current in the ground surface and, from this electric field and from the line multi-wire arrangement, the theory provides the resultant values of induced voltages along the distribution line.

In Rubinstein & Uman (1989) is mathematically demonstrated that the studies presented in Rusck (1957) for resultant electric field computation of return current is correct. This fact has contributed to increase the reliability in relation to method developed by Rusck. Other additional procedures involved with models for induced voltage are also found in Cooray (2003).

An existent question related to this theory is that it estimates induced voltage values for conductors of a multi-wire line taking just into account the conductor geometric localization in relation to incidence point of the atmospheric discharge, that is, the induced voltage values produced in a line composed by several conductors of same height and with a small horizontal spacing, such as in distribution lines, would be equal in each conductor.

Measurements achieved with the reduced model technique (Paula et al., 2001; Salari & Portela, 2007), as well as measurements in fields made in South Africa, demonstrate that the results provided by Rusck's theory is coherent with those obtained by experimental results (Eriksson et al., 1982). Originally, Rusck proposed a current wave to the atmospheric discharge represented by a step function with amplitude *I*. The induced voltage produced by this discharge in relation to an infinite line can be computed by:

$$V(x,t) = U(x,t) + U(-x,t) \tag{1}$$

where:

$$U(x,t) = 30 \cdot I \cdot h \cdot \beta . \frac{(c \cdot t - x)}{[y^2 + \beta^2 (c \cdot t - x)^2]} \cdot \left(1 + \frac{x + \beta^2 (c \cdot t - x)}{\sqrt{(\beta \cdot c \cdot t)^2 + (1 - \beta^2)(x^2 + y^2)}}\right) \tag{2}$$

$$\beta = \frac{v}{c} \approx \sqrt{\frac{1}{1 + \frac{5.10^5}{I}}} \tag{3}$$

In this case, $V(x,t)$ is the induced voltage (V) at a point $x$ of the line; $t$ is the time in seconds; $c$ is the velocity of light in free space (m/s); $I$ is the return-peak current value (A); $h$ is the average height of the distribution line; $y$ is the closest distance between the discharge incidence point and the distribution line (m) and $x$ is a point along the line (m).

Equations (1), (2) and (3) express Rusck's theory basis. In (4) the expression for the maximum induced voltage at the point $x$=0m is given by:

$$V_{max} \approx \frac{38.8 \cdot I \cdot h}{y} \tag{4}$$

From the previous expressions is possible to identify that they provide an analytic form for the computation of induced voltage in a distribution line, whereas other existent theories provide just iterative expressions that have high computational effort to perform the same estimation.

In Fig. 1 is presented the induced voltage at the point $x$=0m for an atmospheric discharge represented by a step function with amplitude $I$=10 kA in relation to an infinite line with 10 meters of height, where the distance between the atmospheric discharge from the distribution line is 100 meters.

In order to illustrate how the proposed formulation in this section is efficient for induced voltage estimation in overhead distribution lines, the induced voltage profile for different positions along the distribution line is presented in Fig. 2.

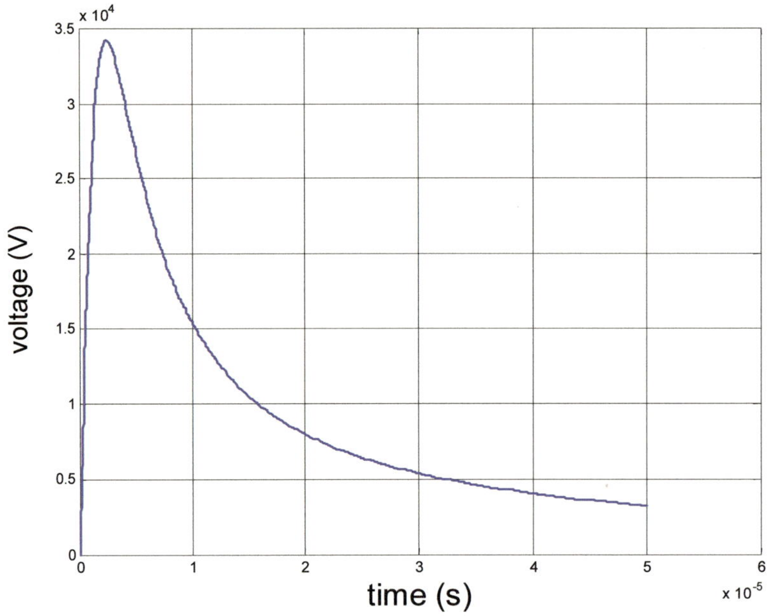


Fig. 1. Induced voltage in relation to the maximum voltage point in infinite line with 10m of height and atmospheric discharge of 10kA in perpendicular distance of 100m from the line.

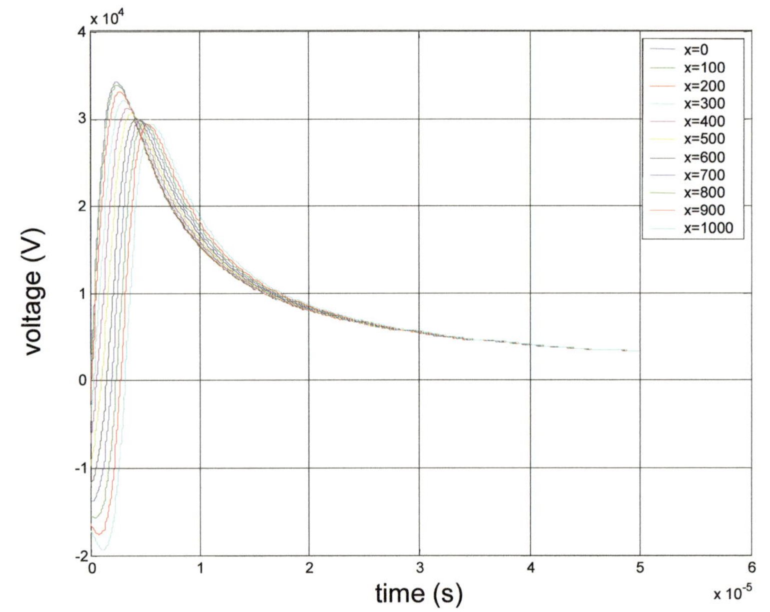


Fig. 2. Induced voltages in infinite distribution line with 10m of height and atmospheric discharge of 10kA in perpendicular distance of 100m from the line in relation to several points along the line.

It is observed from Fig. 2 that the induced voltage waveform modifies in relation to the distance between the maximum voltage point and the measurement point. The alterations in the induced voltage waveforms along the distribution line can be better verified through their parameters, such as maximum induced voltage, rising time, peak time and half-wave time.

For comparative effects, it is assumed as rising time that necessary time for the voltage wavefront to reach 90% of its maximum value, considering half-wave time as that necessary time for the voltage wavefront to reach 50% of peak value after the occurrence of its maximum value. Therefore, Fig. 3 to 6 presents how these parameters are altered in relation to the distance between the maximum voltage point and a point along this conductor.

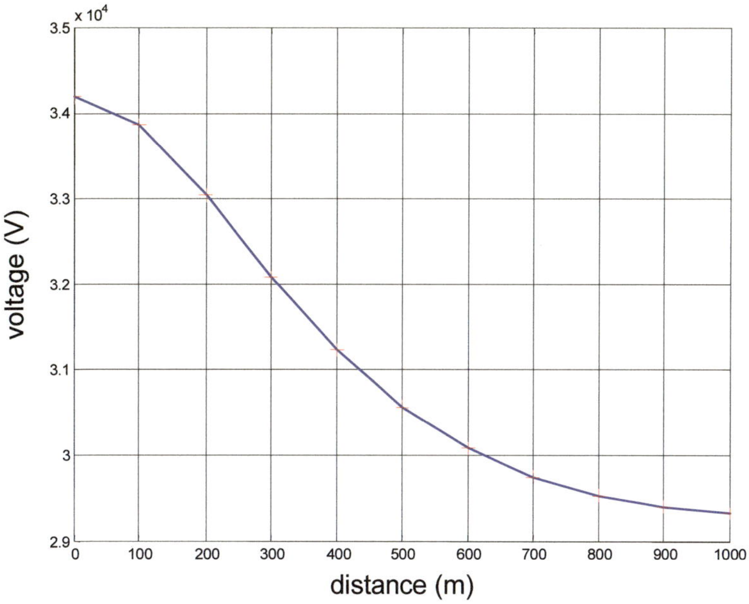


Fig. 3. Maximum induced voltage variation along the line.

From Fig. 3, it is observed that the voltage along the line length reduces at a rate practically linear in relation to the distance from the atmospheric discharge occurrence point. This observation indicates that the voltage wave along the distribution line suffers an attenuation generated from high frequencies involved with the propagation process as well as from energy dissipation in relation to the metallic conductors.

Figs. 4 to 6 illustrate how rising time, peak time and half-wave time alter along the distribution line. We can certify that these three parameters tend to increase at a rate practically constant along the distribution line.

This fact indicates that the voltage waveform loses energy in relation to the distance along the line since that rising time, peak time and half-wave time higher cause voltage gradients more smooth along the line.

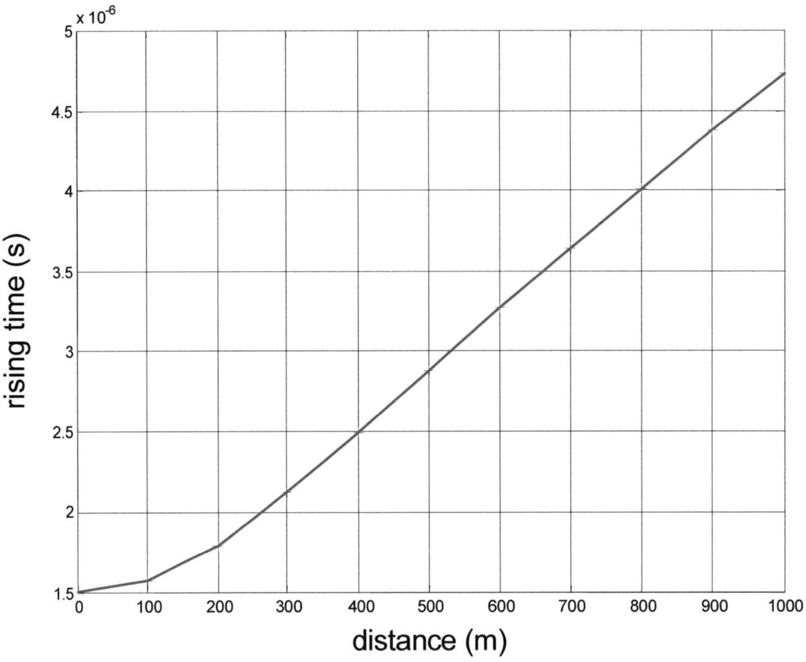


Fig. 4. Rising time variation along the distribution line.

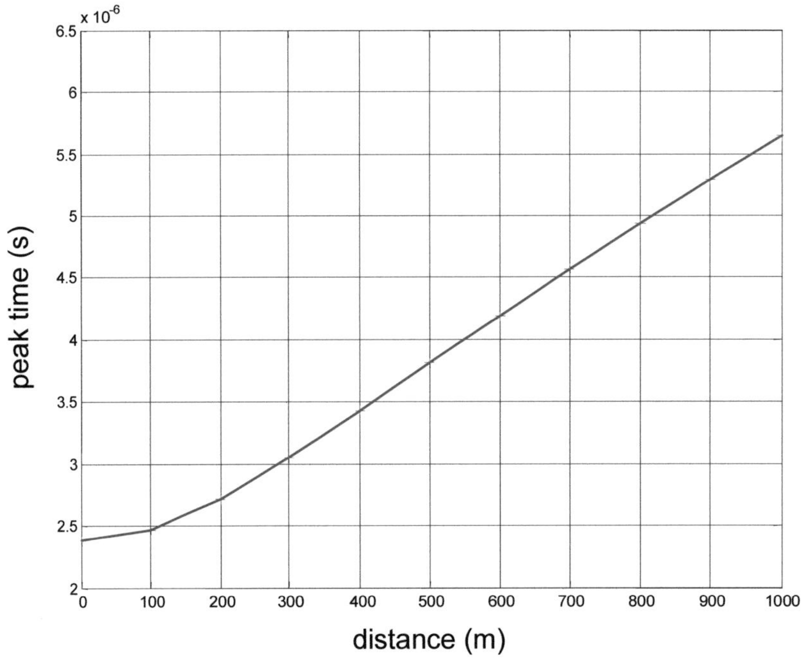


Fig. 5. Peak time variation along the distribution line.

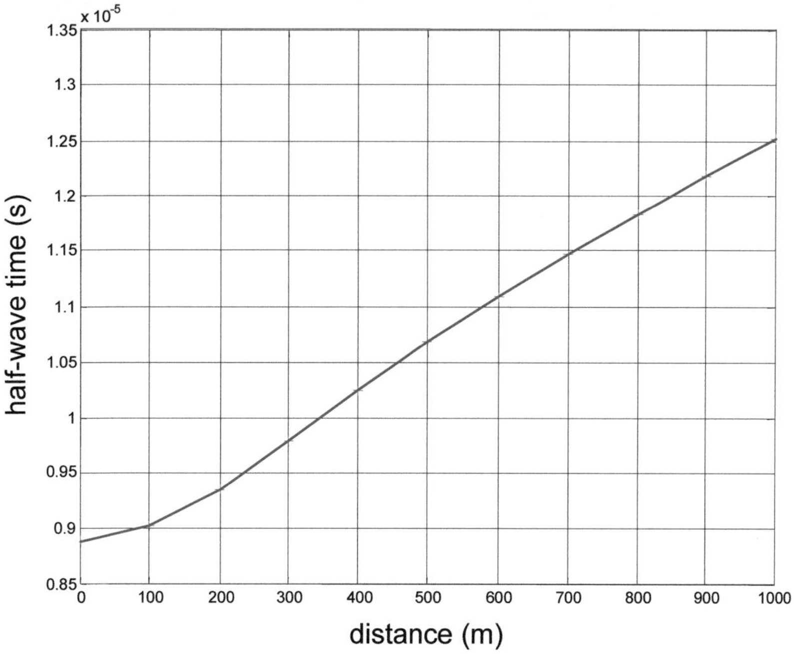


Fig. 6. Half-wave time variation along the distribution line.

From simulations accomplished and presented in this section and taking also into account the formulation proposed in Rusck (1957), it is verified that the obtained results by Rusck's method are coherent with those obtained through field experiments (Eriksson et al., 1982) or even with those results produced using reduced model techniques (Paula et al., 2001; Salari & Portela, 2007).

However, some modifications in this method are necessary in order to transpose this methodology to practical situations involved with real distribution systems. Basically, it is necessary the consideration of current waveforms for the atmospheric discharge similar to those found in the nature. It is needed due to the atmospheric discharge characteristics considered in Rusck's method.

As presented at the beginning of this section, the waveform for the atmospheric discharge current used in Rusck's methodology has been a step function. In the next section, the necessary modifications in the approach proposed in Rusck (1957) are conducted in order to complement the existent theory, becoming it appropriate for practical applications.

Other works involving practical extension of Rusck's formula for maximum lightning-induced voltages that accounts for ground resistivity and improved procedures for the assessment of overhead line indirect lightning performance can also be found in Darveniza (2007) and Borghetti et al. (2007).

## 3. Modification of the conventional theory for induced voltage estimation in practical applications

### 3.1 Generalization of rusck's methodology for generic discharge current waveform

Rusck's formulation presupposes that the atmospheric discharge can be represented by a waveform represented by a step function. However, measurements achieved in field have evidenced that the current waveform characteristics influence in the induced voltage in distribution lines located nearby the discharge occurrence point.

More specifically, parameters such as rising time and current waveform peak time have high correlation with the voltage induction process in distribution lines. Therefore, it is suggested that the induced voltage estimation in distribution lines to be achieved considering a waveform for discharge current near to that found in nature.

An approach often adopted for the atmospheric discharge current modeling can be provided as in (5), that is:

$$i(t) = i_{h1}(t) + i_{h2}(t) + i_{de}(t) \tag{5}$$

where:

$$i_{hm}(t) = \frac{I_{0m}}{\eta_m} \frac{\left(\frac{t}{\tau_{m1}}\right)^{nm}}{1+\left(\frac{t}{\tau_{m1}}\right)^{nm}} \exp\left(-\frac{t}{\tau_{m2}}\right) \tag{6}$$

$$i_{de}(t) = [(1-\exp(\alpha)) - (1-\exp(\beta))] \tag{7}$$

and:

$$\eta_m = \exp\left[-\left(\frac{\tau_{m1}}{\tau_{m2}}\right) \cdot \left(nm\frac{\tau_{m2}}{\tau_{m1}}\right)^{\frac{1}{nm}}\right] \tag{8}$$

Equation (6) is an example of Heidler's functions. An alternative frequently employed in atmospheric discharge modeling is double exponential.

Nevertheless, the modeling through two Heidler's function, as presented in (5), provides a more appropriate approximation for representation of the real phenomenon since the derivative of current at the instant t=0s is null. This fact is proved by innumerous practical cases.

In Fig. 7 is illustrated the current waveform results from modeling presented in this section, where the current has a peak value near to 12kA with a time of $0{,}81 \times 10^{-6}$ s.

Supposing that the system to be linear, it is possible the use of Duhamel's integral (Greenwood, 1992) in order to represent the current waveform through a successive series of steps. Thus, the value of each one of them, which represent the current waveform presented in Fig. 7, can be provided as shown in Fig. 8.

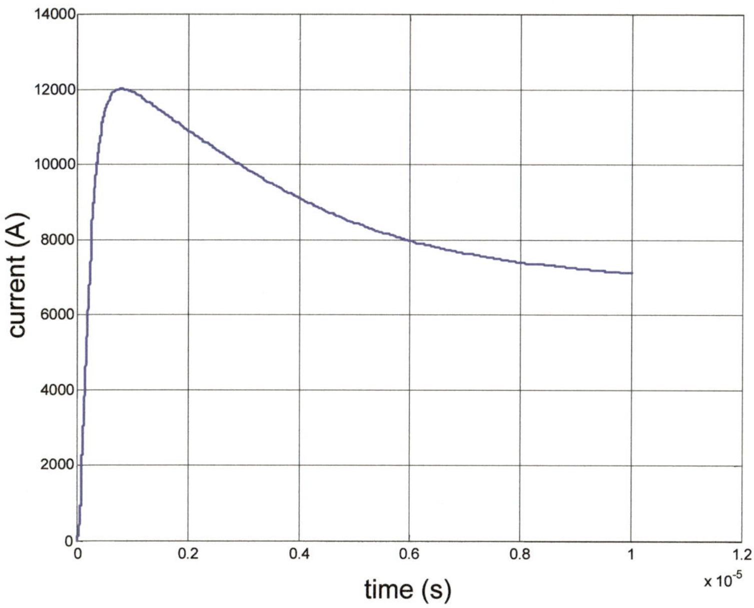


Fig. 7. Current waveform for atmospheric discharge modeling.

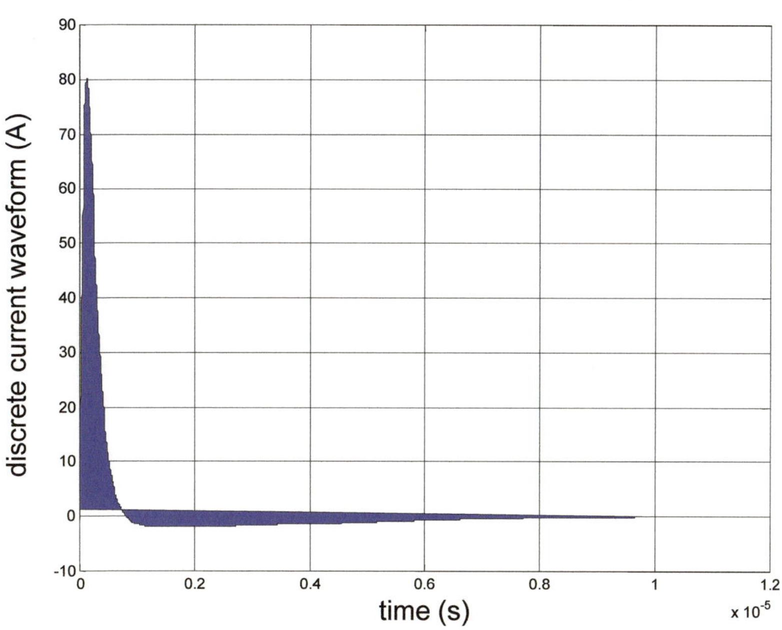


Fig. 8. Discrete current waveform composed by steps.

From this modification, the induced voltage at any point $x$ in the distribution line can be given by the sum of individual contribution in relation to each discrete current component.

Supposing an atmospheric discharge characterized as in Fig. 7, occurring in a distance of 100m from infinite distribution line with 10m of height, the voltage waveform at the point x=0m (point of maximum voltage value) can be represented as in Fig. 9.

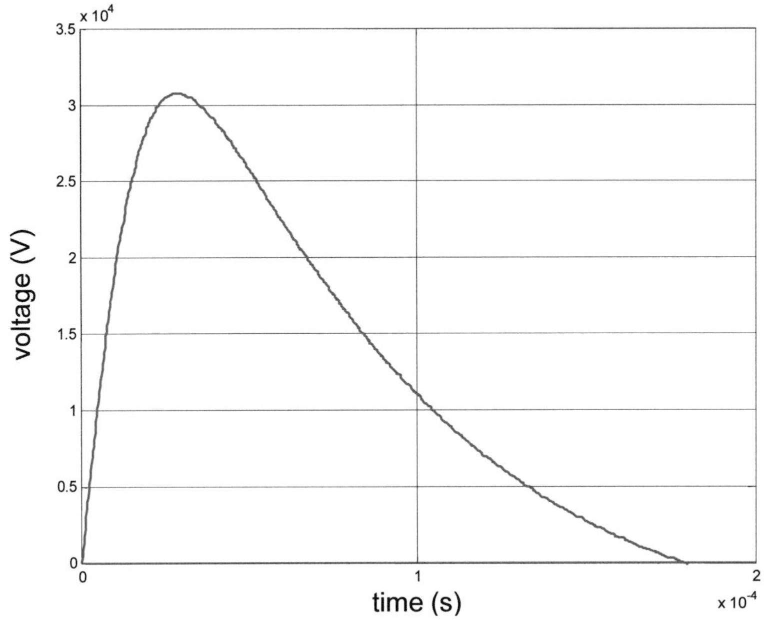


Fig. 9. Induced voltage at the point of maximum voltage value for a current waveform expressed in terms of Heidler's function.

### 3.2 Considerations for induced voltage estimation in finite lines

Rusck's expression for induced voltage calculation in distribution lines is composed of two parcels, which can be observed through the following equation:

$$V(x_0,t) = U(x_0,t) + U(-x_0,t) \tag{9}$$

where $V(x_0,t)$ is the induced voltage at the point $x$ of the line; $U(x_0,t)$ is the induced voltage component due to the load contribution located at the right part of this point and $U(-x_0,t)$ is the induced voltage component due to the load contribution located at the left part of $x_0$.

In Fig. 10 is presented the interpretation of induced voltage proposed in the formulation suggested by Rusck.

In case of a finite line, some modifications in Rusck's theory must be incorporated in order to enable that the induced voltage estimation in any point of the distribution line to be modeled adequately according to real situations.

Hence, we assume a line with termination in $x_1$ with impedance of termination $R_f$ as indicated in Fig. 11.

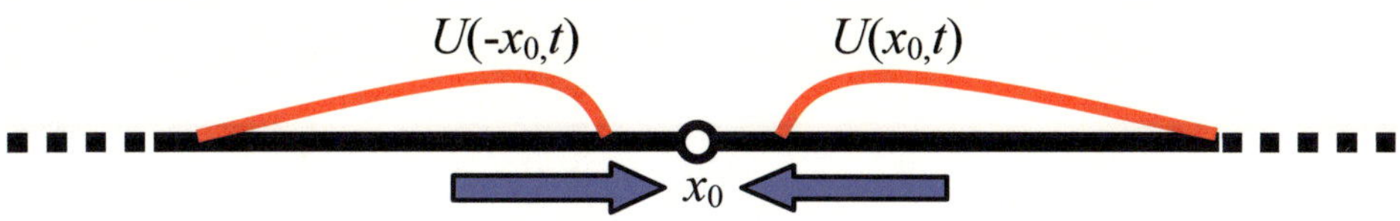


Fig. 10. Induced voltage composition at the point $x_0$ of the line.

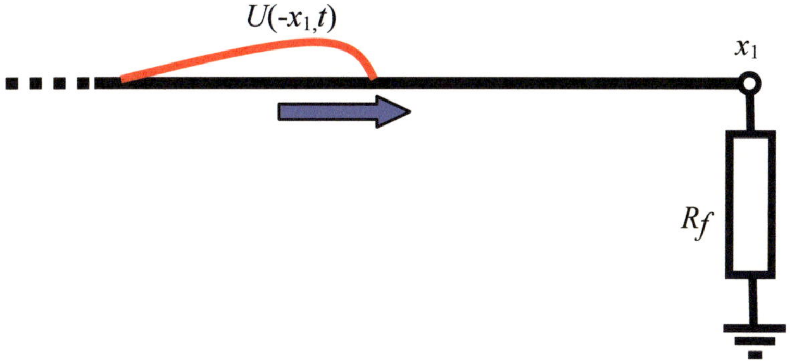


Fig. 11. Induced voltage in a finite line.

If the line was infinite, the voltage at the point $x_1$ would be given by:

$$V(x_1,t) = U(x_1,t) + U(-x_1,t) \tag{10}$$

As there is no line located at the right part of the point $x_1$, there is no contribution of loads coming from the right of $x_1$, that is, the voltage contribution $U(x_1,t)$ is null. As the line has termination impedance, the voltage at the point $x_1$ can be computed as follows:

$$V(x_1,t) = U(-x_1,t) + \Gamma U(-x_1,t) \tag{11}$$

where Γ is the reflection coefficient. The expression to obtain Γ is given by:

$$\Gamma = \frac{R_f - |Z_L|}{R_f + |Z_L|} \tag{12}$$

where $Z_L$ is the characteristic impedance of the distribution line. The numeric value for $Z_L$ is provided by:

$$Z_L = 138 \cdot \log\left(2\frac{h}{r}\right) \tag{13}$$

where $h$ is the height of the distribution line and $r$ is the conductor diameter.

Supposing that the discontinuity at the point $x_1$ to be substituted by a compensation source, the value of this source can be computed according to the following development:

$$V(x_1,t) + \Delta V = U(-x_1,t) + \Gamma U(-x_1,t) \tag{14}$$

$$U(x_1,t)+U(-x_1,t)+\Delta V=U(-x_1,t)+\Gamma U(-x_1,t) \tag{15}$$

$$\Delta V=\Gamma U(-x_1,t)-U(x_1,t) \tag{16}$$

The compensation source of value $\Delta V$ is applied in the point $x_1$, but its effect must be propagated throughout the line, since the non existence of line in the right of $x_1$ alters the induced voltage values along whole line.

In order to compute the voltage at any point $x$, we can sum the induced voltage computed for the point $x$, assuming an infinite line, to the value of the compensation source applied in $x_1$.

However, the compensation source located at $x_1$ suffers a time delay during the trajectory between $x$ and $x_1$, that is:

$$V(x,t)=U(x,t)+U(-x,t)+[\Gamma U(-x_1,t)-U(x_1,t)]u(t-t_f) \tag{17}$$

The function $u(t - t_f)$ is a unit step function and $t_f$ is the travel time between the point $x$ and $x_1$, i.e.:

$$t_f=\frac{|x-x_1|}{v_0} \tag{18}$$

where $v_0$ is the propagation velocity, which for the simulations in question will be assumed as being equal to the velocity of light.

The same procedure can be achieved supposing a discontinuity at the left of $x$. Then, assuming a finite line, with the origin at the point $x_0$ and termination in $x_f$, the induced voltage at a point $x$ along the distribution line can be estimated according to the following expression:

$$\begin{aligned}V(x,t)=U(x,t)+U(-x,t)+[\Gamma_f U(-x_f,t)-U(x_f,t)]\cdot u(t-t_f)+\cdots\\ \cdots+[\Gamma_0 U(x_0,t)-U(-x_0,t)]\cdot u(t-t_0)\end{aligned} \tag{19}$$

The replacement of the line discontinuity effect by a voltage compensation source is an effective procedure, mainly when is desired to produce computational algorithms.

## 4. Expert system for specification of transformers and equipments protection against atmospheric discharges

The expert system proposed in this work, which was developed in order to help in the arresters specification for equipments and distribution transformer protection, has its implementation aspects based on the studies about induced voltages presented in previous sections. Besides using those suggested modifications, the expert system incorporates in a integrated way the databases referent to equipments installed on the distribution lines of Bandeirante Energy, as well as the databases involved with arresters and atmospheric discharge characteristics incident in its concession region.

Therefore, the transformers and equipments protection designs, through this expert system, consider the induced voltage in distribution line where the transformer is installed, the distribution network topology, as well as the atmospheric discharge characteristics of the region.

As the system operates through these databases, before the specification of a determined design, it is necessary that each one of the system elements to be adequately registered. Then, it is presented in Fig. 12, the transformer registration window adequately filled for a distribution transformer of 75kVA.

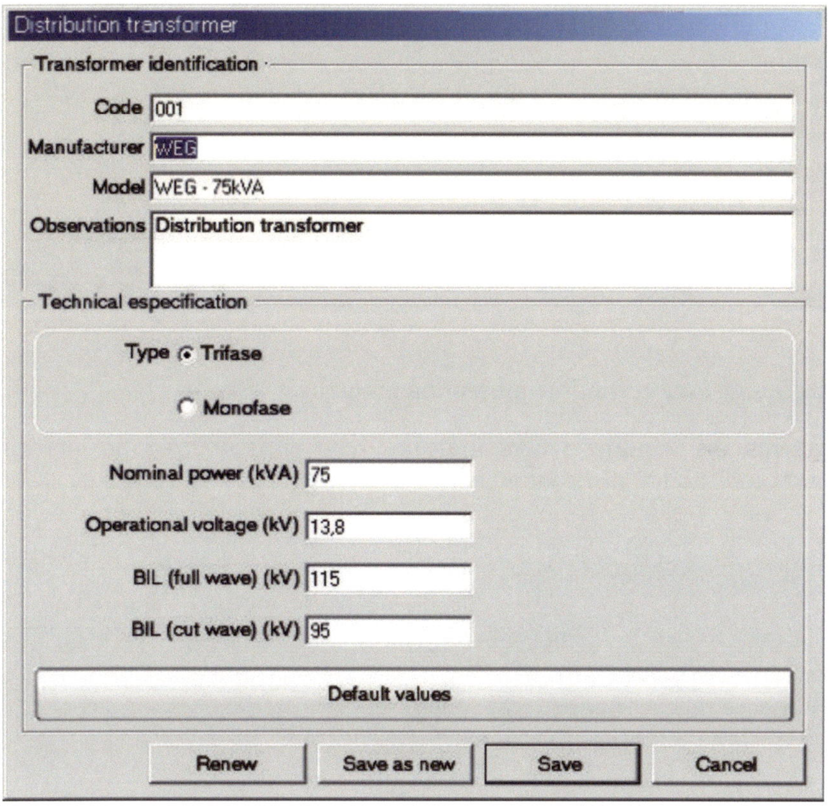


Fig. 12. Transformer registration window.

After registration of each component of the electric system, inclusively of the arresters, the protection design can be registered. Fig. 13 illustrates the project registration window, as well as it emphasizes the preliminary results of simulations.

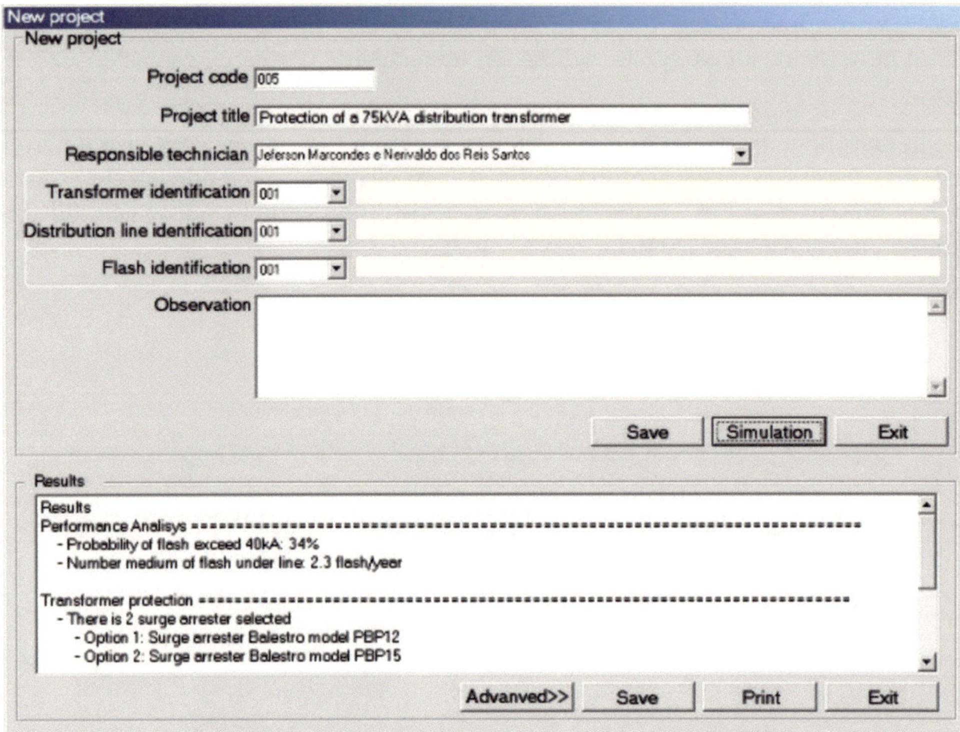


Fig. 13. Project registration window presenting preliminary results.

Fig. 14 presents the window where indicates how each selected arrester can be also employed for protection of distribution network nearby the transformer.

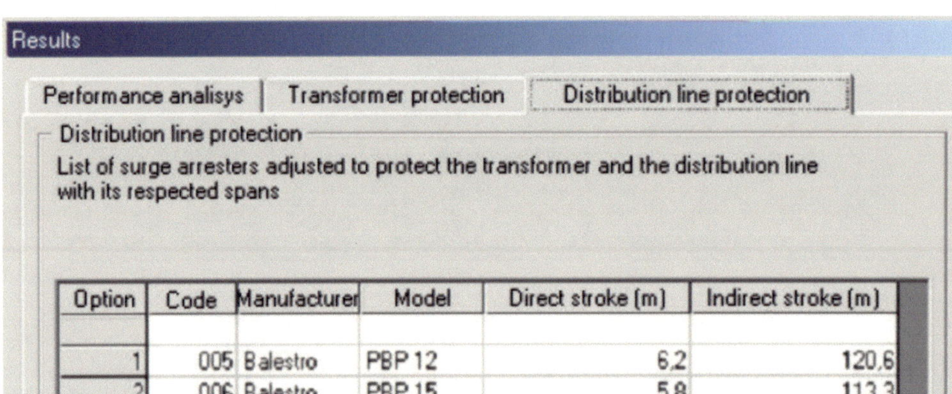


Fig. 14. Window indicating installation distance between arresters aiming the distribution line protection against atmospheric discharges.

## 5. Expert system for optimized design of grounding systems

Other expert system treated in this chapter involves the creation of a computational platform that helps in the specification and decision making regarding the optimized design of grounding systems, which must take into account the particularities of the distribution system under consideration, such as extension of the network, installed equipment and even the performance requirements expected for such system.

However, the effects of lightning should still be considered, since the voltages induced on the line are higher than those where the surge arresters operate, which imply in current flowing to ground.

Thus, analyzing in terms of optimizing the grounding system, the best arrangement must be defined according to the desired type of grounding, which is characterized as a problem of structural optimization. Furthermore, it is of fundamental importance to determine the parameters of the chosen arrangement, such as distance, depth, number of stems etc. The search of these variables characterizes a parametric adjustment problem, whose objective is to determine a grounding system where impedance, and not resistance, is minimal.

A representation of the operation of the expert system for optimization of grounding design can be seen in Fig. 15.

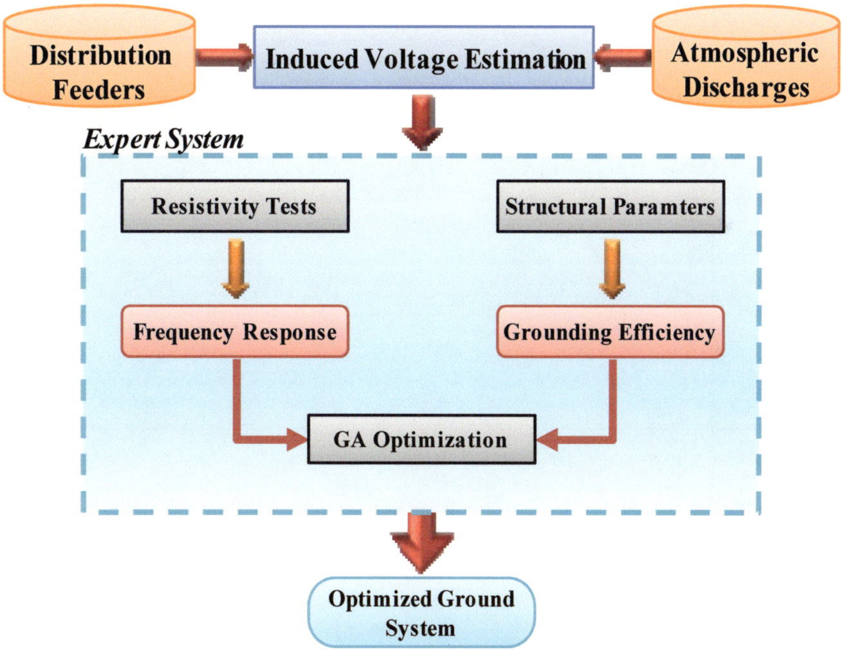


Fig. 15. Diagram representing the expert system for optimized design of grounding systems.

The efficiency of the grounding system must be checked every iteration of the optimization process with the purpose of verifying how the parametric and structural adjustments are improving it.

Thus, at the end of the process, the result should be an optimized grounding system. To evaluate this, the electrical parameters of the grounding system will be initially estimated, taking into account its own structural parameters, such as number of stems, distance between them and their depths.

Once the electrical parameters of the grounding system are known, the characteristic impedance of the grounding can then be calculated. This characteristic impedance is a value that allows relating the propagation of voltage induced by the distribution system to the propagation by the grounding system. To relate both modes of propagation, it is necessary to consider the electrical data of the feeder.

Once the parameters to model the distribution system at high frequencies are known, as well as the characteristic impedance of the grounding system, it is then possible to conduct simulations to verify impulsive voltage in the system.

To illustrate this evaluation procedure, a feeder in which the grounding system is not optimally implemented will be considered. This feeder belongs to the substation BIR of EDP Bandeirante. The induced voltage in the distribution system was calculated by assuming standard data for the lightning. The temporal behavior of the induced voltages is presented in Figure 16.

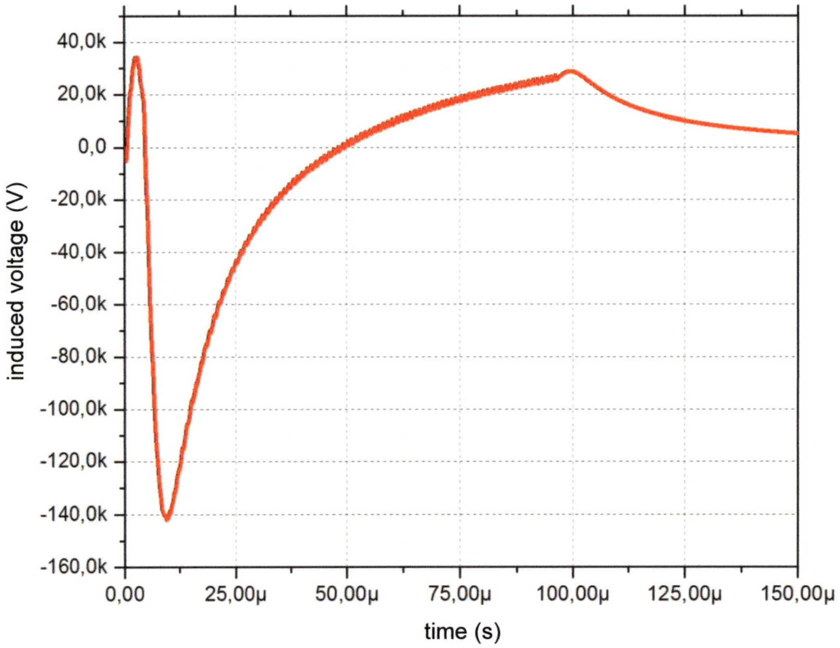


Fig. 16. Behavior of induced voltages for a non-optimized grounding system.

Fig. 16 shows that the peak value of induced voltage to a non-optimized grounding system was above 140 kV (in module). These magnitudes can be compared with those obtained when considering an optimized grounding system.

The graph, in Fig. 17, highlights the behavior of the induced voltage in a distribution system, considering an optimized grounding system and using those same lightning data used for obtaining the results illustrated in Fig. 16. Depending on the optimization of the grounding system, there is a reduction of the peak value of induced voltage, which is now approximately 35 kV.

Besides reduction of four times to the peak value, it is possible to verify that the duration of this electromagnetic event was less than that situation characterized by non-optimized grounding system.

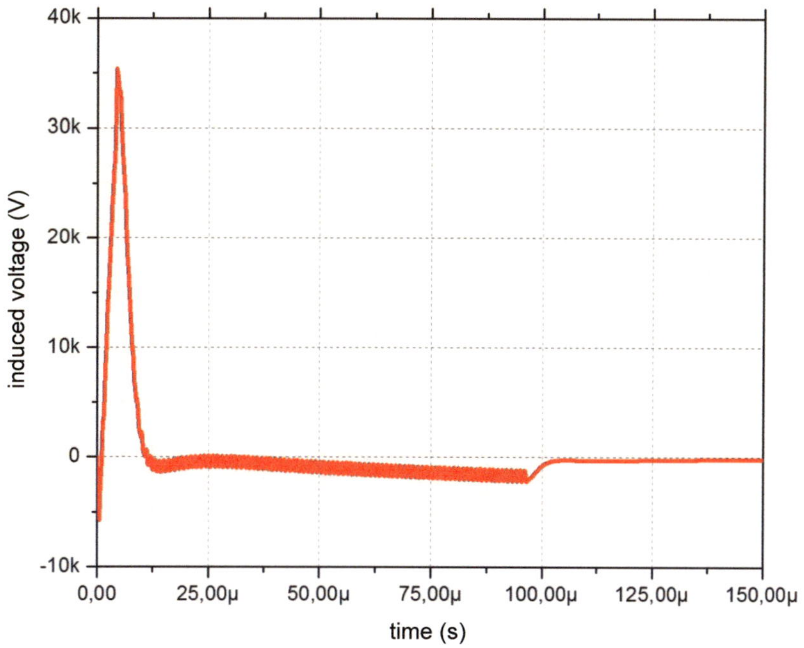


Fig. 17. Behavior of induced voltages for an optimized grounding system.

The expert system for optimizing new designs of grounding systems, called B-TERRA, uses, to start its calculations, the feeders database, which contains structural information, as well as information on lightning that occurred in the analyzed region.

While the database, with information about the feeders, are loaded, the operator can contemplate the evolution of the analysis of lightning, as illustrated in Fig. 18.

The procedures performed by the B-TERRA software allow the identification of the area of influence of lightning on the devices registered in the database of EDP Bandeirante circuits, as indicated by a rectangle highlighted in Fig. 19.

In this figure, it is possible to see an example where the device 2047568 is selected and, consequently, the area of influence of lightning has been highlighted on the screen at the right side of the B-TERRA software.

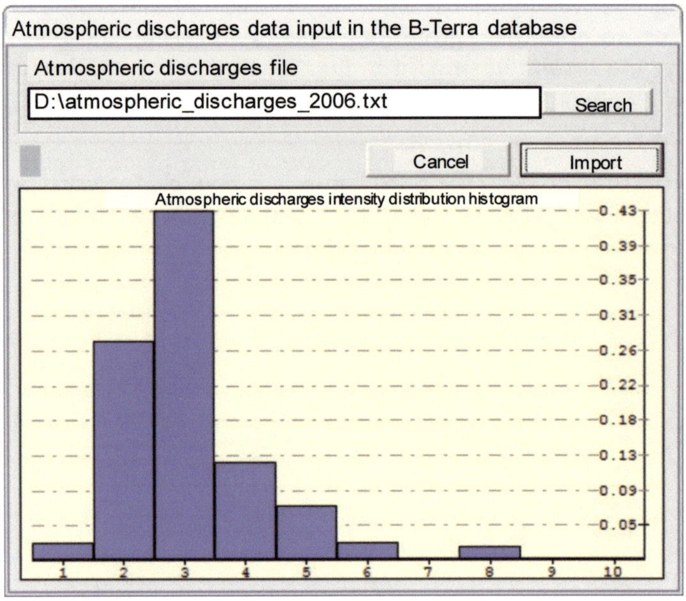


Fig. 18. Results of evolution analysis of lightning intensity.

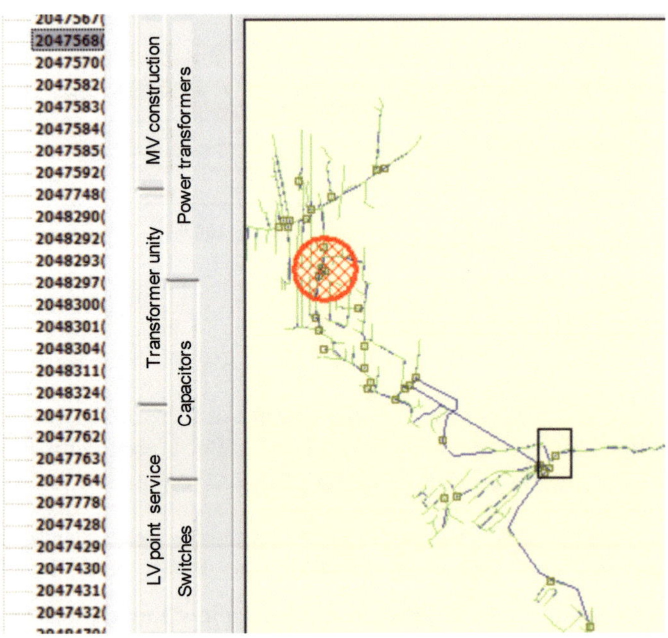


Fig. 19. Area identification where the devices are influenced by the lightning.

After accomplishment of all optimization procedures, through genetic algorithms, B-TERRA software provides as one of its answers the configuration of the best grounding design for the selected device, as shown in Figure 20.

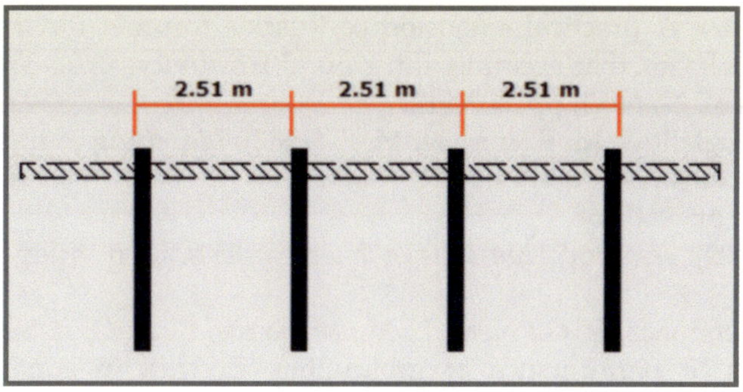


Fig. 20. Output of the B-TERRA software related to the best grounding design for the selected device.

## 6. Conclusion

In this chapter, it has been presented the theoretical development employed to estimate induced voltages in overhead distribution lines supposing a generic discharge current waveform, as well as assuming a finite distribution line.

Taking into account the results provided by the developed technique, an expert system to help in the equipments and distribution transformers protection specification was implemented in order to provide indicatives about the best protection to be adopted to transformers, as well as the best installation distance between arresters, aiming the full protection of the distribution line where these equipments are inserted.

Performance evaluations indicate that the expert system provides coherent results and its practical application contributes to optimize the processes involved with parameters specification related to the equipments and transformers protection.

Additionally, an expert system to assist in the specification of parameters for grounding designs was also implemented. Regarding the grounding system optimized with this tool, we can state that energy to be dissipated on the distribution system is lower than that observed in a non-optimized system, as shown in the charts in Section 5.

The difference in energy between the two cases implies in the energy that flows through the grounding system, i.e., for being better designed the optimized grounding system allows more energy to flow by itself compared to that case of non-optimized system. Experimental evaluations indicate that they provide very consistent results and their practical applications help for optimizing the processes involved with the protection of distribution systems.

## 7. References

Borghetti, A.; Nucci, C. A. & Paolone, M. (2007). An improved procedure for the assessment of overhead line indirect lightning performance and its comparison with the IEEE Std. 1410 method. *IEEE Transactions on Power Delivery*, Vol. 22, No.1, pp. 684-692.

Cooray, G. V. (2003). *The Lightning Flash*. IEE Power & Energy Series, London, UK.

Darveniza, M. (2007). A practical extension of Rusck's formula for maximum lightning-induced voltages that accounts for ground resistivity. *IEEE Transactions on Power Delivery*, Vol. 22, No.1, pp. 605-612.

Eriksson, A. J.; Stringfellow, M. F. & Meal, M. F. (1982). Lightning induced overvoltages on overhead transmission lines. *IEEE Transactions on Power Apparatus and Systems*, Vol. 101, No. 4, pp. 960-968.

Greenwood, A. (1992). *Electrical Transients in Power Systems*. John Wiley & Sons, New York, USA.

Paula, S. C. M.; Mendonça, R. G.; Neto, L. M.; Medeiros, C. A. G. & Silva, R. V. R. (2001). Evaluation of performance of groundings electrics in conditions of lightning current. *Canadian Conference on Electrical and Computer Engineering*, Toronto, Canada, pp. 737-742.

Rubinstein, M. & Uman, M. A. (1989). Methods for calculating the electromagnetic fields from a known source distribution: Application to lightning. *IEEE Transactions on Electromagnetic Compatibility*, Vol. 31, No. 2, pp. 183-189.

Rusck, S. (1957). *Induced Lightning Over-voltage on Power Transmission Lines with Special Reference to Over-voltage Protection of Low Voltage Networks*. Ph.D. Thesis, Stockholm Royal Institute of Technology, Sweden.

Salari, J. C. & Portela, C. (2007). A methodology for electromagnetic transients calculation – an application for the calculation of lightning propagation in transmission lines. *IEEE Transactions on Power Delivery*, Vol. 22, No. 1, pp. 527-536.

# 14

# Intelligent Analysis of Utilization of Special Purpose Machines for Drilling Operations

Majid Tolouei-Rad
*School of Engineering, Edith Cowan University, Perth, Australia*

## 1. Introduction

Drilling and drilling-related operations constitute more than 60% of all machining processes in manufacturing industries. Consequently, it is important to know how to perform these operations properly. With availability of many machining processes capable of performing drilling operations sometimes it is difficult to decide which process would result in a higher profit or a lower unit cost for a given task. Due to increasing global competition, manufacturing industries are now more concerned with their productivity and are more sensitive than ever to their investments with respect to flexibility and efficiency of production equipment (Boothroyd and Knight, 2005, Wecka and Staimer, 2002). Researchers (Ko *et al.*, 2005) believe that increasing the quality of production and reducing cost and time of production are very important factors in achieving higher productivity. Achieving this goal requires reconsidering current production methods that could lead to introduction of new production techniques and more advanced technologies.

In traditional drilling processes a sharp cutting tool with multiple cutting edges is used to cut a round hole in the workpiece material. In non-traditional drilling processes various forms of energy other than sharp cutting tools or abrasive particles are used to remove the material. The energy forms include mechanical, electrochemical, thermal and chemical (Groover, 2010). Generally non-traditional processes incorporate high capital and operating costs. Therefore, when machining economy is of concern manufacturing companies focus on traditional processes. Even within this category, a machining specialist has the choice of using conventional drilling machines, CNC machines, and special purpose machines (SPMs). According to the literature (Groover 2008) when production quantity and variety are low, universal machine tools give the best result. When various components should be produced, CNC is the best option. For the condition of high production quantity with low variety, SPM gives the highest productivity and is considered as the most economic production method. Accordingly, Tolouei-Rad and Zolfaghari (2009) believe that SPMs are superior to computer numerical control (CNC) machines for producing large quantities of similar parts; however, most manufacturers still rely on well-known CNCs for large volume production tasks. This is mainly attributable to the fact that both SPMs and CNCs incorporate high capital costs; SPMs are more productive and CNCs are more flexible. When the part in production is no longer in demand due to frequent market changes, SPMs become idle while CNCs can be easily reprogrammed for producing other parts. Yet the concluding statement could be different when modular SPMs are utilized.

The field of machine tools for generating singular products is well documented; however, the area of specialist machines for dedicated tasks has received less attention (Allen *et al.*, 2010). This is particularly true for modular SPMs that are a new addition to the family of SPMs (Tolouei-Rad and Tabatabaei, 2005). Proper design and utilization of these machines depend upon knowledge, experience, and creativity of SPM designers and machining specialists. Because of modularity in structure, these machines can be applied to the production of a range of parts upon modification. The specific advantages of utilization of this technology have placed them in a superior position in comparison with other machine tools. These advantages include mass production of parts in shorter time, high accuracy of products, uniformity and repeatability of production, elimination of some quality control steps, simultaneous machining of a number of parts, and reduced labour and overhead costs.

The modular principle is very popular in the design of many products such as automobile, home appliances, information devices, industrial equipment, etc. This trend can be considered as one of the great contributions of modular design of machine tools to those working in other industries (Yoshimi, 2008). This article focuses on modular SPMs and for simplicity in the rest of this article modular SPM is referred to as SPM. SPMs do not have a rigid bulky configuration and the machine can be rapidly set up by putting together a number of machining and sliding units, chassis, and other equipment. This is achieved by making use of various types of mechanical fasteners. Once the part in production is no longer in demand, SPMs can be dis-assembled and re-assembled in a different configuration to be used for producing other parts. Properly utilization of SPMs could have a significant impact on the productivity of manufacturing industries; and production improvements of up to 25:1 have been reported (Suhner, 2001). However, the extent of the application of SPM technology in industry is not proportional to its potential impact on productivity improvement. This is mainly attributed to the fact that machining specialists find it difficult to decide when to use SPMs. Making the right decision is a time-consuming task and requires a techno-economical analysis to be performed by expert people. This article addresses a methodology developed to tackle this vital problem. It investigates the possibility and effectiveness of employing artificial intelligent techniques to assist manufacturing firms in feasibility analysis of utilizing SPMs in order to improve productivity. It is important to note that in spite of many publications on production technologies and machine tool design; publications on design and utilization of SPMs are very limited.

Intelligent systems have been extensively used to effectively tackle some real engineering problems in the last three decades. Yet researchers explore new application areas for utilization of various artificial intelligence techniques. Knowledge-based expert systems (KBESs) have proven to be effective for decision making when dealing with qualitative information, hard to capture in a computer program. Accordingly, in the current work a KBES has been developed and used for utilization feasibility analysis of SPMs in different manufacturing settings.

## 2. Fundamentals of SPM technology

Groover (2008) has defined the term "production automation" as the application of electrical, electronic, mechanical, hydraulic and pneumatic systems for rapid and quality productions in large volumes. Automated production techniques are widely used in manufacturing industries for dealing with issues such as high cost of labour, shortage of skilled people, low interest of labour to work in production firms, safety, high cost of raw materials, improved quality, uniformity in the quality of products, low inventory, customers satisfaction, and performing difficult operations. Figure 1 shows a SPM as an example of utilization of automated production techniques in manufacturing. This machine has two work stations, one for drilling and one for tapping. The machine is used for machining the parts shown in the Figure.

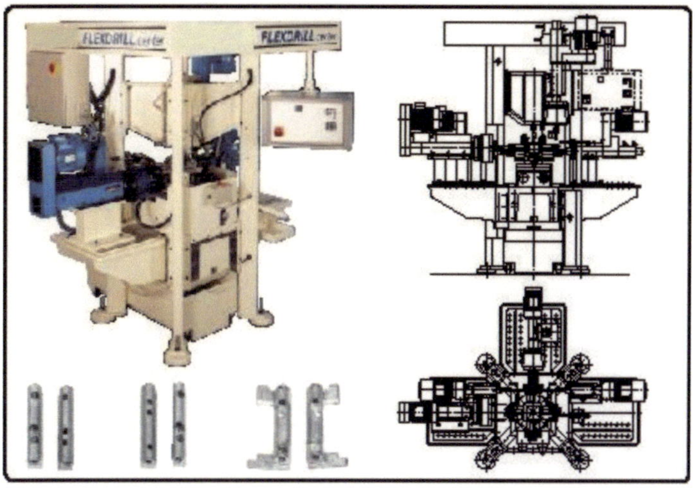

Fig. 1. A two station SPM for drilling and tapping operations with parts being produced (Photo: Suhner, 2001)

Generally SPMs lack the high rigidity found in conventional and CNC machines. Consequently, majority of these machines are used for performing drilling and drilling-related operations such as tapping, reaming, counterboring and countersinking on machinable materials where the magnitude of machining forces is relatively low. This eliminates excessive vibrations of the machine tool due to high cutting forces. However, it should be noted that SPMs are also capable of performing milling and some other machining operations that would result in high cutting forces. In such cases there is a need for stronger chassis, stronger machining and sliding units, and use of special accessories in order to eliminate vibrations when possible.

### 2.1 Machining and sliding units

The units used in SPMs can be divided into two main groups: machining and sliding. A machining unit is equipped with an electro-motor that revolves the spindle by means of pulley and belt systems in order to rotate the cutting tool. Like other machine tools, the connection of cutting tools to the machining unit is accomplished by standard tool holders. Machining units are of three types: quill, power, and CNC. Quill units are used for light drilling and drilling-related operations as they also provide the spindle with a linear feed motion necessary for penetration of the cutting tool into the workpiece. Both the linear and the rotational motions necessary for performing operation are provided simultaneously. Power units are used for drilling, drilling related, and milling operations where large cutting forces exist. Unlike quill units, power units lack the linear feed motion due to presence of significantly larger cutting forces that may cause deflection in the rotating spindle. Consequently, these units are mounted on the sliding units providing them with necessary linear feed motion. Figure 2 shows quill and power units together with tool holders and cutting tools.

Fig. 2. A pneumatic sliding unit with mechanical course adjustment
(Photo: Tolouei-Rad and Zolfaghari, 2009)

Sliding units may carry machining units and provide necessary feed motion of the tool by means of hydraulic/pneumatic actuators, or servomotors. Adjusting the course of motion is provided by use of micro-switches or mechanical limits. Figure 3 shows a pneumatic sliding unit with a mechanical course adjustment device. The sliding plate that carries the machining unit is fastened to the connecting rod of the piston, and therefore, is capable of moving back and forth on the base. Depending on the nature of machining operation and cutting tool motion requirements, machining units can be mounted on the sliding unit such that spindle axis is either along or perpendicular to the sliding direction.

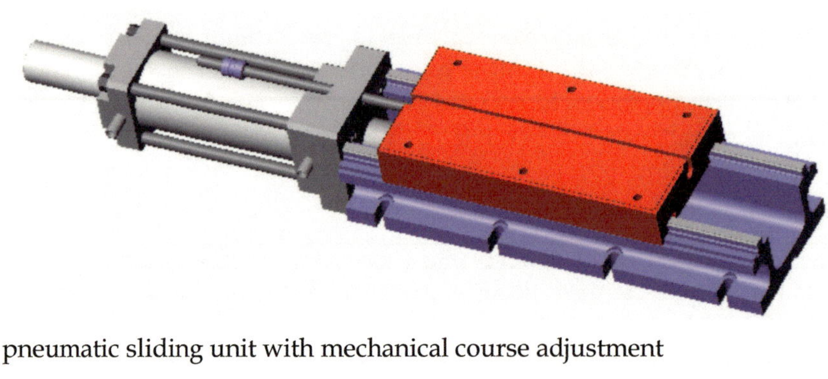

Fig. 3. A pneumatic sliding unit with mechanical course adjustment

CNC machining units are also used for drilling, taping and milling operations precisely as they are equipped with servomotors. CNC units can be programmed for very accurate machining operations when used in conjunction with a controller. Figure 4 shows a two-axis CNC tapping unit. The tapping unit is mounted on the sliding unit where both the units are equipped with servomotors. The servomotor of the tapping unit provides the rotational motion of the cutting tool whereas the servomotor of the sliding unit provides feed motion. When integrated with a control unit, this assembly can be programmed similar to CNC machines.

Fig. 4. Two-axis CNC tapping unit (Photo: Suhner)

### 2.2 Accessories

There exist special stands, adjustable bases, and supports used for positioning and supporting basic machine components. These are also used for preventing or reducing vibrations at the time of machining. Figure 5 shows some of the assembly equipment used to accurately position and support machining units in any position and at any angle.

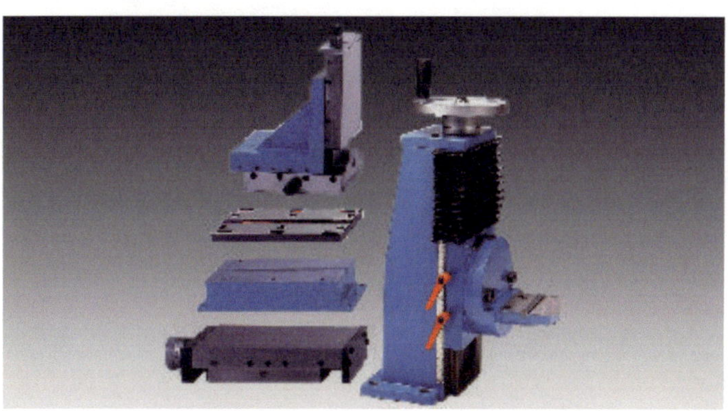

Fig. 5. Special stands, adjustable bases, and supports (Photo: Suhner)

Indexing table is one of the important accessories used in SPMs. Figure 6 shows an indexing table used for positioning the workpiece in different machining stations where the workpiece is machined in a number of rotary stations. After determination of machining steps and the number of working stations, fixtures could be placed on the indexing table. Number of stations could be anything between two and twelve, and is determined on the basis of production volume and technical considerations.

Fig. 6. An indexing table (Photo: Suhner, 2001)

Multi-drill heads provide the possibility of drilling many holes on the same plane simultaneously; thus, reducing machining time significantly. Multi-drill heads are divided into fixed and adjustable types. In fixed multi-drill heads the position of tools are fixed, but in adjustable ones the position of the tools could be adjusted as needed. Angle heads are spindle attachments used to alter the orientation of cutting tool axis relative to the spindle axis. These attachments are used in milling operations. Figure 7 shows different types of multi-drill heads and angle heads used in SPMs.

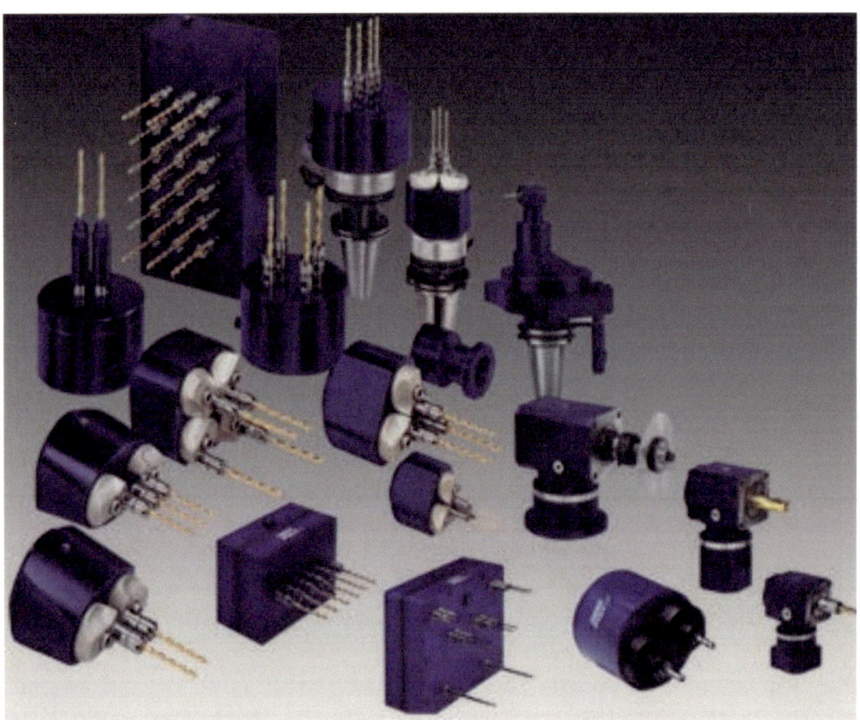

Fig. 7. Various types of multi-drill heads and angle heads (Photo: Suhner)

### 2.3 Machine table, chip removal and coolant system

The table and chassis of the machine are very important considerations in SPMs. Based on technical considerations and machining properties of the workpiece material, the table and chassis are properly designed or selected from the standardized SPM chassis. Due to high machining forces resulting from machining operations the machine table and chassis should be sufficiently rigid to avoid vibrations. It is also very important to consider appropriate coolant and chip removal mechanisms in design of machine table and chassis.

## 3. Design and manufacturing

Because production process is systematic, planning for design and manufacturing has an effective influence on the success of any project (Lutters *et al.*, 2004). The flowchart shown in Figure 8 represents all necessary steps for proper analysis, design and manufacture of SPMs. These steps should be followed in order to achieve feasible results in SPM design and manufacturing.

### 3.1 Technical and economic analysis

As the cost of SPM design and manufacturing is relatively high, critical technical and economic justification of utilization of these machines should be made before any attempt to design and manufacture them. This includes an analysis of machinability of the workpiece, and a comparison of the production costs with other production alternatives considering production volume and machine amortisation period. For technical feasibility analysis a number of questions will be asked and the user needs to answer these questions interactively. These questions investigate quality of workpiece material and its physical and geometrical characteristics to determine whether or not it can be machined with SPMs. The flowchart shown in Figure 9 describes the type of questions asked for technical feasibility analysis. If the answer to any of the questions is "No" then the workpiece is considered to be "Not Suitable" for machining with SPM and its processing will be terminated.

Upon completion of technical feasibility analysis, an economical feasibility analysis is performed. To do so a detailed computation is needed in order to determine the cost of machining a unit of product using SPM. Then the same computation is repeated for traditional and CNC machines in order to achieve a unit cost comparison for different methods, and to find the one that results in a lower cost. For determination of unit cost so many factors are taken into consideration including machining time, production volume, machine cost, cutting tool cost, labour cost, overhead costs, depreciation cost, interest rate, etc. A case study is presented in Section 5 that provides a detailed economic analysis for a sample part. It is noteworthy that sometimes it is necessary to repeat the economic analysis before the final approval of SPM design. This happens when more accurate information on the cost of SPM and required accessories become available. This is represented by a dashed line in the flowchart of Figure 8.

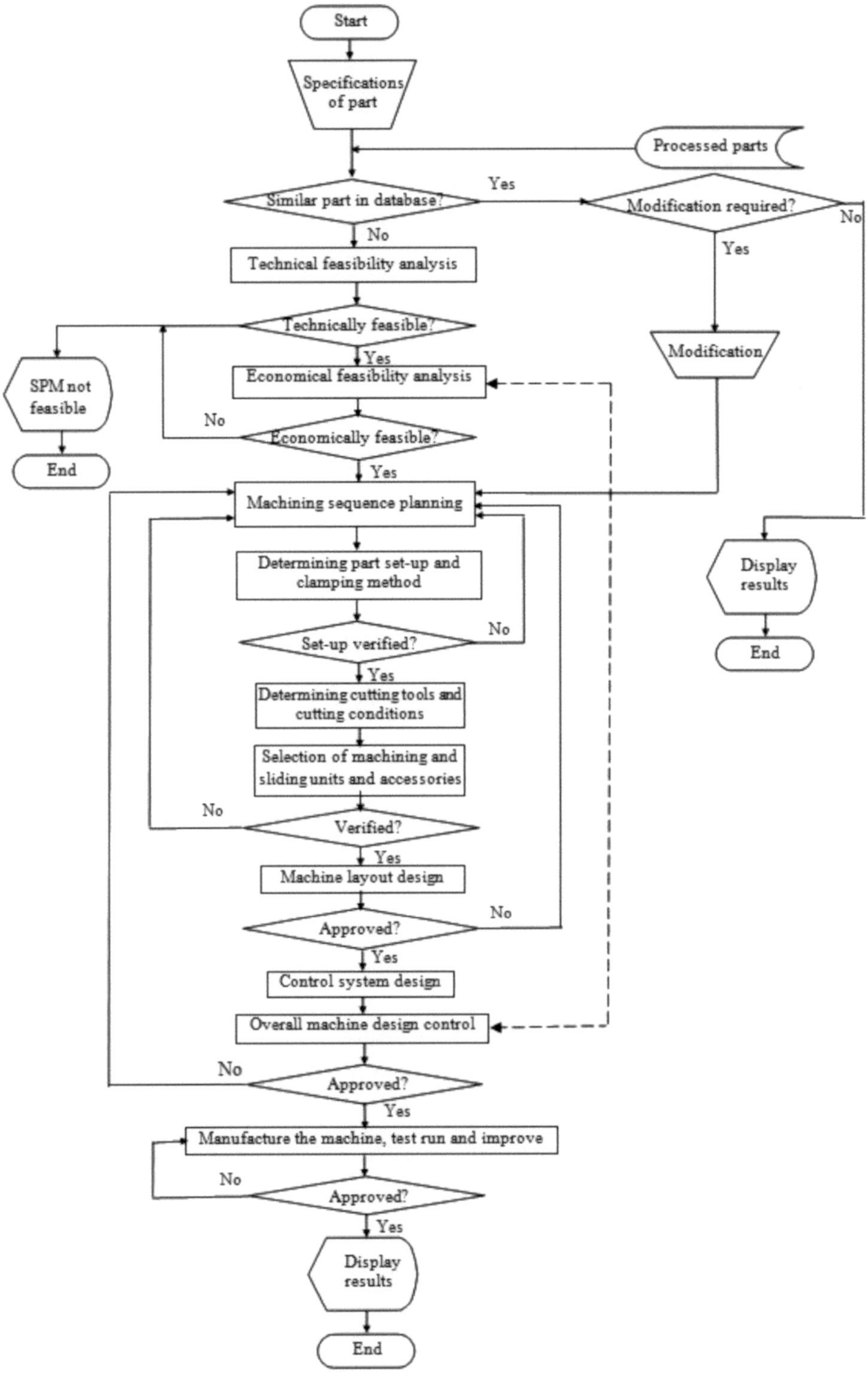


Fig. 8. Flowchart for SPM design and manufacture

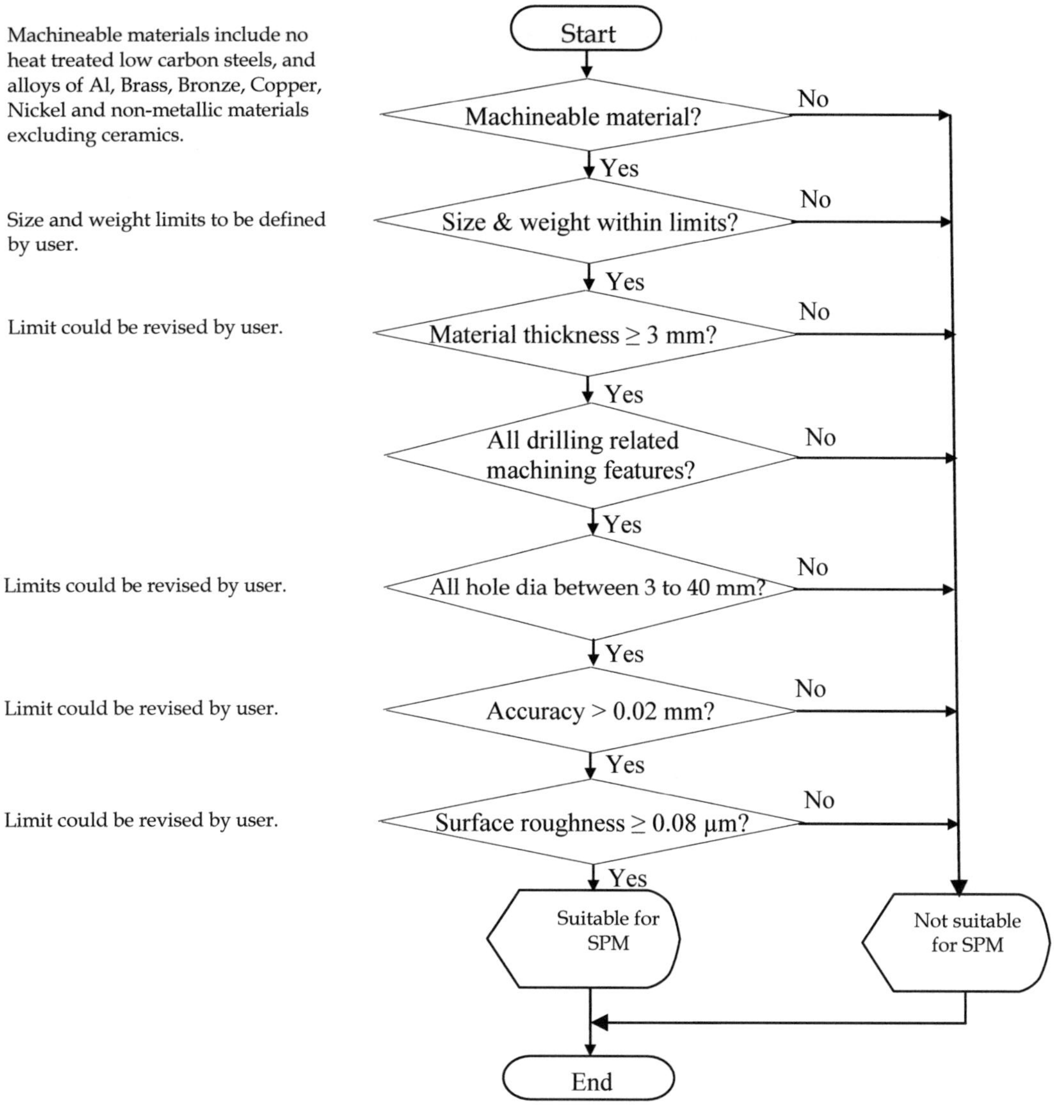


Fig. 9. Flowchart for technical feasibility analysis

### 3.2 Machining sequence planning

Properly determination of machining sequence is a key point in successful SPM utilization. A poor machining sequence plan leads to lower quality of production and/or increased machining times and consequently higher production costs. Often it is possible to combine and perform a number of operations in a single setup lowering machining times and costs while also improving production quality. Indeed machining sequence planning determines the overall configuration of the machine and required machining units and accessories.

### 3.3 Cutting conditions

Properly selection of cutting tools and cutting conditions such as cutting speed, feed, and depth of cut is of great importance in the success of any machining operation. When SPM is in use, due to the stability requirements of the production process in order to produce high quantities of the product, appropriate cutting tools and cutting conditions should be employed. As frequent tool changes influence the productivity of the machine tool, it is suggested to employ long lasting hard material cutting tools made from tungsten carbides and ceramics for high production rates. These tool materials provide longer tool lives and higher production rates. Other important considerations in the selection of cutting tools are the shape and geometry of the tool. Cutting tools are generally divided into standard and special groups. By use of specially designed cutting tools sometimes it is possible to combine different machining operations in a single operation.

### 3.4 Setup and clamping

Machining jigs and fixtures are frequently used to increase the speed and quality of production and to reduce production times and required skill level of machinists. Uniformity of production due to use of jigs and fixtures has an important effect on production quality. Accordingly, properly design and application of jigs and fixtures is very important in SPM utilization. Fixtures used in SPMs are complex as normally a number of machining operations are performed in a single part setup. Fixtures should be designed such that (a) there is adequate tool access to the workpiece in all work stations; (b) the part is easily, quickly, and accurately positioned inside the fixture, and removed from it, and (c) the fixture is rigid enough to withstand large cutting forces applied by multiple cutting tools working on the part simultaneously. In locating the part in the fixture, the most difficult and accurate operation should be considered first in order to achieve the best result. Because there are different machining operations, locating surfaces need to be machined accurately before the workpiece is placed in the fixture. Appropriate measures should be taken for free flow of coolant and chip removal from the fixture.

### 3.5 Machining and sliding units

As described in the previous sections, machining and sliding units are the most important components of SPMs that make the cutting tool capable of rotational and linear motions necessary for cutting. Consequently, the selection of machining units, sliding units and accessories should be accomplished such that following three conditions are met.

1. Previously determined cutting tools are capable of performing all rotational and linear motions necessary for performing corresponding machining operations.
2. Proper cutting conditions such as spindle speed, feed, and depth of cut are provided.
3. Required machining power is provided.

In is important to note that selection of machining and sliding units should always be accomplished after selection of cutting tools and cutting conditions. This is due to the fact that cutting tools' geometry and cutting conditions dictate required powers, velocities, and motions of machining and sliding units.

### 3.6 SPM layout

Generally there are two layouts for SPMs; single-station and multi-station. In the former method the workpiece is held in a fixed position where machining and sliding units are positioned around it such that they can process the part from different directions. The part is machined by a single machining unit or by multiple machining units. In the case of multiple machining units they may process the part simultaneously or in sequence depending on the geometry of the workpiece and machining features. This layout is shown in Figure 10(a). In latter method the workpiece is transferred from one station to another until it is processed in all stations. The number of machining stations varies from two to twelve. Transferring workpiece between stations is performed by rotational or linear motions. The rotational motion is provided by indexing tables and the linear motion can be performed by use of sliding units or other methods. Figures 10 (b) to 10(e) illustrate different multi-station layouts. The layout of the machine and positioning all the machining and sliding units, the number of stations in case of multi-station processing, and workpiece transferring method between stations are decided by machine designers considering technical and productive measures. In general a higher production rate is achieved in the multi-station method because of simultaneous machining of several workpieces in multiple machining stations.

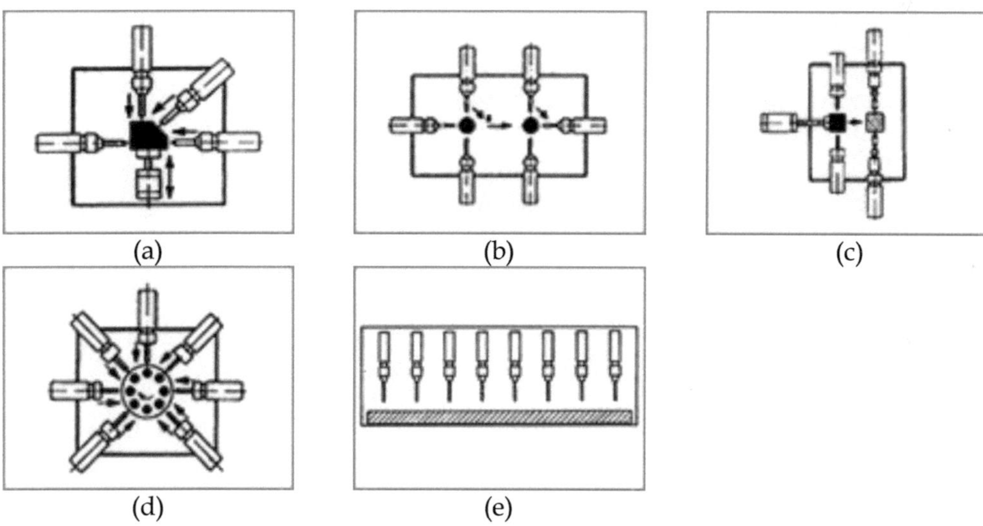


Fig. 10. Different layouts for SPMs; (a) single-station, (b) special application, (c) transfer machine, (d) rotary machine, and (e) in-line drilling machine (Photos: Suhner)

### 3.7 Control system

Before designing the control system, the unit motion diagrams representing reciprocating motions of all units should be prepared. These diagrams explicitly represent speed and magnitude of motion of each unit, exact start/stop times, and its position at any time. As described earlier, the motion of units is often provided by hydraulic and pneumatic cylinders, or servo-motors. Start and stop signals of motion are usually issued by a programmable logic controller (PLC) that is programmed based on the unit motion diagrams.

### 3.8 Approval

Upon completion of preceding steps, it is necessary that all design steps be controlled and inspected by experienced SPM specialists to correct possible errors before sending the machine design to the workshop for manufacturing. These points deserve special consideration at this stage: a) control system and PLC programming, b) types and specifications of machining and sliding units, c) motion diagrams, d) hydraulic and pneumatic systems and servo-systems, e) performance of the machine, and g) possible collision of the moving parts with other moving or fixed parts. As mentioned before, sometimes it becomes necessary to repeat economic considerations of the feasibility of SPM utilization before the machine is built. This is attributable to the fact that initial economic analysis has been made based on the initial estimation. However, when detailed machine design is available a more precise machine cost becomes available that could be different.

### 3.9 Manufacturing and testing

Chassis and table of the machine should be made and assembled considering technical issues. These parts should be sufficiently rigid and equipped with special dampers in order to minimize vibrations resulting from the operation of cutting tools. Generally, thick steel plates and cast iron are used for machine table. Cast irons have good damping character, and therefore, are used for making the machine table to reduce vibrations. Chip removal could be a huge problem in SPMs that cannot be appreciated before the machine is made. The volume of chips produced in SPMs is high and this could reduce effective machining time by half or even less when a proper chip removal mechanism is not considered. In addition, a properly designed coolant system should be used to enhance the lives of cutting tools as frequent tool changes increase machining costs. Then, based on detailed engineering drawings, installation of stands, supports, machining units, sliding units, indexing table and coolant system are performed. Installation of hydraulic and pneumatic systems, wiring, electric power supply to electro-motors, and finally, the control systems are all performed at this stage.

Upon completion of previous steps, machine performance is measured considering required product quality and production volume. Possible issues at this stage are detected and resolved to bring the machine to a more productive state. Producing a reasonable number of quality products is necessary before actual production begins.

## 4. Knowledge-Based Expert System (KBES)

KBESs use rules as the knowledge representation for knowledge coded into the system. The definitions of KBES depend almost entirely on expert systems, which are system that mimic the reasoning of human expert in solving a knowledge intensive problem. Instead of representing knowledge in a declarative, static way as a set of things which are true, KBESs represent knowledge in terms of a set of rules that tells what to do or what to conclude in different situations (Grosan and Abraham, 2011). In this work a KBES has been developed to perform the analysis of SPM utilization and determination of machine layout and its basic components. Its development has been described in this Section.

### 4.1 Knowledge acquisition

The most common obstacle in utilization of SPMs in manufacturing industries is inadequate knowledge of manufacturing engineers and machining specialists with this technology, and the lack of a solid foundation for technical and economic feasibility analysis. This is not an easy task and requires engagement of qualified personnel with reasonable expertise and experience in this field. One needs to do a lot of computations and use various handbooks and assumptions in order to accomplish this task. In recent years artificial intelligence techniques have proven to be capable of restoring human's logic and expertise and efficiently applying this expertise to tackle complicated engineering problems. For example, KBESs have been used to restore human's logic and expertise and efficiently applying this expertise to tackle complicated engineering problems including product design (Myung and Han, 2001), design for assembly (Sanders *et al.*, 2009), and process planning (Patil and Pande, 2002). Accordingly, a KBES has been developed in order to capture the knowledge of SPM specialists in a computer program, and integrate it with a large amount of machining and tooling data restored in the database. This allows less experienced people to use the system developed in order to perform a detailed and accurate analysis of SPM utilization for production tasks. A rule-base has been developed that restores knowledge in the rule-base in the form of *if-then* rules. An example rule is presented here:

*Rule 121:*
*if there are multiple holes of the same diameter and on the same plane,*
*and the minimum centre-to-centre distance is 30 mm,*
*then a multi-drill head can be used in a combined operation,*
*else the holes are to be machined in multiple operations.*

A number of expertise rules have been developed in order to restore qualitative information in the rule-base as shown in Figure 11. One group of rules is specific to determination of workpiece setup such that there is tool access to all machining features in a single setup if possible. Another group of rules determine proper clamping method such that workpiece is securely held in place during machining. A group of rules determine the number of machining stations such that the total number of stations is kept minimal. Determination of required cutting tools and cutting conditions, and required machine power are performed by other groups of rules. Some rules are developed for selection of machining units, sliding units, chassis, and accessories such as multi-drill heads, angle heads, etc.

As can be seen in Figure 11, the KBES developed in this work is also equipped with a database. It contains quantitative information of available cutting tools and corresponding cutting conditions extracted from handbooks, together with characteristics of standard SPM components. Machining and sliding units restored in the database include CNC units (CNCmasters), quill units (MONOmasters), small drilling units with flexible power transmission mechanism (MULTImasters), power units (POWERmasters), and tapping units (TAPmasters). Table 1 represents characteristics of eight MONOmasters restored in the database which include designation, maximum drill diameter when used for drilling low carbon steels, working stroke that determines maximum hole depth, available power and thrust, spindle speeds, and weight for each unit. Other information restored in the database includes characteristics of assembly components for accurately positioning and orienting the units; multi-drill heads (POLYdrills) and angle heads, tool holders, and machine components or standardized chassis. It is noteworthy that the database contains full characteristics of SPM components and three-dimensional (3D) solid models of these components are restored in a feature library of a computer-aided design (CAD) system integrated with the KBES.

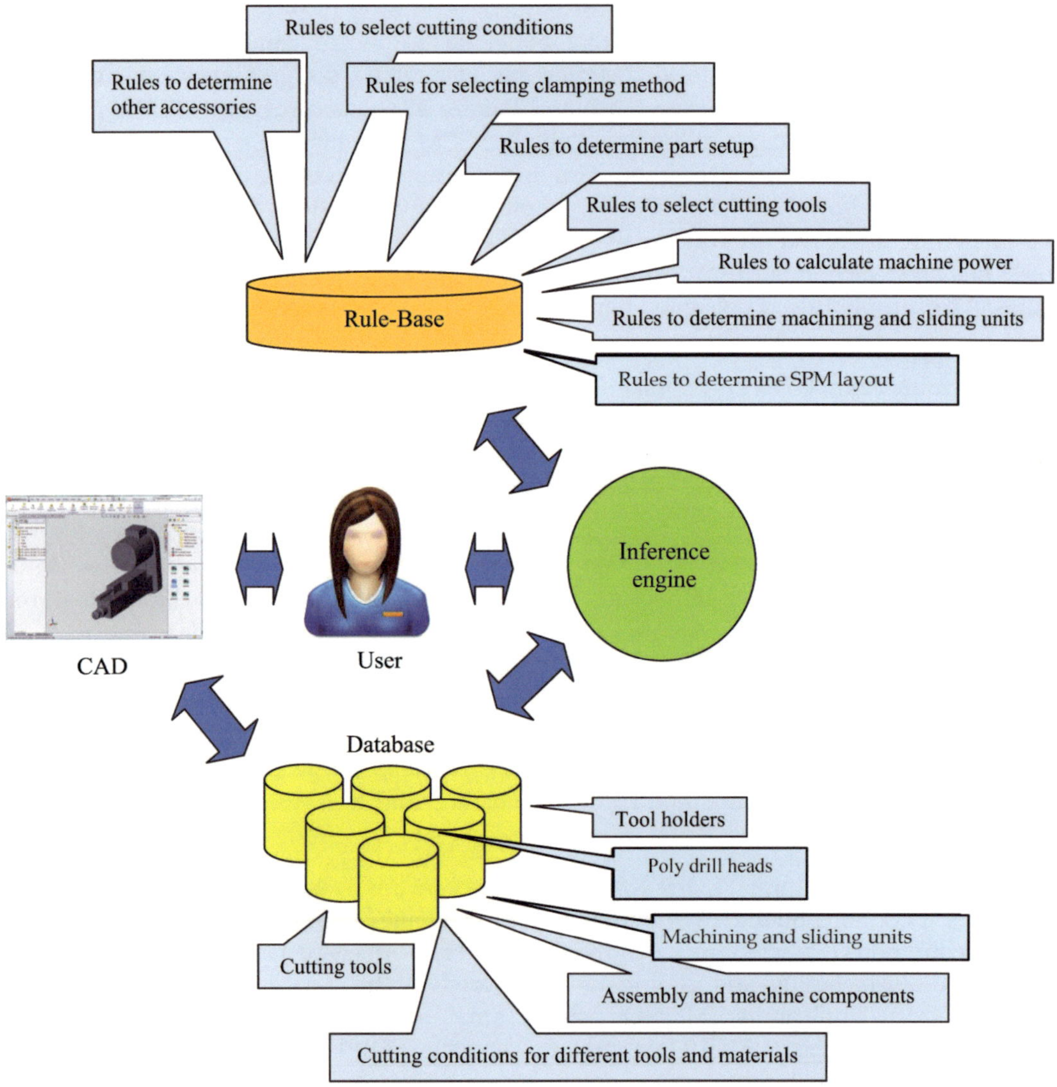


Fig. 11. KBES architecture

| *Designation* | *Drill Dia (mm)* | *Working Stroke (mm)* | *Total Storke (mm)* | *Spindle Speed (rpm)* | *Motor Power (kW)* | *Thrust at 85 psi (N)* | *Unit Weigh t (kg)* | *Configuration* |
|---|---|---|---|---|---|---|---|---|
| BEM03 | 3 | 25 | 40 | 940 to 10,270 | | 380 | 9 |  |
| BEM06 | 6 | 50 | 80 | 550 to 7,730 | 0.37 | 700 | 16 |  |
| BEM06D | 6 | 50 | 80 | 1450 to 11,600 | 0.37 | 700 | 12 |  |
| BEM12 | 12 | 50 | 80 | 35 to 7,730 | 0.75 | 1,470 | 26 |  |
| BEM12D | 12 | 50 | 80 | 90 to 2,900 | 0.75 | 1,470 | 20 |  |
| BEM20 | 20 | 125 | 125 | 360 to 10,000 | 1.5 | | 73 |  |
| BEM25H | 25 | 125 | 125 | 360 to 10,000 | 1.5 | | 108 |  |
| BEM28 | 28 | 200 | 200 | 400 to 2,580 | 2.2 | 8,200 | 150 | 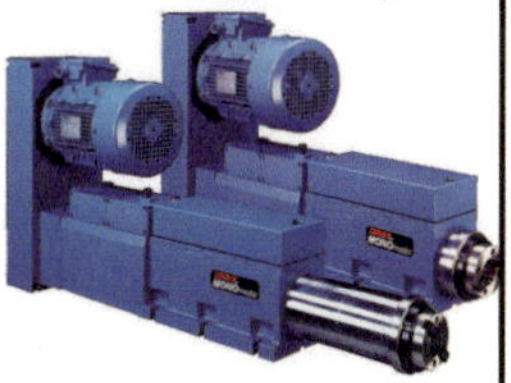 |

Table 1. Database of MONOmasters restored in the database (Photos: Suhner)

The KBES developed is capable of integrating qualitative information of the rule-base with quantitative data of the database and the feature library. It uses forward chaining approach for firing the rules in the rule-base and to achieve the goal. Forward chaining starts with the data available (for example the plane of holes, size of holes, and centre-to centre distance between holes) and uses the inference rules to extract more data until a desired goal (for example the possibility of using multi-drill head) is reached. An inference engine searches the inference rules until it finds one in which the "if" clause is known to be true. It then concludes the "then" clause and adds this information to its data. It continues to do this until a "goal" is reached. The system stores input and output information of the processed workpieces in the database for future use. Therefore, it adds to the extent of its knowledge.

To determine the feasibility of utilization of SPM for a new workpiece, the inference engine first searches the database to find out whether it has been processed before. If so, it uses previously restored information. If not processed before then the inference engine searches for similar workpieces. When a similar workpiece is found then the system provides user with possibility of interactive modification if necessary. When a similar workpiece is not found then it is processed by the system.

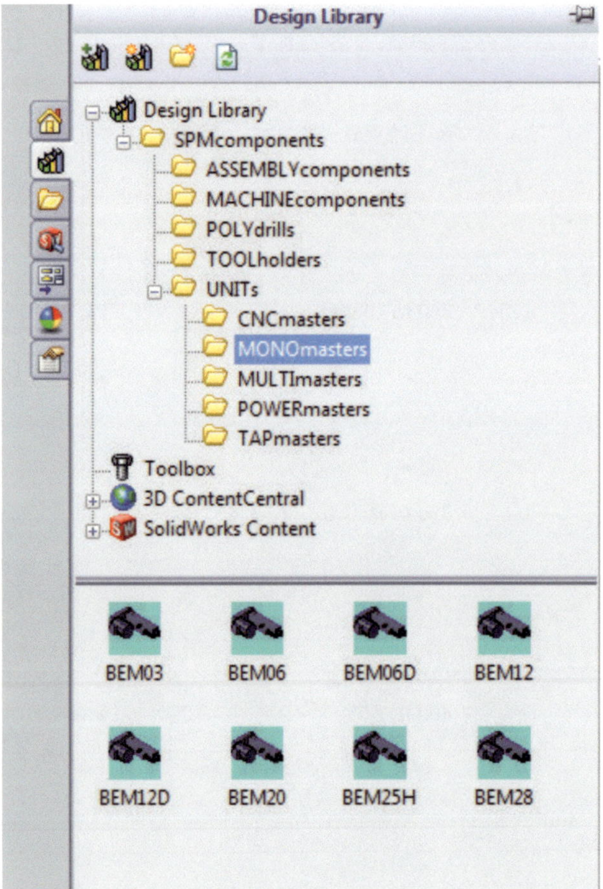


Fig. 12. Developed feature library containing 3D solid models of standardized SPM components

The user consults with the KBES for determination of appropriate machining units and then s/he uses the CAD system for designing the required SPM. The CAD system used in this work is SolidWorks which provides user with a 3D modelling environment. It is customized for SPM design by developing a feature library containing 3D models of standardized SPM components. As shown in Figure 12 the feature library contains a number of folders, each containing a group of SPM components. When the user wishes to insert a component, s/he simply opens the corresponding folder and double clicks on the desired component. Component's model is extracted from the library and can be easily placed in the desired position and orientation within modelling environment. Figure 13 shows different 3D solid models of quill units (MONOmasters) restored in the feature library, and Figure 14 represents the major steps of processing a typical drilling operation and the way that various components of the system are used in different activities.

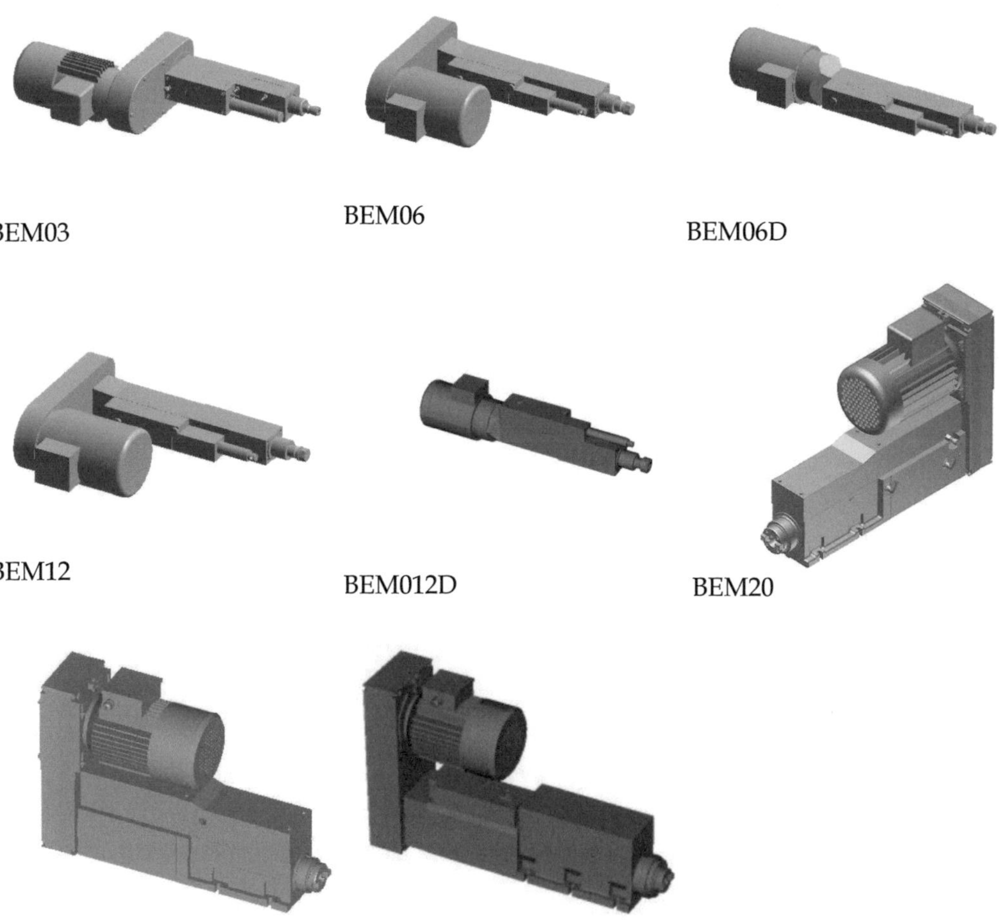


Fig. 13. 3D solid models of eight quill units (MONOmasters) restored in the feature library

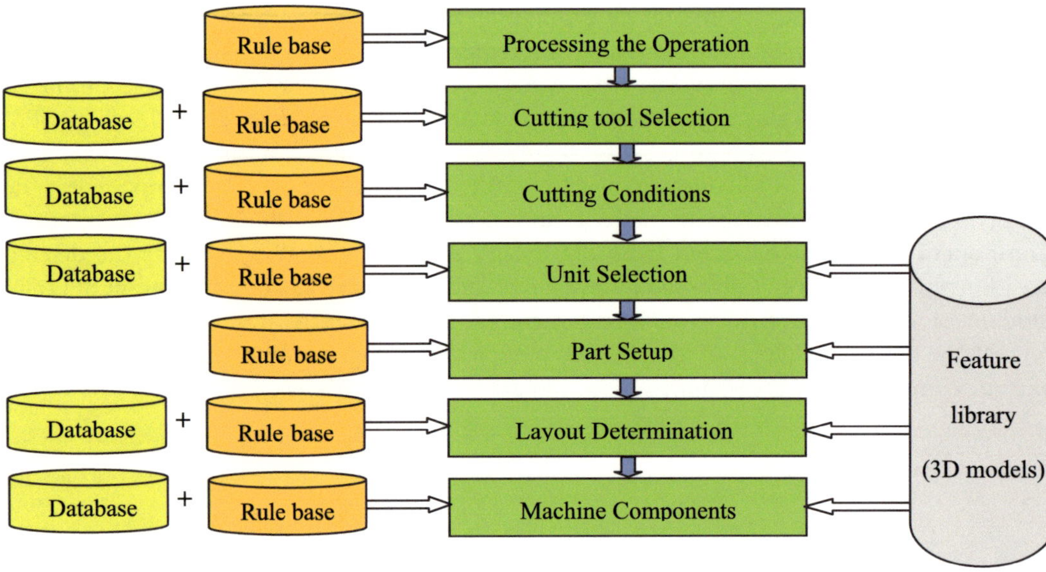


Fig. 14. Different steps in processing a drilling operation

Figure 15 illustrates a BEM12 quill unit extracted from the feature library. SolidWorks provides the user with full freedom in placing the selected models in the desired position

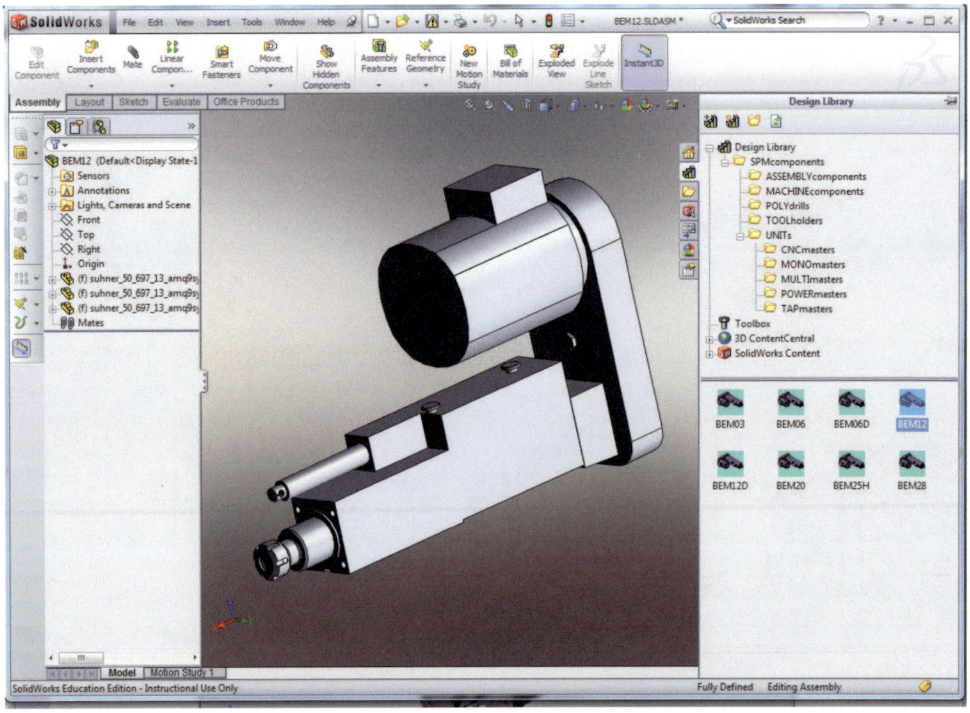


Fig. 15. 3D solid model of a BEM12 quill unit extracted from the feature library while it is being positioned in the modelling environment of SolidWorks

and orientation in a 3D modelling environment. All the models are placed in a similar method that leads to the completion of machine design with many components where any possible part collisions will be detected early at design stage.

## 5. Case study

Figure 16 shows a rotational part 50 mm in diameter and 75 mm in length. As shown in the Figure this part has three machining features: counterboring, drilling, and tapping. The workpiece material is low carbon steel and it has not been subjected to heat treatment processes before. The annual production quantity is 1,500,000 and production will be running for five years. Manufacturer of this part faces three options for production: traditional machines, CNC Chiron machining centre, and SPM. As the part size is small, on the CNC machining centre it is possible to use a pallet carrying 50 parts. Once the pallet is loaded the machine begins processing 50 parts in one setup. Once processing of all 50 parts is completed the pallet will be exchanged with another one that is already loaded with 50 new parts ready for processing. This would significantly reduce machine idle time for loading and unloading.

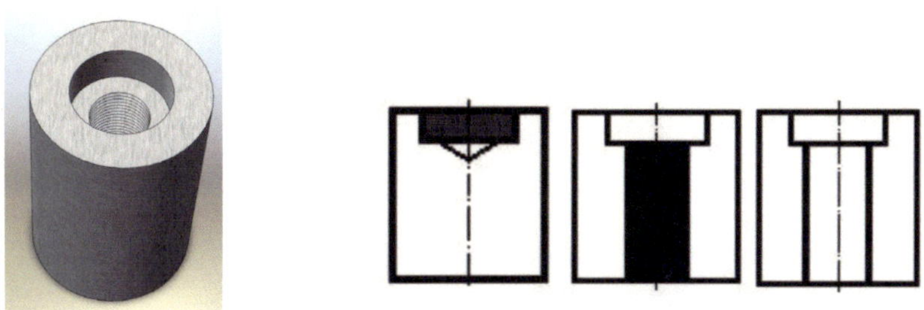

(a) (b)

Fig. 16. (a) The part with three machining features, (b) machining operations of the part from left to right: counterboring, drilling, and tapping

Table 2 compares the times required for performing machining operations on the traditional lathe, CNC Chiron machining centre, and SPM. Total time of machining on traditional lathe and CNC machine are equal to the sum of cutting times plus non-cutting times that include tool changing between processes, loading/unloading, and free movements of cutting tool. As schematically shown in Figure 17, the multi-station SPM for this part has an indexing table with four stations, one for loading/unloading and three for processing. This makes it possible to perform all machining operations simultaneously, one process at each station. Machining units are arranged such that all of the operations can be performed at a single part setup. Accordingly, the total machining time for each part is equal to the longest time needed for a single operation, plus one indexing time. As represented in Table 2, the total time per part on traditional lathe is 50 seconds, on the CNC machine 15.12 seconds, and it is only 6.8 seconds for SPM. Therefore, SPM produces 529.41 parts/hour, a figure remarkably higher than 238.10 for the CNC machine, and significantly higher than 72 for the lathe. Yet it is possible to multiply the output of the SPM when all machining stations are equipped with multi-drill heads.

| | *Lathe* | CNC | SPM |
|---|---|---|---|
| | **Time (sec)** | **Time (sec)** | **Time (sec)** |
| Counterboring time | 5.0 | 3.0 | 3.0 |
| Drilling time | 8.0 | 4.0 | 4.0 |
| Tapping time | 10.0 | 5.0 | 5.0 |
| Cutting time | **23.0** | **12.0** | **5.6**[1] |
| Tool changing per part | 6.0 | 0.12[2] | |
| Free tool traveling per part | 6.0 | 0.6[3] | |
| Indexing time per part | | | 1.2 |
| Loading/unloading | 15.0 | 2.40[4] | 5.0[5] |
| Non-cutting time | **27.0** | **3.12** | **1.2** |
| **Total time per part** | **50.0** | **15.12** | **6.8** |
| **Parts per hour** | **72** | **238.10** | **529.41** |

1: On the SPM the longest operation time determines the time required for each operation
2: Tool changing time for the CNC machine is 3 times of 2 seconds each for 50 pieces (0.12 sec/part)
3: Free tool traveling for the CNC machine is 30 seconds for 50 pieces (0.6 sec/ part)
4: Loading/unloading time of one pallet carrying 50 pieces is 2 minutes (2.4 sec/part)
5: Loading/unloading on the SPM will be performed by an automated system and at the same time machining is in progress in other stations

Table 2. Comparison of machining times for traditional lathe, CNC, and SPM

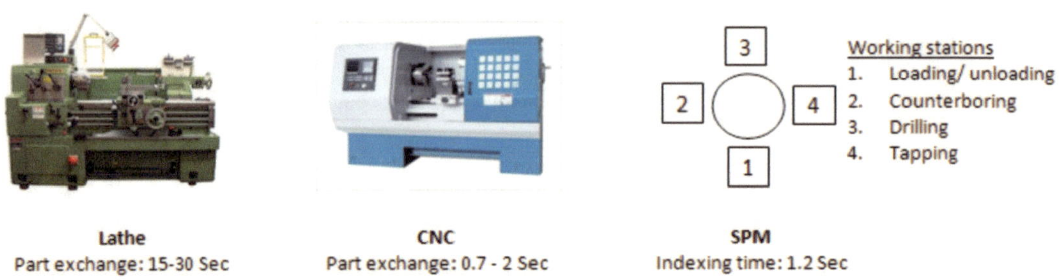


Fig. 17. Part exchange time on traditional lathe, CNC, and SPM.

Table 3 represents machining unit cost for all of the three methods and provides all cost components. When traditional lathe is used there is a need to use seven machines in order to achieve required annual output. This significantly increases labour and overhead costs that would result in a unit cost of $4.7423. In the case of CNC machine there is a need to use two machines in order to achieve the required output. This would reduce the unit cost to $0.5211 that is significantly lower. Yet SPM would further decrease this figure. Due to high productivity of SPMs only one machine with a single operator is needed to achieve the required output. This decreases most cost components including labour and overhead costs. Consequently the cost per part is reduced to only $0.2138. In other words, the use of SPM results in a significant 59% reduction of unit cost in comparison with CNC, and an amazing 95.5% cost reduction is achieved when compared to traditional lathe.

| | | *Lathe* | *CNC* | *SPM* |
|---|---|---|---|---|
| *Production data* | | | | |
| Parts required per year ($D$) | | 1,500,000 | 1,500,000 | 1,500,000 |
| Production cycle ($t$) | | 5 years | 5 years | 5 years |
| Interest rate ($r$) | | 6% | 6% | 6% |
| Max. working hours per year ($H$) | | 3,600 | 3,600 | 3,600 |
| *Machine tool data* | | | | |
| Parts per hour ($p$) | | 72 | 238.10 | 529.41 |
| Machine availability ($a$) | | 90% | 95% | 90% |
| Effective parts per hour ($E$) | $E = p \times a$ | 64.8 | 226.2 | 476.47 |
| Working hours per year ($h$) | $h = D / E$ | 23148.15 | 6,637.17 | 3,148.15 |
| Machines required ($M$) | $M = h / H$ | 6.43 => 7 | 1.84 => 2 | 0.87 => 1 |
| *Wage costs* | | | | |
| Wage rate ($w$) | | $45/h | $45/h | $45/h |
| Machinists required ($R$) | | 7 | 2 | 1 |
| Wage per hour ($W$) | $W = w \times R$ | $315 | $90 | $45 |
| **Wage cost per part ($C^w$)** | $C^w = W/E$ | **$4.4811** | **$0.3979** | **$0.0944** |
| *Cutting tool consumption* | | | | |
| Tool cost per process ($T$) | | $0.0168 | $0.0168 | $0.0168 |
| Number of processes per part ($n$) | | 3 | 3 | 3 |
| **Cutting tool cost per part ($C^t$)** | $C^t = n \times T$ | **$0.0504** | **$0.0504** | **$0.0504** |
| *Electricity consumption costs* | | | | |
| Electricity cost per kWh ($k$) | | $0.15 | $0.15 | $0.15 |
| Machine electricity consumption ($e$) | | 9 kW | 11 kW | 36 kW |
| Total consumption ($d$) | $d = e \times R$ | 63 kW | 22 kW | 36 kW |
| Electricity cost per h ($c$) | $c = k \times d$ | $9.45 | $3.30 | $5.40 |
| **Electricity cost per part ($C^e$)** | $C^e = c / E$ | **$0.1456** | **$0.0146** | **$0.0113** |
| *Machine depreciation costs* | | | | |
| Machine investment cost per unit ($u$) | | $35,900 | $124,800 | $264,678 |
| Total machine investment cost ($U$) | $U = M \times u$ | $251,300 | $249,600 | $264,678 |
| Machine depreciation cost per year ($f$) | $f = U / t$ | $50,260 | $49,920 | $52,935.60 |
| **Depreciation cost/part ($C^m$)** | $C^m = f/D$ | **$0.0335** | **$0.0333** | **$0.0353** |

| | | *Lathe* | *CNC* | *SPM* |
|---|---|---|---|---|
| *Interest costs* | | | | |
| Annual amount subject to interest ($A$) | $A = U$ | $251,300 | $249,600 | $264,678 |
| Interest per year ($i$) | $i = A \times r$ | $17,591 | $17,472 | $18,527.46 |
| **Interest per part ($I$)** | $I = i/D$ | **$0.0117** | **$0.0116** | **$0.0124** |
| *Overhead costs* | | | | |
| Annual overhead costs (trans., rent, etc.) ($v$) | | $30,000 | $20,000 | $15,000 |
| **Overhead cost per part ($O$)** | $O = v/D$ | **$0.02** | **$0.0133** | **$0.01** |
| **Total production cost per part** (excluding the cost of material) | | **$4.7423** | **$0.5211** | **$0.2138** |

Table 3. Machining costs for traditional lathe, CNC, and SPM

## 6. Conclusions

Production quality and low production cost are essential for the success of manufacturers in today's competitive market. SPMs are very useful for producing large quantities of high quality products at low costs. These machines can also be altered to produce similar components when necessary. High accuracy, uniform quality, and large production quantities are important characteristics of SPMs. However, the inadequate knowledge of machining specialists with this technology has resulted in its low utilization in manufacturing firms. In this article a detailed discussion of SPMs, their capabilities and accessories have been described. It also explained the development of a KBES to assist SPM users in deciding whether or not to make use of SPMs for a given production task. An analysis was made on the basis of technical and economical considerations. The case study presented clarified the method of analysis between three methods for producing a typical part. After a detailed discussion and extensive computations it has been concluded that for the given production task SPM would result in a significant 59% reduction of costs when compared to CNC, and an unbelievable 95.5% cost reduction was achieved when compared to traditional lathe. The system described in this work significantly reduces the time and effort needed for decision making on utilization of SPMs and determination of machine layout. In addition, the system developed minimizes the level of expertise required to perform the analysis and eliminates possible human errors.

The current system focuses on drilling and drilling-related operations. More work is needed to cover other machining operations including milling. Also the KBES developed currently works on a standalone basis. Work is in progress to integrate it with the 3D CAD modelling system such that the information could be directly extracted from the CAD system, eliminating the need for manual data input by user. A database of standard

3D components of SPM including machining and sliding units and other accessories has been constructed on Solidworks software platform. This assists SPM designers in the design task, and helps standardization of SPM designs that is of great importance to industries.

## 7. References


Allen J., Axinte D., Roberts P., and Anderson R. (2010) "A review of recent developments in the design of special-purpose machine tools with a view to identification of solutions for portable in situ machining systems," *International Journal of Advanced Manufacturing Technology*, Vol 50, pp. 50:843–857.

Boothroyd, G., and Knight, W.A. (2005) *Fundamentals of Machining and Machine Tools, Third edition,* Taylor & Francis, UK.

Groover, M.P. (2008) *Automation, production systems, and computer integrated manufacturing,* Prentice Hall, NJ, USA.

Groover, M.P. (2010) *"Fundamentals of Modern Manufacturing,"* John Wiley and Sons Inc, 4th edition.

Grosan, C., and Abraham, A., (2011) "Rule-based expert systems," *Intelligent Systems,* Vol. 17, pp. 149-185.

Ko, J., Hu, S J., and Huang, T. (2005) "Reusability assessment for manufacturing systems," *CIRP Annals,* Vol 54, No 1, pp. 113-114.

Lutters, D., Vaneker, T.H.J. and Van Houten, F.J.A.M. (2004) "What-if design: a synthesis method in the design process", *College International pour la Recherche en Productique (CIRP) Annals,* Vol. 53, No. 1, pp. 113-114.

Myung, S., and Han, S. (2001) "Knowledge-based parametric design of mechanical products based on configuration design method," *Expert Systems with Applications,* Vol. 21, Issue 2, pp. 99-107.

Patil, L., and Pande, S. S, (2002) "An intelligent feature process planning system for prismatic parts," International Journal of Production Research, Vol. 40, No. 17, pp. 4431-4447.

Sanders, D., Tan, Y. C., Rogers, I., Tewkesbury, G. E. (2009) "An expert system for automatic design-for-assembly", *Assembly Automation,* Vol. 29 Iss: 4, pp.378 – 388.

Suhner (2001) *"Automation Expert Catalogue,"* Switzerland (Suhner.com)

Tolouei-Rad, M. (2009) "Intelligent design of reconfigureable machines," *World Academy of Science, Engineering and Technology,* Vol. 59, 2009, pp. 278-282.

Tolouei-Rad, M., and Tabatabaei, S. M. (2005) "Design and manufacture of modular special purpose machine tools", *CD-ROM Proceedings of International Conference on Achievements in Manufacturing and Materials Science,* 6-9 Dec 2005, Giliwice-Zakopane, Poland.

Tolouei-Rad, M. & Zolfaghari, S. (2009) "Productivity improvement using Special-Purpose Modular machine tools," *International Journal of Manufacturing Research,* Vol 4, No 2, 2009, pp 219-235.

Wecka M & Staimer D (2002) Parallel Kinematic Machine Tools – Current State and Future Potentials, *CIRP Annals – Manufac. Tech.,* Vol 51, No 2, 2002, pp 671-683

Yoshimi, I., (2008) *"Modular Design for Machine Tools,"* McGraw-Hill Professional Publishing, Blacklick, OH, USA.

15

# Intelligent Biosystems and the Idea of the Joint Synthesis of Goals and Means

Pavel N. Prudkov
*Ecomon Ltd., Moscow, Russia*

## 1. Introduction

Immediately after the appearance of first computers more than sixty years ago, the idea of the creation of artificial intelligence similar to that of humans has inspired activity of thousands of outstanding individuals. Interesting results have been achieved in this endeavor but the situation still seems unsatisfactory. With exception of very narrow domains such as chess playing, intelligent systems cannot compete with humans or even animals. Several factors may be the reason of this situation. In this chapter, I consider one of the most important reasons: there are serious problems in the theory of intelligent systems and, accordingly, in theoretical approaches to the building of artificial intelligence. Therefore, the consideration of fundamental principles of intelligence may be an appropriate method for constructing effective systems of AI.

Although there is no clear definition for the term 'intelligence', it is intuitively understandable that intelligence is an attribute of goal-directed systems. A goal-directed system has various goals, which the system attempts to achieve through interactions with the environment based on diverse methods or means. Intelligence characterizes the efficacy of such systems in the achievement of its goals (Russell & Norvig, 2003). Humans and animals undoubtedly are goal-directed systems and observations of their activities reveal two obvious classes of such systems.

One class that may underlie the activity of nonhuman animals contains goal-directed systems in which basic goals and means are determined jointly in the moment of the creation of a system. A system belonging to this class functions as follows: one or several basic goals are activated along with a broad diversity of means innately associated with those goals. In accordance with the requirements of the situation, one or several of such means are performed and then associations between those goals and means are changed through feedback loops using hard-wired relations between goals and the result of performance or/and those relations generate new means, which are consequences of some changes in ongoing means. It seems that various systems in neural nets, evolutionary computing, reinforcement learning, etc correspond to this class of goal-directed systems (Haykin, 1998; Bäck, 1996; Holland, 1975; Leslie et al, 1996; Sutton & Barto, 1998).

The observation of human actions and introspection allow us to define the other class in which goals and means can be constructed arbitrarily and independently from each other. If a goal is constructed arbitrarily, then searching through all of possible means is the only method for selecting one or several means appropriate to achieve the goal. The efficacy of those means may increase the probability of their usage in similar situations; however, this class does not suggest unequivocal methods based on feedback loops to construct novel means. Various, largely symbolic, systems can be related to this class (Bertino, Piero & Zarria, 2001; Jackson, 1998; Newell, 1990).

Because these classes are so obvious, it is very reasonable to assume that any AI project can be attributed to one of the classes (though some projects may combine characteristics of both). Like other technical systems, AI projects are not intended to imitate their natural counterparts but rather attempt to achieve "natural functionality". The fact that the objective of Artificial Intelligence as a scientific and engineering activity is the full-scale functionality of human intelligence means AI researchers implicitly suggest that humans can be attributed to one or both of these classes. However, in my opinion this supposition is doubtful.

Undoubtedly, like other animals humans have a complex structure of innate goals associated with survival and reproduction. As a result, some scholars attribute humans to the first class of goal-directed systems. For example, behaviorism suggested an innate motivation mechanism in order to establish connections between goals and means through reward and punishment (Heckhausen, 1980). Currently, evolutionary psychology is very explicit in supposing that humans have an innate repertoire of goals and domain-specific modules (Tooby &Cosmides 1992; Tooby, Cosmides & Barrett, 2005). However, the attribution of humans to the first class system is unable to explain the diversity and rapid alterations of actions either at the level of a single individual, or at that of a whole society (Buller, 1998).

This inability hints that humans belong to the second-class systems. The main problem, which faces such systems, is a combinatorial explosion owing to the need to search through the potentially infinite number of possible means. However, people regularly make effective and flexible decisions without being overwhelmed by their decision-making processes. Some ideas to explain how the mind avoids a combinatorial explosion have been suggested (Newell, 1990), but they do not seem satisfactory (Cooper & Shallice, 1995). Moreover, although people are able to apply the strategy of deliberately searching among several conscious alternatives, some problems demonstrate that the thinking system is reluctant to use searching.

Consider, for example the following simplest chess riddle: White: Ke1, Rf2, Rh1; Black: Ka1. White to play and mate in one. When the author (P.P.) was acquainted with the problem he found that many poor chess players (and P.P. himself), who were, of course, familiar with the chess rules, could not solve the riddle or solved it after many attempts. However, any chess program immediately finds the solution: castling O-O. Indeed, since White should mate in one, in order to solve this problem it is necessary to generate each formally possible move for White in the given position, and to test whether this move is the solution. Such a searching procedure is available for the computer program but often not available for a human.

Everyday experience seems to demonstrate that people seldom use searching among possible alternatives. Instead, they prefer (often unconsciously) a routine action. In accordance with this opinion, the dual-processes models (Stanovich & West, 2000; Evans, 2003) have supposed that the mind includes two components. One component uses searching procedures and accordingly is responsible for deliberate actions. The other component, which complies with the systems of the first class, underlies routine, automatic actions. It is suggested that in routine everyday situations, in which, according to such theories, the vast majority of actions is performed, the routine component effectively selects an appropriate action. Searching and planning are involved only in unusual situations. Some unspecified mechanisms constrain searching in those rare cases when the latter is necessary.

In my opinion, however, nonroutine and routine situations are intertwined more strongly than it may be consciously acknowledged. The mind cannot be separated into the two components. For example, if an individual is hungry, she may open her home refrigerator without the clear awareness of this process. However, people usually do not open somebody's refrigerators automatically even if they are hungry. No special intention to inhibit the wish "to open somebody's refrigerator" is necessary in such situations. Obviously, there is no universal routine "not to open somebody's refrigerator", simply because it is very difficult to define unequivocally and finally what refrigerators are permitted to open. Therefore, it is necessary to suggest that ongoing goals somehow control activity when an individual attends to the refrigerator, allowing or forbidding the opening of the latter. In the same manner, ongoing goals unconsciously involve in most of routine situations even when the individual believes that some component of her activity is automatic. With the involvement of ongoing goals in most of everyday situations, the problem of combinatorial explosion becomes unresolved for the dual-processes models.

Whereas, AI research is not intended directly to imitate human intelligence but it seems obvious that a certain view on human intelligence is a very important tacit heuristic to AI researchers and strongly influences AI studies. In my opinion, the analysis of the two conventional classes of goal-directed systems demonstrates that human activity hardly can be derived from these classes and this may be a very serious factor constraining AI research.

I suggest that the standard view on possible classes of goal-directed systems is incomplete and consider a more complex categorization below. I present, based on this classification, a new view on human goal-directed activity as a characteristic of a particular class of goal-directed systems. Some ideas on how this class can be represented in the brain are considered. These ideas form the basis for the simulation of simple models of goal-directed activity. Some proposals on how this novel understanding of humans as goal-directed systems can be used to create intelligent systems are also considered in the article.

## 2. Two-dimensional classification of goal-directed systems and the idea of joint synthesis

The two classes of goal-directed systems are usually considered as two poles of one axis and as a result, it seems that there are no other classes. However, a more profound view on the classes demonstrates that the situation may be more complex. Indeed, the first class contains goal-directed systems in which basic goals and means are constructed innately and together. In the systems of the second-class goals and means can be constructed arbitrarily and separately from each other. It is easy to discern that the words "innately" and "separately" are not antonyms neither are the words "together" and "arbitrarily". This may mean that the two classes are only an apparent projection of a two-dimensional structure, in which one dimension can be characterized as "innate" versus "arbitrary" or "learned" and another dimension as "constructed together" versus "constructed separately". With this assumption, a representation of this structure can be given as the following table.

| | Together | Separately |
|---|---|---|
| Innately | Goals and means are constructed innately and together | Goals and means are constructed innately and separately |
| Arbitrarily | Goals and means are constructed arbitrarily and together | Goals and means are constructed arbitrarily and separately |

Table 1. Classification of goal-directed systems

This results in a more complicated structure with four classes. Prior to the consideration of this structure, it seems useful to raise an issue of whether this classification is fundamental enough. Undoubtedly, there may be many various sources of classification: for example, the diversity of goals or the number of levels in the system can be used to classify. However, obviously, the most important classification should be based on key characteristics of goal-directed systems. In my view, the table reflects such fundamental characteristics because one axis is the capability of a goal-directed system to change and adjust and the second dimension is the relationship between the main components of any goal-directed system, i.e. its goals and means.

It is easy to discern that two cells in the table correspond to the conventional classes but two new classes emerge from the other cells. One new class is goal-directed systems, in which goals and means are constructed innately and separately. Such architecture is, however, logically impossible. Indeed, if basic goals and means of a certain goal-directed system are defined at the moment of the creation of the system, then a common configuration undoubtedly underlies them and they cannot be constructed separately.

The other new class is goal-directed systems, in which goals and means can be constructed arbitrarily and jointly. If one suggests that the construction of a goal and means in such a system is a self-organizing process, which is based on an extremal principle, e.g. that the costs on the synthesis should be minimal, then particular advantages of this class can be easily revealed. Indeed, because the goal and means in a system of this class are constructed jointly, there is no need to search among a potentially infinite set of means to satisfy the given goal; this is a simple solution to the problem of combinatorial explosion. On the other hand, the possibility to synthesize goals and means arbitrarily indicates the actions of the systems belonging to this class may be very flexible and adaptive. With such characteristics of this class, my main idea is that human beings are goal-directed systems in which arbitrary goals and means are synthesized jointly.

One may propose some objections to this hypothesis. First, if a goal and means are constructed together then the means ought to be appropriate for achieving the goal. However, people often understand what goal must be achieved but they cannot suggest appropriate means to achieve the goal. However, it is necessary to note that the joint synthesis is not a method to create the best action (this is impossible due to combinatorial explosion) but a method to create any action (because the number of possible actions is infinite, in principle). To a certain degree, an alternative to the action constructed by the ongoing joint synthesis is not another action but rather its absence. Therefore, the idea of joint synthesis is not hurt by the fact that people are able to imagine, plan, or pursue completely arbitrary even unachievable goals. Because even when the individual thinks that there is no method to achieve the goal, nevertheless an inappropriate method is chosen because the selection of a certain aspect of reality among the infinite number of other possible aspects occurred.

Second, experience teaches us that one goal can be achieved by various methods, ways (this is the principle of equifinality (Bertalanffy, 1968)) and that one method can be applied to achieve various goals. These obvious facts, which underlie one of the two conventional classes, seem inconsistent with the joint synthesis hypothesis (referred to as the JSH hereinafter). In my opinion, the idea that goals and means can be constructed separately is correct at the level of social practice but a psychological illusion at the level of psychological mechanisms of a particular action.

In order to clear this idea, imagine that one needs to achieve the 35th floor of a skyscraper. Firstly, this can be made by means of an elevator. If no elevator can be used (e.g. there is no voltage), it is possible to go upstairs. Finally, if the staircase is destroyed then one can climb on the wall using necessary tools. It seems one invariable goal can be combined with various methods to achieve it. However, the first method is available for everyone because it requires no concentration of mental recourses. The second one can be accepted when there is a serious need to reach the goal. In addition, the last one can be used only under extreme circumstances requiring the strongest concentration of will and energy. In other words, from the position of internal processes each way requires a certain psychological arrangement with special goals and this arrangement is acknowledged by any individual as distinctive from the others. Therefore, a change in the situation results in the alteration of goals at a particular level of the hierarchy of goals. It is reasonable to assume that the interaction between goals and means in the process of the construction of a goal-directed activity is a characteristic of any such activity.

In my opinion, like other psychological illusions, such as, for example, the illusion of the instantaneous reaction to an external stimulus (the understanding that the reaction is not instant, occurred in 1823 only (Corsini & Auerbach, 1998)), the illusion of the separate construction of goals and means results from the fact that it is very difficult to combine the involvement in a particular activity with the simultaneous introspective monitoring of this activity. Indeed, when an individual pursues a particular everyday goal (e.g., shopping at the supermarket) she usually does not pay attention to all variations in the intermediate goals and means necessary for this multi-stage pursuit. As a result, the complex interplay of these intermediate processes is reflected by consciousness and memory only partially, while the success or failure in the achievement of the main goal is usually in the focus of consciousness. In addition, the detailed awareness of each stage in a multi-staged activity is merely impossible because this is able to destroy the activity itself. The result of these circumstances is, in my opinion, a false feeling of the separate formation and change of goals and means.

It is necessary to note that the hypothesis that the mind constructs the goal and means together does not imply that an individual deliberately cannot search through possible options as a method to determine an appropriate means. Indeed, the conscious idea to apply searching along with the awareness of several possible options may be the result of the ongoing synthesis.

The validation of the JSH is easy. Indeed, because the hypothesis suggests that the mind constructs the goal and means of an action jointly following the criterion of minimal construction costs. This means that if there are no explicit preferences to choose among several possible actions then an action requiring minimal mental costs to be constructed is preferable. This action should be selected without intensive searching among probable alternatives. On the other hand, this choice should not be a result of the activation of a routine procedure and can be changed deliberately. A real experimentation to test these suppositions is possible but beyond the scope of this article (Prudkov &Rodina, 1999, Rodina &Prudkov, 2005). Instead, I consider a thought experiment, which, in my opinion, is sufficient to demonstrate the relevance of the JSH.

Imagine that two individuals participate in this experiment, one of them is Experimenter, the other is Subject, accordingly, and the experiment takes place in London. The participants are discussing some problem and at a certain moment, Experimenter asks Subject to give him a pen without specifying the location of the pen. Many people have a pen in their pockets, and it is very probable that Subject is among them. Subject takes the pen out of the pocket and gives it to Experimenter. It is very reasonable to suggest that the construction of this action needs minimal mental costs. In response, however, Experimenter asks, "why did Subject take the pen out of the pocket instead of calling New York?" Subject is astonished by this question and then Experimenter says that there are many pens in New York and Subject could find a pen there. The astonishment of Subject means that his mind did not find among possible alternatives of the pen's location but one may argue that this reflects the fact that Experimenter's request is performed by the activation of a corresponding routine. It is obvious, however, that if Experimenter would merely ask Subject to find a pen in New York then Subject could easily convert this idea to a sequence of actions. Such a rapid adjustment to the situation cannot be provided by a routine. This is the result of a special goal-directed process. In my opinion, this simple situation, which can be easily repeated in reality, demonstrates the appropriateness of the idea of joint synthesis.

Although the joint synthesis is a basic attribute of humans as goal-directed systems, the consideration of this characteristic alone may be insufficient to understand the whole diversity of human actions. Humans, of course, have innate mechanisms necessary for survival and reproduction and those, although are under control from more modern systems, influence actions and therefore, to a certain degree, humans can be considered as the goal-directed systems of the first class. On the other hand, using language and complex social skills, an individual can "emulate" the separation between goals and means. Indeed, by discussing some ideas with other people or by writing the ideas down and afterwards thinking about them, an individual can concentrate either on the goals or on the means of a goal-directed activity. The fact implies, to some extent, humans can be considered as systems with the separate and arbitrary construction of goals and means. However, it is the joint synthesis that determines the involvement of the other classes of goal-directed systems in human actions.

It is usually suggested that a goal-directed activity pursues a clear and unequivocal goal and when the individual acknowledges that the outcome of the process meets its goal then the activity completes. However, in my opinion, the idea of a clear and unequivocal goal seems doubtful. Consider, for example, the situation with Experimenter and Subject above. Obviously, that Subject unconsciously converted the goal "to find a pen" into the goal "to find a pen in the pockets" and as a result, he is astonished by the proposal "to search a pen in New York", though this proposal is consistent with the initial request. Obviously, the supposition "to search for a pen in another room" could astonish Subject to a lesser degree. Similarly, Experimenter would be stunned, if Subject could pull a giant pen (for example, 50 centimeters in length) out of his bag though such a pen meets his request. On the other hand, a pen of a very unusual design but a standard size could wonder Experimenter less. Therefore, it can be assumed that Experimenter and Subject have some distributions of anticipations regarding the result of their goal-directed activities rather than unambiguous goals, but they acknowledge those anticipations only partially.

I suggest that any goal-directed activity is a distribution of anticipations regarding the goal and means of the activity. The activation of some components of this distribution is determined by particular aspects of the situation and the changes in the situation results in the activation of slightly other components of the distribution. The construction and changes in the distribution are based on the criterion of minimal construction costs.

A suggestion that the goal and means of a goal-directed process are some distributions leads to two fundamental conclusions. First, this means that there is no simple procedure to define when the goal is achieved because it may be difficult to find an unequivocal compliance between the distributed representation of the goal and the output of the activity. Therefore, the completion of an ongoing process is the result of the interaction between this process, the situation, and the hierarchy of other processes. In other words, there is no special comparator always able to compare the goal and the output of the activity and as a result, people sometimes do not acknowledge that the result of an ongoing activity does not respond to its initial goal. In my opinion, everyday experience is consistent with this suggestion. Consider, for example, an individual who plans to buy necessary goods at the supermarket. Sometimes the result of such activity is that an individual misses several objects planned. Instead, she purchases other goods but thinks that the goal of the action is achieved.

Second, the vague representation of the goal and method implies that the sustainability of a goal-directed activity can be considered as its relatively autonomous attribute. Indeed, sustainability seems a one-dimensional parameter and hence less variable than multivariate distributions of goals and means that ought to meet the very complex structure of the situation. A proposal of the autonomy of sustainability seems unusual enough but perseveration, i.e., the involuntary and uncontrollable repetitions of a particular action, which is a very frequent attribute of disturbances in goal-directed behavior (Luria, 1966, 1972,1983; Joseph, 1999), clearly favors this proposal. Indeed, perseveration can be considered as the activation of a sustainable component, which, if the goal-directed system is damaged, persists regardless the influence of the situation or other processes.

## 3. Neural basis for the joint synthesis

If the goal and means of a goal-directed activity are constructed together then it is of great importance to understand how this can be implemented in the brain because similar mechanisms can be used to create artificial goal-directed systems. Undoubtedly, human goal-directed activity is very complex and a detailed understanding of it is the beyond scope of this article. Instead, I consider the neural basis of a certain "ideal" goal-directed process suggesting it includes three obvious stages, i.e. initiation, execution, and termination. My approach meets most of the contemporary hypotheses, which consider that the prefrontal cortex (PFC) plays a key role in goal-directed processes (E.K. Miller& Cohen, 2001; Wood& Grafman, 2003). In accordance with this position, I propose that the prefrontal cortex is heavily involved in the construction and maintenance of neural patterns representing goals and means.

It is suggested that the capacity of the PFC to construct and maintain sustainable neural patterns is based on possible reverberatory characteristics of neurons in this structure (Fuster 1997). It can be supposed that owing to such reverberatory properties the emergence of sustainable characteristics of a neural pattern is, to a certain extent, autonomous from the emergence of its other characteristics. In other words, relatively weak changes in neurons of the PFC may be sufficient to make a pattern sustainable but more serious alterations are necessary to form its other characteristics. This underlines a relative autonomy of the sustainability of goal-directed processes at the cognitive level.

It is suggested that the prefrontal cortex can be considered as blackboard architecture. Blackboard architecture consists of a set of specialized or stable processors that interact with each other using a blackboard, consisting of less stable, flexible elements. Some authors (van der Velde& de Kamps 2003, 2006) have suggested the idea that the prefrontal cortex uses this sort of architecture. This idea is consistent with the neural data. For example, this means that most of prefrontal neurons must flexibly adapt its activity to the ongoing task. And 30-80 percents of prefrontal neurons of the monkey show selective responses to some aspect of that task's events (Asaad et al 2000). However, it is necessary to emphasize a distinction between conventional views on blackboard architecture used in AI (Corkill 1991; Craig 1995) and that used in this text. Unlike conventional models, the given model does not suggest an absolute difference between stable processors and flexible elements, i.e. stable processors can be converted to flexible elements and vice versa because both groups comprise of similar neurons and only the level of stability distinguishes them.

It is reasonable to assume that a new goal-directed process emerges from the integration of various sources of information associated with the ongoing situation. So, it is hypothesized that prior to the construction of a new goal-directed process the prefrontal cortex can be considered as a blackboard system in which incoming sensory information and/or ongoing internal processes (emotions, innate drives, other goal-directed processes, especially those at higher levels, etc.) presented as spatiotemporal patterns of neural activity in the PFC and other brain structures are stable processors. Moreover, other ensembles of the PFC comprise a bulletin board with flexible elements. The construction of a new process started from interactions between stable processors and flexible elements and owing to such interactions, the characteristics of flexible elements become similar to some characteristics of stable processors. At the neural level, this means similar frequency or distribution of firing, etc.

and at the cognitive level this means some similar functions. After this, flexible elements with new functions start interacting with each other also exchanging its characteristics. It is reasonable to suggest that the more similar characteristics shared by some elements, the more probability of its interactions. For example, if neuron A has a synapse with neuron B then a probability that the discharge of neuron A results in the discharge of neuron B seems more than the same probability for two neurons that do not share a common synapse. The relationship between the similarity of elements and the probability of its interaction is the substantiation of the criterion of minimal construction costs.

It is reasonable to expect that owing to interactions between elements, the resemblance of elements can be increased. As a result, a pattern joining many elements with similar characteristics gradually emerges and this pattern becomes sustainable. This indicates that the construction of a new process is completed. Although, elements in the pattern have something in common but there are some distinctions among them and this is a prerequisite for the distributed representation for the goal and means.

It is suggested each pattern can be considered as a construction with two interconnected components: one component is responsible for the goal and the other for the means. Such a separation is based on the idea that some neurons in the pattern have mainly local connections within the prefrontal cortex (they comprise the goal component). Other neurons in the pattern are linked to other brain structures (those are the means component). Because the activity of neurons within the PFC is likely more reverberatory and self-sustained than that of neurons linked to other structures, the goal component can be more stable and persistent than the means component.

Once a goal-directed process is constructed, some activation from the means component propagates to other brain structures, which are able to carry out the process, and its performance is initiated (B.T. Miller& D'Esposito 2005). Simultaneously, the components interact with each other; this stabilizes the means component while it receives feedback because of performing the process. Therefore, the fact that the process pursues the goal is a result of the stability in the goal component produced by self-sustainable characteristics of the PFC. It is possible to say that goal-directed processes are self-sustained gates, which amplify appropriate information and diminish inappropriate one. The components are constructed together but their architecture is slightly different. The functioning of components gradually increases these differences and this change may be a basis for an autonomous representation of goals and means in consciousness.

As is emphasized above I do not suggest that the brain includes a special comparator, which monitors when the outcome of the process meets the goal, and then turns the process off. Simply, with the achievement of the goal, the current situation undergoes changes, thus not being able to support the ongoing process with appropriate information. To meet novel requirements of the situation, the construction of another process begins. Probably, more stable processes at a higher level of the goal-directed hierarchy supervising short-term ones also participate in the completion of the ongoing process. Free neural ensembles again become flexible components of the blackboard. It can be hypothesized that a real goal-directed process is a hierarchical multilevel structure joining many of such ideal processes.

## 4. Simulation of a goal-directed activity based on joint synthesis

The hypothesis of joint synthesis and its possible neural implementation can be considered a basis for computer models of goal-directed activity. It is necessary to point out that these models are neither models of a certain aspect of human or animal activity nor implementations of goal-directed activity in the brain. They are simply intended to demonstrate how a goal-directed process can be constructed. The models share a common basis but have certain distinctive characteristics.

### 4.1 A simple model of goal-directed activity (model 1)

The architecture of the model is presented in Figure 1.

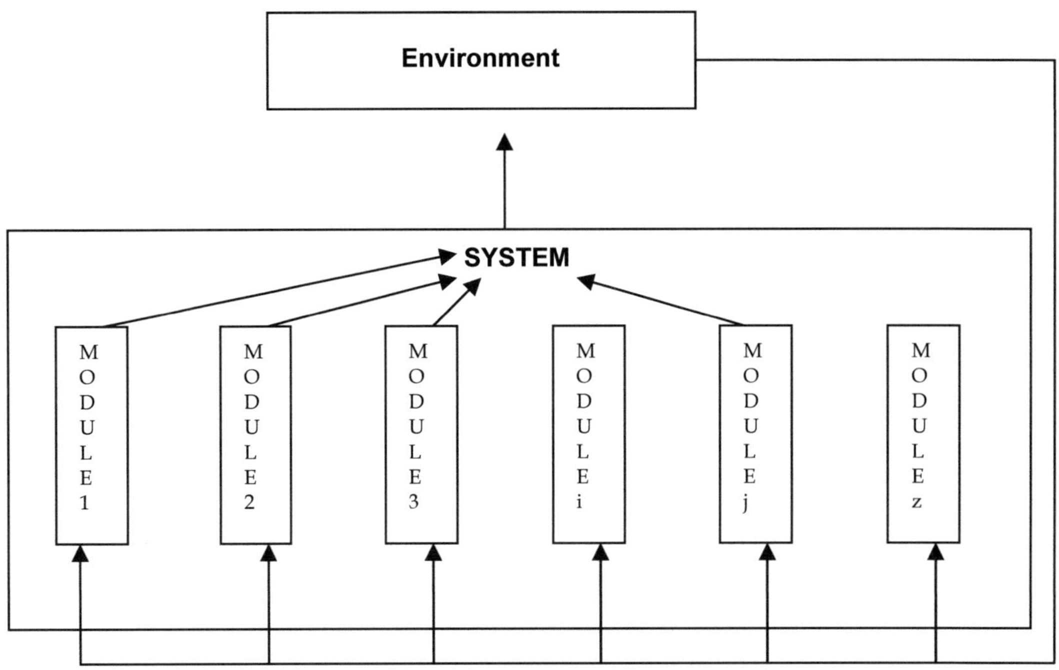


Fig. 1. Architecture of model 1

The model consists of two fractions; one is the system in which a goal-directed activity should be constructed and the other is the environment influencing the state of the system. At the beginning, a new goal-directed process emerges within the system under a certain state of the environment and after changing the environment, the process pursues its goal associated with the initial state of the environment using the means constructed.

The system includes one layer consisting of z autonomous modules and the output of the system is a summation of the outputs of its modules. Each module contains several n-dimension vectors with real numbers as its components. These vectors are an input vector (IV), which is filled by information from the environment (its $k^{th}$ component is $IV^k$, accordingly), a vector of coefficients (CV), and an output vector (OV). The functioning of the vectors is described below. Also, each module has an activation level (AL), a real number from 0 to 1. With the idea of a relative autonomy of sustainability above, this parameter reflects the stability and activity of the module, i.e., as AL increases the functioning of the module becomes more stable.

A fundamental characteristic of modules is that they interact with each other. The functional proximity between two elements is calculated as follows. First, the following characteristic for module i (and j, accordingly) at iteration m is computed

$$me_{i,m} = \frac{\sum_{k=1}^{k=n} |IV_{i,m}{}^{k} - CV_{i,m-1}^{k}|}{n} \tag{1}$$

afterward another parameter is calculated

$$sd_{i,m} = \sqrt{\frac{\sum_{k=1}^{k=n} (|IV_{i,m}{}^{k} - CV_{i,m-1}^{k}| - me_{i,m})^2}{n}} \tag{2}$$

and then the functional proximity between i and j, fp(i,j) is

$$fp(i,j)_m = \left| \frac{sd_{i,m}}{AL_{i,m-1} * me_{i.m}} - \frac{sd_{j,m}}{AL_{j,m-1} * me_{j,m}} \right| \tag{3}$$

The interaction between module i and module j at iteration m occurs if fp(i,m) is less than a threshold (p1) plus a small noise. The fact that modules interacts only if its functional proximity is less than a threshold is an implementation of the idea of minimal construction costs. The result of the interaction between module i and module j is as follows:

$$CV_{i,m}^{k} = CV_{i,m-1}^{k} + \frac{(CV_{i,m-1}^{k} - (CV_{j,m-1}^{k} - IV_{j,m}^{k}) * (1 - AL_{i,m-1})) * p2}{z} \tag{4}$$

$$CV_{j,m}^{k} = CV_{j,m-1}^{k} + \frac{(CV_{j,m-1}^{k} - (CV_{i,m-1}^{k} - IV_{i,m}^{k}) * (1 - AL_{j,m-1})) * p2}{z} \tag{5}$$

It is suggested that modules interact in parallel and the formulae reflect this. Owing to interactions, the activation level of each module (for example, module i at iteration m) is also changed :

$$AL_{i,m} = p3 * AL_{i,m-1} + \frac{t_{i,m} * p4 * (1 - AL_{i,m-1})}{z} \tag{6}$$

where both p3 and p4 <1 and $t_{i,m}$ is the number of interactions between module i and the other modules of the system at iteration m.

It is easy to see that as the AL of a module increases, the components of the module become less prone to change. In addition, if a module did not interact with other modules at the last iteration, its AL should be decreased. Module i is able to influence the environment only if its AL exceeds a threshold (p5) at iteration m, then

$$OV_{i,m}^{k} = \frac{(IV_{i,m}^{k} - CV_{i,m}^{k})}{z}, \text{ otherwise } OV_{i,m}^{k} = 0 \tag{7}$$

The environment is also a n-dimension vector (E) and its k^th component at iteration m is changed by the following formula:

$$E_{m}^{k} = constant_{m}^{k} + noise + \frac{\sum_{i=1}^{i=z} OV_{i,m-1}^{k}}{z} \tag{8}$$

It is not difficult to see that, unlike the analysis of neural mechanisms above, this model does not include special layers to form output. The objective of such a design is to avoid unnecessary difficulties conditioned by complex relations between such layers. These difficulties are able to complicate the understanding of the model's functioning without clearing its main ideas. However, because each module has a complex structure with internal vectors such as CV and OV the model can be useful to understand the functioning of various goal-directed systems.

In all simulations, the number of modules in the system (z) was 300 and the vectors in each module were three-dimensional. Real numbers were used as the stuff of all vectors in the system. A goal-directed activity was constructed as follows. First, 40 modules were considered as stable processors. Its coefficient vectors were filled by a constant plus small noise and its active levels was more than p5 (0.3). The other modules of the system were flexible elements. Its coefficient vectors were randomly filled by numbers from 0 to 100 and its ALs were randomly established at 0,06 plus small noise. Following this initialization, interactions between stable processors and flexible elements started. Five iterations of this process took place and p1 was 0,3. At this stage (stage 1), no outputs from the system influenced the environment. This corresponded to the construction of a goal-directed activity. After this, novel constants were established and the interaction between the system and the environment became possible. This stage (stage 2) meant the functioning of a goal-directed activity.

It is necessary to emphasize that the architecture of the model means stable processors are not a necessary condition for the interaction between the system and the environment. In principle, flexible elements are sufficient to provide the functioning of the system but in this case, the activity of the system must be less stable and persistent. To test this suggestion a special simulation was carried out. In this simulation no stable processors were formed but five iterations similar to those in simulation 1 were performed (stage 1, accordingly). After this, certain constants were selected and the interaction between the system and the environment became possible (stage 2).

In both simulations all constants were 80, in other words, the goal of the activity in simulation 1 entirely met the initial state of its stable processors. After three iterations with such constants at stage 2, in both simulations the constants were forcefully established at 50 during one iteration to estimate the stability of the models to random fluctuations.

Afterwards, the constants were 80 again. Because at any moment all constants were identical, the components of input and coefficients vectors in modules could be averaged within each vector and across all modules. As a result, one number was sufficient to describe the state of coefficients vectors at any iteration. In addition, Al averaged across all modules also was used as a characteristic of the process.

It was suggested that owing to stable processors filled by 80 the coefficient vectors of the model with stable processors (CV-sp) should exceed those of the model without stable processors (CV-wsp) at stage 2. Moreover, CV-sp should be more stable after a sudden fluctuation in the constants of the environment. Also, AL-sp should be more than AL-wsp. The results of both simulations are in figure 2, where for convenience, ALs were multiplied by 100.

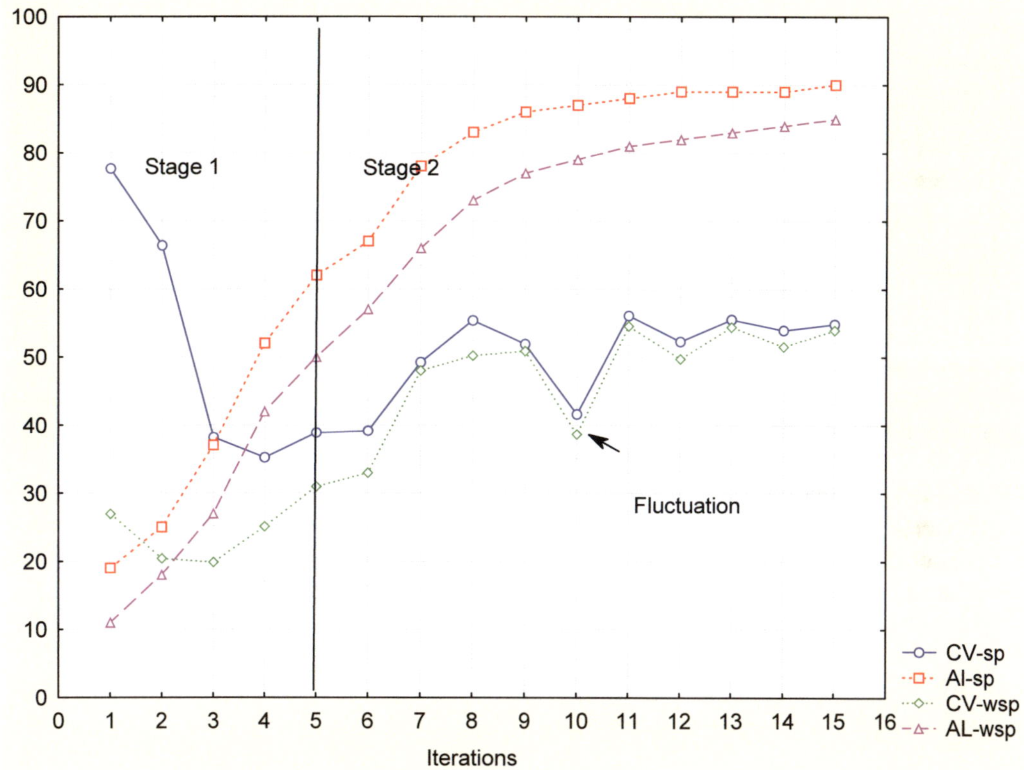


Fig. 2. The comparison of the results of two simulations.

### 4.2 A model with perceptive spot (model 2)

Though model 1 is able to demonstrate some characteristics of goal-directed activity, it seems too primitive for serious actions. Model 2 is more complex, its system has a perceptive spot, which includes the modules whose input vectors are filled by a useful signal from the environment while the input vectors of the other modules are filled by noise. Both a useful signal and noise are real numbers but the amplitude of noise is considerably less. The system is able to move the center of the spot but cannot change its size. The behavior of the system in model 1 is similar to the activity of an insect, which moves in the environment filled by a nutrient with variable concentration. Model 2 is, to some extent, similar to the action of an eye of an animal.

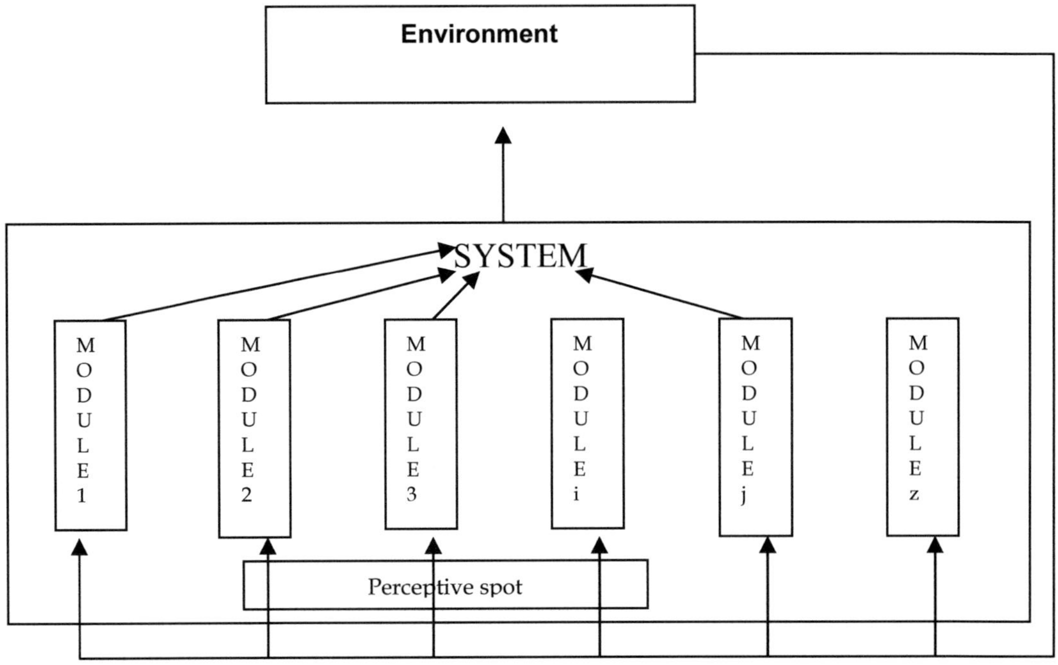


Fig. 3. Architecture of model 2

The modules in this model are similar to those in model 1 but also include a vector of differences (DV), its functioning is described below. In order to avoid the spurious activity of modules filled by noise, a threshold of perception is used, i.e. module i is able to participate in the activity of the system at iteration m only if

$$\frac{AL_{i,m-1} * \sum_{k=1}^{k=n} IV_{i,m}^{k}}{n} \geq p1 \tag{9}$$

The interaction between module *i* and module *j* at iteration *m* occurs if the distance between the modules, i.e. |(i-j)/z| is less than a certain parameter (p2) and the functional proximity i.e.

$$\frac{\sum_{k=1}^{k=n} \left| \left|IV_{i,m}{}^{k} - CV_{i,m-1}^{k}\right| - \left|IV_{j,m}^{k} - CV_{j,m-1}^{k}\right| \right|}{n} \tag{10}$$

is less than a threshold (p3) plus a small noise. The result of the interaction between module *i* and module *j* is as follows:

$$CV_{i,m}^{k} = CV_{i,m-1}^{k} + \frac{(CV_{i,m-1}^{k} - (CV_{j,m-1}^{k} - DV_{j,m-1}^{k}) * (1 - AL_{i,m-1})) * p4}{z} \tag{11}$$

$$CV_{j,m}^{k} = CV_{j,m-1}^{k} + \frac{(CV_{j,m-1}^{k} - (CV_{i,m-1}^{k} - DV_{i,m-1}^{k}) * (1 - AL_{j,m-1})) * p4}{z} \tag{12}$$

Owing to interactions, the characteristics of the vector of differences (DV) of module i at iteration m are also changed as follows :

$$DV_{i,m}^{k} = p5 * (CV_{i,m}^{k} - IV_{i,m}^{k}) + (1 - p5) * DV_{i,m-1}^{k}, \ p5<1 \tag{13}$$

it is possible to say that CV is the long-term memory of a module and DV is its short-term memory.

The modules with AL exceeding a threshold ( p8 in this model or p5 in the previous one) , also, influence the position of the center of perceptive spot. This position (center position or CP) is determined at iteration m as follows:

$$CP_m = CP_{m-1} + p10 * \sum_{i=1}^{i=z} (T_{i,m} - CP_{m-1})$$

and $$T_{i,m} = i / z \text{ if } AL_{i,m} \rangle p8 \text{, otherwise } T_{i,m} = CP_{m-1} . \tag{14}$$

It is suggested the position of the left boundary of the system is 0 and that of the right boundary is 1.

As is emphasized above, only the modules, which are within perceptive spot, are filled by information from the environment, i.e. if $|CP_m - i/z| \le p11$, then for module i at iteration m+1

$$IV_{i,m+1}^{k} = E_m^k + noise$$

and for modules which do not meet this inequality (15)

$$IV_{i,m+1}^{k} = noise .$$

The formulae for computing activation level (AL), output vector OV, and the environment are identical those in model 1.

An idea underlying the usage of model is that under certain circumstances the input vectors of modules i.e. the state of the environment and the vectors of coefficients in the system ought to converge to each other. The results of a simulation intended to test this assumption are presented in table 2. In this simulation as well as in the simulations below, the number of modules in the system (z) was 300 and the vectors in each module were three-dimensional. The constants of environment vector in this simulation were 10, 50, and 90, accordingly. Perceptive spot covered all modules, and each module was able to interact with all of the rest i.e. p2 and p11 were 0,95. The threshold for interactions (p3) was 4,2. The other parameters are in Appendix, they were kept invariable through the other simulations. The values averaged across the components of input vectors were used as the description of the influence of the environment and the averaged components of the vectors of coefficients were considered as the characteristic of change in coefficients. The AL averaged across all modules reflected activity in the whole system.

| Iteration | AL | $IV^1$ | $CV^1$ | $IV^2$ | $CV^2$ | $IV^3$ | $CV^3$ |
|---|---|---|---|---|---|---|---|
| 1 | 0,3 | 15,03 | -3,5 | 55,04 | -3,78 | 94,87 | -3,59 |
| 2 | 0,44 | 23,96 | 1,43 | 80,62 | 11,16 | 137,56 | 21,05 |
| 3 | 0,52 | 31,49 | 4,64 | 104,35 | 20,66 | 177,83 | 36,8 |
| 4 | 0,63 | 35,97 | 8,55 | 119,68 | 32,02 | 204,08 | 55,69 |
| 5 | 0,68 | 36,76 | 10,23 | 124,31 | 37,03 | 212,5 | 64,1 |
| 6 | 0,73 | 36,18 | 11,76 | 124,02 | 41,71 | 212,28 | 71,98 |
| 7 | 0,78 | 34,34 | 12,75 | 120,1 | 44,83 | 205,74 | 77,26 |
| 8 | 0,81 | 32,18 | 13,44 | 114,51 | 47,06 | 196,08 | 81,01 |
| 9 | 0,84 | 30,03 | 13,89 | 108,31 | 48,58 | 186,22 | 83,57 |
| 10 | 0,86 | 27,87 | 14,19 | 102,51 | 49,68 | 176,43 | 85,41 |
| 11 | 0,89 | 25,8 | 14,36 | 96,86 | 50,36 | 167,03 | 86,55 |
| 12 | 0,9 | 24,24 | 14,36 | 91,99 | 50,58 | 158,47 | 86,93 |
| 13 | 0,92 | 23,05 | 14,31 | 87,67 | 50,6 | 151,7 | 86,97 |
| 14 | 0,94 | 22,23 | 14,27 | 84,33 | 50,55 | 146,17 | 86,91 |
| 15 | 0,94 | 21,12 | 14,25 | 81,75 | 50,55 | 141,95 | 86,91 |
| 16 | 0,95 | 20,48 | 14,25 | 79,46 | 50,57 | 138,81 | 86,94 |
| 17 | 0,95 | 19,87 | 14,25 | 78,13 | 50,59 | 135,9 | 86,97 |
| 18 | 0,95 | 19,75 | 14,26 | 76,47 | 50,61 | 133,62 | 87,01 |

$IV^1$, $IV^2$, $IV^3$ are the first, second, and third averaged components of input vectors; $CV^1$, $CV^2$, $CV^3$ are the same components of the vectors of coefficients.

Table 2. Simulation of the convergence between input vectors and vectors of coefficients.

It is easy to see that input vectors and the vectors of coefficients indeed converged, though this process was incomplete probably because, as the mean AL approached to 1, changes in the system became practically impossible.

A goal-directed process was constructed as follows. First, one region of modules (or several regions consecutively) was considered as perceptive spot and the state of modules within this region was changed under a certain state of the environment. The position of the spot could not be changed during this stage. This corresponds to the formation of stable processors. And the modules beyond the spot were considered as flexible elements. At the second stage, perceptive spot covered all modules of the system, which obtained information from a neutral state of the environment. This stage, which corresponds to the interaction between stable processors and flexible elements and the formation of a goal-directed activity, is suggested to be rapid without interacting with the situation. Therefore, at the second stage there was no feedback loop between the system and the environment. A certain distribution of goals and means encoded by coefficient vectors and activation levels resulted from this stage. At the last stage, a new, local perceptive spot was established and the goal-directed process pursued its goal through interactions with the environment. The position of spot was able to change within the third stage.

First, consider the simulation of a goal-directed process with a simple goal. At stage 1, the constants of the environment were 80, 50, and 20. The center of perceptive spot was established at 0,85, the size of perceptive spot (p11) was 0,2. In addition, at this stage, p2 was 0,2 and p3 was 4,2. This stage lasted until the mean AL exceeded 0,2. At stage 2 all constants were 50 and the center of the spot was at 0,5 while p2 and p11 were 0,95 and p3 became 3 at this and last stages. At the start of the last stage all constants were 30, and the center was established at 0,25 while p2 and p11 were 0,2 again.

It was suggested that at stage 3 the process was to move perceptive spot to the right where there were stable processors, thus increasing CP. The state of the vectors of coefficients in the modules within the spot should meet the relationship between the components of coefficient vectors of stable processors caused by the different constants of the environment at stage 1. The components of input and coefficients vectors averaged across the modules within perceptive spot were used to describe the state of the process along with AL averaged across all modules. The results are in table 2

The table shows that at stage 3, the process was increasing CP and the relationship between the components of the vectors of coefficients gradually became similar to that between constants at stage 1. The opposite relationship between the components of input vectors results from formula 7, after inserting a constant as an input vector in it and taking the relationship between the components of CVs into account. Because the constants of the environment were equal at stage 3, the coefficient vectors of the system were influenced by these constants and, as a result, the relationship formed at stage 1 tended to disappear. This corresponds to the completion of the process owing to the influence of the situation. It is important to note that the action of the system cannot be explained by combination of the perseveratory activity of trained modules and the inactivity of untrained ones. The fact that at stage 3 the relationship between the components of the vectors of coefficients was already weakly present at 0,48, considerably beyond the area of modules changed at stage 1 means that a process including most modules indeed was formed at stage 2, while increasing the mean AL at stage 3 implies activity in modules untrained at stage 1.

In another simulation, a process with a complex goal, including two constituents, was formed. In this simulation, stage 1 was divided in two phases. At the first phase, all constants were 20, the center of perceptive spot was at 0, 85, p3 was 4,2 while p2 and p11 were 0,2. After eight iterations this phase was completed, all constants became 80 and the center of perceptive spot was moved to 0,65 without changing p2, p3, and p11. This was the second phase of stage 1 and four iterations were performed. Stage 2 in this simulation was the same as in the previous one. At the beginning of the last stage all constants were 10, and the center was established at 0, 25 while p2 and p11 were 0, 2 again.

It was suggested that the process was to move the center of spot to the right and because there could be two groups of stable processors. The components of the vectors of coefficients within the spot could firstly increase and later decrease but the components of input vectors might change in the opposite direction following formula 7. To some extent, this can be considered as a very primitive form of multilevel activity.

Because at any moment all constants were identical, the components of input and coefficients vectors in modules could be averaged within each vector and across all modules in the spot. As a result, one number was sufficient to describe the state of input or coefficients vectors within the spot at any iteration. In addition, AL averaged across all modules also was used as a characteristic of the process. The results of the simulation are in figure 2, where for convenience, CP and AL were multiplied by 100.

| Iteration | CP | AL | Constant[1] | Constant[2] | Constant[3] | IV[1] | IV[2] | IV[3] | CV[1] | CV[2] | CV[3] |
|---|---|---|---|---|---|---|---|---|---|---|---|
| | | | | | Stage 1 | | | | | | |
| 1 | 0,85 | 0,11 | 80 | 50 | 20 | 85,19 | 54,83 | 24,83 | 3,64 | 3,64 | 3,92 |
| 2 | 0,85 | 0,13 | 80 | 50 | 20 | 84,91 | 55,2 | 25,02 | 11,95 | 8,27 | 4,56 |
| 3 | 0,85 | 0,14 | 80 | 50 | 20 | 84,37 | 55,07 | 24,86 | 22,51 | 14,76 | 6,63 |
| 4 | 0,85 | 0,16 | 80 | 50 | 20 | 88,36 | 57,55 | 25,88 | 29,22 | 19,01 | 8,32 |
| 5 | 0,85 | 0,17 | 80 | 50 | 20 | 91,84 | 59,46 | 27,14 | 33,77 | 22,06 | 9,67 |
| 6 | 0,85 | 0,18 | 80 | 50 | 20 | 94,44 | 61,1 | 28,59 | 37,65 | 24,72 | 10,98 |
| 7 | 0,85 | 0,18 | 80 | 50 | 20 | 95,65 | 62,54 | 28,69 | 40,13 | 26,32 | 11,8 |
| 8 | 0,85 | 0,19 | 80 | 50 | 20 | 95,82 | 61,48 | 28,09 | 42,11 | 27,62 | 12,48 |
| 9 | 0,85 | 0,19 | 80 | 50 | 20 | 95,86 | 61,5 | 27,57 | 43,29 | 28,36 | 12,92 |
| 10 | 0,85 | 0,21 | 80 | 50 | 20 | 95,51 | 61,68 | 28,58 | 44,13 | 28,86 | 13,19 |
| | | | | | Stage 2 | | | | | | |
| 11 | 0,5 | 0,27 | 50 | 50 | 50 | 55,13 | 55,24 | 55,43 | 15,9 | 10,55 | 5,24 |
| 12 | 0,5 | 0,31 | 50 | 50 | 50 | 55,02 | 55,03 | 55,36 | 18,53 | 13,46 | 8,5 |
| 13 | 0,5 | 0,35 | 50 | 50 | 50 | 54,98 | 55,26 | 55,23 | 22,69 | 18,16 | 13,69 |
| 14 | 0,5 | 0,39 | 50 | 50 | 50 | 55,16 | 55,16 | 55,37 | 25,41 | 21,35 | 17,43 |
| | | | | | Stage 3 | | | | | | |
| 15 | 0,25 | 0,4 | 30 | 30 | 30 | 35,15 | 35,25 | 35,34 | 19,74 | 19,79 | 19,89 |
| 16 | 0,33 | 0,4 | 30 | 30 | 30 | 32,36 | 33,76 | 35,65 | 19,42 | 19,55 | 19,73 |
| 17 | 0,39 | 0,41 | 30 | 30 | 30 | 32,49 | 33,77 | 35,07 | 18,99 | 19,19 | 19,23 |
| 18 | 0,43 | 0,41 | 30 | 30 | 30 | 33,1 | 34,59 | 35,79 | 17,86 | 17,96 | 18,18 |
| 19 | 0,48 | 0,42 | 30 | 30 | 30 | 33,38 | 34,52 | 35,28 | 17,75 | 17,44 | 17,12 |
| 20 | 0,51 | 0,42 | 30 | 30 | 30 | 34,03 | 34,19 | 36,29 | 17,85 | 17,1 | 16,35 |
| 21 | 0,55 | 0,42 | 30 | 30 | 30 | 34,42 | 35,37 | 36,28 | 18,04 | 16,88 | 15,55 |
| 22 | 0,57 | 0,43 | 30 | 30 | 30 | 35,72 | 36,51 | 38,02 | 17,82 | 16,49 | 14,83 |
| 23 | 0,6 | 0,43 | 30 | 30 | 30 | 36,07 | 37,1 | 38,73 | 18,05 | 16,49 | 14,58 |
| 24 | 0,61 | 0,43 | 30 | 30 | 30 | 35,94 | 37,92 | 38,61 | 18,34 | 16,68 | 14,82 |
| 25 | 0,62 | 0,43 | 30 | 30 | 30 | 37,52 | 38,04 | 39,53 | 18,4 | 16,77 | 14,98 |
| 26 | 0,63 | 0,44 | 30 | 30 | 30 | 37,32 | 38,14 | 39,41 | 18,66 | 16,96 | 15,26 |
| 27 | 0,64 | 0,44 | 30 | 30 | 30 | 38,42 | 39,43 | 40,34 | 18,65 | 17,11 | 15,68 |
| 28 | 0,64 | 0,44 | 30 | 30 | 30 | 38,17 | 39,83 | 40,62 | 18,8 | 17,32 | 16,08 |
| 29 | 0,65 | 0,44 | 30 | 30 | 30 | 38,59 | 39,65 | 40,52 | 19 | 17,66 | 16,55 |
| 30 | 0,65 | 0,45 | 30 | 30 | 30 | 39,41 | 40,04 | 40,87 | 19,28 | 17,99 | 16,95 |

IV[1], IV[2], IV[3] are the first, second, and third averaged components of input vectors; CV[1], CV[2], CV[3] are the same components of the vectors of coefficients.

Table 3. The simulation of a goal-directed process with a simple goal

In my opinion, all of these simulations demonstrate that the processes constructed can be considered as goal-directed in the sense that there was a state (or states), which each process attempted to achieve using certain means. It is important to note that no innate criterion of functioning was used to construct and perform the processes and that the goals of the processes treated as a source of sustainability and its means were constructed together.

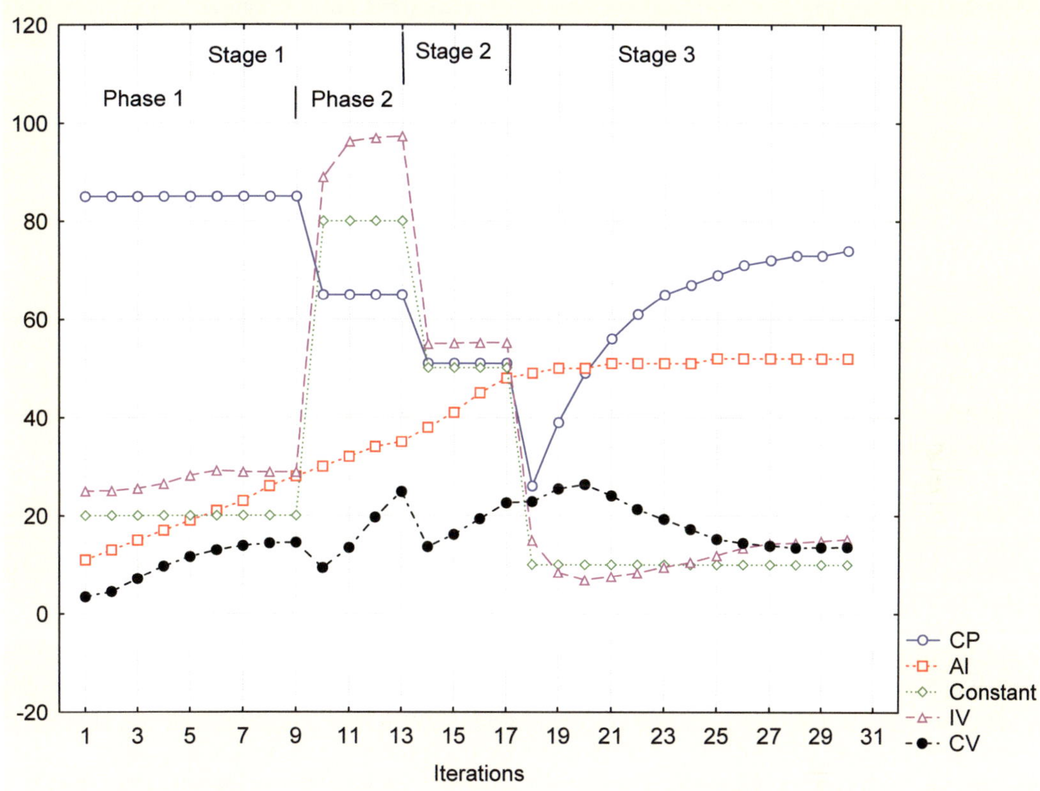


Fig. 4. The simulation of a goal-directed process with a two-constituent goal

Of course, it is easy to see certain shortcomings of the models. For example, the second process in model 2 was able to shift the center of the spot from one constituent to the other only because they were nearby. If the constituents would be established at opposite positions, such a shift would be impossible without changing the criterion of proximity. However, as is pointed out above the models simply are intended to demonstrate how the idea of joint synthesis can be applied to simulate goal-directed activity.

## 5. Future prospects

With the relevance of the idea of joint synthesis to simulate goal-directed activity as shown by the models above, it seems useful to consider some theoretical perspectives of this approach to the construction of intelligent systems. First, it is of importance to note that the consideration of the joint synthesis as the basic class of human activity and intelligence does not mean the abandonment of other classes and approaches. Indeed, successful attempts to achieve natural functionality often are not based on the imitation of a natural architecture – for example, cars can be considered as analogous to horses but cars have no legs, etc.

Similarly, it is not necessary that the joint synthesis is the only way to create full-scale artificial intelligence.

Though the joint synthesis seems appropriate to construct local projects like the models above, I will concentrate on the construction of general artificial intelligence. In my position, the construction of general AI should be a consequence of gradual changes within a system associated with its temporal functioning and complication, i.e. a result of a shift from short – term processes with simple goals and means to long-term processes with multilevel goals and complex methods. It is suggested that, although such a system may have complex innate architecture, the main source of its development is interactions with the system's environment via feedback loops.

The mechanism of joint synthesis is suggested to be a basis for such development. Indeed, because no innate criterion for the construction of goals is used, there are no constraints for the complication of goals. An appropriate means can be constructed for any goal because goals and means are constructed together,. As a result, the system is, in principle, able to adapt to any condition of training. It is suggested that the system can use blackboard architecture with flexible elements, then the formation and/or changes in elements can be considered as learning. The key component of the models above is the functional proximity that determines the possibility of the interaction between modules. It can be supposed that, in the hypothetical system, functional proximity can be dynamically changed in regard with the complexity and diversity of the system's components. The increase in the duration of goal-directed process may result from alterations in something similar to AL in the models above.

It can be suggested that the system should be able to create and use something similar to symbols. The generation of symbols may be performed as follows: because means in the system are constructed along with goals the system should be able to describe input and/or output information caused by these means in the terms consistent with goals and to prescribe a label associated with a goal to a sequence of such descriptions, thus creating symbols. The advantage of this method is that such symbols are grounded in the ongoing activity and therefore they can be used to construct novel goals and means through the involvement of symbols in the system's blackboard. Of course, this mechanism of symbolization can be gradual like changes in the duration of goal-directed processes. That is, at the beginning, the system will prescribe labels for the short sequences of ongoing states and gradually to for the longer and more complex ones.

It seems that the gradual increase in complexity and duration of goal-directed activities is a mechanism underlying human maturation. Indeed, in babyhood, the goal-directed activities of infants can be described as very short-term with primitive means but the activities of adults are long-lasting often life-ranging processes with very complex, hierarchical means and developed language. Therefore, the imitation of gradual human growth may be an effective way to achieve the human complexity of goal-directed activity and intelligence.

Of course, emphasis on the joint synthesis does not imply that other methods cannot be used within the given approach. For example, the criterion of minimal construction costs permits the system to synthesize a goal and means in any situation but if the minimum of costs found by the system is too local then the goal and means synthesized may be inappropriate to the situation. This mechanism seems to be an explanation for the fact that people sometimes are unable to solve simple problems, though their knowledge and skills are sufficient to find the right solution. To avoid similar difficulties an AI system may use the goals and means constructed jointly as a seed point in some cases and afterwards searches for goals and methods that are more suitable.

## 6. Conclusion

Since the advent of first computers, the idea of construction of artificial intelligence similar to that of human beings has driven the work of thousands of brilliant scientists and engineers. However, the result of their activity seems unsatisfactory as compared to, for example, advances in computer hardware. One of the most fundamental reasons for this situation may be that the mechanisms of human intelligence are unclear. Though the imitation of human intelligence is not a necessary characteristic of artificial intelligence, obviously a particular view on human intelligence is a very important heuristic. Therefore, an incorrect understanding of human intelligence can be a serious obstacle to construct intelligent systems. Intelligence is a characteristic of goal-directed systems and two classes of such systems can be easily derived from observations of animals and human beings. In my opinion, the classes that underlie most approaches to the construction of artificial intelligence are not sufficient to explain human activity. A broader classification of goal-directed activities suggests such processes can be described as a two-dimensional structure rather than a one-dimension one. In such structure there is a cell where in my opinion, humans can be located i.e., humans are goal-directed systems that synthesize arbitrary goals and means together. Though the idea of joint synthesis seems contradictory to some aspects of everyday experience, it is consistent with psychological evidence. In addition, there is neural evidence favoring this supposition. Simple computer models demonstrate that the idea of joint synthesis can be applied to simulate goal-directed activity. I suggest that the idea of joint synthesis can be a useful method to advance research in the construction of intelligent systems.

## 7. Appendix

Model 1

$p2=3*10^{-6}$ ; p3=0,99; p4=0,001

Model 2

p1=1; p4=2; p5=0, 3; p6=0,98; p7=0,5; p8=0,3; p9=0,8; p10=0,8

## 8. References


Asaad, W. F., Rainer, G. & Miller, E. K. (2000). Task-specific neural activity in the primate prefrontal cortex. *Journal of Neurophysiology*, 84, 451–459.

Bäck, T. (1996). *Evolutionary Algorithms in Theory and Practice: Evolution Strategies, Evolutionary Programming, Genetic Algorithms.* Oxford Univ. Press.

Bertalanffy, L. von, (1968). *General Systems Theory*.

Bertino, E, Piero, G & Zarria, B.C. (2001*). Intelligent Database Systems.* Addison-Wesley Professional.

Buller, D. J. (1998) DeFreuding evolutionary psychology: adaptation and human motivation, in Hardcastle, V. G., Ed. *Psychology Meets Biology: Connections, Conjectures, Constraints.* MIT Press/Bradford Books. http://cogprints.soton.ac.uk/documents /disk0/00/00/03/26/cog00000326-00/defreud.htm

Cooper, R. P., & Shallice, T. (1995). Soar and the case for unified theories of cognition. *Cognition* , 55,2,:115-49.

Corkill, D.D. (1991). Blackboard Systems. *AI Expert*, 6(9),40-47.

Corsini, R.J. & Auerbach, A.J. (1998). *Concise encyclopedia of psychology*. Wiley.

Craig, I. (1995). *Blackboard Systems.*

Evans, J. St. B. T. (2003). In two minds: dual-process accounts of reasoning. *Trends in Cognitive Sciences* , 10, 454-459.

Fuster, J.M. (1997). Network memory. *Trends Neuroscience*, 20, 451–459

Haykin, S (1998). *Neural Networks: A Comprehensive Foundation*. Prentice Hall

Heckhausen, H. (1980). *Motivation und Handeln.* Springer-Verlag

Jackson, P. (1998). *Introduction to Expert Systems.*

Joseph, R. (1999). Frontal lobe psychopathology: mania, depression, confabulation, catatonia, perseveration, obsessive compulsions, and schizophrenia. *Psychiatry*, 62(2), 138-72.

Holland, J.H. (1975). *Adaptation in natural and artificial systems.* University of Michigan Press, Ann Arbor.

Leslie, K. P. , Littman, M.L & Moore, A.W. (1996). Reinforcement Learning: A Survey. *Journal of Artificial Intelligence Research.* 4, 237–285.

Luria, A.R. (1966). Higher cortical functions in man. Tavistock. Publications, Andover, Hants.

Luria, A.R. (1973). *Foundations of neuropsychology*. Moscow State University Press (in Russian).

Luria, A.R. (1982). Variants of the "frontal" syndrome. In Luria A.R, Homskaya E.D. (eds.), *Functions of the frontal lobes of the brain*, pp. 8-48, Nauka ( in Russian).

Miller, B.T. & D'Esposito, M. (2005). Searching for ''the top'' in top-down control. *Neuron*, 48, 535–538.

Miller, E.K. & Cohen, J.D. (2001). An integrative theory of prefrontal cortex function. *Annual Review Neuroscience*, 24,167–202

Newell, A. (1990*). Unified theories of cognition*. Cambridge, MA: Harvard.

Prudkov, P. N. & Rodina, O.N.(1999). Synthesis of Purposeful Processes. *PSYCOLOQUY* 10(070). psyc.99.10.070.purposeful-processes.1.prudkov.

Rodina, O.N. & Prudkov, P.N. (2005). The principle of joint synthesis in purposeful processes. *MGU Bulletin Psychology*, 2, 77-86 (in Russian).

Russell, S. J. & Norvig, P. (2003). *Artificial Intelligence: A Modern Approach.* Upper Saddle River, NJ: Prentice Hall.

Stanovich, K.E. & West, R.F. (2000). Individual differences in reasoning: Implications for the rationality debate. *Behavioral and Brain Sciences*, 23, 645-726.

Sutton, R. S. & Barto, A.G. (1998). *Reinforcement Learning*: *An Introduction*. MIT Press.

Tooby, J. & Cosmides L., (1992) The psychological foundations of culture, in J. H. Barkow, L. Cosmides, and J. Tooby (eds.) *The Adapted Mind: Evolutionary Psychology and the Generation of Culture* pp. 19-136, NY Oxford University Press.

Tooby, J., Cosmides, L. & Barrett, H. C. (2005). Resolving the debate on innate ideas: Learnability constraints and the evolved interpenetration of motivational and conceptual functions. In Carruthers, P., Laurence, S. & Stich, S. (Eds.), *The Innate Mind: Structure and Content.* NY: Oxford University Press.

Van der Velde, F. & de Kamps, M. (2003). A model of visual working memory in PFC. *Neurocomputing*, 52-54, 419-424.

Van der Velde, F. & de Kamps, M. (2006). Neural blackboard architectures of combinatorial structures in cognition. *Behavioral and Brain Sciences*, 29, 37-70

Wood J.N. & Grafman J. (2003). Human prefrontal cortex: processing and representational perspectives. *Nature Review Neuroscience*, 4, 139–147.

16

# Innovative Intelligent Services for Supporting Cognitively Impaired Older Adults and Their Caregivers

Anelia Mitseva[1], Sofoklis Kyriazakos[2], Antonis Litke[3], Paolo Barone[4], Alessandro Mamelli[4], Nikolaos Papadakis[3] and Neeli R. Prasad[2]
[1]*North Denmark EU-Office/Aalborg Municipality,*
[2]*Center for TeleInFrastructure/Aalborg University,*
[3]*Converge ICT Solutions,*
[4]*Hewlett Packard Italy,*
[1,2]*Denmark*
[3]*Greece*
[4]*Italy*

## 1. Introduction

### 1.1 European pilot project ISISEMD

ISISEMD project started in March 2009 is a European pilot project with the main aim to design, implement and test in real-life conditions innovative intelligent services for older adults with mild cognitive impairments and their formal and family care-givers (ISISEMD, 2009). Their ultimate goal is to improve the Quality of Life of the elderly and to help them to live more independently. The technology service platform is integration of systems from Hewlett Packard (Italy), Alcatel-Lucent (Italy), Converge ICT Solutions (Greece), Eltronic A/S (Denmark) and Socrate Medical (Italy). The service platform has been tested, validated and evaluated in four different European pilot sites (Frederikshavn in Denmark, Lappeenranta in Finland, Trikala in Greece and Belfast in UK) for a duration of more than one year and based on the outcome from the real-life operations and user feedback, it has been optimised, improved and adapted for diverse regional conditions. This has been a very challenging process because the user and functional requirements are very high w.r.t. intuitive user interface with minimum user interaction, diverse needs of the main user groups, personalisation needs, requirements for stable operation despite of the fact that it is a pilot system, but working in real-life conditions and exposed to interruptions in connectivity, hardware failures, human errors, etc.

### 1.2 Understanding the unmet needs of the end-user groups of ISISEMD services

According to the 2009 World Alzheimer Report, the number of people with dementia in Europe is conservatively anticipated to increase by 40% over the next 20 years mainly due to the increase in the ageing population (ALZ, 2009). This means that, due to limited resources, there will be a significant challenge for the social care providers to meet their needs when the illness progresses. Currently, this group of citizens lives in the community and is being taken care of by their families which exposes them to care stress, social isolation, reduced employment and in many cases also leading to health deterioration. There are many types of dementia and for each person the disease develops individually. In general this group of older adults lacks structure of the day, their abstract thinking is drastically reduced, there are risks for home incidents from fire or a food forgotten on the cooker or they can get lost outside their home. All these risks prevent them to live independently and their family care-givers suffer a lot of stress and reduced quality of life. Their Quality of Life (QOL) can be maintained or increased and care stress can be reduced if intelligent technology services give the family care-givers a helping hand to notify about risks in the home or provide support information to the elderly person (EP) about the current day and time, upcoming appointments, etc. ISISEMD services have been initially designed for three main end-user groups - the older adults with mild dementia or mild cognitive impairments, their informal care-givers (partners, closest family, neighbours) and the formal carers.

The holistic approach of the ISISEMD services has a big potential for a positive impact but this requires "a smart system" with very high level of autonomous operation and intelligence of the services so they provide the exact type of home support needed for the specific dyad "elderly-family care-giver", with minimum interaction from the elderly and care-givers part. At the same time, the technology and the services must be "invisible" for the users and require very little or no user interaction at all.

The major contribution of ISISEMD project is that it aims at improving quality of life of fragile user groups by offering home support technology services in a holistic way, fulfilling most of their un-met needs. It involves all relevant end-user groups in the whole process of design, validation and assessment of the intelligent services in real-life conditions and in diverse regional settings. In this way it advances the developments one step closer in understanding the challenges that accompany the process of introducing Information and Communication Technology (ICT) services to older adults with mild cognitive impairments living in the community and their care-givers. Last but not least, it shares hands-on experiences and best practices.

### 1.3 Chapter outline

The challenges listed above were addressed by introducing intelligence in almost all of the services, in data and profile management, in the networking and in the integration and optimisation process. In this chapter we describe the final outcome of 30-month efforts, presented as follows: Section 2 presents a short overview of ISISEMD services. Section 3 focuses on highlighting the intelligent features in the service functionalities. Section 4 describes how ISISEMD project advances State-of-the-Art for intelligent systems and the advantages of ISISEMD system in comparison with other systems. Section 5 gives details how the services were piloted in real-life. Qualitative technical evaluation, service validation and user evaluation for satisfaction and acceptance were carried out and outcome from them is presented in Sections 6, 7 and 8 respectively. The positive impact from the use of the services is depicted with examples of "success stories" and users' statements in Section 9. The chapter is concluded in Section 10.

## 2. ISISEMD service platform – a short overview

The overall architecture of ISISEMD is composed in such a way that on one hand it fulfils the service requirements, and on the other hand it addresses the reality to make the different systems (also identified as x-Servers) to be integrated into a whole with a web-portal functioning as a common entry point for the ISISEMD system. The portal is the actual single point of entrance into the ISISEMD system and is the component responsible for the management of the users as well as the association of users with services and other users. It contains various functional sub-components such as a User Management module, an Authentication and Authorisation module, a Logging module, and a Reporting module. At the user side, the central unit is a computer with a touch screen, which is called Carebox. High level architecture of ISISEMD platform is presented on the figure below.

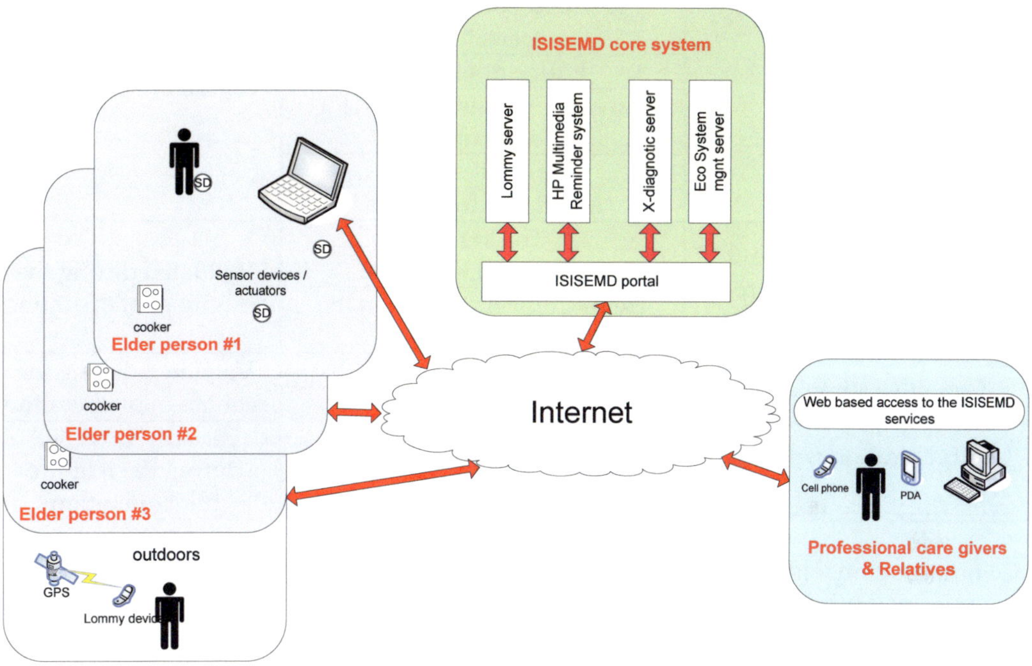


Fig. 1. High level architecture of the ISISEMD service platform

ISISEMD services for cognitively impaired adults include (Table 1): home and personal safety observations; reminders and prompts for basic daily activities - pre-defined reminders exist but there is also the possibility to set up and show personalised "free text reminders"; services for cognitive stimulation (Memory Lane shows a picture slide show on the Carebox and Brain Games that can be played on the Carebox); video communication service with care-givers; location service when the person is out of the home with the help of a simple GPS device called Lommy; emergency contact button in the home (Help button on the Carebox touch screen) and outside the home (panic button on the GPS device).

ISISEMD services for the formal (FCG) and informal care-givers (ICG) include: alerts, notifications, and alarm services which are distributed by mobile phone or email; an overview of daily activities shown on the portal; video-call service for communication with the elderly;

lifestyle pattern information over a period of time and remote doctor service. The added value for the informal care-givers relies on the fact of reducing the care stress towards an elder person and of being able to have the ability to receive information about potentially dangerous situations for their relative. This gives the feeling of safety for the beloved people and to be able to use the services without having any extensive knowledge on ICT - for instance a relative who takes care for the partner can be also a senior citizen. More details for the characteristics of the end-user groups and the added value for them from using the ICT services are provided in (Mitseva et al., 2009).

| Service type | Service name | Validation status |
|---|---|---|
| Home safety | Cooking monitor | Validated during the real-life pilot operation |
| | Smoke/ Fire detection alarm | |
| | Kitchen/Bathroom flood detection | |
| | Fridge door alarm | |
| | Leaving bed during night for long time | |
| | Wake up sensor | |
| | Intelligent front door | |
| Structure of the day and contact to informal care-givers in case of emergency | To Do List, Calendar, Time/Date | Validated during the real-life pilot operation |
| | Help/Contact request on the touch screen | |
| Cognitive stimulation | Brain Games | Validated during the real-life pilot operation |
| | Memory Lane | |
| Communication with care-givers | Videophone | Partially validated during the real-life pilot operation |
| Communication with health and care professionals | Remote Doctor | Demo evaluation |
| | Medication Manager | Not validated during the real-life pilot operation |
| Outdoor safety | Outdoor positioning | Validated during the real-life pilot operation |
| | Panic button with outdoor position | |
| | Fall alarm outdoor | |
| Professional care-givers support | Lifestyle Pattern | Partially validated during the real-life pilot operation |

Table 1. List of ISISEMD services

Similarly, the ISISEMD platform adds value to the social care providers. They can unobtrusively monitor some activities that take place in homes and outdoors through general purpose, off-the-shelf devices. They have the ability to save travel time for performing unnecessary homes visits to the clients and to communicate remotely with the elderly clients using video-call service, and in this way, there is more time for care for more clients.

The table above gives an overview of the ISISEMD services. In the following sections we focus on the intelligent features of the service platform.

## 3. Intelligence in the service platform

One of the advantages of the ISISEMD system is the hidden intelligence in the provided services. The basic idea is to abstract the services and make them transparent so the end users cannot actually realise the system complexity as they may not have much knowledge on ICT and this is not expected either. Drawing on this, the services act and pro-act in such a way that they are to define any critical circumstances that might occur before these actually happen and thus, they try to anticipate any consequences (e.g. the relatives of a person will receive a notification if the person is cooking for longer time than expected, anticipating thus a possible danger of having a fire in the home). This intelligence is possible to implement through a high-end home automation system identified as the Ecosystem.

### 3.1 Home safety services

Home safety services consist of sensors for monitoring the safety in the home environment. They function through sending email/sms to care-givers, posting alarms or notification messages on the web portal in cases of alarm events from the intelligent front door sensor, cooking monitor, fridge door sensor, fire/smoke sensor, flood detection sensor, bed sensors and/or motion detectors.

The Ecosystem part of the Carebox technically consists of a virtual machine that runs a local instance of an Ecosystem Domotics server, which is a reduced set of services and processes tailored for the specific requirements. This server is responsible for monitoring and responding to events from the various input sensors in the patient's home. A special ISISEMD-specific service installed on each Domotics module is responsible for relaying those events up to the central X-Server hub process on the portal-side of the server to be evaluated and acted upon if required. Through this fact, a delegation of intelligence is possible to the first level of reaction so as to increase the efficiency of the whole system.

An example of domotic service operation is explained by the control of the home cooker - the event is triggered by the fact that the person turns on the cooker. This activates an event of setting the appropriate timers that will monitor the duration of the cooker being on. Alert messages will be issued accordingly and the measures will be taken in such a way that will prohibit an accident and preventing fires, etc. Respective workflows are triggered by events captured by other sensors.

Elderly person is staying at home alone and the home is equipped with the aforementioned home automation services for preventing the events that have been mentioned. The services are pre-configured and running in the background without disturbing his daily life. Whenever the events that trigger the services are activated, the workflows will start-up to deliver the services.

#### 3.1.1 Cooking monitor service

The purpose of having installed a cooking monitor in the elderly peoples' homes is significant for the safety of receiving an alarm in case of having forgotten to turn off the cooker. If an elderly has forgotten to turn off the cooker, a care-giver will be able to view the current status displayed on the portal when logging in. For instance, on the service page on the portal, it will be displayed if an elderly has "started cooking", "cooking on" or "not cooking" and the last time when this event took place will also be illustrated. If for instance the cooker has been on for a while or for too long, the system will send the information containing an alert message (email/sms) to the care-giver. At the same time, at elderly's home, a voice message will be played to the elderly person from the Carebox, and a blinking message will turn up on the top part of the Carebox screen to warn him/her about the forgotten activity. The duration for cooking before receiving an alert is to be adjusted depending on the "life style pattern" of the specific elderly person. For example, the time for the duration of a cooker being turned on for a while can be adjusted before it is to trigger an alarm to care-givers. The voice and text message for cooking for a while is a prompt for the elderly to react, defined as first level reaction. Then if the system detects that there is no response from the elderly, an alarm could be sent to care-giver for example that the cooker has not been turned off for more than a pre-defined period of time – this is characterised as the second level reaction. All these events, communicated as cooker on, cooker off, message for cooking for a while or for too long, are posted on the message board on the web portal for overview purpose of the daily activities. The workflow for this service is depicted on Figure 2 below.

Depending on the preferences of the regional care provider and the family care-givers, the cooking monitoring service can work with either one of the three installations - one temperature sensor, with two temperature sensors or with a power relay. In case of two temperature sensors, a threshold for temperature difference can be adjusted from the web portal.

### 3.1.2 Smoke/fire detection service

The purpose of the smoke/fire alarm is to send information for smoke or fire alarm to the web portal. Furthermore, the system notifies the elderly person on the Carebox about the dangerous situation. At the same time it notifies the caregivers by SMS or email. If care-giver accesses this service, a care-giver can see if a fire alarm is in progress, the last time when a fire alarm may have occurred, and if so, the care-giver can view the time when it ended (i.e. it was reset). All these events are posted on the web portal in the list with recent events so the care-giver can see them. If there is event "smoke/fire alarm ON", at the same time the system shows a blinking message on the top line of the Carebox and is "telling" to the elderly person that there is smoke/fire detected in the home and he/she needs to react. This notification is repeated periodically on the Carebox until the event "smoke/fire alarm OFF" is detected by the system. Improvement suggested during the real-life pilot operation for the smoke/fire alarm service was to send one additional SMS - initially the service was designed to send one SMS in case of "alarm on" event but there was a need for similar notification SMS for "alarm off" event and this was implemented. This was needed because of some cases with false alarms during the test period and also due to the fact that very often more than one relative receives SMS alarms but depending on their agreement, one is to react in case of incident. The second SMS was to inform all of them that there is no more danger.

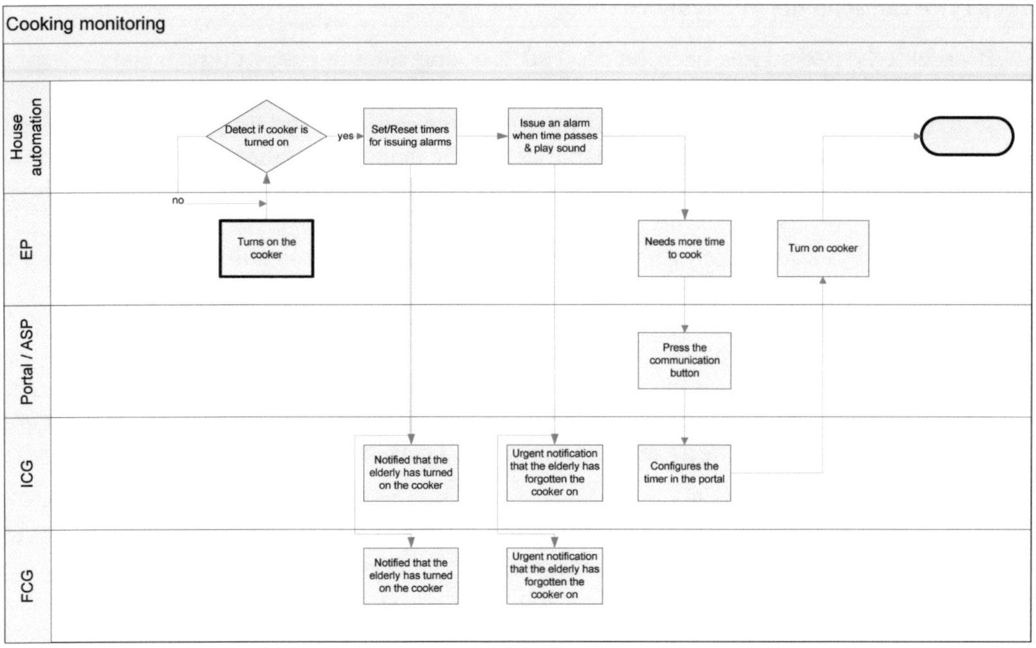


Fig. 2. Workflow for service "cooking monitor"

### 3.1.3 Fridge door service

This service monitors the door of the refrigerator. Once the elderly person opens the refrigerator door, the system will wait for it to be closed after a certain predefined time period. If it is not closed in the specified amount of time, an alert will be issued:

- Letting a caregiver know if the door has been forgotten open for too long - by email or SMS.
- The open, close or alarm events will be posted on the portal
- The following parameter can be adjusted: Time duration, since the fridge door was opened, after which to send an alert to a caregiver that the fridge door has probably been forgotten open (specified in minutes).

If there is an alarm situation, the system shows a blinking message on the top line of the Carebox and is "telling" to the elderly that the fridge door has been opened for too long and he/she needs to react. This notification is repeated periodically on the Carebox until the event "fridge door closed" is detected by the system.

### 3.1.4 Bed service

Alarm is triggered if an elderly has left the bed for a long time during the night. Furthermore, this service allows a caregiver to be notified about disturbances or significant alterations in the patient's sleep pattern. From the service page, a caregiver can view whether the elderly person is in the bed or not, the last time the patient sat or slept on it, and the last time the elderly person got up from the bed.

The service can send the following alerts:

- If an elderly person has been on the bed too long time (a case in which the care-giver assumes that the elderly might be experiencing difficulty or health issues).
- If an elderly person has left the bed too long time during a certain period of time (such as night time) and which might mean that elderly person has fallen down.

The following three parameters can be adjusted:

- Time duration after which an alarm is issued, if an elderly is still in bed (specified in minutes)
- Time duration, during "night time" (see next parameter) after which a care-giver should be alerted if the elderly is out of bed.
- The start and end times of the 'night time' period. These two times tell the service what time is considered to be "night time", i.e. the period during which the care-giver wants to receive alerts if the elderly leaves the bed for a certain time (see previous parameter).

Example of these parameters is when the system raises an alarm if the patient is in bed for longer than 10 hours, and also in case the patient left the bed between 10pm and 6am for longer than one hour (specified as 60 minutes). Since very often the elderly person takes a nap in the afternoon, it was suggested by the regional partners that additional time period of afternoon sleep is defined, similar to the night-time sleep period. However, this could not be implemented in the time frame of the project.

### 3.1.5 Intelligent front door service

This service monitors the status of the elderly's front door and monitors the presence of the elderly in the home with the help of motion detection (and bed sensor information if such a sensor is installed). On the main service page a care-giver can see the status of the front door, as well as the last times it was opened or closed and the last time a movement was recorded in the home.

Line for current status also shows whether the system has assumed that the elderly is present in the home or not at this moment. The system makes this conclusion by monitoring the various sensors, such as cooking sensor, door activity sensor, fridge door activity sensor, motion detection activity sensor. Each time when an activity is detected by one of these sensors it assumes that the elderly is active and in the home. The service also monitors the bed status (if bed sensor is installed), so that if there is no activity but the elderly is sleeping then this too will indicate an elderly's presence in the home. If there is no activity on any of these sensors for a certain amount of time (customisable from the service screen in the web portal) then the system will report to care-givers that the elderly is absent from the home and will make notification accordingly. Alerts are sent if the front door has been opened for more than a certain amount of minutes, when an elderly is absent from the house for certain hours and if an elderly is assumed to be absent from home for too long time.

The front door alarm is a service that can be customised depending on the elderly life pattern. For this purpose, four parameters can be adjusted according to:

- Time duration after which the front door will issue an alert if it stays opened, specified in minutes.

- Time duration of inactivity that determines when the system decides that the patient is out of the home (see above description).
- Time duration after which the system will issue an alert if the elderly is considered inactive (see above description), specified in minutes.
- The start and end times of the "night time" period. These two times tell the service what time is considered to be "night time", i.e. the period during which the care-giver wants to receive alerts if the patient leaves the home.

During the pilot operation, there were some cases when bed sensors could not be used - for example the elderly sleeps on a folding sofa and a bed sensor cannot be installed or if the elderly does not want to have a bed sensor installed due to some health problems. In this case, the current settings of this service cannot allow for optimal operation during the night period. Therefore, one of the suggestions for improvement was for the intelligent front door service to work without considering information from the bed sensor during the night. However, the final solution could not be implemented by the end of the project; instead a temporary solution was found for the special cases.

### 3.2 Carebox for the end-user

The only visible interface toward the ISISEMD platform for the elderly persons is the touch screen-enabled device installed in their homes. The motivations behind the selection of such kind of device are multiple:

1. First of all, it is very difficult for people with cognitive impairments to learn how to interact with new technologies: since they tend to forget what they already know, it would not be effective at all introducing in their life new elements that are not familiar to them
2. In addition, for the same reason described above, the need for direct interaction between them and the system must be reduced to the minimum, if not eliminated
3. Finally, in the cases where such interactions cannot be eliminated, they must be performed in the simplest and more intuitive modality possible

The touch screen-enabled device selected for providing the ISISEMD services for the end user can fulfil the above-mentioned requirements in the way that:

1. The shape, dimensions and aspect of the device are indeed identical to the ones of a television set, an appliance whose diffusion, in the last fifty years, has reached almost every home (at least in the developed countries). This means that it can be introduced in the elderly persons' homes in a natural manner
2. The device can provide different interaction levels; the level for each end-user can be configured (at any time and remotely) by a care-giver based on the level of impairment. In the simplest configuration, no interaction possibilities at all are provided
3. The touch screen modality is currently the simplest and more intuitive technology available to interact with a computing system, which requires a very low level of training and cognitive capabilities

From a functional perspective, the device plays several roles:

- Acts as the collector for all the messages that must be shown to the end-user. Running an intelligent software module, it makes decisions on when a message must be delivered and, based on several static and dynamic parameters - such as the user profile, the configuration made by the care-givers, the importance of the event to be notified, the surrounding context - what the proper formats for the delivery are (e.g. only text, text and audio message, text and sound, etc.)

- Allows the user to proactively use the platform by pressing a single "soft" button on the graphical user interface (GUI) to ask assistance from the care-givers. This can be accomplished by pressing with a finger on a help button which triggers the sending of notification messages in the form of SMS or email, or a button for receiving a video-conference session
- Stimulates the cognitive capabilities of mild-dementia affected people by displaying information that helps them in maintaining the structure of the day (e.g. date and time) and the memories (e.g. slide show of personal pictures meaningful to them). Provides possibility to the elderly to confirm an activity by pressing a single "soft" button on GUI if elderly is able to interact with the system

The intelligent software module running on the device is constantly in communication with a central server module and is capable to enable/disable in real-time every single service provisioned, based on the configuration decided by a care-giver. Accordingly, it repaints the GUI elements displayed on the screen adding or removing them dynamically, for example by adding a new upcoming event in the list of "Next events". In addition to this, the module constantly considers the user context, leveraging the device equipment (e.g. the embedded web camera) or data coming from other devices (e.g. domotic sensors) and takes decisions based on the current situation.

Here follow some examples:

- During the night time the system enters an energy saving mode by turning off the screen. Such modality is interrupted (the screen is displayed again) if movement is detected in the surrounding by the context monitoring module
- Multimedia alarm messages related to dangerous conditions in the home (e.g. a fire alarm or a cooker left on for a long time) are played on the device speakers and shown on the device screen on behalf of the domotic module. In this way, the elderly person can react to the situation (e.g. switching off the cooker) or, in case he/she does not within a pre-configured timeframe, alarm messages are sent to the care-givers and relatives in form of SMS and email
- In case of external conditions that temporarily prevent the module to provide some of the functionalities (e.g. instable network connection), it changes the display layout showing proper notification messages which inform of the unavailability of one or more services. At the same time, a server side module is capable of detecting the error conditions and of alerting the proper actors (for example the service support team) to take action. As soon as the error conditions disappear, the module automatically returns in full-operation mode. Notifications are sent also to the care-givers.

The layout of the GUI displayed on the Carebox and the related contents are strongly dependent on the settings made by the care-givers for each end-user. As already mentioned, the system is quite flexible, so that the care-givers can enable/disable at runtime a different set of services for each user depending on the level of cognitive impairments. Such configuration is made by accessing the web portal. Anyway, there is a core set of essential services that are provisioned to all the end users (since they are strictly related to their safety) that require the delivery of notifications to them by means of the Carebox. Such notifications can be divided into two main categories:

1. Messages coming from the domotic sensors, which are strictly related to the end-user safety
2. Messages configured by the care-givers on the web portal which should help the end user in maintaining the structure of the day

The configuration for messages of type 1 is made by the care-giver by accessing the "Domotic services" section of the web portal, and by filling the proper settings as described in the previous section on domotic-related services.

The configuration for messages of type 2 is made by accessing the "To Do List" and "Calendar" section of the web portal. This section provides the caregivers with a huge set of possibilities for configuring and scheduling the prompt messages that must be shown on the screen of an end user:

- It is possible either to choose among a pre-defined set of commonly used messages or to create custom ones, so called "free text reminders"
- It can be selected the format for the notification: text, audio or both
- It is possible to associate a sound to the message, to catch the end-user´s attention
- It can be defined how many times the message must be played and shown before disappearing from the screen and the interval among repetitions
- The system allows to configure every desired scheduling pattern for the message:
  - One-time only at a specified date and time
  - Recurring message (every day, once a week, once a month, once a year at the same time)
  - Recurring only in specified date ranges
- It is possible for care-givers to specify, for each configured reminder, if a corresponding confirmation button must appear on the Carebox screen together with the message. If the message is not confirmed (e.g. the end user does not press the confirmation button), notifications are sent to the caregiver by SMS and email
- In case the reminder requires confirmation, the care-givers can define on the service page some rules for how and when they want to receive SMS or email messages in case of missing confirmation

Every Carebox is constantly in communication with the server-side module handling the configuration of the reminders and updates in almost real time for every modification, which affects the set of messages to display.

### 3.3 Knowledge and data management

In general knowledge management comprises a range of strategies and practices used in an organisation to identify, create, represent, distribute, and enable adoption of insights and experiences. Such insights and experiences comprise knowledge, either embodied in individuals or embedded in organisational processes or practice.

In ISISEMD platform knowledge is being used in order to assist the care-givers to take the appropriate decisions. Knowledge comprises the aggregated information gathered from various sources (sensors, log data, events, etc) and is being considered in the service provisioning.

A dedicated service directly related with this is a Lifestyle pattern service. This service is not based on one workflow. It is a rather complex service that has to do with monitoring and logging the various events that happen in the domotics and Carebox environment of the elderly and in the sequel applying Business Intelligence in order to derive the patterns and the life style of the elderly. Based on this, important conclusions can be made for further optimisation of the home automations and care-giver strategies can be better adapted.

### 3.4 System optimisation for real-life operation

During the pilot operation, diverse interruptions of the normal system operation were observed due to some real-life factors, e.g. internet disconnection problems, high sensitivity of the touch screen, etc., all of them leading to generating false alarms or service unavailability. Therefore, additional layer of intelligence was introduced by fall back solutions and allowing for a higher tolerance to interruptions without jeopardising the safety of the end user. Also in case of planned technical maintenance operations, messages are sent to all care-givers and in case of portal or x- servers' unavailability, a notification is sent to the technical support team.

## 4. Advancing state-of-the-art for intelligent systems

### 4.1 Service oriented architecture

One of the major challenges for ISISEMD platform is the sustainability in the long-run, which can only be guaranteed if the technology can support a long term evolution, considering the user needs and the competition. Therefore, ISISEMD platform deploys a pure Service Oriented Architecture (SOA) that ensures the service integrity and the extensibility of the platform.

Service level agreement (SLA)-based web service infrastructures are the key for driving automation and system dynamics for ISISEMD platform. Web Services Distributed Management (WSDM) specifications and Web Services (WS)-Management only support a crude description of consumer-centric Quality of Service (QoS) properties not suitable to fully describe ISISEMD application requirements. However, the main challenge for ISISEMD is the specification of a QoS at the various levels in the value chain, including the ability to translate of high-level business objectives to low-level resource provisioning policies. Furthermore, well-defined metrics need to exist at all levels to allow monitoring and reporting of service usage against SLAs.

ISISEMD applications necessarily involve a network of services for their implementation. The application workflows involved, including both data and control flows, can be complex and require explicit support for e-care aspects and constraints.

The use of workflows for "programming in the large" to compose web services has led to significant interest in a standard workflow language within the web services stack. WS-BPEL (BPEL) has major industry support and was created through the agreed merge of their earlier web service composition languages WSFL and XLANG respectively. WS-BPEL and is being promoted as a standard through OASIS (BPEL). The work of the workflow management coalition WfMC (WFMC) with the resulting XPDL standard (XPDL) provides a higher level of abstraction of workflow and aims to provide a format for process design. The focus of BPEL, and most business-oriented workflow languages, is control flow. Extensive research on workflow control patterns has shown that all languages have limitations in terms of what can be easily expressed (AALST, 2003). This insufficient expressivity and lack of rigorous semantics to allow automated checks on correctness and completeness mean that BPEL and related languages are unlikely to be a suitable foundation for ISISEMD.

The scientific community has also conducted considerable research into information and data processing applications that have similarities to some of the ISISEMD applications. However, these languages and tools do not support the constructs needed in ISISEMD and are not designed for Business to Business (B2B) applications that require distributed management, and trust and security based on the emerging industry Web Service standards.

Beyond this, comes research into intelligent, autonomous, goal-oriented and knowledge-based service infrastructures. These infrastructures include facilities for: dynamic negotiation, adaptation and configuration; intelligent scheduling, resource and service selection; and optimised job execution and management. The infrastructure itself is able to decide on how to react in case of unexpected situations using self-organisation, self-management, etc. Of particular relevance to ISISEMD is the use of semantic service descriptions to facilitate autonomic discovery, composition and use of services, for example within an organisation as an approach to resource management.

ISISEMD makes heavy use of emerging web service standards, including the areas of semantic service descriptions, SLAs and agreements, workflow and orchestration, management, trust and security, and transport and messaging. A significant research element of the work includes determining exactly how to apply and extend these standards in order to support ISISEMD applications. A particular challenge is balancing the use of industry standards, which are the key to meeting business to business needs and hence exploitation of the ISISEMD results. The standards that ISISEMD consider and engage with are manifold. Competing proposals from industry vendors may eventually converge through consolidation, but whilst this has the potential to improve interoperability, it often does so at the expense of compromising the specification.

In particular, ISISEMD adopts WS-Convergence where possible and evaluate/build upon/adapt the standards used for management, in particular to enable distributed management of networks of services that deliver real time applications in inter-organisation value-chains. Moreover, it uses Simple Knowledge Organisation System (SKOS) and Web Ontology Language (OWL), for formally describing SLA terms and their relationships, including QoS attributes of e-care applications. In particular, we address the problem of mapping high-level business objectives to low-level resource provisioning policies in a more automated, robust and verifiable way.

### 4.2 Potentials of ISISEMD services and limitations

Summarising the key features and comparing them with the existing solutions available in the market, ISISEMD service platform has the following advantages:

- Different levels of interaction and easy interactive features, allowing the elderly to ask for contact&help, confirm actions, play cognitive stimulation games, receive video calls
- Highly customized and targeting all user groups involved in care provision for a person with mild dementia or cognitive impairments and the person himself
- Integrated system with open architecture that can be easily extended with new features in the future
- Focuses on mild dementia persons in a holistic way, looking at all their needs (home and person safety, promote independence, prevent social isolation, increase quality of life, etc)
- Maintain or increase quality of life not only to persons with mild dementia, but also for the relatives who suffer care stress and are also socially isolated because of caring for the dementia relative
- Able to offer additional services with disease progression

On the other hand studying the competition, following points have to be considered:

- An end-to-end service approach should be addressed, so that this solution can be easily deployed. That includes: helpdesk, formal and informal care-givers, technicians, all accessible through a single entity
- The "breakeven" requires a large number of installations in order to have affordable service cost

## 5. Pilot operation and user evaluations

The pilot operation activities started with final testing of the integrated platform and the beginning of the real-life pilot operation. During 15 months (May 2010-August 2011) the pilots were used by the test users under realistic conditions - older adults in their homes; the professional care-givers in their work tasks, performing their daily work to care for the elderly; the informal care-givers/family, also in their everyday activities to care for the seniors. The services were first tested in a smaller scale, with a few end-users at three of the pilot sites for a period of 3-4 months, in order to identify if any major problems exist before the large scale testing with all users during the rest of the testing period. Small scale pilots were carried out in all of the regions, except in the region of Trikala, with 2-3 home installations in each of the regions.

Since the launch of the services, in three of the regions demo-rooms have been installed and in the fourth region the system was installed in the home of one of the formal care-givers. The demo-rooms existed in addition to the home installations and had the following goals:

- Demonstration of the services to potential test participants and their relatives - they were able to see, and experience the system before deciding to join the controlled study and were convinced that it is very user friendly and also aesthetically acceptable
- In these demo rooms, the formal care-givers were able to try in reality the system and provide final feedback to technical partners for usability and functionality and suggestions for improvement
- Potential end-users were introduced to the services and training was provided to them
- Personnel from care-giver organisations gained hands-on experience with the services and became more confident in usage of the system and learnt how to report technical problems

- Last but not least, the demo rooms were used as living labs because the improvements of the services were carried out in parallel with the pilot operation and in all cases the improvements were first applied and proofed in the demo machines, and then transferred to the home installations of the test users

In August 2010 the partners had a meeting to discuss experiences from the small scale pilot operation and how to make the transition to the full scale pilot operation more efficiently. In this way, the full pilot operation started in September 2010 and continued until the end of the project (August 2011).

To evaluate the effects of using the services in real-life, we followed overall assessment framework and carried out 15-month controlled study in the four European regions involving 71 elderly, 71 informal care-givers and around 15 formal care-givers, assessing baseline and final status of cognitive impairments, daily functioning and quality of life of the older adults. For the informal care-givers, quality of life and care stress were assessed. In the end of the controlled study, all groups were asked to evaluate their satisfaction and acceptability of the ICT services and their importance for care; the potential to promote independence and to increase feeling of safety. In three of regions, except in the region of Frederikshavn, the trial participants were split in intervention and control groups.

Significant results from the pilot operation were achieved even though the roll out of the pilots was more complicated than initially anticipated. There were a number of challenges to be addressed during the real-life pilot operation; some of those were not dependent on the consortium. The partners worked together and in many cases they were resolving technical issues in non-working hours/days based on good will and because of the eagerness to achieve a high impact. The whole process has been a positive learning experience for all of them.

The fact that most of the test users and their relatives are satisfied, feel safer and confident with ISISEMD services, is a significant result that is not measurable. Even somehow sceptical in the beginning, after giving them time to get used to the services, the elderly and their relatives accept the technology and can see the opportunities for positive impact. The relatives can better feel the difference by using the services in comparison with the elderly, because due to the disease, it is difficult for the elderly to think abstractly and understand it.

## 6. Outcome from technical evaluations - non-functional aspects

Technical evaluation was carried out to determine whether the system requirements were fulfilled by testing the services after the components of the system have been integrated into one system. The system evaluation had two aspects: *Functional evaluation* and *Non-functional evaluation*. The purpose of the *functional* tests were to evaluate all the functions that were enabled with the ISISEMD system. The *non-functional* evaluation included aspects such as e.g. scalability, reliability, flexibility. Non-functional requirements were validated based on qualitative and quantitative appropriate measures. More details about the overall assessment framework are presented in (Mitseva, 2010). In the next paragraphs we focus on the non-service specific evaluations which assess the readiness of the system for wider deployment.

### 6.1 Personalisation/customisation

Overall, personalisation/customisation features of the services were highly appreciated by the regional care providers and the end-users because they give possibility for them to map precisely the services to the exact needs of the dyad "elderly-informal care-giver" and fitting the support services in the care-giving and coping strategies.

### 6.2 Robustness of the equipments and connectivity

Carebox: we experienced some issues with the Touch-screen computer due to high touch sensitivity and they have been resolved by context-aware solution. Some few cases related to hardware failures that required replacement of the computer were mainly due to the fact that such device has been designed in "consumer electronic" segment that is not intended to run 24x7 in highly reliable environment. Unstable internet connections were reasons for false alarms and freezing of Carebox screen but they were alleviated by applying more sophisticated filters on bypassing false alarm triggering conditions.

GPS device: we used a simple GPS device called Lommy that is in general very robust and has been already in use in different contexts. The only few issues were the connector for charging the Lommy as it was difficult for use by elderly people; LED indicators, blinking with different colours, were confusing for the elderly and their care-givers; in two of the regions, that had hilly and mountain landscape, problems with the coverage were experienced.

Sensors and RAck MOnitoring System (RAMOS): The type used was Ramos Mini C. It is a very robust device. It is meant to be used both in home and industrial environments. The only one issue was Ramos and Ethernet failures during the installation and then fixed in the installation process. Overall, the problems with RAMOS and sensor devices were related to setup, configuration, placement, and installation, which is more about practical issue than the robustness.

Overall, the equipments to be used when offering ICT services for home support to elderly must be robust and "invisible" i.e. placed in those areas of the home where they are difficult to reach. This will prevent un-wanted disconnections or damages due to some every day activities such as cleaning, dusting, etc. It is best if the wires, RAMOS, routers are hidden in or behind cupboards or in a box. On the contrary, it is best if the Carebox (the Touch screen for the end users) is placed in a kitchen or living room or close to a TV, to make it easer for the elderly to see it and refer to it. It is even more important the equipments and the integrated services to be extensively tested in conditions as close to the real-life operation as possible before installing it in the homes. In this way, specific local issues can be discovered and eliminated. For example we experienced some hardware problems in only one region that were not common to the other three regions.

### 6.3 Scalability

During the ISISEMD pilot operation, it has been shown that the current architecture of ISISEMD portal and X-Server have been able to handle between 30 and 40 end users concurrently. In the future, it would be good to study and make some prediction on ISISEMD's users growth and traffic volume, such that network dimensioning and simulation can be done, and finally to decide the best network architecture.

### 6.4 Response time

During the pilot operation, response time metric is highly related to the services that activate alarms, especially alarms through SMS which is very much dependent on the network operator and SMS service provider. In the beginning of the pilot operation, the SMS service was assigned to normal level but since we observed delays in the delivery, the SMS service level was changed. The problem related to SMS service has been solved by subscribing to highest (and more expensive) service level of the SMS service provider.

### 6.5 Integration/openness

Integration of new hardware (especially sensors), requires some testing period in order to get the correct information reading as expected, e.g. by configuration and correct placement.

Integration of new software modules both on server and client side have been easily done in ISISEMD system since the platform has been designed in such a way that the services provided to end-user can evolve by providing API (Application Programming Interface) to service/software developer.

### 6.6 Manageability/flexibility

The assessment of ISISEMD system for these two parameters show that the platform is very easy and flexible to manage, i.e. in terms of adding/deleting new users, new services, new home installations, and new regions/sub-regions, etc., since it has been designed to support all these requirements. Furthermore, a user manual book written in four different languages (English, Finnish, Danish and Greek) has been provided as a guideline to regions and end users in general.

## 7. Outcome from service validation of the common functionalities of ISISEMD platform

We would like to argue for having carried out a good piece of work, overcoming a number of challenges, and that the final services meet the user expectations and acceptances at a high level supported by the outcome of the user evaluations. Overall, the care-givers were satisfied with the services and consider them important for providing care. Most of the users now state their wish for continuing to use the services after the project end. As suggested by the user feedback, there is even stronger need for service personalisation so they can function in a more intelligent and autonomous way.

Based on the continuous user feedback during the pilot operation, the services were improved where possible. But due to the limited project lifetime and resources, not all additional features suggested by the end-users as improvements could be implemented. However, they can be used for further development of the service platform as a commercial product. Subsequently, we emphasize on some of the suggestions that can be considered as **"wish list for the commercial system"** by the regional partners and by the test persons. We are of the interpretation that the following suggestions could improve the intelligence of the service platform in the next version of the system.

### 7.1 "Wish list" for enhancements for the commercial system

They were related mainly to higher intelligence&personalisation, improved usability and additional services.

#### 7.1.1 Services enhancement for higher intelligence&personalisation

For the purpose of better personalisation, the free text reminders on the Carebox are suggested to be enhanced so they can contain longer text and, with advantage, to make it possible for the elderly him/her self to create their own text reminders, if the elderly is able to do it. It would also be an advantage for the users if the system is able to atomically create voice files for these free text reminders through speech synthesis. The reminders functionality can also be enhanced with more pre-defined reminders and advanced by having additional services such as shopping list reminders for the elderly people.

Other suggestions for enhancing the services and their usability concern implementing even more intelligence into the platform for automatic synchronisation of the calendar service events with the service for home presence. And for the cooker service, it would be an advantage to make separate time settings for the cooker plates and for the oven seeing that users have individual patterns and the oven shows to be used for a longer time than the cooker plates are. Users also suggest for the functionality of the intelligent front door service to be able to work without the bed sensor because there are cases when bed sensor cannot be used.

Further enhancement of the services is to create the possibility of having a small message board on the Carebox that can show to the elderly a SMS message sent by their care-givers mobile devices. In this way, the relatives will be able to send a SMS to the Carebox so the SMS text can be shown on the screen to the elderly person.

#### 7.1.2 Usability enhancement

Some of the first suggestions focused on enhancing usability of the services, the portal and the Carebox - for instance, improving the visual aspect of the portal and the Carebox for enhancing the user interface to be usable by visual, hearing or cognitive impaired users. This will also create the possibility for other people with disabilities (blind/ deaf) to interact with the system.

#### 7.1.3 "Entertainment" features

For the purpose of enhancing satisfaction of the elderly people and their family caregivers, it was suggested to include "entertainment" features - plug-ins for facilitating distribution of relevant information such as local news, the weather forecast, favourite music, etc. These entertainment features are to be accessible and shown on the Carebox screen by assigning for such a service.

#### 7.1.4 Reflections

The automation degree of the services, together with their availability, was seen as a key feature for the family care-givers. Informal caregivers are willing to have very few degree of interaction of the user with the system. This is mainly due to the fact that they understand, on the one hand, that elderly is not able to be familiar with the new technology and on the other hand, they are willing to increase the level of independence of the elderly but without the cost of adding more stress to their daily responsibilities. In addition, elderly cannot handle a lot of interactions with the system, since they are not familiar with the new technology and have somewhat of an aversion to learning. We have also seen that this may discourage use of the system, as the elderly may worry that they will break the technology, so they would rather not use it at all than be the cause of expensive repairs. The users want the system to be as automatic as possible; however, they also want inexpensive technological solutions.

### 7.2 Future work

Future work on the service platform can go in several directions. With respect to the technical side, it comprises mainly on implementing some of the suggested by the end users enhancements of the user interface of the Carebox and the portal. With respect to functionality, it can involve adding new services and enhancing the functionality of the Lifestyle Pattern service to automatically generate (graphical) reports for deviation from normal user behaviour. This service has also potential for improving quality of care for the formal care-providers and saving them time.

With respect to the services support, efforts can be dedicated to offering the services as one complete home-support service including acquiring the equipments, making the home installations, ensuring help-desk support, training the end-users, maintaining the services, etc. For user support, uploading short tutorial video-clips on the web portal for re-enforcing the training process for service setting was a suggestion by the regional partners.

For optimising the installation process, a direction to go is preparing installation software package with all needed settings and defining "a standard service package" in each region with the most desired services that will be initially offered to all elderly who subscribe to the home-support services and further re-assessed and updated if needed.

Taken as a whole, wide scale testing with higher number of test participants, more European regions and for a duration of a couple of years would show delay in institutionalisation and provide more real-life assessments of the services.

## 8. Results from the controlled study

### 8.1 Important aspects of the piloting process

Developing and piloting ICT services for older adults with cognitive impairments or mild dementia and their family care-givers has been a challenging process. A system like the ISISEMD platform is complementary to the daily support provided by the family care-giver and the relative itself is considered a user of the system. In addition, spouses/partners and closest family played a key role in the level of independence of old people with cognitive impairments or mild dementia and also in ISISEMD pilot. In the process of piloting the ICT services, diverse aspects played an important role - such as trust towards technology, complexity of installations and the platform due to the fact that it included high number of services. It is natural for this elderly user group to feel scepticism towards the technology and we took this into consideration in the process. There was a thin line and a trade off between testing the platform with real users while the services were still under improvement and adaptation for the real-life conditions. Finding many volunteers who fit the inclusion criteria and are willing to evaluate the services was another challenge for us. It also took us time to build understandable communication in cross-disciplinary teams because of the different paradigms for the regional and technical partners. By far, the most crucial factors were proved to be the maturity of the services; the thorough testing before installing them in the homes; matching the services to those clients who have the most benefit from them and openness for new technology.

During the trial period, all ethical rights of the citizens were respected and the trials were carried out according to high ethical standards and the national regulations and the privacy of the trial participants and all data related to this were ensured. All applicable national and international laws and acts were respected too. The trial participants were recruited only after approvals from Ethical Committees were granted for each region where it was required and consent forms were signed by all trial participants.

At baseline, for the cohorts combined (intervention and control groups), the female participants were 67.4%, the average age was 78.69 years, having mild to moderate decline in cognition. The assessment on basic daily functioning showed full or high dependency, while instrumental activities of daily living mean score indicated mid-range of dependency. The test group of informal care-givers showed severe effect on their quality of life, but the mean value for cohorts combined was on the border line of severe effect on their quality of life. The care burden indicated that the care-givers were in the mid-range of caregiver-burden effects. Highest percentage of family care-givers was children.

### 8.2 Findings from the final assessments

The controlled study assessed in the end of the 15-month trial period cognitive decline and daily functioning for the elderly persons. For the informal care-givers - care stress. For both groups the impact of the services on the quality of life was investigated. We looked further into domains of which we expected the technology services to make a positive impact. Elderly persons and relatives were also asked for their willingness to use the services after the end of the project and their willingness to pay for the services in general.

User acceptance and satisfaction with the services were evaluated upon with the three main end-user groups and for instance, care-givers were asked about the importance for care and ability for independent living and, overall satisfaction. We observed a difference among the views from the four regions for the services showing a minimum/maximum satisfaction and acceptance among the elderly test users and a difference in the lowest/highest rating among informal care-givers of the services that are important for care giving. This also reflected cultural and care-model differences among the four European regions.

Regarding the feeling of safety, 70% of the elderly felt safer when using the ISISEMD system. Another 20% reported feeling significantly safer. 40% of the informal care-givers report feeling safer, with another 50% of them reporting feeling significantly safer. More than half of the test users reported independent living increases - 51.61% of elderly and 67.74% of informal care-givers. Also 3.23% of the informal care-givers reported it increases more than they thought.

According to the test group's final evaluation, there was a significant decrease of the level of care burden among the informal care-givers after using the ISISEMD services whereas in the control group the informal care-givers burden indicated an increase after the evaluation period. Overall for the test group, 80% of the elderly maintained their basic Activities of Daily Living (ADL) and 40% of the elderly improved their Instrumental Activities of Daily Living (IADL). For the Quality of Life, 70% of the elderly had an improvement in their Quality of Life and 80% of the informal care-givers similarly had an improvement in their Quality of Life. 80% of the informal care-givers had a reduction of care-related stress (care-giver burden) and 0% had an increase in care-related stress.

### 8.3 The view of the formal care-givers

From formal care-givers point of view, at least two thirds of formal care-givers rated the services to be easy to use. In extension, the majority of formal care-givers rated the services to be very important for care. They felt that services were easy to integrate into their existing care routines and were easy to personalise. Three quarters of formal care-givers also provided high ratings for services, in terms of their importance for care-giving.

From the qualitative evaluations, we can draw the conclusions that parameters that were important along the way for piloting the services were service maturity, flexibility and personalisation. Furthermore, the training of the end-users and the intelligence of the services played an important role for the overall satisfaction too, platform stability and service availability and offering the services at earliest stage of the disease.

### 8.4 Acknowledgements for the test users in the pilot

We would like to thank to our test users whom we accept as an equal partner of the consortium. They played a very important role in the process of bringing the services to a mature level and improving them in all aspects in order to meet their needs as best as possible. We can confirm that it is of high importance that the primary user and care-givers are to be motivated towards the usage of aiding technologies in their homes. For the acceptance of the services by the elderly, a key role was played by the family care-giver and the process was much more rapid and easier if the care-givers had previous experience with technology.

## 9. "Success stories" from the pilot

The positive impacts from the use of the services are described below with the words of the real users as success stories and the overall interpretation of these, points towards an improvement in feeling of independence and safety and in communication and social relation between the elderly people and the relatives. Thus, an improved Quality of Life is being observed in reality.

**ISISEMD services form a basis for good communication between the elderly and their relatives.** Hence, the services help the elderly people with mild dementia in the North Region of Denmark to create quick and easy communication with relatives. The Carebox equipped with a help button, is helpful for the elderly in the sense that it is easier to get in touch with relatives whenever it is needed, emergency or not. One case showing the advantages of the ISISEMD Carebox comes into play due to the fact that one elderly with dementia has difficulties to make phone calls to relatives. Instead, by pressing the Carebox help button, the elderly person can easily get into contact with relatives. Contact is simply generated automatically by the system with the help of an SMS that is sent to relatives when the elderly presses the help button.

**The outdoor safety service helps the elderly people with mild dementia to stay healthy** by giving them the possibility to be active outdoors in their everyday lives. One case with an older man from North Region of Denmark reveals the advantage brought by the GPS device. The older man with diabetes who needs to keep his blood pressure down used to be afraid to go outside, as he could get lost. Today, with the GPS device the older man is no longer afraid to go for a walk. He explains, *"I feel more safe because I know that the Lommy will help me to get in contact with my family and then, they can find me if I get lost"*. Neighbours and relatives reveal that they have even observed that the older man is going regularly for walks and that they can see his position on a map if he needs help or gets lost.

**Intelligent door alarms prevent the elderly people from leaving their homes unnoticeably in the winter time -** In Finland, a relative explains the significance of ISISEMD Intelligent door alarm and the impact it has done on both her mother and her self. The relative explains that now she can prevent her mother from going out of the house and getting lost in the cold winter in Finland. The Intelligent front door service sends an alarm message to a relative informing that the door opens and thus, the older person might be leaving the house. According to this, a relative has stated: *"In Finland, this service is very important so that we can be informed if our relatives get lost. It is so cold in the winter and this can be dangerous if the elderly goes outside for a longer period of time"*.

**Bed sensor helps the elderly to alert their families automatically when help is needed during the night -** In Finland, a relative expresses the importance of having a bed sensor installed. The relative explains that her mother has had several incidents of falling down from her bed during the night. The bed sensor sends a signal when an elderly is out of bed for too long, thus a relative or a caregiver will receive an SMS with the alert. In this particular case, the relative explained… *"When I received this message, I went to my mother's house and found her on the floor. I am very happy to have received this SMS so that I could help my mother, even if it was in the middle of the night"*.

**ISISEMD Calendar and To Do List, shown on the ISISEMD Carebox, helps the elderly with mild dementia to live more independently -** With the ISISEMD Carebox the elderly can keep track of the day and time. For instance, in North Ireland, a relative living with her mother states: *"Even if we only have had the Carebox for 10 days, both my mother and I already feel a difference. Normally my mother always calls me several times at work every day being anxious about not knowing the day and time. Now, with the Carebox, my mother is always informed about the day and time and this has helped her to become more confident. "*

**ISISEMD services are beneficial for enhancing the quality of life of the elderly and their relatives -** In Greece relatives taking care of the elderly explain that the services help them to feel safer knowing that their parents have the ISISEMD services installed in their homes. Hence, relatives are aware if the elderly leaves their houses or if they are out of bed for a long time. One relative explains … *"Before having the ISISEMD services we had to travel 30 minutes outside of town every day to check on our relative. Now we feel safer knowing that our* *relative have the ISISEMD services installed and our relative can keep on doing everyday activities and plan their days, independently. "*

## 10. Conclusion

ISISEMD platform with innovative intelligent services is scalable, open-system, validated in real-live environment. The competitive advantage of ISISEMD systems is that it is based on a modular scalable open platform that advances the State-Of-the-Art in the areas of systems for Ambient Assisted Living and can be integrated with other Health or Care Systems. Additional services can be included anytime, resulting in a very powerful platform system.

Last but not least, ISISEMD services have been extensively tested and validated in a pilot operation with 142 end-users (71 elderly and 71 relatives) for 15 months in four regions - in Denmark, Finland, Greece and UK. The final user evaluations, carried out in June 2011, showed high level of user acceptance and satisfaction with the services and willingness to use them after the project ends.

We knew that sceptical users are stoppers against introduction of new technologies. But our experience shows that the elderly and their relatives accept the technology and can see the opportunities for positive impact and added value from the use of the services in their everyday life even when the older adults with mild dementia and their family care-givers were sceptical in the beginning, after giving them time to get used to the technology. It can be expected, that after about one month, the elderly and their family caregivers can get used to the services. The most successful adoption of the services can happen when they are offered as early as possible in the disease. In this way, the technology services can be integrated in the coping and care strategies in the family and elderly has highest chances to learn to refer to the services.

The benefits from using ISISEMD services were depicted in the user acceptance surveys, contributing to the Quality of Life of the end-users. The services improved the elderly ability for self-care by support for their basic daily activities in way that prevents health risks in their homes and promotes independence. They strengthened the daily interaction with their social sphere - partners and relatives, giving them the feeling of safety and improving their relationships. For the family care-givers, the services increased their quality of life and the feeling of safety; reduced their care burden and gave them a piece of mind while saving them time and money.

Potential for direct savings from the usage of the ICT services is foreseen for both the care-provider organisations and informal care-givers. Costs can be saved from time and travel expenses for delivery of warm meals to elderly, performing on-line sessions with use of video-call service instead of physical home-safety visits, visits for administering medications, automatically registering information for such services, etc. The informal care-givers can save time and money for making telephone calls to elderly to check about status or to drive to elderly place or to cook meals for them. The highest potential for savings is at a society level - with delaying the admittance in nursing or dementia care institutions where savings at European level can range from approx. 1300-4000 euro for one person for 12 months.

## 11. Acknowledgment

The work presented in this paper is partially funded by the ICT PSP EU project "ISISEMD - Intelligent system for independent living and self-care of seniors with cognitive problems or mild dementia." Contract Number: ICT-PSP-2-238914, www.isisemd.eu. The authors would like to acknowledge also the contributions of the whole consortium.

## 12. Disclaimer

This paper reflects only the views of the authors and the European Commission is not liable for any use that might be made of the information contained therein.

## 13. References

Aalst, W.; Hofstede, A.; Kiepuszewski, B.; and Barros, A. (2003). "Workflow Patterns Distributed and Parallel Databases, 14(1):551, 2003

ISISEMD Intelligent System for Independent Living and Self-Care of Seniors with Cognitive Problems or Mild Dementia. (2009) http://www.isisemd.eu/. 2009-2012, www.isisemd.eu

Mitseva, A.; Kyriazakos, S.; Litke, A.; Papadakis, N.; Prasad, N. (2009). *ISISEMD: Intelligent System for Independent living and self-care of Seniors with mild cognitive impairment or Mild Dementia,* © The Journal on Information Technology in Healthcare, Volume 7 Issue 6 2009, pp. 383–399, ISSN 1479-649X

Mitseva, A.; Peterson, C.; Dafoulas, G.; Efthymiou, A.; Abildgaard, A.; Bellini, S. (2010). *ISISEMD evaluation framework for impact assessment of ICT pilot services for elderly with mild dementia, living in the community and their relatives.*, Proceedings of NAEC 2010, pp. 123-148, ISBN 9780-0-9820958-3-6, Riva del Garda, Italy, October 7-10, 2010

ALZ http://www.alz.org/national/documents/summary_alzfactsfigures2009.pdf

BPEL http://www.oasis-open.org/committees/tc_home.php?wg_abbrev=wsbpel

WFMC http://www.wfmc.org/

XPDL http://www.wfmc.org/standards/xpdl.htm